Praise for
Guide to Literary Agents

"The right agent can provide entrée to the right editors, and Writer's Digest's annual *Guide to Literary Agents* will help you determine just who those right agents are." **—Amazon.com**

"Provides writers with everything they need to know about agents." **—Writers Write**

"An invaluable tool for writers in search of an agent . . ." **—Library Journal**

"If you, as a writer, don't have an agent yet, and you have a manuscript—novel, nonfiction, screenplay, or teleplay—this is a guide that should be on your desk." **—Writer's Carousel**

"A splendid reference work." **—The Herald**

D1384693

2 0 0 0
GUIDE TO LITERARY AGENTS

500 AGENTS WHO SELL WHAT YOU WRITE

EDITED BY

DONYA DICKERSON

WRITER'S DIGEST BOOKS
CINCINNATI, OHIO

Supervisory Editors: Barbara Kuroff and Kirsten Holm
Production Editor: Ian Bessler

Writer's Digest Books website: www.writersdigest.com

2000 Guide to Literary Agents. Copyright © 2000 by Writer's Digest Books.
Published by F&W Publications, 1507 Dana Ave., Cincinnati, Ohio 45207. Printed and bound
in the United States of America. All rights reserved. No part of this book may be reproduced in
any form or by any electronic or mechanical means including information storage and retrieval
systems without written permission from the publisher, except by reviewers who may quote brief
passages to be printed in a magazine or newspaper.

International Standard Serial Number 1078-6945
International Standard Book Number 0-89879-936-8

Cover designed by Clare Finney
Cover illustration by Jeffrey Pelo

Attention Booksellers: This is an annual directory of F&W Publications.
Return deadline for this edition is April 30, 2001.

contents at a glance

Contents

From the Editor

I talked to several writers this past year while working on the 2000 edition of the *Guide to Literary Agents*. It is an important part of my job, and I enjoy it. I've met published authors who write fulltime, others who schedule their writing around several jobs. Some are bookish and reserved, others are bohemian and eccentric. Each writer I spoke with has a distinct personality. But that never surprises me—writers are supposed to be individuals.

Agents, on the other hand, are often stereotyped. If they're not out to lunch, they're on the phone. They all wear the same gray pinstriped suit and sit behind the same immaculate desk. Yet, while putting together this edition—interviewing agents, collecting information for their listings and organizing the many articles—I was struck by how different the agents in this book are. They all have different personalities, different views on the publishing industry and different priorities for their writers.

These distinctions are good news for you as start your search for representation. When you look through the agents' listings in this book, think about what you need in order to have a productive relationship with an agent. Consider your personal writing goals, and prioritize the qualities you feel are important in a business partner. Find an agent whose individual way of doing business fits your individual personality.

Besides unique personalities, we also understand that all writers have different ways of working. Therefore, we've included several elements in this book so the information it contains can be accessed in multiple ways.

- If you prefer a linear approach, the informative articles will guide you step-by-step through the process of finding an agent. Or, you can reference specific articles as you come to each new stage of your search.
- If lists help you get organized, use the numerous indexes to find agents who specialize in your subject areas, who are open to new writers, or who live near you. If you've read about specific agents or agencies, use the indexes to find their listings.
- If you like to jump right in to the listings, keep your eye open for several new time-saving features that indicate if an agent is appropriate for your work. Openness icons ▢ ◨ ◒ ◎ ◿ in front of each listing let you immediately assess how receptive an agent is to new clients. To determine what subject areas and genres an agent represents, look for the bolded phrases: **Considers these nonfiction areas:** and **Considers these fiction areas:** in each listing. To reduce the time you spend mailing out material, we've also added, under the subhead **How to Contact:**, information indicating if an agent accepts e-mail and fax queries, or considers multiple queries and submissions.

With this information in mind, take a few minutes to browse this book, looking at the listings, and reading the interviews and articles. If you do, you'll soon observe that agents—like writers—have different tastes and talents. Let your own uniqueness determine the best one for you.

Donya Dickerson

literaryagents@fwpubs.com
www.writersdigest.com

Quick Start Guide to Using Your Guide to Literary Agents

Your hand is cramped from writing; your eyes are permanently red from staring at a computer screen. You are eager to start searching for an agent—anxious to see your name on the spine of a book. But before you go directly to the listings of agencies and start sending out query letters, take a few minutes to familiarize yourself with the various resources available in the *Guide to Literary Agents*. By doing so, you will be more prepared for your search, and ultimately save yourself time and unnecessary grief.

START WITH THE ARTICLES

The book is divided into literary and script agents. These two sections begin with feature articles that give advice on the best strategies for contacting agents and provide perspectives on the author/agent relationship. The articles about literary agents are organized into four sections appropriate for each stage of the search process: **Before You Start** (starting on page 6), **Narrowing Your List** (starting on page 16), **Contacting Agents** (starting on page 31) and **Before You Sign** (starting on page 45). You may want to start by reading through each article, then refer back to relevant articles during each stage of your search for an agent.

Because an important part of your search is learning first-hand information from agents and authors, we've provided Insider Reports throughout the book. These personalized interviews with agents and published authors offer both information and inspiration for any writer hoping to find representation.

DECIDE WHAT TYPE OF AGENT YOU NEED

The book is first divided into literary and script agents. For literary agents, the listings are split into two distinct sections: nonfee-charging and fee-charging agents. For script agents, the listings are grouped in one section, and those who charge fees are indicated with a clapper symbol.

Chances are you already know if you need a literary or a script agent, but whether or not you want a nonfee-charging agent or a fee-charging agent may not be as obvious. Reading the feature articles and the introduction to each section of agency listings will help you understand the difference between the two types of agents. In general, nonfee-charging agents earn income from commissions made on manuscript sales. Their focus is selling books, and they typically do not offer editing services or promote books that have already been published. These agents tend to be more selective, often preferring to work with established writers and experts in specific fields.

Fee-charging agents, on the other hand, charge writers for various services (i.e., reading, critiquing, editing, evaluation, consultation, marketing, etc.) in addition to taking a commission on sales. These agents tend to be more receptive to handling the work of new writers. Some of them charge a reading or handling fee only to cover the additional costs of this openness. Those listings charging fees only to previously unpublished writers are preceded by a briefcase symbol. Others offer services designed to improve your manuscript or script. But payment for any of these services rarely ensures representation. If you pay for a critique or edit, request references and sample critiques. If you do approach fee-charging agents, know exactly what their fees will cover—what you'll be getting before any money changes hands.

NARROW YOUR CHOICES

You could send a mass mailing to all the agencies listed in this book, but doing so would be apparent to agents and would most likely turn them off. Instead, use the organizational tools in this book to help determine a core list of agents who would be appropriate for you and your work.

First, determine whether you want a nonfee-charging or a fee-charging agent. Then, depending on the type of material you write and whether you write fiction, nonfiction or scripts, start your search with the following indexes:

Agents Specialties Index: Immediately following each section of listings and striped for quick reference, these indexes should help you compose a list of agents specializing in your areas. For literary agents, this index is divided by nonfiction and fiction subject categories. For script agents, this index is divided into various subject areas specific to scripts and by common script formats. Cross-referencing categories and concentrating on agents interested in two or more aspects of your manuscript might increase your chances of success. Some agencies indicated they are open to all topics and are grouped under the subject heading "open" in each section.

Geographic Index: For writers looking for an agent close to home, this index lists agents state-by-state.

Agencies Indexed by Openness to Submissions: This index lists agencies according to their receptivity to new clients.

Agent Index: Often you will read about an agent who is an employee of a larger agency and you may not be able to locate her business phone or address. We asked agencies to list the agents on staff, then we've listed the agents' names in alphabetical order along with the name of the agency they work for. Find the name of the person you would like to contact and then check the agency listing.

Listing Index: This index lists all agencies and conferences listed in the book.

READING THE LISTINGS IN THIS BOOK

Once you have searched the various indexes and compiled a list of potential agents for your manuscript, you should read the description of each agency on your list, eliminating those that seem inappropriate for your work or your individual needs.

Look at the sample agency listing on page 4. Study it to understand what the information provided in it means. You also may want to refer to the brief introductions before each section of agency listings for other information specific to that particular section.

QUICK REFERENCE ICONS

At the beginning of some listings, you will find one or more of the following symbols for quick identification of features particular to that listing.

- 🔲 Agency new to this edition.
- ✓ Change in address, contact information or phone number.
- $ Agents who charge fees to previously unpublished writers only.
- 🔲 Fee-charging script agent.
- 🔲 Canadian listing.

OPENNESS

Each agency has an icon indicating its openness to submissions. Before contacting any agency, check the listing to make sure it is open to new clients.

- ◻ Newer agency actively seeking clients.
- ◗ Agency seeking both new and established writers.
- ◖ Agency prefers to work with established writers, mostly obtains new clients through referrals.

◎ Agency handling only certain types of work or work by writers under certain circumstances.

⊘ Agency not currently seeking new clients. We include these agencies to let you know they are currently not open to new clients. *Unless you have a strong recommendation from someone well respected in the field, our advice is to avoid approaching these agents.*

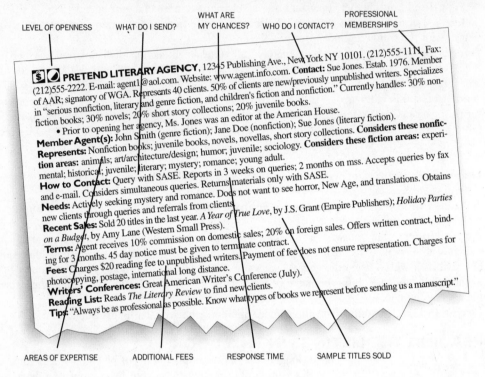

LEVEL OF OPENNESS · WHAT DO I SEND? · WHAT ARE MY CHANCES? · WHO DO I CONTACT? · PROFESSIONAL MEMBERSHIPS

$⊘ PRETEND LITERARY AGENCY, 12345 Publishing Ave., New York NY 10101. (212)555-1111. Fax: (212)555-2222. E-mail: agent1@aol.com. Website: www.agent.info.com. **Contact:** Sue Jones. Estab. 1976. Member of AAR; signatory of WGA. Represents 40 clients. 50% of clients are new/previously unpublished writers. Specializes in "serious nonfiction, literary and genre fiction, and children's fiction and nonfiction." Currently handles: 30% non-fiction books; 30% novels; 20% short story collections; 20% juvenile books.
• Prior to opening her agency, Ms. Jones was an editor at the American House.
Member Agent(s): John Smith (genre fiction); Jane Doe (nonfiction); Sue Jones (literary fiction).
Represents: Nonfiction books; juvenile books, novels, novellas, short story collections. **Considers these nonfiction areas:** animals; art/architecture/design; humor; juvenile; sociology. **Considers these fiction areas:** experimental; historical; juvenile; literary; mystery; romance; young adult.
How to Contact: Query with SASE. Reports in 3 weeks on queries; 2 months on mss. Accepts queries by fax and e-mail. Considers simultaneous queries. Returns materials only with SASE.
Needs: Actively seeking mystery and romance. Does not want to see horror, New Age, and translations. Obtains new clients through queries and referrals from clients.
Recent Sales: Sold 20 titles in the last year. *A Year of True Love*, by J.S. Grant (Empire Publishers); *Holiday Parties on a Budget*, by Amy Lane (Western Small Press).
Terms: Agent receives 10% commission on domestic sales; 20% on foreign sales. Offers written contract, binding for 3 months. 45 day notice must be given to terminate contract.
Fees: Charges $20 reading fee to unpublished writers. Payment of fee does not ensure representation. Charges for photocopying, postage, international long distance.
Writers' Conferences: Great American Writer's Conference (July).
Reading List: Reads *The Literary Review* to find new clients.
Tips: "Always be as professional as possible. Know what types of books we represent before sending us a manuscript."

AREAS OF EXPERTISE · ADDITIONAL FEES · RESPONSE TIME · SAMPLE TITLES SOLD

SUBHEADS

Each listing is broken down into subheads to make locating specific information easier. In the first paragraph, you'll find the information you'll need to contact each agency, including where to send your query letter and who to send it to. You'll also learn if the agency belongs to any professional organization. If an agent is a member of the Association of Authors' Representatives (AAR), they are prohibited from charging reading or evaluating fees. If they are a member of the Writers Guild of America (WGA), they are not permitted to charge a reading fee to WGA members but are allowed to do so to nonmembers. An agent's willingness to work with new or previously unpublished writers is indicated by the percentages given here. The total number of clients an agency represents can also suggest what your status might be in the agency.

Member Agents: Agencies can range from a one-person operation to many agents and junior agents. Often different agents within an agency have specific specialties. Listed here are agents and their individual specialties to help you determine the best agent to query for your work.

Represents: To expedite your search for an agent, only query agents who represent the type of material you write. Under this subhead, agents list what types of manuscripts they are interested in receiving. To help you find those agents more quickly, check the **Agents Specialties Index** immediately following each section of agency listings.

How to Contact: Most agents open to submissions prefer initially to receive a query letter briefly describing your work. (For sample queries, read Queries That Made It Happen on page 35). Some agents ask for an outline or sample chapters, but you should send these only if you are requested to do so. Agents indicate here if they are open to fax or e-mail queries, as well as if they consider simultaneous submissions. Always send a self-addressed stamped envelope (SASE) or postcard for reply. If you have not heard back from an agent within the approximate reporting time given (allowing for holidays and summer vacations), a quick, polite phone call to ask when it will be reviewed would be in order.

Needs: For agents open to a wide-range of subjects, we list here nonfiction, fiction and script areas they are actively seeking as well as subjects they do *not* wish to receive. Also listed is the agent's preferred way of meeting new clients.

Recent Sales: Another way to determine if an agent is appropriate for your manuscript is to look at other titles sold by that agent. Looking at the publisher of those titles can also tell you the caliber of publishing contacts the agent has developed. To give you an idea of how successful an agent has been, we also list the number of titles an agent sold last year. If an agency lists no sales information, we explain why.

Terms: Here you'll find the agent's commission, whether a contact is offered and for how long, and possible office expenses you might have to pay (postage, photocopying, etc.). Most agents receive a 10 to 15 percent commission for domestic sales and a 20 to 25 percent commission for foreign or dramatic sales, with the difference going to the co-agent who places the work.

Fees: A separate subhead is included for agents who do charge fees in addition to their commissions. Often, payment of reading or critique fees does not ensure representation. To better understand the different issues surrounding fee-charging agents, read Agents & Ethics: How to Get Published Without Losing Your Shirt on page 11 and Understanding Fees—What Writers Must Know on page 15 *before* you pay for any services.

Writers' Conferences: The conferences agents attend also give an idea of their professional interests and provide a way for writers to meet agents face-to-face. For more information about a specific conference, check the Writers' Conference section starting on page 292.

Reading List: Learn what magazines and journals agents read to discover potential clients.

Tips: This subhead contains direct quotes from agents revealing even more specifics about what they want and giving you a better sense of agents' personalities.

OTHER RESOURCES

If you don't recognize a symbol or abbreviation, refer to the **Key to Symbols** on the front and back inside covers or the **Table of Acronyms** on page 318. For definitions of unfamiliar words or expressions, check the **Glossary** in the back of the book.

Starting on page 316 are additional resources available for writers including a list of **Professional Organizations** for writers, **Books & Publications of Interest** to further your knowledge about agents, and **Websites of Interest** to guide you to the best sites available for writers on the Internet.

From Page to Personality: What One Agent Looks for in Clients

BY DONALD MAASS

So, what *really* happens in those once-a-week meetings at my agency office during which we comb through the 200 letters and manuscripts we receive each week? Wouldn't you love to be a fly on the wall or a genuine mind reader? What catches our eyes? Do we actually read *each* submission? Do we sneer and laugh? Later—after the serious reading and exploratory phone calls—when I am down to final candidates, the moment of decision, just what is going on in my mind? What am I looking for in a potential client?

I have been at this profession for 19 years. With 100 clients to look after, all chosen with due thought and care, you'd think I know exactly what I am looking for. Yet when I sat down to analyze my own process of analysis for this article, I was surprised by what I learned. What I am actually looking for is not what you might think.

One reassuring discovery: I *am* looking for something. And it's not a case of "I'll know it when I see it." There are criteria. There have to be—otherwise every letter and partial manuscript would be potential gold, and experience has taught me that is not the case. There is a rich vein of fool's gold in them thar' hills.

So, what are the criteria? Now, as soon as I tell you, I know some of you are going to rush straight to your word processors, revise your standard query letters and pack it with avowals of every quality on my list. Go right ahead. Before you do, however, you might give some thought to my points. You may find many of these qualities can only be demonstrated. Avowals alone will not persuade me to sign you up as a client.

Another reassuring fact: There is no such thing as "the ideal client." We are talking here about real people. Writers. Over the years I've come to accept that every one of my clients comes with strengths and weaknesses—positive attributes and flaws making them easy to work with in some ways, more difficult in others. In choosing clients, I try to weigh the mix and make the best possible matches, just as I hope they do in choosing me. My points are not a shopping list; rather, they are factors to be weighed, ingredients in a recipe.

As you read on, bear in mind I am a fiction specialist. Nonfiction agents are sure to apply criteria I do not. For pop psychology, stock market advice, cookbooks and the like, they probably will want bona fide experts and proven self-promoters, possibly even a "reel" of clips from your cable TV show. (You have one, don't you?) They may also need writers to supply them with market analysis that in the fiction game is fairly irrelevant.

So, with that caveat in mind, let's examine what I'm looking for.

Natural writing ability

Duh. But just what does that mean? And how do I uncover that quality, particularly when I have only a query letter on which to go?

DONALD MAASS *founded his New York literary agency in 1980. He represents over 100 novelists and has written 14 pseudonymous novels of his own. He is also the author of* The Career Novelist: A Literary Agent Offers Strategies for Success *(Heinemann, 1996). He is treasurer of the Association of Authors' Representatives, Inc.*

In the fiction business, natural writing ability is, first of all, the ability to draw the reader immediately into the author's world. A great first line helps do that, needless to say. A tougher trick is sustaining the illusion for several hundred pages. When reading only an opening chapter, the ability to grip the imagination over the long haul can be difficult to forecast. Still, in my experience, when an immediate command of the narrative is evident, it often means the rest of the manuscript will be worth a read. Great openings get me excited.

What exactly is "command of the narrative?" Smoothly flowing prose, assured paragraph construction, spare but snapshot-vivid description, believable yet surprising characters, conflict palpable on every page, a great story idea beautifully spun out in all its wonder and complexity. . . . You know, the easy stuff.

Is that your manuscript? Great. Send along a few pages. That is all it takes for me to know whether or not I am in the hands of a natural storyteller. When the writing is confident and skilled, I set down my pencil and feel myself relax. I know I am going for a terrific ride, at least for a time. So, the way to display natural (or practiced) writing ability is to display natural (or practiced) writing ability.

No problem, right?

Now, what if you have honored the preference I state in my listing in this guide and have sent me only a query letter? Can I possibly spot natural fiction ability from that? Not perfectly, of course. I have been fooled by many a concise, smoothly written query. Still, a writer is a writer, and the natural ones infuse even a four-paragraph query with an assurance that suggests natural talent at work or at least the confidence that comes with learned skill.

I do not mean boastful chest pounding. I am talking about the ability to leave things out, to overcome the anxious urge to tell me every last detail about the plot, theme, author's ambitions, and so forth. A brief synopsis of one's story will speak for itself. It is the avoidance of gimmicks or artificially friendly chat. Good queries are brief and businesslike. Good fiction writers know how to get to the point.

Professionalism

You are new at this? That's okay. Everyone has to start somewhere. But in the long process of developing a fiction career, it is extremely helpful for me to be working with an individual who has a professional attitude; that is, someone with at least a little knowledge of the publishing business and realistic expectations about how things are going to happen. Professionalism means treating writing as a business, and being both as passionate and as detached as one would be about any other business. The first clue that a writer is professional? A businesslike query letter.

Professionalism also implies sanity. How nice to deal with writers who can easily express their feelings, needs and concerns; writers who can get answers and resolve conflicts in a straight-forward fashion. Such writers, I know, will have an easier time in the glacially slow, ambiguous and maddeningly imprecise art form-as-industry we call book publishing. On the other hand, emotionally needy, borderline neurotic writers living on the edge of poverty are certain to make my life difficult.

How can I tell whether or not a writer is sane? Believe me, it can be difficult. Getting together with an agent is a lot like dating. All parties put on their best clothes and manners. Compliments abound. It is only after the wedding ceremony, when the honeymoon glow has worn off, that the irritating tics become apparent. Sooner or later both parties notice each other's maddening habits. Eventually, they may even uncover in each other horrifying character flaws. I try to learn as much as I can up front about prospective clients, but, just like every agent and editor, I have to fall in love. That passion is what gets me through the rough patches.

It is worth noting that the query letter is not the stage at which I need to know how much you know or do not know about publishing. I do not need to know your ambitions are high or your expectations are helpfully low. "Mr. Maass, I am going to make you rich beyond your wildest dreams," is equally as off-putting an opening line to a query letter as, "Shucks, Mr.

Maass, I'm no good at selling myself. Forgive my lack of professionalism." Lack of professionalism? It should be plain by now I am *not* looking for that in a potential client.

Put away your hollow hubris and your fake humility. The purpose of your query letter need only be this: To interest me in reading more of your writing. The rest will emerge in time.

Experience

Life experience? That is helpful, but what I mean is writing experience. It is a rare first manuscript that is ready to sell right out of the word processor. Truthfully, I am glad when a writer confesses to several prior efforts in the closet. It suggests the author has taken time to learn the craft of writing. Strangely enough, writers get better with practice.

That said, I must also point out that fiction calls for special skills one does not necessarily acquire while practicing other forms of writing. Some of the worst novel manuscripts my agency gets are from screenwriters. Journalists, technical writers and poets are, in my experience, no more or less apt to be salable novelists than teachers, nurses or computer game designers.

What about writing courses, teachers, mentors, MFAs? Those, too, indicate a writer is serious about craft, as does participation in a critique group, prior short story sales, rewrites based on an editor's comments and so on.

Don't have any of those things to offer me? Hmm. Why not rack up a bit more experience? What can it hurt?

Great ideas and plenty of them

Stop! Get away from that word processor! I know you are suddenly tempted to share with me the bags full of story ideas you have stored up, but do not, repeat, *do not* do it! Don't you prefer to get to know people gradually? Me, too. And that includes you and your writing.

It is much better, I can tell you, to tantalize me with *one* great idea and leave me wanting more. Gypsy Rose Lee understood that principle, I am told, and I have noticed great novelists also practice the art of the tease with their readers. Less is more, so why not start by offering me just one story idea; the one you feel is the best and most representative of your writing?

Even so, a novelist's career is almost never one book long. For me, a prospective client needs to be a fiction writer who seems to have the knack of generating great novel ideas year after year.

All right, so what *is* a great idea? Isn't that subjective? I don't think so. Have you ever said in reaction to a description of a movie, play or book, "Wow, what a great idea. Wish I'd thought of it." If you have, then you know what I mean. A great idea immediately excites. It makes one believe the story behind it must be good. It is succinct. It captures enormous conflicts in a tiny number of words. It evokes time, place, character and problem in its very essence. It is a whole but promises infinitely interesting parts.

There's a reason most agents and I like great ideas: We have to pitch. There's precious little time to get a story across to an editor on the phone, even less in a meeting with a Los Angeles producer. A hundred words or less is the goal. Can't be done? Sure it can. We do it all the time, and it's a rare story that cannot be summarized in a pithy, catchy way.

Some pitch proponents counsel the Hollywood approach: the "*Jurassic Park* meets *Jaws*" formulation. That can work, but I don't find it works well for novels. It makes them sound like movies. In my experience, it is better to find the intriguing element or the unexpected conflict, and build around it a mini-story. Here is how I pitch a mystery novel, *A Clue for the Puzzle Lady*, by my client Parnell Hall:

"Sherry is a young and beautiful puzzle genius who had trouble breaking into the world of crossword puzzle writing because she is young and beautiful, and thus was not taken seriously. So, she got her sweet-looking, gray-haired Aunt Cora to front for her as 'The Puzzle Lady.' Now they are a success. Sherry writes a nationally syndicated crossword puzzle, and Aunt Cora's picture runs with it. Sherry stays in the background; Aunt Cora makes public appearances. All would be well, except that Aunt Cora is not a sweet little old lady, but a lush, a gambler and fancies herself an amateur sleuth. When a murder takes place in their sleepy Connecticut town and the police turn to The Puzzle Lady for help, Sherry must save their puzzle empire by saving Aunt Cora from her unfortunate tendency to stir up trouble."

Okay that is 139 words, but I have made this pitch scores of times. When I do it with a bit of excitement in my voice and a sparkle in my eye, it gets people every time. Notice the pitch does not tell much of the story, but instead focuses on some key contradictions and contrasts. Sherry is a puzzle genius but is dismissed due to her beauty. Aunt Cora, who looks like a sweet little old lady, is a handful. Those contrasts are intriguing. So is the conflict: Aunt Cora wants to investigate a real-life murder, but Sherry needs to keep their puzzle empire intact.

Even when there are not such intriguing hooks to sink, most stories can nevertheless excite interest if only three teasing elements are presented: setting, protagonist, problem. Deliver those three elements succinctly and with the barest embellishment, and you will be surprised at how often people respond with, "Hey, great idea!"

Hard work, discipline, drive

Please don't overdo this one, either. Often writers spend far too many query letter paragraphs (sometimes far too many Chardonnay and Brie party minutes) telling me how important their writing is to them, how they've been writing since the age of six, how they absolutely *have* to write every day, how they have more stories ideas than they will use in a lifetime, how they're committed to doing whatever (no, really, *whatever*) it takes to succeed.

I know. I have heard all that. I take it for granted. Of course you are committed, hard working, creative, ambitious. You have to be in order to complete a novel. If you need to convince yourself you have those attributes that is one thing, but you do not need to convince me.

In any event, hard work, discipline and drive are attributes that show up in other ways. Novelists with drive read positively everything, especially authors who are like them, who may one day be their competition. They know what is good and what is bad about those authors' novels, and they can tell me passionately why they had to write their own stories the way that they did.

Their stories often spring from specific incidents, a moment or image that gripped them and would not let go. They have something urgent to say; not just a theme to "explore," but a moral conclusion to get across. They have confidence. Even big egos. (But gracious manners, the great ones.) They are funny. They are smart. They are mature. Hardworking writers with discipline and drive are writers we want to know better. They are the kind of writers I would want to spend time with even if they were not my clients.

How do I find these things out? In conversation *after* I have read their material and it's clear I have a natural storyteller on my hands. So, save all the talk about how hardworking, disciplined and driven you are until later. If your writing knocks me out, I will probably not need much convincing.

A day job

Oh, heresy! Is this really an *agent* talking? Shouldn't that heading read, "Earning Power" or even "Bestseller Potential"?

Believe it or not, when looking at prospective clients, I do not think much about money. Oh, sure, I can only work with someone if they bring me a manuscript I can sell. (And if I can sell it for tons of money, so much the better.) I do not need to see the price tag pinned to a manuscript in order to decide whether or not I want to represent it.

I am much more interested in the long term, one reason being that in most cases it takes a long time for novelists to make a comfortable living from their writing. Nothing wrong with that. That's the way it is, but how are these writers going to feed their kids in the meantime?

Ah . . . a day job.

Now hold on, you may be thinking, *isn't the idea to sell a novel immediately for as much money as possible so the publisher will put as much behind it as possible?* In some cases, yes. But the majority of novelists need to build. Overpayment for a first novel can easily result in early career death. For many writers it is better to match advances to a book's realistic future earnings. That is one way to bring a publisher back for more and give consumer word-of-mouth time to work.

The whole shebang

So, what is a literary agent looking for in a potential client? Oh, not much. Just everything: natural talent, rational business behavior, hard-won skill, great ideas, determination, discipline, drive and the means to finance the years it may take to find success.

I'll bet you feel that describes you. No doubt it does. But please remember where it all starts: on the page. Without great storytelling, none of the rest matters a damn. Give me a great story, and who knows? Maybe we are a match.

Agents & Ethics: Getting Published Without Losing Your Shirt

BY JEAN V. NAGGAR

Writing is usually a lonely occupation. When at last, after months, even years of wrestling with words and ideas, the writer types in "THE END," prints up the result of mighty labors and feels the thrill of hefting a bulky pile of crisp pages, it would seem that the Herculean task is over. Now, surely, it is merely a matter of locating the right agent, getting the right publisher interested, and the words and ideas, elegantly bound and jacketed, will appear on the shelves of bookstores everywhere.

Easy, right?

Wrong.

These days, the writer must not only create a fine work of the imagination, the aspiring writer must also learn a good deal about how the publishing business works, who the players are, and how to avoid falling into the clutches of a growing number of "agencies" and "editorial services" that survive on fees paid up front and not on commissions from a job well done. Throughout the years, hardworking, reputable literary agents have striven to distinguish their ways of doing business from the ways of the less particular.

A BRIEF HISTORY OF THE ASSOCIATION OF AUTHORS' REPRESENTATIVES

Early in the 1970s, a small group of independent literary agents who had recently moved to agenting from editorial and other positions in publishing houses, began getting together informally to network and to exchange gossip, war-stories and survival tips. The group quickly coalesced into something more formal, and it named itself the Independent Literary Agents Association (ILAA).

This energetic, proactive group of then relatively new agents operated alongside the venerable and respected Society of Authors Representatives (SAR) for some years, maintaining an independent-minded approach to reading fees as it did to other matters.

The SAR had long held its members to a code of appropriate behavior, and in time, a committee formed in the ILAA to discuss many questions of ethical behavior that came up in conversation and in practice. They discussed appropriate behaviors of member agents with each other, with their authors, and with the publishers and editors with whom they dealt. While not wishing in any way to impinge on the free and independent operation of its members, or to create a policing body, certain red-flag issues came up again and again, and the committee decided to develop a code of appropriate behavior for its members.

In 1990, the two associations joined forces and emerged as the Association of Authors' Representatives (AAR), an energized association of literary agents, committed to following high

JEAN V. NAGGAR *is the president of the Jean V. Naggar Literary Agency in New York, and has been working in publishing for 30 years. She was president of Association of Authors' Representatives from 1998 to 1999. A list of member-agents of the AAR, together with a brochure, can be obtained for $7 and a 55¢ SAE by writing to P.O. Box 237201, Ansonia Station, New York NY 10023. The AAR website is www.aar-online.org.*

standards of behavior in their professional dealings, charging no reading fees, and avoiding any situation that might introduce a conflict of interest, although it took some time for some differences in philosophy to be resolved to the satisfaction of all.

The AAR currently numbers some 350 member agents nationwide. Member agents subscribe annually to a code of ethics which is fast becoming a standard in the publishing industry, and concern themselves with following the latest developments in contracts, royalties and the optimal dispensation of all rights.

CREATING AN ETHICAL STANDARD

The Canon of Ethics that developed from this joining is signed yearly by every member of the AAR when dues are paid. It has produced high standards within an unregulated, unlicensed industry. It is notable that publishers have not developed a similar set of ethical guidelines for their behavior, nor are they likely to do so!

Briefly, the Canon of Ethics ensures the following:

- That members maintain two separate bank accounts so there is no commingling of clients' monies and the agency's operating expenses.
- That prompt disclosure and payment are made to clients regarding monies received from both domestic and foreign sales.
- That members are forbidden to charge reading fees to clients or potential clients, directly or indirectly, beyond the customary return postage charges. In an attempt to deflect potential abuses, the Ethics Committee recently extended this provision. Now, in addition, agents who belong to the AAR may not charge fees for reading manuscripts and proposals at writers' conferences.
- That members of the AAR may not receive a secret profit or enter into any arrangement regarding a client's work that might create a conflict of interest.

While providing this very unique standard of ethical behavior authors can depend upon, the AAR still affirms the total independence of its members' individual operations, adoption or rejection of author-agent agreements, commission structures and negotiations with publishers.

Sometimes, an author attempts to involve the cooperation of the Ethics Committee of the AAR in connection with a particular agent who is not an AAR member or for reasons outside the scope of the Canon of Ethics. Most of these matters, however, are not the purview of the Ethics Committee, which was never intended to be a policing body regarding general "agenting" complaints. Any complaints addressing *a member's* supposed violation of the Canon of Ethics are taken very seriously indeed, and no decision is taken without a thorough exploration of all circumstances surrounding the complaint.

COOPERATING TO KEEP UP WITH A CHANGING INDUSTRY

The AAR also works to inform and educate its agenting community on developments within the publishing industry. At present, the contractual and conceptual problems arising from new electronic technologies and the shrinking of publishing venues due to recent consolidations are taking much of the organization's attention. AAR members have formed task forces to work with publishers on these issues, and have organized forums for the discussion of cutting-edge technologies and their impact on all of us. The AAR makes sure its members are equipped with the information they need to make the decisions that best benefit their writers.

The association also appoints individual agents to act as liaisons with all the major writers' organizations. [See page 316 for a list of Professional Organizations.] They keep abreast of issues concerning these writers' communities and, in turn, inform them of AAR developments, maintaining a steady flow of information. It is more important than ever before that authors and agents share information, insights and move forward together into the changing world of today's publishing scene.

MAKING INFORMED CHOICES

Obviously, in choosing an agent, whether through the AAR list or otherwise, there are vast differences in temperament, sensibility, day-to-day practice and personal style to take into account. To gain a sense of the personalities of several agents, read John Baker's *Literary Agents: A Writer's Introduction* (Macmillan). Every writer should choose the agent best suited for her own needs and disposition. By choosing an agent who is an AAR member, a writer can be sure the agent cares about ethical standards enough to sign on to them on a yearly basis, and because admission to membership requires several recommendations and sale of a specific number of books, it also ensures that the AAR agent you approach is respected by her peers and not a fly-by-night operation.

Your writing career is worth all the advance power you can find to fuel it, and although the temptations out there are many, be advised that reputable agents rarely if ever advertise—most reputable agents obtain new clients through referrals and word of mouth. Agents also cannot make promises about getting your work published. And if your book is going to be published, a reputable publisher will be paying you an advance, not the other way around.

There is no more precious a thing than the painstaking creation of a work of the imagination. Writers are the lifeblood of the publishing industry, the only indispensable element in a continuum that links writer to reader. But the publishing industry is becoming increasingly bound by corporate politics and policies, forcing writers to seek out other kinds of feedback. Publishers are also at the mercy of the media, whose enormous hyping of superlative advances and celebrity has created its own quicksand, into which many writers founder, lured by the pot of gold at the end of the rainbow.

USING FREELANCE EDITORS

Just when technology has provided aspiring writers with wonderful tools like "spellcheck" and the ability to restructure a manuscript several times without having to retype the entire work, the publishing industry itself has chosen to batten down the hatches, jettison imprints and editors in droves and consolidate lists—all of which leave little room for the unpublished writer to slip a toe in the door.

Publishing has undergone seismic change. Mergers and consolidations have led to firings and departures of editors, and have caused a general sense of unease among those who are still employed. Departing editors are often not replaced, placing a greater burden on the shoulders of fewer editors, giving them neither the time nor the energy to take on projects that require a lot of editorial work. Unwilling to take risks that might land them among the unemployed, most people in publishing houses hold back on making decisions and choose the path of least resistance.

Consequently, many reputable and not-so-reputable individuals now offer "book-doctoring" services to evaluate material and pummel it into shape before it even reaches the critical eyes of agents and editors. Offering promises of magical editorial input, some of these self-styled "editorial services" exist solely to tease money from the hopeful and empty pockets of the uninformed. The pitfalls are many along the road to publication, and shape-shifting monsters lurk in the deep to seize the unwary and relieve them of their savings.

However, the happier side of this picture is that there *do* exist groups of seasoned professionals, working as individual freelance editors and exercising editorial skills honed from many years spent making decisions at publishing houses. Finding themselves out of a job because of new corporate groupings, they offer an important entrepreneurial opportunity within the changing landscape of the publishing industry. Some of them are beginning to coalesce into associations of their own. Others work alone. They usually do not advertise, and their services are expensive. But they are true publishing professionals and take genuine pleasure in using hard-won skills to help writers find their voices or to pull a publishable work out of chaos.

The question is, how can a writer tell which face of Janus is smiling in her direction? How do you sift the reputable from the disreputable when you live far from the centers of publishing activity and feed on hope to keep your dreams alive? When you have been rejected by an entire flotilla of agents, and someone out there offers you (for a "small" fee) the opportunity to have your manuscript read by a self-styled "professional" or better yet, offers you publication if you will come up with an "advance" toward it, could this be opportunity knocking at the door? Use the following guidelines to help you decide:

Above all, bear in mind that a reputable publisher *will pay you* for the right to publish your book and will not require you to put up your own money.

Finding Reputable Freelance Editors and Literary Agents

- ☑ Read *Publishers Weekly* for several months before you will need the services of either a book doctor or a literary agent, focusing on new agents who come out of substantial publishing (not necessarily agenting) experience.
- ☑ Attend writers' conferences, and ask around for names of freelance editors and agents with whom people have had positive experiences.
- ☑ From freelance editors, request an advance breakdown of fees before signing any contract including the cost of a reading and editorial letter and the cost of a subsequent in-depth editorial job. Beware of empty promises. A freelance editor cannot guarantee you publication.
- ☑ Ask freelance editors if they will provide samples of previous editing jobs, and discuss the level of editing you will receive for the fees you pay.
- ☑ Request a list of published writers who have worked with this editor, and try to check it out by looking at Acknowledgment pages, etc., unless you are fortunate enough to have access to one of these writers.
- ☑ Ask your librarian or local bookseller if the name of the editor you are considering is at all familiar. Librarians and booksellers read *Publishers Weekly* and attend book conventions, where they sometimes meet editors. They can also make inquiries for you and steer you toward a reputable editor.
- ☑ Familiarize yourself with what services a good agent can and should be able to provide.

The Authors Guild and other writers' organizations can provide information about editors and agents. The AAR has also moved consistently, over the years, to help prevent the abuse of authors within the ethical framework for its members. It has never been more important to be wary of golden promises. It has never been more important to enlist the help of a reputable professional.

Happily, writers are hard to discourage. I would only urge you to put as much energy and research into the "tools" with which you hope to achieve publication as you put into writing the work you hope to publish. In achieving a realistic understanding of the limitations and benefits of the publishing industry, and in gaining a sense of the names and roles of the players in that industry, you can avoid costly mistakes and make choices that lead to publication, rather than insolvency.

Understanding Fees—What Writers Must Know

Before starting your search for an agent, it is extremely important to have an understanding of the various fees some agents may charge. Most agents make their living from the commissions they receive after selling their clients' books. Some agents charge additional fees, others do not. This book separates the agency listings into two sections: nonfee-charging agents and fee-charging agents. The following explanations should help you decide which type of agent you want to approach.

Office expenses Many agents—both those who do and do not charge additional fees—ask the author to pay for photocopying, postage, long-distance phone calls, marketing and other expenses. An agent should only ask for office expenses *after* agreeing to represent the writer. These expenses should be discussed upfront, and the writer should receive an accounting for them. This money is sometimes returned upon sale of the manuscript.

Reading fees Agents who do not charge reading fees earn their money from commissions. Agencies that do charge reading fees often do so to cover the cost of additional readers or the time spent reading that could have been spent selling. This practice can save the agent time and open the agency to a larger number of submissions. Paying fees benefits writers because they know at least someone will look at their work. Whether such promises are kept depends upon the honesty of the agency. You may pay a fee and never receive a response from the agent, or you may pay someone who will not submit your manuscript to publishers. In this book, only fee-charging agents who actively make sales are included.

Reading fees vary from $25 to $500 or more. The fee is usually nonrefundable, but some agents refund the money if they take a writer on as a client or if they sell the writer's manuscript. Keep in mind, however, that payment of a reading fee does not ensure representation.

Officially, the AAR (Association of Authors' Representatives) in their Canon of Ethics prohibits members from directly or indirectly charging a reading fee, and the WGA (Writers Guild of America) does not allow WGA signatory agencies to charge a reading fee to WGA members, as stated in the WGA's Artists' Manager Basic Agreement. A signatory may charge you a fee if you are not a member, but most signatory agencies do not charge a reading fee as an across-the-board policy.

Critique fees Sometimes a manuscript will interest an agent, but he will point out areas still needing development. Some agencies offer criticism services for an additional fee. Like reading fees, payment of a critique fee does not ensure representation. When deciding if you will benefit from having someone critique your manuscript, keep in mind that the quality and quantity of comments vary widely. The critique's usefulness will depend on the agent's knowledge of the market. Also be aware that an agent who spends a significant portion of his time commenting on manuscripts will have less time to actively market work he currently represents.

Some agents refer writers to freelance editors or "book doctors." Make sure you research any critiquing service before sending your work, and don't be charmed by fancy brochures and compliments about your writing. Also beware of agents who hurriedly refer you to editorial services. While it is not illegal to make a referral, some agents may abuse this practice.

The WGA has a rule preventing their signatories from making referrals to book doctors, and the AAR frowns on them as well if the agent is receiving financial compensation for making the referral. The WGA believes that, while an agent may have good intentions, it would be too difficult to differentiate those agents trying to help writers from those who have a financial or professional interest in an editing relationship that develops at their suggestion.

Finding the Right Agent: What Every Writer Needs to Know

BY DONYA DICKERSON

A writer's job is to write. A literary agent's job is to find publishers for her clients' books. Any writer who has endeavored to attract the attention of a publishing house knows this is no easy task. But beyond selling manuscripts, an agent must keep track of the ever-changing industry, writers' royalty statements, fluctuating reading habits, and the list continues.

Because publishing houses receive more unsolicited manuscripts each year, securing an agent is becoming more of a necessity. Nevertheless, finding an eager *and* reputable agent is a difficult task. Even the most patient of writers can become frustrated, even disillusioned. Therefore, as a writer seeking agent representation, you should prepare yourself before starting your search. By learning effective strategies for approaching agents, as well as what to expect from an author/agent relationship, you will save yourself time—and quite possibly, heartache. This article provides the basic information on literary agents and how to find one that's best for your writing career.

AN AGENT'S JOB

To start with, agents must find talented clients. And agents are almost always looking for new writers, searching eagerly for the next John Grisham or Danielle Steel. Nevertheless, before an agent will represent you, she must believe in your writing and know an audience exists somewhere who is interested in what you write. You will want an agent who will be sincere when she tells editors your manuscript is the best thing to land on her desk this year.

Knowing editors' tastes and needs

An agent must possess information on a complex web of publishing houses and a multitude of editors to make sure a manuscript is placed in the hands of the right editor. This knowledge is gathered through her relationships with acquisition editors—the people who decide which books to present to their publisher for possible publication. Through her industry connections, an agent not only helps get her clients' work read faster but also learns each editor's specific needs and tastes. A good agent is acutely aware of the specializations of each publishing house and its imprints, knowing that one publisher only wants contemporary romances while another is interested solely in nonfiction books about the military. By networking with editors, an agent also learns more specialized information—which editor is looking for a crafty Agatha Christie-style mystery for the fall catalog, for example.

Tracking changes in publishing

Being attentive to constant market changes and vacillating trends is also a major requirement of an agent's job. She understands what it may mean for her clients when publisher A merges with publisher B and when an editor from house C moves to house D. Or what it means when readers—and therefore editors—are no longer interested in westerns, but instead can't get their hands on enough Stephen King-style suspense novels.

Understanding contracts

When publishers write contracts, they are primarily interested in their own bottom line rather than the best interests of the author. Writers unfamiliar with contractual language may find themselves trapped in a situation that binds them to a publisher with whom they no longer want to work or that prevents them from getting royalties on their first novel until they have written several books. An agent uses his experience to negotiate a contract that benefits the writer while still respecting some of the publisher's needs.

Negotiating subsidiary rights

Beyond publication, a savvy agent keeps in mind other opportunities for your manuscript. If your agent believes your book will also be successful as an audio book, a Book-of-the-Month club selection or even a blockbuster movie, she will take these options into consideration when shopping your manuscript. These additional mediums for your writing are called "subsidiary rights," and part of an agent's job is to keep track of the strengths and weaknesses of different publishers' subsidiary rights offices to determine the deposition of these rights to your work. For more information on specific subsidiary rights, see Making More from Subsidiary Rights on page 45.

Tracking payments

Because an agent only receives payment when the publisher pays the writer, it is in her best interest to make sure the writer is paid on schedule. Some publishing houses are notorious for late payments. Having an agent distances you from any conflict over payment and allows you to spend your time writing instead of on the phone.

Getting your manuscript read faster

Although it may seem like an extra step to send your manuscript to an agent instead of directly to a publishing house, the truth is an agent can prevent writers from wasting months sending manuscripts to the wrong places or being buried in someone's slush pile. Editors rely on agents to save them time as well. With little time to sift through the hundreds of unsolicited submissions arriving weekly in the mail, an editor is naturally going to prefer a work that has already been approved by a qualified reader. For this reason, many of the larger publishers accept agented submissions only.

MAKE SURE YOU ARE READY FOR AN AGENT

With an agent's job in mind, you should ask yourself if you and your work are at a stage where you need an agent. Look at the Ten Step Checklists for Fiction and Nonfiction Writers on the following pages, and judge how prepared you are for contacting an agent. Have you spent enough time researching or polishing your manuscript? Sending an agent an incomplete project not only wastes your time but may turn him off in the process. Literary agents are not magicians. An agent cannot sell an unsaleable property. He cannot solve your personal problems. He will not be your banker, CPA, social secretary or therapist. Instead, he will endeavor to sell your book because that is how he earns his living.

Moreover, your material may not be appropriate for an agent. Most agents do not represent poetry, magazine articles, short stories, or material suitable for academic or small presses—the commission earned does not justify spending time submitting these works. Those agents who do take on such material generally represent authors on larger projects first and send out these smaller items only as a favor for their clients.

If you strongly believe your work is ready to be placed with an agent, make sure you are personally ready to be represented. In other words, before you contact an agent, consider the direction in which your writing career is headed. Besides skillful writers, agencies want clients with the ability to produce more than one book. Most agents will say they represent careers, not

---

Before You Contact An Agent:
A Ten-Step Checklist for Fiction Writers

☑ **Finish your novel** or short story collection. An agent can do nothing for fiction without a finished product.

☑ **Revise your novel.** Have other writers offer criticism to ensure your manuscript is as finished as you believe possible.

☑ **Proofread.** Don't let your hard work go to waste by turning off an agent with typos or poor grammar.

☑ **Publish** short stories or novel excerpts in literary journals, proving to potential agents that editors see quality in your writing.

☑ **Research** to find the agents of writers you admire or whose work is similar to your own.

☑ **Use the indexes** in this book to construct a list of agents open to new writers and looking for your type of fiction (i.e., literary, romance, mystery).

☑ **Rank your list.** Use the listings in this book to determine the agents most suitable for you and your work, and to eliminate inappropriate agencies.

☑ **Write your synopsis.** Completing this step early will help you write your query letter and save you time later when agents contact you.

☑ **Compose your query letter.** As an agent's first impression of you, this brief letter should be polished and to the point.

☑ **Read about the business** of agents so you are knowledgeable and prepared to act on any offer.

---

books. So as you compose your query letter—your initial contact with an agent—mention your potential. Let an agent know if you've already started drafting your second novel. Let him know that for you writing is more than a half-hearted hobby.

THE IMPORTANCE OF RESEARCH

Nobody would buy a used car without at least checking the odometer, and the savvy shopper would consult a buyer's guide, take a test drive, and even ask for a mechanic's opinion. Because you want to obtain the best possible agent for your writing, you should do some research on the business of agents before sending out query letters. Understanding how agents operate will help you find an agent appropriate for your work, as well as know the types of agents to avoid.

We often receive complaints from writers regarding agents *after* the writer has already lost money or their work is tied into a contract with an ineffective agent. If they'd put the same amount of effort into researching agents as they did writing their manuscript, they would have saved themselves unnecessary grief.

The best way to educate yourself is to read all you can about agents and other authors. The articles in this book will give you insight not only on how to contact an agent but also how the author/agent relationship works. Organizations such as the Association of Authors' Representatives (AAR), the National Writers Union (NWU), American Society of Journalists and Authors (ASJA), and Poets & Writers, Inc. all have informational material on agenting. (These, along with other helpful organizations, are listed in the back of this book.) *Publishers Weekly* covers publishing news affecting agents and others in the publishing industry in general; discusses specific events in the "Hot Deals" and "Behind the Bestsellers" columns; and occasionally lists individual authors' agents in the "Forecasts" section.

Even the Internet has a wide-range of sites devoted to agents. Through the different forums provided on the web, you can learn basic information about preparing for your initial contact

> ### Before You Contact An Agent:
> ### A Ten-Step Checklist for Nonfiction Writers
>
> ☑ **Formulate a concrete idea** for your book. Sketch a brief outline making sure you have enough material for an entire book-length manuscript.
>
> ☑ **Research** works on similar topics to understand the competition and determine how yours is unique.
>
> ☑ **Compose sample chapters.** This step should indicate how much time you will need to finish and if your writing needs editorial help.
>
> ☑ **Publish** completed chapters in journals. This validates your work to agents and provides writing samples for later in the process.
>
> ☑ **Polish your outline** to refer to while drafting a query letter and avoid wasting time when agents contact you.
>
> ☑ **Brainstorm** three to four subject categories that best describe your material.
>
> ☑ **Use the indexes in this book** to find agents interested in at least two of your subject areas and looking for new clients.
>
> ☑ **Rank your list.** Narrow your list further by reading the listings of agencies you found in the indexes; organize the list according to your preferences.
>
> ☑ **Write your query.** Describe your premise and your experience professionally and succinctly, to give an agent an excellent first impression of you.
>
> ☑ **Read about the business** of agents so you are knowledgeable and prepared to act on any offer.

or more specific material about individual agents. Keep in mind, however, that not everything printed on the web is a solid fact; you may come across the site of a writer who is bitter because an agent rejected his manuscript. Your best bet is to use the Internet to supplement your other research. For particularly useful sites, refer to the Websites of Interest on page 322.

Through your research, you will discover the need to be wary of some agents. Anybody can go to the neighborhood copy center and order business cards which say she is a literary agent. But that title does not mean she can sell your book. She may ask for a large sum of money, then disappear from society. Becoming knowledgeable about the different types of fees agents may charge is a *crucial* step to take before contacting any agent. Before paying any type of fee, read Understanding Fees—What Writers Must Know on page 15 and the introduction to the Literary Agents: Fee-charging section on page 197.

An agent also may not have any connections with others in the publishing industry. An agent's reputation with editors can be her major strength or weakness. While it's true that even top agents are not able to sell every book they represent, an inexperienced agent who submits too many inappropriate submissions will quickly lose her standing with any editor. It is acceptable to ask an agent for recent sales before she agrees to represent you, but keep in mind that some agents consider this information confidential. If an agent does give you a list of recent sales, you can call the publishers' contracts department to ensure the sale was actually made by that agent.

THE PROS AND CONS OF LOCATION

For years, the major editors and agents were located in New York. If a writer wanted to be published with a big name house, he had to contact a New York agency. But this has changed over time for many reasons. For starters, publishing companies are appearing all over the country—San Francisco, Seattle, Chicago, Minneapolis. And naturally, agents are locating closer to these smaller publishing hubs.

The recent advances in technology have also had an impact on the importance of location. Thanks to fax machines, e-mail, express mail and inexpensive long-distance telephone rates, it's no longer necessary for an agent to live in New York to work closely with a New York publisher. Besides, if a manuscript is truly excellent, a smart editor will not care where the agent lives.

Nevertheless, there are simply more opportunities for agents located in New York to network with editors. They are able to meet face-to-face over lunch. The editor can share his specific needs, and the agent can promote her newest talent. As long as New York remains the publishing capital of the world, the majority of agents will be found there, too.

CONTACTING AGENTS

Once your manuscript is prepared and you have a solid understanding of how literary agents work, the time is right to contact an agent. Your initial contact is the first impression you make on an agent; therefore, you want to be professional and brief.

Because approaching agents is an important topic, we've included several articles on contacting agents in this book: Ways to Contact a Literary Agent on page 31; Targeting Agents: Make the Best Fit With an Agent Who Knows Your Market on page 22; A Checklist for Inquiries and Submissions on page 33; Queries That Made It Happen on page 35; and Outline and Synopsis Workshop on page 40. Follow the advice in these articles when you are making that all-important first contact.

EVALUATE ANY OFFER

Once you've received an offer of representation, you must determine if the agent is right for you. As flattering as any offer may be, you need to be confident that you are going to work well with this person and that this person is going to work hard to sell your manuscript.

You need to know what you should expect once you enter into a business relationship. You should know how much editorial input to expect from your agent; how often she gives updates about where your manuscript has been and who has seen it; and what subsidiary rights the agent represents.

More importantly, you should know when you will be paid. The publisher will send your advance and any subsequent royalty checks directly to the agent. After deducting her commission—usually 10 to 15 percent—your agents will send you the remaining balance. Most agents charge a higher commission of 20 to 25 percent when using a co-agent for foreign, dramatic, or other specialized rights. As you enter into a relationship with an agent, ask for an explanation of her specific commission rates and payment policy.

As your potential partner, you have the right to ask an agent for information that convinces you she knows what she's doing. Be reasonable about what you ask, however. Asking for recent sales is okay; asking for the average size of clients' advances is not. A list of the AAR's suggested questions can be found on page 53. An agent's answers should help you make your decision. If you are polite and she responds with anger or contempt, that tells you something you need to know about what working together would be like.

Evaluate the agent's level of experience. Agencies that have been in the business a while have a larger number of contacts, but new agencies may be hungrier, as well as more open to previously unpublished writers. Talk to other writers about their interactions with specific agents. Writers' organizations such as the National Writers Association (NWA), the American Society of Journalists and Authors (ASJA), and the National Writers Union (NWU) maintain files on agents their members have dealt with, and can share this information by written request or through their membership newsletters.

UNDERSTAND ANY CONTRACT BEFORE YOU SIGN

Some agents offer written contracts, some do not. If your prospective agent does not, at least ask for a "memorandum of understanding" that details the basic relationship of expenses and commissions. If your agent does offer a contract, be sure to read it carefully, and keep a copy for yourself.

The National Writers Union (NWU) has drafted a Preferred Literary Agent Agreement and a pamphlet, *Understand the Author-Agent Relationship*, which is available to members. (Membership is $74 and open to all writers actively pursuing a writing career. See the Resources section on page 316 for their address.) The union suggests clauses that delineate such issues as:

☑ The scope of representation (One work? One work with the right of refusal on the next? All work completed in the coming year? All work completed until the agreement is terminated?)

☑ The extension of authority to the agent to negotiate on behalf of the author

☑ Compensation for the agent, and any co-agent, if used

☑ Manner and time frame for forwarding monies received by the agent on behalf of the client

☑ Termination clause, allowing client to give about 30 days to terminate the agreement

☑ The effect of termination on concluded agreements as well as ongoing negotiations

☑ Arbitration in the event of a dispute between agent and client

IF THINGS DON'T WORK OUT

Because this is a business relationship, it is possible that a time may come when it is beneficial for you and your agent to part ways. Unlike a marriage, you don't need to go through counseling to keep the relationship together. Instead, you end it professionally on terms upon which you both agree.

First check to see if your written agreement spells out any specific procedures. If not, write a brief, businesslike letter, stating that you no longer think the relationship is advantageous and you wish to terminate it. Instruct the agent not to make any new submissions, and give her a 30- to 60-day limit to continue as representative on submissions already under consideration. You can ask for a list of all publishers who have rejected your unsold work, as well as a list of those who are currently considering it. If your agent has made sales for you, she will continue to receive those monies from the publisher, deduct her commission and remit the balance to you. A statement and your share of the money should be sent to you within 30 days. You can also ask that all manuscripts in her possession be returned to you.

FINAL THOUGHTS

Finding an agent is a challenge, but if you want a commercially successful book, it may be a necessary task. Selecting an agent is a task which deserves a lot of time and careful consideration. Above all, it is important to find a person whom you trust and who believes in your work. And now that you know the steps to take to find a literary agent, get started on the right foot and select the right agent for you.

Targeting Agents: Make the Best Fit with an Agent Who Knows Your Market

BY DONYA DICKERSON

As a writer, you are probably familiar with the idea of targeting publishers—identifying a press's interests and successful areas, and sending your work to the appropriate place. You may not realize, however, that you should target agents in the same way. You would never send a science fiction manuscript to a religious publisher, so why send a romance novel to an agent who only represents self-help nonfiction?

There are many benefits to targeting agents. First, you'll save valuable time and effort when sending out query letters. Second, you'll connect with someone who has established relationships with the editors interested in your particular field; who knows the current state of your genre; and who is sensitive to other nuances of your kind of writing.

How do you find an agent appropriate for your manuscript? For starters, refer to the **Agents Specialties Index** following each section of listings in this book. These indexes organize agencies according to the subjects they are interested in receiving. Then, check the individual listings in this book. Under the subhead **Represents**, agents indicate their areas of specialization for both nonfiction and fiction.

If there is a writer whose work is similar to yours, you can find her agent (if she used an agent) by calling her publisher's Contracts Department. Or check the Acknowledgments page of books similar in topic or tone to your manuscript—many writers include their agents' names in their public thank-yous.

Look at the listings in this book for the five agents below, and you'll see that they are specialists. The Virginia Kidd Agency, where James Allen is president, is known for its science fiction and fantasy authors. Pam Hopkins of Hopkins Literary Associates handles only writers of romance and women's fiction. Though his agency is not limited to the suspense/mystery genre, Philip G. Spitzer still considers it one of his main areas. Denise Marcil's agency has a strong emphasis on self-help and self-improvement titles. And Claudia Cross, a member of the larger, more generalized William Morris Agency, represents many of their Christian authors.

For agents, limiting the areas they'll represent has practical consequences. "I handle topics that interest me, and I know the field," explains Marcil. "I have a sense of the competitive books out there in my different areas. I don't think it's essential to specialize, but it makes the job easier. From attracting authors who do those specific topics to focusing on the editors in the houses who buy that type of book—it's a more efficient way to do business."

While some agencies consider any subject, most agents represent a narrow list of specialties. Larger agencies often represent a broad spectrum of material, dividing areas according to each member agent's interests. If you are interested in exploring multiple genres, having separate agents for each area is not necessary. According to Allen, "Most agents expect and require exclusivity with their clients. There are exceptions—like the nuclear physicist who writes within his career field and also writes men's action adventure. Such a person could make use of two agents and plan to market that different genre work under a pseudonym."

In the following roundtable, the agents interviewed not only discuss the importance of targeting agents, but they also share their knowledge of the current state of their areas of specialization. While reading, keep in mind that if you choose your agent carefully, you'll have someone who tracks the ups and downs of your genre, follows your competition and, most importantly, knows the editors who will buy your manuscript. By selecting wisely, you could form a relationship with an agent that lasts your entire career.

JAMES ALLEN, Virginia Kidd Agency, Inc.
Science Fiction and Fantasy Markets

Do science fiction and fantasy writers have a better chance of getting published if they use an agent?

Getting read without an agent is hard. It may sound like I'm puffing agents, but I'm not. It's the publishers making the decisions. It is difficult to find a publishing house that—as policy—will look at unrepresented work. I can remember being shocked better than a decade ago when Bantam Books announced that it—a paperback house—would only look at agented material for their science fiction line. And now, as paperback houses are getting attached to hardcover houses and conglomerates, it is the almost solid rule rather than exception that publishers require agents to be involved.

How have the science fiction and fantasy markets changed in recent years?

As with the rest of publishing, the conglomeration of genre publishing through mergers has gone far toward killing the concept of midlist. With more of the established houses being taken over by faceless corporations, the look to the bottom line has been stronger than ever. However, I see this being balanced out by the slow but steady emergence of small, specialty presses. Also, with the increase in technologies, there is a real burgeoning and growth of alternative "publication." It's a case of publishing still being healthy but changing direction.

Does that mean it is currently easier for a new or an established writer to sell work?

Authors who are known to be big sellers continue to sell well. There is also room to let in new people on the grounds that you have to pay them less up front. The midlist authors are finding it harder to sell new work. I'm seeing trends where houses will give a first timer two shots, maybe three. If there is not a breakout within those three books, they won't pick up number four. In days gone by they would have said, "We will keep on publishing him because if we don't pay him too much he'll do okay."

How do you see the current marketplace for science fiction and fantasy?

Still strong. There is something of a return to "the sense of wonder" type of stories—not tedious old space opera—but the sense of wonder that was central to stories when science fiction was truly new at the beginning of the century. There is not a current special focus that would compare to the effect Stephen King had on the horror genre. Thanks to him everybody had a horror line for awhile, and then they died. And everybody was doing cyberpunk thanks to William Gibson, and that got passé. A narrowly focused concept becomes old fast. There is just so much you can do in a ten-by-ten-foot room, no matter how cool that room is. You can do so much more on a football field. At present there is no ten-by-ten-foot room. We're back to our football field, and everything is wide open.

PAM HOPKINS, Hopkins Literary Associates
Romance Market

Does a romance writer need an agent?

There's a difference of opinion. Many people believe you can do it yourself if you write for one of the category houses like Harlequin or Silhouette. In terms of having access to and an understanding of the market, an agent is always going to be able to provide that and career guidance as well.

Do new or established writers have a better chance in this genre?

I'm not sure today's market favors one over the other. A few years ago, I would have told you an established writer definitely had the edge, but these days, publishing houses are also anxious to start establishing newer voices.

Do romance writers have a better chance of starting a career writing single titles or series?

You can build a career in women's fiction either way. There are many authors who started in category, built a readership and then moved to single titles. They took their readers with them. In other cases, writers had their first sales in single titles and built equally successful careers.

What advice do you have for someone trying to break in to the romance market?

There are a lot of people writing romance and women's fiction so the competition is for a limited number of slots available at each publisher. It is important to target your market, especially if you are writing category romance. You must understand what each line is looking for and write appropriately for that line. The same can be true for single titles; reading extensively from a publisher's list will help you understand what it might be most interested in. You'll get an editor's attention much faster if you send a submission that fits what her house publishes.

How is the current marketplace for romance?

Romance continues to be a strong market in both the contemporary and historical genres. Unlike some other genres, it has not been as affected by the swings of publishing but has remained steady over the last few years. This steadiness is evidenced by statistics provided by the Romance Writers of America indicating that romance novels constitute 40 percent of all popular fiction purchased in the United States.

PHILIP G. SPITZER, Philip G. Spitzer Literary Agency
Suspense and Mystery Markets

Do you think it's necessary for a writer in the mystery/suspense genre to have an agent?

It's a question of getting the book to the best editor for that particular book. It's difficult for writers to keep track of mergers like Dell and Bantam combining—that's going to change a lot.

What qualities do you look for in mystery/suspense submissions?

If a book is well written and character driven, I will tend to want to represent it even knowing it will take me two or three times as long to sell it as it would a plot-driven suspense novel. The market is more plot driven now. Publishers publish down to the reading public, as if they would be less inclined to buy a well-written novel over one that is simplistic. I think that's totally false.

Are there any other trends in the suspense/mystery genre?

Everything is so confused right now. I don't think there are any trends and that's part of what is confusing. Publishers want bestsellers, but nobody knows what they want from a critical point of view. I've never believed in trends. As soon as you have a book that fits a particular trend, the trend is gone. I discourage any writer from writing to a trend.

Is it easier for a new writer or an established writer to sell their work now?

It's easier to sell a first novel than to sell a book by somebody with a poor track record. I have a very good writer whose novel I'm trying to sell now. Two editors said they wanted to buy it, but then they checked on the sales of his last book. The sales were not great in spite of the good reviews. The editors didn't make an offer.

How is the current market for mystery/suspense?

It's very good. Everybody is looking for something new and different, although they often end up publishing the same things.

How do you advise writers who are trying to break into the suspense market?

Don't write to the market, but write the best possible book you can. I've had many experiences seeing writers write to a market or trying to conform to other books that have been successful. The books aren't as good because their hearts weren't in it. I say write the way you want to write.

DENISE MARCIL, The Denise Marcil Literary Agency, Inc.
Self-help and Self-improvement Markets

Is it necessary for a writer wanting to publish in the self-help/self-improvement market to have an agent?

It's always easier if you have an agent. The idea is that an agent knows which editors buy what type of book. There are a number of houses that won't accept unagented submissions. But some houses do buy books directly from the author.

What are currently the hottest subjects?

Health, alternative health—particularly with baby boomers aging—parenting, spiritual self-help. Books for people who are seeking inner peace have surged.

What do you look for in self-help/self-improvement books?

A fresh topic that hasn't been written on extensively or new information on a topic, and an author who has an extensive national outreach. Writers can't be just an expert in the area. They have to be on a seminar circuit, have workshops or regular media exposure, or be able to sell their book long after publication. That's what publishers want these days.

Is it easier for a new or an established writer to sell a book in your field?

A new writer without a track record, and with a good idea and national exposure is easier to sell than someone with a bad track record. We're in a business controlled by computers. Publishers call the bookstore buyers and ask how so-and-so is selling or how a similar book did. It's all numbers.

Is nonfiction easier to sell than fiction?

Absolutely. Publishers think nonfiction is more straightforward. It's easier to quantify who the audience is for nonfiction. It's easier for publishers to do a search on Amazon.com and Books in Print for similar books published. You can't do that with fiction. There's an apprehension on the part of publishers about fiction—what's going to sell?

Are self-help and self-improvement books and health titles growing in popularity?

I've been selling these types of books for 20 years, and I've never seen their popularity wane. I've seen certain areas suddenly become more popular, then overpublished, then no longer popular. But, for me, it's always been a strong area.

CLAUDIA CROSS, William Morris Agency
Christian and Spirituality Markets

Is it becoming more necessary for a writer to have an agent in the Christian market?

Yes. In the past not every author writing for the Christian market had an agent. Now, however, there are more agents who represent these authors. In general, publishers are relying more on agents to determine the potential quality of a manuscript of book project.

Has the religious market changed in recent years? Are there current trends?

It's becoming more sophisticated. Publishers in the Christian market are looking for bigger books, better writing, more high-concept thrillers. The religious reader is also becoming more savvy and is looking for certain kinds of books. For example, I represent an author named Penelope Stokes who exemplifies where the market is going. In the past, she had written a historical fiction series, aimed at women. Her current book, *The Blue Bottle Club* (Word Publishing), is the story of four women. When they're about to graduate from high school they write down their desires—where they think they'll be, what they think they'll do—and put them in a blue bottle. They forget about it and go about their own lives. A number of years later a journalist comes upon this blue bottle. She tracks down the women who are in their late 60s and discovers what they've done with their lives. It's a great concept for a book.

You represent both fiction and nonfiction. Which is currently easier to sell?

Celebrity nonfiction sells well if the celebrity is well known and has an inspiring story to share. Fiction in the Christian market continues to sell well, especially for authors with proven track records. I do think, however, that selling fiction by a first-time writer is getting increasingly difficult.

Is it easier for new or established writers to sell their books?

It is easier to sell work by an established writer. Publishers are more cautious these days when making acquisition decisions.

When you look at a manuscript that comes in, do you consider the secular market?

Definitely. I read a manuscript with an open mind and let the writing, the author's approach and content determine the appropriate market and publisher. There's a fine line between the two markets, but, in general, writers for the Christian market write about faith as an integral part of the plot to encourage readers in their own Christian belief, as opposed to spiritual seeking, which would fit into the general market.

Should a writer consider the broad audience when writing?

I think writers should just write. And depending on where their passion leads them, we'll figure out where their work fits.

Ten Qualities of a Good Agent

BY LORI PERKINS

Finding an agent is a difficult task. Working with the agent you've found is also something you and your agent have to negotiate over time if the relationship is to be truly successful and rewarding for both of you. The following are ten basic skills and relationship expectations that your agent should satisfy for you. If you feel any of them are being seriously fumbled, you should talk with your agent about them—unless they are so serious you decide to leave.

1) Your agent will get back to you within 24 to 48 hours, if it's necessary

When I attend writers' conferences, I am always asked, "Why doesn't my agent return my phone calls?" or "How long should I wait to hear from my agent?"

If the agent in question has agreed to represent you and is not merely someone you hope might represent you, this is a legitimate gripe. Your agent should get back to you regarding any questions or information you might have about submissions, contracts, rights sales, possible future books, and even writerly gossip you've heard. However, if your agent has not gotten back to you because you've sent her something to read, it's probably because she hasn't read it yet. Sometimes she'll have her assistant call you back, or she'll leave you a phone message or send an e-mail.

The agent workload is often colossal. Sometimes we have five existing clients in crisis mode and a major submission going to auction. There's often little time to get back to someone immediately for hand-holding, but we do manage to return important phone calls.

Sometimes your agent has an exceptionally hectic personal life, and she can't get to things as quickly as you would like. A good agent will clue you in to situations before they happen (if she's having elective surgery, going on vacation, or there's an illness in her family). You should be understanding if this is a not a permanent condition. If you're going to be working with someone for a long time, you both will have life crises and joys that will slow you down occasionally.

Sometimes it seems as though your agent is never in the office. Most good agents will tell you their office hours, but you can't expect to reach your agent during nonbusiness hours. A lot of agents take a weekly reading day when they're not in the office (Fridays tend to be the day of choice), and they prefer not to do regular business on that day so they can catch up with their reading workload. If there's a real catastrophe or someone makes an offer on your book, your agent will get back to you, but otherwise you'll have to wait until Monday.

LORI PERKINS *is the founding partner in Perkins, Rubie & Associates, a New York literary agency. She has been a literary agent for 15 years. She is currently team-teaching a class on agenting at NYU's Center for Publishing. Prior to becoming an agent, she was the publisher of* The Uptown Dispatch, *a Manhattan newspaper. She is the author of* The Cheapskate's Guide to Entertaining: How to Throw Fabulous Parties on a Modest Budget *(Carol Publishing). This article is excerpted from* The Insider's Guide to Finding and Keeping an Agent *copyright © by Lori Perkins. Used with permission of Writer's Digest Books, a division of F&W Publications, Inc.*

2) Your agent responds to your work in a timely manner

This is a hard issue to grapple with because most writers feel their agents and editors don't get back to them quickly enough. Even though they know their agent has other clients, they still feel their work should take priority.

If you've sent your agent a brief amount of work (a proposal or three chapters), she should get back to you in two weeks, unless she's out of town or in a crisis of her own. However, it's hard to budget time for full manuscripts, and as long as she lets you know your work is on her schedule, she is doing her job.

Sometimes there's a system or schedule she's working under that puts your book on the back burner, such as she's already selling one vampire novel and wants to place that novel before sending out yours. While this might not be what you want to hear, she's justified in saying she can't send both out at the same time and in waiting until the first one places before reading yours.

3) Your agent knows your genre

This quality is extremely important to your career. Having an agent who isn't well read in the genre in which you're writing makes it much harder to place your work. You may think your work is being taken seriously, only to find your novel is resoundingly rejected because it has the same plot as one of Danielle Steel's novels, but your agent hasn't read Steel, so both you and she didn't know that. (Of course, you should know your genre, too.)

If she's well read in your genre, she may also be able to tell you if something in your novel will just not sell, such as it's set in a prison or that young adult books rarely deal with teen suicide. You can then make changes before the book goes out.

4) Your agent has good contacts and a good reputation in the field

If your agent is respected by the editors in your subject area, your work will be read quicker than the work of other agents who do not have such a positive reputation. If she knows the tastes of individual editors, what they're buying and how much she can expect the book to go for, you're way ahead of the game.

If you ask editors about your agent, you may be surprised to learn that they have less than glowing things to say about her. But the important thing is whether or not they respect her.

Your agent also must have good business contacts with agents in foreign countries, as well as Hollywood agents.

5) Your agent gets your work out there

If your agent tells you your work is on submission, it should be on submission. Unless it's an option, or an exclusive, there should be three copies of your novel making the rounds and five to ten copies of your nonfiction proposal being looked at by editors. She also should follow up the submissions on a regular basis.

If you've sent your agent a number of projects, and they're all in the same genre, she won't be able to send them all out at the same time. She has to give editors the chance to turn down one book before she sends them another one by the same author.

She may also tell you she has another project out with the same group of editors your work will be going to, so she has to wait a while before sending out your material.

There are certain times of the year when your agent may decide to hold back on a project. These times include the Thanksgiving to New Year's slow down, and the months of July and August when everything in the business takes longer. The few times when I've submitted material at this time (because I allowed an author's enthusiasm or financial need to sway me from what I know would be best for his book), I've always regretted it.

6) Your agent has time to give you solid career planning and feedback

You have to decide what you want from your career, and you should be re-evaluating where you are with every contract you sign. It's not your agent's job to tell you where you should be headed, nevertheless she may have some suggestions for your career.

You should be comfortable bouncing ideas off of your agent, and she should give you honest, thoughtful reactions to your book concepts and career goals. You should listen to your agent because she does have a wider perspective on the publishing industry, but ultimately, you have to trust your own judgment.

I recommend never writing a book you don't want to write or will be embarrassed about later on in your career—even if your agent and editor think it will be an instant bestseller. To thine own self be true. While neither one of them will be happy with your decision, they should continue to respect you. After all, it's only one book in their publishing career (they can get someone else to write it if it's such a great idea), and they will have hundreds, if not thousands of books under their belts, while you will have much fewer.

7) You feel your agent understands your needs

Your agent can't understand your needs if you don't tell them to her. Some authors are hesitant to say they'd like concurrent, multiple book contracts so they can write fulltime in two years; or they need extra money this year because their oldest daughter is getting married. They just cross their fingers and hope this year will be better than the last one.

I have been successful in getting extra book contracts for every author of mine who has told me he needed it for a reason in the future (not within a week). Sometimes the writing jobs haven't been as fulfilling as he wanted, but a good agent can usually get you the work, if you tell your agent ahead of time.

Sometimes my authors have told me that even though they are successful in their nonfiction field, what they really want to do is write fiction. It's hard for someone making $100,000 a book to realize they may have to start all over again with fiction and get an advance as low as $5,000 (they may get more because of the success of their nonfiction books, but you can't count on that). Once we've established this fact, I'm willing to work with them to get the novel into shape. Often this shift means relearning the craft of writing because fiction takes different crafting skills than nonfiction. This relearning can be hard on the ego of someone who is a successful writer in another arena, but if they're willing to do the work, I am willing to do my part.

Sometimes a successful genre novelist will tell me he wants to write a more commercial out-of-genre novel or a literary novel, or he wants to go from mass market to hardcover. If the book has promise, I'll work with him to get it to the level he wants. There's no guarantee we will succeed, but I will always give it my best shot.

8) Your agent should believe in you as a writer for the long term

I know of a literary agent who changes writers as often as the color of her nail polish. She would sell a book for a lot of money, and if the book didn't earn out (which it usually didn't), the writer's option would be declined and his career would be close to over. He would go to another agent, who would have to grow his career from the ground up, if she could.

I vowed not to be that kind of agent. I want to work with my authors for the long haul and see their careers grow with mine.

Now this may sound good if you have no book contract, but the down side to this idea is that an agent who wants to work with you for the long term will be thinking about whether your book will earn out. With this in mind, it's not the best thing in the world to get such a large advance for the book that your sales are disappointing. Even if the book sells 60,000 copies in hardcover, if the publisher paid $250,000 for the book, that's a disaster for the publisher.

While I have never turned down a large advance, there's a point at which I start growing nervous for my authors. We had one situation where a 24-year-old first-time author had been offered $200,000. We had another house interested in him, and we could have gotten more money, but this figure was the high reaches of what we could expect his novels to earn. We didn't want him to be a one- or two-book wonder, so we told him this was enough money from the best editor for his book.

On a separate first book I sold, I was told by another agent that I could have gotten a substantial amount more for it. I knew this book alone had changed the author's tax bracket, and that too much more would go directly to the I.R.S. The book earned out and eventually (over four years) earned the additional money the other agent had said it would, but as far as the publishing industry was concerned, my author was a glowing success. We used her strong sales figures to get book contracts over the next ten years earning her more than a million dollars. I doubt she would have had as long a career if we had started at advances too high for the books.

9) Your relationship with your agent is an honest one

If you don't trust your agent or you can't tell your agent what's on your mind, your relationship is doomed. Just as you have to be honest with your lawyer and your accountant, you have to tell your agent what she needs to know.

You also have to be comfortable enough to tell her if something is not working. This doesn't necessarily mean the relationship has to end. Perhaps the two of you can work out a compromise that will improve the relationship.

After representing one of my authors for a few books, she asked if she could discuss something that was bothering her. She said my unbridled enthusiasm for her work and my detailed plans for where I thought I was going to sell it were great, but when things didn't work out, she felt depressed and disappointed. I realized that for her, it was not the best thing for me to say I was going to sell the work here or there, but to just tell her I would send it out right away with enormous enthusiasm. I also explained to her that in order for me to send the work out, I had to believe it would sell to that editor or publisher or magazine. We've worked together for years since then, and I have kept this situation in mind when dealing with other authors as well. Her thoughtful comment actually made me a better agent.

10) You genuinely like and respect your agent, and you believe she feels the same way about you

You don't have to love your agent, but you should like and respect her as a person, not just as an agent. This attitude will make it easier for you to bring up tough subjects and to feel you deserve some of her time.

Some authors choose agents because they are high powered in the publishing industry. They are impressed by what an agent has done for some big-name author and expect the same treatment. But if they don't have the same kind of high-profile career as the established author, they will be second- or third-tier authors on her list. It may be impossible to get her on the phone.

Some agents have a reputation for tenacity and even bitchiness, which can be great for dealing with publishers, but it's not wonderful when it's aimed at the writer. It's hard to maintain a relationship with someone who's always telling you your work is not good enough, or it could always be better, or she's doing you a favor by representing you.

If there's something about your agent that you really don't like and respect (she once told you romance novels are stupid, and you secretly want to write romance novels), the relationship is going to unravel someday. You should find someone who you would feel comfortable inviting to your family gatherings, as well as business meetings. Your agent is your writing partner, and you should never have a partner you can't trust and respect.

Ways to Contact a Literary Agent

Once you and your manuscript are thoroughly prepared, the time is right to contact an agent. Finding an agent can often be as difficult as finding a publisher. Nevertheless, there are three ways to maximize your chances of finding the right agent: obtain a referral from someone who knows the agent; meet the agent in person at a writers' conference; or submit a query letter or proposal.

Referrals

The best way to get your foot in an agent's door is to be referred by one of his clients, or by an editor or another agent he has worked with in the past. Because an agent trusts his clients, he will usually read referred work before over-the-transom submissions. If you are friends with anyone in the publishing business who has connections with agents, ask politely for a referral. However, don't be offended if another writer will not share the name of his agent.

If you don't have a wide network of publishing professionals, use the resources you do have to get an agent's attention.

Conferences

Going to a conference is your best bet for meeting an agent in person. Many conferences invite agents to either give a speech or simply be available for meetings with authors. And agents view conferences as a way to find writers. Often agents set aside time for one-to-one discussions with writers, and occasionally they may even look at material writers bring to the conference. If an agent is impressed with you and your work, she may ask for writing samples after the conference. When you send her your query, be sure to mention the specific conference where you met and that she asked to see your work.

Because this is an effective way to connect with agents, we've asked agents to indicate in their listings which conferences they regularly attend. We've also included a section of conferences, starting on page 292, where you can find out more information about a particular conference, as well as an agent's availability at a specific conference.

Submissions

The most common way to contact an agent is by a query letter or a proposal package. Most agents will accept unsolicited queries. Some will also look at outlines and sample chapters. Almost none want unsolicited complete manuscripts. Check the **How to Contact** subhead in each listing to learn exactly how an agent prefers to be solicited. Never call—let the writing in your query letter speak for itself.

Because a query letter is your first impression on an agent, it should be professional and to the point. As a brief introduction to your manuscript, a query letter should only be one page in length, or at maximum, two pages.

- The first paragraph should quickly state your purpose—you want representation.
- In the second paragraph, mention why you have specifically chosen to query him. Perhaps he specializes in your areas of interest or represents authors you admire. Show him you have done your homework.
- In the next paragraph or two, describe the project, the proposed audience, why your book will sell, etc. Be sure to mention the approximate length and any special features.

- Then, discuss why you are the perfect person to write this book, listing your professional credentials or relative experience.
- Close your query with an offer to send either an outline, sample chapters or the complete manuscript—depending on your type of book.

For examples of actual query letters that led authors straight to publication, see Queries That Made It Happen on page 35. For helpful hints on outlines and synopses, see Outline and Synopsis Workshop on page 40.

Agents agree to be listed in directories such as the *Guide to Literary Agents* to indicate to writers what they want to see and how they wish to receive submissions. As you start to query agents, make sure you follow their individual submission directions. This, too, shows an agent you've done your research. Some agents ask for an outline or sample chapters, but you should send these only if you are requested to do so. Under the **How to Contact** subhead, agents also indicate if they are open to fax or e-mail query letters. Due to the volume of material agents receive, it may take a long time to receive a reply. You may want to query several agents at a time; agents also indicate in their listings if they consider simultaneous queries and submissions. If an agent requests a manuscript, make sure you provide sufficient postage for its return.

Like publishers, agencies have specialties. Some are only interested in novel-length works. Others are open to a wide variety of subjects and may actually have member agents within the agency who specialize in only a handful of the topics covered by the entire agency.

Before querying any agent, first consult the Agent Specialties Indexes in this book for your manuscript's subject, and identify those agents who handle what you write. Then, read the agents' listings to see if they are appropriate for you and for your work. For more information on targeting your submissions see Finding the Right Agent: What Every Writer Needs to Know on page 16 and Targeting Agents: Make the Best Fit With an Agent Who Knows Your Market on page 22.

When an agent queries you

Some agents read magazines or journals to find writers to represent. If you have had an outstanding piece published in a periodical, you may be contacted by an agent wishing to represent you. In such cases, make sure the agent has read your work. Some agents send form letters to writers, and such agents often make their living entirely from charging reading fees, not from commissions on sales.

However, many reputable and respected agents do contact potential clients in this way. For them, you already posses attributes of a good client: you have publishing credits and an editor has validated your work. To receive a letter from a reputable agent who has read your material and wants to represent you is an honor.

A Checklist for Inquiries and Submissions

BY LAURENS R. SCHWARTZ

New authors outnumber agents by 100 million to one. What's a writer to do or not do to attract attention?

Here are some *don'ts:*

☑ Don't send an obvious form letter or a letter with my first name sprinkled throughout—I'll only assume it's from Ed McMahon.

☑ I am not impressed with four-color dingbats, writers with logos, or digitized images of you or what the cover of your book should look like.

☑ Eighty percent of the query letters I receive contain typographical and grammatical errors. I cnt thinck of no reazon for tat. Tanks.

☑ Don't send me a questionnaire. You'll learn all about me if I decide to represent you.

☑ Don't tell me the gas station attendant, your infant or your goldfish read your book and loved it. That everyone you know will buy a copy. That you are a member of 80 writers' groups, organizations, unions and a coffee klatch. That this is your 15th book (if it is, list the publishers and sales for the previous 14, and explain why you don't have an agent). That you will be perfect on Oprah and Leno. That your book should be made into a Movie of the Week, miniseries, theatrical motion picture, direct-to-video and a Broadway musical. That the book has been edited at great expense by a professional editor.

☑ Don't submit a diskette unless specifically requested to do so.

☑ Don't send a manuscript in six-point type, single-spaced, double-sided, bound in leather. It has to be twelve-point type, double-spaced, single-sided, unbound.

☑ Don't falsely tell me you were given my name by a certain editor or publishing house. All I have to do is call to confirm, and I do.

☑ Don't hide the fact that the manuscript has already been shopped around to editors by another agent. It's now on reject lists. Move on to another work.

☑ If you've posted your work on your website or if you've already self-published it, I can only get

---

LAURENS R. SCHWARTZ *has been involved in the entertainment and publishing industry since 1968, and has been involved in numerous motion pictures, television series, books and exploitation of the Web.*

a major publisher to pick it up if you can prove you have substantial hits on the site or huge, regional hard-copy sales.

☑ Don't call long distance, leave a vague message and expect me to return your call. If I do speak with you, be prepared. Ninety percent of the time, an author cannot answer the simple question: "In two sentences, tell me what your work is about." Most agents don't have three hours for an explanation of the work.

☑ Don't try for sympathy. Enclosing a razor blade and threatening suicide should I not want to handle your project, does not work to gain my favor.

☑ Don't send anything without an appropriate SASE if you wish the manuscript returned (or see below). I have yet to discover how to fit a manuscript into a postcard.

☑ Don't send anything overnight, second-day air, or certified or registered mail, return receipt requested. You're a *potential* client, not a client. It takes time to get to anything new. That's life. Regular first-class mail is fine.

☑ After sending your query or requested manuscript, don't call me a dozen times a day. I'll just return your stuff because I know you'll be even worse as a client.

Now some *do's:*

☑ Learn the craft of writing *before* you submit a query or manuscript. Do you understand what you are doing, or are you merely going on "inspiration"?

☑ Do be an expert in your area for a nonfiction proposal. As much as possible, do your research, obtain access to archives and new materials, and secure permissions/releases (if necessary) prior to submitting a proposal.

☑ Do concentrate on carefully nurturing one project. Do not keep churning out proposals and manuscripts.

☑ Make your query letter pithy and focused. I don't want to know about your personal life (unless the proposal is an autobiography). Give me a one- to four-line synopsis of the work and a couple of lines on yourself as a writer if you have credentials.

☑ Do a cost/benefit analysis with regard to postage. If you submit an entire manuscript, for example, you may only need to append a postcard for response. It is probably cheaper to print a fresh copy than to have a beat-up one returned.

☑ Do remember, there are "agencies" that make their money through reading and editing fees instead of sales. They are required to inform you of such fees in advance. Do be careful about those groups.

☑ Do realize, the market is extremely competitive. Keep in mind you may not be a writer, you may be picking the wrong topics, or you may be a writer who will be discovered posthumously. Making money from writing is a skill.

Queries That Made It Happen

BY GLENN L. MARCUM

Imagine it's late, and you're sitting in front of the television hopping from one station to the next looking for something interesting. The picture changes and, suddenly, here's something different, something new. You decide to stay with this channel for a minute or two. And before you know it, you've forgotten the remote. You're engrossed in a new program and want to see more.

That's exactly the effect you want your query letter to have. Your query letter is like a small cable channel hoping to draw in viewers. With the proliferation of channels, it's easy to get lost in the shuffle. Just like the hundreds of letters from other hopeful writers that cross an agent's desk each week, you want to catch her attention, intrigue her before she 'surfs' on to the next. And like those cable channels you have only a small window of opportunity in which to do so, about two minutes or less, so you can't afford to waste those precious milliseconds.

To make the most of this time, you can't afford to be wordy, vague or extreme. Don't make an agent wade through a long and painfully detailed synopsis or your sure-fire marketing plans guaranteed to make your book a bestseller. Avoid long, self-deprecating introductions ("I know you're busy and probably never read unsolicited letters. . . ."), arrogant assertions ("The world is waiting for my book, so you'd better act now!") or vagueness that leaves the agent wondering just what, if anything, your book is about. And *never* write your query by hand or send it on flowery, colored stationery. For a busy agent, flourishes that draw the eye without offering substance aren't helpful; they're annoying.

You must also have a clear idea who you're sending your query to. Don't assume Arthur Bookman is your man simply because the agency bears his name—he may no longer be living or have never existed at all. You'll only embarrass yourself and earn your letter a quick trip to the slush pile.

What agents want is a short letter (one page preferred, maximum two) that introduces you, describes your book and explains why you're the best person to write it. Be creative, but remain focused; the moment you begin to wander you can be sure the agent's attention will, too—right on to the next query. Your letter must be professional in content and appearance as the smallest typographical or grammatical error is glaring under these circumstances. Briefly outline any writing experience you have. Agents want to know whether you've been published or not. Some routinely look for writers who've never been published while others want to see that you have had some success at writing.

On the following pages, you'll find actual queries submitted by authors who went on to find representation and whose agents have sold their books. The authors discuss how they wrote their queries, how they researched which agents to contact and how they knew their agent was the best one for them. The agents also offer their reactions to these letters.

Writing a query letter isn't easy, but take heart. The stories that follow show you're not alone in your agony. And, hopefully, they'll inspire you to write a two-minute 'program' that will catch an agent's eye and keep her hand off the remote.

GLEN MARCUM *is a freelance writer and editor currently based in Kettering, Ohio. Most recently, his work has appeared in* Novel & Short Story Writer's Market, Poet's Market *and* Guide to Literary Agents.

ANN DARBY

Ann Darby, author of *The Orphan Game* (William Morrow and Co.), methodically researched agents before writing her query. "I read Adam Begley's *Literary Agents: A Writer's Guide* (Penguin Books) to get my bearings on what to do."

Ann Darby

She also consulted *A Directory of American Poets and Fiction Writers* (Poets & Writers, Inc.), highlighting any writer who named their agent. "I went through the names, looking for writers whose work I liked, compiling a list of agents and the people they represent. I was looking for someone who would be interested in my work.

"It's difficult as a first-time novelist to have many expectations. You want somebody who's reputable, who you have a good gut feeling about. I felt like a young woman from an earlier century who was determined to get married, and it didn't matter whom the suitor was as long as she got married. You don't know much about these people until you work with them."

With this list of agents in hand, Darby began crafting her letter. "I knew the letter had to convey basic information about me, that I was a serious person and had some achievements as a writer. It also had to engage the reader. As Begley said in his book: 'It's rather like writing a love letter. In that sense it's also very personal.' "

Darby's letter begins with a paragraph from her novel. "I talked to a friend who's not a writer—I felt that was important—and he said: 'I think the only thing you have going for you is your writing, so you should lead with that.' "

Next she prepared a concise synopsis of her novel and ended with a short career outline and publishing history. "I worked on the letter for a long time. I would take a draft to my day job and work on it there. I had a couple of different drafts—some said a bit more, some less."

Darby sent her queries out three at a time. "I created a table and schedule from the list I compiled. I ordered the agents on my list according to whom I thought would most likely like my work." Right away agents requested to see *The Orphan Game*. Darby was discouraged when one agent she was particularly excited about passed on representing her. "Still it was a nice rejection letter. My boss suggested I ask if this agent could recommend another agency."

After sending a thank-you letter, Darby called the agency and was given two recommendations; one of whom, Emma Sweeney of Harold Ober Associates Inc., agreed to represent her. "I sent her the manuscript on Tuesday, and she called me that Saturday. She was excited about my book. We set up a meeting, and I liked her immediately." Five months later *The Orphan Game* was sold to William Morrow and Co. with large print and foreign rights sold soon after.

Darby's advice to authors seeking representation is to not give up. "You have to give yourself the best shot, be really methodical. I've talked to other writers who were discouraged because they'd sent queries to a few people and were rejected. You mustn't take rejection personally. You can't afford to get discouraged or lazy. It's one time you should be really diligent."

SAMPLE QUERY LETTER

Ann Darby
555 Query Lane
Writers Town, MO 25451

December 17, 1997

Ms. Emma Sweeney
Harold Ober Associates
425 Madison Avenue
New York, NY 10017

Dear Ms. Sweeney:

The biggest mistake people make, which Ann Darby did not, is not doing their research. I work at Harold Ober Associates, and we get letters directed to Mr. Harold Ober, who hasn't been alive for 50 years!

I like query letters that are brief and to the point, and this one is. And this is such a perfect paragraph. I read it over several times and that alone gave me enough insight into Darby's writing to know she is a good writer. She had the sense to put her best foot forward.

The year my father was teaching me to drive, the year Jamie died, the year all I could think about was this boy I was dating and what I wanted to do with him in the dark, my father took me to see a Mrs. Rumsen, a woman I'd heard about but never met before. She was a distant relation known in our family for her wayward ways, but when I met her she was widowed and living in a small house on a lot my father hoped someday to turn a profit on. She paid us a little rent and just by living there, my father said, kept vandals off the property.

This is from the opening of my novel, *The Orphan Game*. It is a simple story about Maggie Harris, a teenager who gets pregnant the year her brother dies, and about her family, their ambitions and their anger. The novel is set in the quiet southern California of the 1960s and told for the most part by 3 narrators. Maggie remembers with regret the decisions that made her a single mother. Maggie's mother, absorbed with her household and her dressmaking business, recalls the losses of her own life; and Mrs. Rumsen, the family scapegrace who shelters Maggie during her pregnancy, observes the family with both asperity and forbearance.

Wendy Weil suggested I write you to see if you might be interested in the manuscript. I enclose here a few more pages, from a later section.

I always see something Wendy refers to me because I know it is something she herself loved.

So you'll know something about me: I left school and came to New York to study dance, and for twelve years, I danced, choreographed and waited on many, many tables. Since then, I have earned a B.A. and an M.F.A. from Columbia University and now make my living as a medical editor and science writer. My short stories have appeared in the *Northwest Review, The Malahat Review* and the *Best of StoryQuarterly*, and I've had residencies at The MacDowell Colony, The Ucross Foundation, and The Millay Colony for the Arts.

She gives a sense of professionalism. And I always like when I see a writer has had some fiction published.

If you would like to see the manuscript, please let me know. I would be happy to send it to you.

Sincerely,

Ann Darby

Comments provided by Emma Sweeney of Harold Ober Associates

CAROL THURSTON

Carol Thurston knew the most important element of her novel *The Eye of Horus* (Avon Books) was the story. She had a fascinating and complicated tale involving intertwined narratives in vastly different places and times. "I wasted a lot of time trying to describe what it was about before it dawned on me that I needed to simply *tell* the story." Doing so changed the tone of the letter's writing as well as its content.

Choosing "charged" words such as "inflame" and "obsessed," "glorious" and "inglorious," she attempted to build to the last sentence of the paragraph. "The paragraph that follows is probably anticlimactic, but it served to set the stage for the idea of genetic memory, another hook.

"Then, because I didn't want anyone to think I was dealing with some voodoo concept, I added the proviso 'a thought-provoking possibility.' " Deciding what to leave out

Carol Thurston

Photo by Linda Breland

was also hard. For instance, the fact that the mummy Tashat described in her letter actually does exist. In the end, she decided her fictional account had to stand on its own.

Categorizing her novel wasn't easy. In her opening paragraph, Thurston compares *The Eye of Horus* to two novels in the same ballpark (set in two different time periods) while remaining vastly different. "*The English Patient* was fresh in everyone's mind because of the film, while *The Eight*, though less well known, was an even closer analogy and has been in print for ten years."

For the closing paragraph, Thurston opted for a "short but potent-as-I-could-make-it" summary of her writing experience, work history and academic credentials. She mentions the international market for books similar to hers and "then wrapped up the letter with a nutshell description of my story as 'a tale of political intrigue and a love that echoes through the centuries.' "

She then sent out multiple queries to agents whose names she'd gotten from other writers plus two others she had talked with at writers' conferences, which included Elizabeth Ziemska of Nicholas Ellison, Inc. When Ziemska contacted her by phone, Thurston was immediately impressed by the agent's enthusiasm for the book. "From the beginning, she had a strategy she intended to follow and an unwavering confidence that this book was going to sell—all of which she imparted to me. What a boost that was!"

Thurston then spent a month making revisions at Ziemska's suggestion, even changing the title. "I had changed the title from *The Knot of Isis* to *These Bones Remember* to make it sound more like a mystery. Liz thought it needed an Egyptian title and suggested *The Eye of Horus*, an element that appears in both the historical and modern narratives." With the new title and revisions in place Ziemska went to work, making a sale ten days later to Avon Books. Foreign rights sales to Germany, Spain and Sweden were quickly made in the months that followed.

Thurston recommends attending writers' conferences to learn as much *about* as well as *from* people in publishing. "Some agents, for instance, sound incredibly passive or reactive. I once heard one say she would look only at mysteries and inspirational nonfiction because that's all that was selling. Listen for the differences between agents. It's probably useful to attend more than one conference, too, but not so many that you get jaded or discouraged, especially if what you're writing doesn't fit the popular mold."

SAMPLE QUERY LETTER

Carol Thurston
6611 Author Court
Novelville, NY 10001

May 19, 1997

Elizabeth Ziemska
Nicholas Ellison, Inc.
55 Fifth Avenue, 15th Floor
New York, NY 10003

Dear Ms. Ziemska,

We met briefly last August at the Southwest Writers Conference in Albuquerque, where I was a presenter as well. You mentioned then that you were looking for "good historical fiction," so I would like to briefly describe the novel I just completed, which—like Katherine Neville's *The Eight* or Michael Ondaatje's *The English Patient*—moves back and forth through time.

In 1360 BC Thebes, a daughter is born to the beautiful Nefertiti (once Queen to the heretic Akhenaten) and a powerful priest of Amen. Destined from conception to be a pawn in the priest's attempt to take the throne, this half-royal princess named for the Goddess of Love (Aset to the Egyptians; Isis to the Greeks), instead changes the course of the empire with her picture-stories about greed, sexual politics and even murder in high places. As they spread up and down the Nile, her "cartoons" at first titillate and then inflame an illiterate people. They also cost Aset her life, provoking the man who loves her to commit an act that goes beyond vengeance, bringing the glorious Eighteenth Dynasty to an inglorious end. More than 33 centuries later, medical illustrator Kate McKinnon begins to remember people she cannot have known, places she has never seen and events that never happened—at least not to her. Hired by a Denver museum to create forensic displays for an exhibit, Kate becomes obsessed with the young Lady Tashat after X-rays of her mummy reveal not only a broken, contorted skeleton but the head of an adult male between her legs.

My contemporary protagonists (sleuths, if you will) are a radiologist and medical illustrator who pioneer using the newest medical imaging and reconstruction techniques to "see" into the past, to learn who Tashat really was. Despite their well-honed "rational" instincts, they also must confront mounting evidence of an irrational, at times terrifying, phenomenon—genetic memory. This subplot is not firmly resolved; instead it is presented as a thought-provoking possibility.

I have published two novels (Pocket Books, UK rights to Piatkus and Pan) and a sociological study (University of Illinois Press), as well as a number of freelance articles for newspapers and magazines (e.g., *Psychology Today, Newsday*). As a former newspaper reporter, political speech writer and university professor, I assure you I have thoroughly researched both the historical period and medical technology portrayed in *These Bones Remember*. I also am aware that historical fiction has been wildly popular in Europe (Noah Gordon in Germany, Christian Jacq's five-part novel about Ramses II in France) and that Germany and France together constitute a very big market. I would like to think that my tale of political intrigue and a love that echoes through the centuries to the present would have wide appeal to both American and European readers.

If you are interested in seeing sample chapters and a synopsis, I would be happy to send however much you suggest. In any case, I appreciate your time and consideration of this work.

Sincerely,

Carol Thurston

SASE enclosed

I like that her introduction to me is relatively brief. Her first paragraph is so teeny, and then she gets right into it.

The middle two paragraphs really got to me. I'm interested in science and the way it appears in fiction. I'm also interested in all things Egyptian.

Hello! How could you not look at something like that? I've got to see this book.

It was also nice to see she'd been published. Not to say that's a requirement; I like to discover people who've never been published before but that helped a little bit.

Comments provided by Elizabeth Ziemska of Nicholas Ellison, Inc.

Outline and Synopsis Workshop

BY IAN BESSLER

You've written your Great American Novel or your Nonfiction Tome. After mailing out a punchy, carefully composed query letter, you receive word back that an agent is interested in finding out more about your project. Your task now is to put together a full proposal package. These usually include a cover letter, three sample chapters (or the first 100 pages of a fiction manuscript) and an outline or synopsis. Outline or synopsis? What's the difference?

Agents often use the terms interchangeably, but there is indeed a difference. In general, "outline" refers to nonfiction, while "synopsis" refers to fiction.

Nonfiction is defined by logical and meaningful structure. Your goal when selling a nonfiction project is to detail the logical presentation of facts, ideas and arguments; a nonfiction outline is therefore primarily a structural skeleton showing how each part relates to the whole and in what order the reader encounters each element.

On the other hand, fiction is defined by conflict. Your goal when selling a novel manuscript is to show the characters, the flow of events and how these events are propelled forward by the conflict. A novel synopsis, therefore, is a condensed narrative version of your story from beginning to end that, ideally, reads like your novel, conveys a similar style of writing and sells your novel by grabbing the reader's attention much like the full-scale manuscript.

The nonfiction outline and the novel synopsis are useful means for both the writer and the agent to "step back" from the manuscript and look at the larger outlines of structure and plot.

THE NONFICTION OUTLINE

The nonfiction outline serves as an annotated table of contents and describes the structure of a book that you either have written or intend to write. It is also a tool used to sell that book to an editor or agent, as well as a valuable labor-saving device for you as a writer. It can indicate what you're getting into and guide how you develop the book idea. Creating an outline for your idea can help impose form and point out further avenues of research and development.

If you intend to pitch an idea for a nonfiction book that has not yet been completed, the outline must convince an agent or editor that the proposed idea has been developed in a way that is both wide-ranging and detailed enough to produce a book-length manuscript's worth of material. They need to know your idea will support a book and not just an article. Your outline must also demonstrate you have a clear grasp of the level of research needed to complete the project and deliver the manuscript on time. If you have not thoroughly investigated what is involved in researching the book, you may begin writing only to lose focus when you come across books, people to interview and other areas of research you had not realized were essential to a thorough treatment of your idea.

The following list covers several pointers for generating an outline:

- **DESCRIBE:** Describe what each section of the book does—how it arranges and presents the material you have gathered on the topic—and not the topic itself. For instance, if the topic of the chapter is the Marine Corps boot camp training process, your outline of the chapters should begin with something like this: "The chapter assesses the boot camp

IAN BESSLER *is a production editor for* Poet's Market *and the* Guide to Literary Agents*, and is a fiction writer and musician.*

SAMPLE NONFICTION OUTLINE

Psychedelic Rawk: 1965 to Present

Chapter 1

Designed to Blow Your Mind:
the Psychedelic Sound, the Studio and the Road   23 pages, 10 photos.

The first chapter launches a discussion of the term ''psychedelic''; the corresponding aesthetic and musical features generally considered psychedelic; the associated sound studio technologies; and elements of the live psychedelic music experience. It is divided into three sections.

The first section scrutinizes the aesthetics and musical characteristics of psychedelic rock. It argues that psychedelic music is based on an aesthetic of sound fetishizing radically new, sensual or shocking sound textures, including the perception of familiar sounds as ''strange'' or ''weird'' when placed into new contexts. It argues for a wider interpretation of the term ''psychedelic'' to include any sort of music that allows listeners to defamiliarize themselves with common musical and everyday sounds. As an expansion of this argument, it discusses the inherently slippery and imprecise nature of music terminology and notes the numerous crossover points between psychedelic rock and other genres and schools of musical thought, including ''art rock'' artists such as Frank Zappa, Captain Beefheart, the Velvet Underground and Brian Eno. It expands on these points with a discussion of other common features of psychedelic music, including nonstandard song structures, avant-garde influences, collage, ''found'' sounds, studio chatter and soundscapes.

The second section chronicles the development of specific studio techniques/technologies and the part they have historically played in allowing the expression of the psychedelic aesthetic. It discusses the early multi-track and effects experiments of Les Paul; the innovations of tape loops, phasing, automatic double-tracking and sophisticated mixing techniques refined during mid- to late-Sixties Beatles, Pink Floyd and Jimi Hendrix recording sessions; and modern refinements in sampling, digital effects and computer manipulation of sound.

The third section sketches out a brief overview of the rise of new instrumental and sound-system technology that has made it possible to bring the psychedelic music aesthetic into a live performance context, including new synthesizer technology, the widespread use of small portable effects processors and innovations in PA technology made possible by touring psychedelic bands such as the Grateful Dead and Pink Floyd. This section ends the chapter by scrutinizing other elements of the live psychedelic experience, including the crowd experience, audience participation and musical improvisation, as well visual projections and light shows ranging from the early blobs and phantasms of Haight-Ashbury to modern computerized lighting systems.

Photos: Syd Barrett w/early Pink Floyd, Jefferson Airplane, Brian Eno, Frank Zappa, a photo of the inside of Abbey Road studios in the mid-1960s, Jimi Hendrix in the studio w/engineer Eddie Kramer, Roger Waters onstage w/ Pink Floyd, the early-1970s Grateful Dead onstage w/the Wall of Sound, a crowd of Deadheads, a blob projection from the mid-1960s Fillmore West.

Give each chapter a catchy title to hook interest.

List a page count for the chapter and the number of photos and illustrations you intend to use.

The outline describes what each section does.

Use action-oriented verbs to add spice and interest to the outline.

Use active sentence construction.

Detail any photos you intend to use.

process where recruits are stripped of their individual identities, broken down and then rebuilt as Marines. It is divided into three sections. The first part discusses . . ." Once again, the focus is on what the chapter does (it "assesses"), how it is constructed ("divided into three sections") and what information goes in what sections ("The first part discusses . . ."), rather than on a detailed explication of the topic itself.

- **STAY PRESENT:** Write the outline in the present tense for clarity.
- **STAY ACTIVE:** Avoid using the passive voice whenever possible. Avoid a sentence form like this: "The issue of combat unit cohesion is explored." Instead, use a form more like this: "The chapter explores combat unit cohesion." Consistent use of the active voice maintains clarity and punch in the outline.
- **HOOK:** Give each chapter a hook title with impact and clarity. For example, if the book on Marine training is titled *Parris Island Blues*, a chapter encapsulating Marine Corp history could be titled "The Leatherneck Chronicles."
- **BE VIVID:** Use vivid and active verbs to tell what the chapter does. The chapter doesn't just "talk about" the topic, it *unearths* information, *confronts* the possibilities, *expands* a viewpoint or *blasts* a commonly held misconception. Action verbs can liven up your outline and serve as an additional tool for maintaining the active interest of the agent or editor, but be sure not to repeat the same verb too many times.
- **PHOTOS AND ILLUSTRATIONS:** In the upper right-hand corner of the first page of each chapter outline, give a page count for the chapter and a tally of the number of photos and illustrations you intend to use. At the end of each chapter outline, include a short paragraph detailing any photographs or illustrations incorporated into the chapter.

The example outline on page 41 models the principles listed above:

THE NOVEL SYNOPSIS

A well-written synopsis is an important tool when marketing your novel, and many agents and editors will use it to judge your ability to tell a story. The synopsis is a condensed narrative version of the novel. It should hook the editor or agent by showcasing the central conflict of the book and the interlocking chain of events set off by that conflict. It should incorporate every chapter of your book, and distill every main event, character and plot twist. A synopsis should highlight the element of human drama and emotion that explains *why* the characters in a novel took their particular path. When crafting your synopsis, these pointers form a set of guidelines to lead you through the process of condensing your manuscript:

- **FORMAT:** Type a heading in the upper left-hand corner of the first page, featuring the title of your novel, the genre, an estimated word count for the full manuscript and your name. At the end of the synopsis, type out "THE END" to signify the conclusion of the story.
- **STAY PRESENT:** Write the synopsis in the present tense and third-person point of view. Even if your novel is written in first person, use third person for the synopsis. This allows for consistency and ease in summarizing. Such a summary will also help when an agent pitches the work to an editor.
- **DON'T HOLD BACK:** Tell the entire story, including the ending. Do not tease—tell who lives, who dies, who did it and so on. At this stage of the query process, the agent or editor has already been hooked by your brilliant query letter with the clever teaser, and now they want an overview of the entire project, so don't leave anything out.
- **HOOK:** Start with a hook detailing your primary character and the main conflict of the novel. Give any pertinent information about the lead character, such as age, career, marital status, etc., and describe how that character manifests or is drawn into the primary conflict.
- **SPOTLIGHT:** The first time you introduce a character, spotlight that character by capitalizing his name. If possible, weave the character's initial description into the flow of the text, but don't stray from the narrative with a lengthy or overly-detailed character sketch.

SAMPLE NOVEL SYNOPSIS

Obelisk
Science Fiction
75,000 words
by Maxwell Parker

ARCAS KANE, newly minted agent for the Imperial Galactic Security Apparatus, is eager for promotion within the ranks. Security Apparatus Director DELSIN HISTER, leader of an Imperial faction hostile to the current ruler, sees Kane's ambitions and picks the young man for a mission on the fringe of the galaxy, where archaeologists make a startling discovery.

Buried in the sands of a sparsely populated desert world they find artifacts from times beyond the reckoning of even the oldest histories of the Imperium. The artifacts include obsidian obelisks, perfectly preserved and carved with glyphs and signs. Using bits of lore preserved by the desert planet's nonhuman natives, the scientists decipher part of the message and send news of their discovery.

Kane arrives with the crew of a supply ship and finds the archaeologists murdered, the artifacts destroyed. He searches through bits of surviving scientific data. The obelisks describe a planet, the mythical home system of the human race. The obelisks tell of the abandonment of the home world and the wandering of the human race. They also refer to an ancient doomsday weapon, the source of the destruction.

Kane questions the wary natives. He learns that two of the archaeologists escaped in a ship to retrace the ancient wanderers' steps back to the home planet. He reports in to Hister, who orders Kane to follow.

He departs with the reluctant crew of the supply ship. They spend weeks hopping from world to world, following the trail. Beautiful AVA, the supply ship's executive officer, seduces Kane, and jealous hostility flares between Kane and the ship's captain. Crew members die in mysterious accidents. Suspicion falls on Kane. He suspects a mole among the crew and wonders if he is himself a pawn.

He catches the archaeologists. They find the hulking ruins of a colony generation ship floating lifelessly in orbit around an obscure star system. A search of the colony ship's archives reveals detailed descriptions of the home planet's location and the doomsday device. Hister is shadowing the pursuit. He overtakes them in an Imperial warship. Hister congratulates them on their discovery and urges them all on to the home planet.

Nothing is left of the planet but a charred, sterilized cinder. They detect a beacon in the ruins of a city on the surface. In a bunker beneath the city, they find an artificial intelligence unit waiting for the return of its masters. In between senile harangues by the AI, they coax out the complete history of the war and the formula for the doomsday device.

After returning to orbit, Hister announces that Kane and the others have reached the end of their usefulness and must be liquidated. Hister intends to take the doomsday device information for his own use. Hister's minions lead Kane, Ava and the others away to be ejected from the airlocks. The supply ship's engines explode where it sits docked with the warship. Kane, Ava and one of the archaeologists narrowly escape in a life pod as the ship comes apart at the seams. Hister is sucked into the vacuum of space as the bridge ruptures. Ava reveals her identity as the mole, a spy for the Imperial loyalists. They seal themselves into hibernation pods to wait for rescue by loyalist forces.

THE END

As the synopsis introduces each character, their name is high-lighted where it first appears in all capital letters.

The first two paragraphs introduce major characters and outline the plot set-up and character motivations.

The synopsis retells the narrative in present tense and third person, using active sentence construction.

The synopsis applies extreme compression to the narrative and condenses several chapters comprising weeks of narrative time into two paragraphs.

The entire story is told, including the outcome.

- **CONDENSE:** Don't defeat the purpose of the synopsis by letting it run too long. A workable rule of thumb for calculating the length of the synopsis is to condense every 25 pages of your novel synopsis down to 1 page. If you follow this formula for a 200-page novel manuscript, you should wind up with 8 pages of synopsis. This formula is not set in stone, however, since some agents like to see even more compression and will frequently ask for a two-page synopsis to represent an entire novel. If in doubt, ask the agent what length he prefers, and tailor your synopsis to his requirement, no more, no less.
- **CUT OUT THE FAT:** Be concise. Include only details of the action essential to the story, and excise excessive adjectives and adverbs. Dialogue is rarely used, but at the same time don't be afraid to feature pivotal quotes, descriptive gems or a crucial scene when you know it will enhance the impact of your synopsis at critical points.
- **RETELL:** Work from your manuscript chapter by chapter, and briefly retell the events of each chapter. You should tell one complete account of your book, although you may use paragraphs to represent chapters or sections. Whenever possible, use a style reflecting the tone of the actual novel—if the novel is dark and moody in tone, then a dark and moody tone is called for in the synopsis.
- **BE SEAMLESS:** Do not intrude in the narrative flow with authorial commentary, and do not let the underlying story framework show in your synopsis. Don't use headings such as "Setting" or phrases like "At the climax of the conflict . . ." or "The next chapter begins with . . ." In short, do not let it read like a nonfiction outline. Your goal is to entrance the agent or editor with the story itself and not to break the spell by allowing the supporting scaffolding to show. These elements should already be self-evident and woven into the narrative. You should also avoid reviewing your own story; the agent or the editor will make his own judgment. Your work should hopefully speak for itself.

The example synopsis on page 43 condenses an entire novel in one page. This is an extreme example of compression as noted above but a demonstration of the principles involved.

A FEW LAST BITS

A few final tips to consider:

☑ Include two SASEs with your submission, a #10 business-size SASE for reply and a larger SASE big enough to hold your manuscript, along with enough postage for its return.

☑ Be sure your proposal package is either laser-printed or neatly typed (no dot matrix) on clean paper sufficiently strong to stand up to handling (do not use erasable bond or onionskin). Also, put a blank piece of paper at the end of the manuscript to protect the last page.

☑ Be sure to use proper manuscript format (one-inch margins on all four sides of the page, double-spaced, one-sided and left-justified only).

☑ Resist the urge to cover your manuscript with copyright symbols. Under current copyright law, your work is protected as soon as you put it into tangible form. To many agents and editors, a manuscript sporting copyright symbols is the mark of an amateur.

Not all agents or editors have boiled down an explicit set of nuts-and-bolts guidelines, but the methods outlined in this article will provide you with a repeatable set of steps for framing your ideas with clarity and precision. For further treatments of nonfiction outline issues, refer to *How to Write a Book Proposal*, by Michael Larsen (Writer's Digest Books). For further advice on constructing a synopsis, refer to *Your Novel Proposal: From Creation to Contract*, by Blythe Camenson and Marshall J. Cook (Writer's Digest Books) or *The Marshall Plan for Novel Writing*, by Evan Marshall (Writer's Digest Books).

Making More From Subsidiary Rights

BY BONNIE NADELL

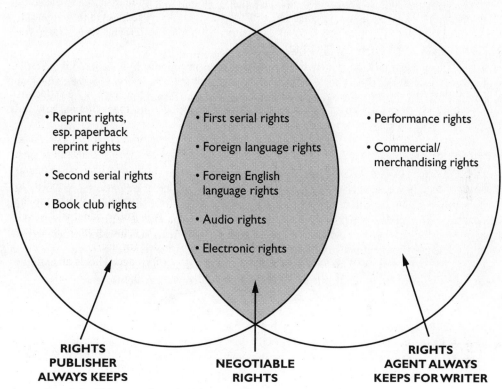

| RIGHTS PUBLISHER ALWAYS KEEPS | NEGOTIABLE RIGHTS | RIGHTS AGENT ALWAYS KEEPS FOR WRITER |

Australian rights?! I never thought I'd see the day when I would be negotiating Australian rights. But I do. Publishing is undergoing some of its deepest structural changes in decades. Where houses were once independent, they are now part of huge international conglomerates. Where a decade ago paperback auctions generated much excitement and income, now paperback editions are usually published inhouse. Perhaps in no other area of publishing are the changes in the industry reflected as much as in subsidiary rights—the all-important rights that are also negotiated when your book is sold.

At one of my early jobs in publishing, in the subsidiary rights department of Simon & Schuster, one of the acknowledged doyennes of the business succinctly explained our job as "exploiting the copyright." What she meant by this phrase was that the purchase of a book in a bookstore is only one of many ways a book can generate income for the publisher and, potentially, royalty payments to the author. The purchase of a manuscript by a publishing house—a transaction where a publisher advances an author money that will be deducted from any future royalties—

BONNIE NADELL *is vice president of Frederick Hill Associates, a literary agency with offices in San Francisco and Los Angeles. She has been an agent for 15 years. Prior to becoming an agent, she worked in the subsidiary rights department at Simon & Schuster.*

also involves the negotiation of rights to these ancillary sources of income, called subsidiary rights. An agent who negotiates these additional rights well earns more money for the writer and helps an author's advance earn out faster, allowing the writer to start earning royalties sooner.

When an agent is negotiating a contract with an American publisher, she is negotiating how to split any income derived from a wide-range of additional sources, which include translation, serialization, audio, electronic and performance rights. Some of these subsidiary rights can be negotiated with the publisher, some the publisher always claims, and some are generally reserved by the agent on behalf of the author.

NON-NEGOTIABLE RIGHTS

The publisher claims as a matter of course the "non-negotiable rights" including reprint rights, second serial rights and book club rights. With all of these rights, you as the author will not receive royalties until after your advance has earned out from book sales or from selling subsidiary rights. Don't assume you will see any income until six months after publication of your book, at the earliest.

Reprint rights

In theory, reprint rights means reprinting your book in any format other than its original one. For the publishing industry, however, it refers to selling the paperback rights after a hardcover is produced. Selling paperback rights used to be a lucrative part of the business. At Simon & Schuster, I saw auctions where paperback rights were sold for over a million dollars with a number of paperback editors bidding against each other. This situation is now a rare occurrence. With the consolidation the industry has undergone, most hardcover publishers have joined with houses who specialize in softcover books. Random House alone has at least seven paperback houses; they are not about to allow those rights to go to a competing publisher.

Most books today are consequently bought in "hard/soft" deals, meaning the same publisher has the rights to produce both hardcover and paperback editions. If a publisher does sell reprint rights, the earnings are generally split 50/50 between author and publisher. However, the author's share is deducted from his advance. A writer only sees paperback money if the hardcover edition earns out from royalties. A hard/soft deal can sometimes be better for a writer since he will receive full royalties on both the hardcover and paperback edition, instead of splitting the paperback royalties with the hardcover publisher as was done in the past.

Book club rights

These rights are always granted to the publisher to sell, and the split is usually 50/50. The author's share is deducted from his advance since book club rights are usually sold before publication. The two major book clubs, the Book-of-the-Month Club and The Literary Guild, compete against each other for major authors and commercial titles. Specialty clubs like the Mystery Guild, History Book Club or cooking and gardening clubs also buy for their audiences.

BOMC and The Guild were set up years ago for readers who did not have access to a local bookstore or who wanted the imprimatur of judges who chose the titles for them. The book clubs are gradually becoming less important due to the rise of Internet booksellers like Amazon.com that can deliver anywhere in the country. Nevertheless, it is considered an honor to have one's book chosen by either club since they are selective in what they choose to offer members (unlike Amazon.com which prides itself on carrying a huge number of titles).

Serial rights

First serial rights are open to negotiation with a publisher, whereas second serial rights are always the domain of the publisher and split in half. First serial rights are excerpts of the book which appear before it is published; second serial rights refer to sections excerpted after publication. The split on first serial is 90/10 in the author's favor, but these monies are also put against the author's advance.

For a number of years, big novels and major nonfiction books were serialized and could create quite a stir with readers. As newspapers and magazines reduced this practice, it is a rare book that gets this treatment. Now, political memoirs or celebrity biographies tend to be the most lucrative and sought-after books by the print media. How-to books, self-help or other service-oriented books also tend to work best for second serial reprints since magazines always need experts for their articles.

Even if the money is not particularly large, serial rights of both kinds are valuable because of the publicity and exposure they give your work. If you don't have an agent, it is better to let the publisher sell first serial rights than approaching newspapers and magazines on your own.

NEGOTIABLE RIGHTS

Confusing as it may sound at first, the term "negotiable rights" does not actually mean the negotiation of rights to a book but instead the negotiation between agent and publisher for the rights to license the copyright to third parties. The rights to do this negotiating either go to the publisher or to the agent on behalf of the author.

Foreign language rights

Foreign language and British rights are a part of publishing where, because there are so many variables, an agent's experience can make a significant difference. There are no hard and fast rules about who gets these rights to sell, but there are certain types of books which "travel" better than others. A book about the future of the Social Security system probably won't be sold outside the United States. For the biography of the pop music icon of the moment, foreign language and British rights could be sold for a great deal. Nevertheless, there are certain guiding principles that come into play when negotiating the ownership of these rights.

When a major publisher sells foreign rights, the split is usually 75/25 in the author's favor. University and small presses, however, generally split all translation rights 50/50. Like reprint rights, these monies are deducted from your advance. You will not see the money until after your American advance earns out. Speaking in broad generalities, if an agent sells the foreign rights to a book, an author gets the money faster since the money paid by the foreign publisher goes directly to the author instead of to the original publisher to be deducted from the author's royalty advance. But for an agent to be successful at selling foreign rights, she should be well connected to the international publishing world. This means attending book fairs in Frankfurt, Germany and London, and being in touch with the scouts who look for books on behalf of major foreign publishers. If your agent is selling foreign rights, she will take a 20 percent commission and split it with the foreign representative who directly negotiates the contract with the foreign publisher for that country.

British rights

For the purposes of publishing, English language rights are generally split between United States and British publishers, with the Americans having the right to sell the book in North America and the Philippines, and the British having the right to sell anywhere else. Australia and New Zealand were once included in British rights, but as Australian publishers become more independent and due to a change in Australian copyright law, it is now possible to divide Australian rights from British rights and sell them separately. British and Australian rights are generally split 80/20 in the author's favor.

Electronic rights

These rights are currently the most fought over part of contracts—not because of their value now, which is minimal—but for their future value. Essentially we are talking about means of reproduction which barely exist, if at all. To slightly formalize the negotiating process that applies to electronic rights, these rights have been divided into two parts: interactive/multimedia rights and computer publishing rights. The former are usually part of any movie or television contract (since video game rights are valuable for studios if the movie takes off).

The latter refer to literally putting the text on a computer screen, and publishers are insistent about keeping these rights. Many agents, however, fight to keep these rights for their clients. The latest invention is electronic books, and publishers want to keep these rights so they can either sell or produce "e-books." These rights, like many others, are split 50/50. Electronic books are rare now but may become popular in the future. Or they may not. CD-ROMs were once touted as the latest thing in publishing, but the manufacturing process proved to be too expensive to catch on with the reading public. (For more information on recent developments in electronic rights, see Harnessing the Power of Electronic Rights on page 49.)

Audio rights

Audiobooks have become increasingly popular in recent years, and most major publishers want to acquire audio rights for their audio divisions. There are several ways an audio deal can be structured. The publisher can acquire audio rights along with the other rights in its contract and pay a bit more as part of the advance, or the publisher can license the audio rights and split the proceeds 50/50 with the writer.

If the publisher has an audio division, it will pay royalties on each audiobook like it does for a print book. But unlike most royalties on books which are based on a percentage of the cover price, royalties for audiobooks are based on a percentage of the *net* proceeds a publisher receives. If the publisher is simply going to license the rights to an audio company, you are better off having your agent sell them because you will see the monies faster and have more control over the process.

RIGHTS RESERVED TO THE AUTHOR

Performance rights

Performance rights, also known as dramatic rights, refer to the ability to license film and television rights to your work. These rights are always reserved to the author and not granted to the publisher. In most cases, a producer or studio will option your work for a period of time in order to develop a script based on your work. You will receive a sum of money for the option if the project goes into production; you are then paid a purchase price.

When you license performance rights, a number of other rights such as video, games and certain merchandise rights are included in the contract. In rare cases, an author will be given the opportunity to help write a script or consult on the screenplay. It is an unusual writer who is skilled at both types of writing and has the ability to work in a group with a producer or studio.

Commercial and merchandising rights

These rights refer to products such as calendars, stationery, dolls, toys or other products which can be created from your work. These rights are rarely licensed, but film companies generally request them as part of their option deal. Publishers hardly ever do anything with these rights so there is no reason to grant them. And if your project has the potential for becoming valuable for such products, these rights are definitely worth keeping and selling yourself.

As a writer, the more you know about the process of negotiating subsidiary rights, the better off you will be. It is important to remember that, although there are protocols, the negotiation of subsidiary rights is as much an art as a science. A savvy agent can make a real difference in helping the copyright of your book be exploited to its full potential—even if it means waking up at five a.m. to hold the auction for the Australian edition.

Harnessing the Power of Electronic Rights

BY KELLY MILNER HALLS

Trying to track and understand electronic rights four years ago, when I first wrote this *Guide to Literary Agents*'s special report, was a little like tracking phantom lightning bolts. Clearly, something was in the air, thunder rumbling in the distance. But there was no way of knowing when or where it would strike, no way to anticipate the sparks or flames yet to come.

THE ELECTRONIC RIGHTS DEBATE BEGINS

In 1997, I found forward-thinking agent Robert Gottlieb—of the famed William Morris Agency—a pioneer blazing a trail for his client, Tom Clancy. As he negotiated one of the first book/CD-ROM/online deals ever contracted, Gottlieb knew that area of publishing was largely untested. "In terms of print versus electronic rights," he said, "electronic rights are obviously much more complicated." Gottlieb recognized, even in its infancy, the issue of electronic rights would be a tough tiger to tame. It would be, he said, like harnessing nature, "raw and ever evolving."

That same year, Sanford Greenburger Associates agent Theresa Park came face-to-face with the beast. When one of her clients was transformed overnight from salesman to million-dollar novelist, electronic rights became her formidable, almost invisible foe.

"One of my worst legal battles was with the movie company that bought the rights to Nicholas Sparks's book, *The Notebook* (Warner)," Park says. "The most contentious action of negotiation revolved around who would retain multimedia rights."

Uncertainty fueled electronic conflict in 1997, according to Park. "Publishers try to cover their bases by drafting wide-sweeping contracts," she said. "It's my job to pare back, to protect the future rights of my authors. How writers will be compensated is pretty much up for grabs when it comes to the Internet, so the best I can do is to keep my authors' options open."

THE INTERNET AS PROMOTIONAL TOOL

By 1998, sheer numbers drove the debate. Nearly two billion cybernauts traversed the information highway, hungry for information. Agents, authors and publishers were poised and eager to fill the void. But in that year, electronic applications seemed to take a promotional turn. Internet commerce, experts agreed, was a concept not yet defined.

"I see this medium as a powerful marketing tool, especially considering the explosion of interest the Internet and America Online have created," said Paul Cirone, assistant to Molly Friedrich, top-tier agent at the Aaron M. Priest Literary Agency. "If you can expose a book to a group of people that might not see it otherwise, why not?"

KELLY MILNER HALLS *is a full-time freelance writer headquartered in Spokane, Washington. Her work is regularly featured in the* Chicago Tribune, Atlanta Journal Constitution, Denver Post *and the* Spokesman-Review, *as well as magazines including* Teen People, Fox Kids, Highlights for Children, FamilyFun, Parenting Teens *and many others. Her sixth and latest book,* I Bought a Baby Chicken, *will be released in Spring 2000 from Boyds Mills Press.*

Internet book havens like Amazon.com (www.amazon.com), AOL's The Book Report (www.-bookreporter.com) and BookWire (www.bookwire.com) volleyed for author exclusives and attention grabbing "scoops." The Book Report's sneak peek at the first two chapters of John Grisham's novel, *The Partner*, hooked 800,000 cyber-surfers in a single online day. In two weeks, 3,200 copies of the book were bought and paid for, securing for The Book Report the prestigious LMP Award for Excellence in Book Publishing.

But professional recognition wasn't the only benefit The Book Report enjoyed. For every book sold through its site, the online review of books received a very modest percentage. The potential for Internet profit quickly ignited industry debate. At issue: Should everyone get a piece of The Book Report pie?

"I see, daily, the powerful effect online book previews and excerpts have on reader choices and opinions," said AOL Network Editorial Director Jesse Kornbluth in 1998. "Given that, I find it amazing and a bit backward that any publisher believes The Book Report should pay for the privilege of promoting its books. When the power of online is better understood," he continued, "I suspect the scales will fall from publishers' eyes, and they will see this is promotion, pure and simple, and not subsidiary rights in any way."

Internet guru and Nicholas Ellison agent Dan Mandel seemed to both back and dispute Kornbluth's stance. "I believe electronic rights as we know them will eventually become almost totally Web based," he said. "And on the Web, content is king. Internet service providers are always looking for outstanding content that will draw in people."

Mandel didn't see promotional previews as cause for serious dispute, but he predicted bigger things to come. "I think we will eventually see the online serial run of novels," he said. "When that happens, electronic rights will shift from subsidiary to primary rights. And as it becomes easier to calculate what material is most appealing, real financial considerations will be at stake."

DOWNLOADING BOOKS FROM THE WEB

Elements of Mandel's prediction came to pass in 1999. Internet publishers like the Hard Shell Word Factory (www.hardshell.com) offered consumers electronic options for a substantial but reasonable fee. "You can buy books two ways," said author Denise Dietz Wiley, whose books *Promises to Keep* and *Footprints in the Butter* are both featured Hard Shell titles. "You can download text directly from the publisher online, adjusting the print on your screen to any font you like. Or you can order disks you insert into your drive."

Credit card payments kept Hard Shell's 1999 investment—including what Dietz Wiley called a fair royalty—secure. But only authors who consciously retained their electronic rights could take advantage of this promising new realm of Internet commerce. Authors who sold electronic rights with their print publications were left out of the modest cash flow.

So noteworthy was the Web's obvious upward momentum in 1999, political icons like former U.S. Congresswoman Pat Schroeder at least tentatively stepped into the Internet ring as the CEO of the Association of American Publishers. "Obviously, we would like to be able to do commerce on the Net like everyone else," Schroeder said. "But it has become so easy to copy anything you put out on the Net that it's difficult to safeguard intellectual properties."

Schroeder endorsed the World Intellectual Property Organization (WIPO) and their proposed string of international Internet treaties as the best possible safeguard. "WIPO legislation is what we need," Schroeder insisted. "And the United States has the most at stake. Our number one export is copyrighted product. Considering how much we have to lose, it's clear if we don't ratify WIPO, no other country will." To Schoeder's delight, the treaty was adopted by the 105th United States Congress.

THE FUTURE OF ELECTRONIC RIGHTS

As the year 2000 unfolds, so will waves of new electronic opportunity, according to author Karen Wiesner. Overwhelmed by the rush of newly launched online publishers, Wiesner joined forces with e-publisher Petals of Life in July 1999 to create *Electronic Publishing: The Definitive Guide*. Available only via CD-ROM and Internet download, Wiesner's project objectively lays out the electronic pros and cons (www.eclectics.com/karenwiesner).

High on the disadvantage list, according to Wiesner, is the current fiscal return. "There's not a lot of money in electronic publishing at the moment," she says, "because the public doesn't know that much about the medium. But it's gaining momentum, and the potential is huge."

How huge? "E-publishers don't give advances," Wiesner says, "but their royalty agreements are generous." The lowest Wiesner has seen is a fat 24 percent. "But I've seen them go as high as 85 percent," she says.

So convinced is Wiesner of the economic potential, she published her guide in electronic form only. "It may come out in print form later," she says, "but this book is about online opportunities. It's geared toward writers already familiar with how things work online. And if you are exploring the CD-ROM while you're online, live links will take you right to the electronic publishers' websites. Doing it electronically was basic common sense."

Gelfman Schneider Literary Agents partner Deborah Schneider believes fiscal gain via the sale of electronic books is little more than a dream on some distant horizon. "My personal opinion is that electronic rights, with relation to e-books, won't represent a real economic consideration until the cost of the electronic book reader follows the Walkman and VCR lead, and drops in price," she says.

THE BATTLE CONTINUES

Nevertheless, the control of electronic rights remains a ferocious industry battle. "It's one of the most contentious issues between agents and publishers today," Schneider admits. "Agents view electronic rights as they would any subsidiary right, as they would any other licensee of primary rights." In other words, most agents believe the author should get 50 percent of the publisher's electronic cut. "But not a single publisher has seen this as a subsidiary rights issue," continues Schneider. "They call it a matter of distribution and offer the author the prevailing royalty in whatever print edition is currently available."

Companies like NuvoMedia work directly with existing print publishers. NuvoMedia's subgroup Rocket eBook CEO and co-founder Martin Eberhard sides with the publisher, rather than Schneider, when it comes to Rocket eBook royalties. "Some e-book vendors are responsible for preparing and maintaining each electronic edition book they offer," Eberhard says. "This kind of system falls under a book licensing contract since the database is owned and administered by the vendor with little control by the publisher."

Distribution at Rocket eBook, according to Eberhard, is different. "Each publisher's book remains on the publisher's own server under the control of the publisher." he says. "When a customer buys a RocketEdition from a Web bookstore, the request goes through NuvoMedia's system, straight to a specific publisher, telling that publisher to deliver the book (in secure electronic form) to the consumer."

According to Schneider, that profit distribution may be unfair to the author of the original work. "As it stands, publishers are selling e-books for a 60 percent discount. Rocket is getting 20 percent, B&N 40 percent, and the publisher is getting the remaining 40 percent. That 40 percent is pure profit," Schneider says, "not production cost. The cost to encrypt a book for electronic transmission is negligible. And Rocket has been assuming the cost of encryption themselves." Awarding half of the publisher's 40 percent share to the author—rather than the traditional print royalty of 10 percent (4 percent of the total cost of the book)—is not unreasonable, according to Schneider.

Why war over the admittedly trickling electronic cash flow? Precedent, Schneider says. "Everyone is fighting hard over these issues now because they don't want to set an unfair precedent the industry will cling to if and when these rights do take on significant value."

Eberhard understands the agent/author's concern. "I think we all recognize that the electronic book will one day be very important," he says. "And I understand agents and authors are concerned about precedent because the first offer publishers made, years ago, was a bad deal, a really low royalty."

But now that Rocket eBooks command the same 11 to 15 percent royalty authors traditionally get for hardcover books, Eberhard would like to see any additional savings distributed to an often overlooked partner in publishing. "If there really is money saved in producing electronic books," Eberhard says, "why not pass that savings on to the guy who shelled out $350 to buy the Rocket eBook reader—the guy who makes it all possible? Now there's a novel notion, isn't it?

"I want the authors to be paid the same fair royalty they get for hardcover books," he says. "I want the publisher to make the same profit margin. Then I want the remainder of the savings passed on to the customer. That sells more books. Anything else is like fighting over a melting ice cube while sitting on an ice machine. It doesn't make much sense."

So the debate over electronic rights continues into the new millennium. And while innovations and options arise almost every day, the best ways to harmoniously use them seem to be just out of reach. If the answers are hazy, one thing remains crystal clear. The Internet is the undisputed wave of the future. And compromise will be the only way to come out on top.

AAR Checklist for Authors

Once you've found an agent

The following is a suggested list of topics to discuss with a literary agent who offers to represent you.

1. Are you a member of the Association of Authors' Representatives?
2. Is your agency a sole proprietorship? A partnership? A corporation?
3. How long have you been in business as an agent?
4. How many people does your agency employ?
5. Of the total number of employees, how many are agents, as opposed to clerical workers?
6. Do you have specialists at your agency who handle movie and television rights? Foreign rights? Do you have sub-agents or corresponding agents overseas and in Hollywood?
7. Do you represent other authors in my area of interest?
8. Who in your agency will actually be handling my work? Will the other staff members be familiar with my work and the status of my business at your agency? Will you oversee or at least keep me apprised of the work your agency is doing on my behalf?
9. Do you issue an agent-author contract? May I review a specimen copy? And may I review the language of the agency clause that appears in contracts you negotiate for your clients?
10. What is your approach to providing editorial input and career guidance for your clients or for me specifically?
11. How do you keep your clients informed of your activities on their behalf? Do you regularly send them copies of publishers' rejection letters or provide them only on request? Do you regularly, or upon request, send out updated activity reports?
12. Do you consult with your clients on any and all offers?
13. Some agencies sign subsidiary contracts on behalf of their clients to expedite processing. Do you?
14. What are your commissions for: 1) basic sales to U.S. publishers; 2) sales of movie and television rights; 3) audio and multimedia rights; 4) British and foreign translation rights?
15. What are your procedures and time frames for processing and disbursing client funds? Do you keep different bank accounts separating author funds from agency revenue?
16. What are your policies about charging clients for expenses incurred by your agency? Will you list such expenses for me? Do you advance money for such expenses? Do you consult with your clients before advancing certain expenditures? Is there a ceiling on such expenses above which you feel you must consult with your clients?
17. How do you handle legal, accounting, public relations or similar professional services that fall outside the normal range of a literary agency's functions?
18. Do you issue 1099 tax forms at the end of each year? Do you also furnish clients upon request with a detailed account of their financial activity, such as gross income, commissions and other deductions, and net income, for the past year?
19. In the event of your death or disability, or the death or disability of the principal person running the agency, what provisions exist for continuing operation of my account, for the processing of money due to me, and for the handling of my books and editorial needs?
20. If we should part company, what is your policy about handling any unsold subsidiary rights to my work that were reserved to me under the original publishing contracts?
21. What are your expectations of me as your client?

22. Do you have a list of Do's and Don'ts for your clients that will enable me to help you do your job better?

(Please bear in mind that most agents are NOT going to be willing to spend the time answering these questions unless they have already read your material and wish to represent you.)

Reprinted by permission of the Association of Authors' Representatives.

Listing Policy and Complaint Procedure

Listings in *Guide to Literary Agents* are compiled from detailed questionnaires, phone interviews and information provided by agents. The industry is volatile and agencies change frequently. We rely on our readers for information on their dealings with agents and changes in policies or fees that differ from what has been reported to the editor of this book. Write to us if you have new information, questions or problems dealing with the agencies listed.

Listings are published free of charge and are not advertisements. Although the information is as accurate as possible, the listings are *not* endorsed or guaranteed by the editor or publisher of *Guide to Literary Agents*. If you feel you have not been treated fairly by an agent or representative listed in *Guide to Literary Agents*, we advise you to take the following steps:

☑ First try to contact the agency. Sometimes one phone call or a letter can clear up the matter.

☑ Document all your correspondence with the agency. When you write to us with a complaint, provide the name of your manuscript, the date of your first contact with the agency and the nature of your subsequent correspondence.

☑ We will enter your letter into our files and attempt to contact the agency.

☑ The number, frequency and severity of complaints will be considered in our decision whether or not to delete the listing from the next edition.

Guide to Literary Agents reserves the right to exclude any agency for any reason.

Literary Agents: Nonfee-charging

Agents listed in this section generate from 98 to 100 percent of their income from commission on sales. They do not charge for reading, critiquing or editing. Sending a query to a nonfee-charging agent means you pay only the cost of postage to have your work considered by an agent with an imperative to find saleable manuscripts: Her income depends on finding the best publisher for your manuscript.

Because her time is more profitably spent meeting with editors, she will have little or no time to critique your writing. Agents who don't charge fees must be selective and often prefer to work with established authors, celebrities or those with professional credentials.

Some agents in this section may charge clients for office expenses such as photocopying, foreign postage, long distance phone calls or express mail services. Make sure you have a clear understanding of what these expenses are before signing any agency agreement. While most agents deduct expenses from the advance or royalties before passing them on to the author, a few agents included in this section charge a low ($100 or less) one-time "marketing" or "handling" fee up front. These agents have a ($) preceding their listing. Agents charging more than $100 in marketing fees are included in the Literary Agents: Fee-charging section.

For a detailed explanation of the agency listings and for more information on how to use the resources in this book, read Quick Start Guide to Using Your *Guide to Literary Agents* on page 2. When reading through this section, use the following key to help you understand specific material in the nonfee-charging listings:

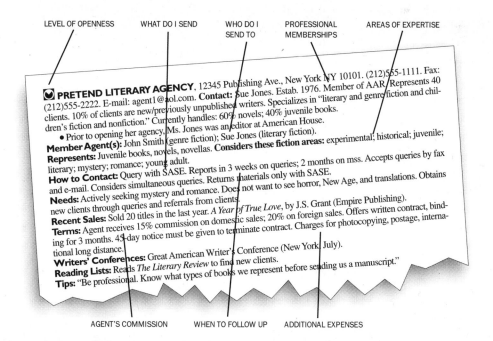

QUICK REFERENCE ICONS

At the beginning of some listings, you will find one or more of the following symbols for quick identification of features particular to that listing.

N Agency new to this edition.

☑ Change in address, contact information or phone number from last year's edition.

⑤ Agents who charge fees to previously unpublished writers only.

❖ Canadian agency.

OPENNESS

Each agency has an icon indicating its openness to submissions. Before contacting any agency, check the listing to make sure it is open to new clients.

◯ Newer agency actively seeking clients.

◑ Agency seeking both new and established writers.

◉ Agency prefers to work with established writers, mostly obtains new clients through referrals.

◎ Agency handling only certain types of work or work by writers under certain circumstances.

⊘ Agency not currently seeking new clients. We include these agencies to let you know they are currently not open to new clients. *Unless you have a strong recommendation from someone well respected in the field, our advice is to avoid approaching these agents.*

SUBHEADS

Each listing is broken down into subheads to make locating specific information easier. In the first section, you'll find contact information for each agency. You'll also learn if they belong to any professional organizations which can tell you a lot about an agency. For example, members of the Association of Authors' Representatives (AAR) are prohibited from charging reading or evaluating fees. Further information is provided which indicates an agency's size, its willingness to work with a new or previously unpublished writer, and its areas of specialization.

Member Agents: Agencies comprised of more than one agent list member agents and their individual specialties to help you determine the most appropriate person for your query letter.

Represents: Make sure you query only agents who represent the type of material you write. Here agencies specify what nonfiction and fiction subjects they consider. To help narrow your search, check the **Agents Specialties Index** that follows the nonfee-charging listings.

How to Contact: Most agents open to submissions prefer initially to receive a query letter briefly describing your work. (See Queries That Made It Happen on page 35.) Some agents ask for an outline and a number of sample chapters, but you should send these only if requested to do so. Here agents also indicate if they accept queries by fax or e-mail, and if they consider simultaneous submissions.

Needs: Here agents list what areas they are currently seeking as well as subjects they do *not* wish to receive. Also listed is the agent's preferred way of meeting new clients.

Recent Sales: To give a sense of the types of material they represent, agents provide specific titles they've sold as well as a sampling of clients' names. Some agents consider their client list confidential and may only share names once they agree to represent you.

Terms: Provided here are details of an agent's commission, whether a contract is offered and for how long, and what additional office expenses you might have to pay. Commissions range from 10 to 15 percent for domestic sales, and 20 to 25 percent for foreign or dramatic sales with the difference going to the co-agent who places the work.

Writers' Conferences: A great way to meet an agent is at a writer's conference. Here agents list the ones they attend. For more information about a specific conference, check the Writers'

Conferences section starting on page 292.

Reading List: Learn what magazines and journals agents read to discover potential clients.

Tips: Agents offer advice and additional instructions to writers looking for representation.

SPECIAL INDEXES AND ADDITIONAL HELP

This book contains several indexes to help facilitate your search for an agent. Use the indexes to help narrow your list of possible agents to query.

Additional Nonfee-charging Agents: Many literary agents are also interested in scripts; some script agents will also consider book manuscripts. Nonfee-charging script agents who primarily sell scripts but also handle at least 10 to 15 percent book manuscripts appear among the listings in this section, with the contact information, breakdown of work currently handled and a note to check the full listing in the script section. Those nonfee-charging script agencies that sell scripts and less than 10 to 15 percent book manuscripts appear at the end of this section on page 168. Complete listings for these agents also appear in the Script Agents section.

Agents Specialties Index: Immediately following this section of listings is an index which organizes agencies according to the subjects they are interested in receiving. This index should help you compose a list of agents specializing in your areas. Cross-referencing categories and concentrating on agents interested in two or more aspects of your manuscript might increase your chances of success. Agencies open to all nonfiction or fiction topics are grouped under the subject heading "open."

Agents Index: Often you will read about an agent who is an employee of a larger agency and you may not be able to locate her business phone or address. Starting on page 341, is a list of agents' names in alphabetical order along with the name of the agency they work for. Find the name of the person you would like to contact and then check the agency listing.

Geographic Index: For writers looking for an agent close to home, this index lists agents state-by-state.

Agencies Indexed by Openness to Submissions: This index lists agencies according to their receptivity to new clients.

Listing Index: This index lists all agencies and conferences listed in the book.

NONFEE-CHARGING AGENTS

CAROLE ABEL LITERARY AGENT, 160 W. 87th St., New York NY 10024. This agency did not respond to our request for information. Query before submitting.

ACACIA HOUSE PUBLISHING SERVICES LTD., 51 Acacia Rd., Toronto, Ontario M4S 2K6 Canada. Phone/fax: (416)484-8356. **Contact:** (Ms.) Frances Hanna. Estab. 1985. Represents 30 clients. Works with a small number of new/unpublished authors. Specializes in contemporary fiction: literary or commercial (no horror, occult or science fiction); nonfiction. Currently handles: 30% nonfiction books; 70% novels.

- Ms. Hanna has been in the publishing business for 30 years, first in London (UK) as a fiction editor with Barrie & Jenkins and Pan Books, and as a senior editor with a packager of mainly illustrated books. She was condensed books editor for 6 years for *Reader's Digest* in Montreal, senior editor and foreign rights manager for (the then) Wm. Collins & Sons (now HarperCollins) in Toronto.

Represents: Nonfiction books, novels. **Considers these nonfiction areas:** animals; biography/autobiography; language/literature/criticism; memoirs; military/war; music/dance/theater/film; nature/environment; travel. **Considers these fiction areas:** action/adventure; detective/police/crime; literary; mainstream; mystery/suspense; thriller/espionage.

How to Contact: Query with outline. Prefers to be only reader. No unsolicited mss. Reports in 3-6 weeks on queries. Returns materials only with SASE.

Needs: Actively seeking "outstanding first novels with literary merit."

Recent Sales: Sold 20 titles in the last year and numerous international rights. Prefers not to share client or sales data.

Terms: Agent receives 15% commission on English language sales; 20% on dramatic sales; 25-30% on foreign language sales. Charges for photocopying.

Writers' Conferences: London International Book Fair (England); BEA (Chicago); Frankfurt Book Fair (Germany).

Tips: "I prefer that writers be previously published, with at least a few articles to their credit. Strongest consideration will be given to those with, say, three or more published books. However, I *would* take on an unpublished writer of outstanding talent."

✓ ◎ **AGENTS INC. FOR MEDICAL AND MENTAL HEALTH PROFESSIONALS**, P.O. Box 4956, Fresno CA 93744. (559)438-8289. Fax: (559)438-1883. **Contact:** Sydney H. Harriet, Ph.D., Psy.D., director. Estab. 1987. Member of APA. Represents 49 clients. 70% of clients are new/previously unpublished writers. Specializes in "writers who have education and experience in the business, legal and health professions. It is helpful if the writer is licensed, but not necessary. Prior nonfiction book publication not necessary. For fiction, previously published fiction is prerequisite for representation." Currently handles: 80% nonfiction books; 20% novels.

 • Prior to becoming an agent and author, Dr. Harriet was a professor of English, psychologist, and radio and television reporter.

Represents: Nonfiction books, novels, multimedia projects. **Considers these nonfiction areas:** law; health/medicine; cooking/food/nutrition; psychology; reference; science/technology; self-help/personal improvement; sociology; sports medicine/psychology; mind-body healing. **Considers these fiction areas:** mystery/suspense; psychological thrillers and commercial fiction. No fantasy or science fiction. Currently representing previously published novelists only.

How to Contact: Query with vita and SASE. Accepts query letters only. Considers simultaneous queries and submissions. Reports in 3-4 weeks on queries; 1 month on mss "we request to read." "Craft must be outstanding since 99% of fiction mss are rejected. We do not respond to book pitches over the phone. Always submit a carefully prepared query or proposal with a SASE."

Needs: Does not want memoirs, autobiographies, stories about overcoming an illness, science fiction, fantasy, religious materials and children's books.

Recent Sales: Sold 5 titles in the last year. *Infantry Soldier*, by George Neil (University of Oklahoma Press); *SAMe, The European Arthritis and Depression Breakthrough*, by Sol Grazi, M.D. and Marie Costa (Prima); *What to Eat if You Have Diabetes*, by Danielle Chase M.S. (Contemporary); *The Red Yeast Diet Breakthrough*, by Maureen Keane, M.S. (Adams Media Corporation); *The Senior Golfer's Answer Book*, by Sol Grazi, M.D. and Syd Harriet, Ph.D., Psy.D. (Batsford-Brassey's).

Terms: Agent receives 15% commission on domestic sales; 20% on foreign sales. Offers written contract, binding for 6-12 months (negotiable).

Writers' Conferences: Scheduled as a speaker at a number of conferences across the country in 2000-2001. "Contact agency to book authors and agents for conferences."

Tips: "Remember, query first. *Do not call to pitch an idea.* The only way we can judge the quality of your idea is to see how you write. Please, unsolicited manuscripts will not be read if they arrive without a SASE. Currently we are receiving more than 200 query letters and proposals each month. Send complete proposal/manuscript only if requested. Please, please, ask yourself why someone would be compelled to buy your book. If you think the idea is unique, spend the time to create a query and then a proposal where every word counts. Fiction writers need to understand that the craft is just as important as the idea. 99% of the fiction is rejected because of sloppy overwritten dialogue, wooden characters, predictable plotting and lifeless narrative. Once you finish your novel, put it away and let it percolate, then take it out and work on fine-tuning it some more. A novel is never finished until you stop working on it. Would love to represent more fiction writers and probably will when we read a manuscript that has gone through a dozen or more drafts. Because of rising costs, we no longer can respond to queries, proposals, and/or complete manuscripts without receiving a return envelope and sufficient postage."

◎ **ALIVE COMMUNICATIONS, INC.,** 1465 Kelly Johnson Blvd., Suite 320, Colorado Springs CO 80920. (719)260-7080. Fax: (719)260-8223. Website: www.alivecom.com. Estab. 1989. Member of AAR, CBA. Represents 100 clients. 5% of clients are new/unpublished writers. Currently handles: 40% nonfiction books; 10% juvenile books; 4% short story collections; 40% novels; 1% syndicated material; 5% novellas.

Member Agent(s): Rick Christian (blockbusters, bestsellers); Greg Johnson (popular/commercial nonfiction and fiction); Kathy Yanni (literary nonfiction and fiction); Jerry "Chip" MacGregor (popular/commercial nonfiction and fiction, new authors with breakout potential).

Represents: Nonfiction books, juvenile books, novels, novellas, poetry, short story collections. **Considers these nonfiction areas:** biography/autobiography; business; child guidance/ parenting; how-to; religious/inspirational; self-help/personal improvement; sports; women's issues/women's studies. **Considers these fiction areas:** action/adventure; contemporary issues; detective/police/crime; family saga; historical; humor/satire; juvenile; literary; mainstream; mystery/suspense; religious/inspirational; thriller/espionage; westerns/frontier; young adult.

How to Contact: Send outline and 3 sample chapters. Include bio/résumé, publishing history and SASE. Considers simultaneous submissions, "if clearly noted in cover letter." Reports in 2 weeks on queries; 1 month on mss. Returns materials only with SASE.

Needs Actively seeking inspirational/literary/mainstream fiction and work from authors with established track record and platforms. Does not want to receive poetry, young adult paperback, scripts, dark themes. Obtains new clients through recommendations from clients and publishers.

Recent Sales: Sold 300 titles in the last year. *Left Behind* series, by Tim LaHaye and Jerry B. Jenkins (Tyndale); *Jerusalem Vigil*, by Bodie and Brock Thoene (Viking).

Terms: Agent receives 15% commission on domestic sales; 15-30% on foreign sales. Offers written contract. 60 days written notice must be given to terminate contract.

Reading List: Reads literary, religious and mainstream journals to find new clients. "Our goal is always the same—to find writers whose use of language is riveting and powerful."

Tips: "Rewrite and polish until the words on the page shine. Provide us with as much personal and publishing history

information as possible. Endorsements and great connections may help, provided you can write with power and passion. Alive Communications, Inc. has established itself as a premiere literary agency and speakers bureau. Based in Colorado Springs, we serve an elite group of authors and speakers, who are critically acclaimed and commercially successful in both Christian and general markets."
Terms: Agent receives 15% commission. Charges for photocopying.

JAMES ALLEN, LITERARY AGENT, P.O. Box 278, Milford PA 18337-0278. **Contact:** James Allen. Estab. 1974. Signatory of WGA. Represents 40 clients. 10% of clients are new/previously unpublished writers. "I handle all kinds of genre fiction (except westerns) and specialize in science fiction and fantasy." Currently handles: 2% nonfiction books; 8% juvenile books; 90% novels.
Represents: Nonfiction books, novels. **Considers these nonfiction areas:** history; true crime/investigative. **Considers these fiction areas:** action/adventure; detective/police/crime; family saga; fantasy; glitz; historical; horror; mainstream; mystery/suspense; romance (contemporary, historical); science fiction; young adult.
How to Contact: Query. Responds in 1 week on queries; 2 months on mss. "I prefer first contact to be a query letter with two- to three-page plot synopsis and SASE with a response time of one week. If my interest is piqued, I then ask for the first four chapters, response time within a month. If I'm impressed by the writing, I then ask for the balance of the manuscript, response time about two months."
Needs: Actively seeking "well-written work by people who at least have their foot in the door and are looking for someone to take them to the next (and subsequent) levels." Does not want to receive "petitions for representation from people who do not yet have even one booklength credit."
Recent Sales: Sold about 35 titles in the last year. *China Sea*, by David Poyer (St. Martin's Press), *Aranur's Tale*, by Tara K. Harper (Del Rey), *The Devil in Ol' Rosie*, by Louise Moeri (Atheneum/S&S). Other clients include Doug Allyn, Judi Lind, Robert Trout, Juanita Coulson and Jan Clark.
Terms: Agent receives 10% commission on domestic print sales; 20% on film sales; 20% on foreign sales. Offers written contract, binding for 3 years "automatically renewed. No reading fees or other up-front charges. I reserve the right to charge for extraordinary expenses (in practice, only the cost of book purchases when I need copies to market a title abroad). I do not bill the author but deduct the charges from incoming earnings."
Tips: *"First time at book length need NOT* apply—only taking on authors who have the foundations of their writing careers in place and can use help in building the rest. A cogent, to-the-point query letter is necessary, laying out the author's track record and giving a brief blurb for the book. The response to a mere 'I have written a novel, will you look at it?' is universally 'NO!' "

LINDA ALLEN LITERARY AGENCY, 1949 Green St., Suite 5, San Francisco CA 94123-4829. (415)921-6437. **Contact:** Linda Allen or Amy Kossow. Estab. 1982. Member of AAR. Represents 35-40 clients. Specializes in "good books and nice people."
Represents: Nonfiction, novels (adult). **Considers these nonfiction areas:** anthropology/archaeology; art/architecture/design; biography; business; child guidance/parenting; computers/electronics; ethnic/cultural interests; gay/lesbian issues; government/politics/law; history; music/dance/theater/film; nature/environment; popular culture; psychology; sociology; women's issues/women's studies. **Considers these fiction areas:** action/adventure; contemporary issues; detective/police/crime; ethnic; feminist; gay; glitz; horror; lesbian; literary; mainstream; mystery/suspense; psychic/supernatural; regional; thriller/espionage.
How to Contact: Query with SASE. Considers simultaneous queries. Reports in 2-3 weeks on queries. Returns materials only with SASE.
Needs: Obtains new clients "by referral mostly."
Recent Sales: Prefers not to share information on specific sales.
Terms: Agent receives 15% commission. Charges for photocopying.

ALLRED AND ALLRED LITERARY AGENTS, (formerly All-Star Talent Agency), 7834 Alabama Ave., Canoga Park CA 91304-4905. (818)346-4313. **Contact:** Robert Allred. Estab. 1991. Represents 5 clients. 100% of clients are new/previously unpublished writers. Specializes in books. Currently handles: books, movie scripts, TV scripts.
  ● Prior to opening his agency, Mr. Allred was a writer, assistant producer, associate director and editorial assistant.
Member Agents: Robert Allred (all); Kim Allred (all).
Represents: Nonfiction books, scholarly books, textbooks, juvenile books, novels, short story collections, syndicated material. **Considers these nonfiction areas:** anthropology/archaeology; art/architecture/design; biography/autobiography; cooking/food/nutrition; crafts/hobbies; current affairs; education; ethnic/cultural interests; health/medicine; history;

FOR EXPLANATIONS OF THESE SYMBOLS,
SEE THE INSIDE FRONT AND BACK COVERS OF THIS BOOK

how-to; humor; interior design/decorating; juvenile nonfiction; language/literature/criticism; military/war; music/dance/theater/film; New Age/metaphysics; photography; popular culture; psychology; religious/inspirational; science/technology; self-help/personal improvement; sociology; sports; true crime/investigative; women's issues/women's studies. **Considers these fiction areas:** action/adventure; confessional; contemporary issues; detective/police/crime; erotica; ethnic; family saga; fantasy; feminist; gay; glitz; historical; horror; humor/satire; juvenile; lesbian; literary; mainstream; mystery/suspense; psychic/supernatural; regional; religious/inspirational; romance (contemporary, gothic, historical, regency); science fiction; sports; thriller/espionage; westerns/frontier; young adult.

Also Handles: Feature film, TV MOW, episodic drama, sitcom, soap opera, theatrical stage play, animation, documentary, variety show. **Considers all script subject areas.**

How to Contact: Query. Book: send first 25 pages. Script: send entire script. For both, include 1-2 page synopsis, cover letter and SASE. "The synopsis must cover the entire length of the project from beginning to end." Considers simultaneous queries and submissions. Reports in 3 weeks on queries; 2 months on mss. Returns materials only with SASE.

Needs: Obtains new clients through recommendations and solicitation.

Recent Sales: Prefers not to share information on specific sales.

Terms: Agent receives 10% commission on domestic sales; 10% on foreign sales with foreign agent receiving additional 10%. Offers written contract, binding for 1 year. 100% of business derived from commissions on ms.

Tips: "A professional appearance in script format, dark and large type and simple binding go a long way to create good first impressions in this business, as does a professional business manner. We must be able to at least estimate the potential of the whole project before we can expend the time reading it in its entirety. Writers who try to sell us with overblown hyperbole or titillate our curiosity by vaguely hinting at a possible outcome do themselves a disservice; agents don't have time for reading sales copy—just tell us what it's about, and let us make the decision about whether we want to see the entire project."

[N] ☉ ALTAIR LITERARY AGENCY, 141 Fifth Ave., Suite 8N, New York NY 10010. (212)505-3320. **Contact:** Nicholas Smith, partner. Estab. 1996. Member of AAR. Represents 75 clients. Specializes in nonfiction with an emphasis on authors who have a direct connection to their topic, and at least a moderate level of public exposure. Currently handles: 95% nonfiction books; 2% juvenile books; 1% multimedia; 2% novels.

Member Agents: Andrea Pedolsky, partner (nonfiction); Nicholas Smith, partner.

Represents: Nonfiction books. **Considers these nonfiction areas:** anthropology/archaeology; art/architecture/design; biography/autobiography; business; child guidance/parenting; ethnic/cultural interests; gay/lesbian issues; government/politics/law; health/medicine; history; how-to; illustrated books; money/finance/economics; music/dance/theater/film; nature/environment; photography; popular culture; popular reference; psychology; religious/inspirational; science/technology; self-help/personal improvement; sociology; sports; women's issues/women's studies. **Considers these fiction areas:** historical; literary. Also interested in book to CD conversion and book to museum exhibition.

How to Contact: Query with SASE. Considers simultaneous queries and submissions. Reports in 2-3 weeks on queries; 1 month on mss.

Needs: Actively seeking solid, well-informed authors who have or are developing a public platform for the subject specialty. Does not want to receive true crime, memoirs, romance novels. Obtains new clients through recommendations, solicitations and author queries.

Recent Sales: *Women of Discovery,* by Milbry Polk and Mary Tiegreen (Crown/Clarkson Potter); *Building a Business the Zen Way,* by Geri Larkin (Ten Speed/Celestial Arts); *Date Smart!,* by David Coleman and Rick Doyle (Prima); *Extreme Science,* by Peter Taylor (McGraw-Hill).

Terms: Agent receives 15% commission on domestic sales; 20% on foreign sales. Offers written contract, exclusive for 1 year. 60 day notice must be given to terminate contract. Charges for photocopying (edits of the proposal/chapters/ms to author, copies of proposal for submissions), postage (correspondence to author, proposals for submission, and marketing book for translation rights. May refer writers to outside editor but receives no compensation for referral.

Tips: "Beyond being able to write a compelling book, have an understanding of the market issues that are driving publishing today."

☉ MIRIAM ALTSHULER LITERARY AGENCY, RR #1 Box 5, 5 Old Post Rd., Red Hook NY 12751. This agency did not respond to our request for information. Query before submitting.

[N] ○ ☉ AMBER LITERARY, 1956 Homestead Duquesne Rd., W. Mifflin PA 15122. (412)469-8293. E-mail: jlaycak@libcom.com. Website: www.freeyellow.com/members/jlaycak/index.html. **Contact:** Jerome E. Laycak. Estab. 1999. Represents 3 clients. 75% of clients are new/unpublished writers. Currently handles: 5% nonfiction books; 5% juvenile books; 70% novels; 10% novellas; 10% poetry.

• Prior to becoming an agent, Mr. Laycak was a newspaper columnist, magazine staff editor and freelance writer.

Member Agents: Jerome Laycak (all areas); William Ray (mainstream fiction); Jeri Spang (poetry, scholarly books, history); Beverly Browe (romance).

Represents: Nonfiction books, juvenile books, scholarly books, novels, novellas, poetry books, short story collections. **Considers these nonfiction areas:** anthropology/archaeology; art/architecture/design; biography/autobiography; child guidance/parenting; computers/electronics; current affairs; education; government/politics/law; history; how-to; humor; juvenile nonfiction; military/war; music/dance/theater/film; psychology; religious/inspirational; sociology; true crime/investigative; women's issues/women's studies. **Considers these fiction areas:** action/adventure; contemporary issues;

detective/police/crime; family saga; fantasy; historical; horror; humor/satire; juvenile; literary; mainstream; mystery; romance; religious/inspirational; science fiction; thriller/espionage; westerns/frontier; young adult.

How to Contact: Query with SASE or e-mail synopsis. Accepts queries by e-mail. Considers simultaneous queries and submissions. Reports in 2 weeks. Returns materials only with SASE.

Needs: Actively seeking all types of mainstream fiction. Does not want to receive movies, TV, scripts, erotica or pornography. Obtains new clients through submissions.

Recent Sales: New agency with no reported sales. Clients include Thomas Rohosky, Jarrod Davis, Linda S. Bingham.

Terms: Agent receives 15% commission on domestic sales; 20% on foreign sales. Offers written contract. 30 day notice must be given to terminate contract. Charges $10 office handling fee.

Tips: "Clarity in synopsis is important. Many first-time writers have excellent story lines but are weak in sentence structure and basic grammar."

BETSY AMSTER LITERARY ENTERPRISES, P.O. Box 27788, Los Angeles CA 90027-0788. **Contact:** Betsy Amster. Estab. 1992. Member of AAR. Represents over 50 clients. 40% of clients are new/unpublished writers. Currently handles: 65% nonfiction books; 35% novels.

● Prior to opening her agency, Ms. Amster was an editor at Pantheon and Vintage for 10 years and served as editorial director for the Globe Pequot Press for 2 years. "This experience gives me a wider perspective on the business and the ability to give focused editorial feedback to my clients."

Represents: Nonfiction books, novels. **Considers these nonfiction areas:** biography/autobiography; business; child guidance/parenting; cyberculture; ethnic/cultural interests; gardening; health/medicine; history; how-to; money/finance/economics; popular culture; psychology; self-help/personal improvement; sociology; women's issues/women's studies. **Considers these fiction areas:** ethnic; literary.

How to Contact: For fiction, send query and first page. For nonfiction, send query only. For both, "include SASE or no response." Reports in 2-4 weeks on queries; 4-8 weeks on mss.

Needs: Actively seeking "outstanding literary fiction (the next Jane Smiley or Wally Lamb) and high profile self-help/psychology." Does not want to receive poetry, children's books, romances, westerns, science fiction. Obtains new clients through recommendations from others, solicitation, conferences.

Recent Sales: *Esperanza's Box of Saints*, by Maria Amparo Escandón; *The Tribes of Palos Verdes*, by Joy Nicholson (St. Martin's); *How to be a Chicana Role Model*, by Michele M. Serros (Riverhead); *The Blessing of a Skinned Knee: Using Jewish Spiritual Wisdom to Solve Everyday Parenting Problems*, by Wendy Mogel (Scribner); *What They Don't Teach You at Film School*, by Camille Landau & Tiare White (Hyperion); *Sports Her Way: Motivating Girls to Start & Stay with Sports*, by Susan M. Wilson (Simon & Schuster); *The Medicine Wheel Garden*, by E. Barrie Kavasch (Bantam).

Terms: Agent receives 15% commission on domestic sales. Offers written contract, binding for 1-2 years. 60 days notice must be given to terminate contract. Charges for photocopying, postage, long distance phone calls, messengers and galleys and books used in submissions to foreign and film agents and to magazines for first serial rights.

Writers' Conferences: Squaw Valley, Maui Writers Conference; Pacific Northwest Conference; San Diego Writers Conference; UCLA Writers Conference.

MARCIA AMSTERDAM AGENCY, 41 W. 82nd St., New York NY 10024-5613. (212)873-4945. **Contact:** Marcia Amsterdam. Estab. 1970. Signatory of WGA. Currently handles: 15% nonfiction books; 70% novels; 10% movie scripts; 5% TV scripts.

● Prior to opening her agency, Ms. Amsterdam was an editor.

Represents: Nonfiction, novels. **Considers these nonfiction areas:** child guidance/parenting, humor, popular culture, self-help/personal improvement. **Considers these fiction areas:** action/adventure; detective; horror; humor; mainstream; mystery/suspense; romance (contemporary, historical); science fiction; thriller/espionage; westerns/frontier; young adult. **Also Handles:** Feature film, TV MOW, sitcom. **Considers these script subject areas:** comedy; mainstream; mystery/suspense; romantic comedy; romantic drama.

How to Contact: Send outline plus first 3 sample chapters and SASE. Reports in 1 month on queries.

Recent Sales: *Rosey In the Present Tense*, by Louise Hawes (Walker); *Flash Factor*, by William H. Lovejoy (Kensington). *TV scripts optioned/sold:* Mad About You, by Jenna Bruce (Columbia Tristar TV).

Terms: Agent receives 15% commission on domestic sales; 20% on foreign sales, 10% on scripts. Offers written contract, binding for 1 year, "renewable." Charges for extra office expenses, foreign postage, copying, legal fees (when agreed upon).

Tips: "We are always looking for interesting literary voices."

BART ANDREWS & ASSOCIATES INC., 7510 Sunset Blvd., Suite 100, Los Angeles CA 90046. (213)851-8158. **Contact:** Bart Andrews. Estab. 1982. Member of AAR. Represents 25 clients. 25% of clients are new/previously unpublished authors. Specializes in nonfiction only, and in the general category of entertainment (movies, TV, biographies, autobiographies). Currently handles: 100% nonfiction books.

Represents: Nonfiction books. **Considers these nonfiction areas:** biography/autobiography; music/dance/theater/film; TV.

How to Contact: Query. Reports in 1 week on queries; 1 month on mss.

Recent Sales: *Roseanne*, by J. Randy Taraborrelli (G.P. Putnam's Sons); *Out of the Madness*, by Rose Books (packaging firm) (HarperCollins).

Terms: Agent receives 15% commission on domestic sales; 15% on foreign sales (after subagent takes his 10%). Offers written contract, "binding on a project-by-project basis." Author/client is charged for all photocopying, mailing, phone calls, postage, etc.

Writers' Conferences: Frequently lectures at UCLA in Los Angeles.

Tips: "Recommendations from existing clients or professionals are best, although I find a lot of new clients by seeking them out myself. I rarely find a new client through the mail. Spend time writing a query letter. Sell yourself like a product. The bottom line is writing ability, and then the idea itself. It takes a lot to convince me. I've seen it all! I hear from too many first-time authors who don't do their homework. They're trying to get a book published and they haven't the faintest idea what is required of them. There are plenty of good books on the subject and, in my opinion, it's their responsibility—not mine—to educate themselves before they try to find an agent to represent their work. When I ask an author to see a manuscript or even a partial manuscript, I really must be convinced I want to read it—based on a strong query letter—because I have no intention of wasting my time reading just for the fun of it."

APPLESEEDS MANAGEMENT, 200 E. 30th St., Suite 302, San Bernardino CA 92404. (909)882-1667. For screenplays and teleplays only, send to 1870 N. Vermont, Suite 560, Hollywood CA 90027. **Contact:** S. James Foiles, executive manager. Estab. 1988. Signatory of WGA, licensed by state of California. 40% of clients are new/previously unpublished writers. Currently handles: 15% nonfiction books; 75% novels; 5% movie scripts; 5% teleplays (MOW).

● This agency reports that it is not accepting unsolicited screenplays and teleplays at this time.

Represents: Nonfiction books, novels. **Considers these nonfiction areas:** film; true crime/investigative. **Considers these fiction areas:** detective/police/crime; fantasy; horror; mystery/suspense; psychic/supernatural; science fiction; true crime/investigative.

Also Handles: Movie scripts, TV MOW, no episodic. Specializes in materials that could be adapted from book to screen; and in screenplays and teleplays.

How to Contact: Query. Reports in 2 weeks on queries; 2 months on mss.

Recent Sales: Prefers not to share in information on specific sales.

Terms: Agent receives 10-15% commission on domestic sales; 20% on foreign sales. Offers written contract, binding for 1-7 years.

Tips: "In your query, please describe your intended audience and distinguish your book/script from similar works."

AUTHENTIC CREATIONS LITERARY AGENCY, 875 Lawrenceville-Suwanee Rd., Suite 310-306, Lawrenceville GA 30043. (770)339-3774. Fax: (770)995-2648. E-mail: marylee@authenticcreations.com. **Contact:** Mary Lee Laitsch. Estab. 1993. Member of Sisters in Crime. Represents 70 clients. 60% of clients are new/previously unpublished writers. Currently handles: 50% nonfiction books; 50% novels.

● Prior to becoming agents, Ms. Laitsch was a librarian and elementary school teacher; Mr. Laitsch was an attorney and a writer.

Member Agents: Mary Lee Laitsch; Ronald E. Laitsch.

Represents: Nonfiction books, scholarly books, novels. **Considers these nonfiction areas:** anthropology/archaeology; biography/autobiography; child guidance/parenting; crafts/hobbies; current affairs; history; how-to; science/technology; self-help/personal improvement; sports; true crime/investigative; women's issues/women's studies. **Considers these fiction areas:** action/adventure; contemporary issues; detective/police/crime; family saga; literary; mainstream; mystery/suspense; romance; sports; thriller/espionage.

How to Contact: Query. Reports in 2 weeks on queries; 2 months on mss. "We prefer not to receive queries by e-mail."

Recent Sales: Sold 18 titles in the last year. Prefers not to share information on specific sales.

Terms: Agent receives 15% commission on domestic sales; 15% on foreign sales. Charges for photocopying and postage.

Tips: "Service to our authors is the key to our success. We work with authors to produce a fine product for prospective publishers."

AUTHORS ALLIANCE INC., 25 Claremont Ave., Suite 3C, New York NY 10027. Phone/Fax: (212)662-9788. E-mail: camp544@aol.com. **Contact:** Chris Crane. Represents 25 clients. 10% of clients are new/previously unpublished writers. Specializes in "biographies, especially of historical figures and big name celebrities and business books." Currently handles: 40% nonfiction books, 30% movie scripts, 30% novels.

● Prior to opening the agency, Chris Crane worked for Bantam Doubleday Dell Publishing and Warner Books.

Represents: Nonfiction books, movie scripts, novels. **Considers these nonfiction areas:** biography/autobiography; business; child guidance/parenting; computers/electronics; cooking/food/nutrition; crafts/hobbies; current affairs; government/politics/law; health/medicine; history; how-to; language/literature/criticism; memoirs; military/war; money/finance/economics; music/dance/theater/film; nature/environment; New Age/metaphysics; psychology; religious/inspirational; self-help/personal improvement; sports; true crime/investigative. **Considers these fiction areas:** contemporary issues; detective/police/crime; glitz; historical; literary; mainstream; mystery/suspense; thriller/espionage.

How to Contact: Published authors should send outline and 3 sample chapters. Reports in 2 weeks on queries; 1 month on mss.

Needs: Actively seeking mainstream and literary fiction/nonfiction. Does not want to receive children's books or poetry. Usually obtains clients through recommendations and queries.

Recent Sales: *License to Steal*, by Scott Gilman (HarperCollins); *Moscow Madness*, by Tim Harper (McGraw-Hill).

Terms: Agent receives 15% commission on domestic sales; 10% on foreign sales. Offers written contract. Charges for postage, photocopying.

N $ ☑ ◎ AUTHORS & ARTISTS GROUP, INC., 19 W. 44th St., New York NY 10036. (212)944-9898. Fax: (212)944-6484. **Contact:** Al Lowman, president. Estab. 1984. Represents 50 clients. 25% of clients are new/unpublished writers. Specializes in celebrity-based autobiographies and self-help books; and any books that bring its readers to "higher ground." Currently handles: 95% nonfiction books; 5% novels.
   • Prior to becoming an agent, Mr. Lowman was an advertising executive.
Member Agents: B.G. Dilworth (nonfiction); Dean Williamson (nonfiction); Al Lowman (president nonfiction).
Represents: Nonfiction books, novels. **Considers these nonfiction areas:** art/architecture/design; biography/autobiography; business; child guidance/parenting; computers/electronics; cooking/food/nutrition; crafts/hobbies; current affairs; education; ethnic/cultural interests; gay/lesbian issues; health/medicine; history; how-to; humor; interior design/decorating; memoirs; money/finance/economics; music/dance/theater/film; nature/environment; New Age/metaphysics; photography; popular culture; psychology; religious/inspirational; science/technology; self-help/personal improvement; sociology; sports; true crime/investigative; women's issues/women's studies. **Considers these fiction areas:** action/adventure; contemporary issues; detective/police/crime; erotica; ethnic; gay/lesbian; horror; humor/satire; mainstream; psychic/supernatural; religious/inspirational; thriller/espionage.
How to Contact: Fax 1 page query. Accepts queries by fax. Considers simultaneous queries. Reports in 3 weeks on queries. Discards unwanted queries and mss.
Needs: Actively seeking fresh full length, adult nonfiction ideas and established novelists. Does not want to receive film and TV scripts, children's stories, poetry or short stories. Obtains new clients through recommendations.
Recent Sales: Sold 20 titles in the last year. *Labelle Cuisine*, by Patti Labelle (Broadway); *Get Skinny on Fabulous Food*, by Suzanne Somers (Crown); *A Bend in the Road is Not the End of the Road*, by Joan Lunden (William Morrow); *Forgive or Forget*, by Mother Love (HarperCollins). Other clients include Sarah, Duchess of York, Diana Ross, Mary Lou Retton.
Terms: Agent receives 15% commission on domestic sales; 20% on foreign sales. Charges for office expenses, postage, photocopying not to exceed $1,000 without permission of author.

N ◎ THE AXELROD AGENCY, INC., 66 Church St., Lenox MA 01240. This agency did not respond to our request for information. Query before submitting.

N ◎ JULIAN BACH LITERARY AGENCY, 22 E. 71st St., New York NY 10021. This agency did not respond to our request for information. Query before submitting.

◎ MALAGA BALDI LITERARY AGENCY, 2112 Broadway, Suite 403, New York NY 10023. (212)579-5075. **Contact:** Malaga Baldi. Estab. 1985. Represents 40-50 clients. 80% of clients are new/previously unpublished writers. Specializes in quality literary fiction and nonfiction. Currently handles: 60% nonfiction books; 40% novels.
   • Prior to opening the agency, Malaga Baldi worked in a bookstore.
Represents: Nonfiction books, novels. **Considers these nonfiction areas:** agriculture/horticulture; animals; anthropology/archaeology; art/architecture/design; biography/autobiography; business; cooking/food; current affairs; ethnic/cultural interests; gay/lesbian issues; government/politics; health/medicine; history; interior design/decorating; language/literature/criticism; memoirs; money/finance/economics; music/dance/theater/film; nature/environment; photography; psychology; science/technology; sociology; travel; true crime/investigative; women's issues/women's studies. **Considers these fiction areas:** action/adventure; contemporary issues; detective; erotica; ethnic; experimental; feminist; gay; historical; lesbian; literary; mainstream; mystery/suspense; regional; thriller.
How to Contact: Query first. Reports after a minimum of 10 weeks. "Please enclose self-addressed stamped jiffy bag or padded envelope with submission. For acknowledgement of manuscript receipt send via certified mail or UPS."
Needs: Actively seeking well-written fiction and nonfiction. Does not want to receive child guidance, crafts, juvenile nonfiction, New Age/metaphysics, sports, family saga, fantasy, glitz, juvenile fiction, picture book, psychic/supernatural, religious/inspirational, romance, science fiction, western or young adult.
Recent Sales: Sold 13 titles in the last year. Prefers not to share information on specific sales.
Terms: Agent receives 15% commission on domestic sales; 20% on foreign sales. Offers written contract. Charges "initial $50 fee to cover photocopying expenses. If the manuscript is lengthy, I prefer the author to cover expense of photocopying."
Tips: "From the day I agree to represent an author, my role is to serve as his or her advocate in contract negotiations and publicity efforts. Along the way, I wear many different hats. To one author I may serve as a nudge, to another a

THE PUBLISHING FIELD is constantly changing! If you're still using this book and it is 2001 or later, buy the newest edition of *Guide to Literary Agents* at your favorite bookstore or order directly from Writer's Digest Books at (800)289-0963.

confidante, and to many simply as a supportive friend. I am also a critic, researcher, legal expert, messenger, diplomat, listener, counselor and source of publishing information and gossip. I work with writers on developing a presentable submission and make myself available during all aspects of a book's publication."

⊘ BALKIN AGENCY, INC., P.O. Box 222, Amherst MA 01004. (413)548-9835. Fax: (413)548-9836. **Contact:** Rick Balkin, president. Estab. 1972. Member of AAR. Represents 50 clients. 10% of clients are new/previously unpublished writers. Specializes in adult nonfiction. Currently handles: 85% nonfiction books; 5% scholarly books; 5% reference books; 5% textbooks.
 • Prior to opening his agency, Mr. Balkin served as executive editor with Bobbs-Merrill Company.
Represents: Nonfiction books, textbooks, reference, scholarly books. **Considers these nonfiction areas:** animals; anthropology/archaeology; biography; current affairs; health/medicine; history; how-to; language/literature/criticism; music/dance/theater/film; nature/environment; popular culture; science/technology; social science; translations; travel; true crime/investigative.
How to Contact: Query with outline/proposal. Reports in 2 weeks on queries; 3 weeks on mss. Returns materials only with SASE.
Needs: Does not want to receive fiction, poetry, screenplays, computer books. Obtains new clients through referrals.
Recent Sales: Prefers not to share information on specific sales.
Terms: Agent receives 15% commission on domestic sales; 20% on foreign sales. Offers written contract, binding for 1 year. Charges for photocopying, trans-Atlantic long-distance calls or faxes and express mail.
Tips: "I do not take on books described as bestsellers or potential bestsellers. Any nonfiction work that is either unique, paradigmatic, a contribution, truly witty or a labor of love is grist for my mill."

⊘ VIRGINIA BARBER LITERARY AGENCY, INC., 101 Fifth Ave., New York NY 10003. This agency did not respond to our request for information. Query before submitting.

⊘ LORETTA BARRETT BOOKS INC., 101 Fifth Ave., New York NY 10003. (212)242-3420. Fax: (212)691-9418. E-mail: lbarbooks@aol.com. President: Loretta A. Barrett. **Contact:** Kirsten Lundell or Loretta A. Barrett. Estab. 1990. Member of AAR. Represents 70 clients. Specializes in general interest books. Currently handles: 25% fiction; 75% nonfiction.
 • Prior to opening her agency, Ms. Barrett was vice president and executive editor at Doubleday for 25 years.
Represents: Considers all areas of nonfiction. Considers these fiction areas: action/adventure; confessional; contemporary issues; detective/police/crime; ethnic; experimental; family saga; feminist; gay; glitz; historical; humor/satire; lesbian; literary; mainstream; mystery/suspense; psychic/supernatural; religious/inspirational; romance; sports; thriller/espionage. "No children's or juvenile."
How to Contact: Query first with SASE. Considers simultaneous queries and submissions. Reports in 4-6 weeks on queries. Returns materials only with SASE.
Recent Sales: *Inviting God to Your Wedding*, by Martha Williamson (Harmony); *Line of Sight*, by Jack Kelly (Hyperion).
Terms: Agent receives 15% commission on domestic sales; 20% on foreign sales. Offers written contract. Charges for shipping and photocopying.
Writers' Conferences: San Diego State University Writer's Conference; Maui Writer's Conference.

⊘ MARGARET BASCH, 850 E. Higgins, #125, Schaumburg IL 60173. (847)240-1199. Fax: (847)240-1845. E-mail: lawlady@aol.com. **Contact:** Margaret Basch. Represents 100 clients. 5% of clients are new/unpublished writers. Currently handles: 40% nonfiction books; 20% juvenile books; 40% novels.
 • Prior to becoming an agent, Ms. Basch was a trial lawyer.
Represents: Currently not accepting new clients.
Recent Sales: Prefers not to share information on specific sales.
Terms: Agent receives 10% commission on domestic sales; 10% on foreign sales. Offers written contract.
Tips: "All of our clients are published and most came from other agents to be with us."

☑ ⊘ THE BEDFORD BOOK WORKS, INC., 17 Adams St., Bedford Hills NY 10507. (914)242-6262. Fax: (914)242-5232. **Contact:** Joel E. Fishman, president. Estab. 1993. Represents 50 clients. 50% of clients are new/previously unpublished writers. Currently handles: 80% nonfiction books, 20% novels.
 • Prior to becoming agents, Mr. Fishman served as senior editor at Doubleday and Mr. Lang worked as Doubleday's foreign rights director.
Member Agents: Joel E. Fishman (narrative nonfiction, category nonfiction and commercial fiction); Kevin Lang (commercial fiction, humor, nonfiction).
Represents: Nonfiction books, novels. **Considers these nonfiction areas:** biography/autobiography; business; current affairs; health/medicine; history; how-to; humor; money/finance/economics; popular culture; psychology; science/technology; sports. **Considers these fiction areas:** contemporary issues; detective/police/crime; mainstream; mystery/suspense; thriller/espionage.
How to Contact: Query. Reports in 2 weeks on queries; 2 months on mss.
Needs: Obtains new clients through recommendations and solicitation.
Recent Sales: *Breathwalk*, by Gurucharan Singh Khalsa and Yogi Bhajan (Broadway); *The Corporate Athlete*, by Jack

insider report

Important advice for beginning—and established—writers

Growing up in a house full of books, Jenny Bent always knew she wanted to be involved in publishing. So when she graduated with a B.A. and M.A. in English literature from Cambridge University, she got a job working for the Sagalyn Agency where she eventually became foreign rights manager. She later worked as an editor for a book packager, then as a bookseller, and now represents her own titles as a literary agent affiliated with the law firm of Graybill & English in Washington, D.C.

Jenny Bent

What's the best way for a writer to find an agent?
Most of my clients have been referred to me by other writers or by other industry professionals. If you don't know anyone in the industry, join a writing group, take writing classes. Work on making connections with people who can help you.

Otherwise, do your homework—check out reference books on agents and find out who accepts work in categories similar to yours. Go to bookstores, and look at the acknowledgments in books. Often writers thank their agents. You can then approach an agent by saying, "You represent so-and-so, and I think my work is similar."

How should a writer contact an agent?
Always approach the agent via a query letter. Never call first unless one of that agent's friends or clients has referred you and told you it's okay to call. The query letter should contain a short synopsis and your biographical information. It's important for the agent to know about you and your writing credentials, and if you are submitting exclusively or simultaneously. Never forget the SASE because many agents won't respond without one.

What are some common mistakes you see beginning writers make?
I turn down most of the unsolicited submissions I get for the simple reason that they are not well written. Beginning writers need to read everything they can get their hands on, and they need to take classes or join writing groups to practice and hone their craft. While I respect artistic vision, I think many beginning writers would benefit from taking the writing advice of their agent or editor. And too many new writers assume their publisher will sufficiently promote and market their books. In fact, writers have to work like crazy to make sure their books are successful.

What are some common mistakes established writers make?

Established writers don't get enough editing. I don't know if it's because they think they don't need it or because editors are getting too busy to edit. If I were a successful, established writer, I would insist on being properly edited, even to the point of hiring an outside editor.

How successful can an agent be outside New York?

In today's information age, it's easy to operate outside New York—in Boston, Los Angeles, D.C., even New Orleans. It's still a good idea for an agent to go to New York and meet with editors as often as possible, but in many ways you are at an advantage if you are outside New York. You can be closer to many of your clients and closer to the kinds of clients you want to attract. For instance, many of the Boston agents work with people affiliated with Harvard, and, here in D.C., I represent doctors and health professionals affiliated with the National Institutes of Health and Georgetown University.

How have you changed as an agent since you started out?

It's a tough business. I've become more cautious about signing projects up, although I'm not sure that's a good thing—it's important to take some chances. I'm also more reluctant to take on clients on the basis of a partial, rather than a complete, novel manuscript.

What kinds of manuscripts are publishers signing up now?

Narrative nonfiction is hot. By narrative nonfiction, I mean wonderfully written nonfiction that tells a story. Health is another hot topic, but it's a crowded field—writers have to be doctors with impressive credentials and new ideas. Within health, alternative health is big, especially nutritional cures.

Is nonfiction or fiction easier to sell?

Nonfiction is easier to sell to publishers, even though fiction sells better to the public. That's because it's much easier for an editor to tell if nonfiction is going to work, as opposed to fiction which is subjective. It's also easier to break out an unknown in nonfiction—if you look at the fiction bestseller list, it's almost entirely made up of "brand-name" writers.

How willing are agents to negotiate contracts with small publishers?

If there is no upfront money, the agent will be doing a lot of work for no money, and that's a deterrent. But I think some agents will negotiate a contract with a small publisher if they think the writer has long-term potential. If the author has an offer from one of these small publishers and is having trouble getting an agent, she should just hire a lawyer who specializes in publishing and pay the lawyer by the hour to negotiate the contract.

What are some of the mistakes writers make in the author-agent relationship?

Authors are often too quick to sign with the first agent who comes along. Unfortunately, there are unscrupulous agents out there, so make sure you thoroughly check out anyone who wants you to sign an agreement. A good source for checking an agent's legitimacy is the website www.agentresearch.com. Get the list of questions that the Association of Authors' Representatives gives out (see page 53), and ask the agent all of them. If the agreement is confusing in any way, have a lawyer who specializes in publishing look it over. Try not to sign any agreement with a time limit. Get one that is open ended and can be canceled at any time by either party.

What makes you want to work with new writers?
One word: credentials. In terms of fiction, it helps if they've published short stories, won contests and have an MFA from a prestigious university. With practical, self-help type nonfiction, I like to see articles, lecturing, advanced degrees and television appearances. The other thing that would make me want to work with an unpublished author is a glowing referral from another client who has read her work. But the most important thing is talent: great writing, tight plot and compelling characters.
—*Anna Olswanger*

Groppel with Bob Andelman (John Wiley & Sons); *The Global Me*, by G. Pascal Zachary (Public Affairs); *Beyond Pleasure and Pain*, by Steven Reiss (Tarcher-Putnam).
Terms: Agent receives 15% commission on domestic sales; 20% on foreign sales. Offers written contract, binding for 1 year with 60 day cancellation clause. Charges for postage and photocopying.
Tips: "Grab my attention right away with your query—not with gimmicks, but with excellent writing."

JENNY BENT, LITERARY AGENT, GRAYBILL & ENGLISH, L.L.C., 1920 N St. NW, #620, Washington DC 20036. Fax: (202)457-0662. E-mail: jenlbent@aol.com. **Contact:** Jenny Bent. Estab. 1997. Represents 40 clients. 50% of clients are new/unpublished writers. Currently handles: 75% nonfiction books; 25% novels.
• Prior to joining her agency Ms. Bent worked as an editor in book publishing and magazines.
Represents: Nonfiction books, novels. **Considers these nonfiction areas:** animals; biography/autobiography; child guidance/parenting; ethnic/cultural interests; gay/lesbian issues; health/medicine; history; language/literature/criticism; New Age/metaphysics; popular culture; psychology; religious/inspirational; science/technology; self-help/personal improvement; women's issues/women's studies. **Considers these fiction areas:** contemporary issues; detective/crime/police (hard-boiled detective); ethnic; family saga; gay/lesbian; literary; romance; suspense.
How to Contact: Query. Send outline/proposal and SASE. "Please always include a bio or résumé with submissions or queries." *No calls please.* Accepts queries by e-mail. Considers simultaneous submissions. Reports in 2 weeks on queries; 1 month on mss. Returns material only with SASE.
Needs: Actively seeking quality fiction from well-credentialed authors. Does not want to receive science fiction, New Age fiction, thrillers, children's, self-help from non-credentialed writers. Obtains new clients through recommendations, solicitations, conferences.
Recent Sales: Sold 15 titles in the last year. *If Men Were Angels*, by Reed Karaim (W.W. Norton); *Angelhead: A Crime Memoir*, by Greg Bottoms (Crown).
Terms: Agent receives 15% commission on domestic sales; 25% on foreign sales. Offers written contract. 30 days notice must be given to terminate contract. Charges for office expenses, postage, photocopying, long distance.
Writer's Conferences: Hurston-Wright (Richmond, VA, summer); Washington Independent Writers Spring Writers Conference (Washington DC, May); Washington Romance Writers Spring Retreat; Virginia Romance Writers Conference (Williamsburg, VA, March).
Reading List: Reads *New Age Journal* and *Psychology Today* to find new clients. Looks for "writers with strong credentials."
Tips: "Since Graybill & English is both a literary agency and a law firm, we can offer our clients essential legal services."

PAM BERNSTEIN & ASSOCIATES, INC., 790 Madison Ave., Suite 310, New York NY 10021. (212)288-1700. Fax: (212)288-3054. **Contact:** Pam Bernstein or Donna Downing. Estab. 1992. Member of AAR. Represents 50 clients. 20% of clients are new/previously unpublished writers. Specializes in commercial adult fiction and nonfiction. Currently handles: 60% nonfiction books; 40% fiction.
• Prior to becoming agents, Ms. Bernstein served as vice president with the William Morris Agency; Ms. Downing was in public relations.
Represents: Considers these nonfiction areas: child guidance/parenting; cooking/food/nutrition; current affairs; health/medicine; how-to; popular culture; psychology; religious/inspirational; self-help/personal improvement; sociology; true crime/investigative; women's issues/women's studies. **Considers these fiction areas:** contemporary issues; ethnic; historical; mainstream; mystery/suspense; romance (contemporary); thriller.
How to Contact: Query. Reports in 2 weeks on queries; 1 month on mss. Include postage for return of ms.
Recent Sales: Sold 25 titles in the last year. *The Bipolar Child*, by Janice and Demitri Papolos (Broadway); *The

Wholeness of a Broken Heart (Riverhead); *The Barefoot Contessa Cookbook* (Clarkson Potter).
Terms: Agent receives 15% commission on domestic sales; 20% on foreign sales. Offers written contract, binding for 3 years, with 30 day cancellation clause. 100% of business is derived from commissions on sales. Charges for postage and photocopying.

$ Ⓞ MEREDITH BERNSTEIN LITERARY AGENCY, 2112 Broadway, Suite 503 A, New York NY 10023. (212)799-1007. Fax: (212)799-1145. Estab. 1981. Member of AAR. Represents approximately 100 clients. 20% of clients are new/previously unpublished writers. Does not specialize, "very eclectic." Currently handles: 50% nonfiction books; 50% fiction.
  • Prior to opening her agency, Ms. Bernstein served in another agency for 5 years.
Member Agents: Meredith Bernstein, Elizabeth Cavanaugh.
Represents: Fiction and nonfiction books.
How to Contact: Query first.
Needs: Obtains new clients through recommendations from others, queries and· at conferences; also develops and packages own ideas.
Recent Sales: *Bone Density Diet Book*, by Dr. George Kessler (Ballantine); *Natural Healing for Dogs and Cats*, by Amy Shujai (Rodale); *Interview with An Angel*, by Linda Nathanson and Stephen Thayer (Dell).
Terms: Agent receives 15% commission on domestic sales; 20% on foreign sales. Charges clients $75 disbursement fee per year.
Writers' Conferences: Southwest Writers Conference (Albuquerque, August); Rocky Mountain Writers Conference (Denver, September); Beaumont (TX, October); Pacific Northwest Writers Conference; Austin League Writers Conference; Willamette Writers Conference (Portland, OR); Lafayette Writers Conference (Lafayette, LA); Surrey Writers Conference (Surrey, BC.); San Diego State University Writers Conference (San Deigo, CA).

Ⓞ DANIEL BIAL AGENCY, 41 W. 83rd St., Suite 5-C, New York NY 10024-5246. (212)721-1786. E-mail: dbialagency@juno.com. **Contact:** Daniel Bial. Estab. 1992. Represents under 50 clients. 15% of clients are new/previously unpublished writers. Currently handles: 95% nonfiction books; 5% novels.
  • Prior to opening his agency, Mr. Bial was an editor for 15 years.
Represents: Nonfiction books, novels. **Considers these nonfiction areas:** animals; anthropology/archaeology; biography/autobiography; business; child guidance/parenting; cooking/food/nutrition; current affairs; ethnic/cultural interests; gay/lesbian issues; government/politics/law; history; how-to; humor; language/literature/criticism; memoirs; military/war; money/finance/economics; music/dance/theater/film; nature/environment; New Age/metaphysics; popular culture; psychology; religious/inspirational; science/technology; self-help/personal improvement; sociology; sports; travel; true crime/investigative; women's issues/women's studies. **Considers these fiction areas:** action/adventure; comic; contemporary issues; detective/police/crime; erotica; ethnic; feminist; gay; humor/satire; literary.
How to Contact: Send outline/proposal. Accepts queries by e-mail. Consider simultaneous queries. Reports in 2 weeks on queries. Returns materials only with SASE.
Needs: Obtains new clients through recommendations, solicitation, "good rolodex, over the transom."
Recent Sales: Prefers not to share information on specific sales.
Terms: Agent receives 15% commission on domestic sales; 20% on foreign sales. Offers written contract, binding for 1 year with 6 week cancellation clause. Charges for overseas calls, overnight mailing, photocopying, messenger expenses.
Tips: "Good marketing is a key to success at all stages of publishing—successful authors know how to market themselves as well as their writing."

Ⓞ BIGSCORE PRODUCTIONS INC., P.O. Box 4575, Lancaster PA 17604. (717)293-0247. E-mail: bigscore@starburstpublishers.com. Website: www.starburstpublishers.com. **Contact:** David A. Robie. Estab. 1995. Represents 5-10 clients. 50% of clients are new/previously unpublished writers.
  • Mr. Robie is also the president of Starburst Publishers, an inspirational publisher that publishes books for both the ABA and CBA markets.
Represents: Specializes in inspirational and self-help nonfiction and fiction.
How to Contact: Query over e-mail. Reports in 1 month on proposals. "Queries *only* accepted at bigscore@starburstpublishers.com. Do not send file attachments!"
Recent Sales: *The Hired Man's Christmas*, by George Givens (Scribner); *Leggett's Antique Atlas 2000*, by David and Kim Leggett (Crown); *My Name Isn't Martha, but I Can Renovate My Home* series, by Sharon Hanby-Robie (Pocket Books); and *If I Only Knew . . . What Would Jesus Do?*, by Joan Hake Robie (Warner Books).
Terms: Agent receives 15% on domestic sales. Offers a written contract, binding for 6 months. Charges for shipping, ms photocopying and preparation, and books for subsidiary rights submissions.
Tips: "Very open to taking on new clients. Submit a well-prepared proposal that will take minimal fine-tuning for presentation to publishers. Nonfiction writers must be highly marketable and media savvy—the more established in speaking or in your profession, the better."

Ⓞ VICKY BIJUR, 333 West End Ave., Apt. 513, New York NY 10023. This agency did not respond to our request for information. Query before submitting.
  • Ms. Bijur is the current president of AAR.

⬤ **DAVID BLACK LITERARY AGENCY, INC.**, 156 Fifth Ave., New York NY 10001. (212)242-5080. Fax: (212)924-6609. **Contact:** David Black, owner. Estab. 1990. Member of AAR. Represents 150 clients. Specializes in sports, politics, novels. Currently handles: 80% nonfiction; 20% novels.
Member Agents: Susan Raihofer (general nonfiction to literary fiction), Gary Morris (commercial fiction to psychology), Joy E. Tutela (general nonfiction to literary fiction).
Represents: Nonfiction books, literary and commercial fiction. **Considers these nonfiction areas:** politics; sports.
How to Contact: Query with outline and SASE. Does not accept queries by fax. Considers simultaneous queries and submissions. Reports in 2 months on queries. Returns unwanted materials only with SASE.
Recent Sales: *Body For Life*, by Bill Phillips with Mike D'Orso (HarperCollins); *Walking with the Wind*, by John Lewis with Mike D'Orso (Simon & Schuster).
Terms: Agent receives 15% commission. Charges for photocopying and books purchased for sale of foreign rights.

▓▓ ⬤ **BLEECKER STREET ASSOCIATES, INC.**, 532 LaGuardia Place, New York NY 10012. (212)677-4492. Fax: (212)388-0001. **Contact:** Agnes Birnbaum. Estab. 1984. Member of AAR, RWA, MWA. Represents 60 clients. 20% of clients are new/previously unpublished writers. "We're very hands-on and accessible. We try to be truly creative in our submission approaches. We've had especially good luck with first-time authors." Currently handles: 65% nonfiction books; 25% novels; 10% syndicated material.
● Prior to becoming an agent, Ms. Birnbaum was an editor at Simon & Schuster, Dutton/Signet and other publishing houses.
Represents: Nonfiction books, novels, short story collections. **Considers these nonfiction areas:** animals; anthropology/archaeology; biography/autobiography; business; child guidance/parenting; computers/electronics; cooking/food/nutrition; current affairs; ethnic/cultural interests; gay/lesbian issues; government/politics/law; health/medicine; history; how-to; humor; juvenile nonfiction; memoirs; military/war; money/finance/economics; nature/environment; New Age/metaphysics; popular culture; psychology; religious/inspirational; science/technology; self-help/personal improvement; sociology; sports; true crime/investigative; women's issues/women's studies. **Considers these fiction areas:** detective/police/crime; erotica; ethnic; family saga; feminist; gay/lesbian; historical; literary; mystery; psychic/supernatural; romance; thriller/espionage.
How to Contact: Query with SASE. Does not accept queries by fax or e-mail. Considers simultaneous queries. Reports in 1 week on queries "if interested"; 1 month on mss. Returns materials only with SASE.
Needs: Does not want to receive science fiction, westerns, poetry, children's books, academic/scholarly/professional books, plays, scripts. Obtains new clients through recommendations from others, queries, conferences. "Plus, I will approach someone with a letter if his/her work impresses me."
Recent Sales: Sold 35 titles in the last year. *Star Spangled Banner*, by Irvin Molotsky (Dutton); *Salt In Your Sock*, by Lillian Beard, M.D. (Times Books); *Sabrina*, by Pat Barnes-Svarney (Archway); *Healing Companion*, by Jeff Kane, M.D. (Harper SF).
Terms: Agent receives 15% commission on domestic sales; 25% on foreign sales if co-agent is used, if not, 15% on foreign sales. Offers written contract, exclusive on all work. 30-day notice must be given to terminate contract. Charges for postage, long distance, fax, messengers, photocopies, not to exceed $150.
Writer's Conferences: PennWriters (Pittsburgh PA, May).
Tips: "Keep query letters short and to the point; include only information pertaining to book or background as writer. Try to avoid superlatives in description. Work needs to stand on its own, so how much editing it may have received has no place in a query letter."

▓▓ ⬤ **REID BOATES LITERARY AGENCY**, 69 Cooks Crossroad, Pittstown NJ 08867. (908)730-8523. Fax: (908)730-8931. E-mail: rboatesla@aol.com. **Contact:** Reid Boates. Estab. 1985. Represents 45 clients. 5% of clients are new/previously unpublished writers. Specializes in general fiction and nonfiction, investigative journalism/current affairs; bios and celebrity autobiographies; serious self-help; literary humor; issue-oriented business; popular science; "no category fiction." Currently handles: 85% nonfiction books; 15% novels; "very rarely accept short story collections."
Represents: Nonfiction books, novels. **Considers these nonfiction areas:** animals; anthropology/archaeology; art/architecture/design; biography/autobiography; business; child guidance/parenting; current affairs; ethnic/cultural interests; government/politics/law; health/medicine; history; language/literature/criticism; nature/environment; psychology; science/technology; self-help/personal improvement; sports; true crime/investigative; women's issues/women's studies. **Considers these fiction areas:** contemporary issues; family saga; mainstream; thriller/espionage.
How to Contact: Query with SASE. Reports in 2 weeks on queries; 6 weeks on mss.
Needs: Obtains new clients through recommendations from others.
Recent Sales: Sold 20 titles in the last year. Prefers not to share information on specific sales.
Terms: Agent receives 15% commission on domestic sales; 20% on foreign sales. Offers written contract, binding "until terminated by either party." Charges for photocopying costs above $50.

⬤ **BOOK DEALS, INC.**, Civic Opera Bldg., 20 N. Wacker Dr., Suite 1928, Chicago IL 60606. (312)372-0227. **Contact:** Caroline Francis Carney. Estab. 1996. Represents 40 clients. 25% of clients are new/previously unpublished writers. Specializes in highly commercial and literary fiction and nonfiction. Currently handles: 75% nonfiction books, 25% fiction.
● Prior to opening her agency, Ms. Carney was editorial director for a consumer book imprint within Times

Mirror and held senior editorial positions in McGraw-Hill and Simon & Schuster.

Represents: Narrative nonfiction, how-to, novels. **Considers these nonfiction areas:** animals; biography/autobiography; business; nutrition; current affairs; ethnic/cultural interests; health/medicine; history; money/finance/economics; popular culture; science/technology; inspirational; popular psychology; and self help. **Considers these fiction areas:** contemporary women's fiction; ethnic; literary; mainstream; white collar crime stories; financial and medical thrillers; urban literature.

How to Contact: Fiction by referral only. Send synopsis, outline/proposal with SASE. Reports in 2-4 weeks on queries.

Needs: Actively seeking well-crafted fiction and nonfiction from authors with engaging voices and impeccable credentials.

Recent Sales: *The Most Important Thing I Know About Love*, by Lorne Adrain (William Morrow); *Usher: The Ultimate Entertainer*, by Marc Malkin (Andrews McMeel); *Yet a Stranger: Why Black Americans Still Don't Feel at Home*, by Deborah Mathis (Warner); *Transforming Practices: How to Find Joy and Satisfaction in Your Legal Life*, by Steve Keeva (Contemporary Book); *A is for Attitude: An Alphabet for Living*, by Pat Russell-McCloud (HarperCollins); *Intuitive Astrology*, by Elizabeth Rose Campbell (Ballantine).

Terms: Agent receives 15% commission on domestic sales; 20% on foreign sales. Offers a written contract. Charges for photocopying and postage.

THE BOOK PEDDLERS, 18326 Minnetonka Blvd., Deephaven MN 55391. This agency did not respond to our request for information. Query before submitting.

BOOKMARK LITERARY AGENCY, 481 Eighth Ave., Suite 1542, New York NY 10001. (212)868-2364. Fax: (212)868-2567. E-mail: bookmarklit@hotmail.com. **Contact:** Liz Martinez DeFranco. Estab. 1999. Represents 10 clients. 20% of clients are new/unpublished writers. Specializes in police writing from the point of view of both the writer and the reader. "We have years of experience working with law enforcement officers and military personnel, which allows us to forge good working relationships with our clients." Currently handles: 20% nonfiction books; 60% novels; 10% textbooks; 10% novellas.

● Prior to becoming an agent, Ms. DeFranco was an editor of fiction and nonfiction for the *Cop Tales*; and gave seminars on getting published for cops.

Member Agents: Dave Williams (military); Donna Decker (textbooks); Liz Martinez DeFranco (all).

Represents: Nonfiction books, novels, textbooks, novellas. **Considers these nonfiction areas:** government/politics/law; military/war; true crime/investigative. **Considers these fiction areas:** detective/police/crime; ethnic; mystery; psychic/supernatural; young adult; fire/arson investigation.

How to Contact: Send outline and 3-5 sample chapters. Accepts queries by e-mail. Considers simultaneous queries and submissions. Reports in 1 month on queries; 3 months on mss. Returns materials only with SASE.

Needs: Actively seeking true crime, mystery fiction, police stories, military works—"Any of these subjects with a twist are most welcome." Also looking for fictional fire/arson investigation stories. Does not want to receive poetry. Obtains new clients through conferences, presentations, referrals.

Recent Sales: New agency with recorded sales. Clients include Peter Holub, Penny James, Jim DeFilippi, Mary Thomas, Ernie Dorling, Nick Mangieri, Keith Bettinger.

Terms: Agent receives 15% commission on domestic sales; 20% on foreign sales. Offers written contract, binding for 1 year. 90 days notice must be given to terminate contract. Charges for marketing expenses, such as photocopying and courier service. "We get approval from the client for any such expenses over $30."—May refer to outside editor, but agency does not receive money for referral.

Writer's Conferences: Police Writers Conference (Williamsburg VA, November); Mystery Writers of America (New York NY, Spring); Boating Writers International (Miami FL, February).

Tips: "We will work with unpublished writers, but the work must be good. If you have a well-written cop story, send it to us first. We can spot potential quickly!"

BOOKS & SUCH, 3093 Maiden Ln., Altadena CA 91001. (626)797-1716. Fax: (626)398-0246. E-mail: jkgbooks@aol.com. **Contact:** Janet Kobobel Grant. Estab. 1996. Associate member of CBA. Represents 20 clients. 10% of clients are new/unpublished writers. Specializes in "general and inspirational fiction, romance, specializes in the Christian booksellers market but is expanding into the ABA market as well as children's and young adult market." Currently handles: 51% nonfiction books, 34% juvenile books, 11% novels, 4% novellas.

● Before becoming an agent, Ms. Grant was an editor for Zondervan and managing editor for Focus on the Family.

Represents: Nonfiction books, juvenile books, novels. **Considers these nonfiction areas:** child guidance/parenting; humor; juvenile nonfiction; religious/inspirational; self-help/personal improvement; women's issues/women's studies.

CHECK THE AGENT SPECIALTIES INDEX to find agents who are interested in your specific nonfiction or fiction subject area.

Considers these fiction areas: contemporary issues; family saga; historical; juvenile; mainstream; picture book; romance; religious/inspirational; young adult.

How to Contact: Query with SASE. Accepts queries by e-mail. Considers simultaneous queries. Reports in 3 weeks on queries; 6 weeks on mss. Returns materials only with SASE.

Needs: Actively seeking "material appropriate to the Christian market or that would crossover to the ABA market as well." Obtains new clients through recommendations and conferences.

Recent Sales: Sold 16 titles in the last year. *The White Pony*, by Sandra Byrd (WaterBrook Press); *Brenda's Gift*, by Cynthia Yates (Broadman & Holman); *What My Dog Taught Me About Life*, by Gary Stanley (Honor Books); *Departures*, by Robin Jones Gunn and Wendy Nentwig (Bethany House). Other clients include Joanna Weaver, Jane Orcutt, Jim Watkins.

Terms: Agent receives 15% commission on domestic and foreign sales. Offers written contract. 2 months notice must be given to terminate contract. Charges for postage, photocopying, fax and express mail.

Writer's Conferences: Romance Writers of America; Mt. Hermon Writers Conference (Mt. Hermon, CA, April 14-18); Glorieta Writers Conference (Glorieta NM, October 17-21).

Tips: "The heart of my motivation is to develop relationships with the authors I serve, to do what I can to shine the light of success on them, and to help be a caretaker of their gifts and time."

☉ GEORGES BORCHARDT INC., 136 E. 57th St., New York NY 10022. (212)753-5785. Fax: (212)838-6518. Estab. 1967. Member of AAR. Represents 200 clients. 10% of clients are new/previously unpublished writers. Specializes in literary fiction and outstanding nonfiction. Currently handles: 60% nonfiction books; 1% juvenile books; 37% novels; 1% novellas; 1% poetry books.

Member Agents: Anne Borchardt, Georges Borchardt, DeAnna Heindel, Lourdes Lopez, Valerie Borchardt.

Represents: Nonfiction books, novels. **Considers these nonfiction areas:** anthropology/archaeology; biography/autobiography; current affairs; history; memoirs; travel; women's issues/women's studies. **Considers literary fiction.** "Must be recommended by someone we know."

How to Contact: Reports in 1 week on queries; 3-4 weeks on mss.

Needs: Obtains new clients through recommendations from others.

Recent Sales: Sold 106 titles in the last year. *Stories*, by T.C. Boyle (Viking/Penguin); *Enduring Love*, by Ian McEwan (Nan Talese/Doubleday); *East of the Mountains*, by David Guterson (Harcourt Brace); and *History of Psychoanalysis*, by Elizabeth Young-Bruehl (Free Press). Also new books by William Boyd, Jack Miles, Elie Wiesel, and first novels by Yannick Murphy and Judy Troy.

Terms: Agent receives 15% commission on domestic and British sales; 20% on foreign sales (translation). Offers written contract. "We charge cost of (outside) photocopying and shipping mss or books overseas."

☉ THE BOSTON LITERARY GROUP, 156 Mount Auburn St., Cambridge MA 02138-4875. (617)547-0800. Fax: (617)876-8474. E-mail: agent@bostonliterary.com. **Contact:** Elizabeth Mack. Estab. 1994. Member of PEN New England. Represents 30 clients. 25% of clients are new/unpublished writers. Currently handles: 95% nonfiction books, 5% scholarly books.

Member Agents: Kristen Wainwright (psychology, health, current events, religion, business); Kerry Nugent-Wells (science, history, memoir, how-to, biography).

Represents: Nonfiction books. **Considers these nonfiction areas:** animals; anthropology/archaeology; art/architecture/design; biography/autobiography; business; child guidance/parenting; current affairs; education; ethnic/cultural interests; gay/lesbian issues; government/politics/law; health/medicine; history; how-to; military/war; money/finance/economics; music/dance/theater/film; nature/environment; photography; popular culture; psychology; religious/inspirational; science/technology; self-help/personal improvement; sociology; true crime/investigative; women's issues/women's studies.

How to Contact: Query with SASE. Accepts queries by e-mail. Considers simultaneous queries. Reports in 6 weeks on queries. Returns materials only with SASE.

Needs: Actively seeking "nonfiction manuscripts that have something new and fascinating to say. Good writing skills are essential." Does not want to receive poetry, cookbooks, children's literature. Obtains new clients through recommendations and magazine and journal articles.

Recent Sales: *Zero: The Biography of a Dangerous Idea*, by Charles Seife (Viking Penguin); *This Is What I've Been Telling You About: Defending the Lives & Minds of Black Children*, by Janie Ward (Free Press); *Managing Creativity: The Science of Enterprise-Wide Innovation*, by Jeff Manzy and Richard Harriman (Harvard Business School Press); *The Healing Power of Faith*, by Dr. Harold Koenig (Simon & Schuster).

Terms: Agent receives 15% commission on domestic sales; 10% on foreign sales. Offers written contract, binding for 1 year. 60 days notice must be given to terminate contract. Charges for expenses associated with manuscript submissions. Makes referrals to editing service. "We work with development editors on promising projects."

☉ THE BARBARA BOVA LITERARY AGENCY, 3951 Gulfshore Blvd., PH1-B, Still Naples FL 34103. (941)649-7237. Fax: (941)649-0757. **Contact:** Barbara Bova. Estab. 1974. Represents 35 clients. Specializes in fiction and nonfiction hard and soft science. Currently handles: 35% nonfiction books; 65% novels.

Represents: Considers these nonfiction areas: biography; business; cooking/food/nutrition; how-to; money/finance/economics; self-help/personal improvement; social sciences; true crimes/investigative; women's issues/women's studies. **Considers these fiction areas:** action/adventure; contemporary issues; detective/police/crime; family saga; glitz; mainstream; mystery/suspense; regional; romance (contemporary); science fiction; thrillers/espionage.

How to Contact: Query with SASE. "Published authors only."
Needs: Obtains new clients only through recommendations from others.
Recent Sales: *Chameleon*, by Shirley Kennett (Kensington); *Enchantment*, by Orson Scott Card (Del Rey); *Ice Covers the Hole*, by Rick Wilber (TOR/Forge); *Following Through*, by Steve Levinson and Pete C. Greider (Kensington); *Immortality*, by Ben Bova (Avon).
Terms: Agent receives 15% commission on domestic sales; handles foreign rights, movies, television, CDs.

◖ BRADY LITERARY MANAGEMENT, P.O. Box 164, Hartland Four Corners VT 05049. **Contact:** Sally Brady. Estab. 1986. Represents 100 clients.
Represents: Nonfiction books, literary and commercial fiction.
How to Contact: Query with SASE. For fiction submit first 50 pages; for nonfiction submit outline and 2 sample chapters. Reports in 6-8 weeks on queries.
Recent Sales: Prefers not to share information on specific sales.
Terms: Agent receives 15% commission on domestic sales; 20% on foreign sales. Charges for extensive international postage and photocopying.

◖ BRANDT & BRANDT LITERARY AGENTS INC., 1501 Broadway, New York NY 10036. (212)840-5760. Fax: (212)840-5776. **Contact:** Carl Brandt, Gail Hochman, Marianne Merola, Charles Schlessiger. Estab. 1913. Member of AAR. Represents 200 clients.
Represents: Nonfiction books, scholarly books, juvenile books, novels, novellas, short story collections. **Considers these nonfiction areas**: agriculture/horticulture; animals; anthropology/archaeology; art/architecture/design; biography/ autobiography; business; child guidance/parenting; cooking/food/nutrition; crafts/hobbies; current affairs; ethnic/cultural interests; gay/lesbian issues; government/politics/law; health/medicine; history; interior design/decorating; juvenile nonfiction; language/literature/criticism; military/war; money/finance/economics; music/dance/theater/film; nature/environment; psychology; science/technology; self-help/personal improvement; sociology; sports; true crime/investigative; women's issues/women's studies. **Considers these fiction areas**: action/adventure; contemporary issues; detective/ police/crime; erotica; ethnic; experimental; family saga; feminist; gay; historical; humor/satire; lesbian; literary; mainstream; mystery/suspense; psychic/supernatural; regional; romance; science fiction; sports; thriller/espionage; westerns/ frontier; young adult.
How to Contact: Query. Prefers to be only reader. Reports in 1 month on queries. Returns materials only with SASE.
Needs: Obtains new clients through recommendations from others or "upon occasion, a really good letter."
Recent Sales: Prefers not to share information on specific sales. Clients include Scott Turow, Carlos Fuentes and Ursula Hegi.
Terms: Agent receives 15% commission on domestic sales; 20% on foreign sales. Charges for "manuscript duplication or other special expenses agreed to in advance."
Tips: "Write a letter which will give the agent a sense of you as a professional writer, your long-term interests as well as a short description of the work at hand."

⊘ THE HELEN BRANN AGENCY, INC., 94 Curtis Rd., Bridgewater CT 06752. This agency did not respond to our request for information. Query before submitting.

⊘ BROADWAY PLAY PUBLISHING, 56 E. 81st St., New York NY 10028-0202. This agency did not respond to our request for information. Query before submitting.

◖ ◖ MARIE BROWN ASSOCIATES INC., 625 Broadway, New York NY 10012. (212)533-5534. Fax: (212)533-0849. E-mail: mbrownlit@aol.com. **Contact:** Marie Brown. Estab. 1984. Represents 60 clients. Specializes in multicultural and African-American writers. Currently handles: 75% nonfiction books; 10% juvenile books; 15% other.
Member Agents: Janell Walden Agyeman, Lisa Davis, Dorothy Branch.
Represents: Considers these nonfiction areas: art; biography; business; ethnic/cultural interests; history; juvenile nonfiction; music/dance/theater/film; religious/inspirational; self-help/personal improvement; women's issues/women's studies. **Considers these fiction areas:** contemporary issues; ethnic; juvenile; literary; mainstream.
How to Contact: Query with SASE. Reports in 6 weeks on queries.
Needs: Obtains new clients through recommendations from others.
Recent Sales: *Waiting in Vain*, by Colin Channer (Ballantine/One World); *Defending the Spirit* and *The Debt*, by Randall Robinson (Dutton); *Gender Talk*, by Johnetta Cole and Beverly Guy Shaftan.
Terms: Agent receives 15% commission on domestic sales; 20% on foreign sales. Offers written contract.

◖ CURTIS BROWN LTD., 10 Astor Place, New York NY 10003-6935. (212)473-5400. Member of AAR; signatory of WGA. **Contact:** Perry Knowlton, chairman; Timothy Knowlton, CEO; Peter L. Ginsberg, president.
Member Agents: Laura Blake Peterson; Ellen Geiger; Emilie Jacobson, vice president; Maureen Walters, vice president; Virginia Knowlton; Timothy Knowlton, COO (film, screenplays, plays); Marilyn Marlow, executive vice president; Ed Wintle (film, screenplays, plays); Andrew Pope; Clyde Taylor; Mitchell Waters; Dave Barber (translation rights).
Represents: Nonfiction books, juvenile books, novels, novellas, short story collections, poetry books. **Considers all categories of nonfiction and fiction.**

Also Handles: Movie scripts, feature film, TV scripts, TV MOW, stage plays. **Considers these script subject areas:** action/adventure; comedy; detective/police/crime; ethnic; feminist; gay; historical; horror; lesbian; mainstream; mystery/suspense; psychic/supernatural; romantic comedy and drama; thriller; westerns/frontier.
How to Contact: No unsolicited mss. Query first with SASE. Reports in 3 weeks on queries; 3-5 weeks on mss (only if requested).
Needs: Obtains new clients through recommendations from others, solicitation, at conferences and query letters.
Recent Sales: Prefers not to share information on specific sales.
Terms: Offers written contract. Charges for photocopying, some postage.

◐ ◎ ANDREA BROWN LITERARY AGENCY, INC., P.O. Box 371027, Montara CA 94037-1027. (650)728-1783. **Contact:** Andrea Brown, president. Estab. 1981. Member of AAR, WNBA, SCBWI and Authors Guild. 10% of clients are new/previously unpublished writers. Specializes in "all kinds of children's books—illustrators and authors." Currently handles: 98% juvenile books; 2% novels.
• Prior to opening her agency, Ms. Brown served as an editorial assistant at Random House and Dell Publishing and as an editor with Alfred A. Knopf.
Member Agents: Andrea Brown, Laura Rennert.
Represents: Juvenile books. **Considers these juvenile nonfiction areas:** animals; anthropology/archaeology; art/architecture/design; biography/autobiography; current affairs; ethnic/cultural interests; history; how-to; juvenile nonfiction; nature/environment; photography; popular culture; science/technology; sociology; sports. **Considers these juvenile fiction areas:** historical; juvenile; picture book; science fiction; young adult.
How to Contact: Query with SASE. Reports in 1-4 weeks on queries; 1-3 months on mss.
Needs: Mostly obtains new clients through recommendations, editors, clients and agents.
Recent Sales: *Bus Driver From the Black Lagoon*, by Mike Thaler (Scholastic); *Foreign Exchange*, by Mel Glenn (Morrow).
Terms: Agent receives 15% commission on domestic sales; 20% on foreign sales. Offers written contract.
Writers' Conferences: Austin Writers League; SCBWI, Orange County Conferences; Mills College Childrens Literature Conference (Oakland CA); Asilomar (Pacific Grove CA); Maui Writers Conference, Southwest Writers Conference; San Diego State University Writer's Conference; Big Sur Children's Writing Workshop (Director).
Tips: Query first. "Taking on very few picture books. Must be unique—no rhyme, no anthropomorphism. Do not call, or fax queries or manuscripts."

◐ PEMA BROWNE LTD., HCR Box 104B, Pine Rd., Neversink NY 12765-9603. (914)985-2936. Website: www.geocities.com/~pemabrowneltd. **Contact:** Perry Browne or Pema Browne ("Pema rhymes with Emma"). Estab. 1966. Member of SCBWI, RWA. Signatory of WGA. Represents 50 clients. Handles selected commercial fiction, nonfiction, romance, business, New Age, reference, pop culture, juvenile and children's picture books. Currently handles: 50% nonfiction books; 35% juvenile books; 10% novels; 5% movie scripts.
• Prior to opening their agency, Mr. Browne was a radio and TV performer; Ms. Browne was a fine artist and art buyer.
Member Agents: Pema Browne (children's fiction and nonfiction, adult nonfiction); Perry Browne (adult fiction and nonfiction).
Represents: Nonfiction books, reference books, juvenile books, novels. **Considers these nonfiction areas:** business; child guidance/parenting; cooking/food/nutrition; ethnic/cultural interests; gay/lesbian issues; health/medicine; how-to; juvenile nonfiction; military/war; money/finance/economics; nature/environment; New Age/metaphysics; popular culture; psychology; religious/inspirational; self-help/personal improvement; sports; true crime/investigative; women's issues/women's studies. **Considers these fiction areas:** action/adventure, contemporary issues; detective/police/crime; ethnic; feminist; gay; glitz; historical; humor/satire; juvenile; lesbian; literary; mainstream; mystery/suspense; picture book; psychic/supernatural; religious/inspirational; romance (contemporary, gothic, historical, regency); science fiction; thriller/espionage; young adult.
How to Contact: Query with SASE. No fax queries. No e-mail queries. Reports in 3 weeks on queries; within 6 weeks on mss. Prefers to be the only reader. "We do not review manuscripts that have been sent out to publishers."Returns materials only with SASE.
Needs: Actively seeking nonfiction, juvenile, middle grade, some young adult, picture books. Obtains new clients through "editors, authors, *LMP*, *Guide to Literary Agents* and as a result of longevity!"
Recent Sales: Sold 25 titles in the last year. *Start Your Own Business in 30 Days*, by Gary J. Grappo (Berkley); *Healing the Trauma From Past Lives*, by Thelma Freedman, Ph.D. (Carol Publ); *Echoes*, by Linda Cargill (Cora Verlag).
Terms: Agent receives 15% commission on domestic sales; 20% on foreign sales.
Tips: "If writing romance, be sure to receive guidelines from various romance publishers. In nonfiction, one must have credentials to lend credence to a proposal. Make sure of margins, double-space and use clean, dark type."

◐ HOWARD BUCK AGENCY, 80 Eighth Ave., Suite 1107, New York NY 10011. (212)807-7855. **Contact:** Howard Buck or Mark Frisk. Estab. 1981. Represents 75 clients. "All-around agency." Currently handles: 75% nonfiction books; 25% novels.
Represents: Nonfiction, novels. Considers all nonfiction and fiction areas except children's, horror, juvenile, picture book, self-help, young adult or science fiction/fantasy.
How to Contact: Query with SASE. Reports in 6 weeks on queries. "We do not read original screenplays."

Needs: Obtains new clients through recommendations from others.

Recent Sales: Prefers not to share information on specific sales.

Terms: Agent receives 15% commission on domestic sales. Offers written contract. Charges for office expenses, postage and photocopying.

⊘ KNOX BURGER ASSOCIATES, LTD., 39½ Washington Square South, New York NY 10012. This agency did not respond to our request for information. Query before submitting.

◎ SHEREE BYKOFSKY ASSOCIATES, INC., 16 W. 36th St., 13th Floor, New York NY 10018. Website: www.users.interport.net/~sheree. **Contact:** Sheree Bykofsky. Estab. 1984. Incorporated 1991. Member of AAR, ASJA, WNBA. Represents "a limited number" of clients. Specializes in popular reference nonfiction. Currently handles: 80% nonfiction; 20% fiction.
- Prior to opening her agency, Ms. Bykofsky served as executive editor of The Stonesong Press and managing editor of Chiron Press. She is also the author or co-author of more than 10 books.

Represents: Nonfiction, commercial and literary fiction. **Considers all nonfiction areas,** especially biography/autobiography; business; child guidance/parenting; cooking/foods/nutrition; current affairs; ethnic/cultural interests; gay/lesbian issues; health/medicine; history; how-to; humor; music/dance/theater/film; popular culture; psychology; inspirational; self-help/personal improvement; true crime/investigative; women's issues/women's studies. "I have wide-ranging interests, but it really depends on quality of writing, originality, and how a particular project appeals to me (or not). I take on very little fiction unless I completely love it—it doesn't matter what area or genre."

How to Contact: Query with SASE. No unsolicited mss or phone calls. Considers simultaneous queries. Reports in 1 week on short queries; 1 month on solicited mss. Returns materials only with SASE.

Needs: Does not want to receive poetry, material for children, screenplays. Obtains new clients through recommendations from others.

Recent Sales: Sold 50 titles in the last year. *Falling Flesh Just Ahead*, by Lee Potts (Longstreet); *Tripping*, by Charles Hayes (Viking).

Terms: Agent receives 15% commission on domestic sales; 15% on foreign sales. Offers written contract, binding for 1 year "usually." Charges for postage, photocopying and fax.

Writers' Conferences: ASJA (NYC); Asilomar (Pacific Grove CA); Kent State; Southwestern Writers; Willamette (Portland); Dorothy Canfield Fisher (San Diego); Writers Union (Maui); Pacific NW; IWWG; and many others.

Tips: "Read the agent listing carefully, and comply with guidelines."

◉ C G & W ASSOCIATES, 252 Stanford Ave. (or P.O. Box 7613), Menlo Park CA 94025-6328. (650)854-1020. Fax: (650)854-1020. E-mail: sallyconley@msn.com. **Contact:** Sally Conley. Estab. 1996. Represents 12 clients. 72% of clients are new/unpublished writers. Specializes in literary and commercial mainstream fiction. Currently handles: 10% nonfiction books; 90% novels.
- Prior to opening her agency, Ms. Conley spent 20 years as co-owner of The Guild Bookstore (Menlo Park, CA) and was a Peace Corps volunteer for women in development from 1993-96.

Represents: Literary and commercial mainstream fiction. **Considers these nonfiction areas:** biography/autobiography; current affairs; ethnic/cultural interests; women's issues/women's studies. **Considers these fiction areas:** action/adventure; confessional; contemporary issues; detective/police/crime; ethnic; family saga; glitz; historical; literary; mainstream; mystery/suspense; regional; romance (contemporary, historical); thriller/espionage.

How to Contact: Query "with first 30 pages and SASE large enough to return pages." Accepts queries by fax. Considers simultaneous queries. Reports in 2 weeks on queries; 2-4 weeks on mss. Returns materials only with SASE.

Needs: Actively seeking "writers with a highly original voice."

Recent Sales: Prefers not to share information on specific sales. Clients include Karl Luntta.

Terms: Agent receives 15% commission on domestic sales; 20% on foreign sales. Offers written contract. 30 days written notice must be given to terminate contract.

Ⓝ ◎ CADDEN, FULLER & BURKHALTER LLP, 2010 Main St., Suite 960, Irvine CA 92614-7204. (949)263-2275. Fax: (949)263-2265. E-mail: 102352.21@compuserve.com. **Contact:** Alton G. Burkhalter. 90% of clients are new/unpublished writers. Specializes in "love and truth-based fiction and nonfiction. Emphasis on personal/spiritual growth."
- Mr. Burkhalter is also an actively practicing lawyer.

Represents: Nonfiction books, scholarly books, novels. **Considers these nonfiction areas:** psychology; religious/inspirational; science/technology; self-help/personal improvement. **Considers these fiction areas:** cartoon/comic; humor/satire; literary; psychic/supernatural; religious/inspirational.

How to Contact: Query. Send outline and 3 sample chapters. Reports in 2 weeks on queries; 1 month on mss.

Needs: Actively seeking "completed manuscripts that have not been shopped by the author." Does not want to receive "inquiries concerning incomplete or previously shopped manuscripts." Obtains new clients through solicitation.

Recent Sales: Sold 2 titles in the last year. Prefers not to share information on specific sales.

Terms: Agent receives 15% commission on domestic sales; 15% on foreign sales. Offers written contract, binding for 6 months. 30 days notice must be given to terminate contract. Charges for "actual expenses."

Tips: "We insist that all manuscripts be independently reviewed by an outside editor or book doctor prior to our submission to any publisher. We bring solid business, legal and accounting support to clients who are generally focused on the creative process."

[N] [O] MARIA CARVAINIS AGENCY, INC., 235 West End Ave., New York NY 10023. (212)580-1559. Fax: (212)877-3486. **Contact:** Maria Carvainis. Estab. 1977. Member of AAR, Authors Guild, ABA, MWA, RWA, signatory of WGA. Represents 35 clients. 10% of clients are new/previously unpublished writers. Currently handles: 34% nonfiction books; 65% novels; 1% poetry books.
- Prior to opening her agency, Ms. Carvainis spent more than 10 years in the publishing industry as a senior editor with Macmillan Publishing, Basic Books, Avon Books, where she worked closely with Peter Mayer and Crown Publishers. Ms. Carvainis has served as a member of the AAR Board of Directors and AAR Treasurer, as well as serving as chair of the AAR Contracts Committee. She presently serves on the AAR Royalty Committee.

Represents: Nonfiction books, novels. **Considers these nonfiction areas:** biography; business; health/medicine; personal memoirs; popular science; women's issues. **Considers these fiction areas:** fantasy; historical; literary; mainstream; mystery/suspense; romance; thriller; children's; young adult.

How to Contact: Query first with SASE. Reports within 2-3 weeks on queries; within 3 months on solicited mss.

Needs: Does not want to receive science fiction. "60% of new clients derived from recommendations or conferences. 40% of new clients derived from letters of query."

Recent Sales: *The Alibi* and *Standoff*, by Sandra Brown (Warner Books); *The Guru Guide to Entrepreneurship*, by Joseph H. Boyett and Jimmie T. Boyett (John Wiley and Sons); *Bearing Witness*, by Michael Kahn (TOR/Forge); *Dark of the Moon*, by P.J. Parrish (Kensington); *Heroin*, by Charlie Smith (W.W. Norton). Other clients include Mary Balogh, David Bottoms, Pam Conrad, Cindy Gerard, Sarah Isidore, Samantha James, Jerome Loving, Kristine Rolofson, William Sessions and Jose Yglesias.

Terms: Agent receives 15% commission on domestic sales; 20% on foreign sales. Offers written contract, binding for 2 years "on a book-by-book basis." Charges for foreign postage and bulk copying.

Writers' Conferences: BEA; Frankfurt Book Fair.

[O] [O] MARTHA CASSELMAN LITERARY AGENCY, P.O. Box 342, Calistoga CA 94515-0342. (707)942-4341. Fax: (707)942-4358. **Contact:** Martha Casselman. Estab. 1978. Member of AAR, IACP. Represents 30 clients. Specializes in "nonfiction, especially food books. Do not send any submission without query."

Represents: Nonfiction proposals only, food-related proposals and cookbooks. **Considers these nonfiction areas:** agriculture/horticulture; anthropology/archaeology; biography/autobiography; cooking/food/nutrition; health/medicine; women's issues/women's studies.

How to Contact: Send proposal with outline, SASE, plus 3 sample chapters. *"Don't send manuscripts!"* Reports in 3 weeks on queries.

Needs: Does not want to receive children's book material. Obtains new clients through referrals.

Recent Sales: Prefers not to share information on specific sales.

Terms: Agent receives 15% commission on domestic sales; 20% on foreign sales (if using subagent). Offers contract review for hourly fee, on consultation with author. Charges for photocopying, overnight and overseas mailings.

Writers' Conferences: IACP, other food-writers' conferences.

Tips: "No tricky letters; no gimmicks; *always* include SASE or mailer, or we can't contact you."

[✓] [O] CASTIGLIA LITERARY AGENCY, 1155 Camino Del Mar, PMB 510, Del Mar CA 92014. (858)755-8761. Fax: (858)755-7063. **Contact:** Julie Castiglia. Estab. 1993. Member of AAR, PEN. Represents 50 clients. Currently handles: 55% nonfiction books; 45% fiction.
- Prior to opening her agency, Ms. Castiglia served as an agent with Waterside Productions, as well as working as a freelance editor and published writer of 3 books.

Represents: Fiction and nonfiction. **Considers these nonfiction areas:** animals; anthropology/archaeology; biography/autobiography; business; child guidance/parenting; cooking/food/nutrition; current affairs; ethnic/cultural interests; finance; health/medicine; history; language/literature/criticism; nature/environment; New Age/metaphysics; psychology; religious/inspirational; science/technology; self-help/personal improvement; sociology; women's issues/women's studies. **Considers these fiction areas:** contemporary issues; ethnic; glitz; literary; mainstream; mystery/suspense; women's fiction especially.

How to Contact: Send outline/proposal plus 2 sample chapters; send synopsis with 2 chapters for fiction. No fax queries. Considers simultaneous queries. Reports in 6-8 weeks on mss. Returns materials only with SASE.

Needs: Does not want to receive horror or science fiction. No screenplays or academic nonfiction. Obtains new clients through solicitations, conferences, referrals.

Recent Sales: Sold 24 titles in the last year. *Mothers Work*, by Rebecca Matthias (Doubleday); *Squeeze the Moment*, by Karen O'Connor (Watebrook/Doubleday); *Outside the Bungalow*, by Doug Keister and Paul Duscherer (Penguin);

IF YOU'RE LOOKING for a particular agent, check the Agents Index to find at which agency the agent works. Then check the listing for that agency in the appropriate section.

The Miracle of Silence, by Ron Rathbun (Berkley); *150 Ways to Boost Your Child's Self-Esteem*, by Karin Ireland (Berkley); *The Marketing Game*, by Eric Sculz (Adams Media).

Terms: Agent receives 15% commission on domestic sales; 20% on foreign sales. Offers written contract. 6 week notice must be given to terminate contract. Charges for excessive postage and copying.

Writers' Conferences: Southwestern Writers Conference (Albuquerque NM August). National Writers Conference; Willamette Writers Conference (OR); San Diego State University (CA); Writers At Work (Utah).

Tips: "Be professional with submissions. Attend workshops and conferences before you approach an agent."

✔ ◠ ◎ **CHARISMA COMMUNICATIONS, LTD.**, 250 W. 54th St., Suite 807, New York NY 10019. (212)832-3020. Fax: (212)867-6906. **Contact:** James W. Grau. Estab. 1972. Represents 10 clients. 20% of clients are new/previously unpublished writers. Specializes in organized crime, Indian casinos, FBI, CIA, secret service, NSA, corporate and private security, casino gaming, KGB. Currently handles: 50% nonfiction books; 20% movie scripts; 20% TV scripts; 10% other.

Member Agents: Phil Howart; Rena Delduca (reader).

Represents: Nonfiction books, novels. **Considers these nonfiction areas:** biography/autobiography; current affairs; government/politics/law; military/war; true crime/investigative. **Considers these fiction areas:** contemporary issues; detective/police/crime; mystery/suspense; religious/inspirational; sports; cult issues.

Also Handles: Movie scripts, TV scripts, feature film, documentary, TV MOW, miniseries.

How to Contact: Send outline/proposal. Reports in 1 month on queries; 2 months on mss.

Needs: New clients are established writers.

Recent Sales: Untitled documentary (Scripps Howard).

Terms: Agent receives 10% commission on domestic sales; variable commission on foreign sales. Offers variable written contract. 100% of business is derived from commissions on sales.

⬛ Ø **JANE CHELIUS LITERARY AGENCY**, 548 Second St., Brooklyn NY 11215. This agency did not respond to our request for information. Query before submitting.

⬛ Ø **FAITH CHILDS LITERARY AGENCY, INC.**, 915 Broadway, Suite 1009, New York NY 10010. This agency did not respond to our request for information. Query before submitting.

Ø **CIRCLE OF CONFUSION LTD.**, 666 Fifth Ave., Suite 303, New York NY 10103. (212)969-0653. Fax: (718)997-0521. E-mail: circleltd@aol.com. **Contact:** Rajeev K. Agarwal, Lawrence Mattis. Estab. 1990. Signatory of WGA. Represents 25 clients. 60% of clients are new/previously unpublished writers. Specializes in screenplays for film and TV. Currently handles: 5% novels; 5% novellas; 90% movie scripts.

• See the expanded listing for this agency in Script Agents.

Ø **CLAUSEN, MAYS & TAHAN, LLC**, 249 W. 34th St., Suite 605, New York NY 10001-2815. (212)239-4343. Fax: (212)239-5248. **Contact:** Stedman Mays, Mary M. Tahan. Estab. 1976. 10% of clients are new/previously unpublished writers. Specializes in nonfiction with a strong backlist.

Member Agents: Stedman Mays; Mary M. Tahan. Associates: Michael Mezzo; Kristy Sottalano.

Represents: Handles mostly nonfiction. **Considers these nonfiction areas:** women's issues, relationships, psychology, memoirs, biography/autobiography, history, true stories, health/medicine, nutrition, how-to, money/finance/economics, spirituality, religious, fashion/beauty/style, humor. Rights for books optioned for TV movies and feature films.

How to Contact: Send queries or outline/proposal with sufficient postage for return for materials. Reports in 3 weeks on queries; 1 month or less after receiving requested proposals and sample chapters.

Recent Sales: *The War Journal of Major Damon "Rocky" Gause*, by Major Damon "Rocky" Gause (Hyperion); *The Official Rent-a-Husband Guide to a Safe, Problem-Free Home*, by Kaile Warren and Jane Maclean Craig (Doubleday); *What the IRS Doesn't Want You to Know*, Marty Kaplan, CPA and Naomi Weiss (Villard); *The Rules II: More Rules to Live and Love By*, by Ellen Fein and Sherrie Schneider (Warner Books); *What Men Want: Three Professional Single Men Reveal to Women What It Takes to Make a Man Yours*, by Bradley Gerstman, Esq., Christopher Pizzo, CPA, and Rich Seldes, M.D. (HarperCollins).

Terms: Agent receives 15% commission on domestic sales; 20% of foreign sales. Charges for postage, shipping and photocopying.

Tips: "Research proposal writing and the publishing process; always study your book's competition; send a proposal and outline instead of complete manuscript for faster response; always pitch books in writing, not over the phone."

Ø **CLIENT FIRST—A/K/A LEO P. HAFFEY AGENCY**, P.O. Box 128049, Nashville TN 37212-8049. (615)463-2388. E-mail: c1@nashville.net. Website: www.c-1st.com or www.nashville.net/~c1. **Contact:** Robin Swensen. Estab. 1990. Signatory of WGA. Represents 21 clients. 25% of clients are new/previously unpublished writers. Specializes in movie scripts and novels for sale to motion picture industry. Currently handles: 40% novels; 60% movie scripts.

• See the expanded listing for this agency in Script Agents.

◠ **THE COHEN AGENCY**, 331 W. 57th St. #176, New York NY 10019. (212)399-9079. Fax: (212)246-4697. **Contact:** Ms. Rob Cohen. Estab. 1994. Member of AAR, signatory of WGA. Represents 35 clients. 10% of clients are new/previously unpublished writers. Specializes in historical romance. Currently handles: 5% nonfiction books; 95% novels.

Member Agents: Rob Cohen (women's fiction).

Represents: Nonfiction books, novels. **Considers these commercial nonfiction areas:** child guidance/parenting; education; ethnic/cultural interests; politics/law; language/literature/criticism; music/dance/theater/film; women's issues/women's studies. **Considers these fiction areas:** contemporary issues; detective/police/crime; ethnic; feminist; historical; literary; mainstream; mystery/suspense; regional; romance (contemporary, historical, regency); science fiction.

How to Contact: Send outline and first 3 sample chapters with SASE. Reports in 6 weeks on queries.

Needs: Actively seeking fiction and very little nonfiction.

Recent Sales: *Heat of the Moment*, by Olga Bicos (Kensington); *Cimarron*, by Shelly Thacker (Bantam Doubleday Dell).

Terms: Agent receives 15% commission on domestic sales; 20% on foreign sales. No written contract.

Writers' Conferences: Romance Writers of America National Conference (July); Annual American Booksellers Association Conference (June).

Tips: Obtains new clients through recommendations from others, solicitation and conferences.

⬤ RUTH COHEN, INC. LITERARY AGENCY, P.O. Box 7626, Menlo Park CA 94025. (650)854-2054. **Contact:** Ruth Cohen or Sally Driscoll. Estab. 1982. Member of AAR, Authors Guild, Sisters in Crime, RWA, SCBWI. Represents 45 clients. 15% of clients are new/previously unpublished writers. Specializes in "quality writing in contemporary fiction, women's fiction, mysteries, thrillers and juvenile fiction." Currently handles: 60% fiction, 35% juvenile, 5% nonfiction.

● Prior to opening her agency, Ms. Cohen served as directing editor at Scott Foresman & Company (now HarperCollins).

Represents: Adult novels, juvenile books. **Considers these nonfiction areas:** ethnic/cultural interests; juvenile nonfiction; women's issues/women's studies. **Considers these fiction areas:** detective/police; ethnic; historical; juvenile; contemporary; thriller; literary; mainstream; mystery/suspense; picture books; romance (historical, long contemporary); young adult.

How to Contact: *No unsolicited mss.* Send outline plus 2 sample chapters. "Please indicate your phone number or e-mail address." *Must include SASE.* Reports in 3 weeks on queries.

Needs: Does not want to receive poetry, westerns, film scripts or how-to books. Obtains new clients through recommendations from others and through submissions.

Recent Sales: Prefers not to share information on specific sales.

Terms: Agent receives 15% commission on domestic sales; 20% on foreign sales, "if a foreign agent is involved." Offers written contract, binding for 1 year "continuing to next." Charges for foreign postage, phone calls, photocopying submissions and overnight delivery of mss when appropriate.

Tips: "As the publishing world merges and charges, there seem to be fewer opportunities for new writers to succeed in the work that they love. We urge you to develop the patience, persistence and perseverance that have made this agency so successful. Prepare a well-written and well-crafted manuscript, and our combined best efforts can help advance both our careers."

⬤ HY COHEN LITERARY AGENCY LTD., P.O. Box 43770, Upper Montclair NJ 07043. (973)783-9494. Fax: (973)783-9867. E-mail: cogency@home.com. **Contact:** Hy Cohen. Estab. 1975. Represents 25 clients. 50% of clients are new/previously unpublished writers. Currently handles: 20% nonfiction books; 5% juvenile books; 75% novels.

Represents: Nonfiction books, novels. **Considers all categories of nonfiction and fiction.**

How to Contact: Send 100 pages with SASE. Reports in about 2 weeks (on 100-page submission).

Needs: Obtains new clients through recommendations from others and unsolicited submissions.

Recent Sales: Prefers not to share information on specific sales.

Terms: Agent receives 10% commission.

Tips: "Send double-spaced, legible scripts and SASE. Good writing helps."

⬤ JOANNA LEWIS COLE, LITERARY AGENT, 404 Riverside Dr., New York NY 10025. This agency did not respond to our request for information. Query before submitting.

⬤ FRANCES COLLIN LITERARY AGENT, P.O. Box 33, Wayne PA 19087-0033. (610)254-0555. **Contact:** Marsha S. Kear. Estab. 1948. Member of AAR. Represents 90 clients. 1% of clients are new/previously unpublished writers. Currently handles: 50% nonfiction books; 1% textbooks; 48% novels; 1% poetry books.

Represents: Nonfiction books, novels. **Considers these nonfiction areas:** anthropology/archaeology; biography/autobiography; health/medicine; history; nature/environment; true crime/investigative. **Considers these fiction areas:** detective/police/crime; ethnic; family saga; fantasy; historical; literary; mainstream; mystery/suspense; psychic/supernatural; regional; romance (historical); science fiction.

How to Contact: Query with SASE. Reports in 1 week on queries; 2 months on mss.

Needs: Obtains new clients through recommendations from others.

Recent Sales: Prefers not to share information on specific sales.

Terms: Agent charges 15% commission on domestic sales; 20% on foreign sales. Offers written contract. Charges for overseas postage for books mailed to foreign agents; photocopying of mss, books, proposals; copyright registration fees; registered mail fees; passes along cost of any books purchased.

Ⓩ COLUMBIA LITERARY ASSOCIATES, INC., 7902 Nottingham Way, Ellicott City MD 21043-6721. This agency is currently not taking on new clients.

Ⓜ COMMUNICATIONS AND ENTERTAINMENT, INC., 2851 S. Ocean Blvd., #5K, Boca Raton FL 33432-8407. (561)391-9575. Fax: (561)391-7922. **Contact:** James L. Bearden. Estab. 1989. Represents 10 clients. 50% of clients are new/previously unpublished writers. Specializes in TV, film and print media. Currently handles: 5% juvenile books; 40% movie scripts; 10% novel; 40% TV scripts.
 • See the expanded listing for this agency in Script Agents.

Ⓜ DON CONGDON ASSOCIATES INC., 156 Fifth Ave., Suite 625, New York NY 10010-7002. **Contact:** Don Congdon, Michael Congdon, Susan Ramer. Estab. 1983. Member of AAR, signatory of WGA. Represents approximately 100 clients. Currently handles: 50% fiction; 50% nonfiction books.
Represents: Nonfiction books, novels. **Considers all nonfiction and fiction areas, especially literary fiction.**
How to Contact: Query. Include SASE. "If interested, we ask for sample chapters and outline." Reports in 1 week on queries; 1 month on mss.
Needs: Obtains new clients through referrals from other authors.
Recent Sales: *The Return of Little Big Man*, by Thomas Berger (Little, Brown); *New Word Order*, by Leslie Savan (Alfred A. Knopf); and *Pulse*, by Edna Buchanan (Avon Books).
Terms: Agent receives 10% commission on domestic sales. Charges for overnight mail, postage and photocopying.
Tips: "Writing a query letter with a self-addressed stamped envelope is a must."

Ⓜ CONNOR LITERARY AGENCY, 2911 West 71st St., Richfield MN 55423. (612)866-1426. Fax: (612)869-4074. **Contact:** Marlene Connor Lynch. Estab. 1985. Represents 50 clients. 30% of clients are new/previously unpublished writers. Specializes in popular fiction and nonfiction. Currently handles: 50% nonfiction books; 50% novels.
 • Prior to opening her agency, Ms. Connor served at the Literary Guild of America, Simon and Schuster and Random House.
Member Agents: Amy Jensen (children's books); Richard Zanders (assistant).
Represents: Nonfiction books, novels, children's books (especially with a minority slant). **Considers these nonfiction areas:** business; child guidance/parenting; cooking/food/nutrition; crafts/hobbies; current affairs; ethnic/cultural interests; government/politics/law; health/medicine; how-to; humor; interior decorating; language/literature/criticism; money/finance/economics; photography; popular culture; self-help/personal improvement; sports; true crime/investigative; women's issues/women's studies. **Considers these fiction areas:** contemporary issues; detective/police/crime; ethnic; experimental; family saga; horror; literary; mystery/suspense; thriller/espionage.
How to Contact: Query with outline/proposal and SASE. Reports in 1 month on queries; 6 weeks on mss.
Needs: Obtains new clients through "queries, recommendations, conferences, grapevine, etc."
Recent Sales: *Essence: 25 Years of Celebrating the Black Woman* (Abrams); *The Marital Compatibility Test*, by Susan Adams (Carol Publishing Group); *We Are Overcome*, by Bonnie Allen (Crown).
Terms: Agent receives 15% commission on domestic sales; 25% on foreign sales. Offers a written contract, binding for 1 year.
Writers' Conferences: Howard University Publishing Institute; BEA; Detroit Writer's Conference; Mid-West Romance Writer's Conference.
Tips: "Seeking previously published writers with good sales records and new writers with real talent."

Ⓩ THE DOE COOVER AGENCY, P.O. Box 668, Winchester MA 01890. (781)721-6000. Fax: (781)721-6727. **Contact:** Doe Coover, president. Estab. 1985. Represents 75 clients. Doe Coover specializes in cookbooks and serious nonfiction, particularly books on social issues. Colleen Mohyde represents fiction (literary and commercial), as well as journalism and general nonfiction. Currently handles: 80% nonfiction; 20% fiction.
 • Prior to becoming agents, Ms. Coover and Ms. Mohyde were editors for over a decade.
Member Agents: Doe Coover (cooking, general nonfiction); Colleen Mohyde (fiction, general nonfiction).
Represents: Nonfiction books, fiction. **Considers these nonfiction areas:** anthropology; biography/autobiography; business; child guidance/parenting; cooking/food; ethnic/cultural interests; finance/economics; health/medicine; history; language/literature/criticism; memoirs; nature/environment; psychology; sociology; travel; true crime; women's issues/women's studies.
How to Contact: Query with outline. Considers simultaneous queries and submissions. All queries must include SASE. Reporting time varies on queries. Returns materials only with SASE.
Needs: Does not want to receive children's books. Obtains new clients through recommendations from others and solicitation.
Recent Sales: Sold 25-30 titles in the last year. *Zuni Cafe Cookbook*, by Judy Rodgers (Scribner); *Appetites*, by Caroline Knapp (Dial). Other clients include Peter Lynch, Eileen McNamara, Deborah Madison, Loretta La Roche, Rick Bayless, Marion Cunningham.
Terms: Agent receives 15% commission on domestic sales; 15% on foreign sales.
Writers' Conferences: BEA (Chicago).

◎ **CORE CREATIONS, INC.**, 9024 S. Sanderling Way, Littleton CO 80126. (303)683-6792. E-mail: agent@eoncity .com. Website: www.eoncity.com/agent. **Contact:** Calvin Rex. Estab. 1994. Represents 10 clients. 70% of clients are new/unpublished writers. Specializes in "bold, daring literature." Agency has strong "experience with royalty contracts and licensing agreements." Currently handles: 30% nonfiction books; 60% novels; 5% novellas; 5% games.

• Prior to becoming an agent, Mr. Rex managed a small publishing house.

Member Agents: Calvin Rex.

Represents: Nonfiction books, novels, novellas. **Considers these nonfiction areas:** gay/lesbian issues; how-to; humor; psychology; true crime/investigative. **Considers these fiction areas:** detective/police/crime; horror; science fiction.

How to Contact: Query with outline/proposal. Reports in 3 weeks on queries; 3 months on mss.

Needs: Usually obtains new clients through recommendations from others, through the Internet and from query letters.

Recent Sales: Prefers not to share information on specific sales.

Terms: Agent receives 15% commission on domestic sales; 20% on foreign sales. Offers written contract. "Either party may terminate contract at any time." Charges for postage (applicable mailing costs).

Writers' Conferences: Steamboat Springs Writers Group (Colorado, July); Rocky Mountain Fiction Writers Colorado Gold Conference.

Tips: "Have all material proofread. Visit our webpage before sending anything."

◑ **ROBERT CORNFIELD LITERARY AGENCY**, 145 W. 79th St., New York NY 10024-6468. (212)874-2465. Fax: (212)874-2641. E-mail: rbcbc@aol.com. **Contact:** Robert Cornfield. Estab. 1979. Member of AAR. Represents 60 clients. 20% of clients are new/previously unpublished writers. Specializes in film, art, literary, music criticism, food, fiction. Currently handles: 60% nonfiction books; 20% scholarly books; 20% novels.

• Prior to opening his agency, Mr. Cornfield was an editor at Holt and Dial Press.

Represents: Nonfiction books, novels. **Considers these nonfiction areas:** animals; anthropology/archaeology; art/ architecture/design; biography/autobiography; cooking/food/nutrition; history; language/literature/criticism; music/ dance/theater/film. **Considers literary fiction.**

How to Contact: Query with SASE. Reports in 2-3 weeks on queries.

Needs: Obtains new clients through recommendations.

Recent Sales: Sold 15-20 titles in the last year. *Mixed Signals*, by Richard Barrios (Routledge); *Multiple Personalties*, by Joan Acorella (Jossey-Bass).

Terms: Agent receives 10% commission on domestic sales; 20% on foreign sales. No written contract. Charges for postage, excessive photocopying.

◑ **CRAWFORD LITERARY AGENCY**, 94 Evans Rd., Barnstead NH 03218. (603)269-5851. Fax: (603)269-2533. **Contact:** Susan Crawford. Estab. 1988. Represents 40 clients. 10% of clients are new/previously unpublished writers. Specializes in celebrity and/or media-based books and authors. Currently handles: 50% nonfiction books; 50% novels.

Member Agents: Susan Crawford, Lorne Crawford (commercial fiction); Scott Neister (scientific/techno thrillers); Kristen Hales (parenting, psychology, New Age, self help).

Represents: Commercial fiction and nonfiction books.

How to Contact: Query with SASE. No fax queries. Considers simultaneous queries; no simultaneous ms submissions. Reports in 3 weeks on queries. Returns materials only with SASE.

Needs: Actively seeking action/adventure stories, medical thrillers, suspense thrillers, celebrity projects, self-help, inspirational, how-to and women's issues. Does not want to receive short stories or poetry. Obtains new clients through recommendations, conferences, and queries.

Recent Sales: *Housebroken*, by Richard Karn and George Mair (HarperCollins); *With Ossie & Ruby*, by Ruby Dee and Ossie Davis (William Morrow); *Psi/Net*, by Billy Dee Williams and Rob MacGregor (TOR/Forge). Other clients include Dr. Avner Hershlag, M.D., John Travolta, Richard Karn, Billy Dee Williams, Ruby Dee and Ossie Davis.

Terms: Agent receives 15% commission on domestic sales; 20% on foreign sales. Offers written contract, binding for 90 days. 100% of business is derived from commissions on sales.

Writers' Conferences: International Film & Writers Workshop (Rockport ME).

◑ **RICHARD CURTIS ASSOCIATES, INC.**, 171 E. 74th St., Suite 2, New York NY 10021. (212)772-7363. Fax: (212)772-7393. E-mail: ltucker@curtisagency.com. Website: www.curtisagency.com. **Contact:** Pam Valvera. Estab. 1969. Member of AAR, RWA, MWA, WWA, SFWA, signatory of WGA. Represents 100 clients. 5% of clients are new/ previously unpublished writers. Specializes in general and literary fiction and nonfiction, as well as genre fiction such as science fiction, romance, horror, fantasy, action-adventure. Currently handles: 50% nonfiction books; 50% novels.

• Prior to opening his agency, Mr. Curtis was an agent with the Scott Meredith Literary Agency for 7 years and has authored over 50 published books.

Member Agents: Amy Victoria Meo, Laura Tucker, Richard Curtis.

Represents: Nonfiction books, scholarly books, novels. **Considers all nonfiction and fiction areas.**

How to Contact: "We do not accept fax or e-mail queries, conventional queries (outline and 3 sample chapters) must be accompanied by SASE." Reports in 1 month on queries; 1 month on mss.

Needs: Obtains new clients through recommendations from others, solicitations and conferences.

Recent Sales: Sold 100 titles in the last year. *Courtney Love: The Real Story*, by Poppy Z. Brite (Simon & Schuster); *Darwin's Radio*, by Greg Bear (Del Rey/Random House); *Expendable*, by James Gardner (Avon). Other clients include Dan Simmons, Jennifer Blake, Leonard Maltin, Earl Mindell and Barbara Parker.

Terms: Agent receives 15% commission on domestic sales; 20% on foreign sales. Offers written contract, binding on a "book by book basis." Charges for photocopying, express, fax, international postage, book orders.
Writers' Conferences: Romance Writers of America; Nebula Science Fiction Conference.

◑ JAMES R. CYPHER, THE CYPHER AGENCY, 616 Wolcott Ave., Beacon NY 12508-4247. (914)831-5677. E-mail: jimcypher@aol.com. Website: pages.prodigy.net/jimcypher/. **Contact:** James R. Cypher. Estab. 1993. Member of HWA, MWA and Authors Guild. Represents 53 clients. 57% of clients are new/previously unpublished writers. Currently handles: 67% nonfiction book; 33% novels.

● Mr. Cypher is a special contributor to Prodigy Service Books and Writing Bulletin Board. Prior to opening his agency, Mr. Cypher worked as a corporate public relations manager for a Fortune 500 multi-national computer company for 28 years.

Represents: Nonfiction books, novels. **Considers these nonfiction areas:** biography/autobiography; business; current affairs; ethnic/cultural interests; gay/lesbian issues; government/politics/law; health/medicine; history; how-to; language/literature/criticism; money/finance/economics; music/dance/theater/film; nature/environment; popular culture; psychology; science/technology; self-help/personal improvement; sociology; sports; true crime/investigative; women's issues/women's studies; travel memoirs. **Considers these fiction areas:** literary; mainstream; crime fiction; horror.
How to Contact: For nonfiction, send outline proposal, 2 sample chapters and SASE. For fiction, send synopsis, 3 sample chapters and SASE. Reports in 2 weeks on queries; 6 weeks on mss.
Needs: Actively seeking a wide variety of topical nonfiction. Does not want to receive humor; pets; gardening; cookbooks; crafts; spiritual; religious or New Age topics. Obtains new clients through referrals from others, networking on online computer services and attending writers' conferences.
Recent Sales: *Storytellers* (horror fiction), by Julie Anne Parks (Design Image Group); *Taco Titan: The Glen Bell Story*, by Debra Lee Baldwin (Summit Publishing Group); *Why Gay Spirituality*, by Toby Johnson, Ph.D. (Alyson Books); *Inside Sudan*, by Donald Petterson (Westview Press).
Terms: Agent receives 15% commission on domestic sales; 20% on foreign sales. Offers written contract, with 30 day cancellation clause. Charges for postage, photocopying, overseas phone calls and faxes. 100% of business is derived from commissions on sales.
Tips: " 'Debut fiction' is very difficult to place in today's tight market, so a novel has to be truly outstanding to make the cut."

◑ DARHANSOFF & VERRILL LITERARY AGENTS, 179 Franklin St., 4th Floor, New York NY 10013. (212)334-5980. Fax: (212)334-5470. Estab. 1975. Member of AAR. Represents 100 clients. 10% of clients are new/previously unpublished writers. Specializes in literary fiction. Currently handles: 25% nonfiction books; 60% novels; 15% short story collections.
Member Agents: Liz Darhansoff, Charles Verrill, Leigh Feldman.
Represents: Nonfiction books, novels, short story collections. **Considers these nonfiction areas:** anthropology/archaeology; biography/autobiography; current affairs; health/medicine; history; language/literature/criticism; nature/environment; science/technology. **Considers literary and thriller fiction.**
How to Contact: Query letter only. Reports in 2 weeks on queries.
Needs: Obtains new clients through recommendations from others.
Recent Sales: *Cold Mountain*, by Charles Frazier (Atlantic Monthly Press); *At Home in Mitford*, by Jan Karon (Viking).

◑ JOAN DAVES AGENCY, 21 W. 26th St., New York NY 10010. (212)685-2663. Fax: (212)685-1781. **Contact:** Jennifer Lyons, director; Heather Currier, assistant. Estab. 1960. Member of AAR. Represents 100 clients. 10% of clients are new/previously unpublished writers. Specializes in literary fiction and nonfiction, also commercial fiction.
Represents: Nonfiction books, novels. **Considers these nonfiction areas:** biography/autobiography; gay/lesbian issues; popular culture; translations; women's issues/women's studies. **Considers these fiction areas:** ethnic; family saga; gay; literary; mainstream.
How to Contact: Query. Considers simultaneous submissions. Reports in 3 weeks on queries; 6 weeks on mss. Returns materials only with SASE.
Needs: Obtains new clients through editors' and author clients' recommendations. "A few queries translate into representation."
Recent Sales: Sold 70 titles in the last year. *Strange Fire*, by Melvin Jules Bukiet (W.W. Norton); *JLVT! Growing Up Female with a Bad Reputation*, by Leora Tannenbaum; and *Candor and Perversion*, by Roger Shattuck (W.W. Norton).
Terms: Agent receives 15% commission on domestic sales; 20% on foreign sales. Offers written contract, on a per book basis. Charges for office expenses. 100% of business is derived from commissions on sales.
Reading List: Reads *The Paris Review*, *Missouri Review*, and *Voice Literary Supplement* to find new clients.

[N] ◑ LIZA DAWSON ASSOCIATES, 240 W. 35th St., Suite 500, New York NY 10001. (212)465-9071. E-mail: ldawson@viconet.com. **Contact:** Liza Dawson. Signatory of WGA; member of SAR, MWA, Women's Media

---

TO FIND AN AGENT near you, check the Geographic Index.

Group. Represents 30 clients. 10% of clients are new/previously unpublished writers. Specializes in readable literary fiction, thrillers, mainstream historicals and women's fiction, academics, historians, doctors, journalists, self-help and psychology. "My specialty is shaping books and ideas so that a publisher will quickly respond." Currently handles: 60% nonfiction books; 40% novels.

• Prior to becoming an agent, Ms. Dawson was an editor for 20 years, spending 11 years at William Morrow as vice president and 2 at Putnam as executive editor.

Represents: Nonfiction books, scholarly books, novels. **Considers these nonfiction areas:** biography/autobiography; business; health/medicine; history; how-to; memoirs; psychology; self-help/personal improvement; sociology; women's issues/women's studies. **Considers these fiction areas:** action/adventure; ethnic; family saga; historical; literary; regional; suspense; thriller/espionage.

How to Contact: Query with SASE. Reports in 2 weeks on queries; 1 month on mss.

Needs: Actively seeking talented professionals. Does not want to receive westerns, science fiction, sports, computers, juvenile. Obtains new clients through recommendations and writers' conferences.

Recent Sales: Sold 11 titles in the first 11 months of business. *Back Roads*, by T.L. O'Dell (Viking); *The Inscription*, by Pamela Binder (Pocket Books).

Terms: Agent receives 15% commission on domestic sales; 20% on foreign sales. Offers written contract. Charges for photocopying and overseas postage.

Writer's Conferences: Pacific Northwest Book Conference (Seattle area, July).

Reading Lists: Reads *The Sun, New York Review of Books, The New York Observer, Utne Reader*, and *The Wall Street Journal* to find new clients.

Tips: "Please include a detailed bio with any query letter, let me know somehow that you've done a little research, that you're not just interested in any agent but someone who is right for you."

DH LITERARY, INC., P.O. Box 990, Nyack NY 10960-0990. (212)753-7942. E-mail: dhendin@aol.com. **Contact:** David Hendin. Estab. 1993. Member of AAR. Represents 50 clients. 20% of clients are new/previously unpublished writers. Specializes in trade fiction, nonfiction and newspaper syndication of columns or comic strips. Currently handles: 60% nonfiction books; 10% scholarly books; 20% fiction; 10% syndicated material.

• Prior to opening his agency, Mr. Hendin served as president and publisher for Pharos Books/World Almanac as well as senior vp and COO at sister company United Feature Syndicate.

Represents: Nonfiction books, novels, syndicated material. **Considers these nonfiction areas:** animals; anthropology/archaeology; biography/autobiography; child guidance/parenting; current affairs; ethnic/cultural interests; government/politics/law; health/medicine; history; how-to; language/literature/criticism; money/finance/economics; nature/environment; popular culture; psychology; science/technology; self-help/personal improvement; true crime/investigative; women's issues/women's studies. **Considers these fiction areas:** literary; mainstream; mystery; thriller/espionage.

How to Contact: Reports in 4-6 weeks on queries. Accepts queries by e-mail, "but no downloads." Considers simultaneous queries. Returns materials only with SASE.

Needs: Obtains new clients through referrals from others (clients, writers, publishers).

Recent Sales: Sold 18-20 titles in the last year. *Pink Flamingo Murders*, by Elaine Viets (Dell); *Age of Anxious Anxiety*, by Tom Tiede (Grove Atlantic); *History of American Etiquette*, by Judith Martin (Norton).

Terms: Agent receives 15% commission on domestic sales; 20% on foreign sales. Offers written contract, binding for 1 year. Charges for out of pocket expenses for postage, photocopying manuscript, and overseas phone calls specifically related to a book.

Tips: "Have your project in mind and on paper before you submit. Too many writers/cartoonists say 'I'm good . . . get me a project.' Publishers want writers with their own great ideas and their own unique voice. No faxed submissions."

DHS LITERARY, INC., 6060 N. Central Expwy., Suite 624, Dallas TX 75206-5209. (214)363-4422. Fax: (214)363-4423. **Contact:** David Hale Smith, president. Estab. 1994. Represents 40 clients. 50% of clients are new/previously unpublished writers. Specializes in commercial fiction and nonfiction for adult trade market. Currently handles: 50% nonfiction books; 50% novels.

• Prior to opening his agency, Mr. Smith was an editor at a newswire service.

Represents: Nonfiction books, novels. **Considers these nonfiction areas:** biography/autobiography; business; child guidance/parenting; computers/electronics; cooking/food/nutrition; current affairs; ethnic/cultural interests; gay/lesbian issues; popular culture; sports; true crime/investigative. **Considers these fiction areas:** detective/police/crime; erotica; ethnic; feminist; gay; historical; horror; literary; mainstream; mystery/suspense; sports; thriller/espionage; westerns/frontier.

How to Contact: Query for fiction; send outline/proposal and sample chapters for nonfiction. Considers simultaneous queries and submissions. Reports in 1 month on queries; 4 months on mss. Returns materials only with SASE, otherwise discards.

Needs: Actively seeking thrillers, mysteries, suspense, etc., and narrative nonfiction. Does not want to receive poetry, short fiction, children's books. Obtains new clients through referrals from other clients, editors and agents, presentations at writers conferences and via unsolicited submissions.

Recent Sales: Sold 29 titles in the last year. *Shooting At Midnight*, by Greg Rucka (Bantam); *Food & Mood*, by Elizabeth Somer (Holt).

Terms: Agent receives 15% commission on domestic sales; 25% on foreign sales. Offers written contract, with 10-day cancellation clause or upon mutual consent. Charges for client expenses, i.e., postage, photocopying. 100% of business is derived from commissions on sales.

Reading List: Reads *Outside Magazine*, STORY, *Texas Monthly*, *Kenyon Review*, *Missouri Review* and *Mississippi Mud* to find new clients. "I like to see good writing in many formats. So I'll often call a writer who has written a good short story, for example, to see if she has a novel."

Tips: "Remember to be courteous and professional, and to treat marketing your work and approaching an agent as you would any formal business matter. When in doubt, always query first—in writing—with SASE."

 DIAMOND LITERARY AGENCY, INC., 3063 S. Kearney St., Denver CO 80222. (303)759-0291. "People who are not yet clients should not telephone." President: Pat Dalton. **Contact:** Jean Patrick. Estab. 1982. Represents 20 clients. 10% of clients are new/previously unpublished writers. Specializes in romance, romantic suspense, women's fiction, thrillers, mysteries. "Only considering new clients who are previously published and romantic suspense or contemporary romance writers (series or single title). Previously unpublished writers with completed romance suspense or contemporary romance manuscripts must have a letter of recommendation from a client, editor or other published author personally known to us." Currently handles: 20% nonfiction books; 80% novels.

Represents: Nonfiction books, novels. **Considers these nonfiction areas with mass market appeal:** business; health/ medicine; money/finance/economics; psychology; self-help/personal improvement. **Considers these fiction areas:** detective/police/crime; family saga; glitz; historical; mainstream; mystery/suspense; romance; thriller/espionage.

How to Contact: Send a SASE for agency information and submission procedures. Considers simultaneous submissions. Reports in 1 month on mss (partials). Returns materials only with SASE.

Needs: *Not likely to consider new clients through mid-2000.* Obtains new clients through "referrals from writers, or someone's submitting saleable material."

Recent Sales: Specializes in romance, including sales to Harlequin and Silhouette. Specifics on request if representation offered.

Terms: Agent receives 15% commission on domestic sales; 20% on foreign sales. Offers written contract, binding for 2 years "unless author is well established." Charges a "$15 submission fee for writers who have not previously published the same type of book." Charges for express and foreign postage. "Writers provide the necessary photostat copies."

Tips: "We represent only clients who are professionals in writing quality, presentation, conduct and attitudes—whether published or unpublished. We consider query letters a waste of time—most of all the writer's, secondly the agent's. Submit approximately the first 50 pages and a complete synopsis for books, along with SASE and standard-sized audiocassette tape for possible agent comments. Nonclients who haven't sold the SAME TYPE of book or script within five years must include a $15 submission fee by money order or cashier's check. Material not accompanied by SASE is not returned."

 SANDRA DIJKSTRA LITERARY AGENCY, PMB 515, 1155 Camino del Mar, Del Mar CA 92014-2605. (619)755-3115. **Contact:** Sandra Zane. Estab. 1981. Member of AAR, Authors Guild, PEN West, Poets and Editors, MWA. Represents 100 clients. 30% of clients are new/previously unpublished writers. "We specialize in a number of fields." Currently handles: 60% nonfiction books; 5% juvenile books; 35% novels.

Member Agents: Sandra Dijkstra.

Represents: Nonfiction books, novels. **Considers these nonfiction areas:** anthropology; biography/autobiography; business; child guidance/parenting; nutrition; current affairs; ethnic/cultural interests; government/politics; health/medi-

---

CLOSE UP with David Hale Smith, DHS Literary, Inc.
. . . On being an agent outside of New York

"My advice for writers is to sign with a *good* agent, period. It doesn't matter where an agent is located, as long as he has the contacts and clout necessary to get your work read by the right editors, and he is experienced enough to help you successfully navigate the whole arc of the publishing process.

"When I decided to start my own agency, I never gave much thought to moving to New York. There are a lot of agents in New York. I thought, 'Why go up against all that competition if I don't have to?' It makes for a lot of travel, but most New York agents I know travel nearly as much as I, since we're all spending our time going after good clients and putting people together to create business opportunities.

"There have always been good agents outside New York. Several of the best agents in the country are in San Francisco, for example. Editors at the major houses are very receptive to agents working outside New York. Once you get a reputation for bringing in good stuff, where you are from is not an issue."

cine; history; literary studies (trade only); military/war (trade only); money/finance/economics; nature/environment; psychology; science/technology; self-help/personal improvement; sociology; sports; true crime/investigative; women's issues/women's studies. **Considers these fiction areas:** contemporary issues; detective/police/crime; ethnic; family saga; feminist; literary; mainstream; mystery/suspense; thriller/espionage.

How to Contact: Send "outline/proposal with sample chapters for nonfiction, synopsis and first 50 pages for fiction and SASE." Reports in 4-6 weeks.

Needs: Obtains new clients primarily through referrals/recommendations, but also through queries and conferences and often by solicitation.

Recent Sales: *The Mistress of Spices*, by Chitra Divakaruni (Anchor Books); *The Flower Net*, by Lisa See (HarperCollins); *Outsmarting the Menopausal Fat Cell*, by Debra Waterhouse (Hyperion).

Terms: Agent receives 15% commission on domestic sales; 20% on foreign sales. Offers written contract, binding for 1 year. Charges for expenses "from years we are *active* on author's behalf to cover domestic costs so that we can spend time selling books instead of accounting expenses. We also charge for the photocopying of the full manuscript or nonfiction proposal and for foreign postage."

Writers' Conferences: "Have attended Squaw Valley, Santa Barbara, Asilomar, Southern California Writers Conference, Rocky Mountain Fiction Writers, to name a few. We also speak regularly for writers groups such as PEN West and the Independent Writers Association."

Tips: "Be professional and learn the standard procedures for submitting your work. Give full biographical information on yourself, especially for a nonfiction project. Always include SASE with correct return postage for your own protection of your work. Query with a 1 or 2 page letter first and always include postage. Nine page letters telling us your life story, or your book's, are unprofessional and usually not read. Tell us about your book and write your query well. It's our first introduction to who you are and what you can do! Call if you don't hear within a reasonable period of time. Be a regular patron of bookstores and study what kind of books are being published. READ. Check out your local library and bookstores—you'll find lots of books on writing and the publishing industry that will help you! At conferences, ask published writers about their agents. Don't believe the myth that an agent has to be in New York to be successful—we've already disproved it!"

◐ **DONADIO AND OLSON, INC.**, (formerly Donadio and Ashworth), 121 W. 27th St., Suite 704, New York NY 10001. (212)691-8077. Fax: (212)633-2837. **Contact:** Neil Olson. Estab. 1970. Member of AAR. Represents approximately 100 clients. Specializes in literary fiction and nonfiction. Currently handles: 40% nonfiction; 50% novels; 10% short story collections.

Member Agents: Edward Hibbert (literary fiction); Neil Olson; Ira Silverberg; Peter Steinberg.

Represents: Nonfiction books, novels, short story collections.

How to Contact: Query with 50 pages and SASE. Considers simultaneous queries and submissions. Returns materials only with SASE.

Recent Sales: Sold over 15 titles in the last year. Prefers not to share information on specific sales.

Terms: Agent receives 15% commission on domestic sales; 20% on foreign sales.

◐ ◑ **JIM DONOVAN LITERARY**, 4515 Prentice St., Suite 109, Dallas TX 75206. **Contact:** Jim Donovan, agent/president; Kathryn McKay. Estab. 1993. Represents 20 clients. 25% of clients are new/unpublished writers. Specializes in commercial fiction and nonfiction. Currently handles: 75% nonfiction; 25% novels.

Member Agents: Jim Donovan (president); Kathryn McKay.

Represents: Nonfiction books; novels. **Considers these nonfiction areas:** biography/autobiography; business; child guidance/parenting; current affairs; health/medicine; history; military/war; money/finance/economics; music/dance/theater/film; nature/environment; popular culture; sports; true crime/investigative. **Considers these fiction areas:** action/adventure; detective/police/crime; historical; horror; literary; mainstream; mystery/suspense; sports; thriller/espionage; westerns/frontier.

How to Contact: For nonfiction, send query letter. For fiction, send 2- to 5-page outline and 3 sample chapters with SASE. Reports in 1 month on queries and mss.

Needs: Does not want to receive poetry, humor, short stories, juvenile, romance or religious work. Obtains new clients through recommendations from others and solicitation.

Recent Sales: Sold 18 titles in the last year. *Daytona*, by Ed Hinton (Warner Books); *All About "All About Eve"*, by Sam Staggs (St. Martin's).

Terms: Agent receives 15% commission on domestic sales; 20% on foreign sales. Offers written contract, binding for 1 year. Written letter must be received to terminate a contract. Charges for "some" postage and photocopying—"author is notified first."

Tips: "The vast majority of material I receive, particularly fiction, is not ready for publication. Do everything you can to get your fiction work in top shape before you try to find an agent. I've been in the book business since 1981, in retail (as a chain buyer), as an editor, and as a published author. I'm open to working with new writers if they're serious about their writing and are prepared to put in the work necessary—the rewriting—to become publishable."

◑ **DOYEN LITERARY SERVICES, INC.**, 1931 660th St., Newell IA 50568-7613. (712)272-3300. President: (Ms.) B.J. Doyen. Estab. 1988. Member of RWA, SCBA. Represents 25 clients. 20% of clients are new/previously unpublished writers. Specializes in nonfiction and handles genre and mainstream fiction mainly for adults. Currently handles: 90% nonfiction books; 2% juvenile books; 8% novels. No poetry books.

• Prior to opening her agency, Ms. Doyen worked as a teacher, guest speaker and wrote and appeared in her own weekly TV show airing in 7 states.

Represents: Nonfiction books, novels. **Considers most nonfiction areas. Considers these fiction areas:** contemporary issues; family saga; historical; literary; mainstream; psychic/supernatural.

How to Contact: Query first with SASE. Considers simultaneous queries. Reports immediately on queries; 2-3 weeks on mss. Returns materials only with SASE.

Needs: Actively seeking business, health, how-to, psychology; all kinds of adult nonfiction suitable for the major trade publishers. Does not want to receive pornography, children's. Prefers fiction from published novelists only.

Recent Sales: *Homemade Money*, by Barbara Brabec (Betterway); *Megahealth*, by Sorenson (Evans); *The Family Guide to Financial Aid for Higher Education*, by Black (Putnam/Perigee).

Terms: Agent receives 15% commission on domestic sales; 20% commission on foreign sales. Offers written contract, binding for 1 year.

Tips: "Our authors receive personalized attention. We market aggressively, undeterred by rejection. We get the best possible publishing contracts. We are very interested in nonfiction book ideas at this time; will consider most topics. Many writers come to us from referrals, but we also get quite a few who initially approach us with query letters. Do *not* use phone queries unless you are successfully published or a celebrity. It is best if you do not collect editorial rejections prior to seeking an agent, but if you do, be up-front and honest about it. Do not submit your manuscript to more than one agent at a time—querying first can save you (and us) much time. We're open to established or beginning writers—just send us a terrific letter with SASE!"

ROBERT DUCAS, The Barn House, 244 Westside Rd., Norfolk CT 06058. (860)542-5733. Fax: (860)542-5469. **Contact:** R. Ducas. Estab. 1981. Represents 55 clients. 15% of clients are new/previously unpublished writers. Specializes in nonfiction, journalistic exposé, biography, history. Currently handles: 70% nonfiction books; 2% scholarly books; 28% novels.

• Prior to opening his agency, Mr. Ducas ran the *London Times* and the *Sunday Times* in the U.S. from 1966 to 1981.

Represents: Nonfiction books, novels, novellas. **Considers these nonfiction areas:** animals; biography/autobiography; business; current affairs; gay/lesbian issues; government/politics/law; health/medicine; history; memoirs; military/war; money/finance/economics; nature/environment; science/technology; sports; travel; true crime/investigative. **Considers these fiction areas:** action/adventure; contemporary issues; detective/police/crime; family saga; literary; mainstream; mystery/suspense; sports; thriller/espionage.

How to Contact: Reports in 2 weeks on queries; 2 months on mss.

Needs: Does not want to receive women's fiction. Obtains new clients through recommendations.

Recent Sales: Sold 10 titles in the last year. Prefers not to share information on specific sales.

Terms: Agent receives 15% commission on domestic sales; 20% on foreign sales. Charges for photocopying and postage. "I also charge for messengers and overseas couriers to subagents."

HENRY DUNOW LITERARY AGENCY, 22 W. 23rd St., 5th Floor, New York NY 10010. This agency did not respond to our request for information. Query before submitting.

DWYER & O'GRADY, INC., P.O. Box 239, Lempster NH 03605-0239. (603)863-9347. Fax: (603)863-9346. E-mail: dosouth@mindspring.com. **Contact:** Elizabeth O'Grady. Estab. 1990. Member of SCBWI. Represents 20 clients. 20% of clients are new/unpublished writers. Represents only writers and illustrators of children's books. Currently handles: 100% juvenile books.

• Prior to opening their agency, Mr. Dwyer and Ms. Grady were booksellers and publishers.

Member Agents: Elizabeth O'Grady (children's books); Jeff Dwyer (children's books).

Represents: Juvenile books. **Considers these nonfiction areas:** juvenile nonfiction. **Considers these fiction areas:** juvenile; picture book; young adult.

How to Contact: *Not accepting new clients.*

Needs: Does not want to receive nonjuvenile submissions. Obtains new clients through referrals or direct approach by agent to writer whose work they've read.

Recent Sales: Sold 13 titles in the last year. *A Gardener's Alphabet*, by Mary Azarian (Houghton Mifflin); *Many Many Moons*, by Mary Azarian (Little Brown); *Hinkley Fire*, by Ted Rose (Houghton Mifflin); *Talkin' 'Bout Bess*, by Earl B. Lewis (Orchard Books). Other clients include Kim Ablon, Mary Azarian, Tom Bodett, Odds Bodkin, Donna Clair, Pat Lowery Collins, Leonard Jenkins, E.B. Lewis, Robert H. Miller, Ted Rose, Rebecca Rule, Steve Schuch, Virginia Stroud, Natasha Tarpley, Zong-Zhou Wang and Rashida Watson.

Terms: Agent receives 15% commission on domestic sales; 20% on foreign sales. Offers written contract. 30 days notice must be given to terminate contract. Charges for "photocopying of longer manuscripts or mutually agreed upon marketing expenses."

Writer's Conferences: Book Expo; American Library Association; Society of Children's Book Writers & Illustrators.

JANE DYSTEL LITERARY MANAGEMENT, One Union Square West, Suite 904, New York NY 10003. (212)627-9100. Fax: (212)627-9313. Website: www.dystel.com. **Contact:** Miriam Goderich, Todd Keithley. Estab. 1994. Member of AAR. Presently represents 200 clients. 50% of clients are new/previously unpublished writers. Specializes in commercial and literary fiction and nonfiction plus cookbooks. Currently handles: 65% nonfiction books; 25% novels; 10% cookbooks.

Member Agents: Stacey Glick, Jessica Jones, Todd Keithley, Charlotte Ho (foreign rights), Jane Dystel, Miriam Goderich, Jo Fagan, Kyong Cho.

Represents: Nonfiction books, novels, cookbooks. **Considers these nonfiction areas:** animals; anthropology/archaeology; biography/autobiography; business; child guidance/parenting; cooking/food/nutrition; current affairs; education; ethnic/cultural interests; gay/lesbian issues; government/politics/law; health/medicine; history; humor; military/war; money/finance/economics; New Age/metaphysics; popular cultures; psychology; religious/inspirational; science/technology; true crime/investigative; women's issues/women's studies. **Considers these fiction areas:** action/adventure; contemporary issues; detective/police/crime; ethnic; family saga; gay; lesbian; literary; mainstream; thriller/espionage.

How to Contact: Query with SASE. Reports in 3 weeks on queries; 6 weeks on mss.

Needs: Obtains new clients through recommendations from others, solicitation, at conferences.

Recent Sales: *The Sparrow* and *Children of God*, by Mary Russell; *Water Carry Me*, by Thomas Moran; *Syrup*, by Maxx Barry.

Terms: Agent receives 15% commission on domestic sales; 19% of foreign sales. Offers written contract on a book to book basis. Charges for photocopying. Galley charges and book charges from the publisher are passed on to the author.

Writers' Conferences: West Coast Writers Conference (Whidbey Island WA, Columbus Day weekend); University of Iowa Writer's Conference; Pacific Northwest Writer's Conference; Pike's Peak Writer's Conference; Santa Barbara Writer's Conference.

N **○** **ANNE EDELSTEIN LITERARY AGENCY**, 404 Riverside Dr., New York NY 10025. This agency did not respond to our request for information. Query before submitting.

○ **◎** **EDUCATIONAL DESIGN SERVICES, INC.**, P.O. Box 253, Wantagh NY 11793-0253. (718)539-4107 or (516)221-0995. President: Bertram L. Linder. Vice President: Edwin Selzer. Estab. 1979. Represents 17 clients. 70% of clients are new/previously unpublished writers. Specializes in textual material for educational market. Currently handles: 100% textbooks.

Represents: Textbooks, scholarly books. **Considers these nonfiction areas:** anthropology/archaeology; business; child guidance/parenting; current affairs; ethnic/cultural interests; government/politics/law; history; juvenile nonfiction; language/literature/criticism; military/war; money/finance/economics; science/technology; sociology; women's issues/women's studies.

How to Contact: Query with outline/proposal or outline plus 1-2 sample chapters. "SASE essential." Reports in 1 month on queries; 4-6 weeks on mss.

Needs: Obtains new clients through recommendations, at conferences and through queries.

Recent Sales: *First Principles of Cosmology*, by E.V. Linder (Addison-Wesley Longman).

Terms: Agent receives 15% commission on domestic sales; 25% on foreign sales. Offers written contract. Charges for photocopying.

✓ **○** **PETER ELEK ASSOCIATES**, Box 223, Canal Street Station, New York NY 10013-2610. (212)431-9368. Fax: (212)966-5768. E-mail: info@theliteraryagency.com. **Contact:** Lauren Macta. Estab. 1979. Represents 20 clients. Specializes in children's picture books, adult nonfiction. Currently handles: 30% juvenile books.

Member Agents: Gerardo Greco (director of project development/multimedia).

Represents: Juvenile books (nonfiction, picture books). **Considers these nonfiction areas:** anthropology; parenting; juvenile nonfiction; nature/environment; popular culture; science; true crime/investigative.

How to Contact: Query with outline/proposal and SASE. Reports in 3 weeks on queries; 5 weeks on mss.

Needs: Obtains new clients through recommendations and studying bylines in consumer and trade magazines and in regional and local newspapers.

Recent Sales: *Legendary Brides*, by Letitia Baldridge (HarperCollins); *Today I Feel Silly*, by Laura Cornell (HarperCollins); *When Animals Speak*, by Barbara Hehner (Barron's); *Secrets in Stone*, by Laurie Coulter (Little, Brown).

Terms: Agent receives 15% commission on domestic sales; 20% on foreign sales. If required, charges for wholesale photocopying, typing, courier charges.

Writers' Conferences: Frankfurt Book Fair (Frankfurt Germany, October); LIBF (England); Bologna Children's Book Fair (Italy); APBA (Sidney, Australia).

Tips: "Do your research thoroughly before submitting proposal. Only fresh and original material considered."

○ **ETHAN ELLENBERG LITERARY AGENCY**, 548 Broadway, #5-E, New York NY 10012. (212)431-4554. Fax: (212)941-4652. E-mail: eellenberg@aol.com. **Contact:** Ethan Ellenberg. Estab. 1983. Represents 70 clients. 10%

of clients are new/previously unpublished writers. Specializes in commercial fiction, especially thrillers and romance/women's fiction. "We also do a lot of children's books." Currently handles: 25% nonfiction books; 75% novels.

• Prior to opening his agency, Mr. Ellenberg was contracts manager of Berkley/Jove and associate contracts manager for Bantam.

Represents: Nonfiction books, novels. **Considers these nonfiction areas:** biography/autobiography; business; child guidance/parenting; cooking/food/nutrition; current affairs; health/medicine; history; juvenile nonfiction; New Age/metaphysics; popular culture; psychology; religious/inspirational; science/technology; self-help/personal improvement; true crime/investigative. **Considers these fiction areas:** detective/police/crime; family saga; fantasy; historical; humor; juvenile; literary; mainstream; mystery/suspense; picture book; romance; science fiction; thriller/espionage; young adult.

How to Contact: Send outline plus 3 sample chapters. Accepts queries by e-mail; does not accept fax queries. Considers simultaneous queries and submissions. Reports in 10 days on queries; 3-4 weeks on mss. Returns materials only with SASE.

Needs: Commercial and literary fiction, children's books, break-through nonfiction. Does not want to receive poetry, westerns, autobiographies.

Recent Sales: Sold over 100 titles in the last year. 2 untitled historical romances, by Bertrice Small (Ballantine and Zebra); *The Prairie Train*, illustrated by Eric Rohmann (Crown); *The Hero of the Herd*, by John McCormack (Crown); *Consulting Demons*, by Louis Pinault (HarperCollins); *Puppy and Me* series, by Julia Noonan (Scholastic); *Threat From The Sea* series, by Mel Odom (Wizards of the Coast); *Soul Collector*, by Maureen Child (Hearst Entertainment/CBS).

Terms: Agent receives 15% on domestic sales; 10% on foreign sales. Offers written contract, "flexible." Charges for "direct expenses only: photocopying, postage."

Writers' Conferences: Attends RWA National and Novelists, Inc.

Tips: "We do consider new material from unsolicited authors. Write a good clear letter with a succinct description of your book. We prefer the first three chapters when we consider fiction. For all submissions you must include SASE for return or the material is discarded. It's always hard to break in, but talent will find a home. We continue to see natural storytellers and nonfiction writers with important books."

NICHOLAS ELLISON, INC., 55 Fifth Ave., 15th Floor, New York NY 10003. (212)206-6050. Fax: (212)463-8718. Affiliated with Sanford J. Greenburger Associates. **Contact:** Elizabeth Ziemska, Jane Mendle. Estab. 1983. Represents 70 clients. Currently handles: 25% nonfiction books; 75% novels.

• Prior to becoming an agent, Mr. Ellison was an editor at Minerva Editions, Harper & Row and editor-in-chief at Delacorte.

Member Agents: Alicka Pistek (foreign rights); Elizabeth Ziemska, Jane Mendle.

Represents: Nonfiction, novels. **Considers most nonfiction areas. Considers literary and mainstream fiction.**

How to Contact: Query with SASE. Reporting time varies on queries.

Needs: Does not want biography or self-help. Usually obtains new clients from word-of-mouth referrals.

Recent Sales: *Plum Island*, by Nelson DeMille (Warner); *The Mermaids Singing*; by Lisa Carey (Avon). Other clients include Olivia Goldsmith, P.T. Deutermann, James Webb.

Terms: Agent receives 15% commission on domestic sales; 20% commission on foreign sales.

ANN ELMO AGENCY INC., 60 E. 42nd St., New York NY 10165. (212)661-2880, 2881. Fax: (212)661-2883. **Contact:** Lettie Lee. Estab. 1961. Member of AAR, MWA, Authors Guild.

Member Agents: Lettie Lee, Mari Cronin (plays); A.L. Abecassis (nonfiction).

Represents: Nonfiction, novels. **Considers these nonfiction areas:** anthropology/archaeology; art/architecture/design; biography/autobiography; business; child guidance/parenting; computers/electronics; cooking/food/nutrition; crafts/hob-

---

 CLOSE UP with Ethan Ellenberg, Ethan Ellenberg Literary Agency
... On contracts

"Contracts are very confusing. Not only is your basic publishing agreement complex—especially the royalty section—but now with electronic rights and other issues erupting, it's becoming a very complex area. Obviously, common sense is your best guide. Read the contract carefully. Try to isolate what is most important. For me, that is mainly income and some legal protection.

"We negotiate electronic rights clauses very carefully. We're trying to keep the royalties comparable to hardcover royalties—or better—because we think the new economic model means publishers should make more money electronically. It's a wait and watch situation because it's an evolving field, but there are some good paradigms. Audio royalties finally shook out, and we have a relatively stable environment there. CD-ROMs was another area where we started with a chaotic free-for-all and ended up with some base royalties. We're an industry that is looking at potential for tremendous technological change."

bies; current affairs; education; health/medicine; history; how-to; juvenile nonfiction; money/finance/economics; music/dance/theater/film; photography; popular culture; psychology; self-help/personal improvement; true crime/investigative; women's issues. **Considers these fiction areas:** action/adventure; contemporary issues; detective/police/crime; ethnic; family saga; feminist; glitz; historical; juvenile; literary; mainstream; mystery/suspense; psychic/supernatural; regional; romance (contemporary, gothic, historical, regency); thriller/espionage; young adult.

How to Contact: Query with outline/proposal. "Letter queries *only* with SASE." No queries by fax. Reports in 10-12 weeks "average" on queries.

Needs: Obtains new clients through referrals.

Recent Sales: Prefers not to share information on specific sales.

Terms: Agent receives 15% commission on domestic sales; 20% on foreign sales. Offers written contract (standard AAR contract). Charges for "special mailings or shipping considerations or multiple international calls. No charge for usual cost of doing business."

Tips: "Query first, and when *asked* only please send properly prepared manuscript. A double-spaced, readable manuscript is the best recommendation. Include SASE, of course."

☑ ⊘ **ES TALENT AGENCY**, 777 Davis St., San Francisco CA 94111. (415)543-6575. Fax: (415)543-6534. **Contact:** Ed Silver. Estab. 1995. Signatory of WGA. Represents 50-75 clients. 70% of clients are new/previously unpublished writers. Specializes in theatrical screenplays, MOWs and miniseries. Currently handles: 50% nonfiction books; 25% movie scripts; 25% novels.
   • See the expanded listing for this agency in Script Agents.

◐ **MARY EVANS INC.**, 242 E. Fifth St., New York NY 10003. (212)979-0880. Fax: (212)979-5344. E-mail: merrylit@aol.com. **Contact:** Tanya McKinnon or Laura Albritton. Member of AAR. Represents 45 clients. Specializes in literary fiction and serious nonfiction. Currently handles: 45% nonfiction books; 5% story collections; 50% novels.

Member Agents: Tanya McKinnon, Mary Evans.

Represents: Nonfiction books, novels. **Considers these nonfiction areas:** biography/autobiography; computers/electronics; current affairs; gay/lesbian issues; government/politics/law; history; nature/environment; popular culture; science/technology. **Considers these fiction areas:** contemporary issues; ethnic; gay; literary.

How to Contact: Query with SASE. Reports in 3-4 week on queries; 1-2 months on mss.

Needs: Actively seeking "professional well-researched nonfiction proposals; literary novels." No children's books. Obtains new clients through recommendations from others.

Recent Sales: *Whiteouts*, by Michael Blaire (Rob Weisbach Books); *Biorealism*, by Robert Frenay (Farrar, Straus & Giroux); *Venus Rituals*, by Vendela Vida (St. Martin's Press).

Terms: Agent receives 15% commission on domestic sales; 20% on foreign sales.

〔N〕 ⊘ **CHARLES EVERITT LITERARY AGENCY, INC.**, 3 School St., Boston MA 02108. (617)973-9422. Fax: (617)624-0313. E-mail: cbela@msn.com. **Contact:** Charles Everitt. Estab. 1997. Represents 22 clients. 80% of clients are new/unpublished writers. Currently handles: 80% nonfiction books, 20% novels.
   • Prior to opening his agency, Mr. Everitt had 35 years of experience in the trade book industry, including 13 years as an editor at Little, Brown, 15 years as president of Globe Pequot Press, and was originally assistant editor at *Publishers Weekly*.

Represents: Nonfiction books, novels. **Considers these nonfiction areas:** agriculture/horticulture; animals; anthropology/archaeology; biography/autobiography; business; child guidance/parenting; current affairs; education; ethnic/cultural interests; government/politics/law; health/medicine; history; memoirs; military/war; money/finance/economics; nature/environment; science/technology; sociology; sports; true crime/investigative. **Considers these fiction areas:** action/adventure; contemporary issues; historical; literary; sports.

How to Contact: Query with SASE. Accepts queries by e-mail and fax. Considers simultaneous queries. Reports in "several days" on queries; 2 months on mss. Returns materials only with SASE.

Needs: Actively seeking contemporary nonfiction. Does not want to receive poetry, science fiction, women's romance, fantasy. Obtains new clients through word-of-mouth, queries, solicitation.

Recent Sales: Sold 9 titles in the last year. *Tender As Hellfire*, by Joe Meno (St. Martin's Press); *Inner Game of Investing* and *A Killing on Wall St.*, by Derrick Niederman (John Wiley & Sons); *God: Stories*, edited by C. Michael Curtis (Houghton Mifflin). Other clients include Ferne Arfin, JoAnne Bennett, G. Cadwallader, R.D. Estes, Aaron Altera, Michael Hallett, Vilma Hunt, Mark Poröbeck, Alan R. Spievack, M.D., Lisa Feinberg Densmore, Erik Wolf, Daniel King, Estate of Stefan Lorant.

Terms: Agent receives 15% commission on domestic sales; 20% on foreign sales. Offers written contract. Charges for photography, overnight mail, postage, long distance phone calls and messengers.

Writer's Conferences: N.E. Writer's Workshop (Boston, June).

⊘ **FALLON LITERARY AGENCY**, 15 E. 26th St., Suite 1609, New York NY 10010. This agency did not respond to our request for information. Query before submitting.

⊘ **FARBER LITERARY AGENCY INC.**, 14 E. 75th St., #2E, New York NY 10021. (212)861-7075. Fax: (212)861-7076. **Contact:** Ann Farber. Estab. 1989. Represents 40 clients. 50% of clients are new/previously unpublished writers. Currently handles: 40% fiction; 15% scholarly books; 45% stage plays.

Represents: Nonfiction books, textbooks, juvenile books, novels, stage plays. **Considers these nonfiction areas:** child guidance/parenting; cooking/food/nutrition; music/dance/theater/film; psychology. **Considers these fiction areas:** action/adventure; contemporary issues; humor/satire; juvenile; literary; mainstream; mystery/suspense; thriller/espionage; young adult.

How to Contact: Send outline/proposal, 3 sample chapters and SASE. Reports in 1 month on queries; 2 months on mss.

Needs: Obtains new clients through recommendations from others.

Recent Sales: *Live a Little*, by Colin Neenan (Harcourt Brace & Co.); *Saving Grandma*, by Frank Schaeffer (The Putnam Berkley Publishing Group, Inc.); *Step on a Crack*, by M.T. Coffin (Avon/Camelot Publishing Co.); *Bright Freedom Song*, by Gloria Houston (Harcourt Brace & Co.).

Terms: Agent receives 15% commission on domestic sales; 20% on foreign sales. Offers written contract, binding for 2 years. Client must furnish copies of ms, treatments and any other items for submission.

Tips: "Our attorney, Donald C. Farber, is the author of many books. His services are available to the agency's clients as part of the agency service at no additional charge."

FEIGEN/PARRENT LITERARY MANAGEMENT, 10158 Hollow Glen Circle, Bel Air CA 90077-2112. (310)271-0606. Fax: (310)274-0503. E-Mail: 104063.3247@compuserve.com. **Contact:** Brenda Feigen, Joanne Parrent. Estab. 1995. Member of PEN USA West, Authors Guild, and LA County Bar Association. Represents 35-40 clients. 20-30% of clients are new/previously unpublished writers. Currently handles: 40% nonfiction books, 25% movie scripts, 30% novels, 5% TV scripts.

● Ms. Feigen is also an attorney and producer; Ms. Parrent is also a screenwriter and author.

Member Agents: Brenda Feigen (books, books-to-film); Joanne Parrent (screenplays).

Represents: Nonfiction books, novels. **Considers these nonfiction areas:** biography/autobiography; business; current affairs; gay/lesbian issues; government/politics/law; health/medicine; how-to; money/finance/economics; memoirs; theater/film; psychology; self-help/personal improvement; women's issues/women's studies. **Considers these fiction areas:** contemporary issues; family saga; feminist; gay; lesbian; literary. "Manuscripts must be less than 75,000 words for a new author."

Also Handles: Feature film, TV MOW. **Considers these script areas:** action/adventure; comedy; contemporary issues; family saga; feminist; lesbian; thriller. "Must be professionally formatted and under 130 pages."

How to Contact: Query only with 2-page synopsis and author bio with SASE. Does not accept queries by fax or e-mail. "Prefers regular mail." Reports in 2-3 weeks on queries; 4-6 weeks on mss. Returns materials only with SASE.

Needs: Actively seeking "material about women, including strong, positive individuals. The material can be fiction, memoir or biographical." Does not want to receive horror, science fiction, religion, pornography; "poetry or short stories unless author has been published by a major house." Usually obtains clients through recommendations from other clients and publishers, through the Internet, and listings in *Literary Market Place*.

Recent Sales: Sold 8 book titles and 2 script projects in the last year. *Rape of Nanking*, by Iris Chang (Basic Books); *The Women's Movement*, by Joanne Parrent (Random House); *Hell's Fire*, by Joe Rosenblum and David Kohn (Praeger); *Tailwind* (working title), by April Oliver (Knopf). **Movie/TV MOW script(s) optioned/sold:** *The Cowboys of Haddington Moor*, by David Martin Anderson (James Coburn, producer).

Terms: Agent receives 15% commission on domestic sales; 20% on foreign sales. Offers written contract, binding for 1 year. Charges for postage, long distance calls, and photocopying.

Tips: "If we like a book or screenplay we will either, at the writer's choice, represent it as agents or offer to produce it ourselves if the material is of real interest to us, personally."

JUSTIN E. FERNANDEZ, AGENT/ATTORNEY, (formerly Justin E. Fernandez Attorney/Agent—Agency for the Digital & Literary Arts, Inc.), P.O. Box 20038, Cincinnati OH 45220. E-mail: lit4@aol.com. **Contact:** Justin E. Fernandez. Estab. 1996. Represents 10-15 clients. 50% of clients are new/previously unpublished writers. Currently handles: 25% nonfiction; 65% fiction; 5% digital/multimedia, 5% other. "We are presently an affiliate agency of AEI, Inc. AEI has offices in Beverly Hills and New York. AEI's web address is www.aeionline.com."

● Prior to opening his agency, Mr. Fernandez, a 1992 graduate of the University of Cincinnati College of Law, served as a law clerk with the Ohio Court of Appeals, Second Appellate District (1992-94), and as a literary agent for Paraview, Inc., New York (1995-96).

Member Agents: Paul A. Franc (associate agent).

Represents: Nonfiction, fiction, screen/teleplays and digital art (virtual reality, music, software, multimedia/Internet-related products). **Considers most nonfiction and fiction genres.**

How to Contact: Query first with SASE (e-mail encouraged). Considers simultaneous queries and submissions. When hard copy is requested, be sure to include a container for the manuscript, with return address and sufficient postage affixed unless recycling is an option.

Needs: Mainstream fiction; pop culture; women's fiction; thrillers; histories; biographies; literary fiction and nonfiction; children's books; computer and Internet-related books; romance novels; African-American and Hispanic fiction; science fiction; gift and humor books; photography, art and design books; popular/mainstream science and philosophy, political science, Eastern religion, gay/lesbian fiction and nonfiction; and material for syndication (columns, cartoon strips, etc.). Usually obtains new clients through referrals or queries from listings.

Recent Sales: Sold 4 titles last year. *By Way of a Wager* and *Seeking Celeste*, by Hayley Ann Solomon (Kensington/Zebra).

Terms: Agent receives 10% commission on domestic sales; 15% on foreign sales; 25% with foreign co-agent. Offers written contract. No fees. Expenses deducted from monies received per contract terms.

Tips: "Proofread, proofread, proofread—50% of submissions have typos, usage errors, or clichés in the first several pages. Manuscripts should be double spaced, with 1-inch margins, 12 point font, and be accompanied by a return package, with sufficient postage attached (not loose) to the package. When sending e-mail follow-up messages, don't assume your name is enough information—identify the submission by title and date and method submitted."

FINESSE LITERARY AGENCY, 655 N. First St., Wood River IL 62095. (618)254-7666. Fax: (618)254-9737. E-mail: angel@mvp.net. Website: users.marz.com/~angel1. **Contact:** Karen Elizabeth Carr. Estab. 1996. Represents 60 clients. 50% of clients are new/unpublished writers. Currently handles: 5% nonfiction books, 30% juvenile books, 15% story collections. 40% novels, 10% novellas.

• Prior to becoming an agent, Ms. Carr worked in law enforcement and ran an answering service for doctors.

Represents: Nonfiction books, juvenile books, scholarly books, novels, textbooks, novellas, poetry books, short story collections. **Considers these nonfiction areas:** animals; art/architecture/design; biography/autobiography; business; child guidance/parenting; computers/electronics; cooking/food/nutrition; crafts/hobbies; education; ethnic/cultural interests; gay/lesbian issues; government/politics/law; health/medicine; history; how-to; humor; interior design/decorating; juvenile nonfiction; language/literature/criticism; memoirs; military/war; money/finance/economics; nature/environment; New Age/metaphysics; photography; popular culture; psychology; religious/inspirational; science/technology; self-help/personal improvement; sociology; sports; true crime/investigative; women's issues/women's studies. **Considers these fiction areas:** action/adventure; cartoon/comic; confessional; contemporary issues; detective/police/crime; erotica; ethnic; experimental; family saga; fantasy; feminist; gay/lesbian; historical; horror; humor/satire; juvenile; literary; mainstream; mystery; picture book; psychic/supernatural; romance; religious/inspirational; science fiction; sports; thriller/espionage; westerns/frontier; young adult.

How to Contact: Send entire ms. Accepts queries by e-mail and fax. Considers simultaneous queries and submissions. Reports in 2 weeks on queries; 1 month on mss. Returns materials only with SASE.

Needs: Actively seeking all new writers of fiction and nonfiction. Obtains new clients through recommendations and website.

Recent Sales: Sold 5 titles in the last year. *The Bear, The Book and the Blanket*, by Kim Farral (Denlingers); *Day World Night World*, by Kim Farral (Denlingers); *Sacrifice For Cause*, by Kim Farral (Denlingers).

Terms: Agent receives 10% commission on domestic sales; 15% on foreign sales. Offers written contract. Charges for postage, photocopying under a 3-plan system.

Tips: "Please send all work in full hard copy by mail not e-mail. Feel free to call agency during business hours."

FIRST BOOKS, 3000 Market St. N.E., #527, Salem OR 97301. (503)588-2224. Fax: (503)588-2818. E-mail: firstbooks@aol.com. Website: www.firstbooks.com. **Contact:** Jeremy Solomon. Estab. 1988. Represents 80 clients. 40% of clients are new/previously unpublished writers. Specializes in book-length fiction and nonfiction for the adult and juvenile markets.

Member Agents: Jeremy Solomon, Bernadette Duperron.

Represents: Nonfiction books, juvenile books, novels.

Needs: Does not want to receive romance novels. Obtains new clients through recommendations from others and website, as well as unsolicited submissions.

How to Contact: Query with SASE. No e-mail queries. Prefers to be only reader. Reports in 2-3 weeks on queries. Returns materials only with SASE.

Recent Sales: Sold 40 titles in the last year. *Mastering the Markets*, by Ari Kiev (John Wiley & Sons); *So Many Strange Things*, by Charise Mericle (Little, Brown & Co.); *Turning Lead Into Gold*, by Robin Pinkley (St. Martin's Press); *How Murray Saved Christmas*, by Mike Reiss (Price Stern Sloan/Penguin-Putnam); *The Same Phrase Describes My Marriage and My Breasts: Before the Kids They Used to Be Such a Cute Couple*, by Amy Krouse Rosenthal (Andrews McMeel Universal).

Terms: Agent receives 15% commission on domestic sales; 20% on foreign sales. Offers written contract, with cancellation on demand by either party.

FITZGERALD LITERARY MANAGEMENT, 84 Monte Alto Rd., Santa Fe NM 87505. Phone/fax: (505)466-1186. **Contact:** Lisa FitzGerald. Estab. 1994. Represents 12 clients. 75% of clients are new/unpublished writers. Represents screenwriters and film rights to novels. Currently represents: 75% movie scripts; 15% film rights to novels; 5% TV scripts; 5% films rights to stage plays.

• See expanded listing for this agency in Script Agents.

JOYCE A. FLAHERTY, LITERARY AGENT, 816 Lynda Court, St. Louis MO 63122-5531. (314)966-3057. **Contact:** Joyce Flaherty. Estab. 1980. Member of AAR, RWA, MWA, Authors Guild. Represents 40 clients. "At this time we are adding only currently published authors." Currently handles: 15% nonfiction books; 85% novels.

• Prior to opening her agency, Ms. Flaherty was a journalist, public relations consultant and executive director of a large suburban Chamber of Commerce.

Member Agents: Joyce A. Flaherty.

Represents: Nonfiction books, novels. **Considers these nonfiction areas:** Americana; animals; child guidance/parenting; collectibles; cookbooks; crafts/hobbies; health/medicine; how-to; memoirs; nature; popular culture; psychology;

self-help/personal improvement; sociology; travel; women's issues. **Considers these fiction areas:** contemporary issues; family saga; feminist; historical; mainstream; military; mystery/suspense; thrillers; women's genre fiction.

How to Contact: Send outline plus 1 sample chapter and SASE. No unsolicited mss. Prefers to be only reader. Reports in 1 month on queries; 2 months on mss unless otherwise agreed on. Returns materials only with SASE.

Needs: Actively seeking "high concept fiction, very commercial; quality works of both fiction and nonfiction. Gripping nonfiction adventure such as *Into Thin Air* and *The Perfect Storm*." Does not want to receive "poetry, novellas, short stories, juvenile, syndicated material, film scripts, essay collections, science fiction, traditional westerns." Obtains new clients through recommendations from editors and clients, writers' conferences and from queries. Preference given to published book authors.

Recent Sales: Sold 50 titles in the last year. *Primary Target*, by Joe Weber (Putnam-Berkley); *Princess*, by Gaelen Foley (Ballantine).

Terms: Agent receives 15% commission on domestic sales.

Writers' Conferences: Often attends Romance Writers of America.

Tips: "Be concise and well focused in a letter or by phone. Always include a SASE as well as your phone number. If a query is a multiple submission, be sure to say so and mail them all at the same time so everyone has the same chance. Know something about the agent beforehand so you're not wasting each other's time. Be specific about word length of project and when it will be completed if not completed at the time of contact. Be brief!"

N **FLANNERY LITERARY**, 1140 Wickfield Court, Naperville IL 60563-3300. (630)428-2682. Fax: (630)428-2683. **Contact:** Jennifer Flannery. Estab. 1992. Represents 33 clients. 90% of clients are new/previously unpublished writers. Specializes in children's and young adult, juvenile fiction and nonfiction. Currently handles: 5% nonfiction books; 95% juvenile books.

● Prior to opening her agency, Ms. Flannery was an editorial assistant.

Represents: Nonfiction books, juvenile books. **Considers these nonfiction areas:** child guidance/parenting; juvenile nonfiction. **Considers these fiction areas:** humor/satire; juvenile; literary; mainstream; mystery/suspense; picture book; young adult.

How to Contact: Query with SASE. Reports in 2-4 weeks on queries; 6-8 weeks on mss; 6-8 weeks on scripts.

Also Handles: Feature film, animation, TV MOW, miniseries, animation. **Considers these script subject areas:** action/adventure; cartoon/animation; comedy; contemporary issues; ethnic; family saga; historical; humor; juvenile; mainstream; mystery/suspense; sports; teen; western/frontier.

Needs: Obtains new clients through referrals and queries.

Recent Sales: Sold over 20 titles in the last year. Prefers not to share information on specific sales.

Terms: Agent receives 15% commission on domestic sales; 20% on foreign sales. Offers written contract, binding for life of book in print, with 30 day cancellation clause. 100% of business is derived from commissions on sales.

Writers' Conferences: SCBWI Fall Conference.

Tips: "Write an engrossing, succinct query describing your work."

PETER FLEMING AGENCY, P.O. Box 458, Pacific Palisades CA 90272. (310)454-1373. **Contact:** Peter Fleming. Estab. 1962. Specializes in "nonfiction books: innovative, helpful, contrarian, individualistic, pro-free market . . . with bestseller big market potential." Currently handles: 100% nonfiction books.

● Prior to becoming an agent, Mr. Fleming worked his way through the University of Southern California at CBS TV City.

Represents: Nonfiction books. **Considers "any nonfiction area with a positive, innovative, helpful, professional, successful approach to improving the world (and abandoning special interests, corruption and patronage)."**

How to Contact: Query with SASE.

Recent Sales: *Launching Your Child in Show Biz*, by Dick Van Patten (General Publishing); *Sexual Compulsion*, by Dr. Paul Fick (Judith Regan-HarperCollins).

Terms: Agent receives 15% commission on domestic sales; 25% on foreign sales. Offers written contract, binding for 1 year. Charges "only those fees agreed to *in writing*, i.e., NY-ABA expenses shared. We may ask for a TV contract, too."

Tips: Obtains new clients "through a *sensational*, different, one of a kind idea for a book usually backed by the writer's experience in that area of expertise. If you give seminars, you can begin by self-publishing, test marketing with direct sales. One of my clients sold 100,000 copies through his speeches and travels, and another writing duo sold over 30,000 copies of their self-published book before we offered it to trade bookstore publishers."

**FOR EXPLANATIONS OF THESE SYMBOLS,
SEE THE INSIDE FRONT AND BACK COVERS OF THIS BOOK**

☑ ◖ **B.R. FLEURY AGENCY**, P.O. Box 149352, Orlando FL 32814-9352. (407)895-8494. Fax: (407)898-3923. E-mail: brfleuryagency@juno.com. **Contact:** Blanche or Margaret. Estab. 1994. Signatory of WGA. Currently handles: 70% books; 30% scripts.
  • See the expanded listing for this agency in Script Agents.

☑ ◖ **THE FOGELMAN LITERARY AGENCY**, 7515 Greenville, Suite 712, Dallas TX 75231. (214)361-9956. Also: 599 Lexington Ave., Suite 2300, New York NY 10022. (212)836-4803. E-mail: info@fogelman.com. Website: www.fogelman.com. **Contact:** Evan Fogelman. Estab. 1990. Member of AAR, signatory of WGA. Represents 100 clients. 2% of clients are new/unpublished writers. Specializes in women's fiction and nonfiction. "Zealous author advocacy" makes this agency stand apart from others. Currently handles: 40% nonfiction books; 10% scholarly books; 40% novels; 10% TV scripts.
  • Prior to opening his agency, Mr. Fogelman was an entertainment lawyer.
Member Agents: Evan Fogelman (nonfiction, women's fiction); Linda Kruger (women's fiction, nonfiction).
Represents: Novels. **Considers these nonfiction areas:** biography/autobiography; business; child guidance/parenting; current affairs; education; ethnic/cultural interests; government/politics/law; health/medicine; popular culture; psychology; sports; true crime/investigative; women's issues/women's studies. **Considers these fiction areas:** historical; literary; mainstream; and all sub-genres of romance.
How to Contact: Query. Considers simultaneous queries and submissions. Reports "next business day" on queries; 6-8 weeks on mss. Returns materials only with SASE.
Needs: Actively seeking "nonfiction of all types; contemporary romances." Does not want to receive children's/juvenile. Obtains new clients through recommendations from others.
Recent Sales: Sold over 50 titles in the last year. Prefers not to share information on specific sales.
Terms: Agent receives 15% commission on domestic sales; 10% on foreign sales. Offers written contract, binding on a project-by-project basis.
Writers' Conferences: Romance Writers of America; Novelists, Inc.
Tips: "Finish your manuscript, and see our website."

◖ **THE FOLEY LITERARY AGENCY**, 34 E. 38th St., New York NY 10016. (212)686-6930. **Contact:** Joan or Joseph Foley. Estab. 1956. Represents 15 clients. Currently handles: 75% nonfiction books; 25% novels.
Represents: Nonfiction books, novels.
How to Contact: Query with letter, brief outline and SASE. Reports promptly on queries.
Needs: Rarely takes on new clients.
Terms: Agent receives 10% commission on domestic sales; 20% on foreign sales. Charges for photocopying, messenger service and unusual expenses (international phone, etc.). 100% of business is derived from commissions on sales.
Tips: Desires *brevity* in querying.

☑ ◖ **FORTHWRITE LITERARY AGENCY**, 23852 W. Pacific Coast Hwy., Suite 701, Malibu CA 90265. (310)456-5698. E-mail: literaryag@aol.com. **Contact:** Wendy Keller. Estab. 1989. Member of Women's National Book Assn., National Speakers Association, Publisher's Marketing Association, National Association for Female Executives, Society of Speakers, Authors & Consultants. Represents 20 clients. 10% of clients are new/previously unpublished writers. Specializes in "serving authors who are or plan to also be speakers. Our sister company is a speaker's bureau." Currently handles: 80% nonfiction books; 20% foreign and other secondary rights.
  • Prior to opening her agency, Ms. Keller was an associate publisher of Los Angeles' second largest Spanish-language newspaper.
Represents: "We handle business books (sales, finance, marketing and management especially); self-help and how-to books on many subjects." **Considers commercial nonfiction in these areas:** business; self-help; how-to; pop psychology; health; alternative health; child care/parenting; inspirational; spirituality; home maintenance and management; cooking; crafts; interior design; art; biography; writing; film; consumer reference; ecology; current affairs; women's studies; economics and history. "Particularly books by speakers and seminar leaders."
Also Handles: Foreign, ancillary, upselling (selling a previously published book to a larger publisher) & other secondary & subsidiary rights.
How to Contact: "Prefer 1 page e-mail query (no attachments)." Query with SASE only. *No unsolicited mss!* Considers simultaneous queries and submissions. Reports in 2 weeks on queries; 6 weeks on ms. Returns materials only with SASE or discards.
Needs: Actively seeking "professional manuscripts by highly qualified authors." Does not want to receive "fiction, get-rich-quick or first person narrative on health topics." Obtains new clients through referrals, recommendations by editors, queries, satisfied authors, conferences etc.
Recent Sales: Sold approximately 32 titles in the last year. *Questions from Earth Answers from Heaven*, by Cher Margolis (St. Martin's Press); *Dancing with Our Souls*, by Irene Lambert (Ballantine); *Secrets of the Executive Search Researchers*, by Nils Rasmussen and Christian Schoyen (AMACOM); *L'Onda Perfetta*, by Sergio Bambaren (Sperling & Kupfer—Italy); *Ein Strand für meine Träume*, by Sergio Bambaren (Kabel—Germany); *The Cult of the Born Again Virgin: How Single Women Are Reclaiming Their Sexual Power*, by Wendy Keller (HEALTH COMMUNICATIONS, Inc.).
Writers' Conferences: BEA, Frankfurt Booksellers' Convention, Maui Writer's Conference, some regional conferences and regularly talks on finding an agent, how to write nonfiction proposals, query writing, creativity enhancement, persevering for creatives.

Tips: "Write only on a subject you know well, and be prepared to show a need in the market for your book. We prefer to represent authors who are already presenting their material publicly through seminars or other media."

✪ FOX CHASE AGENCY, INC., Public Ledget Bldg. 930, Philadelphia PA 19106. This agency did not respond to our request for information. Query before submitting.

✪ LYNN C. FRANKLIN ASSOCIATES, LTD., 1350 Broadway, Suite 2015, New York NY 10018. (212)868-6211. Fax: (212)868-6312. E-mail: agency@fsainc.com. **Contact:** Lynn Franklin and Claudia Nys. Estab. 1987. Member of PEN America. Represents 30-35 clients. 50% of clients are new/previously unpublished writers. Specializes in general nonfiction with a special interest in health, biography, international affairs and spirituality. Currently handles: 90% nonfiction books; 10% novels.
Represents: Nonfiction books. **Considers these nonfiction areas:** biography/autobiography; current affairs; health/medicine; history; memoirs; New Age/metaphysics; psychology; religious/inspirational; self-help/personal improvement; travel. **Considers literary and mainstream commercial fiction.**
How to Contact: Query with SASE. No unsolicited mss. Reports in 2 weeks on queries; 6 weeks on mss.
Needs: Obtains new clients through recommendations from others and from solicitation.
Recent Sales: *No Future Without Forgiveness*, by Archbishop Desmond Tutu (Doubleday).
Terms: Agent receives 15% commission on domestic sales; 20% on foreign sales. Offers written contract, with 60-day cancellation clause. Charges for postage, photocopying, long distance telephone if significant. 100% of business is derived from commissions on sales.

✪ JEANNE FREDERICKS LITERARY AGENCY, INC., 221 Benedict Hill Rd., New Canaan CT 06840. Phone/fax: (203)972-3011. E-mail: jflainc@ix.netcom.com. **Contact:** Jeanne Fredericks. Estab. 1997. Member of AAR. Represents 80 clients. 10% of clients are new/unpublished writers. Specializes in quality adult nonfiction by authorities in their fields. Currently handles: 98% nonfiction books; 2% novels.
   ● Prior to opening her agency, Ms. Fredericks was an agent and acting director with the Susan P. Urstadt Inc. Agency.
Represents: Nonfiction books. **Considers these nonfiction areas:** animals; anthropology/archeaology; art/architecture; biography/autobiography; business; child guidance/parenting; cooking/food/nutrition; crafts/hobbies; current affairs; health/medicine/alternative health; history; horticulture; how-to; interior design/decorating; money/finance/economics; nature/environment; photography; psychology; science; self-help/personal improvement; sports; women's issues. **Considers these fiction areas:** family saga; historical; literary.
How to Contact: Query first with SASE, then send outline/proposal or outline and 1-2 sample chapters with SASE. No fax queries. Accepts queries by e-mail. "If short—no attachments." Considers simultaneous queries and submissions. Reports in 3 weeks on queries; 4-6 weeks on mss. Returns material only with SASE.
Needs: Obtains new clients through referrals, submissions to agency, conferences.
Recent Sales: Sold 22 titles in the last year. *Gaining Ground: Creating Big Gardens in Small Spaces*, by Maureen Gilmer (NTC/Contemporary); *The Book of Five Rungs for Executives*, by Donald Krause (Nicholas Brealey—US & Britain; Meberneuter-Germany; Lyon—Portugal; Makron—Brazil; etc.).
Terms: Agent receives 15% commission on domestic sales; 20% on foreign sales; 25% with foreign co-agent. Offers written contract, binding for 9 months. 2 months notice must be given to terminate contract. Charges for photocopying of whole proposals and mss, overseas postage, priority mail and Federal Express.
Writers' Conferences: PEN Women Conference (Williamsburg VA, February); Connecticut Press Club Biennial Writers' Conference (Stamford CT, April); ASJA Annual Writers' Conference East (New York NY, May); BEA (Chicago, June).
Tips: "Be sure to research the competition for your work and be able to justify why there's a need for it. I enjoy building an author's career, particularly if s(he) is professional, hardworking, and courteous. Aside from eight years of agenting experience, I've had ten years of editorial experience in adult trade book publishing that enables me to help an author polish a proposal so that it's more appealing to prospective editors. My MBA in marketing also distinguishes me from other agents."

✪ SARAH JANE FREYMANN LITERARY AGENCY, (formerly Stepping Stone), 59 W. 71st St., Suite 9B, New York NY 10023. (212)362-9277. Fax: (212)501-8240. **Contact:** Sarah Jane Freymann. Member of AAR. Represents 100 clients. 20% of clients are new/previously unpublished writers. Currently handles: 75% nonfiction books; 2% juvenile books; 23% novels.
Represents: Nonfiction books, novels, lifestyle-illustrated. **Considers these nonfiction areas:** animals; anthropology/archaeology; art/architecture/design; biography/autobiography; business; child guidance/parenting; cooking/food/nutrition; current affairs; ethnic/cultural interests; gay/lesbian issues; health/medicine; history; interior design/decorating; nature/environment; psychology; religious/inspirational; self-help/personal improvement; women's issues/women's studies. **Considers these fiction areas:** contemporary issues; ethnic; literary; mainstream; mystery/suspense; thriller/espionage.
How to Contact: Query with SASE. Reports in 2 weeks on queries; 6 weeks on mss.
Needs: Obtains new clients through recommendations from others.
Recent Sales: *Just Listen*, by Nancy O'Hara (Broadway); *Flavors*, by Pamela Morgan (Viking); *Silent Thunder*, by Katherine Payne (Simon & Schuster); *The Wisdom of Depression*, by Dr. Jonathan Zuess (Crown).

Terms: Agent receives 15% commission on domestic sales; 20% on foreign sales. Offers written contract. Charges for long distance, overseas postage, photocopying. 100% of business is derived from commissions on ms sales.
Tips: "I love fresh new passionate works by authors who love what they are doing and have both natural talent and carefully honed skill."

⊘ CANDICE FUHRMAN LITERARY AGENCY, 2440C Bush St., San Francisco CA 94115. (415)674-7654. Fax: (415)674-4004. This agency did not respond to our request for information. Query before submitting.

Ⓝ Ⓜ SHERYL B. FULLERTON ASSOCIATES, 1095 Amito Ave., Berkeley CA 94705. (510)841-9898. E-Mail: sfullerton@aol.com. Website: www.YouCanWrite.com. **Contact:** Sheryl Fullerton. Estab. 1994. Represents 20 clients. 70% of clients are new/previously unpublished writers. Specializes in nonfiction subject areas. Currently handles: 96% nonfiction books, 3% scholarly books, 1% textbooks.
   • Prior to opening her agency, Ms. Fullerton was an editor, then editor in chief of a college textbook publisher.
Represents: Nonfiction books, scholarly books, textbooks. **Considers these nonfiction areas:** anthropology/archaeology; business/management; current affairs; gay/lesbian issues; ethnic/cultural interests; how-to; New Age/metaphysics; popular culture; psychology; self-help/personal improvement; sociology; women's issues/women's studies.
How to Contact: Query with description and bio. Accepts queries by e-mail. Considers simultaneous queries. Reports in 2 weeks on queries; 1 month weeks on mss. Returns materials only with SASE.
Needs: Actively seeking psychology, business/management, popular culture and lesbian/gay nonfiction. Does not want to receive health/medicine, inspirational or parenting. Usually obtains clients through recommendations and referrals, and through previous contacts.
Recent Sales: Sold 10 titles in the last year. *Coming Home to Your Body*, by Johanna Putuoi; *Work Less, Make More*, by Jennifer White; *Small Wonders*, by Joan Lovett; *Still Groovin'*, by Ruth Beckford; *Terms of Engagement*, by Richard Axelrod; *Burritos*, by David Thomsen and Derek Wilson; *The Alchemy of Fear*, by Kay Gilley.
Terms: Agent receives 15% commission on domestic sales; 20% on foreign sales. Offers a written contract binding for 1 year, then renewable. 60 days notice must be given to terminate contract. Charges for reimbursement of phone calls, postage, photocopies.
Tips: "With SASE, I will provide guidelines for writing a book proposal. Visit our website, YouCanWrite.com."

Ⓜ MAX GARTENBERG, LITERARY AGENT, 521 Fifth Ave., Suite 1700, New York NY 10175-0038. (212)860-8451. Fax: (973)535-5033. E-mail: gartenbook@prodigy.net. **Contact:** Max Gartenberg. Estab. 1954. Represents 30 clients. 5% of clients are new writers. Currently handles: 90% nonfiction books; 10% novels.
Represents: Nonfiction books. **Considers these nonfiction areas:** agriculture/horticulture; animals; art/architecture/design; biography/autobiography; child guidance/parenting; current affairs; health/medicine; history; military/war; money/finance/economics; music/dance/theater/film; nature/environment; psychology; science/technology; self-help/personal improvement; sports; true crime/investigative; women's issues/women's studies.
How to Contact: Query. Reports in 2 weeks on queries; 6 weeks on mss.
Needs: Obtains new clients "primarily by recommendations from others, but occasionally by following up on good query letters."
Recent Sales: *Dreamers: In Search of the Nez Percé*, by Martin Stadius (Caxton Press); *A Newer World*, by David Roberts (Simon & Schuster); *Harry and Ruth*, by Howard Owen (Permanent Press).
Terms: Agent receives 15% commission on first domestic sale, 10% commission on subsequent domestic sales; 15-20% on foreign sales.
Tips: "This is a small agency serving established writers, and new writers whose work it is able to handle are few and far between. Nonfiction is more likely to be of interest here than fiction, and category fiction not at all of interest."

Ⓜ GELFMAN SCHNEIDER LITERARY AGENTS, INC., 250 W. 57th St., New York NY 10107. (212)245-1993. Fax:(212)245-8678. **Contact:** Deborah Schneider. Estab. 1981. Member of AAR. Represents 150 clients. 10% of clients are new/unpublished writers.
Represents: "We represent adult, general, hardcover fiction and nonfiction, literary, commercial, and some mysteries."
How to Contact: Query with SASE. Reports in 2-3 weeks on queries; 6-8 weeks on mss.
Needs: Obtains new clients through recommendations and referrals. No romances, science fiction, westerns or children's books.
Recent Sales: Prefers not to share information on specific sales.
Terms: 15% commission on domestic sales; 20% on foreign sales. Offers written contract. Charges for photocopying, messengers and couriers.

◎ GHOSTS & COLLABORATORS INTERNATIONAL, Division of James Peter Associates, Inc., P.O. Box 772, Tenafly NJ 07670. (201)568-0760. Fax: (201)568-2959. E-mail: bertholtje@compuserve.com. **Contact:** Bert Holtje. Parent agency established 1971. Parent agency is a member of AAR. Represents 54 clients. Specializes in representing only published ghost writers and collaborators, nonfiction only. Currently handles: 100% nonfiction books.
   • Prior to opening his agency, Mr. Holtje was a book packager.
Represents: Nonfiction collaborations and ghost writing assignments.
Recent Sales: Prefers not to share information on specific sales. Clients include Alan Axelrod, Carol Turkington, George Mair, Brandon Toropov, Alvin Moscow, Richard Marek, Susan Shelly.

Terms: Agent receives 15% commission on domestic sales; 20% on foreign sales. Offers written contract.

Tips: "We would like to hear from professional writers who are looking for ghosting and collaboration projects. We invite inquiries from book publishers who are seeking writers to develop house-generated ideas, and to work with their authors who need professional assistance."

$ ✍ THE SEBASTIAN GIBSON AGENCY, P.O. Box 13350, Palm Desert CA 92255-3350. (760)837-3726. Fax: (619)322-3857. **Contact:** Sebastian Gibson. Estab. 1995. 100% of clients are new/previously unpublished writers. Specializes in fiction.

Represents: Nonfiction books, novels. **Considers these nonfiction areas:** animals; anthropology/archaeology; biography/autobiography; business; cooking/food/nutrition; current affairs; government/politics/law; health/medicine; history; military/war; music/dance/theater/film; nature/environment; photography; popular culture; psychology; science/technology; sociology; sports; travel; true crime/investigative; women's issues/women's studies. **Considers these fiction areas:** action/adventure; contemporary issues; detective/police/crime; ethnic; experimental; family saga; glitz; historical; mainstream; regional; romance (contemporary, gothic, historical, regency); science fiction; sports; thriller/espionage.

How to Contact: Send outline and 3 sample chapters; "$10 bush-league, small-potato, hardly-worth-mentioning handling fee is requested as each year we receive more and more submissions and we wish to give each of them the time they deserve." SASE required for a response. No fax or e-mail queries. Considers simultaneous queries and submissions. Reports in 3 weeks. "Writers should not be overly demanding or with unrealistic time constraints." Returns materials only with SASE.

Needs: Actively seeking sports books, thrillers, contemporary fiction, detective/police/crime and psychological suspense, as well as business and financial books. Does not want to receive autobiographies, poetry, short stories, pornography. Obtains new clients through advertising, queries, book proposals, and through the representation of entertainment clients.

Recent Sales: Prefers not to share information on specific sales.

Terms: Agent receives 10% commission on domestic sales; 20% on foreign sales. Offers written contract, with 30 day cancellation notice. Charges for postage, photocopying and express mail fees charged only against sales.

Writer's Conference: BEA (Chicago, June); Book Fair (Frankfurt); London Int'l Book Fair (London).

Tips: "We look for manuscripts with fresh characters whose dialogue and pacing jump off the page. With the well-edited book that contains new and exciting story lines, and locations that grab at the imagination of the reader, we can see that you become a published author. No bribes necessary, just brilliant writing. We're also interested in nonfiction business and financial books, books for investors and books by industry leaders. Consider hiring a freelance editor to make corrections and assist you in preparing book proposals. Try to develop unusual characters in your novels, and novel approaches to nonfiction. Manuscripts should be clean and professional looking and without errors. Do not send unsolicited manuscripts or disks. Save your money and effort for redrafts. Don't give up. We want to help you become published. But your work must be very readable without plot problems or gramatical errors. Do not send sample chapters or book proposals until you've completed at least your fourth draft. Unless you're famous, don't send autobiographies. We are looking primarily for all categories of fiction with unusual characters, new settings and well-woven plots. Key tip: Make the first page count and your first three chapters your best chapters. An author should have something to say that either pulls on your emotions, or sparks you interest in such a way as to have a profound effect on the reader."

✍ THE GISLASON AGENCY, 219 Main St. SE, Suite 506, Minneapolis MN 55414-2160. (612)331-8033. Fax: (612)331-8115. E-mail: gislasonbj@aol.com. **Contact:** Barbara J. Gislason. Estab. 1992. Member of Minnesota State Bar Association, Art & Entertainment Law Section (Former Chair), Internet Committee, Minnesota Intellectual Property Law Association Copyright Committee (Former Chair), SFWA, MWA, RWA, Sisters In Crime, University Film Society (Board Member) and Neighborhood Justice (Board Member). 50% of clients are new/previously unpublished writers. "The Gislason Agency represents published and unpublished mystery, science fiction, fantasy, romance and law-related works and is seeking submissions in all categories. The Gislason Agency is also committed to expanding in the nonfiction market." Currently handles: 10% nonfiction books; 90% fiction.

● Ms. Gislason became an attorney in 1980, and continues to practice Art & Entertainment Law and has been nationally recognized as a leading American attorney.

Member Agents: Barbara Grey (mystery); Jocelyn Pihlaja (romance); Deborah Sweeney (fantasy, science fiction); Karen Butak (fantasy, science fiction); Anitra Budd (nonfiction).

Represents: Fiction, nonfiction. **Considers these nonfiction areas:** medicine/alternative medicine; spirituality; science; self-help; animals; biography; popular psychology; sociology; politics/law. **Considers these fiction areas:** fantasy; law related; mystery/suspense; romance; science fiction.

How to Contact: Fiction: query with synopsis and first 3 chapters. SASE required. Nonfiction: query with proposal and sample chapters. Reports in 1 month on queries, 3 months on mss. "Multicultural submissions are welcome."

Needs: Do not send personal memoirs, poetry or children's books. Obtains half of new clients through recommendations

---

ALWAYS INCLUDE a self-addressed, stamped envelope (SASE) for reply or return of your query or manuscript.

from other authors and editors, contacts made at conferences, television and radio shows, and half from *Guide to Literary Agents*, *Literary Market Place* and other reference books.

Recent Sales: *Night Fires* (3 book deal), by Linda Cook (Kensington); *A Deadly Shaker Spring* (3 book deal), by Deborah Woodworth (Avon). Clients include Robert Kline, Paul Lake, Joan Verba, Marjorie DeBoer and Kathryn Harwig.

Terms: Agent receives 15% commission on domestic sales; 20% on foreign sales. Offers written contract, binding for 1 year with option to renew. Charges for photocopying and postage.

Writers' Conferences: Dark & Stormy Nights; Boucheron; Minicon; Romance Writers of America; Midwest Fiction Writers; University of Wisconsin Writer's Institute. Also attend state and regional writers conferences.

Tips: "Cover letter should be well written and include a detailed synopsis (if fiction) or proposal (if nonfiction), the first three chapters and author information. Appropriate SASE required. We are looking for a great writer with a poetic, lyrical or quirky writing style who can create intriguing ambiguities. We expect a well-researched, imaginataive and fresh plot that reflects a familiarity with the applicable genre. If submitting a nonfiction work, explain how the submission differs from and adds to previously published works in the field. Scenes with sex and violence must be intrinsic to the plot. Remember to proofread, proofread, proofread. If the work was written with a specific publisher in mind, this should be communicated. In addition to owning an agency, Ms. Gislason practices law in the area of Art and Entertainment and has a broad spectrum of entertainment industry contacts."

GOLDFARB & ASSOCIATES, 1501 M St. NW, Washington DC 20005-2902. (202)466-3030. Fax: (202)293-3187 (no queries by fax). E-mail: rglawlit@aol.com. **Contact:** Ronald Goldfarb. Estab. 1966. Represents "hundreds" of clients. "Minority" of clients are new/previously unpublished writers. Specializes primarily in nonfiction but has a growing interest in well-written fiction. "Given our D.C. location, we represent many journalists, politicians and former federal officials. We arrange collaborations. We also represent a broad range of nonfiction writers and novelists." Currently handles: 75% nonfiction books; 25% fiction. Increasing TV and movie deals.

● Ron Goldfarb's book (his ninth), *Perfect Villains, Imperfect Heroes*, was published by Random House. Other books include *TV or not TV: Courts, Television, and Justice* (NYU Press), 1998.

Member Agents: Ronald Goldfarb, Esq. (nonfiction), Robbie Anna Hare.

Represents: Nonfiction, fiction. **Considers all nonfiction areas. Considers these adult fiction areas:** action/adventure; contemporary issues; detective/police/crime; ethnic; feminist; glitz; literary; mainstream; mystery/suspense; thriller/espionage.

How to Contact: Send outline or synopsis plus 1-2 sample chapters (include SASE if return requested). Reports in 1 month on queries; 2 months on mss.

Needs: Actively seeking "fiction with literary overtones; strong nonfiction ideas." Does very little children's fiction or poetry." Obtains new clients mostly through recommendations from others.

Recent Sales: Sold approximately 35 titles in the last year. *Crimes of War*, by Roy Gutman, David Rieff (Norton); *Plato or Prozac*, by Lou Marinoff (HarperCollins); *Agent of Destiny*, by John S.D. Eisenhower (Free Press). Other clients include Congressman John Kasich, Diane Rehm, Susan Eisenhower, Dan Moldea, Roy Gutman, Chuck Negron of Three Dog Night, Carrie Brown.

Terms: Charges for photocopying, long distance phone calls and postage.

Writers' Conferences: Washington Independent Writers Conference; Medical Writers Conference; VCCA; participate in many ad hoc writers' and publishers' groups and events each year.

Tips: "We are a law firm which can help writers with related legal problems, Freedom of Information Act requests, libel, copyright, contracts, etc. As published authors ourselves, we understand the creative process."

FRANCES GOLDIN, 57 E. 11th St., New York NY 10003. This agency did not respond to our request for information. Query with SASE before submitting.

GOODMAN ASSOCIATES, 500 West End Ave., New York NY 10024-4317. (212)873-4806. **Contact:** Elise Simon Goodman. Estab. 1976. Member of AAR. Represents 100 clients. "Presently accepting new clients on a very selective basis."

● Arnold Goodman is current chair of the AAR Ethics Committee.

Member Agents: Elise Simon Goodman, Arnold P. Goodman.

Represents: Nonfiction, novels. **Considers most adult nonfiction and fiction areas.** No "poetry, articles, individual stories, children's or YA material."

How to Contact: Query with SASE. Reports in 10 days on queries; 1 month on mss.

Recent Sales: Prefers not to share information on specific sales.

Terms: Agent receives 15% commission on domestic sales; 20% on foreign sales. Charges for certain expenses: faxes, toll calls, overseas postage, photocopying, book purchases.

GOODMAN-ANDREW-AGENCY, INC., 1275 N. Harper, #7, West Hollywood CA 90046. (323)656-3785. Fax: (323)656-3975. **Contact:** Sasha Goodman. Estab. 1992. Represents 25 clients. 50% of clients are new/previously unpublished writers. Currently handles: 50% nonfiction books; 50% novels.

Represents: Nonfiction books, novels. **Considers these nonfiction areas:** agriculture/horticulture; anthropology/archaeology; art/architecture/design; biography/autobiography; business; child guidance/parenting; cooking/food/nutrition; current affairs; education; ethnic/cultural interests; gay/lesbian issues; government/politics/law; health/medicine;

history; how-to; language/literature/criticism; music/dance/theater/film; nature/environment; popular culture; psychology; self-help/personal improvement; sociology; sports; true crime/investigative; women's issues/women's studies. **Considers these fiction areas:** contemporary issues; ethnic; gay; lesbian; literary; mainstream. "Not big on genre fiction."
How to Contact: Send outline and 2 sample chapters. Considers simultaneous queries and submissions. Reports in 3 weeks on queries; 3 months on mss. Returns materials only with SASE.
Recent Sales: Sold 10 titles in the last year. *Person or Persons Unknown*, by Bruce Alexander (Putnam); *Taking Charge When You're Not In Control*, by Patricia Wiklund, Ph.D. (Ballantine).
Terms: Agent receives 15% commission. Offers written contract. Charges for postage.
Writers' Conferences: Pacific Northwest (Seattle, July).
Tips: "Query with 1-page letter, brief synopsis and 2 chapters. Patience, patience, patience. Always enclose return postage/SASE if you want your material returned. Otherwise, say you do not. Remember the agent is receiving dozens of submissions per week so try to understand this, and be patient and courteous."

☑ ◖ **CARROLL GRACE LITERARY AGENCY**, P.O. Box 10938, St. Petersburg FL 33733. (727)865-2099.
Contacts: Pat Jozwiakowski, Sunny Mays. Estab. 1998. Represents 30 clients. 100% of clients are new/unpublished writers. "We understand how difficult it is for a new writer to obtain an agent or a publisher. We want to guide careers and encourage our clients to their top potential by offering our experience and knowledge." Currently handles: 40% nonfiction books; 10% scholarly books; 50% novels.
Member Agents: Sunny Mays (acquisitions director); Pat Jozwiakowski (agent).
Represents: Nonfiction books, scholarly books, novels. **Considers these nonfiction areas:** art; biography/autobiography; cooking/food/nutrition; crafts/hobbies; education; health/medicine; history; how-to; interior design/decorating; photography; true crime/investigative; women's issues/women's studies. **Considers these fiction areas:** action/adventure; detective/police/crime; family saga; fantasy; historical; horror; literary; mainstream; mystery/suspense (amateur sleuth, cozy, culinary); psychic/supernatural; romance (contemporary, gothic, historical, regency); thriller/espionage; westerns/frontier.
How to Contact: Query with SASE. Send outline and first 5 sample chapters. Reports in 4-6 weeks on queries, 6-8 weeks on mss.
Needs: Actively seeking romance, fantasy, mystery/suspense, psychic supernatural, timeswept (romance w/time travel).
Recent Sales: New agency with no recorded sales.
Terms: Agent receives 15% commission on domestic sales; 20% on foreign sales. Offers written contract, binding on book-by-book basis. 90 days notice must be given to terminate contract. Charges for photocopying, international and express postage, and faxes.
Tips: "Make sure your manuscript is as near to finished as possible—be neat and orderly. Study manuscript formatting, check your manuscript for spelling, grammar and punctuation errors."

🅽 ◙ **ASHLEY GRAYSON LITERARY AGENCY**, 1342 18th St., San Pedro CA 90732. This agency did not respond to our request for information. Query before submitting.

◙ **SANFORD J. GREENBURGER ASSOCIATES, INC.**, 55 Fifth Ave., New York NY 10003. (212)206-5600. Fax: (212)463-8718. **Contact:** Heide Lange. Estab. 1945. Member of AAR. Represents 500 clients.
Member Agents: Heide Lange, Faith Hamlin, Beth Vesel, Theresa Park, Elyse Cheney, Dan Mandel.
Represents: Nonfiction books, novels. **Considers all nonfiction areas. Considers these fiction areas:** action/adventure; contemporary issues, detective/police/crime; ethnic; family saga; feminist; gay; glitz; historical; humor/satire; lesbian; literary; mainstream; mystery/suspense; psychic/supernatural; regional; sports; thriller/espionage.
How to Contact: Query first. Reports in 3 weeks on queries; 2 months on mss.
Needs: Does not want to receive romances or westerns.
Recent Sales: Sold 200 titles in the last year. Prefers not to share information on specific sales. Clients include Andrew Ross, Margaret Cuthbert, Nicholas Sparks, Mary Kurcinka, Linda Nichols, Edy Clarke and Peggy Claude Pierre.
Terms: Agent receives 15% commission on domestic sales; 20% on foreign sales. Charges for photocopying, books for foreign and subsidiary rights submissions.

◖ **ARTHUR B. GREENE**, 101 Park Ave., 26th Floor, New York NY 10178. (212)661-8200. Fax: (212)370-7884.
Contact: Arthur Greene. Estab. 1980. Represents 20 clients. 10% of clients are new/previously unpublished writers. Specializes in movies, TV and fiction. Currently handles: 25% novels; 10% novellas; 10% short story collections; 25% movie scripts; 10% TV scripts; 10% stage plays; 10% other.
• See the expanded listing for this agency in Script Agents.

◖ **RANDALL ELISHA GREENE, LITERARY AGENT**, 620 S. Broadway, Suite 210, Lexington KY 40508-3150. (606)225-1388. **Contact:** Randall Elisha Greene. Estab. 1987. Represents 20 clients. 30% of clients are new/previously unpublished writers. Specializes in adult fiction and nonfiction only. No juvenile or children's books. Currently handles: 50% nonfiction books; 50% novels.
• Prior to opening his agency, Mr. Greene worked at Doubleday & Co. as an editor.
Represents: Nonfiction books, novels. **Considers these nonfiction areas:** agriculture/horticulture; biography/autobiography; business; current affairs; ethnic; government/politics/law; health; history; memoirs; psychology; true crime/investigative. **Considers these fiction areas:** contemporary issues; detective/police/crime; ethnic; family saga; humor/

Agent and first-time author land hot deal

Every so often, an aspiring writer's commitment and perseverance come into conjunction with the knowledge and expertise
of a literary agent to spawn the sort of book deal writers dream
about. After making the leap from secretarial jobs and substitute
teaching to full-time writing, Linda Nichols of Tacoma, Washington labored over the manuscript for *Handyman*, a novel about a
depressed and harried housewife who goes to a therapist. What
she doesn't realize is the man to whom she pours out her worries
is actually a handyman contracted to do work on the office.

Linda Nichols

Photo by Perler Photography

Nichols carefully composed a query letter outlining the premise of *Handyman* and mailed it to agent Theresa Park of Sanford
J. Greenburger Associates, Inc. Charmed by the query letter,
Park requested the full manuscript. Nichols sent it on a Friday
and received an enthusiastic reply: "She called me Monday morning and said she loved it. She
also said the Hollywood co-agent was in town, and she was going to give him a copy. He was
going to read it that night in his hotel room. I was stunned, and I said to her, 'Does this mean
you want to represent me?' And she said, 'Yes!'" Park quickly brokered a six-figure deal with
Jackie Cantor and Leslie Schnur of Delacorte Press. Soon after, Hollywood co-agents Howie
Sanders and Richard Green of United Talent Agency optioned the movie rights to Universal/
Dreamworks.

Having landed an agent and a publishing deal, Nichols now stands poised in anticipation of
the January, 2000 release of *Handyman*. In the meantime, she agreed to answer a few questions:

How did you get involved in novel writing?
I wrote during college and didn't do much writing after that. I married after college, had three
boys, and chose to stay home while raising them. Probably seven years ago, when the youngest
went to school, I got back into writing and received regular article assignments from a local
parenting magazine. Then, I joined a writers' workshop and started concentrating on fiction,
which is my first love. At the same time, I thought if I wanted an income I was going to need
a job. I began taking the prerequisites for our nursing program here at Tacoma Community
College. But then I thought, "I want to finish a novel."

How did you come up with the premise for the novel?
I was watching a romantic comedy on television, and I thought, "I could do one of those." I
imagined a scenario where a woman would be in an intimate relationship that involved a
mistaken identity. I came up with the idea of a woman mistaking someone else for her therapist,
and then I asked myself questions like, "What would be the most ridiculous person to mistake

for your therapist?" I chose to make the hero somebody who worked with his hands and was a loser with women.

What led you to give up your day job and write fulltime?

A first grader in my son's class had written a novel. He's a bright kid, very gifted. I asked him, "What novel did you write?"— thinking he'd tell me he wrote a 30-page story—and he said he wrote a 150-page sequel to *Star Wars*. I thought, "If a first grader can write a novel, I can write a novel, too."

I also read this quote about Coleridge, that said his life showed the supreme tragedy of indiscipline, that he never disciplined himself to write the things he wanted to write. He said, 'I have a whole book that's complete save transcription.' That really struck me, because I had all these books that were in my head and needed to be written down.

You've written two novels besides *Handyman*. What sort of revision process did you go through before you felt ready to contact an agent?

Every time I reread *Handyman*, I end up revising it. It's been revised seven or eight times. I felt like I needed to go through the novel with a fine tooth comb. I thought my first three novels were probably going to be practice. I gave the first one to my writing teacher and asked her to critique it. She said, "You know, this is a cute story. You could do something with this." She suggested some revisions. I made them, and then I contacted agents.

Did you consider selling the manuscript to a publishing house yourself without using an agent?

It seemed to me that every now and then lightning would strike, and somebody would get lucky by sending a manuscript to a publisher, but it didn't seem to happen very often. Also, a woman in my writing class told us about her daughter who wrote a young adult fiction book, and had laboriously—I believe it was for three or four years—networked her way through writers' conferences to sell her book to a publisher. Finally, she got an agent and sold it within a month. I thought, "They know their business. It's like going to a specialist at the doctor."

What criteria did you have when you chose which agents to approach?

I tried to find agents interested in the kind of book I'd written, which was very mainstream, very commercial. I felt as though I was without a genre. It isn't a romance. As far as I understand, romances have strict criteria. My book doesn't fit those, and I didn't know if it would find a home.

How did you approach writing your query letter?

The only type of queries I'd written were for magazine articles, so I studied books on writing fiction queries. I thought, "This book is going to sell itself or not. It's not me they're buying here." I don't think there is anything magical about the query. Your query letter should be the best you can do. I took that to heart. I asked myself, "What would I put on the jacket of my book if somebody flipped it open. What would I put on there to draw them into book?" I gave a brief synopsis of each character and the set-up, and then I ended with a couple of questions. I think the query is important, but more important is the book you're selling.

What kind of preparation did you put into the physical presentation of the manuscript?

I sent Park a clean, professional-looking manuscript. In my writers' workshop, that's one thing we hold each other accountable to. You can have the best idea in the world, but if it looks sloppy or unprofessional, you're not going to make a good impression.

Had you given any thought to the possibility of working on a script version?

The agents from United Talent Agency, which also represents quite a few screenwriters, directors and actors, showed it to both a screenwriter and director. Both decided they wanted to do it. They were clear with me that when you sell movie rights, you sell them. They may ask me something now and then out of courtesy, but it's out of my hands.

Do you have any other advice for writers, especially concerning agents?

I would advise everybody to get an agent. The publishing world has changed to such an extent that if you're serious about your writing, that's the way you're going to get published, other than an incredible lucky break. I feel that Theresa more than earns her commission.

—*Ian Bessler*

---

satire; literary; mainstream; mystery/suspense; regional; romance (contemporary); thriller/espionage.
How to Contact: Query with SASE only. Reports in 1 month on queries; 2 months on mss. *No unsolicited mss.*
Recent Sales: Prefers not to share information on specific sales.
Terms: Agent receives 15% commission on domestic sales; 20% on foreign sales and performance rights. Charges for extraordinary expenses such as photocopying and foreign postage.

⊘ MAXINE GROFFSKY LITERARY AGENCY, 2 Fifth Ave., New York NY 10011. This agency did not respond to our request for information. Query before submitting.

◐ THE GROSVENOR LITERARY AGENCY, (formerly Deborah Grosvenor Literary Agency), 5510 Grosvenor Lane, Bethesda MD 20814. (301)564-6231. Fax: (301)581-9401. **Contact:** Deborah C. Grosvenor. Estab. 1995. Member of Nat'l Press Club. Represents 30 clients. 5% of clients are new/previously unpublished writers. Currently handles: 90% nonfiction books, 10% novels.
 • Prior to opening her agency, Ms. Grosvenor was a book editor for 18 years.
Represents: Nonfiction books, novels. **Considers these nonfiction areas:** animals; anthropology/archaeology; art/architecture/design; biography/autobiography; business; child guidance/parenting; current affairs; government/politics/law; health/medicine; history; how-to; language/literature/criticism; military/war; money/finance/economics; music/dance/theater/film; nature/environment; New Age/metaphysics; photography; popular culture; psychology; religious/inspirational; science/technology; self-help/personal improvement; sociology; translations; true crime/investigative; women's issues/women's studies. **Considers these fiction areas:** contemporary issues; detective/police/crime; family saga; gay; historical; lesbian; literary; mainstream; mystery/suspense; romance (contemporary, gothic, historical); thriller/espionage.
How to Contact: Send outline/proposal for nonfiction; send outline and 3 sample chapters for fiction. Reports in 1 month on queries; 2 months on mss. Returns materials only with SASE.
Needs: Obtains new clients almost exclusively through recommendations from others.
Recent Sales: *Dixie: A Personalized Portrait of the South*, by Curtis Wilkie (Scribner); *The Fortune Hunters: The Dazzling Marriages of our Day and the Women Who Made Them*, by Charlotte Hays (St. Martin's).
Terms: Agent receives 15% commission on domestic sales; 20% on foreign sales. Offers a written contract with a 10-day cancellation clause.

Ⓝ ◐ REESE HALSEY NORTH, 98 Main St., PMB 704, Tiburon CA 94920. (415)789-9191. Fax: (415)789-9177. E-mail: bookgirl@worldnet.att.net. **Contact:** Kimberley Cameron. Estab. 1957. Member of AAR, signatory of WGA. Represents 40 clients. 30% of clients are new/previously unpublished writers. Specializes in mystery, literary and mainstream fiction, excellent writing. Currently handles: 30% nonfiction books; 70% fiction.
 • The Reese Halsey Agency has an illustrious client list largely of established writers, including the estate of Aldous Huxley and has represented Upton Sinclair, William Faulkner and Henry Miller. Ms. Cameron has recently opened a Northern California office and all queries should be addressed to her at the Tiburon office.

Member Agents: Doris Halsey (by referral only, LA office); Kimberley Cameron (Reese Halsey North).
Represents: Fiction and nonfiction. **Considers these nonfiction areas:** biography/autobiography; current affairs; history; language/literature/criticism; memoirs; popular culture; spiritualism; true crime/investigative; women's issues/women's studies. **Considers these fiction areas:** action/adventure; contemporary issues; detective/police/crime; ethnic; family saga; historical; literary; mainstream; mystery/suspense; science fiction; thriller/espionage; women's fiction.
How to Contact: Query with SASE. Reports in 3 weeks on queries; 3 months on mss.
Recent Sales: Prefers not to share information on specific sales.
Terms: Agent receives 15% commission on domestic sales of books. Offers written contract, binding for 1 year. Requests 6 copies of ms if representing an author.
Writers' Conferences: BEA and various writer conferences, Maui Writers Conference.
Reading List: Reads *Glimmer Train*, *The Sun* and *The New Yorker* to find new clients. Looks for "writing that touches the heart."
Tips: Obtains new clients through recommendations from others and solicitation. "Please send a polite, well-written query and include a SASE with it!"

N ⊘ JEANNE K. HANSON LITERARY AGENCY, 5441 Woodcrest Dr., Edina MN 55424-1649. This agency did not respond to our request for information. Query before submitting.

⊘ HARDEN CURTIS ASSOCIATES, 850 Seventh Ave., Suite 405, New York NY 10019. This agency did not respond to our request for information. Query with SASE before submitting.

⊘ HARRIS LITERARY AGENCY, P.O. Box 6023, San Diego CA 92166. (619)697-0600. Fax: (619)697-0610. E-mail: hlit@adnc.com. Website: www.HarrisLiterary.com. **Contact:** Barbara J. Harris. Estab. 1998. Represents 60 clients. 65% of clients are new/previously unpublished writers. Specializes in mainstream fiction. Currently handles: 40% nonfiction books; 60% novels.
Member Agents: Barbara J. Harris (nonfiction); Norman J. Rudenberg (fiction).
Represents: Nonfiction books, novels. **Considers these nonfiction areas:** biography/autobiography; health/medicine; how-to; humor; science/technology; self-help. **Considers these fiction areas:** action/adventure; detective/police/crime; humor/satire; juvenile; mainstream; mystery/suspense; science fiction; thriller/espionage.
How to Contact: Query with SASE. "The initial query should contain a one- to two-page description plus the author's pertinent biography, neatly typed in 12 point font with accurate spelling and proper punctuation. Make sure it is clear and succinct. Tell what the work is about and do not add hype. Include the ending and tell us how many words and pages are in your work." Accepts queries by e-mail. "Do not query by sending long e-mail messages. Tell about your work in 200-300 words." Reports in 2 weeks on queries; 1 month on mss. Returns materials only with SASE.
Needs: Usually obtains new clients through directory, recommendations and internet listing.
Recent Sales: Sold 6 titles in the last year. *The Sweep of the Second Hand*, by Dean Monti (Academy Chicago Publishers); *Caught in the Web*, by Ron Joseph (Bervia Publishing).
Terms: Agent receives 15% commission on domestic sales; 20% on foreign sales. Offers written contract. 30 days notice must be given to terminate contract. Charges for photocopying, postage.
Writers' Conferences: BEA (Chicago, June), BEA (Los Angeles, May).
Tips: "Professional guidance is imperative in bringing along new writers. In the highly competitive publishing arena, strict guidelines must be adhered to."

N ◎ THE JOY HARRIS LITERARY AGENCY, INC., 156 Fifth Ave., Suite 617, New York NY 10010. (212)924-6269. Fax: (212)924-6609. E-mail: jhlitagent@aol.com. **Contact:** Joy Harris. Member of AAR. Represents 150 clients. Currently handles: 50% nonfiction books; 50% novels.
Member Agents: Kassandra Duane, Leslie Daniels.
Represents: Considers "adult-type books, not juvenile." **Considers all fiction areas except fantasy; juvenile; science frition; westerns/frontier.**
How to Contact: Query with outline/proposal and SASE. Reports in 2 months on queries. "No unsolicited manuscripts, just query letters."
Needs: Obtains new clients through recommendations from clients and editors.
Recent Sales: Sold 10 titles in the last year. Prefers not to share information on specific sales.
Terms: Agent receives 15% commission on domestic sales; 20% on foreign sales. Charges for extra office expenses.

♥ JOHN HAWKINS & ASSOCIATES, INC., 71 W. 23rd St., Suite 1600, New York NY 10010. (212)807-7040. Fax: (212)807-9555. E-mail: jhawkasc@aol.com. **Contact:** John Hawkins, William Reiss. Estab. 1893. Member of AAR. Represents over 100 clients. 5-10% of clients are new/previously unpublished writers. Currently handles: 40% nonfiction books; 20% juvenile books; 40% novels.
Member Agents: Warren Frazier, Anne Hawkins, Moses Cardona, Elly Sidel.
Represents: Nonfiction books, juvenile books, novels. **Considers all nonfiction areas except computers/electronics; religion/inspirational; translations. Considers all fiction areas except confessional; erotica; romance.**
How to Contact: Query with outline/proposal. Accepts queries by e-mail. Reports in 1 month on queries. Returns materials only with SASE.
Needs: Obtains new clients through recommendations from others.

Recent Sales: *Blonde*, by Joyce Carol Oates (HarperCollins); *House of Leaves*, by Mark Danielewski (Pantheon); *The Living Blood*, by Tananarive Due (Pocket Books).
Terms: Agent receives 15% commission on domestic sales; 20% on foreign sales. Charges for photocopying.

◑HEACOCK LITERARY AGENCY, INC., 1523 Sixth St., Suite #14, Santa Monica CA 90401-2514. (310)393-6227. **Contact:** Rosalie Grace Heacock. Estab. 1978. Member of AAR, Authors Guild, SCBWI. Represents 60 clients. 10% of clients are new/previously unpublished writers. Currently handles: 100% nonfiction books.
Represents: Adult nonfiction books, children's picture books. **Considers these nonfiction areas:** anthropology; art/architecture/design; biography; business; health/medicine (including alternative health); hiking; history; how-to; language/literature/criticism; music; nature/environment; popular culture; psychology; inspirational; science/technology; self-help/personal improvement; sociology; spirituality/metaphysics; women's issues/women's studies. **Considers limited selection of top children's book authors; no beginners.**
How to Contact: Query with SASE. "No multiple queries, please." Prefers to be only readers. Reports in 3 weeks on queries; 2 months on mss. Returns materials only with SASE.
Needs: Does not want to receive scripts. Obtains new clients through "referrals from present clients and industry sources as well as mail queries."
Recent Sales: Sold 25 titles in the last year. Prefers not to share information on specific sales.
Terms: Agent receives 15% commission on domestic sales; 25% on foreign sales, "if foreign agent used; if sold directly, 15%." Offers written contract, binding for 1 year. Charges for actual expense for telephone, postage, packing, photocopying. "We provide copies of each publisher submission letter and the publisher's response." 95% of business is derived from commission on ms sales.
Writers' Conferences: Maui Writers Conference; Santa Barbara City College Annual Writer's Workshop; Pasadena City College Writer's Forum; UCLA Symposiums on Writing Nonfiction Books; Society of Children's Book Writers and Illustrators, Southwest Writers Conference (Albuquerque).
Reading List: Reads "all trade journals, also literary magazines and environmental periodicals" to find new clients. Looks for "new ways to solve old problems."
Tips: "Take time to write an informative query letter expressing your book idea, the market for it, your qualifications to write the book, the 'hook' that would make a potential reader buy the book. Always enclose SASE; we cannot respond to queries without return postage. Our primary focus is upon books which make a contribution."

N◑ RICHARD HENSHAW GROUP, 132 W. 22nd St., 4th Floor, New York NY 10011. (212)414-1172. Fax: (212)721-4208. E-mail: rhgagents@aol.com. Website: www.rich.henshaw.com. **Contact:** Rich Henshaw. Estab. 1995. Member of AAR, SinC, MWA, HWA, SFWA. Represents 35 clients. 20% of clients are new/previously unpublished writers. Specializes in thrillers, mysteries, science fiction, fantasy and horror. Currently handles: 20% nonfiction books; 10% juvenile books; 70% novels.
● Prior to opening his agency, Mr. Henshaw served as an agent with Richard Curtis Associates, Inc.
Represents: Nonfiction books, juvenile books, novels. **Considers these nonfiction areas:** animals; biography/autobiography; business; child guidance/parenting; computers/electronics; cooking/food/nutrition; current affairs; gay/lesbian issues; government/politics/law; health/medicine; how-to; humor; juvenile nonfiction; military/war; money/finance/economics; music/dance/theater/film; nature/enrironment; New Age/metaphysics; popular culture; psychology; science/technology; self-help/personal improvement; sociology; sports; true crime/investigative; women's issues/women's studies. **Considers these fiction areas:** action/adventure; detective/police/crime; ethnic; family saga; fantasy; glitz; historical; horror; humor/satire; juvenile; literary; mainstream; psychic/supernatural; science fiction; sports; thriller/espionage; young adult.
How to Contact: Query with SASE. Reports in 3 weeks on queries; 6 weeks on mss.
Needs: Obtains new clients through recommendations from others, solicitation, at conferences and query letters.
Recent Sales: Sold 17 titles in the last year. *Out For Blood*, by Dana Stabenow (Dutton/Signet); *Deadstick*, by Megan Mallory Rust (Berkley); *And Then There Were None*, by Stephen Solomita (Bantam); *The Well Trained Mind*, by Susan Wise Bauer and Jessie Wise (W.W. Norton).
Terms: Agent receives 15% commission on domestic sales; 20% on foreign sales. No written contract. Charges for photocopying manuscripts and book orders. 100% of business is derived from commission on sales.
Tips: "Always include SASE with correct return postage."

☑◑ THE JEFF HERMAN AGENCY LLC, 332 Bleecker St., New York NY 10014. (212)941-0540. E-mail: jeff@jeffherman.com. Website: www.jeffherman.com. **Contact:** Jeffrey H. Herman. Estab. 1985. Member of AAR. Represents 100 clients. 10% of clients are new/previously unpublished writers. Specializes in adult nonfiction. Currently handles: 85% nonfiction books; 5% scholarly books; 5% textbooks; 5% novels.
● Prior to opening his agency, Mr. Herman served as a public relations executive.
Member Agents: Deborah Levine (vice president, nonfiction book doctor).
Represents: Considers these nonfiction areas: business; computers; health; history; how-to; politics; popular psychology; popular reference; recovery; self-help; spirituality.
How to Contact: Query with SASE. Reports in 2 weeks on queries; 1 month on mss.
Recent Sales: *Joe Montana On the Magic of Making Quarterback*, by Joe Montana (Henry Holt); *A Man Named Dave*, by Dave Peizel (Dutton).
Terms: Agent receives 15% commission on domestic sales. Offers written contract.

◑ SUSAN HERNER RIGHTS AGENCY, P.O. Box 303, Scarsdale NY 10583-0303. (914)725-8967. Fax: (914)725-8969. **Contact:** Susan Herner or Sue Yuen. Estab. 1987. Represents 100 clients. 30% of clients are new/unpublished writers. Eager to work with new/unpublished writers. Currently handles: 60% nonfiction books; 40% novels.
Member Agents: Sue Yuen (romance, thrillers, fantasy).
Represents: Adult nonfiction books, novels. **Consider these nonfiction areas:** anthropology/archaeology; biography/autobiography; business; child guidance/parenting; cooking/food/nutrition; current affairs; ethnic/cultural interests; gay/lesbian issues; government/politics/law; health/medicine; history; how-to; language/literature/criticism; nature/environment; New Age/metaphysics; popular culture; psychology; religious/inspirational; science/technology; self-help/personal improvement; sociology; true crime/investigative; women's issues/women's studies. "I'm particularly interested in women's issues, popular science, and feminist spirituality." **Considers these fiction areas:** action/adventure; contemporary issues; detective/police/crime; ethnic; family/saga; fantasy; feminist; glitz; historical; horror; literary; mainstream; mystery; romance (contemporary, gothic, historical, regency); science fiction; thriller; "I'm particularly looking for strong women's fiction."
How to Contact: Query with outline, sample chapters and SASE. Considers simultaneous queries. Reports in 1 month on queries. Returns materials only with SASE.
Recent Sales: *Feng Shui For Lovers*, by Raphael Simons (Crown); *Catch A Dream*, by Mary Jane Meier (Signet).
Terms: Agent receives 15% commission on domestic sales; 20% on dramatic sales; 20% on foreign sales. Charges for extraordinary postage, handling and photocopying. "Agency has two divisions: one represents writers on a commission-only basis; the other represents the rights for small publishers and packagers who do not have in-house subsidiary rights representation. Percentage of income derived from each division is currently 80-20."
Writers' Conferences: Vermont League of Writers (Burlington, VT); Gulf States Authors League (Mobile, AL).

◑ FREDERICK HILL ASSOCIATES, 1842 Union St., San Francisco CA 94123. (415)921-2910. Fax: (415)921-2802. **Contact:** Irene Moore. Estab. 1979. Represents 100 clients. 50% of clients are new/unpublished writers. Specializes in general nonfiction, fiction.
Member Agents: Fred Hill (president), Bonnie Nadell (vice president); Irene Moore (associate).
Represents: Nonfiction books, novels. **Considers these nonfiction areas:** biography/autobiography; cookbooks; current affairs; government/politics/law; language/literature/criticism; women's issues/women's studies. **Considers literary and mainstream fiction.**
How to Contact: Query with SASE. Considers simultaneous queries. Returns materials only with SASE.
Recent Sales: *The Alternate*, by John Martel (Dutton); *Dark Lady*, by Richard North Patterson; *Brief Interviews with Hideous Men*, by David Foster Wallace (Little, Brown).
Terms: Agent receives 15% commission on domestic sales; 15% on dramatic sales; 20% on foreign sales. Charges for photocopying.

◐ JOHN L. HOCHMANN BOOKS, 320 E. 58th St., New York NY 10022-2220. (212)319-0505. Director: John L. Hochmann. **Contact:** Theodora Eagle. Estab. 1976. Represents 23 clients. Member of PEN. Specializes in nonfiction books. "Writers must have demonstrable eminence in field or previous publications." Prefers to work with published/established authors. Currently handles: 80% nonfiction; 20% textbooks.
Member Agents: Theodora Eagle (popular medical and nutrition books).
Represents: Nonfiction trade books, college textbooks. **Considers these nonfiction areas:** anthropology/archaeology; art/architecture/design; biography/autobiography; cooking/food/nutrition; current affairs; gay/lesbian issues; government/politics/law; health/medicine; history; military/war; music/dance/theater/film; sociology.
How to Contact: Query first with detailed chapter outline, titles and sample reviews of previously published books and SASE. Reports in 1 week on queries; 1 month on solicited mss.
Needs: Obtains new clients through recommendations from authors and editors.
Recent Sales: *Granite and Rainbow: The Life of Virginia Woolf*, by Mitchell Leaska (Farrar, Straus & Giroux); *The Low Fat African-American Cookbook*, by Ruby Banks-Payne (Contemporary).
Terms: Agent receives 15% commission on domestic sales; 25% on foreign sales.
Tips: "Detailed outlines are read carefully; letters and proposals written like flap copy get chucked. We make multiple submissions to editors, but we do not accept multiple submissions from authors. Why? Editors are on salary, but we work for commission, and do not have time to read manuscripts on spec."

◐ BERENICE HOFFMAN LITERARY AGENCY, 215 W. 75th St., New York NY 10023. (212)580-0951. Fax: (212)721-8916. "No fax queries." **Contact:** Berenice Hoffman. Estab. 1978. Member of AAR. Represents 55 clients.
Represents: Nonfiction, novels. **Considers all nonfiction areas and most fiction areas.** No romance.
How to Contact: Query with SASE and 2 sample chapters. Reports in 3-4 weeks on queries.

TO RECEIVE REGULAR TIPS AND UPDATES about writing and Writer's Digest publications via e-mail, send an e-mail with "SUBSCRIBE NEWSLETTER" in the body of the message to "newsletter-request@writersdigest.com."

Needs: Usually obtains new clients through referrals from people she knows.

Recent Sales: Prefers not to share information on specific sales.

Terms: Agent receives 15% on domestic sales. Sometimes offers written contract. Charges for out of the ordinary postage, photocopying.

⚫ BARBARA HOGENSON AGENCY, 165 West End Ave., Suite 19-C, New York NY 10023. (212)874-8084. Fax: (212)362-3011. **Contact:** Barbara Hogenson or Sarah Feider. Estab. 1994. Member of AAR, signatory of WGA. Represents 60 clients. 5% of clients are new/previously unpublished writers. Currently handles: 35% nonfiction books; 15% novels; 15% movie scripts; 35% stage plays.
- See the expanded listing for this agency in Script Agents.

⦂N⦂ ◗ ◎ HOPKINS LITERARY ASSOCIATES, PMB 327, 2117, Buffalo Rd., Rochester NY 14624-1507. (716)429-6559. E-mail: pamhopkins@aol.com. **Contact:** Pam Hopkins. Estab. 1996. Member of AAR, RWA. Represents 30 clients. 5% of clients are new/unpublished writers. Specializes in women's fiction particularly historical, contemporary and category romance as well as mainstream work. Currently handles: 100% novels.

Represents: Novels. **Considers these fiction areas:** historical; mainstream; romance.

How to Contact: Send outline and 3 sample chapters. Does not accept queries by e-mail. Considers simultaneous queries and submissions. Reports in 2 weeks on queries; 1 month on mss. Returns material only with SASE.

Needs: Obtains new clients through recommendations from others, solicitations and conferences.

Recent Sales: Sold 50 titles in the last year. *Winds of Autumn*, by Merline Lovelace (MIRA); *Love in the Shadows*, by Madeline Archer (Bantam); *The Doctor's Wife*, by Cheryl St. John (Harlequin); *Great Caesar's Ghost*, by Cynthia Sterling (Berkley). Other clients include Maggie Price, Shari Anton, Lynda Cooper, Jodi O'Donnell, Victoria Malvey and Jillian Hart.

Terms: Agent receives 15% commission on domestic sales; 20% on foreign sales. No written contract. 30 day written notice must be given to terminate verbal contract.

Writers' Conferences: Romance Writers of America.

⦂N⦂ ⚫ INFINITY MANAGEMENT INTERNATIONAL, 425 N. Robertson Blvd., Los Angeles CA 90048. (310)276-9321. Fax: (310)276-1706. **Contact:** Jon Karas. Estab. 1990. Member of Conference of Personal Managers. Represents 75 clients. 10% of clients are new/unpublished writers. Currently handles: 5% nonfiction books; 15% novels; 60% movie scripts; 20% TV scripts.
- See the expanded listing for this agency in Script Agents.

⚫ INTERNATIONAL CREATIVE MANAGEMENT, 40 W. 57th St., New York NY 10019. (212)556-5600. Fax: (212)556-5665. West Coast office: 8942 Wilshire Blvd., Beverly Hills CA 90211. (310)550-4000. Fax: (310)550-4100. **Contact:** Literary Department. Member of AAR, signatory of WGA.

Member Agents: Esther Newberg and Amanda Urban, department heads; Lisa Bankoff; Kristine Dahl; Mitch Douglas; Suzanne Gluck; Sloan Harris; Heather Schroder; Denise Shannon; Richard Abate.

Terms: Agent receives 10% commission on domestic sales; 15% on UK sales; 20% on translations.

⚫ J DE S ASSOCIATES INC., 9 Shagbark Rd., Wilson Point, South Norwalk CT 06854. (203)838-7571. **Contact:** Jacques de Spoelberch. Estab. 1975. Represents 50 clients. Currently handles: 50% nonfiction books; 50% novels.
- Prior to opening his agency, Mr. de Spoelberch was a publishing editor at Houghton Mifflin.

Represents: Nonfiction books, novels. **Considers these nonfiction areas:** biography/autobiography; business; current affairs; ethnic/cultural interests; government/politics/law; health/medicine; history; military/war; New Age; self-help/personal improvement; sociology; sports; translations. **Considers these fiction areas:** detective/police/crime; historical; juvenile; literary; mainstream; mystery/suspense; New Age; westerns/frontier; young adult.

How to Contact: Query with SASE. Reports in 2 months on queries.

Needs: Obtains new clients through recommendations from authors and other clients.

Recent Sales: Prefers not to share information on specific sales.

Terms: Agent receives 15% commission on domestic sales; 20% on foreign sales. Charges for foreign postage and photocopying.

◗ JABBERWOCKY LITERARY AGENCY, P.O. Box 4558, Sunnyside NY 11104-0558. (718)392-5985. **Contact:** Joshua Bilmes. Estab. 1994. Member of SFWA. Represents 40 clients. 25% of clients are new/previously unpublished writers. "Agency represents quite a lot of genre fiction and is actively seeking to increase amount of nonfiction projects." Currently handles: 25% nonfiction books; 5% scholarly books; 65% novel; 5% other.

Represents: Nonfiction books, scholarly books, novels. **Considers these nonfiction areas:** biography/autobiography; business; cooking/food/nutrition; current affairs; gay/lesbian issues; government/politics/law; health/medicine; history; humor; language/literature/criticism; military/war; money/finance/economics; music/dance/theater/film; nature/environment; popular culture; science/technology; sociology; sports; true crime/investigative; women's issues/women's studies. **Considers these fiction areas:** action/adventure; cartoon/comic; contemporary issues; detective/police/crime; ethnic; family saga; fantasy; gay; glitz; historical; horror; humor/satire; lesbian; literary; mainstream; psychic/supernatural; regional; science fiction; sports; thriller/espionage.

How to Contact: Query with SASE. Considers simultaneous queries and submissions. Reports in 2 weeks on queries. Returns materials only with SASE.

Needs: Obtains new clients through recommendation by current clients, solicitation, "and through intriguing queries by new authors."

Recent Sales: Sold 20 titles in the last year. *Shakespeare's Christmas*, by Charlaine Harris (Dell); *Deathstalker Destiny*, by Simon Green (Roc); *Chance of Command*, by Elizabeth Moon (Baen); *Lupus: Alternate Therapies*, by Sharon Moore (Brassey's). Other clients include Tanya Hutt, Kristine Smith, Edo van Belkom.

Terms: Agent receives 12.5% commission on domestic sales; 20% on foreign sales. Offers written contract, binding for 1 year. Charges for book purchases, photocopying, international book/ms mailing, international long distance.

Writers' Conferences: Malice Domestic (Washington DC, May); World SF Convention (Chicago, August); Icon (Stony Brook NY, April).

Reading list: Reads *New Republic*, *Analog* and various newspapers to find new clients.

Tips: "In approaching with a query, the most important things to me are your credits and your biographical background to the extent its relevant to your work. I (and most agents I believe) will ignore the adjectives you may choose to describe your own work. Please send query letter only with SASE; no manuscript material unless requested."

Ø MELANIE JACKSON AGENCY, 250 W. 57th St., Suite 1119, New York NY 10107. This agency did not respond to our request for information. Query before submitting.

Ø JAMES PETER ASSOCIATES, INC., P.O. Box 772, Tenafly NJ 07670-0751. (201)568-0760. Fax: (201)568-2959. E-mail: bertholtje@compuserve.com. **Contact:** Bert Holtje. Estab. 1971. Member of AAR. Represents 54 individual authors and 5 corporate clients (book producers). 15% of clients are new/previously unpublished writers. Specializes in nonfiction, all categories. "We are especially interested in general, trade and reference." Currently handles: 100% nonfiction books.

   ● Prior to opening his agency, Mr. Holtje was a book packager, and before that, president of an advertising agency with book publishing clients.

Represents: Nonfiction books. **Considers these nonfiction areas:** anthropology/archaeology; art/architecture/design; biography/autobiography; business; child guidance/parenting; current affairs; ethnic/cultural interests; gay/lesbian issues; government/politics/law; health/medicine; history; language/literature/criticism; memoirs (political or business); military/war; money/finance/economics; music/dance/theater/film; popular culture; psychology; self-help/personal improvement; travel; women's issues/women's studies.

How to Contact: Send outline/proposal and SASE. Prefers to be only reader. Reports in 3-4 weeks on queries. Returns materials only with SASE.

Needs: Actively seeking "good ideas in all areas of adult nonfiction." Does not want to receive "children's and young adult books, poetry, fiction." Obtains new clients through recommendations from other clients and editors, contact with people who are doing interesting things, and over-the-transom queries.

Recent Sales: Sold 34 titles in the last year. *Patton on Management*, by Dr. Alan Axelrod (Prentice-Hall); *Out of the Ordinary: A Biographical Dictionary of Women Explorers*, by Sarah Purcell and Edward Purcell (Routledge); *Ace Your Mid Terms and Finals—A 5-book series*, by The Ian Samuel Group (McGraw-Hill).

Terms: Agent receives 15% commission on domestic sales; 20% on foreign sales. Offers written contract on a per book basis.

Ø JANKLOW & NESBIT ASSOCIATES, 598 Madison Ave., New York NY 10022. This agency did not respond to our request for information. Query before submitting.

[N] Ø JCA LITERARY AGENCY, 27 W. 20th St., Suite 1103, New York NY 10011. (212)807-0888. Fax: (212)807-0461. **Contact:** Jeff Gerecke, Tony Outhwaite. Estab. 1978. Member of AAR. Represents 100 clients. 20% of clients are new/unpublished writers. Currently handles: 48% nonfiction books; 2% scholarly books; 50% novels.

Member Agents: Jeff Gerecke; Tony Outhwaite.

Represents: Nonfiction books, scholarly books, novels. **Considers these nonfiction areas:** animals; anthropology/archaeology; art/architecture/design; biography/autobiography; business; child guidance/parenting; computers/electronics; current affairs; ethnic/cultural interests; gay/lesbian issues; government/politics/law; health/medicine; history; language/literature/criticism; memoirs; military/war; money/finance/economics; music/dance/theater/film; nature/environment; New Age/metaphysics; photography; popular culture; psychology; science/technology; sociology; sports; translations; true crime/investigative; women's issues/women's studies. **Considers these fiction areas:** action/adventure; confessional; contemporary issues; detective/police/crime; ethnic; experimental; family saga; feminist; gay/lesbian; glitz; historical; horror; humor/satire; literary; mainstream; mystery; sports; thriller/espionage; westerns/frontier.

How to Contact: Query with SASE. Does not accept queries by fax or e-mail. Considers simultaneous queries and

CHECK THE INSIDER REPORTS throughout this section for first-hand information about working with agents.

submissions. "We occasionally may ask for an exclusive look." Reports in 2 weeks on queries; 6 weeks on mss. Returns materials only with SASE.

Needs: Does not want to receive screenplays, poetry, children's books, science fiction/fantasy, genre romance. Obtains new clients through recommendations, solicitations, conferences.

Recent Sales: *The Lost Glass Plates of Wilfred Eng*, by Thomas Orton (Counterpoint); *Sharp Shooter*, by David Healey (The Berkley Publishing Group/Jove); *A Healthy Place to Die*, by Peter King (St. Martin's Press). Other clients include Ernest J. Gaines, W.E.B. Griffin, Polly Whitney, David J. Garrow.

Terms: Agent receives 15% commission on domestic sales; 20% on foreign sales. No written contract. "We work with our clients on a handshake basis." Charges for postage on overseas submissions, photocopying, mss for submission, books purchased for subrights submission, and bank charges, where applicable. "We deduct the cost from payments received from publishers."

Tips: "We do not ourselves provide legal, accounting, or public relations services for our clients, although some of the advice we give falls somewhat into these realms. In cases where it seems necessary we will recommend obtaining outside advice or assistance in these areas from professionals who are not in any way connected to the agency."

N ◐ JLA LITERARY AGENCY, 5704 Gist Ave., Baltimore MD 21215-3508. (410)578-0468. Fax: (410)578-0237. E-mail: jlaagency@aol.com. **Contact:** Jeffrey O'Bomeghie. Estab. 1999. Represents 12 clients. 60% of clients are new/unpublished writers. Specializes in literary fiction and nonfiction. "We are especially interested in mainstream works." Currently handles: 40% nonfiction books; 40% novels; 20% movie scripts.

 • Prior to becoming an agent, Mr. O'Bomeghie was a newspaper editor and creative writing instructor.

Member Agents: Jeffrey O'Bomeghie (fiction); Emma Ikharo (nonfiction); Jay Lace AG.

Represents: Nonfiction books, novels. **Considers these nonfiction areas:** biography/autobiography; business; cooking/food/nutrition; current affairs; education; government/politics/law; health/medicine; history; how-to; humor; memoirs; money/finance/economics; music/dance/theater/film; New Age/metaphysics; popular culture; psychology; religious/inspirational; science/technology; self-help/personal improvement; sports; translations; true crime/investigative. **Considers these fiction areas:** action/adventure; confessional; detective/police/crime; erotica; glitz; horror; humor/satire; literary; mainstream; mystery; psychic/supernatural; regional; romance; religious/inspirational; science fiction; sports; thriller/espionage.

Also Handles: Movie scripts, feature film. **Considers these script subject areas:** action/adventure; contemporary issues; detective/police/crime; ethnic; horror; mainstream; mystery/suspense; romantic comedy; romantic drama; science fiction; thriller/espionage.

How to Contact: Query with SASE. Accepts queries by e-mail. Considers simultaneous queries and submissions. Reports in 3 days on queries; 2 weeks on mss. Discards unwanted queries and mss.

Needs: Actively seeking literary fiction and nonfiction with mainstream appeal. Does not want to receive erotica, children's books, experimental fiction or picture books. Obtains new clients through recommendations from others, solicitations, conferences.

Recent Sales: New agency with no reported sales.

Terms: Agent receives 15% commission on domestic sales; 20% on foreign sales. Offers written contract, binding for 3 months. 60 day notice must be given to terminate contract.

Tips: "Make your manuscript look as professional as possible. Be patient."

✓ ◐ JOY LITERARY AGENCY, PO Box 957-856, Hoffman Estates IL 60195-7856. (847)310-0003. Fax: (847)310-0893. E-mail: joyco2@juno.com. **Contact:** Carol Joy. Represents 15 clients. 95% of clients are new/unpublished writers. Currently handles: 30% nonfiction books; 10% juvenile books; 10% scholarly books; 50% novels.

 • Prior to becoming an agent, Ms. Joy was a bookstore owner for eight years.

Represents: Nonfiction books, juvenile books, scholarly books, novels. **Considers these nonfiction areas:** biography/autobiography; cooking/food/nutrition; education; health/medicine; how-to; juvenile nonfiction; nature/environment; religious/inspirational; self-help/personal improvement; sociology; women's issues/women's studies. **Considers these fiction areas:** action/adventure; contemporary issues; literary; mainstream; religious/inspirational; suspense; thriller/espionage; westerns/frontier; young adult.

How to Contact: Query with outline/proposal and SASE. Reports in 2 weeks on queries; 1 month on mss.

Needs: Obtains new clients through queries by mail only.

Recent Sales: Prefers not to share information on specific sales.

Terms: Agent receives 15% commission on domestic sales. Offers written contract, binding for 2 years. 30 days notice must be given to terminate contract.

Writer's Conferences: Write-to-Publish (Wheaton IL, June); Christian Writers (Chicago IL, July); Bloomingdale Writers (Bloomingdale IL, September).

Tips: "Proofread carefully. Always include SASE. We are willing to look at a new writer's material and often give personal brief critiques for no extra charge."

✓ ◐ THE KELLOCK COMPANY INC., Lakeview Center, PMB 359, 1440 Coral Ridge Dr., Coral Springs FL 33071-5433. (954)255-0336. Fax: (954)255-3467. E-mail: kellock@aol.com. **Contact:** Alan C. Kellock. Estab. 1990. Represents 60 clients. 15% of clients are new/previously unpublished writers. Specializes in a broad range of practical and informational nonfiction, including illustrated works. Represents authors, packagers, and smaller publishers to larger print and electronic publishers and third party sponsors. "Many of our clients are not career writers but people who are highly successful in other walks of life." Currently handles: 100% nonfiction books.

● Prior to opening his agency, Mr. Kellock served as Director of Sales & Marketing with Harcourt Brace, Vice President Marketing with Waldenbooks and President and Publisher for Viking Penguin.

Member Agents: Loren Kellock (licensing).

Represents: Nonfiction books. **Considers these nonfiction areas:** anthropology/archaeology; art/architecture/design; biography/autobiography; business; child guidance/parenting; crafts/hobbies; current affairs; education; ethnic/cultural interests; government/politics/law; health/medicine; history; how-to; humor; interior design/decorating; military/war; money/finance/economics; music/dance/theater/film; nature/environment; photography; popular culture; psychology; religious/inspirational; self-help/personal improvement; sociology; sports; women's issues/women's studies.

How to Contact: Query with SASE. Reports in 1 week on queries.

Needs: Obtains most new clients through referrals, but all queries are carefully considered.

Recent Sales: *Learn By Doing* books (Macmillan Computer Publishing); *Nice Job!* (Ten Speed); *You've Got E-Mail Business!* Maximum Press).

Terms: Agent receives 15% commission on domestic sales; 25% on foreign and multimedia sales. Offers written contract. Charges for postage, photocopying.

Writer's Conferences: BEA (Chicago, May); Frankfurt (Germany, October).

◪ **NATASHA KERN LITERARY AGENCY**, P.O. Box 2908, Portland OR 97208-2908. (503)297-6190. Website: www.natashakern.com. **Contact:** Natasha Kern. Estab. 1986. Member of RWA, MWA, SinC. "A full service agency." Specializes in commercial fiction and nonfiction for adults.

● Prior to opening her agency, Ms. Kern worked as an editor and publicist for New York publishers.

Represents: Nonfiction books, novels. **Considers these nonfiction areas:** animals; anthropology/archaeology; biography/autobiography; business; child guidance/parenting; current affairs; education; ethnic/cultural interests; health/medicine; nature/environment; New Age/metaphysics; popular culture; psychology; science/technology; self-help/personal improvement; women's issues/women's studies; women's spirituality; gardening; personal finance; investigative journalism. **Considers these fiction areas:** detective/police/crime; ethnic; feminist; historical; mainstream; mystery/suspense; romance (contemporary, historical); medical, technical and historical thrillers; magical realism; inspirational fiction and romance; novels of the West.

How to Contact: "Send a detailed, one-page query with a SASE, including the submission history, writing credits and information about how complete the project is. If requested, for fiction send a two- to three-page synopsis, in addition to the first three chapters; for nonfiction, submit a proposal consisting of an outline, two chapters, SASE, and a note describing market and how project is different or better than similar works. Also send a blurb about the author and information about the length of the manuscript. For category fiction, a five- to ten-page synopsis should be sent with the chapters." Reports in 2 weeks on queries.

Needs: Does not want to receive sports, true crime, scholarly works, coffee-table books, war memoirs, software, photography, poetry, short stories, children's, horror, fantasy, science fiction, stage plays or traditional Westerns.

Recent Sales: Sold 46 titles in the last year. *Act Like An Owner*, by Bob Blonchek and Marty O'Neill (Van Nostrand); *Patterns of Love*, by Robin Hatcher (HarperCollins); *A Rose in Scotland*, by Joan Overfield (Avon).

Terms: Agent receives 15% commission on domestic sales; splits 20% on foreign sales; splits 15% on film rights.

Writer's Conference: RWA National Conference; Santa Barbara Writer's Conference; Golden Triangle Writer's Conference and many regional conferences.

☑ ◪ **LOUISE B. KETZ AGENCY**, 1485 First Ave., Suite 4B, New York NY 10021-1363. (212)535-9259. Fax: (212)249-3103. E-mail: ketzagency@aol.com. **Contact:** Louise B. Ketz. Estab. 1983. Represents 25 clients. 15% of clients are new/previously unpublished writers. Specializes in science, business, sports, history and reference. Currently handles: 100% nonfiction books.

Represents: Nonfiction books only. **Considers these nonfiction areas:** biography; business; current affairs; history; military/war; money/finance/economics; science/technology; sports.

How to Contact: Send outline and 2 sample chapters plus author bio with qualifications for authorship of work. Reports in 6 weeks.

Needs: Obtains new clients through recommendations and idea development.

Recent Sales: *Soccer for Juniors*, by Robert Pollock.

Terms: Agent receives 15% commission on all sales.

☑ ◎ **VIRGINIA KIDD AGENCY, INC.**, 538 E. Harford St., P.O. Box 278, Milford PA 18337-0728. (717)296-6205. Fax: (717)296-7266. **Contact:** James Allen. Estab. 1965. Member of SFWA, SFRA, SFTA. Represents 80 clients. Specializes in "science fiction but we do not limit ourselves to it."

● Prior to opening her agency, Ms. Kidd was a ghost writer, pulp writer and poet.

Member Agents: Virginia Kidd; James Allen; Christine Cohen.

Represents: Fiction. **Considers these fiction areas:** speculative fiction, science fiction, fantasy (special interest in non-traditional fantasy), mystery, literary, mainstream, feminist, glitz, suspense, historical, young adult. **Specializes in science fiction.**

How to Contact: Query with SASE. Reports in 1 week on queries; 4-6 weeks on mss.

Needs: Occasionally obtains new clients through recommendations from others.

Recent Sales: Sold about 50 titles in the last year. *The Telling*, by Ursula K. Le Guin (Harcourt Brace); *The Tower* *and the Hive*, by Anne McCaffrey (Del Rey); *Midas*, by Wolfgang Jeschke (TOR/Forge); *Interlopers*, by Alan Dean Foster (Penguin Putnam); also film rights to the Company series by Kage Baker to Showtime. Other clients include Gene Wolfe, R.A. Lafferty, Joe L. Hensley, William Tenn, Al Coppel and Allan W. Eckert.

Terms: Agent receives 10% commission on domestic sales; 20% on foreign sales. Offers written contract, binding until canceled by either party. 30 days notice must be given to terminate contract.

Tips: "If you have a novel of speculative fiction, romance, or mainstream that is *really extraordinary*, please query me, including a synopsis, a cv and a SASE."

KIDDE, HOYT & PICARD, 335 E. 51st St., New York NY 10022. (212)755-9461. Fax: (212)223-2501. **Contact:** Katharine Kidde, Laura Langlie. Estab. 1980. Member of AAR. Represents 80 clients. Specializes in mainstream fiction and nonfiction. Currently handles: 15% nonfiction books; 5% juvenile books; 80% novels.

 • Prior to becoming agents, Ms. Kidde was an editor/senior editor at Harcourt Brace, New American Library and Putnam; Ms. Langlie worked in production and editorial at Kensington and Carroll & Graf.

Member Agents: Kay Kidde (mainstream fiction, general nonfiction, romances, literary fiction); Laura Langlie (romances, mysteries, literary fiction, general nonfiction).

Represents: Nonfiction books, novels. **Considers these nonfiction areas:** the arts; biography; current events; ethnic/cultural interests; gay/lesbian issues; history; language/literature/criticism; memoirs; popular culture; psychology; self-help/personal improvement; sociology; women's issues. **Considers these fiction areas:** contemporary; detective/police/crime; feminist; gay; glitz; historical; humor; lesbian; literary; mainstream; mystery/suspense; romance (contemporary, historical, regency); thriller.

How to Contact: Query. Reports in a few weeks on queries; 3-4 weeks on mss. Returns materials only with SASE.

Needs: Actively seeking "strong mainstream fiction." Does not want to receive "male adventure, science fiction, juvenile, porn, plays or poetry." Obtains new clients through query letters, recommendations from others, "former authors from when I was an editor at NAL, Harcourt, etc.; listings in *LMP*, writers' guides."

Recent Sales: *Night Bus*, by Janice Law (Forge/TOR); *False Witness*, by Lelia Kelly (Kensington); *She Captains*, by Joan Druett (Simon & Schuster); *Tying Down the Wind*, by Eric Pinder (Tarcher/Putnam). Other clients include Michael Cadmum, Jim Oliver, Patricia Cabot, Bethany Campbell, Robin Hathaway, Mignon F. Ballard and Mark Miano.

Reading List: Reads literary journals and magazines, *Harper's*, STORY, *DoubleTake*, etc. to find new clients.

Terms: Agent receives 15% commission on domestic sales; 20% on foreign sales. Charges for photocopying.

Tips: "We look for beautiful stylistic writing, and that elusive treasure, a good book (mostly fiction). As former editors, we can help launch authors."

KIRCHOFF/WOHLBERG, INC., AUTHORS' REPRESENTATION DIVISION, 866 United Nations Plaza, #525, New York NY 10017. (212)644-2020. Fax: (212)223-4387. Director of Operations: John R. Whitman. **Contact:** Lisa Pulitzer-Voges. Estab. 1930s. Member of AAR, AAP, Society of Illustrators, SPAR, Bookbuilders of Boston, New York Bookbinders' Guild, AIGA. Represents 50 authors. 10% of clients are new/previously unpublished writers. Specializes in juvenile through young adult trade books and textbooks. Currently handles: 5% nonfiction books; 80% juvenile books; 5% novels; 5% novellas; 5% young adult.

 • Kirchoff/Wohlberg has been in business for over 50 years.

Member Agents: Liza Pulitzer-Voges (juvenile and young adult authors).

Represents: "We are interested in any original projects of quality that are appropriate to the juvenile and young adult trade book markets. *But, we take on very few new clients as our roster is full.*"

How to Contact: "Send a query that includes an outline and a sample; SASE required." Reports in 1 month on queries; 2 months on mss. Please send queries to the attention of Liza Pulitzer-Voges.

Needs: Obtains new clients through recommendations from authors, illustrators and editors.

Recent Sales: Sold over 50 titles in the last year. Prefers not to share information on specific sales.

Terms: Agent receives standard commission "depending upon whether it is an author only, illustrator only, or an author/illustrator book." Offers written contract, binding for not less than 1 year.

THE KIRKLAND LITERARY AGENCY INC., P.O. Box 50608, Amarillo TX 79159-0608. (806)356-0216. **Contact:** Dee Pace, submissions director. Estab. 1993. Member of AAR, RWA and Sisters in Crime. Represents 60 clients. 15% of clients are new/previously unpublished writers. Specializes in romance. Also represents mystery and mainstream novels. "Our specialty is women's fiction and extremely selective nonfiction. We offer our clients a quarterly report detailing any activity/correspondence made on their behalf in that given quarter." Currently handles: 5% nonfiction books; 95% novels.

Member Agent: Jean Price.

Represents: Considers novel-length women's fiction and nonfiction.

How to Contact: *By invitation only.* Reports in 6 weeks on queries; 3 months on mss.

Needs: Obtains new clients through referrals or conferences.

Recent Sales: Sold 65 titles in the last year. Prefers not to share information on specific sales.

Terms: Agent receives 15% commission on domestic sales; 20% on foreign sales. Offers written or verbal contract, binding for 1 year, with 30 day cancellation clause.

Writers' Conferences: National RWA conference (July).

Tips: "Write toward publishers' guidelines, particularly concerning maximum and minimum word count."

insider report

Agent helps writer navigate the rocky road of publishing

Award-winning science fiction author Octavia Butler always knew she wanted to make her living as a writer. She began writing when she was 10 and started submitting stories for publication at the young age of 13. Stubbornness and a passionate commitment to writing has kept this shy author at the top of her genre for over 25 years. The author of 11 novels and a book of short stories, Butler has learned the value of a good agent and a supportive publishing house.

Publishing since the mid-1970s, Butler began with her five-volume *Patternist* series about an elite group of mentally linked telepaths. Her most popular novel, *Kindred*, about a contemporary black woman sent back in time to a slave plantation in the antebellum South, was published in 1979. Next Butler published her science fiction *Xenogenisis* trilogy in the late 1980s. Her most recent novel series began with *Parable of the Sower* (1993), named a *New York Times* Notable Book of the Year. In 1998 she published a sequel, *Parable of the Talents*, named one of the best books of 1998 by *Publishers Weekly*. She has won the Hugo Award twice and a Nebula award, and in 1995 was awarded a $295,000 MacArthur Foundation fellowship "Genius Award." Here Butler talks about working with agents and her relationship with different publishers:

Octavia Butler

Photo by Miriam Berkley

You sold your first three novels without an agent. Why did you choose Doubleday as your original publisher?
Doubleday was willing to take a chance publishing new writers because it had a subscription arrangement with schools and libraries. My first three books were almost completely written by the time Doubleday took my first book. I had been laid off, and between looking for another job and generally writing as fast as I could, I was pretty busy. I managed to get two and a half novels done that year. It was the only time that ever happened.

Your novel *Kindred* is not science fiction, even though people categorize you as a science fiction writer. Did you have any trouble selling it to a publisher?
Kindred sold to Doubleday's general fiction department. I tried to sell it elsewhere because for each of my first 3 novels my advance was $1,750. I was just dying to get out. About that time an agent named Felicia Eth at Writers House wrote me, asking if I needed an agent. She submitted *Kindred* all over the place but couldn't sell it because people couldn't figure out where to place it. They didn't know how to sell it. It's obviously not science fiction although people assume it is because it involves time travel. It went to 15 publishers before my agent sold it to Doubleday.

You only published one more book with Doubleday, *Wild Seed*. What made you decide to switch publishing houses at that point?

Doubleday sold the paperback rights to *Wild Seed* for something like $4,000, which meant I got $2,000 minus the agent's commission. And I hit the ceiling! I didn't want that to happen again. I left Doubleday with the next book, *Clay's Ark*, in the desperate hope that I could earn enough to live on. I went to St. Martin's, but they didn't do any advertising.

Next came your *Xenogenisis* trilogy with Warner. How would you compare your relationship with Warner to other publishers?

Warner paid me a pretty decent advance. But the books got very little advertising except as science fiction. I had been trying to convince people since *Kindred* that I had more than a science fiction audience. I had just begun with a new agent, Merrillee Heifetz, at Writers House. Merrillee told me about a new small press, Four Walls Eight Windows. I did *Parable of the Sower* with them and then *Bloodchild and Other Stories* (1995). And then my editor left them for Seven Stories Press. I left to be with the same editor.

You have commented that you have three audiences: a feminist audience, a black audience and a science fiction audience. These audiences also overlap. Do you feel your agent understands your different audiences?

Yes. Merrillee is the reason I hooked up with Four Walls Eight Windows. It would not have occurred to me to go to a small publisher. I didn't even know about this small publisher and

Following her agent's advice that small-sized presses can give more individual attention, award-winning author Octavia Butler sold her book, *Parable of the Talents*, to Seven Stories Press. With her new publisher's emphasis on marketing, the book became a *Los Angeles Times* Bestseller.

wouldn't have discovered them on my own. They had almost no money at that point, so I got a very small advance. I went from finally getting decent advances to getting tiny ones again. But on the other hand, they were willing to market my work to whomever as opposed to just trying to keep me in science fiction. That was really important. Their books are reviewed by people who might not normally review science fiction. And they are willing to send me out on tour, and no one had done that before. I think I reached a lot of audiences I wouldn't have otherwise reached if I had stayed with one of the larger, strictly science fiction publishers.

What are the biggest advantages of working with an agent?
It certainly is a good thing if you don't know the business. It's a good way to hang onto your foreign and subsidiary rights, and have somebody actively peddling those rights because there were years when I lived off subsidiary rights. It's nice to have somebody looking after your interests. Plus I find it difficult to just push people off, so I refer them to my agent. And when I hooked up with my first agent, my money went up considerably.
—*Tricia Waddell*

N **◉** **JEFFREY M. KLEINMAN, ESQ., OF GRAYBILL & ENGLISH L.L.C.**, 1920 N. St., NW, #620, Washington DC 20036. (202)861-0106. Fax: (202)457-0662. E-mail: jmkagent@aol.com. Website: www.expertbiz.com/jmk/. **Contact:** Jeff Kleinman. Estab. 1998. 50% of clients are new/unpublished writers. Specializes in narrative nonfiction; nonfiction; fiction.
• Prior to becoming an agent, Mr. Kleinman was an attorney.
Represents: Nonfiction books, scholarly books, novels. **Considers these nonfiction areas:** agriculture/horticulture; animals; anthropology/archaeology; art/architecture/design; biography/autobiography; business; child guidance/parenting; computers/electronics; cooking/food/nutrition; crafts/hobbies; current affairs; current affairs; education; ethnic/cultural interests; gay/lesbian issues; government/politics/law; health/medicine; history; how-to; humor; interior design/decorating; language/literature/criticism; money/finance/economics; music/dance/theater/film; nature/environment; photography; popular culture; psychology; science/technology; self-help/personal improvement; sociology; translations; true crime/investigative; women's issues/women's studies. **Considers these fiction areas:** action/adventure; cartoon/comic; contemporary issues; erotica; ethnic; family saga; fantasy; feminist; gay/lesbian; glitz; historical; horror; humor/satire; literary; mainstream; psychic/supernatural; regional; science fiction; thriller/espionage. Also considers multimedia tie-ins with literary projects.
How to Contact: Query with SASE, outline/proposal, or send outline and 3 sample chapters. Accepts queries by e-mail. Considers simultaneous queries and submissions. Reports in 2 weeks on queries; 1 month on mss. Returns materials only with SASE.
Needs: Does not want to receive military, romance, sports, children's literature or poetry. Obtains new clients through recommendations and solicitations.
Recent Sales: Sold 2 titles in the last year. *Walrus on My Table*, by Guglielmo and Lynn (St. Martin's Press); *Chaos to Calm*, by Heininger and Weiss (Perigee/Putnam).
Terms: Agent receives 15% commission on domestic sales; 20% on foreign sales. Offers written contract. 30 day notice must be given to terminate contract. Charges for postage, long distance and photocopying.
Writer's Conferences: Baltimore Writers (Baltimore MD, September); Mid-Atlantic Creative Nonfiction Summer Writer's Conference (Baltimore MD, August); Chesterfield Writer's Workshop (Chesterfield VA, March).
Reading List: Reads *Smithsonian Magazine*, *Zoetrope* and *Salon.com* to find new clients. Looks for "great ideas and solid writing."

◉ **HARVEY KLINGER, INC.**, 301 W. 53rd St., New York NY 10019. (212)581-7068. Fax: (212)315-3823. **Contact:** Harvey Klinger. Estab. 1977. Member of AAR. Represents 100 clients. 25% of clients are new/previously unpublished writers. Specializes in "big, mainstream contemporary fiction and nonfiction." Currently handles: 50% nonfiction books; 50% novels.
Member Agents: David Dunton (popular culture, parenting, home improvement, thrillers/crime); Laurie Liss (literary fiction, human interest, politics, women's issues).
Represents: Nonfiction books, novels. **Considers these nonfiction areas:** biography/autobiography; cooking/food/nutrition; health/medicine; psychology; science/technology; self-help/personal improvement; spirituality; sports; true crime/investigative; women's issues/women's studies. **Considers these fiction areas:** action/adventure; detective/police/crime; family saga; glitz; literary; mainstream; thriller/espionage.

How to Contact: Query with SASE. "We do not accept queries by fax or e-mail." Reports in 1 month on queries; 2 months on mss.
Needs: Obtains new clients through recommendations from others.
Recent Sales: Sold 20 titles in the last year. *Secrets About Life Every Woman Should Know*, by Barbara De Angelis (Hyperion); *Torn Jeans: Levi Strauss and the Denim Dynasty*, by Ellen Hawkes (Lisa Drew Books/Scribner); *The Looking Glass*, by Richard Paul Evans (Simon & Schuster); *The Women of Troy Hill*, by Clare Ansberry (Harcourt Brace); *Exit Music: The Radiohead Story*, by Mac Randall (Dell).
Terms: Agent receives 15% commission on domestic sales; 25% on foreign sales. Offers written contract. Charges for photocopying manuscripts, overseas postage for mss.

◖ THE KNIGHT AGENCY, P.O. Box 550648, Atlanta GA 30355. Or: 2407 Matthews St., Atlanta GA 30319. (404)816-9620. E-mail: deidremk@aol.com. Website: www.knightagency.net. **Contact:** Deidre Knight. Estab. 1996. Member of RWA, AAR, Authors Guild. Represents 30 clients. 40% of clients are new/previously unpublished writers. Currently handles: 50% nonfiction books; 50% novels.
Represents: Nonfiction books, novels. **Considers these nonfiction areas:** biography/autobiography; business; child guidance/parenting; computers/electronics; cooking/food/nutrition; current affairs; ethnic/cultural interests; health/medicine; history; how-to; money/finance/economics; music/dance/theater/film; popular culture; psychology; religious/inspirational; self-help/personal improvement; sports; true crime/investigative; women's issues/women's studies. **Considers these fiction areas:** ethnic; literary; mainstream; mystery/suspense; regional; religious/inspirational; romance (contemporary, historical, inspirational); women's fiction; commercial fiction.
How to Contact: Query with SASE. Considers simultaneous queries and submissions. Reports in 2 weeks on queries; 6 weeks on mss.
Needs: "We are looking for a wide variety of fiction and nonfiction. In the nonfiction area, we're particularly eager to find personal finance, business investment, pop culture, self-help/motivational and popular reference books. In fiction, we're always looking for romance, women's fiction, ethnic and commercial fiction."
Recent Sales: Sold 20 titles in the last year. *Panic-Proof Parenting*, by Debra Holtzman (NTC/Contemporary); *Simple Strategies for Electronic Daytrades*, by Tori Turner (Adams Media); and *Abbey Road to Zapple Records: A Beatles Encyclopedia*, by Judson Knight (Taylor Publishing).
Terms: Agent receives 15% commission on domestic sales; 25% on foreign sales. Offers written contract, binding for 1 year. 60 days notice must be given to terminate contract. Charges clients for photocopying, postage, overnight courier expenses.

◖ LINDA KONNER LITERARY AGENCY, 10 W. 15th St., Suite 1918, New York NY 10011-6829. (212)691-3419. E-mail: ldkonner@cs.com. **Contact:** Linda Konner. Estab. 1996. Member of AAR, ASJA. Signatory of WGA. Represents 50 clients. 5-10% of clients are new/unpublished writers. Specializes in health, self-help, how-to. Currently handles: 100% nonfiction books.
Represents: Nonfiction books (adult only). **Considers these nonfiction areas:** business; child care/parenting; diet/nutrition; gay/lesbian issues; health/medicine; how-to; personal finance; popular culture; psychology; relationships; self-help/personal improvement; women's issues.
How to Contact: Query with SASE. Send outline or proposal with sufficient return postage. Reports in 3-4 weeks.
Needs: Obtains new clients through recommendations from others and occasional solicitation among established authors/journalists.
Recent Sales: Sold 15 titles in the last year. *Fattitudes*, by Jeffrey Wilbert Ph.D. and Norean Wilbert R.N. (St. Martin's); *The Dating Bible*, by Sherry Amatenstein (Adams Media).
Terms: Agent receives 15% commission on domestic sales; 25% on foreign sales. Offers written contract. Charges clients $75 one-time fee for domestic expenses; additional expenses may be incurred for foreign sales.
Writers' Conferences: American Society of Journalists and Authors (New York City, May).
Reading List: Reads *New York Times Magazine* and women's magazines to find new clients.

◖ ELAINE KOSTER LITERARY AGENCY, LLC, 55 Central Park West, Suite 6, New York NY 10023. (212)362-9488. Fax: (212)712-0164. **Contact:** Elaine Koster. Member of Women's Media Group and Publishers' Lunch Club. Represents 30 clients. 25% of clients are new/unpublished writers. Specializes in quality fiction and nonfiction. Currently handles: 30% nonfiction books; 70% novels.
● Prior to opening her agency, Ms. Koster was president and publisher of Dutton NAL.
Represents: Nonfiction books, novels. **Considers these nonfiction areas:** biography/autobiography; business; child guidance/parenting; cooking/food/nutrition; current affairs; ethnic/cultural interests; gay/lesbian issues; health/medicine; history; how-to; money/finance/economics; nature/environment; New Age/metaphysics; popular culture; psychology; self-help/personal improvement; women's issues/women's studies. **Considers these fiction areas:** action/adventure; confessional; contemporary issues; detective/police/crime; ethnic; family saga; feminist; gay/lesbian; glitz; historical; literary; mainstream; mystery (amateur sleuth, cozy, culinary, malice domestic); regional; suspense; thriller/espionage.
How to Contact: Query with outline, 3 sample chapters and SASE. No e-mail or fax queries. Prefers to be only reader. Reports in 3 weeks on queries; 1 month on mss. Returns materials only with SASE.
Needs: Does not want to receive juvenile, screenplays. Obtains new clients through recommendations from others.
Recent Sales: *Brown-Eyed Girl*, by Virginia Swift (HarperCollins); *Colors of the Mountain*, by Da Chen (Random House); *The Beryllium Murder*, by Camille Minichino (Morrow).

Terms: Agent receives 15% commission on domestic sales; 20% on foreign sales. Offers written contract, 60 days notice must be given to terminate contract. Charges for photocopying, messengers, express mail, books and book galley, ordered from publisher to exploit other rights, overseas shipment of mss and books, overseas phone and fax charges.
Tips: Obtains new clients through recommendation from others.

● **BARBARA S. KOUTS, LITERARY AGENT**, P.O. Box 560, Bellport NY 11713. (516)286-1278. **Contact:** Barbara Kouts. Estab. 1980. Member of AAR. Represent 50 clients. 10% of clients are new/previously unpublished writers. Specializes in adult fiction and nonfiction and children's books. Currently handles: 20% nonfiction books; 60% juvenile books; 20% novels.
Represents: Nonfiction books, juvenile books, novels. **Considers these nonfiction areas:** biography/autobiography; child guidance/parenting; current affairs; ethnic/cultural interests; health/medicine; history; juvenile nonfiction; music/ dance/theater/film; nature/environment; psychology; self-help/personal improvement; women's issues/women's studies.
Considers these fiction areas: contemporary issues; family saga; feminist; historical; juvenile; literary; mainstream; mystery/suspense; picture book; young adult.
How to Contact: Query with SASE. Reports in 2-3 days on queries; 4-6 weeks on mss.
Needs: Obtains new clients through recommendations from others, solicitation, at conferences, etc.
Recent Sales: *Dancing on the Edge*, by Han Nolan (Harcourt Brace); *Cendrillon*, by Robert San Souci (Simon & Schuster).
Terms: Agent receives 10% commission on domestic sales; 20% on foreign sales. Charges for photocopying.
Tips: "Write, do not call. Be professional in your writing."

● **IRENE KRAAS AGENCY**, 220 Copper Trail, Santa Fe NM 87505. (505)474-6212. Fax: (505)474-6216. Estab. 1990. Member of Authors Guild. Represents 30 clients. 75% of clients are new/unpublished writers. Specializes in fiction only, middle grade through adult. No romance, short stories, plays or poetry. Currently handles: 30% juvenile books; 70% novels.
Represents: Fiction—adult and juvenile (middle grade and up). **Considers these fiction areas:** action/adventure; detective/police/crime; ethnic; family saga; juvenile; literary; mainstream; mystery/suspense; science fiction; thriller/ espionage; young adult.
How to Contact: Send cover letter and first 30 pages. Must include return postage and/or SASE. Does not accept e-mail queries. Considers simultaneous submissions. Returns materials only with SASE.
Needs: Actively seeking "books that are well written with commercial potential." Obtains new clients through recommendations from others, conferences.
Recent Sales: *Songs of Power*, by Hilari Bell (Hyperion); *The Astrologer* series, by Denise Vitola (Ace); *Estate Planning Resource Book*, by Dawn Bradley Berry (Lowell House). Other clients include Brett Davis, Linda George, Christopher Farran, Terry England and Duncan Long.
Terms: Agent receives 15% commission on domestic sales; 20% on foreign sales. Offers written contract, binding for 1 year "but can be terminated at any time for any reason with written notice." Charges for photocopying and postage.
Writers' Conferences: Southwest Writers Conference (Albuquerque); Pacific Northwest Conference (Seattle); Vancouver Writers Conference (Vancouver BC).

⊘ **STUART KRICHEVSKY LITERARY AGENCY, INC.**, One Bridge St., Suite 26, Irvington NY 10533. This agency did not respond to our request for information. Query before submitting.

ℕ ⊘ ◎ **THE CANDACE LAKE AGENCY**, 9200 Sunset Blvd., Suite 820, Los Angeles CA 90069. (310)247-2115. Fax: (310)247-2116. E-mail: clagency@earthlink.net. **Contact:** Ryan Lewis. Estab. 1977. Signatory of WGA, member of DGA. 50% of clients are new/previously unpublished writers. Specializes in screenplay and teleplay writers. Currently handles: 20% novels; 40% movie scripts; 40% TV scripts.
 ● See the expanded listing for this agency in Script Agents.

● **PETER LAMPACK AGENCY, INC.**, 551 Fifth Ave., Suite 1613, New York NY 10176-0187. (212)687-9106. Fax: (212)687-9109. E-mail: renbopla@aol.com. **Contact:** Loren G. Soeiro. Estab. 1977. Represents 50 clients. 10% of clients are new/previously unpublished writers. Specializes in commercial fiction, male-oriented action/adventure, thrillers/suspense, contemporary relationships, distinguished literary fiction, nonfiction by a recognized expert in a given field. Currently handles: 20% nonfiction books; 80% novels.
Member Agents: Peter Lampack (psychological suspense, action/adventure, literary fiction, nonfiction, contemporary relationships); Sandra Blanton (foreign rights); Loren G. Soeiro (literary and commercial fiction, mystery, suspense, nonfiction, narrative nonfiction, high-concept thrillers).
Represents: Nonfiction books, novels. **Considers these nonfiction areas:** anthropology/archaeology; art/architecture/ design; biography/autobiography; business; current affairs; government/politics/law; health/medicine; history; money/ finance/economics; music/dance/theater/film; popular culture; high profile true crime/investigative; women's issues.
Considers these fiction areas: action/adventure; contemporary relationships; detective/police/crime; family saga; historical; literary; mainstream; mystery/suspense; thriller/espionage.
How to Contact: Query with SASE. *No unsolicited mss.* Do not fax queries. Reports in 3 weeks on queries; 2 months on mss.
Needs: Actively seeking literary and commercial fiction, thrillers, mysteries, suspense, psychological thrillers, high-

concept. Does not want to receive romance, science fiction, western, academic material. Obtains new clients from referrals made by clients.

Recent Sales: *Atlantis Found*, by Clive Cussler (Putnam); *The Lamorna Wink*, by Martha Grimes (Viking); *Give Me Liberty*, by Gerry Spence (St. Martin's); *After the Fall* by Judith Kelman.

Terms: Agent receives 15% commission on domestic sales; 20% on foreign sales.

Writers' Conferences: BEA (Chicago, June).

Tips: "Submit only your best work for consideration. Have a very specific agenda of goals you wish your prospective agent to accomplish for you. Provide the agent with a comprehensive statement of your credentials: educational and professional."

◙ **SABRA ELLIOTT LARKIN**, Bly Hollow Rd., Cherry Plain NY 12040-0055. Phone/fax: (518)658-3065. E-mail: becontree@taconic.net. **Contact:** Sabra Larkin. Estab. 1996. Represents 10 clients. 90% of clients are new/unpublished writers. Currently handles: 80% nonfiction books; 20% novels.

● Prior to opening her agency, Ms. Larkin worked for over 30 years in publishing: 5 years in editorial at Dutton; 7 years at Ballantine Books in publicity and advertising; 10 years at Avon Books; and 10 years at Putnam Berkley as vice president of Publicity, Promotion, Advertising and Public Relations

Represents: Nonfiction books, scholarly books, novels, illustrated books/(adult) art and photography. **Considers these nonfiction areas:** agriculture/horticulture; animals; anthropology/archeology; art/architecture/design; biography/autobiography; business; cooking/food/nutrition; current affairs; education; ethnic/cultural interests; government/politics/law; health/medicine; history; how-to; interior design/decorating; language/literature/criticism; money/finance/economics; music/dance/theater/film; nature/environment; photography; popular culture; psychology; religious/inspirational; science/technology; self-help/personal improvement; true crime/investigative; women's issues/women's studies. **Considers these fiction areas:** action/adventure; contemporary issues; detective/police/crime; ethnic; experimental; family saga; glitz; historical; humor/satire; literary; mainstream; mystery/suspense; regional; romance (contemporary, historical); thriller/espionage.

How to Contact: Query with SASE. Send outline and 2-3 sample chapters with return postage. Accepts queries by e-mail. Considers simultaneous queries; prefers to be only reader for ms submissions. Reports in 1 month on queries; 2 months on mss. Returns materials only with SASE.

Needs: Obtains new clients through recommendations from others and queries.

Recent Sales: Sold 1 title in the last year. Clients include James Chlovechok, Steve Stargen, Ernest Barker.

Terms: Agent receives 15% commission on domestic sales; 20% on foreign sales. Offers written contract, binding for 5 years. 60 days notice must be given to terminate contract. Charges for postage and photocopying of mss. "Copies of receipts for dollar amounts are supplied to clients. Not applicable to contracted clients."

◙ **MICHAEL LARSEN/ELIZABETH POMADA LITERARY AGENTS**, 1029 Jones St., San Francisco CA 94109-5023. (415)673-0939. E-mail: larsenpoma@aol.com. Website: www.Larsen-Pomada.com. **Contact:** Mike Larsen or Elizabeth Pomada. Estab. 1972. Members of AAR, Authors Guild, ASJA, NWA, PEN, WNBA, California Writers Club. Represents 100 clients. 40-45% of clients are new/unpublished writers. Eager to work with new/unpublished writers. Currently handles: 70% nonfiction books; 30% novels.

● Prior to opening their agency, both Mr. Larsen and Ms. Pomada were promotion executives for major publishing houses. Mr. Larsen worked for Morrow, Bantam and Pyramid (now part of Berkley), Ms. Pomada worked at Holt, David McKay, and The Dial Press.

Member Agents: Michael Larsen (nonfiction), Elizabeth Pomada (fiction, books of interest to women).

Represents: Adult nonfiction books, novels. **Considers these nonfiction areas:** anthropology/archaeology; art/architecture/design; biography/autobiography; business; cooking/food/nutrition; current affairs; ethnic/cultural interests; futurism; gay/lesbian issues; government/politics/law; health/medicine; history; how-to; humor; interior design/decorating; language/literature/criticism; memoirs; money/finance/economics; music/dance/theater/film; nature/environment; New Age/metaphysics; parenting; photography; popular culture; psychology; religious/inspirational; science/technology; self-help/personal improvement; sociology; sports; travel; true crime/investigative; women's issues/women's studies. **Considers these fiction areas:** action/adventure; contemporary issues; detective/police/crime; ethnic; experimental; family saga; fantasy; feminist; gay; glitz; historical; humor/satire; lesbian; literary; mainstream; mystery/suspense; psychic/supernatural; religious/inspirational; romance (contemporary, gothic, historical).

How to Contact: Query with synopsis and first 10 pages of completed novel. Reports in 6-8 weeks on queries. For nonfiction, "please read Michael's book *How to Write a Book Proposal* (Writer's Digest Books) and then mail or e-mail the title of your book and a promotion plan." Always include SASE. Send SASE for brochure and title list.

Needs: Actively seeking commercial and literary fiction. "Fresh voices with new ideas of interest to major publishers. Does not want to receive children's books, plays, short stories, screenplays, pornography.

Recent Sales: *Black Raven* (10th book in the Deverry Series), by Katharine Kerr (Bantam/Spectra); *If Life Is a Game, These Are The Rules*, by Cherie Carter-Scott (Broadway Books); *The Center at the Edge, Seeking the Inner Meaning of Outer Space*, by Wyn Wachhorst (Basic Books).

Terms: Agent receives 15% commission on domestic sales; 15% on dramatic sales; 20-30% on foreign sales. May charge for printing, postage for multiple submissions, foreign mail, foreign phone calls, galleys, books, and legal fees.

Writers' Conferences: Book Expo America; Santa Barbara Writers Conference (Santa Barbara); Maui Writers Conference (Maui); ASJA.

Tips: "We have very diverse tastes. We look for fresh voices and new ideas. We handle literary, commercial and genre fiction, and the full range of nonfiction books."

THE MAUREEN LASHER AGENCY, P.O. Box 888, Pacific Palisades CA 90272-0888. (310)459-8415. **Contact:** Ann Cashman. Estab. 1980.
- Prior to becoming an agent, Ms. Lasher worked in publishing in New York.

Represents: Nonfiction books, novels. **Considers these nonfiction areas:** animals; anthropology/archaeology; art/architecture/design; biography/autobiography; business; child guidance/parenting; cooking/food/nutrition; current affairs; ethnic/cultural interests; government/politics/law; health/medicine; history; how-to; nature/environment; popular culture; psychology; science/technology; self-help/personal improvement; sociology; sports; true crime/investigative; women's issues/women's studies. **Considers these fiction areas:** action/adventure; contemporary issues; detective/police/crime; family saga; feminist; historical; literary; mainstream; sports; thriller/espionage.

How to Contact: Send outline/proposal and 1 sample chapter with SASE.

Recent Sales: *My Life as a Dog*, by Moose (aka Eddie from Frasier) (HarperCollins); *Never Too Late: A Prosecutor's Story*, by Bobby DeLaughter (Scribner); *Untitled companion book to PBS series*, by Regina Campbell (Morrow); *Relax, This Won't Hurt*, by Judith Reichman (Morrow).

Terms: No information provided. Does not charge a reading fee or offer criticism service.

LAWYER'S LITERARY AGENCY, INC., One America Plaza, 600 W. Broadway, San Diego CA 92101. (619)696-3300. Fax: (619)696-3808. E-mail: allenetling@interim.com. **Contact:** H. Allen Etling. Estab. 1994. Represents 10 clients. 50% of clients are new/previously unpublished writers. Specializes in true crime, including trial aspect written by attorneys, and lawyer biographies and autobiographies. Currently handles: 90% nonfiction books; 10% fiction.

Represents: Fiction, nonfiction books, movie scripts, TV scripts. **Considers these nonfiction areas:** biography/autobiography (of lawyers); law; true crime/investigative. **Considers these fiction areas:** thriller (political, science fiction).

Also Handles: Feature film; TV MOW. **Considers these script subject areas:** detective/police/crime; mystery/suspense.

How to Contact: Books: query with outline and 3 sample chapters. Scripts: Send outline and 3 sample scenes. Reports in 30 days.

Needs: Obtains new clients through recommendations from others.

Recent Sales: *Undying Love: A Key West Love Story*, by Ben Harrison (New Horizon Press).

Terms: Agent receives 15% commission on domestic sales; does not handle foreign rights. Offers written contract for 1 year, with 30 day cancellation clause.

Tips: "Many of the best real stories are true crime stories—including depiction of the crime, background of the participants, official investigation by authorities, defense/prosecution preparation and the trial. There are hundreds of intriguing cases that occur annually in the US and not all of them are handled by attorneys who are household names. We are looking for the most compelling of these stories where there is also a good chance of selling TV movie/feature movie rights. Manuscripts can entail one case or multiple cases. Those involving multiple cases would probably resemble an attorney's biography. The story or stories can be told by defense and prosecution attorneys alike."

LAZEAR AGENCY INCORPORATED, 2 Carlson Pkwy. Suite 350, Plymouth MN 55447. (612)249-1500. Fax: (612)249-1460. E-mail: lazear@lazear.com. Website: www.literaryagent.com/Lazear/index.html. **Contact:** Editorial Board. Estab. 1984. Represents 250 clients. Currently handles: 60% nonfiction books; 10% juvenile books; 30% novels; 2.5% movie and TV scripts; 2.5% syndicated material.
- The Lazear Agency opened a New York office in September 1997.

Member Agents: Jonathon Lazear; Wendy Lazear, Christi Cardenas, Anne Blackstone.

Represents: Nonfiction books, novels, juvenile books, syndicated material, new media with connection to book project. **Considers all nonfiction areas. Considers all fiction areas.**

Also Handles: Feature film, television programming.

How to Contact: Query with outline/proposal and SASE. Accepts queries by fax. Considers simultaneous queries and submissions. Reports in 3 weeks on queries; 1 month on ms; 1 month on scripts. Highly selective. No phone calls or faxes. Returns materials only with SASE.

Needs: Obtains new clients through recommendations from others, "through the bestseller lists, word-of-mouth."

Recent Sales: Sold over 100 titles in the last year. *Reason for Hope*, by Jane Goodall with Phillip Berman (Warner); *The Old Neighborhood*, by Ray Suarez (FreePress/Simon & Schuster); *Smart Money*, by Chris Farrell (Random House); *Home & Away*, by Scott Simon (Hyperion).

Terms: Agent receives 15% commission on domestic sales; 20% on foreign sales. Offers written contract, binding "for term of copyright." Charges for "photocopying, international express mail, bound galleys and finished books used for subsidiary rights sales. No fees charged if book is not sold."

Reading List: Reads STORY, *The New Yorker*, *The Kenyon Review*, *Harper's* and *Virginia Quarterly* to find new clients. Looks for "originality, broad interest."

Tips: "The writer should first view himself as a salesperson in order to obtain an agent. Sell yourself, your idea, your concept. Do your homework. Notice what is in the marketplace. Be sophisticated about the arena in which you are writing."

☑ **SARAH LAZIN**, 126 Fifth Ave., Suite 300, New York NY 10011. This agency did not respond to our request for information. Query with SASE before submitting.

☑ **THE NED LEAVITT AGENCY**, 70 Wooster St., New York NY 10012. This agency did not respond to our request for information. Query before submitting.

☑ ☺ **LESCHER & LESCHER LTD.**, 47 E. 19th St., New York NY 10003. (212)529-1790. Fax: (212)529-2716.
Contact: Robert or Susan Lescher, Michael Choate. Estab. 1966. Member of AAR. Represents 150 clients. Currently handles: 80% nonfiction books; 20% fiction.
Represents: Nonfiction books, fiction. Considers mysteries and cookbooks. No screenplays or science fiction.
How to Contact: Query with SASE.
Recent Sales: Prefers not to share information on specific sales. Clients include Neil Sheehan, Madeleine L'Engle, Calvin Trillin, Judith Vierst and Thomas Perry.
Terms: Agent receives 15% commission on domestic sales; 20-25% on foreign sales.
Needs: Usually obtains new clients through recommendations from others.

☑ ☑ ◎ **LEVANT & WALES, LITERARY AGENCY, INC.**, 108 Hayes St., Seattle WA 98109-2808. (206)284-7114. Fax: (206)284-0190. E-mail: waleslit@aol.com. **Contact:** Elizabeth Wales or Adrienne Reed. Estab. 1988. Member of AAR, Pacific Northwest Writers' Conference, Book Publishers' Northwest. Represents 65 clients. Specializes in mainstream nonfiction and fiction, as well as narrative nonfiction and literary fiction. Currently handles: 60% nonfiction books; 40% novels.
   • Prior to becoming an agent, Ms. Wales worked at Oxford University Press and Viking Penguin.
Represents: Nonfiction books, novels. **Considers these nonfiction areas:** animals; biography/autobiography; business; current affairs; education; ethnic/cultural interests; gay/lesbian issues; health; language/literature/criticism; lifestyle; memoirs; nature; New Age; popular culture; psychology; science; self-help/personal improvement; women's issues/ women's studies—open to creative or serious treatments of almost any nonfiction subject. **Considers these fiction areas:** cartoon/comic/women's; ethnic; experimental; feminist; gay; lesbian; literary; mainstream (no genre fiction).
How to Contact: Query first with SASE. "To Query: Please send cover letter, writing sample (no more than 30 pp.) and SASE." Accepts queries by e-mail. "Only short queries, no attachments." Considers simultaneous queries and submissions. Reports in 3 weeks on queries; 6 weeks on mss. Returns materials only with SASE.
Recent Sales: Sold 14 titles in the last year. *The Amazon.com Way*, by Robert Spector (HarperCollins); *The Kid*, by Dan Savage (Dutton); *Memoir of My Life with Animals*, by Brenda Peterson (Norton); *Harvest Son*, by David Mascmoto (Norton).
Terms: Agent receives 15% commission on domestic sales. "We make all our income from commissions. We offer editorial help for some of our clients and help some clients with the development of a proposal, but we do not charge for these services. We do charge, after a sale, for express mail, manuscript photocopying costs, foreign postage and outside USA telephone costs."
Writers' Conferences: Pacific NW Writers Conference (Seattle, July).
Tips: "We are interested in published and not-yet-published writers. Especially encourages writers living in the Pacific Northwest, West Coast, Alaska and Pacific Rim countries."

☒ ☺ **JAMES LEVINE COMMUNICATIONS, INC.**, 307 Seventh Ave., 19th Floor, New York NY 10001. (212)337-0934. Fax: (212)337-0948. E-mail: levineja@aol.com. Estab. 1989. Represents 150 clients. 33⅓% of clients are new/previously unpublished writers. Specializes in business, psychology, parenting, health/medicine, narrative nonfiction. Currently handles: 90% nonfiction books; 10% fiction.
Member Agents: James Levine; Daniel Greenberg; Arielle Eckstut (narrative nonfiction, psychology, spirituality, religion, women's issues).
   • Prior to opening his agency, Mr. Levine served as Vice President of the Bank Street College of Education.
Represents: Nonfiction books, novels. **Considers these nonfiction areas:** animals; art/architecture/design; biography/ autobiography; business; child guidance/parenting; computers/electronics; cooking/food/nutrition; gardening; gay/lesbian issues; health/medicine; money/finance/economics; nature/environment; New Age/metaphysics; psychology; religious/inspirational; science/technology; self-help/personal improvement; sociology; sports; women's issues/women's studies. **Considers these fiction areas:** contemporary issues; literary; mainstream.
How to Contact: Send outline/proposal plus 1 sample chapter. Reports in 2 weeks on queries; 1 month on mss.
Needs: Obtains new clients through client referrals.
Recent Sales: *Our Dumb Century*, by The Onion (Crown); *Customers.Com*, by Patricia Seybold (Times Books); *Lipstick*, by Gwen Macsai (HarperCollins); *Working Wounded*, by Bob Rosner (Warner).
Terms: Agent receives 15% commission on domestic sales; 20% on foreign sales. Offers written contract; length of

---

FOR INFORMATION ON THE CONFERENCES agents attend, refer to the conference section in this book.

time varies per project. Does not charge reading fee. Charges for out-of-pocket expenses—telephone, fax, postage and photocopying—directly connected to the project.

Writers' Conferences: ASJA Annual Conference (New York City, May).

Tips: "We work closely with clients on editorial development and promotion. We work to place our clients as magazine columnists and have created columnists for *McCall's* and *Child*. We work with clients to develop their projects across various media—video, software, and audio."

N̄ ◎ PAUL S. LEVINE LITERARY AGENCY, 1054 Superba Ave., Venice CA 90291-3940. (310)450-6711. Fax: (310)450-0181. E-mail: pslevine@ix.netcom.com. **Contact:** Paul S. Levine. Estab. 1996. Member of the Attorney-State Bar of California. Represents over 100 clients. 75% of clients are new/unpublished writers. Currently handles: 30% nonfiction books; 30% novels; 10% movie scripts; 30% TV scripts.

• Prior to becoming an agent, Mr. Levine was an entertainment law attorney for almost 20 years and has represented both authors and publishers. "I know the book business from both sides of the table."

Represents: Nonfiction books, novels. **Considers these nonfiction areas:** art/architecture/design; biography/autobiography; business; child guidance/parenting; computers/electronics; cooking/food/nutrition; crafts/hobbies; current affairs; education; ethnic/cultural interests; gay/lesbian issues; government/politics; health/medicine; history; how-to; humor; interior design/decorating; language/literature/criticism; memoirs; military/war; money/finance/economics; music/dance/theater/film; nature/environment; New Age/metaphysics; photography; popular culture; psychology; religious/inspirational; science/technology; self-help/personal improvement; sociology; sports; true crime/investigative; women's issues/women's studies. **Considers these fiction areas:** action/adventure; cartoon/comic; confessional; contemporary issues; detective/police/crime; erotica; ethnic; experimental; family saga; fantasy; feminist; gay/lesbian; glitz; historical; horror; humor/satire; literary; mainstream; mystery; picture book; psychic/supernatural; regional; romance; religious/inspirational; sports; thriller/espionage; westerns/frontier; young adult.

Also Handles: Movie scripts, feature film, episodic drama, TV scripts, TV MOW, sitcom, documentary, syndicated material, miniseries, animation. **Considers these script subject areas:** action/adventure; biography/autobiography; cartoon/animation; comedy; contemporary issues; detective/police/crime; erotica; ethnic; experimental; family saga; fantasy; feminist; gay/lesbian; glitz; historical; horror; juvenile; mainstream; multimedia; mystery/suspense; psychic/supernatural; religious/inspirational; romantic comedy; romantic drama; science fiction; sports; teen; thriller/espionage; western/frontier.

How to Contact: Query with SASE. Accepts queries by fax and e-mail. Considers simultaneous queries and submissions. Reports in 1 day on queries; 2 months on mss. Returns materials only with SASE.

Needs: Actively seeking commercial fiction and nonfiction. Does not want to receive science fiction or children's material. Obtains new clients through writers conferences, referrals, listings on various websites and through listings in directories.

Recent Sales: Sold 10 book titles and 20 script projects in the last year. Prefers not to share information on specific sales.

Terms: Agent receives 15% commission on domestic sales; 20% on foreign sales. Offers written contract. Charges for messengers, long distance, postage. "Only when incurred. No advance payment necessary."

Writer's Conferences: California Lawyers for the Arts (Los Angeles CA); "Colorado Gold Conference" (Rocky Mountain Fiction Writers (Lakewood CO); "Hollywood Pitch Workshop" (Los Angeles CA): National Writers Club (Los Angeles CA); "Selling to Hollywood" Writer's Connection (Glendale CA); "Spotlight on Craft" Willamette Writers Conference (Portland OR); Women In Animation (Los Angeles CA); and many others.

◎ ◎ ELLEN LEVINE LITERARY AGENCY, INC., 15 E. 26th St., Suite 1801, New York NY 10010. (212)889-0620. Fax: (212)725-4501. **Contact:** Ellen Levine, Elizabeth Kaplan, Diana Finch, Louise Quayle. Estab. 1980. Member of AAR. Represents over 100 clients. 20% of clients are new/previously unpublished writers. Currently handles: 55% nonfiction books; 5% juvenile books; 40% fiction.

Represents: Nonfiction books, juvenile books, novels, short story collections. **Considers these nonfiction areas:** anthropology; biography; current affairs; health; history; memoirs; popular culture; psychology; science; women's issues/women's studies; books by journalists. **Considers these fiction areas:** literary; mystery; women's fiction, thrillers.

How to Contact: Query with SASE. Reports in 3 weeks on queries, if SASE provided; 6 weeks on mss, if submission requested.

Needs: Obtains new clients through recommendations from others.

Recent Sales: *The Day Diana Died*, by Christopher Andersen (William Morrow); *Maxing Out: Why Women Sabotage Their Financial Security*, by Colette Dowling (Little, Brown).

Terms: Agent receives 15% commission on domestic sales; 20% on foreign sales. Charges for overseas postage, photocopying, messenger fees, overseas telephone and fax, books ordered for use in rights submissions.

Tips: "My three younger colleagues at the agency (Louise Quayle, Diana Finch and Elizabeth Kaplan) are seeking both new and established writers. I prefer to work with established writers, mostly through referrals."

✓ ◎ KAREN LEWIS & COMPANY, P.O. Box 741623, Dallas TX 75374-1623. (972)772-5260. Fax: (972)772-5276. E-mail: bashaoo@aol.com. Signatory of WGA. **Contact:** Karen Lewis. Estab. 1995. Represents 35 clients. 25% of clients are new/previously unpublished writers. Currently handles: 40% nonfiction books; 60% novels.

• Prior to opening her agency, Ms. Lewis served as a creative writing instructor.

Member Agents: Karen Lewis; Tracy Bisere.

Represents: Nonfiction books, juvenile books, novels. **Considers these nonfiction areas:** ethnic/cultural interests; gay/lesbian issues; juvenile nonfiction; New Age/metaphysics; self-help/personal improvement; women's issues/women's studies. **Considers these fiction areas:** action/adventure; detective/police/crime; erotica; ethnic; literary; mainstream; mystery/suspense; science fiction; thriller/espionage.

How to Contact: Query. Accepts queries by fax and e-mail. Considers simultaneous queries and submissions. Reports in 1 month on queries; 6-8 weeks on mss. Returns materials only with SASE.

Needs: Obtains new clients through "conferences and referrals from people I know."

Recent Sales: Sold 22 titles in the last year. Prefers not to share information on specific sales "until client relationship is established."

Terms: Agent receives 15% commission on domestic sales; 20% on foreign sales. Offers written contract, binding for 1 year, with 30-day cancellation clause. Charges for photocopying and postage. Sometimes makes referrals to editing services. 100% of business is derived from commissions on sales.

Writers' Conferences: Southwest Writers (Albuquerque NM), Romance Writer's of America. Austin Writers' League.

Reading List: "Sometimes we check Internet sites. We look for a fresh new voice with something unique to say."

Tips: "Write a clear letter succinctly describing your book. Be sure to include a SASE. If you receive rejection notices, don't despair. Keep writing! A good book will always find a home."

◖ ROBERT LIEBERMAN ASSOCIATES, 400 Nelson Rd., Ithaca NY 14850-9440. (607)273-8801. E-mail: RHL1 0@cornell.edu. **Contact:** Robert Lieberman. Estab. 1993. Represents 30 clients. 50% of clients are new/previously unpublished writers. Specializes in university/college level textbooks, CD-ROM/software and popular tradebooks in science, math, engineering, economics and others. Currently handles: 20% nonfiction books; 80% textbooks.

Represents: Scholarly books, textbooks. **Considers these nonfiction areas:** agriculture/horticulture; anthropology/ archaeology; art/architecture/design; business; computers/electronics; education; health/medicine; memoirs (by authors with high public recognition); money/finance/economics; music/dance/theater/film; nature/environment; psychology; science/technology; sociology; college, high school and middle school level textbooks.

How to Contact: Send initial inquiries by mail with SASE or e-mail. E-mail preferred. Prefers to be the only reader. Reports in 2 weeks on queries; 1 month on mss. Will not respond to mail queries without SASE.

Needs: Does not want to receive fiction, self-help or screenplays. Obtains new clients through referrals.

Recent Sales: Sold 20 titles in the last year. Prefers not to share information on specific sales.

Terms: Agent receives 15% commission on domestic sales; 20% on foreign sales. Offers written contract, binding for open-ended length of time, with 30 day cancellation clause. "Fees are changed only when special reviewers are required." 100% of business is derived from commissions on sales.

Tips: "The trade books we handle are by authors who are highly recognized in their fields of expertise. Client list includes Nobel prize winners and others with high name recognition, either by the public or within a given area of expertise."

◖ RAY LINCOLN LITERARY AGENCY, Elkins Park House, Suite 107-B, 7900 Old York Rd., Elkins Park PA 19027. (215)635-0827. **Contact:** Mrs. Ray Lincoln. Estab. 1974. Represents 30 clients. 35% of clients are new/previously unpublished writers. Specializes in biography, nature, the sciences, fiction in both adult and children's categories. Currently handles: 30% nonfiction books; 20% juvenile books; 50% novels.

Member Agents: Jerome A. Lincoln.

Represents: Nonfiction books, scholarly books, juvenile books, novels. **Considers these nonfiction areas:** animals; anthropology/archaeology; art/architecture/design; biography/autobiography; business; child guidance/parenting; cooking/food/nutrition; crafts/hobbies; current affairs; ethnic/cultural interests; gay/lesbian issues; government/politics/law; health/medicine; history; horticulture; interior design/decorating; juvenile nonfiction; language/literature/criticism; money/finance/economics; music/dance/theater/film; nature/environment; psychology; science/technology; self-help/ personal improvement; sociology; sports; women's issues/women's studies. **Considers these fiction areas:** action/ adventure; contemporary issues; detective/police/crime; ethnic; family saga; fantasy; feminist; gay; historical; humor/ satire; juvenile; lesbian; literary; mainstream; mystery/suspense; psychic/supernatural; regional; romance (contemporary, gothic, historical); sports; thriller/espionage; young adult.

How to Contact: Query first with SASE, then on request send outline, 2 sample chapters and SASE. "I send for balance of manuscript if it is a likely project." Reports in 2 weeks on queries; 1 month on mss.

Needs: Obtains new clients usually from recommendations.

Recent Sales: *Best Halloween Ever*, by Barbara Robinson (HarperCollins); *Daddy and Me*, by Jerry Spinelli (Knopf); *The Mummy's Smile*, by Susan Katz (Simon & Schuster).

Terms: Agent receives 15% commission on domestic sales; 20% on foreign sales. Offers written contract, binding "but with notice, may be cancelled." Charges only for overseas telephone calls. "I request authors to do manuscript photocopying themselves. Postage, or shipping charge, on manuscripts accepted for representation by agency."

Tips: "I always look for polished writing style, fresh points of view and professional attitudes."

◖ LINDSTROM LITERARY GROUP, 871 N. Greenbrier St., Arlington VA 22205-1220. (703)522-4730. Fax: (703)527-7624. E-mail: lindlitgrp@aol.com. **Contact:** Kristin Lindstrom. Estab. 1994. Represents 13 clients. 30% of clients are new/previously unpublished writers. Currently handles: 50% nonfiction books; 50% novels.

Represents: Nonfiction books; novels. **Considers these nonfiction areas:** biography/autobiography; narrative nonfiction; current affairs; ethnic/cultural interests; history; memoirs; popular culture; psychology; science/technology. **Consid-**

ers these **fiction areas:** action/adventure; contemporary issues; detective/police/crime; ethnic; historical; mainstream; thriller/espionage.

How to Contact: For fiction, send first 3 chapters and outline with SASE to cover return of ms if desired. For nonfiction, send outline/proposal with SASE. Reports in 8 weeks on queries; 8-10 weeks on mss.

Needs: Obtains new clients through references, guide listing.

Recent Sales: *Lucky Man*, by Tony Dunbar (Dell Publishing); *Five Card Stud*, by Elizabeth Gunn (Walker & Co.).

Terms: Agent receives 15% commission on domestic sales; 20% on foreign sales; 20% on performance rights sales. Offers written contract. Charges for marketing and mailing expense, express mail, UPS, etc.

Tips: "Include biography of writer. Send enough material for an overall review of project scope."

WENDY LIPKIND AGENCY, 165 E. 66th St., New York NY 10021. (212)628-9653. Fax: (212)628-2693. **Contact:** Wendy Lipkind. Estab. 1977. Member of AAR. Represents 60 clients. Specializes in adult nonfiction. Currently handles: 80% nonfiction books; 20% novels.

Represents: Nonfiction, novels. **Considers these nonfiction areas:** biography; current affairs; health/medicine; history; science; social history, women's issues/women's studies. **Considers mainstream and mystery/suspense fiction.** No mass market originals.

How to Contact: For nonfiction, query with outline/proposal. For fiction, query with SASE only. Reports in 1 month on queries. Returns materials only with SASE.

Needs: Usually obtains new clients through recommendations from others.

Recent Sales: *Secret Lessons*, by Dr. Thomas Verny (Simon & Schuster); *Sin & Syntax: How to Craft Wickedly Effective Prose*, by Constance Hale (Broadway Books).

Terms: Agent receives 15% commission on domestic sales; 20% on foreign sales. Sometimes offers written contract. Charges for foreign postage, messenger service, photocopying, transatlantic calls and faxes.

Tips: "Send intelligent query letter first. Let me know if you sent to other agents."

LITERARY AND CREATIVE ARTISTS, INC., 3543 Albemarle St. NW, Washington DC 20008-4213. (202)362-4688. Fax: (202)362-8875. E-mail: leadc1@aol.com. **Contact:** Muriel Nellis, Jane Roberts. Estab. 1982. Member of AAR, Authors Guild, associate member of American Bar Association. Represents over 75 clients. Currently handles: 70% nonfiction books; 15% novels; 10% audio/video; 5% film/TV.

Member Agents: Muriel Nellis, Jane Roberts, Leslie Toussaint.

Represents: Nonfiction, novels, audio, film/TV rights. **Considers these nonfiction areas:** biography; business; cooking; health; how-to; human drama; lifestyle; medical; memoir; philosophy; politics.

How to Contact: Query with outline, bio and SASE. *No unsolicited mss.* Reports in 3 weeks on queries. "While we prefer published writers, it is not required if the proposed work has great merit." Requires exclusive review of requested material; no simultaneous submissions.

Recent Sales: *Eleanor Rushing*, by Patty Friedman (Counterpoint); *The Career Battle Plan*, by Keith Block, M.D. (Bantam); *How to Know God*, by Deepak Chopra (Harmony Books).

Terms: Agent receives 15% commission on domestic sales; 20% on dramatic sales; 25% on foreign sales. Charges for long-distance phone and fax, photocopying and shipping.

THE LITERARY GROUP, 270 Lafayette St., #1505, New York NY 10012. (212)274-1616. Fax: (212)274-9876. E-mail: litgrpfw@aol.com. Website: www.literarygroup.com. **Contact:** Frank Weimann. Estab. 1985. Represents 150 clients. 75% of clients are new/previously unpublished writers. Specializes in nonfiction (true crime; biography; sports; how-to). Currently handles: 60% nonfiction books; 40% novels.

Member Agents: Frank Weimann (fiction, biography); Jim Hornfischer (serious nonfiction); Jessica Wainwright (women's issues, romance, how-to); Brian Rago (how-to's, cookbooks).

Represents: Nonfiction books, novels. **Considers these nonfiction areas:** animals; anthropology/archaeology; biography/autobiography; business; child guidance/parenting; cookbooks; crafts/hobbies; current affairs; education; ethnic/cultural interests; gay/lesbian issues; government/politics/law; health/medicine; history; how-to; humor; juvenile nonfiction; language/literature/criticism; memoirs; military/war; money/finance/economics; music/dance/theater/film; nature/environment; New Age/metaphysics; popular culture; psychology; religious/inspirational; science/technology; self-help/personal improvement; sociology; sports; true crime/investigative; women's issues/women's studies. **Considers these fiction areas:** action/adventure; cartoon/comic; contemporary issues; detective/police/crime; ethnic; family saga; fantasy; feminist; gay; horror; humor/satire; lesbian; mystery/suspense; psychic/supernatural; romance (contemporary, gothic, historical, regency); sports; thriller/espionage; westerns/frontier; young adult.

How to Contact: Query with outline plus 3 sample chapters. Accepts queries by e-mail. Prefers to be only reader.

THE PUBLISHING FIELD is constantly changing! If you're still using this book and it is 2001 or later, buy the newest edition of *Guide to Literary Agents* at your favorite bookstore or order directly from Writer's Digest Books at (800)289-0963.

Reports in 1 week on queries; 1 month on mss. Returns materials only with SASE.
Needs: Obtains new clients through referrals, writers' conferences, query letters.
Recent Sales: Sold about 75 titles in the last year. *Bird Watching*, by Larry Bird (Warner); *October Sky*, by Homer Hickam (Dell); *Paris Never Leaves You*, by Adreana Robbins (Forge Tor); *Mutiny at Almack's*, by Judith Lansdowne (Zebra). Other clients include Ed McMahon, Sam Giancana.
Terms: Agent receives 15% commission on domestic sales; 20% on foreign sales. Offers written contract, which can be cancelled after 30 days.
Writers' Conferences: Detroit Women's Writers (MI); Kent State University (OH); San Diego Writers Conference (CA).

◐ STERLING LORD LITERISTIC, INC., 65 Bleecker St., New York NY 10012. (212)780-6050. Fax: (212)780-6095. **Contact:** Peter Matson. Estab. 1952. Signatory of WGA. Represents over 600 clients. Currently handles: 50% nonfiction books, 50% novels.
Member Agents: Peter Matson; Sterling Lord; Jody Hotchkiss (film scripts); Philippa Brophy; Chris Calhoun; Jennifer Hengen; Charlotte Sheedy; George Nicholson; Neeti Madan.
Represents: Nonfiction books, novels. "Literary value considered first."
How to Contact: Query. Reports in 1 month on mss.
Needs: Obtains new clients through recommendations from others.
Recent Sales: Prefers not to share information on specific sales.
Terms: Agent receives 15% commission on domestic sales; 20% on foreign sales. Offers written contract. Charges for photocopying.

☑ ◐ NANCY LOVE LITERARY AGENCY, 250 E. 65th St., New York NY 10021-6614. (212)980-3499. Fax: (212)308-6405. **Contact:** Nancy Love or Sherrie Sutton. Estab. 1984. Member of AAR. Represents 60-80 clients. Specializes in adult nonfiction and mysteries. Currently handles: 90% nonfiction books; 10% mysteries and thrillers.
Member Agents: Nancy Love, Sherrie Sutton.
Represents: Nonfiction books, fiction ("Mysteries and thrillers only!"). **Considers these nonfiction areas:** animals; biography/autobiography; child guidance/parenting; cooking/food/nutrition; current affairs; ethnic/cultural interests; government/politics/law; health/medicine; history; how-to; memoirs; nature/environment; New Age/metaphysics; popular culture; psychology; science/technology; self-help/personal improvement; sociology; travel (armchair only, no how-to travel); true crime/investigative; women's issues/women's studies. **Considers these fiction areas:** mystery/suspense; thriller/espionage.
How to Contact: "For nonfiction, send a proposal, chapter summary and sample chapter. For fiction, query first. Considers simultaneous queries. Reports in 3 weeks on queries; 6 weeks on mss. Returns materials only with SASE.
Needs: Actively seeking health and medicine (including alternative medicine); parenting; spiritual and inspirational. Does not want to receive novels other than mysteries and thrillers. Obtains new clients through recommendations and solicitation.
Recent Sales: Sold 20 titles in the last year. *Cubans in America*, by Roger Hernandez and Alex Anton (Kensington); *The Family Bond*, by Susan Kuczmarski (NTC/Contemporary); Next 2 books in Gale Grayson mystery series, by Teri Holbrook (Bantam).
Terms: Agent receives 15% commission on domestic sales; 20% on foreign sales. Offers written contract. Charges for photocopying, "if it runs over $20."
Tips: Needs an exclusive on fiction. Nonfiction author and/or collaborator must be an authority in subject area. Submissions will be returned only if accompanied by a SASE.

◐ LOWENSTEIN ASSOCIATES, INC., 121 W. 27th St., Suite 601, New York NY 10001. (212)206-1630. Fax: (212)727-0280. President: Barbara Lowenstein. Estab. 1976. Member of AAR. Represents 150 clients. 20% of clients are new/unpublished writers. Specializes in multicultural books (fiction and nonfiction), medical experts, commercial fiction, especially suspense, crime and women's issues. "We are a full-service agency, handling domestic and foreign rights, film rights, and audio rights to all of our books." Currently handles: 60% nonfiction books; 40% novels.
Member Agents: Barbara Lowenstein (president); Nancy Yost (agent); Eileen Cope (agent); Norman Kurz (business affairs).
Represents: Nonfiction books, novels. **Considers these nonfiction areas:** animals; anthropology/archaeology; biography/autobiography; business; child guidance/parenting; craft/hobbies; current affairs; education; ethnic/cultural interests; gay/lesbian issues; government/politics/law; health/medicine; history; how-to; humor; language/literature/criticism/; memoirs; money/finance/economics; music/dance/theater/film; nature/environment; New Age/metaphysics, popular culture; psychology; religious/inspirational; science/technology; self-help/personal improvement; sociology; sports; travel; true crime/investigative; women's issues/women's studies. **Considers these fiction areas:** contemporary issues; detective/police/crime; erotica; ethnic; feminist; gay; historical; lesbian; literary mainstream; mystery/suspense; romance (contemporary, historical, regency); medical thrillers.
How to Contact: Send query with SASE, "otherwise will not respond." For fiction, send outline and 1st chapter. No unsolicited mss. "Please do not send manuscripts." Prefers to be only reader. Reports in 6 weeks on queries. Returns materials only with SASE.
Needs: Obtains new clients through "referrals, journals and magazines, media, solicitations and a few conferences."
Recent Sales: Sold approximately 75 titles in the last year. *Getting Everything You Can out of All You've Got*, by Jay

Abraham (St. Martin's); *Work As a Spiritual Practice*, by Lewis Richmond (Broadway); *Acts of Malice*, by Perri O'Shaughnessy (Delacorte). Other clients include Gina Barkhordar Nahai, Ishmael Reed, Michael Waldholz, Myrlie Evers Williams, Barry Yourgrau, Deborah Crombie, Jan Burke and Leslie Glass.

Terms: Agent receives 15% commission on domestic sales; 20% on foreign sales; 20% on dramatic sales. Offers written contract on a book-by-book basis. Charges for large photocopy batches and international postage.

Writer's Conference: Malice Domestic; Bouchercon.

Tips: "Know the genre you are working in and READ!"

☑ LUKEMAN LITERARY MANAGEMENT LTD., 501 Fifth Avenue, New York NY 10017. **Contact:** Noah Lukeman. Estab. 1996. Represents 100 clients. 10% of clients are new/previously unpublished writers. Currently handles: 50% nonfiction books; 10% short story collections; 40% novels.

● Prior to opening his agency, Mr. Lukeman worked at William Morrow, Farrar, Straus & Giroux and Delphinium Books.

Represents: Nonfiction books, novels, novellas, short story collections. **Considers these nonfiction areas:** animals; anthropology/archaeology; art/architecture/design; biography/autobiography; business; child guidance/parenting; cooking/food/nutrition; current affairs; health/medicine; language/literature/criticism; military/war; money/finance/economics; music/dance/theater/film; nature/environment; New Age/metaphysics; photography; popular culture; psychology; religious/inspirational; self-help/personal improvement; translations; true crime/investigative; women's issues/women's studies. **Considers these fiction areas:** action/adventure; contemporary issues; experimental; horror; literary; mainstream; thriller/espionage.

How to Contact: Send query letter only with SASE. Reports in 1 month on queries.

Needs: Does not want to receive poetry, children's or young adult.

Recent Sales: Sold 30 titles in the last year. *Wake of the Perdido Star*, by Gene Hackman and Daniel Lenihan (Newmarket Press); *Dead Run: America's Only Mass Escape From Death Row*, by Joe Jackson and William Burke (Times Books); *Having Everything*, by John L'Heureux (Grove/Atlantic); *Teaching Creative Writing*, by Carol Bly (Anchor Books); *Nude in Tub*, by G.K. Wuroi (Algonquin Books); *Your Pain is Real*, by Emile Hiesiger, M.D. with Kathleen Brady (Regan Books); *30 Days to a More Spiritual Life*, by Shana Aborn (Doubleday); *How to Teach Your Dog to Talk*, by Captain Haggerty (Simon & Schuster/Fireside Books).

Terms: Agent receives 15% commission on domestic sales; 20% on foreign sales. Offers written contract.

Tips: "Include SASE. Be patient. Don't call. For my full thoughts on writing, see my book *The First Five Pages: A Writer's Guide to Getting out of the Rejection Pile* (Simon & Schuster/Fireside Books)."

✓ ☑ DONALD MAASS LITERARY AGENCY, 157 W. 57th St., Suite 703, New York NY 10019. (212)757-7755. **Contact:** Donald Maass, Jennifer Jackson or Michelle Brummer. Estab. 1980. Member of AAR, SFWA, MWA, RWA. Represents over 100 clients. 5% of clients are new/previously unpublished writers. Specializes in commercial fiction, especially science fiction, fantasy, mystery, romance, suspense. Currently handles: 100% novels.

● Prior to opening his agency, Mr. Maass served as an editor at Dell Publishing (NY) and as a reader at Gollancz (London).

Member Agents: Donald Maass (mainstream, literary, mystery/suspense, science fiction); Jennifer Jackson (commercial fiction: especially romance, science fiction, fantasy, mystery/suspense); Michelle Brummer (fiction: literary, contemporary, feminist, science fiction, fantasy).

Represents: Novels. **Considers these fiction areas:** detective/police/crime; fantasy; historical; horror; literary; mainstream; mystery/suspense; psychic/supernatural; romance (historical, paranormal, time travel); science fiction; thriller/espionage.

How to Contact: Query with SASE. Considers simultaneous queries and submissions. Returns materials only with SASE. Reports in 2 weeks on queries, 3 months on mss (if requested following query).

Needs: Actively seeking "to expand the literary portion of our list and expand in romance and women's fiction." Does not want to receive nonfiction, children's or poetry.

Recent Sales: Sold over 100 titles in the last year. *The Twisted Root*, by Anne Perry (Fawcett Columbine); *A Clue for the Puzzle Lady*, by Parnell Hall (Bantam); *Midnight Robber*, by Nalo Hopkinson (Warner Aspect); *The Avalanche Soldier*, by Susan Matthews (Avon Eos); *Confluence II: Ancient of Days*, by Paul McAuley (Avon Eos).

Terms: Agent receives 15% commission on domestic sales; 20% on foreign sales. Charges for large photocopying orders and book samples, "after consultation with author."

Writers' Conferences: Donald Maass: World Science Fiction Convention, Frankfurt Book Fair, Pacific Northwest Writers Conference, Bouchercon, and others. Jennifer Jackson: World Science Fiction and Fantasy Convention, RWA National, and others. Michelle Brummer: ReaderCon, World Science Fiction Convention and Luna Con.

Tips: "We are fiction specialists, also noted for our innovative approach to career planning. Few new clients are accepted, but interested authors should query with SASE. Subagents in all principle foreign countries and Hollywood. No nonfiction or juvenile works considered."

☑ GINA MACCOBY LITERARY AGENCY, P.O. Box 60, Chappaqua NY 10514. (914)238-5630. **Contact:** Gina Maccoby. Estab. 1986. Represents 35 clients. Currently handles: 33% nonfiction books; 33% juvenile books; 33% novels. Represents illustrators of children's books.

Represents: Nonfiction, juvenile books, novels. **Considers these nonfiction areas:** biography; current affairs; ethnic/cultural interests; history; juvenile nonfiction; pop culture; women's issues/women's studies. **Considers these fiction**

insider report

Agents compete for powerful memoir

Sometimes passion, fierce determination and faith are all you need to get your first break. Talent doesn't hurt either. First-time author Andrew X. Pham has all this and more. "As a writer you're living such a difficult life. You have to believe in yourself," says Pham, and he did just that. In 1998, with only $40 left to his name, he had a choice between buying food or stamps to send his manuscript to agents. As a compromise, he bought a six-pack, some chips and printed his manuscript single-spaced to save on paper and postage. He took the first 3 chapters of his manuscript, a short query letter of only 3 sentences, and mailed it to 25 agents he researched in a directory. Ten agents requested his entire manuscript. Upon reading it, all ten agencies asked to represent him.

Andrew X. Pham

Pham admits he was shocked by the overwhelming response but says he was willing to do whatever it took to publish his book, even if he had to hand deliver it to agents. This unflagging level of determination has not only served Pham in his writing career but in his life as well.

Few writers have traveled farther in mind and body than Pham to lay their experiences down in print. Escaping Vietnam in a boat with his family at the end of the Vietnam War, Pham was ten when he arrived in the United States. His father, who had been a POW of the Vietcong, settled the family on the West Coast. Pham's sister ran away from home, returning years later as a post-operative transsexual. When she committed suicide, Pham's life irrevocably changed. He quit his job as an engineer, sold all his possessions and embarked on a grueling bicycle journey to come to terms with his sister's death, his family's history and his own cultural identity. His year-long bicycle journey took him through the Mexican desert, 1,000 miles of Japan, and ended 2,357 miles later in Saigon. He chronicled his emotional journey in his memoir, *Catfish and Mandala: A Two-Wheeled Voyage Through the Landscape and Memory of Vietnam*, published by Farrar, Straus & Giroux.

It took Pham nine months to write the book, which began as a travelogue but quickly became much more. "When I was writing the travelogue it just didn't feel right. I got about halfway through and realized I was dealing with all these personal issues and guilt over my sister's suicide," he says. At the time he was living in a horrible apartment, and the only place he could write was in a tiny closet. "I had a picture of my sister and my travels in there. One day I just cracked and started crying. Then I started writing."

Pham, who has been a freelance writer for nine years, learned his craft by taking every writing assignment imaginable. "I've written practically everything: business plans, term papers, technical manuals and a lot for newspapers," he says. His real training ground was freelancing as a restaurant critic for an alternative weekly newspaper. "I learned to say the same thing over and over again, and make it interesting. You come to value the reader a little bit more. You know you need to get to the point while taking the time to savor the common things. Since I freelanced for a living, each word I produced had to earn some sort of cash. You value your words a little bit more that way." In *Publishers Weekly*, both Pham's agent and editor praised his "exquisite" writing and the astonishing "quality of the book."

The agent Pham chose to represent him was Jandy Nelson at Manus & Associates. After interviewing each prospective agency carefully, Pham chose Nelson because she seemed to understand his book best. "With each agency, I listened to what they had to say, what they thought about the manuscript, what they thought needed changing. I was trying something rather new stylistically, and I deal with many issues at once. Once the agent shared a similar vision, I knew I had found the right one. Jandy really knows the market." Nelson sent Pham's book to several publishers, receiving a quick response and substantial offer from Farrar, Straus & Giroux.

With the success of such bestsellers as *Angela's Ashes* and *Tuesdays with Morrie*, memoirs are hot in publishing and popular with the public. "There has always been a lot of interest in personal stories," says Pham. "Memoirs bring you one step closer. People today are more open to ethnic diversity. Readers are interested in someone else's story, someone else's tragedy." However, Pham admits *Catfish & Mandala* was an intense and challenging book to write. "Telling the truth was the most agonizing part. You don't know where the borders of your story begin and other peoples' end. And you don't know if the borders are negotiable—what is your truth versus theirs." But, in the end, Pham believes what made his book so sought after is that it's a good story. "I set out to learn something writing this book, and I did. That message is more important to me than the tragedies or what happened on my adventure. Maybe that's what people like about it."

Pham, who is already hard at work on a novel, is not letting his first success distract him from writing. "I've read from other first-time writers that the industry goes through new writers like woodchips," he says. "Nobody will see my new book until I'm done. That way I don't get any pressure. I've been suffering and have gone without for a long time. Now I have enough food to eat for a year so I'm not going to feel stressed."

Ultimately, it is Pham's admiration for literature that compels him to write. "Literature has inspired me to do things I wouldn't have otherwise. Go the extra step," he advises new writers. "Do what everyone else is *not* doing. Go all the way." While waiting for that first break, Pham urges writers to write everyday. "Pick the best hours of the day for yourself. People can never pay you enough for those hours. Everybody has a certain time in their day when they feel at their best, their sharpest and most creative. Writers should save those hours for themselves. Once you devote those hours to your writing, the time will come when success will find you."

—*Tricia Waddell*

areas: juvenile; literary; mainstream; mystery/suspense; thriller/espionage; young adult.

How to Contact: Query with SASE. "Please, no unsolicited mss." Considers simultaneous queries and submisssions. Reports in 2 months. Returns materials only with SASE.

Needs: Usually obtains new clients through recommendations from own clients.

Recent Sales: Sold 18 titles in the last year. *Vicksburg*, by Don Miller (Simon & Schuster); *The Art of Keeping Cool*, by Janet Taylor Lisle (DK Ink).

Terms: Agent receives 15% commission on domestic sales; 25% on foreign sales. Charges for photocopying. May recover certain costs such as airmail postage to Europe or Japan or legal fees.

◑ ROBERT MADSEN AGENCY, 1331 E. 34th St., Suite #1, Oakland CA 94602-1032. (510)223-2090. **Contact:** Robert Madsen. Senior Editor: Kim Van Nguyen. Estab. 1992. Represents 5 clients. 100% of clients are new/previously unpublished writers. Currently handles: 25% nonfiction books; 25% fiction books; 25% movie scripts; 25% TV scripts.

• Prior to opening his agency, Mr. Madsen was a writing tutor and worked in sales.

Represents: Nonfiction books, fiction. **Considers all nonfiction and fiction areas.** "Willing to look at subject matter that is specialized, controversial, even unpopular, esoteric and outright bizarre. However, it is strongly suggested that authors query first, to save themselves and this agency time, trouble and expense."

Also Handles: Feature film, TV scripts, radio scripts, video, stage plays. **Considers all script subject areas.**

How to Contact: Query with SASE. Considers simultaneous queries and submissions. Reports in 2-4 weeks. Returns materials only with SASE.

Needs: Obtains new clients through recommendations, or by query.

Recent Sales: Sold 1 book title in the last year. *The Art of War*, by Wei Li (International). Clients include Theresa Ohmit.

Terms: Agent receives 10% commission on domestic sales; 20% on foreign sales. Offers written contract, binding for 3 years.

Tips: "Be certain to take care of business basics in appearance, ease of reading and understanding proper presentation and focus. Be sure to include sufficient postage and SASE with all submissions."

◑ ◓ CAROL MANN AGENCY, 55 Fifth Ave., New York NY 10003. (212)206-5635. Fax: (212)675-4809. E-mail: cmlass@aol.com. **Contact:** Carol Mann. Estab. 1977. Member of AAR. Represents over 100 clients. 25% of clients are new/previously unpublished writers. Specializes in current affairs; self-help; psychology; parenting; history. Currently handles: 70% nonfiction books; 30% novels.

Member Agents: Gareth Esersky (contemporary nonfiction); Jim Fitzgerald (literary, cinematic, Internet projects).

Represents: Nonfiction books. **Considers these nonfiction areas:** anthropology/archaeology; art/architecture/design; biography/autobiography; business; child guidance/parenting; current affairs; ethnic/cultural interests; government/politics/law; health/medicine; history; money/finance/economics; psychology; self-help/personal improvement; sociology; women's issues/women's studies. **Considers literary fiction.**

How to Contact: Query with outline/proposal and SASE. Reports in 3 weeks on queries.

Needs: Actively seeking "nonfiction: pop culture, business and health; fiction: literary fiction." Does not want to receive "genre fiction (romance, mystery, etc.)."

Recent Sales: *Radical Healing*, by Rudolph Ballentine, M.D. (Harmony); *Timbuktu*, by Paul Auster (Holt); *Stopping Cancer Before It Starts*, by American Institute for Cancer Research (Golden). Other clients include Dr. William Julius Wilson, Barry Sears (*Mastering The Zone*), Dr. Judith Wallerstein, Lorraine Johnson-Coleman (*Just Plain Folks*), Pulitzer Prize Winner Fox Butterfield and James Tobin, NBCC Award Winner for *Ernie Pyle* (Free Press).

Terms: Agent receives 15% commission on domestic sales; 20% on foreign sales. Offers written contract.

Tips: "No phone queries. Must include SASE for reply."

☑ ◑ ◓ MANUS & ASSOCIATES LITERARY AGENCY, INC., 375 Forest Ave., Palo Alto CA 94301. (650)470-5151. Fax: (650)470-5159. E-mail: manuslit@manuslit.com. Website: www.manuslit.com. **Contact:** Jillian Manus. Also: 417 E. 57th St., Suite 5D, New York NY 10022. (212)644-8020. Fax: (212)644-3374. **Contact:** Janet Manus. Estab. 1985. Member of AAR. Represents 75 clients. 30% of clients are new/previously unpublished writers. Specializes in commercial literary fiction, narrative nonfiction, thrillers, health, pop psychology, women's empowerment. "Our agency is unique in the way that we not only sell the material, but we edit, develop concepts and participate in the marketing effort. We specialize in large, conceptual fiction and nonfiction, and always value a project that can be sold in the TV/feature film market." Currently handles: 55% nonfiction books; 5% juvenile books; 40% novels.

• Prior to becoming agents, Jillian Manus was associate publisher of two national magazines and director of development at Warner Bros. and Universal Studios; Janet Manus has been a literary agent for 20 years.

Member Agents: Jandy Nelson (self-help, health, memoirs, narrative nonfiction, literary fiction, multicultural fiction, thrillers); Jill Maverick (self-help, health, memoirs, dramatic nonfiction, women's fiction, commercial literary fiction, Southern writing, thrillers); Stephanie Lee (self-help, memoirs, dramatic nonfiction, commercial literary fiction, multicultural fiction, quirky/edgy fiction).

Represents: Nonfiction books, novels. **Considers these nonfiction areas**: biography/autobiography; business; child guidance/parenting; computers/electronics; current affairs; ethnic/cultural interests; health/medicine; how-to; memoirs; money/finance/economics; nature/environment; popular culture; psychology; science/technology; self-help/personal improvement; women's issues/women's studies; dramatic/narrative nonfiction; Gen X and Gen Y issues. **Considers these**

fiction areas: literary; thriller/espionage; women's fiction; commercial literary fiction; multicultural fiction; Southern fiction; quirky/edgy fiction.

How to Contact: Query with SASE. Accepts queries by fax and e-mail. If requested, send outline and 2-3 sample chapters. Considers simultaneous queries and submissions. Reports in 6-8 weeks on queries; 6 weeks on mss. Returns materials only with SASE.

Needs: Actively seeking high-concept thrillers, commercial literary fiction, women's fiction, celebrity biographies, memoirs, multicultural fiction, popular health, women's empowerment. Does not want to receive horror, science fiction/fantasy, romance, westerns, young adult, children's, poetry, cookbooks, magazine articles. Usually obtains new clients through recommendations from editors, clients and others; conferences; and unsolicited materials.

Recent Sales: *Catfish & Mandala*, by Andrew X. Pham (Farrar, Straus & Giroux); *Jake & Mimi*, by Frank Baldwin (Little, Brown); *Wishing Well*, by Paul Pearsall, Ph.D. (Hyperion); *Balancing the Equation*, by Dr. Lorraine Zappart (Pocket Books/Simon & Schuster). Other clients include Marcus Allen, Carlton Stowers, Alan Jacobson, Ann Brandt, Dr. Richard Marrs, Mary Loverde, Lisa Huang Fleishman, Judy Carter, Daryl Ott Underhill, Glen Klein.

Terms: Agent receives 15% commission on domestic sales; 20-25% on foreign sales. Offers written contract, binding for 2 years. 60 days notice must be given to terminate contract. Charges for copying and postage.

Writer's Conferences: Maui Writers Conference (Maui HI, Labor Day); San Diego Writer's Conference (San Diego CA, January); Willamette Writers Conference (Willamette OR, July).

Tips: "Research agents using a variety of sources, including *LMP*, guides, *Publishers Weekly*, conferences and even acknowledgements in books similar in tone to yours."

☑ ◖ **MARCH TENTH, INC.**, 4 Myrtle St., Haworth NJ 07641-1740. (201)387-6551. Fax: (201)387-6552. E-mail: schoron@aol.com. **Contact:** Sandra Choron, president; Harry Choron, vice president. Estab. 1982. Represents 40 clients. 30% of clients are new/unpublished writers. "Writers must have professional expertise in the field in which they are writing." Prefers to work with published/established writers. Currently handles: 75% nonfiction books; 25% fiction.

Represents: Nonfiction books, fiction. **Considers these nonfiction areas:** biography/autobiography; current affairs; health/medicine; history; humor; language/literature/criticism; music/dance/theater/film; popular culture. **Considers these fiction areas:** confessional; ethnic; family saga; historical; horror; humor/satire; literary; mainstream.

How to Contact: Query with SASE. Considers simultaneous queries. Does not read unsolicited mss. Reports in 1 month. Returns materials only with SASE.

Recent Sales: *Lynyrd Skynyrd*, by Lee Ballinger (Avon); *Moon: The Story of Keith Moon*, by Tony Fletcher (Avon); *Songs*, by Bruce Springsteen (Avon).

Terms: Agent receives 15% commission on domestic sales; 20% on dramatic sales; 20% on foreign sales. Charges writers for postage, photocopying, overseas phone expenses.

◒ **THE DENISE MARCIL LITERARY AGENCY, INC.**, 685 West End Ave., New York NY 10025. Currently not accepting submissions.

◖ **ELAINE MARKSON LITERARY AGENCY**, 44 Greenwich Ave., New York NY 10011. (212)243-8480. Fax: (212)691-9014. Estab. 1972. Member of AAR and WGA. Represents 200 clients. 10% of clients are new/unpublished writers. Specializes in literary fiction, commercial fiction, trade nonfiction. Currently handles: 35% nonfiction books; 55% novels; 10% juvenile books.

Member Agents: Geri Thoma, Sally Wofford-Girand, Elizabeth Sheinkman, Elaine Markson.

Represents: Quality fiction and nonfiction.

How to Contact: Obtains new clients by recommendation only.

Recent Sales: *The First Horseman*, by John Case (Ballantine); *Life, the Movie*, by Neal Gabler (Knopf); *The Hidden Jesus*, by Donald Spoto (St. Martins).

Terms: Agent receives 15% commission on domestic sales; 20% on foreign sales. Charges for postage, photocopying, foreign mailing, faxing, and other special expenses.

◖ **THE EVAN MARSHALL AGENCY**, 6 Tristam Place, Pine Brook NJ 07058-9445. (973)882-1122. Fax: (973)882-3099. E-mail: evanmarshall@thenovelist.com. Website: www.thenovelist.com. **Contact:** Evan Marshall. Estab. 1987. Currently handles: 50% nonfiction books; 50% novels.

● Prior to opening his agency, Mr. Marshall served as an editor with New American Library, Everest House, and Dodd, Mead & Co., and then worked as a literary agent at The Sterling Lord Agency.

Represents: Nonfiction books, novels. **Considers these nonfiction areas:** animals; biography/autobiography; business; child guidance/parenting; cooking/food/nutrition; crafts/hobbies; current affairs; government/politics/law; health/medicine; history; how-to; humor; interior design/decorating; language/literature/criticism; military/war; money/finance/economics; music/dance/theater/film; nature/environment; New Age/metaphysics; psychology; religious/inspirational; science/technology; self-help/personal improvement; true crime/investigative; women's issues/women's studies. **Considers these fiction areas:** action/adventure; contemporary issues; detective/police/crime; erotica; ethnic; family saga; glitz; historical; horror; humor/satire; literary; mainstream; mystery/suspense; psychic/supernatural; religious/inspirational; romance (contemporary, gothic, historical, regency); science fiction; thriller/espionage; westerns/frontier.

How to Contact: Query with SASE. Reports in 1 week on queries; 2 months on mss.

Needs: Obtains many new clients through referrals from clients and editors.

Recent Sales: *All Fall Down*, by Erica Spindler (Mira); *The Brides of Durango: Elise*, by Bobbi Smith (Leisure); *The Resurrectionist*, by Mark Graham (Avon); *Hook*, by C.J. Songer (Scribner); *Mood to Murder*, by Joyce Christmas (Fawcett).
Terms: Agent receives 15% on domestic sales; 20% on foreign sales. Offers written contract.

ELISABETH MARTON AGENCY, One Union Square Room 612, New York NY 10003-3303. This agency did not respond to our request for information. Query before submitting.

HAROLD MATSON CO. INC., 276 Fifth Ave., New York NY 10001. This agency did not respond to our request for information. Query before submitting.

JED MATTES, INC., 2095 Broadway, Suite 302, New York NY 10023-2895. This agency did not respond to our request for information. Query before submitting.

MARGRET McBRIDE LITERARY AGENCY, 7744 Fay Ave., Suite 201, La Jolla CA 92037. (858)454-1550. Fax: (858)454-2156. Estab. 1980. Member of AAR, Authors Guild. Represents 50 clients. 15% of clients are new/unpublished writers. Specializes in mainstream fiction and nonfiction.
• Prior to opening her agency, Ms. McBride served in the marketing departments of Random House and Ballantine Books and the publicity departments of Warner Books and Pinnacle Books.
Represents: Nonfiction books, novels, audio, video film rights. **Considers these nonfiction areas:** biography/autobiography; business; child guidance/parenting; cooking/food/nutrition; current affairs; ethnic/cultural interests; gay/lesbian issues; government/politics/law; health/medicine; history; how-to; money/finance/economics; music/dance/theater/film; popular culture; psychology; religious/inspirational; science/technology; self-help/personal improvement; sociology; sports; true crime/investigative; women's issues/women's studies. **Considers these fiction areas:** action/adventure; detective/police/crime; ethnic; historical; humor; literary; mainstream; mystery/suspense; thriller/espionage; westerns/frontier.
How to Contact: Query with synopsis or outline. Considers simultaneous queries. *No unsolicited mss.* Reports in 6 weeks on queries. Returns materials only with SASE.
Needs: Does not want screenplays.
Recent Sales: Sold 20 titles in the last year. *Special Circumstances*, by Sheldon Siegel (Bantam); *Instant Emotional Healing*, by George Pratt Ph.D. and Peter Lambrou Ph.D. (Broadway); *Leadership by the Book*, by Ken Blanchard (Morrow).
Terms: Agent receives 15% commission on domestic sales; 10% on dramatic sales; 25% on foreign sales charges for overnight delivery and photocopying.

GERARD McCAULEY, P.O. Box 844, Katonah NY 10536. (914)232-5700. Fax: (914)232-1506. Estab. 1970. Member of AAR. Represents 60 clients. 5% of clients are new/previously unpublished writers. Specializes in history, biography and general nonfiction. Currently handles: 65% nonfiction books; 15% scholarly books; 20% college level textbooks.
Represents: *Currently not accepting new clients.*
How to Contact: Query with SASE. Reports in 1 month on queries; 2 months on mss.

CLOSE UP with Evan Marshall, The Evan Marshall Agency
... **On advances**

"Beginning writers who demand unreasonably large advances and refuse to accept anything less, run a strong risk of not getting published at all. A writer must start somewhere, and in many cases, that somewhere is an advance in the mid four figures. Writers who are just in it for the money should know there are far less speculative ways to get rich.

"Established writers often insist on unreasonably high advances because they believe publishers promote only those books for which they've paid high advances. There is some truth to this idea, but a high advance can also bite an author back. If a publisher is persuaded to pay a high advance and the book never earns this advance back, the publisher is left with a book that has made little or no money, or has lost money. In most of these cases, the publisher then drops the author.

"As an agent, I aim for an advance high enough that the publisher will have to get behind the book, yet reasonable in terms of what the book is likely to earn out. Then everyone is happy, and the author's career at the publishing house may build further."

Needs: Obtains new clients through recommendations.
Recent Sales: *Lewis and Clark*, by Ken Burns; *American Sphinx*, by Joseph Ellis; *Approaching Fury*, by Stephen Oates.
Terms: Agent receives 15% commission on domestic sales; 20% on foreign sales. Charges for "postage for all submissions and photocopying."
Tips: "Always send a personal letter—not a form letter with recommendations from published writers. Will not read manuscripts and proposals sent simultaneously to several agencies and publishers."

⊘ ANITA D. McCLELLAN ASSOCIATES, 50 Stearns St., Cambridge MA 02138. This agency did not respond to our request for information. Query before submitting.

◖ RICHARD P. McDONOUGH, LITERARY AGENT, 34 Pinewood, Irvine CA 92604-3274. (949)654-5480. Fax: (949)654-5481. E-mail: cestmoi@msn.com. **Contact:** Richard P. McDonough. Estab. 1986. Represents over 30 clients. Specializes in nonfiction for general market and literary fiction. Currently handles: 80% nonfiction books; 20% fiction.
Represents: Nonfiction books, novels.
How to Contact: Query with outline and SASE. Does not accept queries by fax or e-mail. Considers simultaneous queries; no simultaneous submissions. Reports in 2 weeks on queries; 2 months on mss. Returns materials only with SASE.
Needs: Does not want to receive genre material.
Recent Sales: Sold 10 titles in the last year. *Muddy Waters* (biography), by Robert Gordon (Little, Brown & Co.); *Untitled* book of essays, by Thomas Lynch.
Terms: Agent receives 15% commission on domestic sales; 15% on dramatic sales; 15% on foreign sales. Charges for photocopying; postage for sold work only.

◑ HELEN McGRATH, 1406 Idaho Ct., Concord CA 94521. (925)672-6211. **Contact:** Helen McGrath. Estab. 1977. Currently handles: 50% nonfiction books; 50% novels.
Represents: Nonfiction books, novels. **Considers these nonfiction areas:** biography; business; current affairs; health/medicine; history; how-to; military/war; psychology; self-help/personal improvement; sports; women's issues/women's studies. **Considers these fiction areas:** contemporary issues; detective/police/crime; literary; mainstream; mystery/suspense; psychic/supernatural; romance; science fiction; thriller/espionage.
How to Contact: Query with proposal and SASE. *No unsolicited mss.* Reports in 2 months on queries.
Terms: Agent receives 15% commission on domestic sales. Sometimes offers written contract. Charges for photocopying.
Needs: Usually obtains new clients through recommendations from others.

Ⓝ ◑ McHUGH LITERARY AGENCY, 1033 Lyon Rd., Moscow ID 83843-9167. (208)882-0107. Fax: (847)628-0146. E-mail: elisabetmch@turbonet.com. **Contact:** Elisabet McHugh. Estab. 1994. Represents 81 clients. 40% of clients are new/unpublished writers. Currently handles: 80% nonfiction books, 20% novels.
 ● Prior to opening her agency, Ms. McHugh was a full-time writer for 14 years.
Represents: Nonfiction books; novels. **Considers these nonfiction areas:** animals; anthropology/archaeology; biography/autobiography; business; child guidance/parenting; cooking/food/nutrition; current affairs; health/medicine; history; how-to; military/war; nature/environment; science/technology; self-help/personal improvement; true crime/investigative; investing, alternative medicine. **Considers these fiction areas:** historical; mainstream; mystery; romance; thriller/espionage.
How to Contact: Query by e-mail. Returns materials only with SASE.
Needs: Does not want to receive children's books, poetry, science fiction, fantasy.
Recent Sales: Sold 35 titles in the last year. *Natural Prostate Healers: A Breakthrough Program for Preventing and Treating Common Prostate Problems*, by Michael Fillon (Prentice Hall); *Lighten Up: Lowfat Cooking in Fifteen Minutes*, by Ginny Clark (Warner); *Crimson Sky: The Air Battle for Korea*, by John Bruning (Brassey's, Inc.); *The Ten Commandments of Small-Business Success*, by Marguerite Kirk (Bookhome Publishing).
Terms: Agent receives 15% commission on domestic sales; 20% on foreign sales. Offers written contract. "Client must provide all copies of manuscripts needed for submissions."
Tips: "Be professional."

Ⓝ ⊘ CLAUDIA MENZA LITERARY AGENCY, 1170 Broadway, New York NY 10001. This agency did not respond to our request for information. Query before submitting.

Ⓝ ⊘ HELEN MERRILL, LTD., 425 W. 23 St., 1F, New York NY 10011. This agency did not respond to our request for information. Query before submitting.

⊘ ◑ DORIS S. MICHAELS LITERARY AGENCY, INC., 1841 Broadway, Suite #903, New York NY 10023. (212)265-9474. **Contact:** Doris S. Michaels. Estab. 1994. Member of WNBA, AAR. Represents 30 clients. 50% of clients are new/previously unpublished writers. Currently handles: 40% nonfiction books; 60% novels.

● Prior to opening her agency, Ms. Michaels was an editor for Prentice-Hall, consultant for Prudential-Bache, and an international consultant for the Union Bank of Switzerland.

Member Agents: Faye Bender.

Represents: Nonfiction books, novels. **Considers these nonfiction areas:** biography/autobiography; business; current affairs; ethnic/cultural interests; health; history; how-to; money/finance/economics; music/dance/theater/film; nature/environment; self-help/personal improvement; sports; women's issues/women's studies. **Considers these fiction areas:** action/adventure; contemporary issues; family saga; feminist; historical; literary; mainstream.

How to Contact: Query with SASE. Considers simultaneous queries. *No phone calls or unsolicited mss.* Reports ASAP on queries with SASE; no answer without SASE. Returns materials only with SASE.

Needs: Obtains new clients through recommendations from others, solicitation and at conferences.

Recent Sales: *How To Be A Rainmaker*, by Jeffrey J. Fox (Hyperion); *The Neatest Little Guide to Making Money Online*, by Jason Kelly (Plume). Other clients include Maury Allen, Wendy Rue, Karin Abarbanel and Eva Shaw.

Terms: Agent receives 15% commission on domestic sales; 20% on foreign sales. Offers written contract, binding for 1 year, with 30 day cancellation clause. Charges for office expenses including deliveries, postage, photocopying and fax. 100% of business is derived from commissions on sales.

Writers' Conferences: BEA (Chicago, June); Frankfurt Book Fair (Germany, October); London Book Fair; Society of Southwestern Authors; San Diego State University Writers' Conference; Willamette Writers' Conference; International Women's Writing Guild; American Society of Journalists and Authors.

〔N〕 ◉ MARTHA MILLARD LITERARY AGENCY, 293 Greenwood Ave., Florham Park NJ 07932. (973)593-9233. Fax: (973)593-9235. E-mail: marmillink@aol.com. **Contact:** Martha Millard. Estab. 1980. Member of AAR, SFWA. Represents 50 clients. 2% of clients are new/unpublished writers. Currently handles: 25% nonfiction books, 10% story collections, 65% novels.

● Prior to opening her agency, Ms. Millard worked in editorial departments of several publishers and was vice president at another agency for four and a half years.

Represents: Nonfiction books, novels. **Considers these nonfiction areas:** art/architecture/design; biography/autobiography; business; child guidance/parenting; cooking/food/nutrition; current affairs; education; ethnic/cultural interests; health/medicine; history; how-to; juvenile nonfiction; memoirs; money/finance/economics; music/dance/theater/film; New Age/metaphysics; photography; popular culture; psychology; self-help/personal improvement; true crime/investigative; women's issues/women's studies. Considers fiction depending on writer's credits and skills.

How to Contact: Query with SASE. Does not accept queries by fax or e-mail. Reports in 2 weeks on queries; 1 month on mss. Returns materials only with SASE.

Needs: Obtains new clients through referrals from other clients or editors.

Recent Sales: Sold 45 titles in the last year. *The Old Bone Road*, by M. Swanwick (Avon); *3 Fishing Mysteries*, by V. Houston (Berkley Prime Crime); *Chainsaw*, by John Byrne (Harper Business); *Crisis of the Real*, by Andy Crundberg (Aperture). Other clients include Elizabeth Hand, Denise Lang, William Gibson, Dr. Marc Weissbluth, Julia Scully, Sean Stewart, Peter Heck, Shirley Rousseau-Murphy.

Terms: Agent receives 15% commission on domestic sales; 20% on foreign sales. Offers written contract, negotiated individually.

✓ ◉ MAUREEN MORAN AGENCY, Park West Station, P.O. Box 20191, New York NY 10025-1518. (212)222-3838. Fax: (212)531-3464. E-mail: maureenm@erols.com. **Contact:** Maureen Moran. Represents 30 clients. Specializes in women's book-length fiction in all categories. Currently handles: 100% novels.

● Prior to opening her agency, Ms. Moran worked for Donald MacCampbell (from whom she purchased the agency).

Represents: Novels.

How to Contact: Query with outline and SASE; does not read unsolicited mss. Reports in 1 week on queries. Returns materials only with SASE.

Needs: Does not want to receive science fiction, fantasy or juvenile books.

Recent Sales: *Bed & Breakfast Mysteries*, by Mary Daheim (Avon); *Romance*, by Julianna Morris (Silhouette).

Terms: Agent receives 10% commission on domestic sales; 15-20% on foreign sales. Charges for extraordinary photocopying, courier and messenger, and bank wire fees, by prior arrangement with author.

Tips: "The agency does not handle unpublished writers."

〔N〕 ⊘ HOWARD MORHAIM LITERARY AGENCY, 841 Broadway, Suite 604, New York NY 10003. This agency did not respond to our request for information. Query before submitting.

◉ WILLIAM MORRIS AGENCY, INC., 1325 Ave. of the Americas, New York NY 10019. (212)586-5100. West Coast Office: 151 El Camino Dr., Beverly Hills CA 90212. **Contact:** Mel Berger, vice president. Member of AAR.

Member Agents: Owen Laster; Robert Gottlieb; Mel Berger; Matt Bialer; Claudia Cross; Joni Evans; Tracy Fisher; Marcy Posner; Dan Strone; Helen Breitwieser.

Represents: Nonfiction books, novels.

How to Contact: Query with SASE. Does not accept queries by fax or e-mail.

Recent Sales: Prefers not to share information on specific sales.

Terms: Agent receives 10% commission on domestic sales; 20% on foreign sales.

⚫ **HENRY MORRISON, INC.**, 105 S. Bedford Rd., Suite 306A, Mt. Kisco NY 10549. (914)666-3500. Fax: (914)241-7846. **Contact:** Henry Morrison. Estab. 1965. Signatory of WGA. Represents 48 clients. 5% of clients are new/previously unpublished writers. Currently handles: 5% nonfiction books; 5% juvenile books; 85% novels; 5% movie scripts.
Represents: Nonfiction books, novels. **Considers these nonfiction areas:** anthropology/archaeology; biography; government/politics/law; history; juvenile nonfiction. **Considers these fiction areas:** action/adventure; detective/police/crime; family saga.
How to Contact: Query. Reports in 2 weeks on queries; 3 months on mss.
Needs: Obtains new clients through recommendations from others.
Recent Sales: Sold 10 titles in the last year. *Untitled*, by Robert Ludlum (St. Martin's); *The Pearl*, by Eric Lustbader (TOR); *Burnt Sienna*, by David Morrell (Warner Books); *Rock & Scissors*, by Steve Samuel (Simon & Schuster). Other clients include Joe Gores, Samuel R. Delany, Beverly Byrnne, Patricia Keneally-Morrison and Molly Katz.
Terms: Agent receives 15% commission on domestic sales; 25% on foreign sales. Charges for ms copies, bound galleys and finished books for submission to publishers, movie producers, foreign publishers.

⚫ **MULTIMEDIA PRODUCT DEVELOPMENT, INC.**, 410 S. Michigan Ave., Suite 724, Chicago IL 60605-1465. (312)922-3063. Fax: (312)922-1905. E-mail: mpdinc@aol.com. **Contact:** Jane Jordan Browne, president. Estab. 1971. Member of AAR, RWA, MWA, SCBWI. Represents 175 clients. 2% of clients are new/previously unpublished writers. "We are generalists looking for professional writers with finely honed skill in writing. We are partial to authors who are promotion savvy. We work closely with our authors through the entire publishing process, from proposal to after publication." Currently handles: 60% nonfiction books; 38% novels; 1% movie scripts.
   • Prior to opening her agency Ms. Browne served as the Managing Editor, then as head of the juvenile department for Hawthorn Books, Senior Editor for Thomas Y. Crowell, adult trade department and General Editorial and Production Manager for Macmillan Educational Services, Inc.
Member Agents: Scott A. Mendel (generalist); Amy Harmon (juvenile).
Represents: Nonfiction books, novels. **Considers these nonfiction areas:** agriculture/horticulture; animals; anthropology/archaeology; biography/autobiography; business; child guidance/parenting; cooking/food/nutrition; crafts/hobbies; current affairs; ethnic/cultural issues; health/medicine; how-to; humor; juvenile nonfiction; memoirs; money/finance; nature; popular culture; psychology; religious/inspirational; science/technology; self-help/personal improvement; sociology; sports; travel; true crime/investigative; women's issues/women's studies. **Considers these fiction areas:** contemporary issues; detective/police/crime; ethnic; family saga; glitz; historical; juvenile; literary; mainstream; mystery/suspense; picture book; religious/inspirational; romance (contemporary, gothic, historical, regency, western); sports; thriller/espionage.
How to Contact: Query "by mail with SASE required." Considers simultaneous queries. Reports within 1 week on queries; 6 weeks on mss. *"No unsolicited mss accepted."* Returns materials only with SASE.
Needs: Actively seeking highly commercial mainstream fiction and nonfiction. Does not want to receive poetry, short stories, plays, screenplays, articles.
Recent Sales: Sold 50 titles in the last year. *Five Novellas*, by Francine Rivers (Tyndale House); *Cruising for Murder*, by Susan Sussman with Sarajane Avidon (St. Martin's); *The Buccaneers*, by Iain Lawrence (Delacorte); *Purgatory Ridge*, by William Kent Krueger (Pocket).
Terms: Agent receives 15% commission on domestic sales; 20% on foreign sales. Offers written contract, binding for 2 years. Charges for photocopying, overseas postage, faxes, phone calls.
Writers' Conferences: BEA (Chicago, June); Frankfurt Book Fair (Frankfurt, October); RWA (Washington DC, July); CBA (New Orleans).
Tips: Obtains new clients through "referrals, queries by professional, marketable authors. If interested in agency representation, be well informed."

⚫ **DEE MURA ENTERPRISES, INC.**, 269 W. Shore Dr., Massapequa NY 11758-8225. (516)795-1616. Fax: (516)795-8797. E-mail: samurai5@ix.netcom.com. **Contact:** Dee Mura, Ken Nyquist. Estab. 1987. Signatory of WGA. 50% of clients are new/previously unpublished writers. "We work on everything, but are especially interested in literary fiction and commercial fiction, in true life stories, true crime, women's stories and issues and unique nonfiction." Currently handles: 25% nonfiction books; 10% scholarly books; 15% juvenile books; 25% novels; 25% movie scripts.
   • Prior to opening her agency, Ms. Mura was a public relations executive with a roster of film and entertainment clients; and worked in editorial for major weekly news magazines.
Represents: Nonfiction books, scholarly books, juvenile books. **Considers these nonfiction areas:** agriculture/horticulture; animals; anthropology/archaeology; biography/autobiography; business; child guidance/parenting; computers/electronics; current affairs; education; ethnic/cultural interests; gay/lesbian issues; government/politics/law; health/medicine; history; how-to; humor; juvenile nonfiction; memoirs; military/war; money/finance/economics; nature/environment; science/technology; self-help/personal improvement; sociology; sports; travel; true crime/investigative; women's issues/women's studies. **Considers these fiction areas:** action/adventure; contemporary issues; detective/police/crime; ethnic; experimental; family saga; fantasy; feminist; gay; glitz; historical; humor/satire; juvenile; lesbian; literary; mainstream; mystery/suspense; psychic/supernatural; regional; romance (contemporary, gothic, historical, regency); science fiction; sports; thriller/espionage; westerns/frontier; young adult.
Also Handles: Feature film, documentary, animation, TV MOW, miniseries, episodic drama, sitcom, variety show, animation. **Considers these script subject areas:** action/adventure; cartoon/animation; comedy; contemporary issues;

detective/police/crime; family saga; fantasy; feminist; gay; glitz; historical; horror; humor; juvenile; mainstream; mystery/suspense; psychic/supernatural; religious/inspirational; romantic comedy and drama; science fiction; sports; teen; thriller; western/frontier.

How to Contact: Query with SASE. Accepts queries by e-mail. Considers simultaneous queries. Reports in approximately 2 weeks on queries. Returns materials only with SASE.

Needs: Actively seeking "unique nonfiction manuscripts and proposals; novelists that are great storytellers; contemporary writers with distinct voices and passion." Does not want to receive "ideas for sitcoms, novels, film, etc.; queries without SASEs." Obtains new clients through recommendations from others and queries.

Recent Sales: Sold over 40 book titles and over 35 script projects in the last year. Prefers not to share information on specific sales.

Terms: Agent receives 15% commission on domestic sales; 20-25% on foreign sales. Offers written contract. Charges for photocopying, mailing expenses and office supplies directly pertaining to writer, overseas and long distance phone calls and faxes.

Tips: "Please include a paragraph on writer's background even if writer has no literary background and a brief synopsis of the project. We enjoy well-written query letters that tell us about the project and the author."

◖ JEAN V. NAGGAR LITERARY AGENCY, 216 E. 75th St., Suite 1E, New York NY 10021. (212)794-1082. **Contact:** Jean Naggar. Estab. 1978. Member of AAR, Women's Media Group and Women's Forum. Represents 100 clients. 20% of clients are new/previously unpublished writers. Specializes in mainstream fiction and nonfiction, literary fiction with commercial potential. Currently handles: 35% general nonfiction books; 5% scholarly books; 15% juvenile books; 45% novels.

Member Agents: Frances Kuffel (literary fiction and nonfiction, New Age); Alice Tasman (spiritual/New Age, medical thrillers, commercial/literary fiction); Anne Engel (academic-based nonfiction for general readership).

Represents: Nonfiction books, novels. **Considers these nonfiction areas among others:** biography/autobiography; child guidance/parenting; current affairs; government/politics/law; health/medicine; history; juvenile nonfiction; memoirs; New Age/metaphysics; psychology; religious/inspirational; self-help/personal improvement; sociology; travel; women's issues/women's studies. "We would, of course, consider a query regarding an exceptional mainstream manuscript touching on any area." **Considers these fiction areas:** action/adventure; contemporary issues; detective/police/crime; ethnic; family saga; feminist; historical; literary; mainstream; mystery/suspense; psychic/supernatural; thriller/espionage.

How to Contact: Query with SASE. Prefers to be only reader. Reports in 24 hours on queries; approximately 2 months on mss. Returns materials only with SASE.

Needs: Obtains new clients through recommendations from publishers, editors, clients and others, and from writers' conferences.

Recent Sales: *The Young Irelanders*, by Ann Moore (N.A.L.); *Empires of Sand*, by David Ball (Bantam); *Hotel Alleluja*, by Lucinda Roy (HarperCollins); *The Missing Moment*, by Robert Pollack (Houghton Mifflin); *Fiona Range*, by Mary McGarry Morris (Viking-Penguin); *La Cucina*, by Lily Prior (HarperCollins).

Terms: Agent receives 15% commission on domestic sales; 20% on foreign sales. Offers written contract. Charges for overseas mailing; messenger services; book purchases; long-distance telephone; photocopying. "These are deductible from royalties received."

Writers' Conferences: Willamette Writers Conference; Pacific Northwest Writers Conference; Breadloaf Writers Conference; Virginia Women's Press Conference (Richmond VA), Marymount Manhattan Writers Conference.

Tips: "Use a professional presentation. Because of the avalanche of unsolicited queries that flood the agency every week, we have had to modify our policy. We will now only guarantee to read and respond to queries from writers who come recommended by someone we know. Our areas are general fiction and nonfiction, no children's books by unpublished writers, no multimedia, no screenplays, no formula fiction, no mysteries by unpublished writers."

◖ RUTH NATHAN, 53 E. 34th St., New York NY 10016. Phone/fax: (212)481-1185. Estab. 1980. Member of AAR and Authors Guild. Represents 6 clients. Specializes in art, decorative arts, fine art; theater; film; show business. Currently handles: 60% nonfiction books; 40% novels.

Represents: Nonfiction books, novels. **Considers these nonfiction areas:** art/architecture/design; biography/autobiography; theater/film. **Considers some historical fiction.**

How to Contact: Query with SASE. Reports in 2 weeks on queries; 1 month on mss.

Recent Sales: *A Booke of Days*, by Stephen Rivele (Macmillan London); *Kurt Weill in the Year 2000*, by Foster Hirsch (A.A. Knopf).

Terms: Agent receives 15% commission on domestic sales; 20% on foreign sales. Charges for office expenses, postage, photocopying, etc.

Tips: "Read carefully what my requirements are before wasting your time and mine."

CHECK THE AGENT SPECIALTIES INDEX to find agents who are interested in your specific nonfiction or fiction subject area.

◢ ◎ **NATIONAL WRITERS LITERARY AGENCY, a division of NWA**, 3140 S. Peoria #295, Aurora CO 80014. (303)751-7844. Fax: (303)751-8593. E-mail: aajwiii@aol.com. **Contact:** Andrew J. Whelchel III. Estab. 1987. Represents 52 clients. 20% of clients are new/previously unpublished writers. Currently handles: 60% nonfiction books; 20% juvenile books; 12% novels; 1% novellas; 1% poetry; 6% scripts.
Member Agents: Andrew J. Whelchel III (screenplays, nonfiction); Jason S. Cangialosi (nonfiction); Shayne Sharpe (novels, screenplays, fantasy).
Represents: Nonfiction books, juvenile books, textbooks. **Considers these nonfiction areas:** animals; biography/autobiography; child guidance/parenting; education; government/politics/law; how-to; juvenile nonfiction; popular culture; science/technology; sports; travel. **Considers these fiction areas:** action/adventure; juvenile; mainstream; picture book; science fiction; sports; young adult.
How to Contact: Query with outline. Accepts queries by e-mail. Considers simultaneous queries. Reports in 1-2 weeks on queries; 1-2 months on mss. Returns materials only with SASE.
Needs: Actively seeking "music, business, cutting edge novels, pop culture, compelling true stories, science and technology." Does not want to receive "concept books, westerns, over published self-help topics." Obtains new clients at conferences or over the transom.
Recent Sales: Sold 12 titles in the last year. *Escapade*, by Natalie Cosby (Orly Adelson Productions); *Love One Another* (3 book series), by Gloria Chisholm (Waterbrook Press/Random House).
Terms: Agent receives 15% commission on domestic sales; 20% on foreign sales; 10% on film. Offers written contract, binding for 1 year with 30-day termination notice.
Writers' Conferences: National Writers Association (Denver, CO, 2nd weekend in June); Sandpiper (Miami, FL, 1st weekend in October).
Reading List: Reads *Popular Mechanics, The Futurist, Industry Standard, Money, Rolling Stone, Maxim, Details, Spin* and *Buzz* to find new clients.
Tips: "Query letters should include a great hook just as if you only had a few seconds to impress us. A professional package gets professional attention. Always include return postage!"

☑ ◢ ☻ **KAREN NAZOR LITERARY AGENCY**, Opera Plaza, PMB 124, 601 Van Ness Ave., Suite E, San Francisco CA 94102. (415)682-7676. Fax: (415)682-7666. E-mail: agentnazor@aol.com (queries only). **Contact:** Karen Nazor. Estab. 1991. Represents 35 clients. 15% of clients are new/previously unpublished writers. Specializes in "good writers! Mostly nonfiction—arts, culture, politics, technology, civil rights, etc." Currently handles: 75% nonfiction books; 10% electronic; 10% fiction.
  ● Prior to opening her agency, Ms. Nazor served a brief apprenticeship with Raines & Raines and was assistant to Peter Ginsberg, president of Curtis Brown Ltd.
Member Agents: Kris Ashley (literary and commercial fiction).
Represents: Nonfiction books, novels, novellas. **Considers these nonfiction areas:** biography; business; computers/electronics; current affairs; ethnic/cultural interests; government/politics/law; history; how-to; music/dance/theater/film; nature/environment; parenting; photography; popular culture; science/technology; sociology; sports; travel; women's issues/women's studies. **Considers these fiction areas:** cartoon/comic; contemporary issues; ethnic; feminist; literary; regional; women's.
How to Contact: Query (preferred) or send outline/proposal (accepted). Accepts queries by e-mail. Considers simultaneous queries and submissions. Reports in 2 weeks on queries; up to 2 months on mss. Returns materials only with SASE.
Needs: Obtains new clients from referrals from editors and writers; online; teaching classes on publishing; newspaper article on agency.
Recent Sales: Sold 12 titles in the last year. *The Secret Life of Dust*, by Hannah Holmes (John Wiley & Sons); *Childhood and Adolescent Obsessive Compulsive Disorder*, by Mitzi Waltz (O'Reilly).
Terms: Agent receives 15% commission on domestic sales; 20% on foreign sales. Offers written contract. Charges for express mail services and photocopying costs.
Tips: "I'm interested in writers who want a long term, long haul relationship. Not a one-book writer, but a writer who has many ideas, is productive, professional, passionate and meets deadlines!"

Ⓝ ◢ **NEW CENTURY LITERARY AGENCY**, Box 7113, The Woodlands TX 77387-7113. (409)295-5357. Fax: (409)295-0409. E-mail: bookagts@lcc.net. Website: www.authorsandpublishers.org/newcentlitagcy. **Contact:** Thomas Fensch or Sharon Wanslee. Estab. 1998. Represents 25 clients. 80% of clients are new/unpublished writers. Specializes in general nonfiction. Currently handles: 100% nonfiction books.
  ● Prior to opening their agency, Mr. Fensch was an editor, book critic and professor; Ms. Wanslee was an editor and art therapy teacher.
Member Agents: Thomas Fensch; Sharon Wanslee.
Represents: Nonfiction books, juvenile books. **Considers these nonfiction areas:** animals; biography/autobiography; business; child guidance/parenting; cooking/food/nutrition; current affairs; education; ethnic/cultural interests; government/politics/law; history; how-to; humor; juvenile nonfiction; language/literature/criticism; memoirs; military/war; money/finance/economics; mustic/dance/theater/film; nature/environment; popular culture; psychology; self-help/personal improvement; sociology; sports; true crime/investigative; women's issues/women's studies.
How to Contact: Query with SASE. Does not accept queries by fax or e-mail. Considers simultaneous queries. See website. "This is an interactive site—authors can query us through the website and describe their projects to us. This

is the best way to contact us." Reports in 3 weeks on queries; 1 month on mss. Returns material only with SASE.
Needs: Actively seeking biographies/memoirs; business and personal success; communication/journalism; current affairs; parenting; popular culture; history; multi-cultural (Hispanic); how-to; southwestern and mountain states subjects; sports; trends; women's issues/women's health; selected children's books. Does not want to receive computer books; gothic romances; horror novels; poetry; science fiction; screenplays; westerns or anything of a nonbook-length nature. Obtains new clients through listings in reference books, conferences.
Recent Sales: New agency with pending sales.
Terms: Agent receives 15% commission on domestic sales; 20% on foreign sales. Offers written contract. Charges for photocopying, express mail and other office expenses if over $100.
Tips: "Be aware of the marketing potential of your book. Publishers won't ask 'is it well written?' (They assume it is.) They will ask 'how can we sell it?' "

◐ NEW ENGLAND PUBLISHING ASSOCIATES, INC., P.O. Box 5, Chester CT 06412-0645. (203)345-READ and (203)345-4976. Fax: (203)345-3660. E-mail: nepa@nepa.com. Website: www.pcnet.nepa.com/~nepa. **Contact:** Elizabeth Frost-Knappman, Edward W. Knappman, Kristine Sciavi, Ron Formica, or Victoria Harlow. Estab. 1983. Member of AAR, ASJA, Authors Guild, Connecticut Press Club. Represents over 100 clients. 15% of clients are new/ previously unpublished writers. Specializes in adult nonfiction books of serious purpose.
Represents: Nonfiction books. **Considers these nonfiction areas:** biography/autobiography; business; child guidance/ parenting; government/politics/law; health/medicine; history; language/literature/criticism; military/war; money/finance/ economics; nature/environment; psychology; science/technology; personal improvement; sociology; true crime/investigative; women's issues/women's studies. **"Occasionally considers crime fiction."**
How to Contact: Send outline/proposal with SASE. Considers simultaneous queries. Reports in 3 weeks on queries; 5 weeks on mss. Returns materials only with SASE.
Recent Sales: Sold 50 titles in the last year. *The Woman's Migraine Survival Handbook*, by Christina Peterson and Christine Adamec (HarperCollins); *Dreams in the Key of Blue, A Novel*, by John Philpin (Bantam); *Ice Blink: The Mysterious Fate of Sir John Franklin's Lost Polar Expedition*, by Scott Cookman (Wiley); *Susan Sontag*, by Carl Rollyson and Lisa Paddock (Norton).
Terms: Agent receives 15% commission on domestic sales; 20% foreign sales (split with overseas agent). Offers written contract, binding for 6 months.
Writers' Conferences: BEA (Chicago, June); ALA (San Antonio, January); ALA (New York, July).
Tips: "Send us a well-written proposal that clearly identifies your audience—who will buy this book and why."

◐ NINE MUSES AND APOLLO INC., 2 Charlton St., New York NY 10014-4909. (212)243-0065. **Contact:** Ling Lucas. Estab. 1991. Represents 50 clients. 10% of clients are new/previously unpublished writers. Specializes in nonfiction. Currently handles: 90% nonfiction books; 10% novels.
 ● Ms. Lucas formerly served as a vice president, sales & marketing director and associate publisher of Warner Books.
Represents: Nonfiction books. **Considers these nonfiction areas:** animals; biography/autobiography; business; current affairs; ethnic/cultural interests; health/medicine; language/literature/criticism; psychology; spirituality; women's issues/ women's studies. **Considers these fiction areas:** commercial; ethnic; literary.
How to Contact: Send outline, 2 sample chapters and SASE. Reports in 1 month on mss.
Needs: Does not want to receive children's and young adult material.
Recent Sales: Sold 12 titles in the last year. *The Prayer Party*, by Carolyn Manji (Harmony); *Essential Spirituality*, by Roger Walsh M.D., Ph.D. (Wiley); and *Utne Reader's Visionaries*, by The Utne Reader (Morrow).
Terms: Agent receives 15% commission on domestic sales; 20-25% on foreign sales. Offers written contract. Charges for photocopying proposals and mss.
Tips: "Your outline should already be well developed, cogent, and reveal clarity of thought about the general structure and direction of your project."

◐ THE BETSY NOLAN LITERARY AGENCY, 224 W. 29th St., 15th Floor, New York NY 10001. (212)967-8200. Fax: (212)967-7292. **Contact:** Donald Lehr, president. Estab. 1980. Represents 200 clients. 10% of clients are new/unpublished writers. Works with a small number of new/unpublished authors. Currently handles: 90% nonfiction books; 10% novels.
Member Agents: Donald Lehr, Carla Glasser, Jennifer Alperen.
Represents: Nonfiction books. Query with outline. No fax queries. Considers simultaneous and submissions. Reports in 3 weeks on queries; 2 months on mss. Returns materials only with SASE.
Recent Sales: Sold 30 titles in the last year. *Desperation Dinners*, by Beverly Mills and Alicia Ross (Workman); *Bridgehampton Weekends*, by Ellen Wright (William Morrow).
Terms: Agent receives 15% commission on domestic sales; 20% on foreign sales.

◎ NONFICTION PUBLISHING PROJECTS, 12 Rally Court, Fairfax CA 94930. This agency did not respond to our request for information. Query before submitting.

✓ ◎ THE NORMA-LEWIS AGENCY, 311 W. 43rd St., Suite 602, New York NY 10036. (212)664-0807. **Contact:** Norma Liebert. Estab. 1980. 50% of clients are new/previously unpublished writers. Specializes in juvenile books (pre-school to high school). Currently handles: 60% juvenile books; 40% adult books.

Represents: Juvenile and adult nonfiction and fiction, miniseries, documentaries, movie scripts, TV scripts, radio scripts, stage plays. **Considers these nonfiction areas:** art/architecture/design; biography/autobiography; child guidance/parenting; cooking/food/nutrition; crafts/hobbies; current affairs; ethnic/cultural interests; government/politics/law; health/medicine; history; juvenile nonfiction; music/dance/theater/film; nature/environment; photography; popular culture; self-help/personal improvement; true crime/investigative; women's issues/women's studies. **Considers these fiction areas:** action/adventure; contemporary issues; detective/police/crime; family saga; historical; horror; humor/satire; juvenile; mainstream; mystery/suspense; picture book; romance (contemporary, gothic, historical, regency); thriller/espionage; westerns/frontier; young adult.

How to Contact: Query with SASE. Prefers to be only reader. Reports in 6 weeks. Returns materials only with SASE.

Recent Sales: *Viper Quarry* and *Pitchfork Hollow*, both by Dean Feldmeyer (Pocket Books).

Terms: Agent receives 15% commission on domestic sales; 20% on foreign sales.

NORTHWEST LITERARY SERVICES, 4570 Walkley Ave., #8, Montreal, Quebec H4B 2K6 Canada. (514)487-0960. **Contact:** Brent Laughren. Estab. 1986. Represents 20 clients. 20% of clients are new/previously unpublished writers. Currently handles: 45% nonfiction books; 55% novels.

• Prior to becoming an agent, Mr. Laughren was a freelance editor, creative writing instructor, librarian, archivist and journalist.

Represents: Nonfiction books, novels. **Considers these nonfiction areas:** agriculture/horticulture; animals; biography/autobiography; child guidance/parenting; cooking/food/nutrition; ethnic/cultural interests; how-to; memoirs; nature/environment; New Age/metaphysics; self-help/personal improvement; translations; travel; true crime/investigative; women's issues/women's studies. **Considers these fiction areas:** action/adventure; confessional; contemporary issues; detective/police/crime; ethnic; experimental; family saga; feminist; historical; humor/satire; literary; mainstream; mystery/suspense; psychic/supernatural; romance; science fiction; thriller/espionage; westerns/frontier.

How to Contact: Query with outline/proposal. Reports in 1 month on queries; 2 months on mss.

Needs: Obtains new clients through recommendations.

Recent Sales: Prefers not to share information on specific sales. Clients include Ann Diamond and Bryanna Clark Grugan.

Terms: Agent receives 15% on domestic sales; 20% on foreign sales. Offers written contract.

Tips: "Northwest Literary Services will no longer be charging reading fees but now prefers to work with established writers."

HAROLD OBER ASSOCIATES, 425 Madison Ave., New York NY 10017. (212)759-8600. Fax: (212)759-9428. Estab. 1929. Member of AAR. Represents 250 clients. 10% of clients are new/previously unpublished writers. Currently handles: 35% nonfiction books; 15% juvenile books; 50% novels.

Member Agents: Phyllis Westberg, Wendy Schmalz, Emma Sweeney, Chris Byrne.

Represents: Nonfiction books, juvenile books, novels. **Considers all nonfiction and fiction subjects.**

How to Contact: Query letter *only* with SASE; faxed queries are not read. Reports in 1 week on queries; 3 weeks on mss.

Needs: Obtains new clients through recommendations from others.

Recent Sales: Prefers not to share information on specific sales.

Terms: Agent receives 15% commission on domestic sales; 20% on foreign sales. Charges for photocopying and express mail or package services.

FIFI OSCARD AGENCY INC., 24 W. 40th St., New York NY 10018. (212)764-1100. **Contact:** Ivy Fischer Stone, Literary Department. Estab. 1956. Member of AAR, signatory of WGA. Represents 108 clients. 5% of clients are new/unpublished writers. Specializes in literary novels, commercial novels, mysteries and nonfiction, especially celebrity biographies and autobiographies. Currently handles: 40% nonfiction books; 40% novels; 5% movie scripts; 10% stage plays; 5% TV scripts.

Member Agents: Carolyn French (plays).

Represents: Nonfiction books, novels, movie scripts, stage plays.

How to Contact: Query with outline and SASE. Prefers to be only reader. Reports in 1 week on queries if SASE enclosed. No unsolicited mss please. Returns materials only with SASE.

Recent Sales: *Dead Center*, by James MacGregor Burns and Georgia J. Sorenson (Scribner); *Get a Life*, by William Shatner (Pocket Books); *Groucho Marx, Private Eye*, by Ron Goulart (St. Martin's Press); **Movie/TV MOW scripts optioned/sold:** *Wit*, by Margaret Edson (The Wit L.L.C.).

Terms: Agent receives 15% commission on domestic sales; 10% on dramatic sales; 20% on foreign sales. Charges for photocopying expenses.

Tips: "Writer must have published articles or books in major markets or have screen credits if movie scripts, etc."

OTITIS MEDIA, 1926 DuPont Ave. S., Minneapolis MN 55403. (612)377-4918. Fax: (612)377-3046. E-mail: brbotm19@skypoint.com. **Contact:** Hannibal Harris. Signatory of WGA. Currently handles: novels; nonfiction books.

Represents: Nonfiction books, novels. **Considers these nonfiction areas:** anthropology/archaeology; biography/autobiography; health/medicine; history; humor; military/war; music/dance/theater/film; photography; true crime/investigative. **Considers these fiction areas:** historical; humor/satire; mainstream; thriller/espionage.

How to Contact: Send query. "We prefer e-mail queries, not phone queries." Considers simultaneous queries. Returns materials only with SASE.

Recent Sales: Prefers not to share information on specific sales.

Terms: Agent receives 15% on domestic sales; 20% on foreign sales. Offers written contract. "We prefer that the writer supply additional copies of all manuscripts."

Tips: "Seminars or classes in creative writing alone are insufficient to attract our attention. You should be constantly writing and rewriting before you submit your first work. Correct format, spelling and grammar are essential. We shall respond quickly to a query letter containing a one page outline, a list of your writing credits, and the opening ten pages of only *one* work at a time. Forget the SASE. We do not return manuscripts. Please, in your query letter, try not to be cute, clever, or hardsell. Save us all the time of having to read about what your relatives, friends, teachers, paid 'editors' or gurus think about your story. Nor do we need a pitch about who will want this book or movie, spend money for it and how much it will earn for writer, editor/producer, and agent. You should, in a few short paragraphs, be able to summarize the work to the point where we'll ask for more. We are appalled to receive works whose cover page is dated and who indicate that this is a first draft. No producer or editor is likely to read a first draft of anything. Please don't call us. We'll contact you if we want more."

PARAVIEW, INC., 1674 Broadway, Suite 4B, New York NY 10019. E-mail: paraview@inch.com. **Contact:** Sandra Martin. Estab. 1988. Represents 120 clients. 50% of clients are new/previously unpublished writers. Specializes in spiritual, New Age and paranormal. Currently handles: 90% nonfiction books; 10% scholarly books.

Member Agents: Sandra Martin (nonfiction); Lisa Hagan (fiction and nonfiction).

Represents: Nonfiction and fiction books. **Considers all nonfiction areas. Considers these fiction areas:** action/adventure; contemporary issues; ethnic; feminist; historical; literary; mainstream; psychic/supernatural; regional; romance; thriller/espionage.

How to Contact: Query with synopsis, author bio and SASE. Reports in 1 month on queries; 3 months on mss.

Recent Sales: *The Coming Global Superstorm*, by Art Bell and Whitley Strieber (Pocket Books); *UFOs, JFK & Elvis: Conspiracies You Don't Have to Be Crazy to Believe*, by Richard Belzer (Ballantine); *Writings On the Wall*, by Paula Roberts (Element); *Dog Whisperer*, by Paul Owens (Adams Media); *Wicca for Women*, by Sirona Knight (Carol); *Cyberflirt*, by Susan Rabin (Dutton).

Needs: Obtains new clients through recommendations from editors mostly.

Terms: Agent receives 15% commission on domestic sales; 20% on foreign sales. Charges for photocopying and delivery.

Writers' Conferences: BEA (Chicago, June); E3—Electronic Entertainment Exposition.

Tips: "New writers should have their work edited, critiqued and carefully reworked prior to submission. First contact should be via regular mail."

THE RICHARD PARKS AGENCY, 138 E. 16th St., 5th Floor, New York NY 10003. (212)254-9067. **Contact:** Richard Parks. Estab. 1988. Member of AAR. Currently handles: 50% nonfiction books; 5% young adult books; 40% novels; 5% short story collections.

• Prior to opening his agency, Mr. Parks served as an agent with Curtis Brown, Ltd.

Represents: Nonfiction books, novels. **Considers these nonfiction areas:** animals; anthopology/archaeology; art/architecture/design; biography/autobiography; business; child guidance/parenting; cooking/food/nutrition; crafts/hobbies; current affairs; ethnic/cultural interests; gay/lesbian issues; government/politics; health/medicine; history; horticulture; how-to; humor; language/literature/criticism; memoirs; military/war; money/finance/economics; music/dance/theater/film; nature/environment; popular culture; psychology; science/technology; self-help/personal improvement; sociology; travel; women's issues/women's studies. **Considers fiction by referral only.**

How to Contact: Query by mail only with SASE. No call, faxes or e-mails, please. "We will not accept any unsolicited material." Reports in 2 weeks on queries. Returns materials only with SASE.

Needs: Actively seeking narrative nonfiction. Does not want to receive unsolicited material. Obtains new clients through recommendations and referrals.

Recent Sales: *A House Named Brazil*, by Audrey Schulman (Bard Books); *Chasing Che*, by Patrick Symmes (Vintage); *Exiting Nirvana*, by Clara Claiborne Park (Little, Brown); *User*, by Blake Nelson (Incommunicado); *Frames Per Second*, by Bill Eidson (TOR); *Double Dealer*, by Barbara Taylor McCafferty and Beverly Taylor Herald (Kensington).

Terms: Agent receives 15% commission on domestic sales; 20% on foreign sales. Charges for photocopying or any unusual expense incurred at the writer's request.

KATHI J. PATON LITERARY AGENCY, 19 W. 55th St., New York NY 10019-4907. (212)265-6586. E-mail: kpjlitbiz@aol.com. **Contact:** Kathi Paton. Estab. 1987. Specializes in adult nonfiction. Currently handles: 65% nonfiction books; 35% fiction.

Represents: Nonfiction, novels, short story collections. **Considers these nonfiction areas:** business; child guidance/

TO FIND AN AGENT near you, check the Geographic Index.

parenting; inspirational; personal investing; how-to; nature/environment; psychology; women's issues/women's studies. **Considers literary and mainstream fiction; short stories.**

How to Contact: For nonfiction, send proposal, sample chapter and SASE. For fiction, send first 40 pages, plot summary or 3 short stories and SASE. Accepts queries by e-mail. Considers simultaneous queries and submissions. Returns materials only with SASE.

Needs: Usually obtains new clients through recommendations from other clients.

Recent Sales: *Future Wealth*, by McInerney and White (St. Martin's Press); *White Trash, Red Velvet*, by Donald Secreast (HarperCollins); *The Home Environmental Sourcebook*, by Andrew Davis and Paul Schaffman (Holt).

Terms: Agent receives 15% commission on domestic sales; 20% on foreign sales. Offers written contract. Charges for photocopying.

Writers' Conferences: Attends major regional panels, seminars and conferences.

Tips: "Write well."

♥ RODNEY PELTER, 129 E. 61st St., New York NY 10021. (212)838-3432. **Contact:** Rodney Pelter. Estab. 1978. Represents 10 clients.

Represents: Nonfiction books, novels. **Considers all nonfiction areas. Considers most fiction areas.** No juvenile; romance; science fiction.

How to Contact: Query with SASE. No unsolicited mss. Reports in 3 months.

Needs: Usually obtains new clients through recommendations from others.

Recent Sales: Prefers not to share information on specific sales.

Terms: Agent receives 15% commission on domestic sales; 20% on foreign sales. Offers written contract. Charges for foreign postage, photocopying.

◎ PERKINS, RUBIE & ASSOCIATES, 240 W. 35th St., Suite 500, New York NY 10001. (212)279-1776. Fax: (212)279-0927. **Contact:** Lori Perkins, Peter Rubie. Estab. 1997. Member of AAR, HWA. Represents 130 clients. 15% of clients are new/previously unpublished writers. Perkins specializes in horror, dark thrillers, literary fiction, pop culture, Latino and gay issues (fiction and nonfiction). Rubie specializes in crime, science fiction, fantasy, off-beat mysteries, history, literary fiction, dark thrillers, narrative nonfiction. Currently handles: 60% nonfiction books; 40% novels.

● Lori Perkins is the author of *The Cheapskate's Guide to Entertaining; How to Throw Fabulous Parties on a Budget* (Carol Publishing) and *Insider's Guide to Getting an Agent* (Writer's Digest Books). Prior to becoming an agent, she taught journalism at NYU. Mr. Rubie is the author of 2 novels and several nonfiction books, including *The Elements of Storytelling* (John Wiley) and *How to Tell a Story* (Writer's Digest Books).

Represents: Nonfiction books, novels. **Considers these nonfiction areas:** art/architecture/design; current affairs; commercial academic material; ethnic/cultural interests; music/dance/theater/film; science; "subjects that fall under pop culture—TV, music, art, books and authors, film, current affairs etc." **Considers these fiction areas:** detective/police/crime; ethnic; fact-based historical fiction; fantasy; horror; literary; mainstream; mystery/suspense; psychic/supernatural; science fiction; dark thriller.

How to Contact: Query with SASE. Reports in 3-6 weeks on queries with SASE; 10 weeks on mss.

Needs: Obtains new clients through recommendations from others, solicitation, at conferences, etc.

Recent Sales: *Mary Rogers*, by Randal Silvis (St. Martins); *Terrorists of Irustan*, by Louise Marley (Berkley); *The Science of Star Wars*, by Jeanne Cavelos (St. Martin's); *Smoker*, by Gregory Rucka (Bantam).

Terms: Agent receives 15% commission on domestic sales; 20% on foreign sales. Offers written contract, only "if requested." Charges for photocopying.

Tips: "Sometimes we come up with book ideas and find authors (*Coupon Queen*, for example). Be professional. Read *Publishers Weekly* and genre-related magazines. Join writers' organizations. Go to conferences. Know your market and learn your craft."

✔ ◑ STEPHEN PEVNER, INC., 248 W. 73rd St., 2nd Floor, New York NY 10023. (212)496-0474. Also: 450 N. Rossmore Ave., Los Angeles CA 90004. (323)464-5546. Fax: (323)464-5588. E-mail: spevner@aol.com. **Contact:** Stephen Pevner. Estab. 1991. Member of AAR. Represents under 50 clients. 50% of clients are new/previously unpublished writers. Specializes in motion pictures, novels, humor, pop culture, urban fiction, independent filmmakers. Currently handles: 25% nonfiction books; 25% movie scripts; 25% novels; TV scripts; stage plays.

Represents: Nonfiction books, novels, movie scripts, TV scripts, stage plays. **Considers these nonfiction areas:** biography/autobiography; ethnic/cultural interests; gay/lesbian issues; history; humor; language/literature/criticism; memoirs; music/dance/theater/film; New Age/metaphysics; photography; popular culture; religious/inspirational; sociology; travel. **Considers these fiction areas:** cartoon/comic; contemporary issues; erotica; ethnic; experimental; gay; glitz; horror; humor/satire; lesbian; literary; mainstream; psychic/supernatural; thriller/espionage; urban.

Also Handles: Feature film, documentary, animation; TV MOW, miniseries, episodic drama; theatrical stage plays. **Considers these script subject areas:** comedy; contemporary issues; detective/police/crime; gay; glitz; horror; humor; lesbian; mainstream; romantic comedy and drama; teen; thriller.

How to Contact: Query with outline/proposal. Reports in 2 weeks on queries; 1 month on mss.

Needs: Actively seeking urban fiction, popular culture, screenplays and film proposals. Obtains new clients through recommendations from others.

Recent Sales: *Your Friends and Neighbors*, by Bash; *The Vagina Monologues*, by Eve Ensler; *Guide to Life*, by The Five Lesbian Brothers; *Noise From the Underground*, by Michael Levine. Other clients include Richard Linklater

(*Slacker, Dazed & Confused, Before Sunrise*); Gregg Araki (*The Living End, Doom Generation*); Tom DiCillo (*Living in Oblivion*); Genvieve Turner/Rose Troche (*Go Fish*); Todd Solondz (*Welcome to the Dollhouse*); Neil LaBute (*In the Company of Men*).

Terms: Agent receives 15% commission on domestic sales; 20% on foreign sales. Offers written contract, binding for 1 year, with 6 week cancellation clause. 100% of business is derived from commissions on sales.

Tips: "Be persistent, but civilized."

PINDER LANE & GARON-BROOKE ASSOCIATES, LTD., 159 W. 53rd St., Suite 14E, New York NY 10019-6005. (212)489-0880. **Contact:** Jean Free, vice president. Member of AAR, signatory of WGA. Represents 80 clients. 20% of clients are new/previously unpublished writers. Specializes in mainstream fiction and nonfiction. Currently handles: 25% nonfiction books; 75% novels.

Member Agents: Nancy Coffey, Dick Duane, Robert Thixton, Jean Free.

Represents: Nonfiction books, novels. **Considers these nonfiction areas:** biography/autobiography; child guidance/parenting; gay/lesbian issues; health/medicine; history; memoirs; military/war; music/dance/theater/film; psychology; self-help/personal improvement; true crime/investigative. **Considers these fiction areas:** contemporary issues; detective/police/crime; family saga; fantasy; gay; literary; mainstream; mystery/suspense; romance; science fiction.

How to Contact: Query with SASE. Reports in 3 weeks on queries; 2 months on mss.

Needs: Does not want to receive screenplays, TV series teleplays or dramatic plays. Obtains new clients through referrals and from queries.

Recent Sales: Sold 15 titles in the last year. *Nobody's Safe*, by Richard Steinberg (Doubleday); *The Kill Box*, by Chris Stewart (M. Evans); *Return to Christmas*, by Chris Heimerdinger (Ballantine).

Terms: Agent receives 15% on domestic sales; 30% on foreign sales. Offers written contract, binding for 3-5 years.

Tips: "With our literary and media experience, our agency is uniquely positioned for the current and future direction publishing is taking. Send query letter first giving the essence of the manuscript and a personal or career bio with SASE."

ARTHUR PINE ASSOCIATES, INC., 250 W. 57th St., New York NY 10019. (212)265-7330. Fax: (212)265-4650. Estab. 1966. Represents 100 clients. 25% of clients are new/previously unpublished writers. Specializes in fiction and nonfiction. Currently handles: 60% nonfiction; 40% novels.

Member Agents: Richard Pine; Arthur Pine; Lori Andiman; Sarah Piel.

Represents: Nonfiction books, novels. **Considers these nonfiction areas:** business; current affairs; health/medicine; money/finance/economics; psychology; self-help/personal improvement. **Considers these fiction areas:** detective/police/crime; family saga; literary; mainstream; romance; thriller/espionage.

How to Contact: Send outline/proposal. Reports in 3 weeks on queries. "All correspondence must be accompanied by a SASE. Will not read manuscripts before receiving a letter of inquiry."

Needs: Obtains new clients through recommendations from others.

Recent Sales: *Cat and Mouse*, by James Patterson (Little, Brown & Warner Books); *Numbered Account*, by Christopher Reich (Delacorte); *Eight Weeks to Optimum Health*, by Andrew Weil, M.D. (Knopf).

Terms: Agency receives 15% commission on domestic sales; 20% on foreign sales. Offers written contract. Charges for photocopying.

Tips: "Our agency will consider exclusive submissions only. All submissions must be accompanied by postage or SASE."

PREFERRED ARTISTS TALENT AGENCY, (formerly HWA Talent Reps), 16633 Ventura Blvd., Suite 1421, Encino CA 91436. (818)990-0305. Fax: (818)990-2736. **Contact:** Kimber Wheeler. Estab. 1985. Signatory of WGA. 90% of clients are new/previously unpublished writers. Currently handles: 90% movie scripts, 10% novels.

● See the expanded listing for this agency in Script Agents.

AARON M. PRIEST LITERARY AGENCY, 708 Third Ave., 23rd Floor, New York NY 10017. (212)818-0344. Fax: (212)573-9417. **Contact:** Aaron Priest or Molly Friedrich. Estab. 1974. Member of AAR. Currently handles: 25% nonfiction books; 75% fiction.

Member Agents: Lisa Erbach Vance, Paul Cirone, Wendy Sherman.

Represents: Nonfiction books, fiction.

How to Contact: Query only (must be accompanied by SASE). Unsolicited mss will be returned unread.

Recent Sales: *Absolute Power*, by David Baldacci (Warner); *Three To Get Deadly*, by Janet Evanovich (Scribner); *How Stella Got Her Groove Back*, by Terry McMillan (Viking); *Day After Tomorrow*, by Allan Folsom (Little, Brown); *Angela's Ashes*, by Frank McCourt (Scribner); *M as in Malice*, by Sue Grafton (Henry Holt).

Terms: Agent receives 15% commission on domestic sales. Charges for photocopying, foreign postage expenses.

SUSAN ANN PROTTER LITERARY AGENT, 110 W. 40th St., Suite 1408, New York NY 10018. (212)840-0480. **Contact:** Susan Protter. Estab. 1971. Member of AAR. Represents 40 clients. 5% of clients are new/unpublished writers. Writer must have book-length project or ms that is ready to be sold. Works with a very small number of new/unpublished authors. Currently handles: 40% nonfiction books; 60% novels; occasional magazine article or short story (for established clients only).

● Prior to opening her agency, Ms. Protter was associate director of subsidiary rights at Harper & Row Publishers.

Agent Molly Friedrich: powerhouse

Molly Friedrich is one of a handful of literary agents in New York who has the power to propel her clients from the breadline to the bank line. Over the past 21 years, she's made dozens of megadollar deals and has become one of the most sought-after representatives in the literary world, and her client list is heavy with household names.

Friedrich's first job in the industry was as an intern with Doubleday; later, she worked in Anchor Press's publicity department. Agent Aaron Priest—making it very clear that he didn't intend to train another agent for his office—hired her as his assistant in January 1978. Friedrich carried out a clandestine apprenticeship, observing her boss at work and acquainting herself with key players at each publishing house. A few months after Friedrich was hired, her boss drove cross-country with his family to explore a possible move to California. When he reached his destination, he called his assistant for an office update; what she told him changed her job description abruptly. In the time it took him to drive coast-to-coast, she had sold three books.

The contacts Friedrich made as an assistant became the foundation of her success as an agent. "This is a very social business," she says. "The absolute job of the agent is to know who's buying what and what's happening with them; if I didn't know that, I might as well not get up in the morning. You have to know who's on a honeymoon, who's just lost an auction and is flush with money to spend. All this is done over lunch."

Friedrich chooses her potential buyers very carefully, and the market varies with every book. After carefully assessing a book's potential, Friedrich chooses a small group of editors who are appropriate for the manuscript. If several are interested, she'll set up an auction: each editor offers a confidential bid to Friedrich. "I'm working for the author, and the author has final say over which bid will be taken. Money isn't the only factor—sometimes an author will meet with an editor and feel they don't have a mutual understanding of the material—then that publisher would be out of the running."

Friedrich receives about 200 queries a week, either an introductory-letter-plus-synopsis or a letter that combines the two. Of these, five percent will be good, and of those, four percent "are just not for me." Friedrich will recommend other agents in this case, though she's cautious about making promises beyond her control. "When I read a manuscript, I know if I want to represent it in the first five pages," she says. "When I read the single-spaced manuscript of Frank McCourt's *Angela's Ashes*, I set it down after a few pages and said, 'This is it, this is why I'm an agent.' It's that quick." If she feels a book shows great potential but needs more work, she'll send it to up to three editors and get their feedback for the author.

Meeting and representing great writers requires building a reputation over time, developing "different arteries." "My writers come to me in complex and elaborate ways," says Friedrich. "The first short story collection I sold, by Maxine Claire, is an example. She did a reading of her work somewhere, and a woman came up to her and said, 'Do you have more of those? If so, send them to Molly Friedrich. Tell her Jackie sent you.' I read the stories—I really loved them—and I sent the manuscript out to four or five editors and got offers. To this day, I still don't know who Jackie is."

Author Frances Park sent queries for her tale of two Korean girls, *When My Sister Was Cleopatra Moon* to several agents, including Friedrich. "She knew her stuff—she knew who my clients were and what I had been doing. Some authors really do keep up with *Publishers Weekly!*" Two other agents wanted the book, but Park chose to wait for Friedrich to finish reading the manuscript. "You're my dream agent," she wrote. Friedrich liked the "aggressively charming" story and placed the book within a few weeks.

Friedrich has worked with several first-time authors. New writers often come to her notice via query letters. "Not the ones with pale purple script or a photo of an author holding her cat. People have sent macadamia nuts, artwork—any number of things to get us to look at their manuscripts. But it's the writing that counts. I look for queries that aren't generic; if it's personable and interesting, I'll read it. A good query should be like the letter you write to the sister you still get along with, telling her about the novel you've written and why it works for you. It shows your personality."

Friedrich believes a good author will not have to wait to be published posthumously. "Unfortunately, a lot of bad writing is published, and that confuses people; some authors see bad writing and wonder why their work isn't on the bookstands. Writers need to read the best examples of published work and strive for it. A great writer will be published, and a great book stays in your mind. I read *To Kill a Mockingbird* when I was very young, and I still remember it. But if you ask me to tell you the plot, I'd ramble on about a lawyer in the South, big case, etc. Why does an outstanding book stay in our memories? It's a combination of plot, characters and an original voice." Friedrich further defines her three touchstones: "By plot, I mean a fresh cast on a plot—there are no new plots; characters who are fully realized; and, most important, an original voice. Read any passage from *Bonfire of the Vanities*, any passage—whether he's describing furniture or the weather—and you'll know within minutes that it's Tom Wolfe. That's an original voice."

Though Friedrich favors "long, flawed, ambitious novels," she's placed two short story collections: "They were so good, I had to represent them." One of those short story collections was *The Girls' Guide to Hunting and Fishing* (Viking), by Melissa Bank. At some point, Friedrich believes, a good author will reach critical mass, so that anything he or she writes will sell, and people will ask each other if they've read the new "Lorrie Moore" rather than referring to the book by title. "That's the agent's dream," she says.

To what does she attribute her great success? "If you have good material even a bad agent can sell it. A good agent can do a little better, and a great agent can make a difference in a writer's life."

Friedrich chivalrously rejects naming a favorite author or book she has represented. "How could I choose between Terry Macmillan's *Mama* or Jane Smiley's *A Thousand Acres*? I loved both those books. I only represent books I love. My client list is closed, but if I come upon something good enough, I'll represent it. A good agent has to be accessible."

When submitting work to an agent, Friedrich suggests that, "Writers should think of quality first, rather than form. A great writer is destined to be published, and if you're good enough, you can break every rule."

—*Joanne Miller*

Represents: Nonfiction books, novels. **Considers these nonfiction areas:** biography; health/medicine; memoirs; psychology; science. **Considers these fiction areas:** crime; mystery; science fiction, thrillers. **Also considers most general novel categories.** Does not want to receive westerns, romance, fantasy, children's books, young adult novels, screenplays, plays, poetry, Star Wars or Star Trek.

How to Contact: *Not currently accepting new clients.* Send short query with brief description of project/novel, publishing history and SASE. Reports in 3 weeks on queries; 2 months on solicited mss. "Please do not call; mail queries only. No bound manuscripts. Double-spaced and single-sided only."

Recent Sales: *Teenage Body Book*, by K. McCoy, Ph.D. and C. Wibhelsman, MD. (Perigree/Putnam); *The Pickup Artist*, by Cary Bisson (TOR); *Spirit of the Sun Child*, by Lyn Armistead McKee (NAL/Penguin); *Five Steps to Finding Chronic Pain*, by Art Klein (Robinson).

Terms: Agent receives 15% commission on domestic sales; 15% on TV, film and dramatic sales; 25% on foreign sales. "If we request to see your manuscript, there is a $10 handling fee requested to cover cost of returning materials should they not be suitable." Charges for long distance, photocopying, messenger, express mail, airmail expenses.

Tips: "Please send neat and professionally organized queries. Make sure to include an SASE or we cannot reply. We receive up to 200 queries a week and read them in the order they arrive. We usually reply within two weeks to any query. Please, do not call. If you are sending a multiple query, make sure to note that in your letter."

○ **QUICKSILVER BOOKS-LITERARY AGENTS**, 50 Wilson St., Hartsdale NY 10530-2542. Phone/fax: (914)946-8748. **Contact:** Bob Silverstein. Estab. 1973 as packager; 1987 as literary agency. Represents 50 clients. 50% of clients are new/previously unpublished writers. Specializes in literary and commercial mainstream fiction and nonfiction (especially psychology, New Age, holistic healing, consciousness, ecology, environment, spirituality, reference). Currently handles: 75% nonfiction books; 25% novels.

● Prior to opening his agency, Mr. Silverstein served as senior editor at Bantam Books and Dell Books/Delacorte Press.

Represents: Nonfiction books, novels. **Considers these nonfiction areas:** anthropology/archaeology; biography; business; child guidance/parenting; cooking/food/nutrition; current affairs; ethnic/cultural interests; health/medicine; history; how-to; literature; memoirs; nature/environment; New Age/metaphysics; popular culture; psychology; inspirational; science/technology; self-help/personal improvement; sociology; sports; true crime/investigative; women's issues/women's studies. **Considers these fiction areas:** action/adventure; glitz; mystery/suspense; thrillers.

How to Contact: Query. Authors are expected to supply SASE for return of mss and for query letter responses. Considers simultaneous queries. Reports in up to 2 weeks on queries; up to 1 month on mss. Returns materials only with SASE.

Needs: Actively seeking commercial mainstream fiction and nonfiction in most categories. Does not want to receive "science fiction; pornography; poetry; single-spaced manuscripts!!" Obtains new clients through recommendations, listings in sourcebooks, solicitations, workshop participation.

Recent Sales: Sold 14 titles in the last year. *Beating Arthritis Naturally*, by Ellen Brown (Doubleday); *Autobiography of Dick Gregory*, by Dick Gregory with Shelia Moses (Longstreet Press); *The Winds of Time*, by Victor Daniels (Eagle Brook/Morrow).

Terms: Agent receives 15% commission on domestic sales; 20% on foreign sales. Offers written contract, "only if requested. It is open ended, unless author requests time frame, usually one year."

Writers' Conferences: National Writers Union Conference (Dobbs Ferry NY, April).

🔲○ **RAINES & RAINES**, 71 Park Ave., Suite 44A, New York NY 10016. This agency did not respond to our request for information. Query before submitting.

🔲● **CHARLOTTE CECIL RAYMOND, LITERARY AGENT**, 32 Bradlee Rd., Marblehead MA 01945. **Contact:** Charlotte Cecil Raymond. Estab. 1983. Currently handles: 100% nonfiction books.

Represents: Nonfiction books. **Considers these nonfiction areas:** biography; current affairs; ethnic/cultural/gender interests; history; nature/environment; psychology; sociology. No self-help/personal improvement.

How to Contact: Query with outline/proposal and SASE. Reports in 2 weeks on queries; 6 weeks on mss.

Recent Sales: Prefers not to share information on specific sales.

Terms: Agent receives 15% commission on domestic sales. 100% of business derived from commissions on ms sales.

🔲○◎ **REAL CRIMINALS**, 122 E. 7th St., #4FW, New York NY 10009. (212)477-3579. E-mail: marti.hohmann @worldnet.att.net. **Contact:** Marti Hohmann. Represents 2 clients. Specializes in true crime, erotica, World Wide Web expertise. Currently handles: 50% nonfiction books; 25% story collections; 25% novels.

● Prior to becoming an agent, Marti Hohmann was editor-in-chief at Masquerade Books.

Represents: Considers these nonfiction areas: true crime/investigative. **Considers these fiction areas:** detective/police/crime; erotica; mystery. Also handles website sponsorship.

How to Contact: Send outline/proposal. Accepts queries by e-mail. Prefers to be only reader. Reports in 1 month. Returns material only with SASE.

Needs: Actively seeking true crime mss and screenplays, and erotic fiction. Obtains new clients through referrals.

Recent Sales: New agency with no reported sales.

Terms: Agent receives 10% commission on domestic sales; 15% on foreign sales. Offers written contract. 6-month notice must be given to terminate contract. Editing service included with representation. 0% of business is derived from editing service.

✓ ⊘ ◉ **HELEN REES LITERARY AGENCY**, 123 N. Washington St., 5th Floor, Boston MA 02114. (617)723-5232, ext. 233 or 222. **Contact:** Joan Mazmanian. Estab. 1981. Member of AAR. Represents 50 clients. 50% of clients are new/previously unpublished writers. Specializes in general nonfiction, health, business, world politics, autobiographies, psychology, women's issues. Currently handles: 60% nonfiction books; 40% novels.
Represents: Nonfiction books, novels. **Considers these nonfiction areas:** biography/autobiography; business; current affairs; government/politics/law; health/medicine; history; money/finance/economics; women's issues/women's studies. **Considers these fiction areas:** contemporary issues; historical; literary; mainstream; mystery/suspense; thriller/espionage.
How to Contact: Query with outline plus 2 sample chapters and SASE. Reports in 2 weeks on queries; 3 weeks on mss.
Needs: Obtains new clients through recommendations from others, solicitation, at conferences, etc.
Recent Sales: *The Mentor*, by Sebastian Stuart (Bantam); *Managing the Human Animal*, by Nigel Nicholson (Times Books); *Just Revenge*, by Alan Dershowitz (Warner).
Terms: Agent receives 15% commission on domestic sales; 20% on foreign sales.

✓ ⊘ **THE NAOMI REICHSTEIN LITERARY AGENCY**, PMB 136, 333 S. State St., Suite V, Lake Oswego OR 97034-3961. (503)636-7575. **Contact:** Naomi Wittes Reichstein. Estab. 1997. Specializes in "literary fiction, serious nonfiction, history, cultural issues, the arts, how-to, science, the environment, psychology, literature, memoirs, creative nonfiction, self-help."
Represents: Nonfiction books, novels. **Considers these nonfiction areas:** animals; anthropology/archaeology; art/architecture/design; biography/autobiography; business; child guidance/parenting; computers/electronics; cooking/food/nutrition; crafts/hobbies; current affairs; education; ethnic/cultural interests; gay/lesbian issues; government/politics/law; health/medicine; history; how-to; interior design/decorating; language/literature/criticism; money/finance/economics; music/dance/theater/film; nature/environment; popular culture; psychology; science/technology; self-help/personal improvement; sociology; sports; true crime/investigative; women's issues/women's studies. **Considers these fiction areas:** literary; mainstream; mystery/suspense; thriller.
How to Contact: "Query with 1-page letter and SASE. No phone calls, faxes or unsolicited manuscripts. Queries sent without SASE will not be answered." Considers simultaneous queries and submissions, with notification. Reports in 1 month on queries; 6 weeks on mss. Returns materials only with SASE.
Needs: Usually obtains new clients "through recommendations from editors, writers, workshop directors and clients of the agency. I also consider non-referred queries." Authors should have been published previously or else (for nonfiction) be expert in the areas in which they write.
Recent Sales: *The Stranger's Craft*, by Kim Todd (W.W. Norton & Co.); *Aleph Beit Cards*, by Richard Seidman (St. Martin's Press).
Terms: Agent receives 15% commission on domestic sales; 20% on foreign sales. "I don't charge fees, but I may deduct reimbursement out of earnings for documented out-of-pocket expenses such as international calls and faxes, international postage and courier services, domestic messenger services, bank fees for international transfers and wiring funds to clients, charges for photocopying manuscripts, proposals and publicity materials for submission, certified and registered mail, and legal fees authorized by clients. If earnings are insufficient to support such deductions, I might send a bill to the client."
Tips: "In book proposals for nonfiction, I look for originality, quality of writing, consciousness of market, and authorial background. I value organization, grace of expression, seriousness and credibility, not gimmicks or 'overselling.' In fiction, I look for beautiful writing, engaging characters, and plots that draw me in. I am attracted to queries that are courteous and carefully proofread (a meticulous query indicates a meticulous writer) and that tell me in some detail what the books say rather than how good they are or how appropriate for film. Writers are well advised to learn from the existing publishing guides and, if possible, from other writers which agents handle the genres in which they are writing. And it's always wise to obtain references."

◉ **JODY REIN BOOKS, INC.**, 7741 S. Ash Court, Littleton CO 80122. (303)694-4430. **Contact:** Winnefred Dollar. Estab. 1994. Member of AAR and Authors Guild. Specializes in commercial nonfiction. Currently handles: 80% nonfiction books; 20% literary fiction.

**FOR EXPLANATIONS OF THESE SYMBOLS,
SEE THE INSIDE FRONT AND BACK COVERS OF THIS BOOK**

• Prior to opening an agency, Jody Rein worked for 13 years as an acquisitions editor for Contemporary Books, Bantam/Doubleday/Dell and Morrow/Avon.

Represents: Nonfiction books; literary novels. **Considers these nonfiction areas:** animals; business; child guidance/parenting; current affairs; ethnic/cultural interests; government/politics/law; health/medicine; history; how-to; humor; music/dance/theater/film; nature/environment; popular culture; psychology; religious/inspirational; science/technology; self-help/personal improvement; sociology; women's issues/women's studies. **Considers these fiction areas:** literary.

How to Contact: Query with SASE. Responds in 6 weeks on queries; 2 months on mss.

Needs: Obtains new clients through recommendations from others.

Recent Sales: *Think Like a Genius*, by Todd Siler (Bantam); *The ADDed Dimension*, by Kate Kelly (Scribner); *Beethoven's Hair*, by Russell Martin (Broadway Books); *Heart of Oak Sea Classics*, by Dean King (Holt).

Terms: Agent receives 15% commission on domestic sales; 25% on foreign sales. Offers a written contract. Charges for express mail, overseas expenses and ms photocopying.

Tips: "Do your homework before submitting. Make sure you have a marketable topic *and* the credentials to write about it. We want well-written books on exciting nonfiction topics that have broad appeal. Authors must be well established in their fields, and have strong media experience."

RENAISSANCE LITERARY AGENCY, (formerly Renaissance—H.N. Swanson), 9220 Sunset Blvd., Suite 302, Los Angeles CA 90069. (310)858-5365. **Contact:** Joel Gotler. Member of SAG, AFTRA, DGA. Represents 250 clients. 10% of clients are new/previously unpublished writers. Specializes in selling movies and TV rights from books. Currently handles: 90% novels; 10% movie and TV scripts.

Member Agents: Irv Schwartz, partner (TV writers); Joel Gotler, partner (film rights); Allan Nevins, partner (book publishing).

Represents: Nonfiction books, novels. **Considers these nonfiction areas:** biography/autobiography; history; film; true crime/investigative. **Considers these fiction areas:** action/adventure; contemporary issue; detective/police/crime; ethnic; family saga; fantasy; historical; humor/satire; literary; mainstream; mystery/suspense; science fiction; thriller/espionage.

Also Handles: Feature film. **Considers these script subject areas:** action/adventure; cartoon/animation; comedy; contemporary issues; detective/police/crime; erotica; ethnic; experimental; family saga; fantasy; feminist; gay; historical; horror; juvenile; lesbian; mainstream; mystery/suspense; psychic/supernatural; regional; romantic comedy and drama; science fiction; sports; teen; thriller/espionage; westerns;frontier.

Recent Sales: *The Late Marilyn Monroe*, by Don Wolfe (Dutton); *Movie scripts optioned/sold: I Was Amelia Earhart*, by Jane Mendohlson (New Line); *The Night Watchman*, by James Ellroy (New Regency); *Rockwood*, by Jere Cunningham (Imagine Ent.); *Scripting assignments: Merlin*, by David Stevens (RHI); *Moby Dick*, by Ben Fitzgerald (Hallmark).

How to Contact: Query with outline and SASE. Reports in 2 weeks on queries; 1 month on mss.

Needs: Obtains news clients through recommendations from others.

Terms: Agent receives 10% commission on domestic books; 10% on film sales.

JODIE RHODES LITERARY AGENCY, 8840 Villa La Jolla Dr., Suite 315, La Jolla CA 92037-1957. (858)625-0544. Website: www.writers.net.literaryagent.com. **Contact:** Jodie Rhodes, president. Estab. 1998. Represents 27 clients. 80% of clients are new/unpublished writers. Currently handles: 35% nonfiction books; 15% juvenile books; 50% novels.

• Prior to opening her agency, Ms. Rhodes was a university level creative writing teacher, workshop director, published novelist and Vice President Media Director at the N.W. Ayer Advertising Agency.

Member Agents: Jodie Rhodes, president (women's books, literary fiction, military, mystery, suspense); Clark McCutcheon (fiction); Bob McCarter (nonfiction); Dan Press (electronic, film, television and foreign rights).

Represents: Nonfiction books, juvenile books, novels. **Considers these nonfiction areas:** animals, anthropology/archaeology; biography/autobiography; business; child guidance/parenting; computers/electronics; cooking/food/nutrition; crafts/hobbies; current affairs; education; ethnic/cultural interests; gay/lesbian issues; government/politics/law; health/medicine; history; how-to; juvenile nonfiction; language/literature/criticism; memoirs; military/war; money/finance/economics; music/dance/theater/film; nature/environment; New Age/metaphysics; popular culture; psychology; religious/inspirational; science/technology; self-help/personal improvement; sports; true crime/investigative; women's issues/women's studies; books that teach people how to use and benefit from the Internet. **Considers these fiction areas:** action/adventure; contemporary issues; detective/police/crime; ethnic; family saga; fantasy; feminist; gay/lesbian; historical; juvenile; literary; mainstream; mystery; psychic/supernatural; regional; romance; science fiction; sports; thriller/espionage; westerns/frontier; young adult.

How to Contact: Query with brief synopsis, plus first 50 pages. Does not accept queries by fax or e-mail. Considers simultaneous queries and submissions. Reports in 10 days on queries; 1 month on mss. Returns materials only with SASE.

Needs: Actively seeking "writers passionate about their books with a talent for richly textured narrative and an eye for details." Does not want to receive erotica, horror, scholarly. Obtains new clients through "agent sourcebooks, Internet websites, writers who read my magazine columns, conferences, recommendations."

Recent Sales: *Infidelity: Memoir in Two Parts*, by Ann Beardman (Election Press); *Attitude Is Everything*, by Morgan Cirket (Markowski International Publishers); *Women Sing the Blues*, by Kate Hart (Election Press).

Terms: Agent receives 15% commission on domestic sales; 20% on foreign sales. Offers written contract, binding for

1 year. 60 day written notice must be given to terminate contract. Charges for fax, photocopying, phone calls and postage. "Charges are itemized and sent to writer with submission report status."
Writer's Conferences: Southern California Writers Conference (San Diego, mid-February); SDSU Writers Conference (San Diego, mid-January).
Tips: "Think your book out before you write it. Do your research, know your subject matter intimately, write vivid specifics, not bland generalities. Care deeply about your book. Don't imitate other writers. Find your own voice. We never take on a book we don't believe in and we go the extra mile for our writers. We welcome talented new writers and work to build their careers."

◙ ANGELA RINALDI LITERARY AGENCY, P.O. Box 7877, Beverly Hills CA 90212-7877. (310)842-7665. Fax: (310)837-8143. E-mail: e2arinaldi@aol.com. **Contact:** Angela Rinaldi. Estab. 1994. Member of AAR. Represents 40 clients. Currently handles: 50% nonfiction books; 50% novels.
 • Prior to opening her agency, Ms. Rinaldi was an editor at New American Library, Pocket Books and Bantam, and the manager of book development of *The Los Angeles Times*.
Represents: Nonfiction books, novels, TV and motion picture rights. **Considers these nonfiction areas:** biography/ autobiography; business; child guidance/parenting; food/nutrition; current affairs; health/medicine; money/finance/economics; popular culture; psychology; self-help/personal improvement; sociology; true crime/investigative; women's issues/women's studies. **Considers literary and commercial fiction.**
How to Contact: For fiction, send the first 100 pages and brief synopsis. For nonfiction, query first or send outline/ proposal, include SASE for both. Reports in 4-6 weeks. Accepts queries by e-mail. Considers simultaneous queries and submissions. "Please advise if this is a multiple submission to another agent." Returns materials only with SASE.
Needs: Actively seeking commercial and literary fiction. Does not want to receive scripts, category romances, children's books, westerns, science fiction/fantasy and cookbooks.
Recent Sales: *The Starlite Drive-In*, by Marjorie Reynolds (William Morrow & Co.); *Twins: Pregnancy, Birth and The First Year of Life*, by Agnew, Klein and Ganon (HarperCollins); *The Thyroid Solution*, by Dr. Ridha Arem; *Quiet Time*, by Stephanie Kane (Bantam).
Terms: Agent receives 15% commission on domestic sales; 20% on foreign sales. Offers written contract. Charges for photocopying ("if client doesn't supply copies for submissions"). 100% of business is derived from commissions on sales. Foreign, TV and motion picture rights for clients only.

◙ ANN RITTENBERG LITERARY AGENCY, INC., 14 Montgomery Place, Brooklyn NY 11215. (718)857-1460. Fax: (718)857-1484. **Contact:** Ann Rittenberg, president. Associate: Silver Tyler. Estab. 1992. Member of AAR. Represents 35 clients. 40% of clients are new/previously unpublished writers. Specializes in literary fiction and literary nonfiction. Currently handles: 50% nonfiction books; 50% novels.
Represents: Considers these nonfiction areas: biography; gardening; memoir; social/cultural history; travel; women's issues/women's studies. **Considers this fiction area:** literary.
How to Contact: Send outline, 3 sample chapters and SASE. Reports in 4-6 weeks on queries; 6-8 weeks on mss.
Needs: Obtains new clients only through referrals from established writers and editors.
Recent Sales: Prefers not to share information on specific sales.
Terms: Agent receives 15% commission on domestic sales; 20% on foreign sales. Offers written contract. Charges for photocopying only.

◙ RIVERSIDE LITERARY AGENCY, 41 Simon Keets Rd., Leyden MA 01337. (413)772-0840. Fax: (413)772-0969. **Contact:** Susan Lee Cohen. Estab. 1991. Represents 40 clients. 20% of clients are new/previously unpublished writers.

 CLOSE UP with Angela Rinaldi, Angela Rinaldi Literary Agency
  ... On being an editor before becoming an agent

"Having been an editor for several major houses gave me an insider's perspective. I have access not only to the criteria for acquiring an author's work but also to the publishing process, including marketing. I think like an editor—and a publisher—when I decide to represent an author, and I'm able to use that experience when I approach a publishing house.

"My experience showed me how agents were perceived in the industry and how important an agent's reputation is. Agents are judged by editorial staffs on a daily basis by the quality of their submissions and are known for the type of material they represent. Editors use agents as their first readers, trusting them to weed out the unpublishable material. Novels that come in poorly written, and nonfiction proposals that are thin and not well thought out, reflect poorly on agents. Editors have lists of 'A' agents whose submissions they will look at immediately."

Represents: Nonfiction books, novels. Very selective.
How to Contact: Query with outline and SASE. Reports in 2 months.
Terms: Agent receives 15% commission. Offers written contract.
Needs: Mainly accepts new clients through referrals.
Recent Sales: *Awakening to the Sacred*, by Lama Surya Das (Broadway); *Jim Morrison's Adventures in the Afterlife*, by Mick Farren (St. Martin's).

BJ ROBBINS LITERARY AGENCY, 5130 Bellaire Ave., North Hollywood CA 91607-2908. (818)760-6602. Fax: (818)760-6616. **Contact:** (Ms.) B.J. Robbins. Estab. 1992. Member of Executive Committee, PEN American Center West. Represents 40 clients. 80% of clients are new/previously unpublished writers. Currently handles: 50% nonfiction books; 50% novels.
Represents: Nonfiction books, novels. **Considers these nonfiction areas:** biography/autobiography; child guidance/parenting; current affairs; education; ethnic/cultural interests; government/politics/law; health/medicine; how-to; humor; memoirs; music/dance/theater/film; nature/environment; popular culture; psychology; self-help/personal improvement; sociology; sports; true crime/investigative; women's issues/women's studies. **Considers these fiction areas:** contemporary issues; detective/police/crime; ethnic; family saga; literary; mainstream; mystery/suspense; sports; thriller/espionage.
How to Contact: Send outline/proposal and 3 sample chapters with SASE. Considers simultaneous queries and submissions. Reports in 2 weeks on queries; 6 weeks on mss. Returns materials only with SASE.
Needs: Obtains new clients mostly through referrals, also at conferences.
Recent Sales: Sold 10 titles in the last year. *Please, Please, Please*, by Renée Swindle (Dial Press); *girl.com*, by Katherine Tarbox (Dutton); *Quickening*, by Laura Catherine Brown (Random House).
Terms: Agent receives 15% commission on domestic sales; 20% on foreign sales. Offers written contract, with 3 months notice to terminate if project is out on submission. Charges for postage and photocopying only. 100% of business is derived from commissions on sales.
Writers' Conferences: Squaw Valley Fiction Writers Workshop (Squaw Valley CA, August); UCLA Writer's Conference.

THE ROBBINS OFFICE, INC., 405 Park Ave., New York NY 10022. (212)223-0720. Fax: (212)223-2535. **Contact:** Kathy P. Robbins, owner. Specializes in selling serious nonfiction, poetry, commercial and literary fiction.
Member Agents: Bill Clegg.
Represents: Serious nonfiction, literary and commercial fiction and poetry. **Considers these nonfiction areas:** biography, political commentary; criticism; memoirs; investigative journalism.
How to Contact: Accepts submissions by referral only.
Recent Sales: *King of the World*, by David Remnick (Random House); *Men in the Off Hours*, by Anne Carson (Knopf); *A Beautiful Mind*, by Sylvia Nasar (Simon & Schuster); *Dating Big Bird*, by Laura Zigman (The Dial Press); *War Boy*, by Kief Hillsbery (Rob Weisbach Books).
Terms: Agent receives 15% commission on all domestic, dramatic and foreign sales. Bills back specific expenses incurred in doing business for a client.

FLORA ROBERTS, 157 W. 57th St., Penthouse A, New York NY 10019. This agency did not respond to our request for information. Query before submitting.

ROBINSON TALENT AND LITERARY MANAGEMENT, (formerly the Robinson Talent and Literary Agency), 1101 S. Robertson Blvd., Suite 21, Los Angeles CA 90035. (310)278-0801. Fax: (310)278-0807. **Contact:** Margaretrose Robinson. Estab. 1992. Signatory of WGA, franchised by DGA/SAG. Represents 150 clients. 10% of screenwriting clients are new/previously unpublished writers; all are WGA members. "We represent screenwriters, playwrights, novelists and producers, directors." Currently handles; 15% novels; 40% movie scripts; 40% TV scripts; 5% stage plays.
    ● See the expanded listing for this agency in Script Agents.

LINDA ROGHAAR LITERARY AGENCY, INC., 133 High Point Dr., Amherst MA 01002. (413)256-1921. Fax: (413)256-2636. E-mail: lroghaar@aol.com. **Contact:** Linda L. Roghaar. Estab. 1996. Represents 31 clients. 50% of clients are new/unpublished writers. Specializes in women's issues, spirituality, history, self-help and mystery. Currently handles: 90% nonfiction books; 10% novels.
    ● Prior to opening her agency, Ms. Roghaar worked in retail bookselling for 5 years and as a publisher's sales rep for 15 years.
Represents: Nonfiction books, novels. **Considers these nonfiction areas:** animals; anthropology/archaeology; biography/autobiography; education; history; nature/environment; popular culture; religious/inspirational; self-help/personal improvement; women's issues/women's studies. **Considers these fiction areas:** mystery (amateur sleuth, cozy, culinary, malice domestic).
How to Contact: Query with SASE. Reports in 2-4 weeks on queries; 6-12 weeks on mss.
Needs: Actively seeking self-help; spirituality; women's; mystery. Does not want to receive horror; romance; science fiction. Obtains new clients through recommendations from others, workshops.

Recent Sales: Sold 18 titles in the last year. *Refrigerator Rights*, by Dr. Will Miller (Delacorte); *Love Always, Patsy* (Penguin Putnam/Berkley).

Terms: Agent receives 15% commission on domestic sales; negotiable on foreign sales. Offers written contract, binding for negotiable time.

RITA ROSENKRANZ LITERARY AGENCY, 285 Riverside Drive, #5E, New York NY 10025-5227. (212)749-7256. **Contact:** Rita Rosenkranz. Estab. 1990. Represents 30 clients. 20% of clients are new/unpublished writers. "Agency focuses on adult nonfiction. Stresses strong editorial development and refinement before submitting to publishers, and brainstorms ideas with authors." Currently handles: 98% nonfiction books; 2% novels.

● Prior to opening her agency, Rita Rosenkranz worked as an editor in major New York publishing houses.

Represents: Nonfiction. **Considers these nonfiction areas:** animals; anthropology/archaeology; art/architecture/design; biography/autobiography; business; child guidance/parenting; computers/electronics; cooking/food/nutrition; crafts/hobbies; current affairs; ethnic/cultural interests; gay/lesbian issues; government/politics/law; health/medicine; history; how-to; humor; interior design/decorating; language/literature/criticism; military/war; money/finance/economics; music/dance/theater/film; nature/environment; New Age/metaphysics; photography; popular culture; psychology; religious/inspirational; science/technology; self-help/personal improvement; sports; women's issues/women's studies.

How to Contact: Send outline/proposal with SASE. Reports in 2 weeks on queries.

Needs: "Actively seeking authors who are well paired with their subject, either for professional or personal reasons." Obtains new clients through word of mouth, solicitation and conferences.

Recent Sales: Sold 30 titles in the last year. Prefers not to share information on specific sales.

Terms: Agent receives 15% commission on domestic sales; 20% on foreign sales. Offers written contract, binding for 3 years. 60 days written notice must be given to terminate contract. Charges for photocopying. Makes referrals to editing service.

Tips: "Identify the current competition for your project to make sure the project is valid. A strong cover letter is very important."

ⓝ ∅ ROSENSTONE/WENDER, 3 E. 48th St., New York NY 10017. This agency did not respond to our request for information. Query before submitting.

ⓜ THE GAIL ROSS LITERARY AGENCY, (formerly Lichtman, Trister, Singer & Ross), 1666 Connecticut Ave. NW, #500, Washington DC 20009. (202)328-3282. Fax: (202)328-9162. **Contact:** Robin Pinnel. Estab. 1988. Member of AAR. Represents 200 clients. 75% of clients are new/previously unpublished writers. Specializes in adult trade nonfiction. Currently handles: 90% nonfiction books; 10% novels.

Member Agents: Gail Ross (nonfiction); Howard Yoon.

Represents: Nonfiction books, novels. **Considers these nonfiction areas:** anthropology/archaeology; biography/autobiography; business; cooking/food/nutrition; education; ethnic/cultural interests; gay/lesbian issues; government/politics/law; health/fitness; humor; money/finance/economics; nature/environment; psychology; religious/inspirational; science/technology; self-help/personal improvement; sociology; sports; true crime/investigative. **Considers these fiction areas:** ethnic; feminist; gay; literary.

How to Contact: Query with SASE. Reports in 1 month.

Needs: Obtains new clients through referrals.

Recent Sales: Prefers not to share information on specific sales.

Terms: Agent receives 15% commission on domestic sales; 25% on foreign sales. Charges for office expenses (i.e., postage, copying).

ⓐ ⓞ CAROL SUSAN ROTH, LITERARY REPRESENTATION, 1824 Oak Creek Dr., Palo Alto CA 94304. (650)323-3795. E-mail: carol@authorsbest.com. **Contact:** Carol Susan Roth. Estab. 1995. Represents 30 clients. 10% of clients are new/unpublished writers. Specializes in spirituality, health, personal growth, business. Currently handles: 100% nonfiction books.

● Prior to opening her agency, Ms. Roth was trained as a psychotherapist, motivational coach, conference producer and promoter for bestselling authors (e.g. Scott Peck, Bernie Siegal, John Gray).

Represents: Nonfiction books. **Considers these nonfiction areas:** business; health/medicine; New Age/metaphysics; religious/inspirational; self help/personal improvement.

How to Contact: Send proposal with SASE. No e-mail queries. Considers simultaneous queries and submissions. Reports in 1 week on queries. *"No phone calls please."* Returns materials only with SASE.

Needs: Actively seeking previously published authors—experts in health, spirituality, personal growth, business. Does not want to receive fiction. Obtains new clients through queries, current client referral.

Recent Sales: Sold 12 titles in the last year. *Yoga Gems*, by Georg Feverstein (Bantam); *Kids Health*, by Nemours Foundation (NTC/Contemporary); *Simple Wicca* (Conari); *Filthy Rich* (Bard Press).

Terms: Agent receives 15% commission on domestic sales; 20% on foreign sales. Offers written contract, binding for 3 years. 60 days notice must be given to terminate contract. Offers a proposal development and marketing consulting service on request. Charges $150/hour for service. Service is separate from agenting services.

Writers' Conferences: Maui Writer's Conference (Maui, HI, September 1999).

Reading List: Reads *Yoga, New Age, People, Men's Health* and *Inquiring Mind* to find new clients. Looks for "ability to write and self-promote."

Tips: "Have charisma, content and credentials—solve an old problem in a new way. I prefer clients with extensive seminar and media experience."

N ◑ JANE ROTROSEN AGENCY LLC, 318 E. 51st St., New York NY 10022. (212)593-4330. Fax: (212)935-6985. E-mail: jrotrosen@aol.com. **Contact:** Jane Rotrosen. Estab. 1974. Member of AAR and Authors Guild. Represents over 100 clients. Currently handles: 30% nonfiction books; 70% novels.
Member Agents: Andrea Cirillo; Ruth Kagle; Annelise Robey; Margaret Ruley; Stephanie Tade.
Represents: Nonfiction books, novels. **Considers these nonfiction areas:** biography/autobiography; business; child guidance/parenting; cooking/food/nutrition; current affairs; health/medicine; how-to; humor; money/finance/economics; nature/environment; popular culture; psychology; self-help/personal improvement; sports; true crime/investigative; women's issues/women's studies. **Considers these fiction areas:** action/adventure; detective/police/crime; family saga; historical; horror; mainstream; mystery; romance; thriller/espionage; women's fiction.
How to Contact: Query with SASE. Does not accept queries by fax or e-mail. Considers simultaneous queries and submissions. Reports in 2 weeks on queries; 7 weeks on mss. Returns materials only with SASE.
Recent Sales: Sold 120 titles in the last year. Prefers not to share information on specific sales.
Terms: Agent receives 15% commission on domestic sales; 20% on foreign sales. Offers written contract, binding for 3 years. 60-days notice must be given to terminate contract. Charges for photocopying, express mail, overseas postage and book purchases.

◐ THE DAMARIS ROWLAND AGENCY, 510 E. 23rd St., #8-G, New York NY 10010-5020. (212)475-8942. Fax: (212)358-9411. **Contact:** Damaris Rowland or Steve Axelrod. Estab. 1994. Member of AAR. Represents 50 clients. 10% of clients are new/previously unpublished writers. Specializes in women's fiction. Currently handles: 75% novels, 25% nonfiction.
Represents: Nonfiction books, novels. **Considers these nonfiction areas:** animals; cooking/food/nutrition; health/medicine; nature/environment; New Age/metaphysics; religious/inspirational; women's issues/women's studies. **Considers these fiction areas:** detective/police/crime; historical; literary; mainstream; psychic/supernatural; romance (contemporary, gothic, historical, regency).
How to Contact: Send outline/proposal with SASE. Reports in 6 weeks.
Needs: Obtains new clients through recommendations from others, at conferences.
Recent Sales: *The Perfect Husband*, by Lisa Gardner (Bantam); *Soul Dating To Soul Mating, On The Path To Spiritual Partnership*, by Basha Kaplan and Gail Prince (Putnam Books); *My Dearest Enemy*, by Connie Brockway (Dell).
Terms: Agent receives 15% commission on domestic sales; 20% on foreign sales. Offers written contract, with 30 day cancellation clause. Charges only if extraordinary expenses have been incurred, e.g., photocopying and mailing 15 ms to Europe for a foreign sale. 100% of business is derived from commissions on sales.
Writers' Conferences: Novelists Inc. (Denver, October); RWA National (Texas, July), Pacific Northwest Writers Conference.

◐ PESHA RUBINSTEIN LITERARY AGENCY, INC., 1392 Rugby Rd., Teaneck NJ 07666-2839. (201)862-1174. Fax: (201)862-1180. E-mail: peshalit@aol.com. **Contact:** Pesha Rubinstein. Estab. 1990. Member of AAR, RWA, MWA, SCBWI. Represents 35 clients. 25% of clients are new/previously unpublished writers. Specializes in commercial fiction and nonfiction and children's books. Currently handles: 30% juvenile books; 70% novels.
● Prior to opening her agency, Ms. Rubenstein served as an editor at Zebra and Leisure Books.
Represents: Commercial fiction, juvenile books, picture book illustration. **Considers these nonfiction areas:** child guidance/parenting; contemporary issues. **Considers these fiction areas:** detective/police/crime; ethnic; glitz; humor; juvenile; mainstream; mystery/suspense; picture book; psychic/supernatural; romance (contemporary, historical); spiritual adventures.
How to Contact: Send query, first 10 pages and SASE. Reports in 2 weeks on queries; 6 weeks on requested mss.
Needs: Does not want to receive poetry or westerns.
Recent Sales: *Freedom School*, by Amy Littlesugar (Philomel); *Excavation*, by James Rollins (Avon).
Terms: Agent receives 15% commission on domestic sales; 20% on foreign sales. Offers written contract. Charges for photocopying and overseas postage. No weekend or collect calls accepted.
Tips: "Keep the query letter and synopsis short. Please send first ten pages of manuscript rather than selected chapters from the manuscript. I am a stickler for correct grammar, spelling and punctuation. The work speaks for itself better than any description can. Never send originals. A phone call after one month is acceptable. Always include a SASE covering return of the entire package with the submission."

◐ RUSSELL & VOLKENING, 50 W. 29th St., #7E, New York NY 10001. (212)684-6050. Fax: (212)889-3026.
Contact: Joseph Regal or Jennie Dunham. Estab. 1940. Member of AAR. Represents 140 clients. 10% of clients are new/previously unpublished writers. Specializes in literary fiction and narrative nonfiction. Currently handles: 40% nonfiction books; 15% juvenile books; 3% short story collections; 40% novels; 2% novellas.
Member Agents: Timothy Seldes (nonfiction, literary fiction); Joseph Regal (literary fiction, thrillers ,nonfiction); Jennie Dunham (literary fiction, nonfiction, children's books).
Represents: Nonfiction books, juvenile books, novels, novellas, short story collections. **Considers these nonfiction areas:** anthropology/archaeology; art/architecture/design; biography/autobiography; business; cooking/food/nutrition; current affairs; education; ethnic/cultural interests; gay/lesbian issues; government/politics/law; health/medicine; history;

juvenile nonfiction; language/literature/criticism; military/war; money/finance/economics; music/dance/theater/film; nature/environment; photography; popular culture; psychology; science/technology; sociology; sports; true crime/investigative; women's issues/women's studies. **Considers these fiction areas:** action/adventure; detective/police/crime; ethnic; juvenile; literary; mainstream; mystery/suspense; picture book; sports; thriller/espionage; young adult.
How to Contact: Query with SASE. Reports in 1 week on queries; 6-8 weeks on mss.
Needs: Obtains new clients through "recommendations of writers we already represent."
Recent Sales: *For the Time Being*, by Annie Dillard (Knopf); *A Patchwork Planet*, by Anne Tyler (Knopf); *Living in Hope and History*, by Nadine Gordimer (Farrar, Straus & Giroux); *Lanterns*, by Marian Wright Edelman (Beacon Press).
Terms: Agent receives 10% commission on domestic sales; 20% on foreign sales. Charges for "standard office expenses relating to the submission of materials of an author we represent, e.g., photocopying, postage."
Tips: "If the query is cogent, well written, well presented and is the type of book we'd represent, we'll ask to see the manuscript. From there, it depends purely on the quality of the work."

THE SAGALYN AGENCY, 4825 Bethesda Ave., Suite 302, Bethesda MD 20814. (301)718-6440. Fax: (301)718-6444. Estab. 1980. Member of AAR. Currently handles: 50% nonfiction books; 25% scholarly books; 25% novels.
How to Contact: Send outline/proposal.
Recent Sales: Prefers not to share information on specific sales.

SAGE ACRE MARKETING & PUBLISHING SOLUTIONS, 55 Western Ave., Cohoes NY 12047-3916. (518)238-2765. E-mail: sageacre@prodigy.net. Website: www.sageacre.com. **Contact:** Christopher Anzalone. Represents 25 clients. 90% of clients are new/unpublished writers. Specializes in new and emerging authors, and project development. Currently handles: 45% nonfiction books; 5% scholarly books; 50% novels.
 • Prior to becoming an agent, Mr. Anzalone had 12 years of publishing experience in sales, marketing, editorial development and editorial acquisitions.
Represents: Nonfiction books, scholarly books, novels, textbooks. **Considers these nonfiction areas:** anthropology/archaeology; art/architecture/design; biography/autobiography; business; child guidance/parenting; current affairs; education; ethnic/cultural interests; gay/lesbian issues; government/politics/law; health/medicine; history; language/literature/criticism; money/finance/economics; popular culture; psychology; sociology; true crime/investigative; women's issues/women's studies. **Considers these fiction areas:** contemporary issues; ethnic; feminist; gay/lesbian; historical; literary; mainstream; romance.
How to Contact: Query with SASE. Accepts queries by e-mail (no more than 5 pages). Considers simultaneous queries and submissions. Reports in 1 month on queries; 2 months on mss. Returns materials only with SASE.
Needs: Actively seeking serious nonfiction: historical, biographical. Serious fiction: literary fiction, romance, women's interest.
Recent Sales: *Parents Who Love Too Much*, by Fogarty (Prima); *Encyclopedia of Supreme Court Quotations*, by Anzalone (ME Sharpe).
Terms: Agent receives 15% commission on domestic sales; 20% on foreign sales. Offers written contract, binding for 1 year. 30 day notice must be given to terminate contract. Charges for postage and photocopying. "No reading or editorial fees."
Tips: "Be particularly diligent on writing mechanics and market expectations for your chosen genre."

VICTORIA SANDERS LITERARY AGENCY, 241 Avenue of the Americas, New York NY 10014-4822. (212)633-8811. Fax: (212)633-0525. **Contact:** Victoria Sanders and/or Diane Dickensheid. Estab. 1993. Member of AAR, signatory of WGA. Represents 75 clients. 25% of clients are new/previously unpublished writers. Currently handles: 50% nonfiction books; 50% novels.
Represents: Nonfiction, novels. **Considers these nonfiction areas:** biography/autobiography; current affairs; ethnic/cultural interests; gay/lesbian issues; govenment/politics/law; history; humor; language/literature/criticism; music/dance/theater/film; popular culture; psychology; translations; women's issues/women's studies. **Considers these fiction areas:** action/adventure; contemporary issues; ethnic; family saga; feminist; gay; lesbian; literary; thriller/espionage.
How to Contact: Query with SASE. Considers simultaneous queries. Reports in 1 week on queries; 1 month on mss. Returns materials only with SASE.
Needs: Obtains new clients through recommendations, "or I find them through my reading and pursue."
Recent Sales: Sold 15 titles in the last year. *Blindsighted*, by Karin Slaughter (Morrow); *Redemption Song*, by Dr. Bertice Berry (Doubleday).
Terms: Agent receives 15% commission on domestic sales; 20% on foreign sales. Offers written contract binding at will. Charges for photocopying, ms, messenger, express mail and extraordinary fees. If in excess of $100, client approval is required.
Tips: "Limit query to letter, no calls, and give it your best shot. A good query is going to get a good response."

ALWAYS INCLUDE a self-addressed, stamped envelope (SASE) for reply or return of your query or manuscript.

SANDUM & ASSOCIATES, 144 E. 84th St., New York NY 10028-2035. (212)737-2011. Fax number on request. Managing Director: Howard E. Sandum. Estab. 1987. Represents 35 clients. 20% of clients are new/unpublished writers. Specializes in general nonfiction. Currently handles: 80% nonfiction books; 20% novels.
Represents: Nonfiction books, literary novels.
How to Contact: Query with proposal, sample pages and SASE. Do not send full ms unless requested. Reports in 2 weeks on queries.
Recent Sales: Prefers not to share information on specific sales.
Terms: Agent receives 15% commission. Agent fee adjustable on dramatic and foreign sales. Charges writers for photocopying, air express, long-distance telephone/fax.

JACK SCAGNETTI TALENT & LITERARY AGENCY, 5118 Vineland Ave., #102, North Hollywood CA 91601. (818)762-3871. **Contact:** Jack Scagnetti. Estab. 1974. Signatory of WGA, member of Academy of Television Arts and Sciences. Represents 50 clients. 50% of clients are new/previously unpublished writers. Specializes in film books with many photographs. Currently handles: 20% nonfiction books; 70% movie scripts; 10% TV scripts.
 • See the expanded listing for this agency in Script Agents.

SCHIAVONE LITERARY AGENCY, INC., 236 Trails End, West Palm Beach FL 33413-2135. Phone/fax: (561)966-9294. E-mail: profschia@aol.com. Website: members.aol.com/profschia/index.html. **Contact:** James Schiavone, Ed.D. Estab. 1997. Member of the National Education Association. Represents 30 clients. 2% of clients are new/unpublished writers. Specializes in celebrity biography and autobiography. Currently handles: 50% nonfiction books; 49% novels; 1% textbooks.
 • Prior to opening his agency, Mr. Schiavone was a full professor of developmental skills at the City University of New York and author of 5 trade books and 3 textbooks.
Represents: Nonfiction books, juvenile books, scholarly books, novels, textbooks. **Considers these nonfiction areas:** animals; anthropology/archaeology; biography/autobiography; child guidance/parenting; current affairs; education; ethnic/cultural interests; gay/lesbian issues; government/politics/law; health/medicine; history; how-to; humor; juvenile nonfiction; language/literature/criticism; military/war; nature/environment; popular culture; psychology; science/technology; self-help/personal improvement; sociology; true crime/investigative. **Considers these fiction areas:** contemporary issues; ethnic; family saga; historical; horror; humor/satire; juvenile; literary; mainstream; young adult.
How to Contact: Send outline/proposal. Considers simultaneous queries and submissions. Reports in 2 weeks on queries; 6 weeks on mss. Returns materials only with SASE.
Needs: Actively seeking serious nonfiction and literary fiction. Does not want to receive poetry. Usually obtains new clients through recommendations from others, solicitation, conferences.
Recent Sales: Sold 3 titles in the last year. *Dire Straits*, by Beatrice Moon (Hypeluxo Productions). Clients include Mark Littleton, Nickolas Gerstner and John Moffitt.
Terms: Agent receives 15% commission on domestic sales; 20% on foreign sales. Offers a written contract. May be terminated by either party notifying the other in writing. Contract is on a "per project" basis. Charges for long distance, photocopying, postage and special handling. Dollar amount varies with each project depending on level of activity.
Writers' Conferences: Key West Literary Seminar (Key West FL, January).
Tips: "I prefer to work with published/established authors. I will consider marketable proposals from new/unpublished writers. We are dedicated to making sales."

BLANCHE SCHLESSINGER AGENCY, 433 Old Gulph Rd., Penn Valley PA 19072. (610)664-5513. Fax: (610)664-5959. E-mail: bmschless@home.com. **Contact:** Blanche Schlessinger. Estab. 1984. "Small agency that works primarily with published writers."
Represents: Nonfiction books, fiction. **Considers these nonfiction areas:** biography/autobiography; business; cooking/food/nutrition; parenting; gardening; health/medicine; how-to; lifestyle; self-help/personal improvement; memoirs; true crime/investigative. **Considers these fiction areas:** adult commercial and literary fiction by referral only.
How to Contact: For nonfiction: submit letter, author's credentials, outline and 1-3 sample chapters. No queries or proposals by e-mail or fax. Reports in 10 days on queries; 4-6 weeks on mss. *SASE essential for reply.*
Needs: Does not want to receive science fiction, horror, poetry, screenplays or children's. *Obtains new clients primarily through recommendations from others.*
Recent Sales: *Michener and Me: A Memoir*, by Herman Silverman (Running Press); *Raising Your 11-14 Year Old in an Age of Chat Rooms and Navel Rings*, by Dr. Susan Panzavine (Facts on File); *100 Vegetables and How They Got Their Names*, by William Ways Weaver (Algonquin Books).
Terms: Agent receives 15% commission on domestic sales; 20% on foreign sales. Offers written contract. Charges for office expenses (long distance telephone, mailing expenses, copying and bound galleys).

SUSAN SCHULMAN, A LITERARY AGENCY, 454 W. 44th St., New York NY 10036-5205. (212)713-1633/4/5. Fax: (212)581-8830. E-mail: schulman@aol.com. **Contact:** Susan Schulman, president. Estab. 1979. Member of AAR, Dramatists Guild, Women's Media Group, signatory of WGA. 10-15% of clients are new/unpublished writers. Prefers to work with published/established authors; works with a small number of new/unpublished authors. Specializes in self-help, New Age, spirituality and books for, by and about women's issues including family, careers, health and spiritual development. "And, most importantly, we love working with writers." Currently handles: 70% nonfiction books; 20% novels; 10% stage plays.

Member Agents: Susan Schulman (self-help, New Age, spirituality); Christine Morin (children's books, ecology, natural sciences and business books); Bryan Leifert (plays and pitches for film).
Represents: Nonfiction, fiction, plays, emphasizing contemporary women's fiction and nonfiction books of interest to women. **Considers these nonfiction areas:** anthropology/archaeology; biography/autobiography; child guidance/parenting; current affairs; education; ethnic/cultural interests; gay/lesbian issues; government/politics/law; health/medicine; history; how-to; juvenile nonfiction; money/finance/economics; music/dance/theater/film; nature/environment; New Age/metaphysics; popular culture; psychology; religious/inspirational; self-help/personal improvement; sociology; translations; true crime/investigative; women's issues/women's studies. **Considers these fiction areas:** contemporary issues; detective/police/crime; historical; lesbian; literary; mainstream; mystery/suspense; young adult.
Also Handles: Feature film, stage plays. **Considers these script subject areas:** comedy; contemporary issues; detective/police/crime; feminist; historical; mainstream; psychic/supernatural; religious/inspirational; mystery/suspense; teen.
How to Contact: Query with outline/proposal and SASE. Accepts queries by fax and e-mail. Considers simultaneous queries. Reports in 1 week on queries; 6 weeks on mss. Returns materials only with SASE.
Recent Sales: *Mockingbird*, by Walter Tevis (New Line); *The English Patient*, by Michael Ondaate (Saul Zaentz); *Voodoo Dreams*, by Jewell Parker Rhodes (Steve Tisch Co.).
Terms: Agent receives 15% commission on domestic sales; 10-20% on dramatic sales; 7½-10% on foreign sales (plus 7½-10% to co-agent). Charges for special messenger or copying services, foreign mail and any other service requested by client.
Writers' Conferences: Florida Studio Theater Artists Weekend (Sarasota, April); SCBWI (Simi Valley CA); Entertainment Expo (New York City).

◖ LAURENS R. SCHWARTZ AGENCY, 5 E. 22nd St., Suite 15D, New York NY 10010-5325. (212)228-2614. **Contact:** Laurens R. Schwartz. Estab. 1984. Represents 100 clients.
Represents: "General mix of nonfiction and fiction. Also handles movie and TV tie-ins, all licensing and merchandising. Works world-wide. *Very* selective about taking on new clients. Only takes on 2-3 new clients per year."
How to Contact: No unsolicited mss. Reports in 1 month.
Recent Sales: Prefers not to share information on specific sales. "Have had 18 best-sellers."
Terms: Agent receives 15% commission on domestic sales; up to 25% on foreign sales. "No fees except for photocopying, and that fee is avoided by an author providing necessary copies or, in certain instances, transferring files on diskette—must be IBM compatible." Where necessary to bring a project into publishable form, editorial work and some rewriting provided as part of service. Works with authors on long-term career goals and promotion.
Tips: "Do not like receiving mass mailings sent to all agents. Be selective—do your homework. Do not send *everything* you have ever written. Choose *one* work and promote that. *Always* include an SASE. *Never* send your only copy. *Always* include a background sheet on yourself and a *one*-page synopsis of the work (too many summaries end up being as long as the work)."

◎ SCOVIL CHICHAK GALEN LITERARY AGENCY, 381 Park Ave. South, Suite 1020, New York NY 10016. (212)679-8686. Fax: (212)679-6710. **Contact:** Russell Galen. Estab. 1993. Member of AAR.
Member Agents: Russell Galen; Jack Scovil; Kathleen Anderson; Jill Grinberg; Anna Ghosh; Denise DeMars; Alexander Smithline.
Recent Sales: *Red Sky at Morning*, by Paul Garrison (Avon); *Last Man Standing*, by Jack Olsen; *Soul of the Fire*, by Terry Goodkind (TOR).
Terms: Charges for photocopying and postage.

✓ ⑤ ◉ SEBASTIAN LITERARY AGENCY, PMB #406, 1560 Van Ness Ave., San Francisco CA 94109. (415)921-8043. Fax: (415)921-8632. E-mail: harperlb@aol.com (query only—no attachments). **Contact:** Laurie Harper. Estab. 1985. Member of AAR. Represents approximately 50 clients. Specializes in business, psychology and health.
Represents: Trade nonfiction only at this time (no scholarly). "No children's or YA." **Considers these nonfiction areas:** biography; business; child guidance/parenting; consumer reference; current affairs; ethnic/cultural interests; government/politics/law; health/medicine; money/finance/economics; psychology; self-help/personal improvement; sociology; women's issues/women's studies.
How to Contact: Taking new clients selectively; mainly by referral. Reports in 3 weeks on queries; 6 weeks on mss.
Needs: Obtains new clients mostly through "referrals from authors and editors, but some at conferences and some from unsolicited queries from around the country."
Recent Sales: *The Warren Buffet Portfolio*, by Robert Hagstrom, Jr. (John Wiley); *Executive Thinking: The Dream, The Vision, The Mission Achieved*, by Leslie Kossoff (Davies-Black Publisher); *Fast Forward Leadership*, by Louellen Essex and Mitchell Kusy (Pitman/Pearson); *Bald in the Land of Big Hair: Confessions of a Slightly Imperfect Woman*, by Joni Rodgers (HarperCollins).
Terms: Agent receives 15% commission on domestic sales; 20% on foreign sales. Offers written contract.
Fees: No reading fees. Charges a $100 annual administration fee for clients and charges for photocopies of ms for submission to publisher.
Writers' Conferences: ASJA (Los Angeles, February).

✓ ◖ SEDGEBAND LITERARY ASSOCIATES, 7312 Martha Lane, Fort Worth TX 76112. (817)996-3652. E-mail: sedgeband@aol.com. Website: members.home.net/sedgeband. **Contact:** David Duperre or Ginger Norton. Estab.

1997. 90% of clients are new/unpublished writers. Agency looking for new writers who have patience and are willing to work hard. Currently handles: 90% novels; 10% novellas.

Member Agents: David Duperre (science fiction/fantasy, all genres); Ginger Norton (mystery/horror, all genres); S. Norton (horror).

Represents: Nonfiction books, juvenile books, novels, novellas. **Considers these nonfiction areas:** biography/autobiography; ethnic/cultural interests; history; true crime/investigative. **Considers these fiction areas:** action/adventure; contemporary issues; erotica; ethnic; experimental; fantasy; horror; juvenile; literary; mainstream; mystery; psychic/supernatural; romance; science fiction; suspense.

How to Contact: Query with synopsis and SASE. Accepts queries by e-mail. Considers simultaneous queries and submissions. Reports in 2 weeks on queries; 2 months on mss. Returns materials only with SASE.

Needs: Actively seeking science fiction, fantasy, all types of mystery; Does not want to receive any religious material unless it pertains to angels. Obtains new clients through queries, the internet, and referral.

Recent Sales: Prefers not to share information on specific sales.

Terms: Agent receives 15% commission on domestic sales; 20% on foreign sales. Offers written contract, binding for 6 months to a year. Notice must be given to terminate contract. Charges for postage, photocopies, long distance calls. "Please query for any additional charges."

Tips: "We spend 18 hours a day working for our clients and we do not stop until we accomplish our goal. Simply put, we care about people and books, not just money. Do not send a rude query, it will get you rejected no matter how good of a writer you might be. And if we ask to review your work, don't wait to send it for several months. Send it as soon as possible. Also, it is better to wait for a contract offer before asking a lot of questions about publication and movie rights."

Ⓔ LYNN SELIGMAN, LITERARY AGENT, 400 Highland Ave., Upper Montclair NJ 07043. (201)783-3631. **Contact:** Lynn Seligman. Estab. 1985. Member of Women's Media Group. Represents 32 clients. 15% of clients are new/previously unpublished writers. Specializes in "general nonfiction and fiction. I do illustrated and photography books and represents several photographers for books." Currently handles: 85% nonfiction books; 10% novels; 5% photography books.

● Prior to opening her agency, Ms. Seligman worked in the subsidiary rights department of Doubleday and Simon & Schuster and served as an agent with Julian Bach Literary Agency (now IMG Literary Agency).

Represents: Nonfiction books, novels, photography books. **Considers these nonfiction areas:** anthropology/archaeology; art/architecture/design; biography/autobiography; business; child guidance/parenting; cooking/food/nutrition; current affairs; education; ethnic/cultural interests; government/politics/law; health/medicine; history; how-to; humor; interior design/decorating; language/literature/criticism; money/finance/economics; music/dance/theater/film; nature/environment; photography; popular culture; psychology; science/technology; self-help/personal improvement; sociology; translations; true crime/investigative; women's issues/women's studies. **Considers these fiction areas:** contemporary issues; detective/police/crime; ethnic; fantasy; feminist; gay; historical; horror; humor/satire; lesbian; literary; mainstream; mystery/suspense; romance (contemporary, gothic, historical, regency); science fiction.

How to Contact: Query with letter or outline/proposal, 1 sample chapter and SASE. Considers simultaneous queries. Reports in 2 weeks on queries; 2 months on mss. Returns materials only with SASE.

Needs: Obtains new clients usually from other writers or from editors.

Recent Sales: Sold 10 titles in the last year. *Twice Blessed*, by Joan Leonard (St. Martin's); *A Desperate Game*, by Barbara Pierce (Kensington); *Investing for Teens*, by Janet Bamford (Bloomberg Press).

Terms: Agent receives 15% commission on domestic sales; 25% on foreign sales. Charges for photocopying, unusual postage or telephone expenses (checking first with the author), express mail.

✓ ⑤ Ⓔ THE SEYMOUR AGENCY, 475 Miner St. Rd., Canton NY 13617. (315)386-1831. Fax: (315)386-1037. Website: www.slic.com/marysue. **Contact:** Mary Sue Seymour or Mike Seymour. Estab. 1992. Represents 65 clients. 20% of clients are new/previously unpublished writers. Currently handles: 50% nonfiction books; 5% scholarly books; 5% textbooks; 40% novels.

● Ms. Seymour is a retired NYS certified teacher. Mr. Seymour has an M.A. from St. Lawrence University in Potsdam.

Represents: Fiction and nonfiction. **Considers these nonfiction areas:** art/architecture/design; juvenile nonfiction; religious/inspirational. **Considers these fiction areas:** action/adventure; detective/police/crime; ethnic; glitz; historical; horror; humor/satire; mainstream; mystery/suspense; religious/inspirational; romance (contemporary, gothic, historical, medieval, regency); vampire; westerns/frontier. Will read any well thought out nonfiction proposals, and any good fiction in any genre.

How to Contact: Query with first 50 pages and synopsis. No faxed queries. Considers simultaneous queries and submissions. Reports in 2 months on queries; 3 months on mss. Returns materials only with SASE.

Needs: Nonfiction and well-written novels. No screenplays, short stories or poetry.

Recent Sales: Sold 27 titles in the last year. *Halloween Knight* and *One Knight in Venice*, by Tori Phillips (Harlequin Historicals); *Strategic Interviewing: A Guide for Executives*, by Joan Curtis (Quorum Books); *Papa Was A Boy in Gray*, by Mary Schaller (Thomas Publications); *Marriage By Design*, by Jill Metcalf (Leisure Books).

Terms: Agent receives 12½% (published authors) to 15% (unpublished authors) commission on domestic sales; 20% on foreign sales. Offers written contract, binding for 1 year. Offers criticism service for prospective clients only. Seymour Agency offers inhouse editing for first 50 pages of selected mss. Author is encouraged to resubmit after rewrite.

Tips: "Send query, synopsis and first 50 pages. If you don't hear from us, you didn't send SASE. We are looking for nonfiction and romance—women in jeopardy, suspense, contemporary, historical, some regency and any well-written fiction and nonfiction."

⊘ CHARLOTTE SHEEDY AGENCY, 65 Bleecker St., New York NY 10012. This agency did not respond to our request for information. Query before submitting.

✔ ⊘ THE SHEPARD AGENCY, Premier National Bank Bldg., Suite 3, 1525 Rt. 22, Brewster NY 10509. (914)279-2900 or (914)279-3236. Fax: (914)279-3239. E-mail: shepardagency-ldi@mindspring.com. **Contact:** Jean or Lance Shepard. Specializes in "some fiction; nonfiction: business, biography, homemaking; inspirational; self-help." Currently handles: 75% nonfiction books; 5% juvenile books; 20% novels.
Represents: Nonfiction books, scholarly books, novels. **Considers these nonfiction areas:** agriculture; horticulture; animals; biography/autobiography; business; child guidance/parenting; computers/electronics; cooking/food/nutrition; crafts/hobbies; current affairs; government/politics/law; health/medicine; history; interior design/decorating; juvenile nonfiction; language/literature/criticism; money/finance/economics; music/dance/theater/film; nature/environment; psychology; religious/inspirational; self-help/personal improvement; sociology; sports; women's issues/women's studies. **Considers these fiction areas:** contemporary issues; family saga; historical; humor/satire; literary; regional; sports; thriller/espionage.
How to Contact: Query with outline, sample chapters and SASE. Reports in 6 weeks on queries; 2 months on mss.
Needs: Obtains new clients through referrals and listings in various directories for writers and publishers.
Recent Sales: *Crane's Wedding Blue Book*, by Steven Feinberg (Simon & Schuster).
Terms: Agent receives 15% on domestic sales. Offers written contract. Charges for extraordinary postage, photocopying and long-distance phone calls.
Tips: "Provide information on those publishers who have already been contacted, seen work, accepted or rejected same. Provide complete bio and marketing information."

⊘ ◎ THE ROBERT E. SHEPARD AGENCY, 4111 18th St., Suite 3, San Francisco CA 94114-2407. (415)255-1097. E-mail: query@shepardagency.com. Website: www.shepardagency.com. **Contact:** Robert Shepard. Estab. 1994. Authors Guild associate member. Represents 25 clients. 25% of clients are new/unpublished writers. Specializes in nonfiction, particularly key issues facing society and culture. Other specialties include personal finance, business, gay/lesbian subjects. Currently handles 90% nonfiction books; 10% scholarly books.
● Prior to opening his agency, Mr. Shepard "spent eight and a half years in trade publishing (both editorial and sales/marketing management). I also consulted to a number of major publishers on related subjects."
Represents: Nonfiction books. **Considers these nonfiction areas:** business; current affairs; ethnic/cultural interests; gay/lesbian issues; government/politics/law; history; money/finance/economics; popular culture; science/technology; sociology; sports; women's issues/women's studies.
How to Contact: Query with SASE. E-mail encouraged; phone and fax strongly discouraged. Considers simultaneous queries and submissions. Reports in 2-4 weeks on queries; 4-6 weeks on mss and proposals. Returns materials only with SASE.
Needs: Actively seeking "works in current affairs by recognized experts; also business, personal finance, and gay/lesbian subjects." Does not want to receive autobiography, highly visual works, fiction. Obtains new clients through recommendations from others, solicitation.
Recent Sales: Sold 8 titles in the last year. *Wine and War*, by Donald and Petie Kladstrup (Broadway Books); *Word Freak*, by Stefan Fatsis (Houghton Mifflin Co.); *Untitled on Early Retirement*, by John F. Wasik (Henry Holt & Co.); *Talking Money With Jean Chatzky*, by Jean Sherman Chatzky (Warner Books); *Islam's Challenge*, by Anthony Shadid (Westview Press); *Between Sodom and Eden*, by Lee Walzer (Columbia University Press).
Terms: Agent receives 15% commission on domestic sales; 20% on foreign sales. Offers written contract, binding for term of project or until cancelled. 30 days notice must be given to terminate contract. Charges "actual expenses for phone/fax, photocopying, and postage only if and when project sells, against advance."
Reading List: Reads *Chronicle of Higher Education*, "certain professional publications and a wide range of periodicals" to find new clients. Looks for "a fresh approach to traditional subjects or a top credential in an area that hasn't seen too much trade publishing in the past. And, of course, superb writing."
Tips: "We pay attention to detail. We believe in close working relationships between author and agent and between author and editor. Regular communication is key. Please do your homework! There's no substitute for learning all you can about similar or directly competing books and presenting a well-reasoned competitive analysis. Don't work in a vacuum; visit bookstores, and talk to other writers about their own experiences."

◖ THE SHUKAT COMPANY LTD., 340 W. 55th St., Suite 1A, New York NY 10019-3744. (212)582-7614. Fax: (212)315-3752. Estab. 1972. Member of AAR. Currently handles: dramatic works.
How to Contact: Query with outline/proposal or 30 pages and SASE.

◖ ROSALIE SIEGEL, INTERNATIONAL LITERARY AGENCY, INC., 1 Abey Dr., Pennington NJ 08534. (609)737-1007. Fax: (609)737-3708. **Contact:** Rosalie Siegel. Estab. 1977. Member of AAR. Represents 35 clients. 10% of clients are new/previously unpublished writers. Specializes in foreign authors, especially French, though diminishing. Currently handles: 45% nonfiction books; 45% novels; 10% young adult books and short story collections.

Needs: Obtains new clients through referrals from writers and friends.

Recent Sales: Prefers not to share information on specific sales.

Terms: Agent receives 15% commission on domestic sales; 20% on foreign sales. Offers written contract, with 60 day cancellation clause. Charges for photocopying. 100% of business is derived from commissions.

Tips: "I'm not looking for new authors in an active way."

☑ ◑ **JACQUELINE SIMENAUER LITERARY AGENCY**, P.O. Box 1039, Barnegat NJ 08005. (609)607-1780. **Contact:** Jacqueline Simenauer. Estab. 1990. Member of Authors Guild, Authors League, NASW. Represents 30-35 clients. 40% of clients are new/previously unpublished writers. Specializes in strong commercial nonfiction such as popular psychology, health/medicine, self-help/personal improvement, women's issues, how-to. Currently handles: 95% nonfiction books; 5% novels.

- Prior to opening her agency, Ms. Simenauer co-authored several books for Doubleday, Simon & Schuster and Times Books.

Members Agents: Jacqueline Simenauer (nonfiction); Fran Pardi (fiction); Deborah Herr (New Age/alternative medicine/spirituality).

Represents: Nonfiction books, novels. **Considers these nonfiction areas:** child guidance/parenting; current affairs; education; health/medicine; how-to; money/finance; New Age/metaphysics; nutrition; popular culture; psychology; religious/inspirational; self-help/personal improvement; true crime/investigative; travel; women's issues/women's studies. **Considers these fiction areas:** contemporary issues; family saga; feminist; gay; glitz; historical; literary; mainstream; mystery/suspense; psychic/supernatural; romance (contemporary); thriller/espionage.

How to Contact: Query with SASE. Reports in 4-6 weeks on queries.

Needs: Actively seeking strong commercial nonfiction, but "will look at some fiction." Does not want to receive poetry, crafts, children's books. Obtains new clients through recommendations from others; advertising in various journals, newsletters, publications, etc. and professional conferences.

Recent Sales: *The Joys of Fatherhood*, by Marcus Goldman, M.D. (Prima); *Bride's Guide to Emotional Survival*, by Rita Bigel Casher, Ph.D. (Prima); *Fasting and Eating in Health*, by Dr. Joel Fuhrman (St. Martin's Press).

Terms: Agent receives 15% commission on domestic sales; 20% on foreign sales. "There are no reading fees. However, we have a special Breakthrough Program for the first-time author who would like an in-depth critique of his/her work by our freelance editorial staff. There is a charge of $2 per page for this service, and it is completely optional." Charges for postage, photocopying, phone, fax. 5% of business is derived from reading or criticism fees.

◐ **EVELYN SINGER LITERARY AGENCY INC.**, P.O. Box 594, White Plains NY 10602-0594. Fax: (914)948-5565. **Contact:** Evelyn Singer. Estab. 1951. Represents 30 clients. 10% of clients are new/previously unpublished writers. Specializes in nonfiction (adult/juvenile, adult suspense).

- Prior to opening her agency, Ms. Singer served as an associate in the Jeanne Hale Literary Agency.

Represents: Nonfiction books, juvenile books (for over 4th grade reading level), novels. (No textbooks). **Considers these nonfiction areas:** anthropology/archaeology; biography; business; child guidance; current affairs; ethnic/cultural interests; government/politics/law; health/medicine; how-to; juvenile nonfiction; money/finance/economics; nature/environment; psychology; inspirational; science; self-help; women's issues/women's studies. **Considers these fiction areas:** contemporary issues; detective/police/crime; ethnic; feminist; historical; literary; mainstream; mystery/suspense; regional; thriller/espionage.

How to Contact: Query with SASE. Reports in 2-3 weeks on queries; 6-8 weeks on mss. "SASE must be enclosed for reply or return of manuscript."

Needs: Obtains new clients through recommendations only.

Recent Sales: *Cloud House*, by Nancy Covert Smith and Tamara Beech (Avon); *Cruel As The Grave*, by John Armistead (Recorded Books); *The Black Cowboy*, by Franklin Folsom (Editorial Cruïlla).

Terms: Agent receives 15% commission on domestic sales; 20% on foreign sales. Offers written contract, binding for 3 years. Charges for long-distance phone calls, overseas postage ("authorized expenses only").

Tips: "I am accepting writers who have earned at least $20,000 from freelance writing. SASE must accompany all queries and material for reply and or return of ms. Enclose biographical material and double-spaced book outline or chapter outline. List publishers queried and publication credits."

◑ **IRENE SKOLNICK LITERARY AGENCY**, 22 W. 23rd St., 5th Floor, New York NY 10010. (212)727-3648. Fax: (212)727-1024. E-mail: sirene35@aol.com. **Contact:** Irene Skolnick. Estab. 1993. Member of AAR. Represents 45 clients. 75% of clients are new/previously unpublished writers.

Represents: Adult nonfiction books, adult fiction. **Considers these nonfiction areas:** biography/autobiography; current affairs. **Considers these fiction areas:** contemporary issues; historical; literary.

How to Contact: Query with SASE, outline and sample chapter. No unsolicited mss. Accepts queries by fax. Considers

simultaneous queries and submissions. Reports in 1 month on queries. Returns materials only with SASE.
Recent Sales: Sold 15 titles in the last year. *An Equal Music*, by Vikram Seth; *Kaaterskill Falls*, by Allegra Goodman; *Taking Lives*, by Michael Pye.
Terms: Agent receives 15% commission on domestic sales; 20% on foreign sales. Sometimes offers criticism service. Charges for international postage, photocopying over 40 pages.

BEVERLEY SLOPEN LITERARY AGENCY, 131 Bloor St. W., Suite 711, Toronto, Ontario M5S 1S3 Canada. (416)964-9598. Fax: (416)921-7726. E-mail: slopen@inforamp.net. Website: www.slopenagency.on.ca. **Contact:** Beverly Slopen. Estab. 1974. Represents 60 clients. 40% of clients are new/previously unpublished writers. "Strong bent towards Canadian writers." Currently handles: 60% nonfiction books; 40% novels.
   • Prior to opening her agency, Ms. Slopen worked in publishing and as a journalist.
Represents: Nonfiction books, scholarly books, novels, occasional college texts. **Considers these nonfiction areas:** anthropology/archaeology; biography/autobiography; business; child guidance/parenting; cooking/food/nutrition; current affairs; psychology; sociology; true crime/investigative; women's issues/women's studies. **Considers these fiction areas:** detective/police/crime; literary; mystery/suspense.
How to Contact: Query with SASE. Accepts queries by e-mail, "if short." Reports in 2 months. Returns materials only with SASE (or SAE with IRCs). Canadian postage only.
Needs: Actively seeking "serious nonfiction that is accessible and appealing to the general reader." Does not want to receive fantasy, science fiction or children's.
Recent Sales: Sold 25 titles in the last year. *Walking Since Daybreak*, by Modris Eksteins (Houghton Mifflin). Other clients include historians Modris Eksteins, Michael Marrus, Timothy Brook, critic Robert Fulford.
Terms: Agent receives 15% commission on domestic sales; 10% on foreign sales. Offers written contract, binding for 2 years. 90 days notice must be given to terminate contract.
Tips: "Please, no unsolicited manuscripts."

SMITH-SKOLNIK LITERARY, 303 Walnut St., Westfield NJ 07090. Specializes in literary fiction. Query with SASE before submitting.

MICHAEL SNELL LITERARY AGENCY, P.O. Box 1206, Truro MA 02666-1206. (508)349-3718. **Contact:** Michael Snell. Estab. 1978. Represents 200 clients. 25% of clients are new/previously unpublished authors. Specializes in how-to, self-help and all types of business and computer books, from low-level how-to to professional and reference. Currently handles: 90% nonfiction books; 10% novels.
   • Prior to opening his agency, Mr. Snell served as an editor at Wadsworth and Addison-Wesley for 13 years.
Member Agents: Michael Snell (business, management, computers); Patricia Smith (nonfiction, all categories).
Represents: Nonfiction books. **Open to all nonfiction categories,** especially business, health, law, medicine, psychology, science, women's issues.
How to Contact: Query with SASE. Reports in 1 week on queries; 2 weeks on mss.
Needs: Actively seeking "strong book proposals in any nonfiction area where a clear need exists for a new book. Especially self-help, how-to books on all subjects, from business to personal well-being." Does not want to receive "complete manuscripts; considers proposals only. No fiction. No children's books." Obtains new clients through unsolicited mss, word-of-mouth, *LMP* and *Guide to Literary Agents*.
Recent Sales: *Topgrading: Hiring the Best People*, by Brad Smart (Prentice Hall); *A Good Night's Sleep*, by Frank Buda (Caroll).
Terms: Agent receives 15% on domestic sales; 15% on foreign sales.
Tips: "Send a half- to a full-page query, with SASE. Brochure 'How to Write a Book Proposal' available on request and SASE." Suggest prospective clients read Michael Snell's book, *From Book Idea to Bestseller* (Prima, 1997).

SOBEL WEBER ASSOCIATES, 146 E. 19th St., New York NY 10003. (212)420-8585. Fax:(212)505-1017. **Contact:** Nat Sobel, Judith Weber. Represents 125 clients. 15% of clients are new/unpublished writers. "We edit every book before submitting it to publishers, even those of books under contract. For fiction, that may mean two or three drafts of the work."

SPECTRUM LITERARY AGENCY, (formerly Blassingame Spectrum Corp.), 111 Eighth Ave., Suite 1501, New York NY 10011.. (212)691-7556. **Contact:** Eleanor Wood, president. Represents 75 clients. Currently handles: 90% fiction; 10% nonfiction books.
Member Agents: Lucienne Diver.
Represents: Considers these fiction areas: contemporary issues; fantasy; historical; romance; mainstream; mystery/suspense; science fiction. **Considers select nonfiction.**
How to Contact: Query with SASE. Reports in 2 months on queries.
Needs: Obtains new clients through recommendations from authors and others.
Recent Sales: Prefers not to share information on specific sales.
Terms: Agent receives 10% commission on domestic sales. Charges for photocopying and book orders.

THE SPIELER AGENCY, 154 W. 57th St., 13th Floor, Room 135, New York NY 10019. (212)757-4439. Fax: (212)333-2019. **Contact:** Ada Muellner. West Coast office: contact Victoria Shoemaker, principal agent, 1328

Sixth Street, #3, Berkeley CA 94710. (510)528-2616. Fax: (510)528-8117. Estab. 1981. Represents 160 clients. 2% of clients are new/previously unpublished writers.

• Prior to opening his agency, Mr. Spieler was a magazine editor.

Member Agents: Joe Spieler; John Thornton (nonfiction); Lisa M. Ross (fiction/nonfiction).

Represents: Nonfiction, literary fiction and children's books. **Considers these nonfiction areas:** biography/autobiography; business; child guidance/parenting; cooking/food/nutrition; current affairs; ethnic/cultural interests; gay/lesbian issues; government/politics/law; history; memoirs; money/finance/economics; sociology; travel; women's studies. **Considers these fiction areas:** ethnic; family saga; feminist; gay; humor/satire; lesbian; literary.

How to Contact: Query with SASE. Considers simultaneous queries. Reports in 2 weeks on queries; 5 weeks on mss. Returns materials only with SASE.

Needs: Obtains new clients through recommendations and occasionally through listing in *Guide to Literary Agents*.

Recent Sales: *I'll Be Home Late Tonight*, by Susan Thames (Villard); *Our Stolen Future*, by Theo Colburn, et. al. (Dutton); *The Dance of Change*, by Peter Senge, et. al. (Doubleday); *The Seventh Child: A Lucky Life*, by Freddie Mae Baxter and Gloria Miller (Knopf).

Terms: Agent receives 15% commission on domestic sales. Charges for long distance phone/fax, photocopying, postage.

Writers' Conferences: London Bookfair; BEA.

◖ PHILIP G. SPITZER LITERARY AGENCY, 50 Talmage Farm Lane, East Hampton NY 11937. (516)329-3650. Fax: (516)329-3651. E-mail: spitzer516@aol.com. **Contact:** Philip Spitzer. Estab. 1969. Member of AAR. Represents 60 clients. 10% of clients are new/previously unpublished writers. Specializes in mystery/suspense, literary fiction, sports, general nonfiction (no how-to). Currently handles: 50% nonfiction books; 50% novels.

• Prior to opening his agency, Mr. Spitzer served at New York University Press, McGraw-Hill and the John Cushman Associates literary agency.

Represents: Nonfiction books, novels. **Considers these nonfiction areas:** biography/autobiography; business; current affairs; ethnic/cultural interests; government/politics/law; health/medicine; history; language/literature/criticism; military/war; music/dance/theater/film; nature/environment; popular culture; psychology; sociology; sports; true crime/investigative. **Considers these fiction areas:** contemporary issues; detective/police/crime; literary; mainstream; mystery/suspense; sports; thriller/espionage.

How to Contact: Send outline plus 1 sample chapter and SASE. Reports in 1 week on queries; 6 weeks on mss.

Needs: Usually obtains new clients on referral.

Recent Sales: *Angels Flight*, by Michael Connelly (Little, Brown); *Heartwood*, by James Lee Burke (Hyperion); *Eva Le Gallienne*, by Helen Sheehy (Knopf); *Dancing After Hours*, by Andre Dubus (Knopf).

Terms: Agent receives 15% commission on domestic sales; 20% on foreign sales. Charges for photocopying.

Writers' Conferences: BEA (Chicago).

✓ ◖ NANCY STAUFFER ASSOCIATES, P.O. Box 1203, Darien CT 06820. (203)655-3717. Fax: (203)655-3704. E-mail: nanstauf@earthlink.net. **Contact:** Nancy Stauffer Cahoon. Estab. 1989. Member of Writers At Work and the Entrada Institute. 10% of clients are new/previously unpublished writers. Currently handles: 45% nonfiction books; 60% fiction.

Represents: Literary fiction, short story collections, nonfiction books. **Considers these nonfiction areas:** animals; biography/autobiography; current affairs; ethnic/cultural interests; popular culture; self-help/personal improvement; narrative nonfiction. **Considers these fiction areas:** contemporary issues; literary; mainstream; regional.

How to Contact: Fiction: Send query letter with first 20 pages. Nonfiction: Send query letter with table of contents. Does not accept queries by fax or e-mail. Considers simultaneous queries and submission. Returns materials only with SASE.

Needs: Obtains new clients primarily through referrals from existing clients.

Recent Sales: *Dear John Wayne*, by Sherman Alexie (Grove/Atlantic); *Delirium of the Brain*, by William C. Harris (St. Martin's Press).

Terms: Agent receives 15% commission on domestic sales; 20% on foreign and film/TV sales.

Writers' Conferences: Writers At Work and Entrada; and the Radcliffe Publishing Course.

✓ ◔ ◖ STERNIG & BYRNE LITERARY AGENCY, 3209 S. 55, Milwaukee WI 53219-4433. (414)328-8034. Fax: (414)328-8034. E-mail: jackbyrne@aol.com. **Contact:** Jack Byrne. Estab. 1950s. Member of SFWA and MWA. Represents 30 clients. 20% of clients are new/unpublished writers. "We have a small, friendly, personal, hands-on teamwork approach to marketing." Currently handles: 5% nonfiction books; 40% juvenile books; 50% novels; 5% short stories.

Member Agents: Jack Byrne.

Represents: Nonfiction books, juvenile books, novels. **Considers these nonfiction areas:** biography/autobiography; juvenile nonfiction; popular culture. **Considers these fiction areas:** action/adventure; fantasy; glitz; horror; juvenile; mystery/suspense; psychic/supernatural; religious/inspirational; science fiction; thriller/espionage; young adult.

How to Contact: Query with SASE. Considers simultaneous queries; no simultaneous submissions. Reports in 3 weeks on queries; 3 months on mss. Returns materials only with SASE. "No SASE equals no return."

Needs: Actively seeking science fiction/fantasy. Does not want to receive romance, poetry, textbooks, highly specialized nonfiction.

Recent Sales: Sold 12 titles in the last year. Prefers not to share information on specific sales. Clients include Betty Ren Wright, Lyn McComchie, Lenard Daniel Houarner, Andre Norton.

Terms: Agent receives 15% commission on domestic sales; 20% on foreign sales. Offers written contract, open/non binding. 60 days notice must be given to terminate contract.

Reading List: Reads *Publishers Weekly, Locus, Science Fiction Chronicles,* etc. to find new clients. Looks for "whatever catches my eye."

Tips: "Don't send first drafts; have a professional presentation . . . including cover letter; know your field (read what's been done . . . good and bad)."

◯ ROBIN STRAUS AGENCY, INC., 229 E. 79th St., New York NY 10021. (212)472-3282. Fax: (212)472-3833. E-mail: springbird@aol.com. **Contact:** Robin Straus. Estab. 1983. Member of AAR. Specializes in high-quality fiction and nonfiction for adults. Currently handles: 65% nonfiction books; 35% novels.
   • Prior to becoming an agent, Robin Straus served as a subsidiary rights manager at Random House and Double-day and worked in editorial at Little, Brown.

Represents: Nonfiction, novels. **Considers these nonfiction areas:** animals; anthropology/archaeology; art/architecture/design; biography/autobiography; child guidance/parenting; cooking/food/nutrition; current affairs; ethnic/cultural interests; government/politics/law; health/medicine; history; language/literature/criticism; music/dance/theater/film; nature/environment; popular culture; psychology; science/technology; sociology; women's issues/women's studies. **Considers these fiction areas:** contemporary issues; family saga; historical; literary; mainstream; thriller/espionage.

How to Contact: Query with sample pages. "Will not download e-mail inquiries." SASE ("stamps, not metered postage") required for response and return of material submitted. Reports in 1 month on queries and mss.

Needs: Takes on very few new clients. Most new clients obtained through recommendations from others.

Recent Sales: Prefers not to share information on specific sales.

Terms: Agent receives 15% commission on domestic sales; 20% on foreign sales. Offers written contract when requested. Charges for "photocopying, UPS, messenger and foreign postage, etc. as incurred."

⊘ GUNTHER STUHLMANN, AUTHOR'S REPRESENTATIVE, P.O. Box 276, Becket MA 01223-0276. Estab. 1954. "We are taking on few new clients at this time."

✓ ⊘ ◎ SUITE A MANAGEMENT, 1101 S. Robertson Blvd., Suite 210, Los Angeles CA 90035. (310)278-0801. Fax: (310)278-0807. E-mail: suite-a@juno.com. Website: www.suite-a-management.com. **Contact:** Lloyd D. Robinson. Estab. 1996. Represents 50 clients. 15% of clients are new/unpublished writers. Representing writers, producers and directors of Movies of the Week for Network and Cable, Features with Budgets under 10Mil and Pilots/Series. Included among clients are a large percentage of novelists whose work is available for adaptation to screen and television. Currently handles: 40% movie scripts; 20% novels; 10% animation; 15% TV scripts; 10% stage plays; 5% multimedia.
   • See the expanded listing for this agency in Script Agents.

🅽 ⊘ SUNSHINE LITERARY AGENCY, P.O. Box 1060, Mims FL 32754-1060. (407)383-4799. Fax: (407)267-8076. E-mail: sunshine@gwc.net. **Contact:** Gail Grimard. Estab. 1998. Member of PAS. Represents 40 clients. 90% of clients are new/unpublished writers. Currently handles: 20% nonfiction books; 5% juvenile books; 2% story collections; 70% novels; 3% poetry.

Member Agents: Steve Greene, Gail Grimard.

Represents: Nonfiction books, juvenile books, novels, poetry books, short story collections. **Considers these nonfiction areas:** biography/autobiography; business; child guidance/parenting; ethnic/cultural interests; health/medicine; juvenile nonfiction; military/war; money/finance/economics; New Age/metaphysics; psychology; religious/inspirational; self-help/personal improvement. **Considers these fiction areas:** action/adventure; contemporary issues; detective/police/crime; family saga; fantasy; historical; horror; humor/satire; juvenile; literary; mainstream; mystery; psychic/supernatural; romance; religious/inspirational; science fiction; thriller/espionage; young adult.

How to Contact: Send entire ms. Accepts queries by e-mail. Considers simultaneous queries and submissions. Reports in 2 weeks on queries; 1 month on mss. Returns materials only with SASE.

Needs: Actively seeking nonfiction, short story collections, children's stories. Does not want to receive pornography, screen plays, movie scripts. Obtains new clients through recommendations from others, queries.

Recent Sales: Sold 1 title in the last year. *Pappy's War,* by John Paris (Merriam Press).

Terms: Agent receives 10% commission on domestic sales; 20% on foreign sales. Offers written contract, binding for 6 months. 30 notice must be given to terminate contract. Charges for postage, photocopying, long-distance calls, etc. (averages $20-25 per month).

Tips: "Be sure to include a one-page synopsis or overview double-spaced with submissions. We update our clients every two months via mail to keep them informed of what progress is being made on their manuscripts."

✓ ◖ THE SWAYNE AGENCY LITERARY MANAGEMENT & CONSULTING, INC., 337 E. 54th St., New York NY 10022. (212)391-5438. E-mail: lswayne@swayneagency.com. Website: www.swayneagency.com. **Contact:** Lisa Swayne. Estab. 1997. Represents 75 clients. Specializes in authors who participate in multimedia: book publishing, radio, movies and television, and information technology. Currently handles: 80% nonfiction books; 20% fiction.

• Prior to opening her agency, Lisa Swayne was a senior agent at Adler & Robin Books and an editor at G.P. Putnam's Sons.

Member Agents: Lisa Swayne (technology-related fiction/nonfiction, women's issues, gay/lesbian issues, literary fiction, self help, health/fitness).

Represents: Nonfiction books, novels, computer technology books. **Considers these nonfiction areas:** business; computers/electronics; current affairs; ethnic/cultural interests; gay/lesbian issues; how-to; popular culture; self-help/personal improvement; women's issues/women's studies. **Considers these fiction areas:** contemporary issues; ethnic; literary; mystery; suspense; thriller/espionage.

How to Contact: Query with outline/proposal and SASE. *No fax queries.* Reports in 4-6 weeks on all submissions.

Needs: Actively seeking technology related nonfiction—particularly aimed at women or business; literary novels. Does not want to receive westerns, romance novels, science fiction, children's books. Obtains new clients through recommendations by colleagues and clients.

Recent Sales: Sold 50 titles in the last year. *Healing Mudras,* by Sabrina Mesko (Ballantine); *Citizen Greenspan,* by Justin Martin (Perseus Books); *Nurturing the Writer's Self,* by Bonni Goldberg (Penguin Putnam).

Terms: Agent receives 15% commission on domestic sales; 20% on foreign sales. Offers written contract, binding for 1 year. 60 days notice must be given to terminate contract.

Reading List: Reads *Red Herring, Business 2.0, Fast Company, Wall Street Journal, New York Observer, The Industry Standard, Glimmer Train* to find new clients. Looks for cutting edge business, technology topics and trends and up and coming fiction authors.

✔ ☑ SYDRA TECHNIQUES CORP., 481 Eighth Ave., E24, New York NY 10001. (212)631-0009. Fax: (212)631-0715. E-mail: sbuck@virtualnews.com. **Contact:** Sid Buck. Estab. 1988. Signatory of WGA. Represents 30 clients. 80% of clients are new/unpublished writers. Currently handles: 30% movie scripts; 10% novels; 30% TV scripts; 10% nonfiction books; 10% stage plays; 10% multimedia.

• See the expanded listing for this agency in Script Agents.

Ⓝ ☑ THE JOHN TALBOT AGENCY, 540 W. Boston Post Rd., PMB 266, Mamaroweck NY 10543-3437. (914)381-9463. **Contact:** John Talbot. Estab. 1998. Member of the Authors Guild. Represents 40 clients. 15% of clients are new/unpublished writers. Specializes in literary and commercial fiction, and general nonfiction. Currently handles: 35% nonfiction books; 65% novels.

• Prior to becoming an agent, Mr. Talbot was a book editor at Simon & Schuster and Putnam Berkley. One of Mr. Talbot's clients recently had her novel selected for the Book of the Month Club.

Represents: Nonfiction books, novels. **Considers these nonfiction areas:** general and narrative nonfiction. **Considers these fiction area:** literary; suspense.

How to Contact: Query with SASE. Does not accept queries by fax or e-mail. Considers simultaneous queries. Reports in 1 month on queries; 2 months on mss.

Needs: Actively seeking suspense and literary fiction, "particularly by writers who are beginning to publish in magazines and literary journals." Also narrative nonfiction, especially outdoor adventure and spirituality. Does not want to receive children's books, science fiction, fantasy, westerns, poetry or screenplays. Obtains new clients through referrals, queries and conferences.

Recent Sales: Sold 25 titles in the last year. *Deep Sound Channel,* by Joe Buff (Bantam); *Lily of the Valley,* by Suzanne Strempek Sheen (Pocket Books); *The Fuck-Up,* by Arthur Nersesian (Pocket Books/MTV); *The Complete Idiot's Guide to Fantasy Baseball,* by Michael Zimmerman (Macmillan). Other clients include Robert Drake, Julio Esquivel, Charles Jaco, Clarence Major, Doris Meredith, Peter Telep, Barrett Tillman.

Terms: Agent receives 15% commission on domestic sales; 20% on foreign sales. Offers written contract. 2 weeks notice must be given to terminate contract. Charges for photocopying, overnight delivery, additional copies of books needed for use in sale of subsidiary rights, and fees incurred for submitting mss or books overseas.

Writers' Conferences: Florida Suncoast Writers Conference (St. Petersburg FL, February).

Tips: "I run an editorially-driven agency and bring the perspective of having been in the corporate book publishing industry for 14 years."

☑ ROSLYN TARG LITERARY AGENCY, INC., 105 W. 13th St., New York NY 10011. (212)206-9390. Fax: (212)989-6233. E-mail: roslyntarg@aol.com. **Contact:** Roslyn Targ. Original agency estab. 1945; name changed to Roslyn Targ Literary Agency, Inc. in 1970. Member of AAR. Represents approximately 100 clients.

Member Agents: B. Jones.

Represents: Nonfiction books, novels, juvenile books, self-help.

How to Contact: No mss without queries first. Query with outline, proposal, curriculum vitae, and SASE. Prefers to be only reader.

Needs: Obtains new clients through recommendations, solicitation, queries.

Recent Sales: *How to Have an Out-Of-Body Experience in 30 Days* and *How to Have Lucid Dreams in 30 Days,* by Keith Harary, Ph.D. and Pamela Weintraub (St. Martin's Press); *Blowing Zen,* by Ray Brooks (H.J. Kramer); *A Season of Passion: Men and Women Talk About Love, Sex and Romance After 60,* by Zenith Gross (New World Library); *African-American Humor: An Anthology,* by Mel Watkins (Lawrence Hill Books).

Terms: Agent receives 15% commission on domestic sales; 20% on foreign sales. Charges standard agency fees (bank charges, long distance, postage, photocopying, shipping of books, overseas long distance and shipping, etc.).

Tips: "This agency reads on an exclusive basis only."

[N] [ ] [◐] REBECCA TAYLOR, LITERARY AGENT, 8491 Hospital Dr., PMB 196, Douglasville GA 30134. (770)947-8263. E-mail: atllitagnt@aol.com. **Contact:** Rebecca Taylor. Estab. 1998. Member of Board of Directors of Georgia Writers Inc. Represents 12 clients. 65% of clients are new/unpublished writers. Currently handles: 10% nonfiction books; 60% juvenile books; 30% novels.
   • Prior to opening her agency, Ms. Taylor was an administrative assistant and apprentice agent.
Represents: Nonfiction books, juvenile books, novels.**Considers these nonfiction areas:** cooking/food/nutrition; juvenile nonfiction; women's issues/women's studies. **Considers these fiction areas:** contemporary issues; family saga; feminist; juvenile; literary fiction; picture book; romance; young adult.
How to Contact: Send outline and 3-5 sample chapters. Does not accept queries by fax or e-mail. Considers simultaneous queries and submissions. Reports in 6 weeks on queries; 2 months on mss. Returns materials only with SASE.
Needs: Actively seeking women's fiction, romance and literary fiction. Does not want to receive screenplays, poetry or science fiction. Obtains new clients through recommendations from clients, conferences.
Recent Sales: New agency with no reported sales. Clients include Valerie Norris, Pamela Levine, June Bowman, Sally Coup.
Terms: Agent receives 15% commission on domestic sales; 20% on foreign sales. Offers written contract. 30 days notice must be given to terminate contract. Charges for unpublished clients for photocopying and postage.
Tips: "I am not afraid to break the rules when necessary, and I feel this industry needs that right now. I have found my previous experience and passion for what I do, coupled with my fresh attitude and unique perspective has been an advantageous distinction. I am currently looking for quality children's picture books and young adult material, and well-written, tasteful romance novels, women's fiction and literary fiction, all written with a fresh perspective and new ideas. I expect my clients to be flexible to constructive criticism, while remaining confident in their ability and attitude."

[$] [♥] PATRICIA TEAL LITERARY AGENCY, 2036 Vista Del Rosa, Fullerton CA 92831-1336. (714)738-8333. **Contact:** Patricia Teal. Estab. 1978. Member of AAR, RWA, Authors Guild. Represents 60 clients. Specializes in women's fiction and commercial how-to and self-help nonfiction. Currently handles: 10% nonfiction books; 90% novels.
Represents: Nonfiction books, novels. **Considers these nonfiction areas:** animals; biography/autobiography; child guidance/parenting; health/medicine; how-to; psychology; self-help/personal improvement; true crime/investigative; women's issues. **Considers these fiction areas:** glitz, mainstream, mystery/suspense, romance (contemporary, historical).
How to Contact: Published authors only. Query with SASE. Considers simultaneous queries. Reports in 10 days on queries; 6 weeks on requested mss. Returns materials only with SASE.
Needs: Does not want to receive poetry, short stories, articles, science fiction, fantasy, regency romance. Usually obtains new clients through recommendations from authors and editors or at conferences.
Recent Sales: Sold 35 titles in the last year. *The Orchid Hunter*, by Jill Marie Landis (Jove); *A Thanksgiving to Remember*, by Margaret Watson (Harlequin/Silhouette).
Terms: Agent receives 10-15% commission on domestic sales; 20% on foreign sales. Offers written contract, binding for 1 year. Charges $35 postage fee for first book, none thereafter.
Writers' Conferences: Romance Writers of America conferences; Asilomar (California Writers Club); Bouchercon; BEA (Chicago, June); California State University San Diego (January); Hawaii Writers Conference (Maui).
Reading List: Reads *Publishers Weekly*, *Romance Report* and *Romantic Times* to find new clients. "I read the reviews of books and excerpts from authors' books."
Tips: "Include SASE with all correspondence."

[✓] [♥] IRENE TIERSTEN LITERARY AGENCY, (formerly Jet Literary Associates, Inc.), 540 Ridgewood Rd., Maplewood NJ 07040. (973)762-4024. Fax: (973)762-0349. E-mail: tiersten@ix.netcom.com. **Contact:** Irene Tiersten. Prefers to work with published/established authors.
Represents: Adult fiction and nonfiction, young adult fiction and nonfiction. No poetry.
How to Contact: Reports in 2 weeks on queries; 1 month on mss.
Recent Sales: *The Lost Deep Thoughts*, by Jack Handey (Hyperion/Disney); *Mysteries of the Opposite Sex*, by David Feldman (Little, Brown); *Traveling Light*, by Katrina Kittle (Warner Books); *Night Flyers*, by Elizabeth Jones (Pleasant/American Girl Series); *Unsuspecting Angel*, by Beverly Bird (Harlequin/Silhouette).
Terms: Agency receives 15% commission on domestic sales; 15% on dramatic sales; 25% on foreign and translation sales (split with co-agents abroad). Charges for international phone and postage expenses.

[✓] [♥] [◎] TOAD HALL, INC., RR 2, Box 16B, Laceyville PA 18623. (717)869-2942. Fax: (717)869-1031. E-mail: toadhallco@aol.com. Website: www.toadhallinc.com. **Contact:** Sharon Jarvis, Anne Pinzow. Estab. 1982. Member of AAR. Represents 35 clients. 10% of clients are new/previously unpublished writers. Specializes in popular nonfiction, some category fiction. Prefers New Age, paranormal, unusual but popular approaches. Currently handles: 50% nonfiction books; 40% novels; 5% movie scripts; 5% ancillary projects.
   • Prior to becoming an agent, Ms. Jarvis was an acquisitions editor.
Member Agents: Sharon Jarvis (fiction, nonfiction); Anne Pinzow (TV, movies); Roxy LeRose (unpublished writers).
Represents: Nonfiction books. **Considers these nonfiction areas:** animals; anthropology/archaeology; business; child guidance/parenting; cooking/food/nutrition; crafts/hobbies; health/medicine; how-to; nature/environment; New Age/

metaphysics; popular culture; religious/inspirational; self-help/personal improvement. **Considers these fiction areas:** historical; mystery/suspense; romance (contemporary, historical, regency); science fiction.

Also Handles: Feature film; TV MOW, episodic drama. **Considers these script areas:** action/adventure; comedy; contemporary issues; detective/police/crime; ethnic; family saga; fantasy; feminist; historical; horror; juvenile; mainstream; mystery/suspense; romantic comedy; science fiction.

How to Contact: Query with SASE. "No fax or e-mail submissions considered." Reports in 3 weeks on queries; 3 months on mss. For scripts, send outline/proposal with query. "We only handle scripts written by our clients who have published material agented by us." Reports in 3 weeks on queries; 3 months on mss.

Needs: Does not want to receive poetry, short stories, essays, collections, children's books. Obtains new clients through recommendations from others, solicitation, at conferences.

Recent Sales: Sold 6 titles in the last year. *The Face of Time*, by Camille Bacon-Smith (DAW); *Against All Odds*, by Barbara Riefe (TOR); *Herbal Medicine*, by Mary Atwood (Sterling); *Blood on The Moon* by Sharman DiVono (movie option to ABC).

Terms: Agent receives 15% commission on domestic sales; 10% on foreign sales. Offers written contract, binding for 1 year. Charges for photocopying and special postage (i.e., express mail). 100% of business is derived from commissions on sales.

Tips: "Pay attention to what is getting published. Show the agent you've done your homework!"

ANN TOBIAS—A LITERARY AGENCY FOR CHILDREN'S BOOKS, 307 S. Carolina Ave., S.E., Washington DC 20003. (202)543-1043. **Contact:** Ann Tobias. Estab. 1988. Member of Children's Book Guild of Washington, Women's National Book Association, SCBWI. Represents 25 clients. 50% of clients are new/unpublished writers. Currently handles 100% juvenile books.
- Prior to opening her agency, Ms. Tobias worked as a children's book editor at Harper, William Morrow and Scholastic.

Represents: Juvenile books. **Considers this nonfiction area:** juvenile nonfiction. **Considers these fiction areas:** picture book texts; mid-level and young adult novels; poetry; illustrated mss.

How to Contact: Send entire ms with SASE. Considers simultaneous queries and submissions. Reports immediately on queries; in 2 months on mss. Returns materials only with SASE.

Needs: Actively seeking material for children. Obtains new clients through recommendations from editors. "Read a few books out of the library on how literary agents do business before approaching one."

Recent Sales: Sold 12 titles in the last year. Prefers not to share information on specific sales.

Terms: Agent receives 15% commission on domestic sales; 20% on foreign sales. No written contract. Charges for photocopying, overnight mail, foreign postage, foreign telephone.

Reading List: Reads *Horn Book*, *Bulletin for the Center of the Book* and *School Library Journal* to find new clients. "These are review media and they keep me up to date on who is being published and by what company."

Tips: "As a former children's book editor I believe I am of special help to my clients, as I understand the practices of the children's book publishing field."

SUSAN TRAVIS LITERARY AGENCY, P.O. Box 3670, Burbank CA 91508-3670. (818)557-6538. Fax: (818)557-6549. **Contact:** Susan Travis. Estab. 1995. Represents 10 clients. 60% of clients are new/previously unpublished writers. Specializes in mainstream fiction and nonfiction. Currently handles: 70% nonfiction books; 30% novels.
- Prior to opening her agency, Ms. Travis served as an agent with the McBride Agency and prior to that worked in the Managing Editors Department of Ballantine Books.

Represents: Nonfiction books, novels. **Considers these nonfiction areas:** business; child guidance/parenting; cooking/food/nutrition; ethnic/cultural interests; health/medicine; how-to; nature/environment; popular culture; psychology; self-help/personal improvement; women's issues/women's studies. **Considers these fiction areas:** contemporary issues; ethnic; historical; literary; mainstream; romance (historical).

How to Contact: Query first with SASE. Reports in 3 weeks on queries; 4-6 weeks on mss.

Needs: Actively seeking mainstream nonfiction. Does not want to receive science fiction, poetry or children's books. Obtains new clients through referrals from existing clients, and mss requested from query letters.

Recent Sales: Prefers not to share information on specific sales.

Terms: Agent receives 15% commission on domestic sales; 20% on foreign sales. Offers written contract, binding for 1 year, with 60 day cancellation clause. Charges for photocopying of mss and proposals if copies not provided by author. 100% of business is derived from commissions on sales.

N **SCOTT TREIMEL NEW YORK**, 434 Lafayette St., New York NY 10003. (212)505-8353. Fax: (212)505-0664. E-mail: mescottyt@earthlink.net. **Contact:** Scott Treimel. Estab. 1995. Represents 20 clients. 30% of

---

TO RECEIVE REGULAR TIPS AND UPDATES about writing and Writer's Digest publications via e-mail, send an e-mail with "SUBSCRIBE NEWSLETTER" in the body of the message to "newsletter-request@writersdigest.com."

clients are new/unpublished writers. Specializes in children's book from concept board books through young adult novels: tightly focused segment of the trade and educational markets. Currently handles: 100% juvenile books.

● Prior to becoming an agent, Mr. Treimel was a rights agent for Scholastic, Inc., a book packager and rights agent for United Feature Syndicate; and the founding director of Warner Bros. Worldwide Publishing.

Represents: Juvenile books, picture books, middle grade. **Considers all juvenile nonfiction areas. Considers all juvenile fiction areas.**

How to Contact: Query with SASE. For picture books, send entire ms. Does not accept queries by fax or e-mail. Prefers to be only reader. Prefers "30 day exclusive read on manuscripts/request." Reports in 2 weeks on queries; 1 month on mss. Returns materials only with SASE or discards.

Needs: Actively seeking picture book illustrators, picture book authors, first chapter books, middle-grade fiction and nonfiction, young adult fiction. Obtains new clients through recommendations and queries.

Recent Sales: Sold 24 titles in the last year. Prefers not to share information on specific sales.

Terms: Agent receives 15% commission on domestic sales; 20% on foreign sales. Offers verbal or written contract, "binding on a contract by contract basis." Charges for photocopying, overnight/express postage, messengers and book orders.

Writers' Conferences: Society of Children's Book Writers & Illustrators (Los Angeles, August).

◩ **2M COMMUNICATIONS LTD.**, 121 W. 27 St., #601, New York NY 10001. (212)741-1509. Fax: (212)691-4460. **Contact:** Madeleine Morel. Estab. 1982. Represents 40 clients. 20% of clients are new/previously unpublished writers. Specializes in adult nonfiction. Currently handles: 100% nonfiction books.

Represents: Nonfiction books. **Considers these nonfiction areas:** biography/autobiography; child guidance/parenting; ethnic/cultural interests; gay/lesbian issues; health/medicine; memoirs; music/dance/theater/film; self-help/personal improvement; travel; women's issues/women's studies.

How to Contact: Query with SASE. Reports in 1 week on queries.

Needs: Obtains new clients through recommendations from others, solicitation.

Recent Sales: *Irish Heritage Cookbook* (Chronicle Books); *Excruciating History of Dentistry* (St. Martin's); *Safe Shopper's Bible for Kids* (Macmillan); *Dewey Beats Truman* (Avon).

Terms: Agent receives 15% commission on domestic sales; 20% on foreign sales. Offers written contract, binding for 2 years. Charges for postage, photocopying, long distance calls and faxes.

◩◯◩ **UNITED TRIBES**, 240 W. 35th St., #500, New York NY 10001. (212)534-7646. Fax: (212)534-7035. E-mail: janguerth@aol.com. Website: www.unitedtribes.com. **Contact:** Jan-Erik Guerth. Estab. 1998. Represents 20 clients. 30% of clients are new/unpublished writers. Specializes in the "Spirituality of Everyday Life" and ethnic, social, gender and cultural issues; comparative religions; self-help and wellness; science and arts; history and politics; nature and travel; and any fascinating future trends. Currently handles: 90% nonfiction books, 10% novels.

● Prior to becoming an agent, Mr. Guerth was a comedian, journalist, radio producer and film distributor.

Represents: Nonfiction books, novels. **Considers these nonfiction areas:** anthropology/archaeology; art/architecture/design; biography/autobiography; business; child guidance/parenting; cooking/food/nutrition; current affairs; education; ethnic/cultural interests; gay/lesbian issues; government/politics/law; health/medicine; history; how-to; language/literature/criticism; memoirs; money/finance/economics; music/dance/theater/film; nature/enviornment; popular culture; psychology; religious/inspirational; science/technology (popular); self-help/personal improvement; sociology; translations; women's issues/women's studies. **Considers these fiction areas:** ethnic; historical; religious/inspirational.

How to Contact: Send outline and 3 sample chapters with SASE, include résumé. Accepts queries by e-mail. Prefers to be only reader. Reports in 2 weeks on queries; 1 month on mss. Returns materials only with SASE.

Needs: Obtains new clients through recommendations from others, solicitations and conferences.

Recent Sales: Prefers not to share information on specific sales.

Terms: Agent receives 15% commission on domestic sales; 20% on foreign sales.

◩ **THE RICHARD R. VALCOURT AGENCY, INC.**, 177 E. 77th St., PHC, New York NY 10021-1934. Phone/fax: (212)570-2340. President: Richard R. Valcourt. Estab. 1995. Represents 50 clients. 20% of clients are new/previously unpublished writers. Specializes in intelligence and other national security affairs; domestic and international politics. Currently handles: 100% nonfiction books.

● Prior to opening his agency, Mr. Valcourt was a journalist, editor and college political science instructor. He is also editor-in-chief of the *International Journal of Intelligence* and a faculty member at American Military University in Virginia.

Represents: Nonfiction books and scholarly books. **Considers these nonfiction areas:** biography; current affairs; government/politics/law; history; memoirs; military/war.

How to Contact: Query with SASE. No queries by fax. Prefers to be only reader. Reports in 1 week on queries; 1 month on mss. Returns materials only with SASE.

Needs: Represents exclusively academics, journalists and professionals in the categories listed. Obtains new clients through active recruitment and recommendations from others.

Recent Sales: *Fixing The Spy Machine: An Insider's View on Overhauling U.S. Intelligence*, by Arthur S. Hulnick (Praeger); *Freedom Radios: How Radio Free Europe and Radio Liberty Broke the Soviet Information Blockade*, by Arch Puddington (University Press of Kentucky).

Reading List: Reads *The New Republic, The Nation, The Weekly Standard, Commentary, International Journal of*

Intelligence and *Intelligence and National Security* to find new clients. Looks for "expertise in my highly-specialized concentrations."

Terms: Agent receives 15% commission on domestic sales; 20% on foreign sales. Offers written contract. Charges for extensive photocopying, express mail and overseas telephone expenses.

◐ **VAN DER LEUN & ASSOCIATES**, 22 Division St., Easton CT 06612. (203)259-4897. **Contact:** Patricia Van der Leun, president. Estab. 1984. Represents 30 clients. Specializes in fiction, science, biography. Currently handles: 60% nonfiction books; 40% novels.

   • Prior to opening her agency, Ms. Van der Leun was a professor of Art History.

Represents: Nonfiction books, novels. **Considers these nonfiction areas:** current affairs; ethnic; history; cookbooks; literary; memoirs; travel. **Considers all fiction areas except science fiction.**

How to Contact: Query with SASE. Reports in 2 weeks on queries; 1 month on mss.

Recent Sales: Sold 9 titles in the last year. *War Crimes*, by Aryeh Neier (Times Books); *The Extraterrestrial Encyclopedia*, by David Darling (Times Books); *Sea of Memory*, by Erri de Luca (Ecco Press).

Terms: Agent receives 15% on domestic sales; 25% on foreign sales. Offers written contract.

Tips: "We are interested in high-quality, serious writers only."

◨ ◐ **RALPH VICIANANZA, LTD.**, 111 Eighth Ave., Suite 1501, New York NY 10011. This agency did not respond to our request for information. Query before submitting.

◨ ◐ **DAVID VIGLIANO LITERARY AGENCY**, 584 Broadway, Suite 809, New York NY 10012. This agency did not respond to our request for information. Query before submitting.

☑ ◐ **THE VINES AGENCY, INC.**, 648 Broadway, Suite 901, New York NY 10012. (212)777-5522. Fax: (212)777-5978. E-mail: jvtva@mindspring.com. **Contact:** James C. Vines or Gary Neuwirth. Estab. 1995. Member of AAR, signatory of WGA. Represents 52 clients. 2% of clients are new/previously unpublished writers. Specializes in mystery, suspense, science fiction, mainstream novels, screenplays, teleplays. Currently handles: 50% nonfiction books; 50% novels.

   • Prior to opening his agency, Mr. Vines served as an agent with the Virginia Literary Agency.

Member Agents: James C. Vines; Gary Neuwirth; Ali Ryan (women's fiction and nonfiction, mainstream).

Represents: Nonfiction books, novels. **Considers these nonfiction areas:** business; biography/autobiography; current affairs; ehnic/cultural interests; history; how-to; humor; military/war; memoirs; money/finance/economics; nature/environment; New Age/metaphysics; photography; popular culture; psychology; religious/inspirational; science/technology; self help/personal improvement; sociology; sports; translations; travel; true crime/investigative; women's issues/women's

---

🏆 **CLOSE UP** with James C. Vines, The Vines Agency, Inc.
. . . On rapid changes in publishing

"I guide my clients through the rapid changes in publishing by being sure I have all the latest information about the business. For example, editors change jobs very frequently these days, and being able to recommend and offer a new manuscript to an editor on the first day of her new job often results in a great sale!

"Since I stay in close touch with all editors, I know what each one is looking for and can usually offer them the right book at the right time. This strategy is especially important in the current marketplace, with large publishers constantly consolidating and thereby reducing the total number of buyers.

"I am also extremely passionate about electronic rights, which I believe will become a major revenue stream for my clients. I absolutely refuse to do deals that pay no advance to the author, and I believe that by holding out for electronic publishing deals that actually pay advances, my clients are positioned perfectly to enter the electronic publishing marketplace at the right moment.

"I decided to become an agent because I love authors. I have a good business sense, which is something I've discovered most authors lack. I enjoy being near creative artists and sharing in their triumphs. What I find most satisfying about this profession is that I have the ability to help great authors achieve their best work. Because I so strongly believe in my clients and their works, I'm able to obtain the best possible business arrangements for them in this very competitive marketplace."

studies. **Considers these fiction areas:** action/adventure; contemporary issues; detective/police/crime; ethnic; feminist; horror; humor/satire; experimental; family saga; gay; lesbian; historical; literary; mainstream; mystery/suspense; psychic/supernatural; regional; romance (contemporary, historical); science fiction; sports; thriller/espionage; westerns/frontier; women's fiction.

Also Handles: Feature film, TV scripts, stage plays. **Considers these script subject areas:** action/adventure; comedy; detective/police/crime; ethnic; experimental; feminist; gay; historical; horror; lesbian; mainstream; mystery/suspense; romance (comedy, drama); science fiction; teen; thriller; westerns/frontier.

How to Contact: Send outline and first 3 chapters with SASE. Accepts queries by fax and e-mail. "Maximum of one page by fax or e-mail." Considers simultaneous queries and submissions. Reports in 2 weeks on queries; 1 month on mss. Returns materials only with SASE.

Needs: Obtains new clients through query letters, recommendations from others, reading short stories in magazines and soliciting conferences.

Recent Sales: Sold 46 book titles and 5 script projects in the last year. *California Fire and Life*, by Don Winslow (Random House); *Sugar*, by Bernice McFadden (Doubleday). *Script(s) optioned/sold: Ninth Life*, by Jay Colvin (Miramax).

Terms: Agent receives 15% commission on domestic sales; 20% on foreign sales. Offers written contract, binding for 1 year, with 30 days cancellation clause. Charges for foreign postage, messenger services and photocopying. 100% of business is derived from commissions on sales.

Writers' Conferences: Maui Writer's Conference.

Tips: "Do not follow up on submissions with phone calls to the agency. The agency will read and respond by mail only. Do not pack your manuscript in plastic 'peanuts' that will make us have to vacuum the office after opening the package containing your manuscript. Always enclose return postage."

◉ MARY JACK WALD ASSOCIATES, INC., 111 E. 14th St., New York NY 10003. (212)254-7842. **Contact:** Danis Sher. Estab. 1985. Member of AAR, Authors Guild, SCBWI. Represents 35 clients. 5% of clients are new/previously unpublished writers. Specializes in literary works, juvenile. Currently handles: adult and juvenile fiction and nonfiction, including some original film/TV scripts.

 • This agency is not currently accepting queries or submissions.

Member Agents: Danis Sher. Foreign rights representative: Lynne Rabinoff, Lynne Rabinoff Associates.

Represents: Nonfiction books, juvenile books, novels, novellas, short story collections, movie scripts, TV scripts. **Considers these nonfiction areas:** biography/autobiography; current affairs; ethnic/cultural interests; history; juvenile nonfiction; language/literature/criticism; music/dance/theater/film; nature/environment; photography; sociology; translations; true crime/investigative. **Considers these fiction areas:** action/adventure; contemporary issues; detective/police/crime; ethnic; experimental; family saga; feminist; gay; glitz; historical; juvenile; literary; mainstream; mystery/suspense; picture book; satire; thriller; young adult.

How to Contact: Query with SASE. Reports in 2 months. Will request more if interested.

Needs: Obtains new clients through recommendations from others.

Recent Sales: *Cactus Tracks & Cowboy Philosophy*, by Baxter Black (Crown); *2099* Series (6 books), by John Peel (Scholastic, Inc.); *The Longest Ride*, by Denise Lewis Patrick (Henry Holt & Co.).

Terms: Agent receives 15% commission on domestic sales; 15-30% on foreign sales. Offers written contract, binding for 1 year.

▣ ◉ WALLACE LITERARY AGENCY, INC., 177 E. 70 St., New York NY 10021. (212)570-9090. **Contact:** Lois Wallace. Estab. 1988. Represents 50 clients. 0% of clients are new/previously unpublished writers. Specializes in fiction and nonfiction by good writers.

Represents: Nonfiction books, novels. **Considers these nonfiction areas:** anthropology/archaeology, biography/autobiography, current affairs, history, literature. **Considers these fiction areas:** literary, mainstream, mystery/suspense.

How to Contact: Send outline, 1 (at the most 2) sample chapter, reviews of previously published books, curriculum vitae, return postage. Reports in 3 weeks on queries with material.

Needs: Does not want to receive children's books, cookbooks, how-to, photography, poetry, romance, science fiction or self-help.

Recent Sales: Prefers not to share information on specific sales.

Terms: Agent receives 10-15% commission on domestic sales; 20% on foreign sales. Offers written contract; binding until terminated with notice. Charges for photocopying, book shipping (or ms shipping) overseas, legal fees (if needed, with writer's approval), galleys and books needed for representation and foreign sales.

Tips: Obtains new clients through "recommendations from editors and writers we respect."

◉ JOHN A. WARE LITERARY AGENCY, 392 Central Park West, New York NY 10025-5801. (212)866-4733. Fax: (212)866-4734. **Contact:** John Ware. Estab. 1978. Represents 60 clients. 40% of clients are new/previously unpublished writers. Currently handles: 75% nonfiction books; 25% novels.

 • Prior to opening his agency, Mr. Ware served as a literary agent with James Brown Associates/Curtis Brown, Ltd. and as an editor for Doubleday & Company.

Represents: Nonfiction books, novels. **Considers these nonfiction areas:** animals; anthropology; biography; current affairs; government/politics/law; history (including oral history, Americana and folklore); investigative journalism; language; music; nature/environment; popular culture; psychology and health (academic credentials required); science;

sports; travel; true crime; women's issues/women's studies; 'bird's eye' views of phenomena. **Considers these fiction areas:** accessible literate noncategory fiction; detective/police/crime; mystery/suspense; thriller/espionage.
How to Contact: Query by letter first only, include SASE. Reports in 2 weeks on queries.
Recent Sales: *The Ice Master,* by Jennifer Niven McJunkin (Hyperion); *Looks Like a Million,* by M.H. Dunlop (William Morrow); *The Lost Explorer,* by Conrad Anker and David Roberts (Simon & Schuster); *The Immortal Class of Chicago,* by Travis Culley (Villard/Random House). Other clients include Jon Krakauer, Jack Womack and Caroline Fraser.
Terms: Agent receives 15% commission on domestic sales; 15% on dramatic sales; 20% on foreign sales. Charges for messenger service, photocopying, extraordinary expenses.
Tips: "Writers must have appropriate credentials for authorship of proposal (nonfiction) or manuscript (fiction); no publishing track record required. Open to good writing and interesting ideas by new or veteran writers."

N: Ø HARRIET WASSERMAN LITERARY AGENCY, 137 E. 36th St., New York NY 10016. This agency did not respond to our request for information. Query before submitting.

Ø WATKINS LOOMIS AGENCY, INC., 133 E. 35th St., Suite 1, New York NY 10016. (212)532-0080. Fax: (212)889-0506. **Contact:** Katherine Fausset. Estab. 1908. Represents 150 clients. Specializes in literary fiction, London/UK translations, nonfiction.
Member Agents: Nicole Aragi (associate); Gloria Loomis (president); Katherine Fausset (assistant agent).
Represents: Nonfiction books, novels. **Considers these nonfiction areas:** art/architecture/design; biography/autobiography; current affairs; ethnic/cultural interests; gay/lesbian issues; history; nature/environment; popular culture; science/technology; translations; true crime/investigative; women's issues/women's studies; journalism. **Considers these fiction areas:** contemporary issues; ethnic; gay; literary; mainstream; mystery/suspense.
How to Contact: Query with SASE. Reports within 1 month on queries.
Recent Sales: Prefers not to share information on specific sales. Clients include Walter Mosley, Edwidge Danticat, Katharine Weber and Junot Díaz.
Terms: Agent receives 15% commission on domestic sales; 20% on foreign sales.

✓ $ Ø SANDRA WATT & ASSOCIATES, 1750 N. Sierra Bonita, Hollywood CA 90046-2423. (323)851-1021. Fax: (323)851-1046. E-mail: rondvart@aol.com. Estab. 1977. Signatory of WGA. Represents 55 clients. 15% of clients are new/previously unpublished writers. Specializes in "books to film" and scripts: film noir; family; romantic comedies; books: women's fiction, young adult, mystery, commercial nonfiction. Currently handles: 40% nonfiction books; 60% novels.
● Prior to opening her agency, Ms. Watt was vice president of an educational publishing compoany.
Member Agents: Sandra Watt (scripts, nonfiction, novels); Pricilla Palmer (adult, YA, children's).
Represents: Nonfiction books, novels. **Considers these nonfiction areas:** agriculture/horticulture; animals; anthropology/archaeology; art/architecture/design; crafts/hobbies; current affairs; how-to; humor; language/literature/criticism; memoirs; nature/environment; New Age/metaphysics; popular culture; psychology; reference; religious/inspirational; self-help/personal improvement; sports; travel; true crime/investigative; women's issues/women's studies. **Considers these fiction areas:** contemporary issues; detective/police/crime; family saga; mainstream; mystery/suspense; regional; religious/inspirational; thriller/espionage; women's mainstream novels.
How to Contact: Query with SASE. Accepts queries by fax and e-mail. Considers simultaneous queries and submissions. Reports in 2 weeks on queries; 2 months on mss. Returns materials only with SASE.
Needs: Does not want to receive "first 'ideas' for finished work." Obtains new clients through recommendations from others, referrals and "from wonderful query letters. Don't forget the SASE!"
Recent Sales: Sold 8 titles in the last year. *Risk Factor,* by Charles Atkins (St. Martin's Press); *Love is the Only Answer* (Putnam).
Terms: Agent receives 15% commission on domestic sales; 25% on foreign sales. Offers written contract, binding for 1 year. Charges one-time nonrefundable marketing fee of $100 *for unpublished authors.*

Ø SCOTT WAXMAN AGENCY, INC., 1650 Broadway, Suite 1011, New York NY 10019. (212)262-2388. Fax: (212)262-0119. E-mail: giles@interport.net. Website: www.scottwaxmanagency.com. **Contact:** Giles Anderson. Estab. 1997. Member of AAR. Represents 60 clients. 50% of clients are new/unpublished writers. Specializes in "both commercial fiction and nonfiction. We are particularly strong in the areas of crime fiction, sports and religion. Will look at literary fiction." Currently handles: 60% nonfiction books; 40% novels.
● Prior to opening his agency, Mr. Waxman was editor for five years at HarperCollins.
Member Agents: Scott Waxman (all categories of nonfiction, commercial fiction); Giles Anderson (literary fiction, commercial fiction).
Represents: Nonfiction books, novels. **Considers these nonfiction areas:** biography/autobiography; business; ethnic/

CHECK THE INSIDER REPORTS throughout this section for first-hand information about working with agents.

cultural interests; health/medicine; history; money/finance/economics; popular crime; religious/inspirational; self-help/personal improvement; sports. **Considers these fiction areas:** action/adventure; ethnic; historical; literary; hard-boiled detective; religious/inspirational; romance (contemporary, historical); sports; suspense.

How to Contact: Query with SASE. Accepts queries by e-mail. Considers simultaneous queries. Reports in 2 weeks on queries; 4-6 weeks on mss. Discards unwanted or unsolicited mss. Returns materials only with SASE.

Needs: Actively seeking strong, high-concept commercial fiction, narrative nonfiction. Obtains new clients through recommendations, writers conferences, Internet, magazines.

Recent Sales: Sold 40 titles in the last year. *Mid-Life Irish*, by Frank Gannon (Wagner); *All Good Things*, by John Reed (Delacorte); *She Got Game*, by Cynthia Cooper (Warner Books); *Cinderella Story*, by Bill Murray (Doubleday).

Terms: Agent receives 15% commission on domestic sales; 20% on foreign sales. Offers written contract. 60 days notice must be given to terminate contract. Charges for photocopying, express mail, fax, international postage, book orders. Refers to editing services for clients only. 0% of business is derived from editing service.

Writers' Conferences: Celebration of Writing in the Low Country (Beaufort SC, August 6-9, 1999); Golden Triangle Writers Guild Conference (Beaumont TX, October 1999); FIU/Seaside Writers Conference (FL, October).

Reading List: Reads *Witness*, *Boulevard*, *Literal Latté*, *Mississippi Review*, *Zoetrope*, and many others to find new clients.

● WECKSLER-INCOMCO, 170 West End Ave., New York NY 10023. (212)787-2239. Fax: (212)496-7035. **Contact:** Sally Wecksler. Estab. 1971. Represents 25 clients. 50% of clients are new/previously unpublished writers. "However, I prefer writers who have had something in print." Specializes in nonfiction with illustrations (photos and art). Currently handles: 60% nonfiction books; 15% novels; 25% juvenile books.

• Prior to becoming an agent, Ms. Wecksler was an editor at *Publishers Weekly*; publisher with the international department of R.R. Bowker; and international director at Baker & Taylor.

Member Agents: Joann Amparan (general, children's books), S. Wecksler (general, foreign rights/co-editions, fiction, illustrated books, children's books, business).

Represents: Nonfiction books, novels, juvenile books. **Considers these nonfiction areas:** art/architecture design; biography/autobiography; business; current affairs; history; juvenile nonfiction; literary; music/dance/theater/film; nature/environment; photography. **Considers these fiction areas:** contemporary issues; historical; juvenile; literary; mainstream; picture book.

How to Contact: Query with outline plus 3 sample chapters and SASE. Include brief bio. Reports in 1 month on queries; 2 months on mss.

Needs: Actively seeking "illustrated books for adults or children with beautiful photos or artwork." Does not want to receive "science fiction or books with violence." Obtains new clients through recommendations from others and solicitations.

Recent Sales: Sold 11 titles in the last year. *Do's & Taboos—Women in International Business*, and *Do's & Taboos—Humor Around the World*, by Roger E. Axtell (Wiley); *Color Series*, by Candace Whitman (Abbeville).

Terms: Agent receives 12-15% commission on domestic sales; 20% on foreign sales. Offers written contract, binding for 3 years.

Tips: "Make sure a SASE is enclosed. Send three chapters and outline, clearly typed or word processed, double-spaced, written with punctuation and grammar in approved style. *We do not like to receive presentations by fax.*"

⊘ THE WENDY WEIL AGENCY, INC., 232 Madison Ave., Suite 1300, New York NY 10016. This agency did not respond to our request for information. Query before submitting.

⊘ CHERRY WEINER LITERARY AGENCY, 28 Kipling Way, Manalapan NJ 07726-3711. (732)446-2096. Fax: (732)792-0506. E-mail: cherry8486@aol.com. **Contact:** Cherry Weiner. Estab. 1977. Represents 40 clients. 10% of clients are new/previously unpublished writers. Specializes in science fiction, fantasy, westerns, mysteries (both contemporary and historical), historical novels, Native American works, mainstream, all the genre romances. Currently handles: 2-3% nonfiction books; 97% novels.

• This agency is not currently looking for new clients except by referral or by personal contact at writers' conferences.

Represents: Nonfiction books, novels. **Considers these nonfiction areas:** self-help/improvement, sociology. **Considers these fiction areas:** action/adventure; contemporary issues; detective/police/crime; family saga; fantasy; glitz; historical; mainstream; mystery/suspense; psychic/supernatural; romance; science fiction; thriller/espionage; westerns/frontier.

How to Contact: Query with SASE. Does not accept queries by fax or e-mail. Prefers to be only reader. Reports in 1 week on queries; 2 months on mss. Returns materials only with SASE or discards.

Recent Sales: *Problem of Spiteful Spiritualist*, by Roberta Rogow (St. Martin's Press); *Nobility*, by Tim McGuire (Dorchester Publishing); *Cherokee Dragon*, by Robert J. Conley (St. Martin's Press).

Terms: Agent receives 15% on domestic sales; 15% on foreign sales. Offers written contract. Charges for extra copies of mss "but would prefer author do it"; 1st class postage for author's copies of books; Express Mail for important document/manuscripts.

Writers' Conferences: Western Writers Convention; SF Conventions, Fantasy Convention.

Tips: "Meet agents and publishers at conferences. Establish a relationship, then get in touch with them reminding them of meetings and conference."

◐ THE WEINGEL-FIDEL AGENCY, 310 E. 46th St., 21E, New York NY 10017. (212)599-2959. **Contact:** Loretta Weingel-Fidel. Estab. 1989. Specializes in commercial, literary fiction and nonfiction. Currently handles: 75% nonfiction books; 25% novels.

• Prior to opening her agency, Ms. Weingel-Fidel was a psychoeducational diagnostician.

Represents: Nonfiction books, novels. **Considers these nonfiction areas:** art/architecture/design; biography/autobiography; investigative; memoirs; music/dance/theater/film; psychology; science; sociology; travel; women's issues/women's studies. **Considers these fiction areas:** contemporary issues; literary; mainstream.

How to Contact: Referred writers only. *No unsolicited mss.*

Needs: Obtains new clients through referrals. Actively seeking investigative journalism. Does not want to receive genre fiction, self-help, science fiction, fantasy.

Recent Sales: *The New Rabbi*, by Stephen Fried (Bantam); and *Brand New House*, by Katherine Salant (Clarkson Potter).

Terms: Agent receives 15% on domestic sales; 20% on foreign sales. Offers written contract, binding for 1 year automatic renewal. Bills back to clients all reasonable expenses such as UPS, express mail, photocopying, etc.

Tips: "A very small, selective list enables me to work very closely with my clients to develop and nurture talent. I only take on projects and writers I am extremely enthusiastic about."

✓ ◉ WEST COAST LITERARY ASSOCIATES, PMB 337, 1534 Plaza Lane, Burlingame CA 94010. E-mail: wstlit@aol.com. **Contact:** Richard Van Der Beets. Estab. 1986. Member of Authors League of America, Authors Guild. Represents 40 clients. 50% of clients are new/previously unpublished clients. Currently handles: 20% nonfiction books; 80% novels.

• Prior to opening his agency, Mr. Van Der Beets served as a professor of English at San Jose State University.

Represents: Nonfiction books, novels. **Considers these nonfiction areas:** biography/autobiography; current affairs; ethnic/cultural interests; government/politics/law; history; language/literature/criticism; music/dance/theater/film; nature/environment; psychology; true crime/investigative; women's issues/women's studies. **Considers these fiction areas:** action/adventure; contemporary issues; detective/police/crime; experimental; historical; literary; mainstream; mystery/suspense; regional; romance (contemporary and historical); science fiction; thriller/espionage; westerns/frontier.

How to Contact: Query first with SASE. Accepts queries by e-mail. Considers simultaneous queries and submissions. Reports in 2 weeks on queries; 1 month on mss. Returns materials only with SASE.

Needs: Actively seeking mystery, suspense, thriller. Does not want to receive self-help, humorous nonfiction.

Recent Sales: "Send SASE for list of sales."

Terms: Agent receives 10% commission on domestic sales; 20% commission on foreign sales. Offers written contract, binding for 6 months. Charges $75-95 marketing and materials fee, depending on genre and length. Fees are refunded in full upon sale of the property.

Writers' Conferences: California Writer's Conference (Asilomar).

Tips: "Query with SASE for submission guidelines before sending material."

◐ RHODA WEYR AGENCY, 151 Bergen St., Brooklyn NY 11217. (718)522-0480. **Contact:** Rhoda A. Weyr, president. Estab. 1983. Member of AAR. Prefers to work with published/established authors. Specializes in general nonfiction and fiction.

• Prior to starting her agency, Ms. Weyr was an agent at William Morris and a foreign correspondent.

Represents: Nonfiction books, novels.

How to Contact: Query with outline, sample chapters and SASE.

Recent Sales: Sold over 21 titles in the last year. Prefers not to share information on specific sales.

Terms: Agent receives 15% commission on domestic sales; 20% on foreign sales. Charges for "heavy duty copying or special mailings (e.g., Fed Ex etc.)."

✓ ◐ WIESER & WIESER, INC., 25 E. 21 St., 6th Floor, New York NY 10010. (212)260-0860. **Contact:** Olga Wieser. Estab. 1975. 30% of clients are new/previously unpublished writers. Specializes in mainstream fiction and nonfiction. Currently handles: 50% nonfiction books; 50% novels.

Member Agents: Jake Elwell (history, military, mysteries, romance, sports, thrillers); Olga Wieser (psychology, fiction, pop medical, literary fiction).

Represents: Nonfiction books, novels. **Considers these nonfiction areas:** business; cooking/food/nutrition; current affairs; health/medicine; history; money/finance/economics; nature/environment; psychology; sports; true crime/investigative. **Considers these fiction areas:** contemporary issues; detective/police/crime; historical; literary; mainstream; mystery/suspense; romance; thriller/espionage.

How to Contact: Query with outline/proposal and SASE. Reports in 2 weeks on queries.

Needs: Obtains new clients through queries, authors' recommendations and industry professionals.

FOR INFORMATION ON THE CONFERENCES agents attend, refer to the conference section in this book.

Recent Sales: *Cutting* , by Steven Levenkron (Norton); *Hocus Corpus*, by James N. Tucker, M.D. (Dutton/Signet); *Grinning in Her Mashed Potatoes*, by Margaret Moseley (Berkley); *The Kamikazes*, by Edwin P. Hoyt (Burford Books); and *Angels & Demons*, by Dan Brown (Pocket).
Terms: Agent receives 15% commission on domestic sales; 20% on foreign sales. Offers written contract. "No charge to our clients or potential clients." Charges for photocopying and overseas mailing.
Writers' Conferences: BEA; Frankfurt Book Fair.

✓ ⊘ **WITHERSPOON & ASSOCIATES, INC.**, 157 W. 57th St., #700, New York NY 10019. (212)889-8626. Fax: (212)696-0650. **Contact:** Ross Kramer. Estab. 1990. Represents 150 clients. 20% of clients are new/previously unpublished writers. Currently handles: 50% nonfiction books; 45% novels; 5% short story collections.
 • Prior to becoming an agent Ms. Witherspoon was a writer and magazine consultant.
Member Agents: Maria Massie; Kimberly Witherspoon; David Forrer; Ross Kramer.
Represents: Nonfiction books, novels. **Considers these nonfiction areas:** anthropology/archaeology; biography/auto-biography; business; current affairs; ethnic/cultural interests; gay/lesbian issues; government/politics/law; health/medicine; history; memoirs; money/finance/economics; music/dance/theater/film; science/technology; self-help/personal improvement; travel; true crime/investigative; women's issues/women's studies. **Considers these fiction areas:** contemporary issues; detective/police/crime; ethnic; family saga; feminist; gay; historical; lesbian; literary; mainstream; mystery/suspense; thriller/espionage.
How to Contact: Query with SASE. Reports in 3 weeks on queries; no unsolicited mss.
Needs: Obtains new clients through recommendations from others, solicitation and conferences.
Recent Sales: Prefers not to share information on specific sales.
Terms: Agent receives 15% commission on domestic sales; 20% on foreign sales. Offers written contract.
Writers' Conferences: BEA (Chicago, June); Frankfurt (Germany, October).

⊘ **AUDREY A. WOLF LITERARY AGENCY**, 1001 Connecticut Ave. NW, Washington DC 20036. This agency did not respond to our request for information. Query before submitting.

⊘ **THE WONDERLAND PRESS, INC.**, 160 Fifth Avenue, Suite 723, New York NY 10010-7003. (212)989-2550. E-mail: litraryagt@aol.com. **Contact:** John Campbell. Estab. 1985. Member of the American Book Producers Association. Represents 24 clients. Specializes in high-quality nonfiction, illustrated, reference, how-to and entertainment books. Currently handles: 90% nonfiction books; 10% novels.
 • The Wonderland Press is also a book packager and "in a very strong position to nurture strong proposals all the way from concept through bound books."
Represents: Nonfiction books, novels. **Considers these nonfiction areas:** art/architecture/design; biography/autobiography; enthnic/cultural interests; gay/lesbian issues; health/medicine; history; how-to; interior design/decorating; language/literature/criticism; photography; popular culture; psychology; self-help/personal improvement. **Considers these fiction areas:** action/adventure; literary; picture book; thriller.
How to Contact: Send outline/proposal. Reports in 3-5 days on queries; 1-2 weeks on mss.
Needs: Does not want to receive poetry, memoir, children or category fiction.
Recent Sales: Sold 38 titles in the last year. *Body Knots*, by Howard Schatz (Rizzoli); *Nude Body Nude*, by Beverly Ornstein (HarperCollins); *501 Great Things About Being Gay*, by Edward Taussig (Andrews McMeel). "Almost all of our new authors come to us by referral. Often they 'find' us by researching the books we have sold for our other clients."
Terms: Agent receives 15% commission on domestic sales. Offers written contract. 30-90 days notice must be given to terminate contract. Offers criticism service, included in 15% commission. Charges for photocopying, long-distance telephone, overnight express-mail, messengering.
Tips: "We welcome submissions from new authors, but proposals must be unique, of high commercial interest and well written. Follow your talent. Write with passion. Know your market. Submit your work without apologizing for its mistakes, typos, incompleteness, etc. We want to see your best work."

⊘ **ANN WRIGHT REPRESENTATIVES**, 165 W. 46th St., Suite 1105, New York NY 10036-2501. (212)764-6770. Fax: (212)764-5125. **Contact:** Dan Wright. Estab. 1961. Signatory of WGA. Represents 23 clients. 30% of clients are new/unpublished writers. Prefers to work with published/established authors; works with a small number of new/unpublished authors. "Eager to work with any author with material that we can effectively market in the motion picture business worldwide." Specializes in "books or screenplays with strong motion picture potential." Currently handles: 50% novels; 40% movie scripts; 10% TV scripts.
 • See the expanded listing for this agency in Script Agents.

⊘ **WRITERS HOUSE**, 21 W. 26th St., New York NY 10010. (212)685-2400. Fax: (212)685-1781. Estab. 1974. Member of AAR. Represents 280 clients. 50% of clients were new/unpublished writers. Specializes in all types of popular fiction and nonfiction. No scholarly, professional, poetry or screenplays. Currently handles: 25% nonfiction books; 35% juvenile books; 40% novels.
Member Agents: Albert Zuckerman (major novels, thrillers, women's fiction, important nonfiction); Amy Berkower (major juvenile authors, women's fiction, art and decorating, psychology); Merrilee Heifetz (quality children's fiction, science fiction and fantasy, popular culture, literary fiction); Susan Cohen (juvenile and young adult fiction and nonfic-

tion, Judaism, women's issues); Susan Ginsburg (serious and popular fiction, true crime, narrative nonfiction, personality books, cookbooks); Fran Lebowitz (juvenile and young adult, popular culture); Michele Rubin (serious nonfiction); Karen Solem (contemporary and historical romance, women's fiction, narrative nonfiction, horse and animal books); Robin Rue (commercial fiction and nonfiction, YA fiction); Jennifer Lyons (literary, commercial fiction, international fiction, nonfiction and illustrated).

Represents: Nonfiction books, juvenile books, novels. **Considers these nonfiction areas:** animals; art/architecture/ design; biography/autobiography; business; child guidance/parenting; cooking/food/nutrition; health/medicine; history; interior design/decorating; juvenile nonfiction; military/war; money/finance/economics; music/dance/theater/film; nature/environment; psychology; science/technology; self-help/personal improvement; true crime/investigative; women's issues/women's studies. **Considers any fiction area.** "Quality is everything."

How to Contact: Query. Reports in 1 month on queries.

Needs: Obtains new clients through recommendations from others.

Recent Sales: *The New New Thing*, by Michael Lewis (Norton); *The First Victim*, by Ridley Pearson (Hyperion); *Into the Garden*, by V.C. Andrews (Pocket); *Fearless*, by Francine Pascal (Pocket).

Terms: Agent receives 15% commission on domestic sales; 20% on foreign sales. Offers written contract, binding for 1 year.

Tips: "Do not send manuscripts. Write a compelling letter. If you do, we'll ask to see your work."

⬛ⓒ WRITERS HOUSE, (West Coast Office), 3368 Governor Dr. #224F, San Diego CA 92122. (619)678-8767. Fax: (619)678-8530. **Contact:** Steven Malk.
  • See Writers House listing above for more information.

Represents: Nonfiction, fiction, picture books, young adult, occasional adult books.

ⓒ WRITERS' PRODUCTIONS, P.O. Box 630, Westport CT 06881-0630. (203)227-8199. **Contact:** David L. Meth. Estab. 1982. Represents 25 clients. Specializes in literary-quality fiction and nonfiction, and children's books. Currently handles: 40% nonfiction books; 60% novels.

Represents: Nonfiction books, novels. Literary quality fiction. "Especially interested in children's work that creates a whole new universe of characters and landscapes that goes across all media, i.e.—between Hobbits and Smurfs. Must be completely unique and original, carefully planned and developed."

How to Contact: Send query letter only with SASE. Reports in 1 week on queries; 1 month on mss.

Needs: Obtain new clients through word of mouth.

Recent Sales: Prefers not to share information on specific sales.

Terms: Agent receives 15% on domestic sales; 25% on foreign sales; 25% on dramatic sales; 25% on new media or multimedia sales. Offers written contract. Charges for electronic transmissions, long-distance calls, express or overnight mail, courier service, etc.

Tips: "Send only your best, most professionally prepared work. Do not send it before it is ready. We must have SASE for all correspondence and return of manuscripts. No telephone calls, please."

☑ⓒ WRITERS' REPRESENTATIVES, INC., 116 W. 14th St., 11th Floor, New York NY 10011-7305. (212)620-9009. E-mail: glen@writersreps.com. **Contact:** Glen Hartley or Lynn Chu. Estab. 1985. Represents 100 clients. 5% of clients are new/previously unpublished writers. Specializes in serious nonfiction. Currently handles: 90% nonfiction books; 10% novels.
  • Prior to becoming agents Ms. Chu was a lawyer and Mr. Hartley worked at Simon & Schuster, Harper & Row and Cornell University Press.

Member Agents: Lynn Chu; Glen Hartley.

Represents: Nonfiction books, novels. **Considers literary fiction.**

How to Contact: "Nonfiction submissions should include book proposal, detailed table of contents and sample chapter(s). For fiction submissions send sample chapters—not synopses. All submissions should include author biography and publication list. SASE required." Does not accept unsolicited mss.

Needs: Actively seeking serious nonfiction and quality fiction. Does not want to receive motion picture/television screenplays.

Recent Sales: *The Animals Within*, by Sherwin B. Nuland, M.D. (Simon & Schuster); *Why We Buy*, by Paco Underhill (Simon & Schuster); *How to Read and Why*, by Harold Bloom.

Terms: Agent receives 15% commission on domestic sales; 20% on foreign sales. "We charge for out-of-house photocopying as well as messengers, courier services (e.g., Federal Express), etc."

Tips: Obtains new clients "recommended by our clients. Always include a SASE that will ensure a response from the agent and the return of material submitted."

ⓒ MARY YOST ASSOCIATES, INC., 59 E. 54th St. 72, New York NY 10022. This agency did not respond to our request for information. Query before submitting.

ⓒ ZACHARY SHUSTER AGENCY, Boston Office: 45 Newbury St., Boston MA 02116. (617)262-2400. Fax: (617)262-2468. E-mail: toddshus@aol.com. **Contact:** Todd Shuster. Also: New York Office: 244 Fifth Ave., 11th Floor, New York NY 10001. Phone: (212)532-5666. Fax: (212)532-5888. **Contact:** Cherie Burns, Jennifer Gates. Estab. 1996. Represents 75 clients. 20% of clients are new/unpublished writers. Specializes in journalist-driven narrative nonfiction,

insider report

Going on instincts and playing author's advocate

Agent Steven Malk's conference appearances have been known to cause whispering among the writers in the crowd. He's a guy in his mid-twenties? What could he possibly know about children's books? What conference-goers don't know (until he tells them) is that Malk has been surrounded by children's books and authors his whole life. His mother owns The White Rabbit Children's Bookstore in La Jolla, California (www.whiterabbit-childbooks. com), and his grandmother opened one of the world's first children's bookstores in Johannesburg, South Africa, in the 1950s. "How many people can say they're the third generation of something?" he says.

Steven Malk

Malk, an agent for New York-based Writers House, works out of San Diego. He reads all the manuscripts he receives, speaks at a number of Society of Children's Book Writers and Illustrators conferences, and has led several online chats for children's writers. Recent and upcoming work from his authors include *Video* (Greenwillow), the second novel from Karen Romano Young, author of the well-received *The Beetle and Me: A Love Story*; *I Hate to Go to Bed* (Harcourt), by author/illustrator Katie Davis; award-winning novelist Franny Billingsley's *The Folk Keeper* (Atheneum); Elise Primavera's *Auntie Claus*, Harcourt's lead fall title featured in New York Saks Fifth Avenue Christmas window displays; and *Stop Pretending: What Happened When My Big Sister Went Crazy*, a young adult poetry collection by Sonya Sones (HarperCollins).

Here Malk talks about the advantages of having an agent, offers tips on choosing one, reveals what impresses him in a submission, and shares his advice to unpublished writers.

How did working at your mom's bookstore affect your career path?
I could not overstate how important it was. I started working there when I was 16, and I continued all through high school and college. I loved it and I developed strong instincts. Matching up customers with books was great experience—it's similar to what I do now with publishers. I learned how to read people's tastes, as well as how to pitch books. It's a great store with a great selection, so I learned everything that was out there and developed a strong sense about what I like and don't like.

How did you end up becoming an agent? Why did agenting interest you?
After working at The White Rabbit for a while, I realized I wanted to be in publishing, but I wasn't sure if I wanted to be an editor or an agent. I interned for the Sandra Dijkstra Agency when I was still in college, and then worked there fulltime as soon as I graduated. It seemed like the best of all worlds. These days, agents do a lot of editorial work. I get to be involved

in the business side of things and I can be very creative. I'm involved in every single facet of an author's career.

How do you maintain relationships with editors and get a feel for their tastes and interests?

That's really important. I do have to get a feel for an editor's personality and what she likes, further than "she likes to do novels." It's something that's learned; it takes a little while; it's trial and error. I start to get a sense, the more I deal with an editor, of what she likes. If she buys something from me or if she turns something down, it's all educational. I start to see a pattern and get an idea of her taste. There are certain editors I work with more than others. I have a really good idea, if I have a certain type of project, who I'm going to send it to—if I have a young picture book as opposed to an edgy novel or a longer picture book.

You probably don't have an "average" day, do you?

Every day is different. I can tell you this—I'm not sitting in the office all day reading manuscripts. A lot of writers think that. I'm most likely talking to a couple of editors. On any given day, I might be negotiating a contract. Or I'm sending a project out. I'm writing a pitch letter. I'm making my submission list of editors. I'm calling editors and pitching something. I'm following up on a project. Or I'm dealing with subsidiary rights. There's so much involved.

Why should an author have an agent?

There are a lot of reasons. It's different for every person. I don't think it's going to work for every single author necessarily. If you're a control freak, you shouldn't have an agent. You relinquish a certain amount of control of your career. You have to do a lot of research when deciding if you want an agent. You should decide why you want an agent and what you expect from an agent. You really have to find someone you like and trust. You should feel like you and your agent share a common vision.

An agent is going to be able to place your work, and not just place your work with a house, but place your work with the right editor and the right house. The response time is going to be quicker. I can say with a lot of confidence that the offer an agent gets for you is going to be higher. And you're going to have an expert negotiating your contract for you. Placing manuscripts is what agents do for a living. It's our job to know what's going on and who's publishing what and how much money authors are getting.

The most important thing to keep in mind is that an agent is someone who's working for you and is in your corner; he's your advocate. Editors are ultimately working for their company, so as nice and friendly as they may be, it's not in their best interest to get you a great deal.

Your agent is only going to be making money if you're making money. With companies merging these days, editors are losing their jobs or changing companies. Even though an author-editor relationship might seem stable, you never know when it's going to end or change. Having an agent, someone you know and trust, someone who's working for you and is in your corner no matter what, is extremely valuable.

Can it be just as difficult to find an agent as it is to find a publisher?

It can be really hard to find an agent. You have to do your research. All agents are different. I'm not the right agent for everyone. I have my own style—everyone has his own style—so you have to do your homework. Some agents are biased against first-time authors and don't really want to take them on. I love to work with first-time authors. I don't care if someone's published 60 books or none.

What makes you excited about a manuscript when you read it?

It's hard to define—it's my instincts. Some might look at a manuscript and think about what niche it would fall into, what market; try to define it. I don't care about that stuff—whether it's "marketable" or not doesn't matter to me. What matters is how much it speaks to me, and whether or not it has a voice, and voice itself is hard to define. I look for books I can't stop thinking about. They can be funny, or really haunting or sad, or just very well written. But whatever they are, the books I take on tend to stay with me—days later, I'll still be thinking about them. That's when I know I want to represent something.

Have you "discovered" authors at conferences?

At the 1998 SCBWI conference in Los Angeles, I found two. One was Sonya Sones. Her book *Stop Pretending* (HarperCollins) came out in Fall 1999. That's a perfect example. When I got that book, I read it in one sitting. I didn't even get up, I just called her and said, "I want to represent this—this is going to be a huge book." It's young adult poetry about a really difficult subject. It's not, on the fact of it, the most marketable story. I totally go on my instincts, and that was such an easy call—talk about voice. And it's so moving.

I also met Bruce Hale. Harcourt bought his three-book Chet Gecko series. It's also been optioned as a television series. The first book comes out Spring 2000. Again, there's a really great voice. His and Sonya's could not be more different. Sonya's is a serious, intense book, and Bruce's is fun and humorous.

What's your final advice to a writer looking for an agent?

Be professional. It's amazing to me how many people don't send a SASE, or write their cover letters in pencil with things misspelled, or send me something, then three weeks later send a whole new draft saying, "I sent you the wrong story." I like a good cover letter—it makes an impression on me. But your work's going to speak for itself no matter what.

—Alice Pope

---

literary and commercial fiction. Currently handles: 35% nonfiction books; 5% juvenile books; 5% scholarly books; 45% novels; 5% story collections; 5% movie scripts.

● "Our principals include two former publishing and entertainment lawyers, a journalist and an editor/agent."

Member Agents: Esmond Harmsworth (commercial fiction, history, science, adventure); Todd Shuster (narrative and prescriptive nonfiction, biography, memoirs); Lane Zachary (biography, memoirs, literary fiction); Cherie Burns (celebrity books, nonfiction); Jennifer Gates (literary fiction, nonfiction); Rochelle Lurie (nonfiction).

Represents: Nonfiction books, novels, movie scripts. **Considers these nonfiction areas:** animals; biography/autobiography; business; current affairs; gay/lesbian issues; government/politics/law; health/medicine; history; how-to; juvenile nonfiction; language/literature/criticism; memoirs; money/finance/economics; music/dance/theater/film; psychology; science/technology; self-help/personal improvement; sports; true crime/investigative; women's issues/women's studies. **Considers these fiction areas:** contemporary issues; detective/police/crime; ethnic; feminist; gay; historical; lesbian; literary; mainstream; mystery/suspense; romance (contemporary, gothic, historical, regency); thriller/espionage; young adult.

How to Contact: Send query letter and 50 page sample of ms. Reports in 8-12 weeks on mss.

Needs: Actively seeking narrative nonfiction, mystery, commerical and literary fiction, romance novels, memoirs, history, biographies. Does not want to receive poetry. Obtains new clients through recommendations from others, solicitation, conferences.

Recent Sales: *The Science Behind The X-Files*, by Anne Simon (Simon & Schuster); *Tracking El Niño*, by Madeleine Nash (Warner); and *Waiting*, by Ha Jin (Alfred A. Knopf). Other clients include Leslie Epstein, David Mixner.

Terms: Agent receives 15% commission on domestic sales; 20% on foreign sales. Offers written contract, binding for 1 work only. 30 days notice must be given to terminate contract.

Tips: "We work closely with all our clients on all editorial and promotional aspects of their works."

◨ SUSAN ZECKENDORF ASSOC. INC., 171 W. 57th St., New York NY 10019. (212)245-2928. **Contact:** Susan Zeckendorf. Estab. 1979. Member of AAR. Represents 15 clients. 25% of clients are new/previously unpublished writers. Currently handles: 50% nonfiction books; 50% fiction.

● Prior to opening her agency, Ms. Zeckendorf was a counseling psychologist.

Represents: Nonfiction books, novels. **Considers these nonfiction areas:** art/architecture/design; biography/autobiography; child guidance/parenting; health/medicine; history; music/dance; psychology; science; sociology; women's issues/women's studies. **Considers these fiction areas:** contemporary issues; detective/police/crime; ethnic; family saga; glitz; historical; literary; mainstream; mystery/suspense; thriller/espionage.

How to Contact: Query with SASE. Considers simultaneous queries and submissions. Reports in 10 days on queries; 3 weeks mss. Obtains new clients through recommendations, listings in writer's manuals. Returns materials only with SASE.

Needs: Actively seeking mysteries, literary fiction, mainstream fiction, thrillers, social history, parenting, classical music, biography. Does not want to receive science fiction, romance. "No children's books."

Recent Sales: Sold 6 titles in the last year. *The Four Hundred: New York in the Gilded Age*, by Jerry E. Patterson (Rizzoli); *The Power of Myth in Storytelling*, by James N. Frey (St. Martin's).

Terms: Agent receives 15% commission on domestic sales; 20% on foreign sales. Charges for photocopying, messenger services.

Writers' Conferences: Central Valley Writers Conference; the Tucson Publishers Association Conference; Writer's Connection; Frontiers in Writing Conference (Amarillo, TX); Golden Triangle Writers Conference (Beaumont TX); Oklahoma Festival of Books (Claremont OK); Mary Mount Writers Conference.

Tips: "We are a small agency giving lots of individual attention. We respond quickly to submissions."

Additional Nonfee-charging Agents

The following nonfee-charging agencies have indicated they are *primarily* interested in handling the work of scriptwriters, but also handle less than 10 to 15 percent book manuscripts. After reading the listing (you can find the page number in the Listings Index), send a query to obtain more information on needs and manuscript submissions policies.

Above the Line Agency	Miller Co., The Stuart M.	Vegas Literary Agency
Cinema Talent International	Picture of You, A	Wauhob Agency, Donna
Epstein-Wyckoff and Associates	Shapiro-Lichtman-Stein	
Larchmont Literary Agency	Sherman & Associates, Ken	

Agents Specialties Index: Nonfee-charging

The subject index is divided into fiction and nonfiction subject categories for Nonfee-charging Literary Agents. To find an agent interested in the type of manuscript you've written, see the appropriate sections under subject headings that best describe your work. Check the Listings Index for the page number of the agent's listing or refer to the section of Nonfee-charging Literary Agents preceding this index. Agents who are open to most fiction, nonfiction or script subjects appear under the "Open to all Categories" heading.

NONFEE-CHARGING LITERARY AGENTS/FICTION

Action/Adventure: Acacia House Publishing Services Ltd.; Alive Communications, Inc.; Allen Literary Agency, Linda; Allen, Literary Agent, James; Allred and Allred Literary Agents; Amber Literary; Amsterdam Agency, Marcia; Authentic Creations Literary Agency; Authors & Artists Group, Inc.; Baldi Literary Agency, Malaga; Barrett Books Inc., Loretta; Bial Agency, Daniel; Bova Literary Agency, The Barbara; Brandt & Brandt Literary Agents Inc.; Browne Ltd., Pema; Buck Agency, Howard; C G & W Associates; Communications and Entertainment, Inc.; Crawford Literary Agency; Dawson Associates, Liza; Donovan Literary, Jim; Ducas, Robert; Dystel Literary Management, Jane; Elmo Agency Inc., Ann; ES Talent Agency; Everitt Literary Agency, Inc., Charles; Farber Literary Agency Inc.; Finesse Literary Agency; Fleury Agency, B.R.; Gibson Agency, The Sebastian; Goldfarb & Associates; Grace Literary Agency, Carroll; Greenburger Associates, Inc., Sanford J.; Greene, Arthur B.; Halsey North, Reese; Harris Literary Agency; Harris Literary Agency, Inc., The Joy; Hawkins & Associates, Inc., John; Henshaw Group, Richard; Herner Rights Agency, Susan; Hogenson Agency, Barbara; Infinity Management International; Jabberwocky Literary Agency; JCA Literary Agency, Inc.; JLA Literary Agency; Joy Literary Agency; Kleinman, Esq. of Graybill & English L.L.C., Jeffrey M.; Klinger, Inc., Harvey; Koster Literary Agency, LLC, Elaine; Kraas Agency, Irene; Lampack Agency, Inc., Peter; Larkin, Sabra Elliott; Larsen/Elizabeth Pomada Literary Agents, Michael; Lasher Agency, The Maureen; Levine Literary Agency, Paul S.; Lewis & Company, Karen; Lincoln Literary Agency, Ray; Lindstrom Literary Group; Literary Group, The; Lukeman Literary Management Ltd.; Marshall Agency, The Evan; McBride Literary Agency, Margret; Michaels Literary Agency, Inc., Doris S.; Morrison, Inc., Henry; Mura Enterprises, Inc., Dee; Naggar Literary Agency, Jean V.; National Writers Literary Agency; Norma-Lewis Agency, The; Northwest Literary Services; Paraview, Inc.; Pelter, Rodney; Pevner, Inc., Stephen; Quicksilver Books-Literary Agents; Renaissance Literary Agency; Rhodes Literary Agency, Jodie; Rotrosen Agency LLC, Jane; Russell & Volkening; Sanders Literary Agency, Victoria; Scagnetti Talent & Literary Agency, Jack; Sedgeband Literary Associates; Seymour Agency, The; Sternig & Byrne Literary Agency; Sunshine Literary Agency; Van der Leun & Associates; Vines Agency, Inc., The; Wald Associates, Inc., Mary Jack; Waxman Agency, Inc., Scott; Weiner Literary Agency, Cherry; West Coast Literary Associates; Wonderland Press, Inc., The; Wright Representatives, Ann; Zeckendorf Assoc. Inc., Susan

Cartoon/Comic: Bial Agency, Daniel; Buck Agency, Howard; Cadden, Fuller & Burkhalter LLP; Communications and Entertainment, Inc.; Finesse Literary Agency; Harris Literary Agency, Inc., The Joy; Hawkins & Associates, Inc., John; Jabberwocky Literary Agency; Kleinman, Esq. of Graybill & English L.L.C., Jeffrey M.; Levant & Wales, Literary Agency, Inc.; Levine Literary Agency, Paul S.; Literary Group, The; Nazor Literary Agency, Karen; Pelter, Rodney; Pevner, Inc., Stephen; Van der Leun & Associates; Vines Agency, Inc., The

Confessional: Allred and Allred Literary Agents; Barrett Books Inc., Loretta; Buck Agency, Howard; C G & W Associates; Finesse Literary Agency; Harris Literary Agency, Inc., The Joy; JCA Literary Agency, Inc.; JLA Literary Agency; Koster Literary Agency, LLC, Elaine; Levine Literary Agency, Paul S.; March Tenth, Inc.; Northwest Literary Services; Pelter, Rodney; Van der Leun & Associates

Contemporary Issues: Alive Communications, Inc.; Allen Literary Agency, Linda; Allred and Allred Literary Agents; Amber Literary; Authentic Creations Literary Agency; Authors Alliance, Inc.; Authors & Artists Group, Inc.; Baldi Literary Agency, Malaga; Barrett Books Inc., Loretta; Bedford Book Works, Inc., The; Bent, Literary Agent, Jenny; Bernstein & Associates, Inc., Pam; Bial Agency, Daniel; Boates Literary Agency, Reid; Books & Such; Bova Literary Agency, The Barbara; Brandt & Brandt Literary Agents Inc.; Brown Associates Inc., Marie; Browne Ltd., Pema; Buck Agency, Howard; C G & W Associates; Castiglia Literary Agency; Charisma Communications, Ltd.; Cohen Agency, The; Communications and Entertainment, Inc.; Connor Literary Agency; Dijkstra Literary Agency, Sandra; Doyen Literary Services, Inc.; Ducas, Robert; Dystel Literary Management, Jane; Elmo Agency Inc., Ann; ES Talent Agency; Everitt Literary Agency, Inc., Charles; Farber Literary Agency Inc.; Feigen/Parrent Literary Management; Finesse Literary Agency; Flaherty, Literary Agent, Joyce A.; Freymann Literary Agency, Sarah Jane; Gibson Agency, The Sebastian; Goldfarb & Associates; Goodman-Andrew-Agency, Inc.; Greenburger Associates, Inc., Sanford J.; Greene, Literary Agent, Randall Elisha; Grosvenor Literary Agency, The; Halsey North, Reese; Harris Literary Agency, Inc., The Joy; Hawkins & Associates, Inc., John; Herner Rights Agency, Susan; Hogenson Agency, Barbara; Jabberwocky Literary Agency; JCA Literary Agency, Inc.; Joy Literary Agency; Kidde, Hoyt & Picard; Kleinman, Esq. of Graybill & English L.L.C., Jeffrey M.; Koster Literary Agency, LLC, Elaine; Kouts, Literary Agent, Barbara S.; Lampack Agency, Inc., Peter; Larkin, Sabra Elliott; Larsen/Elizabeth Pomada Literary Agents, Michael; Lasher Agency, The Maureen; Levine Communications, Inc., James; Levine Literary Agency, Paul S.; Lincoln Literary Agency, Ray; Lindstrom Literary Group; Literary Group, The; Lowenstein Associates, Inc.; Lukeman Literary Management Ltd.; Marshall Agency, The Evan; McGrath, Helen; Michaels Literary Agency, Inc., Doris S.; Multimedia Product Development, Inc.; Mura Enterprises, Inc., Dee; Naggar Literary Agency, Jean V.; Nazor Literary Agency, Karen; Norma-Lewis Agency, The; Northwest Literary Services; Paraview, Inc.; Pelter, Rodney; Pevner, Inc., Stephen; Pinder Lane & Garon-Brooke Associates, Ltd.; Rees Literary Agency, Helen; Renaissance Literary Agency; Rhodes Literary Agency, Jodie; Robbins Literary Agency, BJ; Sage Acre Marketing & Publishing Solutions; Sanders Literary Agency, Victoria; Scagnetti Talent & Literary Agency, Jack; Schiavone Literary Agency, Inc.; Schulman, A Literary Agency, Susan; Sedgeband Literary Associates; Seligman, Literary Agent, Lynn; Shepard Agency, The; Simenauer Literary Agency, Jacqueline; Singer Literary Agency Inc., Evelyn; Skolnick Literary Agency, Irene; Spectrum Literary Agency; Spitzer Literary Agency, Philip G.; Stauffer Associates, Nancy; Straus Agency, Inc., Robin; Sunshine Literary Agency; Swayne Agency Literary Management & Consulting, Inc., The; Taylor, Literary Agent, Rebecca; Travis Literary Agency, Susan; Van der Leun & Associates; Vines Agency, Inc., The; Wald Associates, Inc., Mary Jack; Watkins Loomis Agency, Inc.; Watt & Associates, Sandra; Wecksler-Incomco; Weiner Literary Agency, Cherry; Weingel-Fidel Agency, The; West Coast Literary Associates; Wieser & Wieser, Inc.; Witherspoon & Associates, Inc.; Zachary Shuster Agency; Zeckendorf Assoc. Inc., Susan

Detective/Police/Crime: Acacia House Publishing Services Ltd.; Alive Communications, Inc.; Allen Literary Agency, Linda; Allen, Literary Agent, James; Allred and Allred Literary Agents; Amber Literary; Amsterdam Agency, Marcia; Appleseeds Management; Authentic Creations Literary Agency; Authors Alliance, Inc.; Authors & Artists Group, Inc.; Baldi Literary Agency, Malaga; Barrett Books Inc., Loretta; Bedford Book Works, Inc., The; Bent, Literary Agent, Jenny; Bial Agency, Daniel; Bleecker Street Associates; Bookmark Literary Agency; Bova Literary Agency, The Barbara; Brandt & Brandt Literary Agents Inc.; Browne Ltd., Pema; Buck Agency, Howard; C G & W Associates; Charisma Communications, Ltd.; Cohen Agency, The; Cohen, Inc. Literary Agency, Ruth; Collin Literary Agent, Frances; Connor Literary Agency; Core Creations, Inc.; Cypher, The Cypher Agency, James R.; DHS Literary, Inc.; Diamond Literary Agency, Inc.; Dijkstra Literary Agency, Sandra; Donovan Literary, Jim; Ducas, Robert; Dystel Literary Management, Jane; Ellenberg Literary Agency, Ethan; Elmo Agency Inc., Ann; ES Talent Agency; Finesse Literary Agency; Fleury Agency, B.R.; Gibson Agency, The Sebastian; Goldfarb & Associates; Grace Literary Agency, Carroll; Greenburger Associates, Inc., Sanford J.; Greene, Arthur B.; Greene, Literary Agent, Randall Elisha; Grosvenor Literary Agency, The; Halsey North, Reese; Harris Literary Agency; Harris Literary Agency, Inc., The Joy; Hawkins & Associates, Inc., John; Henshaw Group, Richard; Herner Rights Agency, Susan; Hogenson Agency, Barbara; Infinity Management International; J de S Associates Inc.; Jabberwocky Literary Agency; JCA Literary Agency, Inc.; JLA Literary Agency; Kern Literary Agency, Natasha; Kidde, Hoyt & Picard; Klinger, Inc., Harvey; Koster Literary Agency, LLC, Elaine; Kraas Agency, Irene; Lampack Agency, Inc., Peter; Larkin, Sabra Elliott; Larsen/Elizabeth Pomada Literary Agents, Michael; Lasher Agency, The Maureen; Levine Literary Agency, Paul S.; Lewis & Company, Karen; Lincoln Literary Agency, Ray; Lindstrom Literary Group; Literary Group, The; Lowenstein Associates, Inc.; Maass Literary Agency, Donald; Marshall Agency, The Evan; McBride Literary Agency, Margret; McGrath, Helen; Morrison, Inc., Henry; Multimedia Product Development, Inc.; Mura Enterprises, Inc., Dee; Naggar Literary Agency, Jean V.; Norma-Lewis Agency, The; Northwest Literary Services; Pelter, Rodney; Perkins, Rubie & Associates; Pinder Lane & Garon-Brooke Associates, Ltd.; Pine Associates, Inc, Arthur; Real Criminals; Renaissance Literary Agency; Rhodes Literary Agency, Jodie; Robbins Literary Agency, BJ; Rotrosen Agency LLC, Jane; Rowland Agency, The Damaris; Rubenstein Literary Agency,

Inc., Pesha; Russell & Volkening; Scagnetti Talent & Literary Agency, Jack; Schulman, A Literary Agency, Susan; Seligman, Literary Agent, Lynn; Seymour Agency, The; Singer Literary Agency Inc., Evelyn; Slopen Literary Agency, Beverley; Spitzer Literary Agency, Philip G.; Sunshine Literary Agency; Van der Leun & Associates; Vines Agency, Inc., The; Wald Associates, Inc., Mary Jack; Wallace Literary Agency, Inc.; Ware Literary Agency, John A.; Watt & Associates, Sandra; Weiner Literary Agency, Cherry; West Coast Literary Associates; Wieser & Wieser, Inc.; Witherspoon & Associates, Inc.; Wright Representatives, Ann; Zachary Shuster Agency; Zeckendorf Assoc. Inc., Susan

Erotica: Allred and Allred Literary Agents; Authors & Artists Group, Inc.; Baldi Literary Agency, Malaga; Bial Agency, Daniel; Bleecker Street Associates; Brandt & Brandt Literary Agents Inc.; Buck Agency, Howard; DHS Literary, Inc.; ES Talent Agency; Finesse Literary Agency; Harris Literary Agency, Inc., The Joy; Infinity Management International; JLA Literary Agency; Kleinman, Esq. of Graybill & English L.L.C., Jeffrey M.; Levine Literary Agency, Paul S.; Lewis & Company, Karen; Lowenstein Associates, Inc.; Marshall Agency, The Evan; Pelter, Rodney; Pevner, Inc., Stephen; Real Criminals; Sedgeband Literary Associates; Van der Leun & Associates

Ethnic: Allen Literary Agency, Linda; Allred and Allred Literary Agents; Amster Literary Enterprises, Betsy; Authors & Artists Group, Inc.; Baldi Literary Agency, Malaga; Barrett Books Inc., Loretta; Bent, Literary Agent, Jenny; Bernstein & Associates, Inc., Pam; Bial Agency, Daniel; Bleecker Street Associates; Book Deals, Inc.; Bookmark Literary Agency; Brandt & Brandt Literary Agents Inc.; Brown Associates Inc., Marie; Browne Ltd., Pema; Buck Agency, Howard; C G & W Associates; Castiglia Literary Agency; Cohen Agency, The; Cohen, Inc. Literary Agency, Ruth; Collin Literary Agent, Frances; Connor Literary Agency; Daves Agency, Joan; Dawson Associates, Liza; DHS Literary, Inc.; Dijkstra Literary Agency, Sandra; Dystel Literary Management, Jane; Elmo Agency Inc., Ann; Evans Inc., Mary; Finesse Literary Agency; Fleury Agency, B.R.; Freymann Literary Agency, Sarah Jane; Gibson Agency, The Sebastian; Goldfarb & Associates; Goodman-Andrew-Agency, Inc.; Greenburger Associates, Inc., Sanford J.; Greene, Literary Agent, Randall Elisha; Halsey North, Reese; Harris Literary Agency, Inc., The Joy; Hawkins & Associates, Inc., John; Henshaw Group, Richard; Herner Rights Agency, Susan; Hogenson Agency, Barbara; Jabberwocky Literary Agency; JCA Literary Agency, Inc.; Kern Literary Agency, Natasha; Kleinman, Esq. of Graybill & English L.L.C., Jeffrey M.; Knight Agency, The; Koster Literary Agency, LLC, Elaine; Kraas Agency, Irene; Larkin, Sabra Elliott; Larsen/Elizabeth Pomada Literary Agents, Michael; Levant & Wales, Literary Agency, Inc.; Levine Literary Agency, Paul S.; Lewis & Company, Karen; Lincoln Literary Agency, Ray; Lindstrom Literary Group; Literary Group, The; Lowenstein Associates, Inc.; March Tenth, Inc.; Marshall Agency, The Evan; McBride Literary Agency, Margret; Multimedia Product Development, Inc.; Mura Enterprises, Inc., Dee; Naggar Literary Agency, Jean V.; Nazor Literary Agency, Karen; Nine Muses and Apollo; Northwest Literary Services; Paraview, Inc.; Pelter, Rodney; Perkins, Rubie & Associates; Pevner, Inc., Stephen; Renaissance Literary Agency; Rhodes Literary Agency, Jodie; Robbins Literary Agency, BJ; Ross Literary Agency, The Gail; Rubenstein Literary Agency, Inc., Pesha; Russell & Volkening; Sage Acre Marketing & Publishing Solutions; Sanders Literary Agency, Victoria; Schiavone Literary Agency, Inc.; Sedgeband Literary Associates; Seligman, Literary Agent, Lynn; Seymour Agency, The; Singer Literary Agency Inc., Evelyn; Spieler Agency, The; Swayne Agency Literary Management & Consulting, Inc., The; Travis Literary Agency, Susan; United Tribes; Van der Leun & Associates; Vines Agency, Inc., The; Wald Associates, Inc., Mary Jack; Watkins Loomis Agency, Inc.; Waxman Agency, Inc., Scott; Witherspoon & Associates, Inc.; Zachary Shuster Agency; Zeckendorf Assoc. Inc., Susan

Experimental: Baldi Literary Agency, Malaga; Barrett Books Inc., Loretta; Brandt & Brandt Literary Agents Inc.; Buck Agency, Howard; Connor Literary Agency; ES Talent Agency; Finesse Literary Agency; Fleury Agency, B.R.; Gibson Agency, The Sebastian; Harris Literary Agency, Inc., The Joy; Hawkins & Associates, Inc., John; JCA Literary Agency, Inc.; Kidd Agency, Inc., Virginia; Larkin, Sabra Elliott; Larsen/Elizabeth Pomada Literary Agents, Michael; Levant & Wales, Literary Agency, Inc.; Levine Literary Agency, Paul S.; Lukeman Literary Management Ltd.; Manus & Associates Literary Agency; Mura Enterprises, Inc., Dee; Northwest Literary Services; Pelter, Rodney; Pevner, Inc., Stephen; Rhodes Literary Agency, Jodie; Sedgeband Literary Associates; Van der Leun & Associates; Vines Agency, Inc., The; Wald Associates, Inc., Mary Jack; West Coast Literary Associates

Family Saga: Alive Communications, Inc.; Allen, Literary Agent, James; Allred and Allred Literary Agents; Amber Literary; Authentic Creations Literary Agency; Barrett Books Inc., Loretta; Bent, Literary Agent, Jenny; Bleecker Street Associates; Boates Literary Agency, Reid; Books & Such; Bova Literary Agency, The Barbara; Brandt & Brandt Literary Agents Inc.; Buck Agency, Howard; C G & W Associates; Collin Literary Agent, Frances; Connor Literary Agency; Daves Agency, Joan; Dawson Associates, Liza; Diamond Literary Agency, Inc.; Dijkstra Literary Agency, Sandra; Doyen Literary Services, Inc.; Ducas, Robert; Dystel Literary Management, Jane; Ellenberg Literary Agency, Ethan; Elmo Agency Inc., Ann; Feigen/Parrent Literary Management; Finesse Literary Agency; Flaherty, Literary Agent, Joyce A.; Fleury Agency, B.R.; Fredericks Literary Agency, Inc., Jeanne; Gibson Agency, The Sebastian; Grace Literary

Agency, Carroll; Greenburger Associates, Inc., Sanford J.; Greene, Literary Agent, Randall Elisha; Grosvenor Literary Agency, The; Halsey North, Reese; Harris Literary Agency, Inc., The Joy; Hawkins & Associates, Inc., John; Henshaw Group, Richard; Herner Rights Agency, Susan; Jabberwocky Literary Agency; JCA Literary Agency, Inc.; Kleinman, Esq. of Graybill & English L.L.C., Jeffrey M.; Klinger, Inc., Harvey; Koster Literary Agency, LLC, Elaine; Kouts, Literary Agent, Barbara S.; Kraas Agency, Irene; Lampack Agency, Inc., Peter; Larkin, Sabra Elliott; Larsen/Elizabeth Pomada Literary Agents, Michael; Lasher Agency, The Maureen; Levine Literary Agency, Paul S.; Lincoln Literary Agency, Ray; Literary Group, The; March Tenth, Inc.; Marshall Agency, The Evan; Michaels Literary Agency, Inc., Doris S.; Morrison, Inc., Henry; Multimedia Product Development, Inc.; Mura Enterprises, Inc., Dee; Naggar Literary Agency, Jean V.; Norma-Lewis Agency, The; Northwest Literary Services; Pelter, Rodney; Pinder Lane & Garon-Brooke Associates, Ltd.; Pine Associates, Inc, Arthur; Renaissance Literary Agency; Rhodes Literary Agency, Jodie; Robbins Literary Agency, BJ; Rotrosen Agency LLC, Jane; Sanders Literary Agency, Victoria; Scagnetti Talent & Literary Agency, Jack; Schiavone Literary Agency, Inc.; Shepard Agency, The; Simenauer Literary Agency, Jacqueline; Spieler Agency, The; Straus Agency, Inc., Robin; Sunshine Literary Agency; Taylor, Literary Agent, Rebecca; Van der Leun & Associates; Vines Agency, Inc., The; Wald Associates, Inc., Mary Jack; Watt & Associates, Sandra; Weiner Literary Agency, Cherry; Witherspoon & Associates, Inc.; Zeckendorf Assoc. Inc., Susan

Fantasy: Allen, Literary Agent, James; Allred and Allred Literary Agents; Amber Literary; Appleseeds Management; Carvainis Agency, Inc., Maria; Collin Literary Agent, Frances; Communications and Entertainment, Inc.; Ellenberg Literary Agency, Ethan; Finesse Literary Agency; Fleury Agency, B.R.; Gislason Agency, The; Grace Literary Agency, Carroll; Hawkins & Associates, Inc., John; Henshaw Group, Richard; Herner Rights Agency, Susan; Infinity Management International; Jabberwocky Literary Agency; Kidd Agency, Inc., Virginia; Kleinman, Esq. of Graybill & English L.L.C., Jeffrey M.; Larsen/Elizabeth Pomada Literary Agents, Michael; Levine Literary Agency, Paul S.; Lincoln Literary Agency, Ray; Literary Group, The; Maass Literary Agency, Donald; Mura Enterprises, Inc., Dee; Pelter, Rodney; Perkins, Rubie & Associates; Pinder Lane & Garon-Brooke Associates, Ltd.; Renaissance Literary Agency; Rhodes Literary Agency, Jodie; Sedgeband Literary Associates; Seligman, Literary Agent, Lynn; Spectrum Literary Agency; Sternig & Byrne Literary Agency; Sunshine Literary Agency; Van der Leun & Associates; Weiner Literary Agency, Cherry

Feminist: Allen Literary Agency, Linda; Allred and Allred Literary Agents; Baldi Literary Agency, Malaga; Barrett Books Inc., Loretta; Bial Agency, Daniel; Bleecker Street Associates; Brandt & Brandt Literary Agents Inc.; Brown Associates Inc., Marie; Browne Ltd., Pema; Buck Agency, Howard; Cohen Agency, The; DHS Literary, Inc.; Dijkstra Literary Agency, Sandra; Elmo Agency Inc., Ann; Feigen/Parrent Literary Management; Finesse Literary Agency; Flaherty, Literary Agent, Joyce A.; Goldfarb & Associates; Greenburger Associates, Inc., Sanford J.; Harris Literary Agency, Inc., The Joy; Hawkins & Associates, Inc., John; Herner Rights Agency, Susan; JCA Literary Agency, Inc.; Kern Literary Agency, Natasha; Kidd Agency, Inc., Virginia; Kidde, Hoyt & Picard; Kleinman, Esq. of Graybill & English L.L.C., Jeffrey M.; Koster Literary Agency, LLC, Elaine; Kouts, Literary Agent, Barbara S.; Larsen/Elizabeth Pomada Literary Agents, Michael; Lasher Agency, The Maureen; Levant & Wales, Literary Agency, Inc.; Levine Literary Agency, Paul S.; Lincoln Literary Agency, Ray; Literary Group, The; Lowenstein Associates, Inc.; Michaels Literary Agency, Inc., Doris S.; Mura Enterprises, Inc., Dee; Naggar Literary Agency, Jean V.; Nazor Literary Agency, Karen; Northwest Literary Services; Pelter, Rodney; Rhodes Literary Agency, Jodie; Ross Literary Agency, The Gail; Sage Acre Marketing & Publishing Solutions; Sanders Literary Agency, Victoria; Seligman, Literary Agent, Lynn; Simenauer Literary Agency, Jacqueline; Singer Literary Agency Inc., Evelyn; Spieler Agency, The; Taylor, Literary Agent, Rebecca; Van der Leun & Associates; Vines Agency, Inc., The; Wald Associates, Inc., Mary Jack; Witherspoon & Associates, Inc.; Wright Representatives, Ann; Zachary Shuster Agency

Gay: Allen Literary Agency, Linda; Allred and Allred Literary Agents; Authors & Artists Group, Inc.; Baldi Literary Agency, Malaga; Barrett Books Inc., Loretta; Bent, Literary Agent, Jenny; Bial Agency, Daniel; Bleecker Street Associates; Brandt & Brandt Literary Agents Inc.; Brown Associates Inc., Marie; Browne Ltd., Pema; Buck Agency, Howard; Daves Agency, Joan; DHS Literary, Inc.; Dystel Literary Management, Jane; Evans Inc., Mary; Feigen/Parrent Literary Management; Finesse Literary Agency; Goodman-Andrew-Agency, Inc.; Greenburger Associates, Inc., Sanford J.; Grosvenor Literary Agency, The; Harris Literary Agency, Inc., The Joy; Hawkins & Associates, Inc., John; Jabberwocky Literary Agency; JCA Literary Agency, Inc.; Kidde, Hoyt & Picard; Kleinman, Esq. of Graybill & English L.L.C., Jeffrey M.; Koster Literary Agency, LLC, Elaine; Larsen/Elizabeth Pomada Literary Agents, Michael; Levant & Wales, Literary Agency, Inc.; Levine Literary Agency, Paul S.; Lincoln Literary Agency, Ray; Literary Group, The; Lowenstein Associates, Inc.; Mura Enterprises, Inc., Dee; Perkins, Rubie & Associates; Pevner, Inc., Stephen; Pinder Lane & Garon-Brooke Associates, Ltd.; Rhodes Literary Agency, Jodie; Ross Literary Agency, The Gail; Sage Acre Marketing & Publishing Solutions; Sanders Literary Agency,

Victoria; Seligman, Literary Agent, Lynn; Simenauer Literary Agency, Jacqueline; Spieler Agency, The; Van der Leun & Associates; Vines Agency, Inc., The; Wald Associates, Inc., Mary Jack; Watkins Loomis Agency, Inc.; Witherspoon & Associates, Inc.; Wright Representatives, Ann; Zachary Shuster Agency

Glitz: Allen Literary Agency, Linda; Allen, Literary Agent, James; Allred and Allred Literary Agents; Authors Alliance, Inc.; Barrett Books Inc., Loretta; Bova Literary Agency, The Barbara; Browne Ltd., Pema; Buck Agency, Howard; C G & W Associates; Castiglia Literary Agency; Diamond Literary Agency, Inc.; Elmo Agency Inc., Ann; Gibson Agency, The Sebastian; Goldfarb & Associates; Greenburger Associates, Inc., Sanford J.; Harris Literary Agency, Inc., The Joy; Hawkins & Associates, Inc., John; Henshaw Group, Richard; Herner Rights Agency, Susan; Jabberwocky Literary Agency; JCA Literary Agency, Inc.; JLA Literary Agency; Kidd Agency, Inc., Virginia; Kidde, Hoyt & Picard; Kleinman, Esq. of Graybill & English L.L.C., Jeffrey M.; Klinger, Inc., Harvey; Koster Literary Agency, LLC, Elaine; Larkin, Sabra Elliott; Larsen/Elizabeth Pomada Literary Agents, Michael; Levine Literary Agency, Paul S.; Marshall Agency, The Evan; Multimedia Product Development, Inc.; Mura Enterprises, Inc., Dee; Pelter, Rodney; Pevner, Inc., Stephen; Quicksilver Books-Literary Agents; Rubenstein Literary Agency, Inc., Pesha; Seymour Agency, The; Simenauer Literary Agency, Jacqueline; Sternig & Byrne Literary Agency; Teal Literary Agency, Patricia; Van der Leun & Associates; Wald Associates, Inc., Mary Jack; Weiner Literary Agency, Cherry; Zeckendorf Assoc. Inc., Susan

Historical: Alive Communications, Inc.; Allen, Literary Agent, James; Allred and Allred Literary Agents; Altair Literary Agency; Amber Literary; Authors Alliance, Inc.; Baldi Literary Agency, Malaga; Barrett Books Inc., Loretta; Bernstein & Associates, Inc., Pam; Bleecker Street Associates; Books & Such; Brandt & Brandt Literary Agents Inc.; Brown Associates Inc., Marie; Browne Ltd., Pema; Buck Agency, Howard; C G & W Associates; Carvainis Agency, Inc., Maria; Cohen Agency, The; Cohen, Inc. Literary Agency, Ruth; Collin Literary Agent, Frances; Communications and Entertainment, Inc.; Dawson Associates, Liza; DHS Literary, Inc.; Diamond Literary Agency, Inc.; Donovan Literary, Jim; Doyen Literary Services, Inc.; Ellenberg Literary Agency, Ethan; Elmo Agency Inc., Ann; ES Talent Agency; Everitt Literary Agency, Inc., Charles; Finesse Literary Agency; Flaherty, Literary Agent, Joyce A.; Fleury Agency, B.R.; Fredericks Literary Agency, Inc., Jeanne; Gibson Agency, The Sebastian; Grace Literary Agency, Carroll; Greenburger Associates, Inc., Sanford J.; Grosvenor Literary Agency, The; Halsey North, Reece; Harris Literary Agency, Inc., The Joy; Hawkins & Associates, Inc., John; Henshaw Group, Richard; Herner Rights Agency, Susan; Hogenson Agency, Barbara; Hopkins Literary Associates; J de S Associates Inc.; Jabberwocky Literary Agency; JCA Literary Agency, Inc.; Kern Literary Agency, Natasha; Kidd Agency, Inc., Virginia; Kidde, Hoyt & Picard; Kleinman, Esq. of Graybill & English L.L.C., Jeffrey M.; Koster Literary Agency, LLC, Elaine; Kouts, Literary Agent, Barbara S.; Lampack Agency, Inc., Peter; Larkin, Sabra Elliott; Larsen/Elizabeth Pomada Literary Agents, Michael; Lasher Agency, The Maureen; Levine Literary Agency, Paul S.; Lincoln Literary Agency, Ray; Lindstrom Literary Group; Lowenstein Associates, Inc.; Maass Literary Agency, Donald; March Tenth, Inc.; Marshall Agency, The Evan; McBride Literary Agency, Margret; McHugh Literary Agency; Michaels Literary Agency, Inc., Doris S.; Multimedia Product Development, Inc.; Mura Enterprises, Inc., Dee; Naggar Literary Agency, Jean V.; Nathan, Ruth; Norma-Lewis Agency, The; Northwest Literary Services; Otitis Media; Paraview, Inc.; Pelter, Rodney; Perkins, Rubie & Associates; Rees Literary Agency, Helen; Renaissance Literary Agency; Rhodes Literary Agency, Jodie; Rotrosen Agency LLC, Jane; Rowland Agency, The Damaris; Sage Acre Marketing & Publishing Solutions; Scagnetti Talent & Literary Agency, Jack; Schiavone Literary Agency, Inc.; Schulman, A Literary Agency, Susan; Seligman, Literary Agent, Lynn; Seymour Agency, The; Shepard Agency, The; Simenauer Literary Agency, Jacqueline; Singer Literary Agency Inc., Evelyn; Skolnick Literary Agency, Irene; Spectrum Literary Agency; Straus Agency, Inc., Robin; Sunshine Literary Agency; Toad Hall, Inc.; Travis Literary Agency, Susan; United Tribes; Van der Leun & Associates; Vines Agency, Inc., The; Wald Associates, Inc., Mary Jack; Waxman Agency, Inc., Scott; Wecksler-Incomco; Weiner Literary Agency, Cherry; West Coast Literary Associates; Wieser & Wieser, Inc.; Witherspoon & Associates, Inc.; Zachary Shuster Agency; Zeckendorf Assoc. Inc., Susan

Horror: Allen Literary Agency, Linda; Allen, Literary Agent, James; Allred and Allred Literary Agents; Amber Literary; Amsterdam Agency, Marcia; Appleseeds Management; Authors & Artists Group, Inc.; Connor Literary Agency; Core Creations, Inc.; Cypher, The Cypher Agency, James R.; DHS Literary, Inc.; Donovan Literary, Jim; Finesse Literary Agency; Fleury Agency, B.R.; Grace Literary Agency, Carroll; Greene, Arthur B.; Hawkins & Associates, Inc., John; Henshaw Group, Richard; Herner Rights Agency, Susan; Infinity Management International; Jabberwocky Literary Agency; JCA Literary Agency, Inc.; JLA Literary Agency; Kleinman, Esq. of Graybill & English L.L.C., Jeffrey M.; Levine Literary Agency, Paul S.; Literary Group, The; Lukeman Literary Management Ltd.; Maass Literary Agency, Donald; March Tenth, Inc.; Marshall Agency, The Evan; Norma-Lewis Agency, The; Perkins, Rubie & Associates; Pevner, Inc., Stephen; Rotrosen Agency LLC, Jane; Schiavone Literary Agency, Inc.; Sedgeband Literary Associates; Seligman, Literary Agent, Lynn; Seymour Agency, The; Sternig & Byrne Literary Agency; Sunshine Literary Agency; Van der Leun & Associates; Vines Agency, Inc., The

Humor/Satire: Alive Communications, Inc.; Allred and Allred Literary Agents; Amber Literary; Amsterdam Agency, Marcia; Authors & Artists Group, Inc.; Barrett Books Inc., Loretta; Bial Agency, Daniel; Brandt & Brandt Literary Agents Inc.; Browne Ltd., Pema; Cadden, Fuller & Burkhalter LLP; ES Talent Agency; Farber Literary Agency Inc.; Finesse Literary Agency; Flannery Literary; Fleury Agency, B.R.; Greenburger Associates, Inc., Sanford J.; Greene, Literary Agent, Randall Elisha; Harris Literary Agency; Henshaw Group, Richard; Hogenson Agency, Barbara; Jabberwocky Literary Agency; JCA Literary Agency, Inc.; JLA Literary Agency; Kidde, Hoyt & Picard; Kleinman, Esq. of Graybill & English L.L.C., Jeffrey M.; Larkin, Sabra Elliott; Larsen/Elizabeth Pomada Literary Agents, Michael; Levine Literary Agency, Paul S.; Lincoln Literary Agency, Ray; Literary Group, The; March Tenth, Inc.; Marshall Agency, The Evan; McBride Literary Agency, Margret; Mura Enterprises, Inc., Dee; Norma-Lewis Agency, The; Northwest Literary Services; Otitis Media; Pevner, Inc., Stephen; Renaissance Literary Agency; Rubenstein Literary Agency, Inc., Pesha; Schiavone Literary Agency, Inc.; Seligman, Literary Agent, Lynn; Seymour Agency, The; Spieler Agency, The; Sunshine Literary Agency; Van der Leun & Associates; Vines Agency, Inc., The; Wright Representatives, Ann

Juvenile: Alive Communications, Inc.; Allred and Allred Literary Agents; Amber Literary; Books & Such; Brown Associates Inc., Marie; Brown Literary Agency, Inc., Andrea; Browne Ltd., Pema; Cohen, Inc. Literary Agency, Ruth; Dwyer & O'Grady, Inc.; Elek Associates, Peter; Ellenberg Literary Agency, Ethan; Elmo Agency Inc., Ann; Farber Literary Agency Inc.; Finesse Literary Agency; Fitzgerald Literary Management; Flannery Literary; Harris Literary Agency; Hawkins & Associates, Inc., John; Henshaw Group, Richard; J de S Associates Inc.; Kirchoff/Wohlberg, Inc., Authors' Representation Division; Kouts, Literary Agent, Barbara S.; Kraas Agency, Irene; Lincoln Literary Agency, Ray; Maccoby Literary Agency, Gina; Multimedia Product Development, Inc.; Mura Enterprises, Inc., Dee; National Writers Literary Agency; Norma-Lewis Agency, The; Rhodes Literary Agency, Jodie; Rubenstein Literary Agency, Inc., Pesha; Russell & Volkening; Schiavone Literary Agency, Inc.; Sedgeband Literary Associates; Sternig & Byrne Literary Agency; Sunshine Literary Agency; Targ Literary Agency, Inc., Roslyn; Taylor, Literary Agent, Rebecca; Tiersten Literary Agency, Irene; Tobias—A Literary Agency for Children's Books, Ann; Treimel New York, S©ott; Van der Leun & Associates; Vines Agency, Inc., The; Wald Associates, Inc., Mary Jack; Wecksler-Incomco; Writers' Productions

Lesbian: Allen Literary Agency, Linda; Allred and Allred Literary Agents; Baldi Literary Agency, Malaga; Barrett Books Inc., Loretta; Brandt & Brandt Literary Agents Inc.; Browne Ltd., Pema; Buck Agency, Howard; Dystel Literary Management, Jane; Feigen/Parrent Literary Management; Goodman-Andrew-Agency, Inc.; Greenburger Associates, Inc., Sanford J.; Grosvenor Literary Agency, The; Harris Literary Agency, Inc., The Joy; Hawkins & Associates, Inc., John; Jabberwocky Literary Agency; Kidde, Hoyt & Picard; Koster Literary Agency, LLC, Elaine; Larsen/Elizabeth Pomada Literary Agents, Michael; Levant & Wales, Literary Agency, Inc.; Lincoln Literary Agency, Ray; Literary Group, The; Lowenstein Associates, Inc.; Mura Enterprises, Inc., Dee; Pelter, Rodney; Perkins, Rubie & Associates; Pevner, Inc., Stephen; Sanders Literary Agency, Victoria; Schulman, A Literary Agency, Susan; Seligman, Literary Agent, Lynn; Spieler Agency, The; Van der Leun & Associates; Vines Agency, Inc., The; Witherspoon & Associates, Inc.; Wright Representatives, Ann; Zachary Shuster Agency

Literary: Acacia House Publishing Services Ltd.; Alive Communications, Inc.; Allen Literary Agency, Linda; Allred and Allred Literary Agents; Altair Literary Agency; Amber Literary; Amster Literary Enterprises, Betsy; Authentic Creations Literary Agency; Authors Alliance, Inc.; Baldi Literary Agency, Malaga; Barrett Books Inc., Loretta; Bent, Literary Agent, Jenny; Bial Agency, Daniel; Black Literary Agency, David; Bleecker Street Associates; Book Deals, Inc.; Borchardt Inc., Georges; Brandt & Brandt Literary Agents Inc.; Brown Associates Inc., Marie; Browne Ltd., Pema; Buck Agency, Howard; C G & W Associates; Cadden, Fuller & Burkhalter LLP; Carvainis Agency, Inc., Maria; Castiglia Literary Agency; Cohen Agency, The; Cohen, Inc. Literary Agency, Ruth; Collin Literary Agent, Frances; Congdon Associates, Inc., Don; Connor Literary Agency; Cornfield Literary Agency, Robert; Cypher, The Cypher Agency, James R.; Darhansoff & Verrill Literary Agents; Daves Agency, Joan; DH Literary, Inc.; DHS Literary, Inc.; Dijkstra Literary Agency, Sandra; Donovan Literary, Jim; Doyen Literary Services, Inc.; Ducas, Robert; Dystel Literary Management, Jane; Ellenberg Literary Agency, Ethan; Ellison Inc., Nicholas; Elmo Agency Inc., Ann; ES Talent Agency; Evans Inc., Mary; Everitt Literary Agency, Inc., Charles; Farber Literary Agency Inc.; Feigen/Parrent Literary Management; Finesse Literary Agency; Flannery Literary; Fleury Agency, B.R.; Fogelman Literary Agency, The; Franklin Associates, Ltd., Lynn C.; Fredericks Literary Agency, Inc., Jeanne; Freymann Literary Agency, Sarah Jane; Gelfman Schneider Literary Agents, Inc.; Goldfarb & Associates; Goodman-Andrew-Agency, Inc.; Grace Literary Agency, Carroll; Greenburger Associates, Inc., Sanford J.; Greene, Literary Agent, Randall Elisha; Grosvenor Literary Agency, The; Halsey North, Reese; Harris Literary Agency, Inc., The Joy; Hawkins & Associates, Inc., John; Henshaw

Group, Richard; Herner Rights Agency, Susan; Hill Associates, Frederick; Hogenson Agency, Barbara; J de S Associates Inc.; Jabberwocky Literary Agency; JCA Literary Agency, Inc.; JLA Literary Agency; Joy Literary Agency; Kidd Agency, Inc., Virginia; Kidde, Hoyt & Picard; Kleinman, Esq. of Graybill & English L.L.C., Jeffrey M.; Klinger, Inc., Harvey; Knight Agency, The; Koster Literary Agency, LLC, Elaine; Kouts, Literary Agent, Barbara S.; Kraas Agency, Irene; Lampack Agency, Inc., Peter; Larkin, Sabra Elliott; Larsen/Elizabeth Pomada Literary Agents, Michael; Lasher Agency, The Maureen; Levant & Wales, Literary Agency, Inc.; Levine Communications, Inc., James; Levine Literary Agency, Inc., Ellen; Levine Literary Agency, Paul S.; Lewis & Company, Karen; Lincoln Literary Agency, Ray; Lowenstein Associates, Inc.; Lukeman Literary Management Ltd.; Maass Literary Agency, Donald; Maccoby Literary Agency, Gina; Mann Agency, Carol; Manus & Associates Literary Agency; March Tenth, Inc.; Markson Literary Agency, Elaine; Marshall Agency, The Evan; McBride Literary Agency, Margret; McDonough, Literary Agent, Richard P.; McGrath, Helen; Michaels Literary Agency, Inc., Doris S.; Multimedia Product Development, Inc.; Mura Enterprises, Inc., Dee; Naggar Literary Agency, Jean V.; Nazor Literary Agency, Karen; Nine Muses and Apollo; Northwest Literary Services; Paraview, Inc.; Paton Literary Agency, Kathi J.; Pelter, Rodney; Perkins, Rubie & Associates; Pevner, Inc., Stephen; Pinder Lane & Garon-Brooke Associates, Ltd.; Pine Associates, Inc, Arthur; Rees Literary Agency, Helen; Reichstein Literary Agency, The Naomi; Rein Books, Inc., Jody; Renaissance Literary Agency; Rhodes Literary Agency, Jodie; Rittenberg Literary Agency, Inc., Ann; Robbins Literary Agency, BJ; Ross Literary Agency, The Gail; Rowland Agency, The Damaris; Russell & Volkening; Sage Acre Marketing & Publishing Solutions; Sanders Literary Agency, Victoria; Sandum & Associates; Schiavone Literary Agency, Inc.; Schulman, A Literary Agency, Susan; Sedgeband Literary Associates; Seligman, Literary Agent, Lynn; Shepard Agency, The; Simenauer Literary Agency, Jacqueline; Singer Literary Agency Inc., Evelyn; Skolnick Literary Agency, Irene; Slopen Literary Agency, Beverley; Spieler Agency, The; Spitzer Literary Agency, Philip G.; Stauffer Associates, Nancy; Straus Agency, Inc., Robin; Sunshine Literary Agency; Swayne Agency Literary Management & Consulting, Inc., The; Talbot Agency, The John; Taylor, Literary Agent, Rebecca; Travis Literary Agency, Susan; Van der Leun & Associates; Vines Agency, Inc., The; Wald Associates, Inc., Mary Jack; Wallace Literary Agency, Inc.; Ware Literary Agency, John A.; Watkins Loomis Agency, Inc.; Waxman Agency, Inc., Scott; Wecksler-Incomco; Weingel-Fidel Agency, The; West Coast Literary Associates; Wieser & Wieser, Inc.; Witherspoon & Associates, Inc.; Wonderland Press, Inc., The; Wright Representatives, Ann; Writers' Productions; Writers' Representatives, Inc.; Zachary Shuster Agency; Zeckendorf Assoc. Inc., Susan

Mainstream: Acacia House Publishing Services Ltd.; Agents Inc. for Medical and Mental Health Professionals; Alive Communications, Inc.; Allen Literary Agency, Linda; Allen, Literary Agent, James; Allred and Allred Literary Agents; Amber Literary; Amsterdam Agency, Marcia; Authentic Creations Literary Agency; Authors Alliance, Inc.; Authors & Artists Group, Inc.; Baldi Literary Agency, Malaga; Barrett Books Inc., Loretta; Bedford Book Works, Inc., The; Bernstein & Associates, Inc., Pam; Black Literary Agency, David; Boates Literary Agency, Reid; Book Deals, Inc.; Books & Such; Bova Literary Agency, The Barbara; Brandt & Brandt Literary Agents Inc.; Brown Associates Inc., Marie; Browne Ltd., Pema; Buck Agency, Howard; C G & W Associates; Carvainis Agency, Inc., Maria; Castiglia Literary Agency; Cohen Agency, The; Cohen, Inc. Literary Agency, Ruth; Collin Literary Agent, Frances; Crawford Literary Agency; Cypher, The Cypher Agency, James R.; Daves Agency, Joan; DH Literary, Inc.; DHS Literary, Inc.; Diamond Literary Agency, Inc.; Dijkstra Literary Agency, Sandra; Donovan Literary, Jim; Doyen Literary Services, Inc.; Ducas, Robert; Dystel Literary Management, Jane; Ellenberg Literary Agency, Ethan; Ellison Inc., Nicholas; Elmo Agency Inc., Ann; ES Talent Agency; Farber Literary Agency Inc.; Finesse Literary Agency; Fitzgerald Literary Management; Flaherty, Literary Agent, Joyce A.; Flannery Literary; Fleury Agency, B.R.; Fogelman Literary Agency, The; Franklin Associates, Ltd., Lynn C.; Freymann Literary Agency, Sarah Jane; Gelfman Schneider Literary Agents, Inc.; Gibson Agency, The Sebastian; Goldfarb & Associates; Goodman-Andrew-Agency, Inc.; Grace Literary Agency, Carroll; Greenburger Associates, Inc., Sanford J.; Greene, Literary Agent, Randall Elisha; Grosvenor Literary Agency, The; Halsey North, Reese; Harris Literary Agency; Harris Literary Agency, Inc., The Joy; Hawkins & Associates, Inc., John; Henshaw Group, Richard; Herner Rights Agency, Susan; Hill Associates, Frederick; Hogenson Agency, Barbara; Hopkins Literary Associates; J de S Associates Inc.; Jabberwocky Literary Agency; JCA Literary Agency, Inc.; JLA Literary Agency; Joy Literary Agency; Kern Literary Agency, Natasha; Kidd Agency, Inc., Virginia; Kidde, Hoyt & Picard; Kleinman, Esq. of Graybill & English L.L.C., Jeffrey M.; Klinger, Inc., Harvey; Knight Agency, The; Koster Literary Agency, LLC, Elaine; Kouts, Literary Agent, Barbara S.; Kraas Agency, Irene; Lampack Agency, Inc., Peter; Larkin, Sabra Elliott; Larsen/Elizabeth Pomada Literary Agents, Michael; Lasher Agency, The Maureen; Levant & Wales, Literary Agency, Inc.; Levine Communications, Inc., James; Levine Literary Agency, Paul S.; Lewis & Company, Karen; Lincoln Literary Agency, Ray; Lindstrom Literary Group; Lipkind Agency, Wendy; Lowenstein Associates, Inc.; Lukeman Literary Management Ltd.; Maass Literary Agency, Donald; Maccoby Literary Agency, Gina; March Tenth, Inc.; Markson Literary Agency, Elaine; Marshall Agency, The Evan; McBride Literary Agency, Margret; McGrath, Helen; McHugh Literary Agency; Michaels Literary Agency, Inc., Doris S.;

Multimedia Product Development, Inc.; Mura Enterprises, Inc., Dee; Naggar Literary Agency, Jean V.; National Writers Literary Agency; Nine Muses and Apollo; Norma-Lewis Agency, The; Northwest Literary Services; Otitis Media; Paraview, Inc.; Paton Literary Agency, Kathi J.; Pelter, Rodney; Perkins, Rubie & Associates; Pevner, Inc., Stephen; Pinder Lane & Garon-Brooke Associates, Ltd.; Pine Associates, Inc, Arthur; Rees Literary Agency, Helen; Reichstein Literary Agency, The Naomi; Renaissance Literary Agency; Rhodes Literary Agency, Jodie; Robbins Literary Agency, BJ; Rotrosen Agency LLC, Jane; Rowland Agency, The Damaris; Rubenstein Literary Agency, Inc., Pesha; Russell & Volkening; Sage Acre Marketing & Publishing Solutions; Sandum & Associates; Scagnetti Talent & Literary Agency, Jack; Schiavone Literary Agency, Inc.; Schlessinger Agency, Blanche; Schulman, A Literary Agency, Susan; Sedgeband Literary Associates; Seligman, Literary Agent, Lynn; Seymour Agency, The; Simenauer Literary Agency, Jacqueline; Singer Literary Agency Inc., Evelyn; Spectrum Literary Agency; Spitzer Literary Agency, Philip G.; Stauffer Associates, Nancy; Straus Agency, Inc., Robin; Sunshine Literary Agency; Teal Literary Agency, Patricia; Travis Literary Agency, Susan; Van der Leun & Associates; Vines Agency, Inc., The; Wald Associates, Inc., Mary Jack; Wallace Literary Agency, Inc.; Ware Literary Agency, John A.; Watkins Loomis Agency, Inc.; Watt & Associates, Sandra; Wecksler-Incomco; Weiner Literary Agency, Cherry; Weingel-Fidel Agency, The; West Coast Literary Associates; Wieser & Wieser, Inc.; Witherspoon & Associates, Inc.; Wright Representatives, Ann; Zachary Shuster Agency; Zeckendorf Assoc. Inc., Susan

Mystery/Suspense: Acacia House Publishing Services Ltd.; Agents Inc. for Medical and Mental Health Professionals; Alive Communications, Inc.; Allen Literary Agency, Linda; Allen, Literary Agent, James; Allred and Allred Literary Agents; Amber Literary; Amsterdam Agency, Marcia; Appleseeds Management; Authentic Creations Literary Agency; Authors Alliance, Inc.; Baldi Literary Agency, Malaga; Barrett Books Inc., Loretta; Bedford Book Works, Inc., The; Bernstein & Associates, Inc., Pam; Bleecker Street Associates; Bookmark Literary Agency; Bova Literary Agency, The Barbara; Brandt & Brandt Literary Agents Inc.; Brown Associates Inc., Marie; Browne Ltd., Pema; Buck Agency, Howard; C G & W Associates; Carvainis Agency, Inc., Maria; Castiglia Literary Agency; Charisma Communications, Ltd.; Cohen Agency, The; Cohen, Inc. Literary Agency, Ruth; Collin Literary Agent, Frances; Connor Literary Agency; Dawson Associates, Liza; DH Literary, Inc.; DHS Literary, Inc.; Diamond Literary Agency, Inc.; Dijkstra Literary Agency, Sandra; Donovan Literary, Jim; Ducas, Robert; Ellenberg Literary Agency, Ethan; Elmo Agency Inc., Ann; ES Talent Agency; Farber Literary Agency Inc.; Finesse Literary Agency; Flaherty, Literary Agent, Joyce A.; Flannery Literary; Fleury Agency, B.R.; Freymann Literary Agency, Sarah Jane; Gelfman Schneider Literary Agents, Inc.; Gislason Agency, The; Goldfarb & Associates; Grace Literary Agency, Carroll; Greenburger Associates, Inc., Sanford J.; Greene, Arthur B.; Greene, Literary Agent, Randall Elisha; Grosvenor Literary Agency, The; Halsey North, Reese; Harris Literary Agency; Harris Literary Agency, Inc., The Joy; Hawkins & Associates, Inc., John; Herner Rights Agency, Susan; Hogenson Agency, Barbara; Infinity Management International; J de S Associates Inc.; JCA Literary Agency, Inc.; JLA Literary Agency; Joy Literary Agency; Kern Literary Agency, Natasha; Kidd Agency, Inc., Virginia; Kidde, Hoyt & Picard; Knight Agency, The; Koster Literary Agency, LLC, Elaine; Kouts, Literary Agent, Barbara S.; Kraas Agency, Irene; Lampack Agency, Inc., Peter; Larkin, Sabra Elliott; Larsen/Elizabeth Pomada Literary Agents, Michael; Lescher & Lescher Ltd.; Levine Literary Agency, Inc., Ellen; Levine Literary Agency, Paul S.; Lewis & Company, Karen; Lincoln Literary Agency, Ray; Lipkind Agency, Wendy; Literary Group, The; Love Literary Agency, Nancy; Lowenstein Associates, Inc.; Maass Literary Agency, Donald; Maccoby Literary Agency, Gina; Marshall Agency, The Evan; McBride Literary Agency, Margret; McGrath, Helen; McHugh Literary Agency; Multimedia Product Development, Inc.; Mura Enterprises, Inc., Dee; Naggar Literary Agency, Jean V.; Norma-Lewis Agency, The; Northwest Literary Services; Pelter, Rodney; Perkins, Rubie & Associates; Pinder Lane & Garon-Brooke Associates, Ltd.; Protter Literary Agent, Susan Ann; Quicksilver Books-Literary Agents; Real Criminals; Rees Literary Agency, Helen; Reichstein Literary Agency, The Naomi; Renaissance Literary Agency; Rhodes Literary Agency, Jodie; Robbins Literary Agency, BJ; Roghaar Literary Agency, Inc., Linda; Rotrosen Agency LLC, Jane; Rubenstein Literary Agency, Inc., Pesha; Russell & Volkening; Scagnetti Talent & Literary Agency, Jack; Schulman, A Literary Agency, Susan; Sedgeband Literary Associates; Seligman, Literary Agent, Lynn; Seymour Agency, The; Simenauer Literary Agency, Jacqueline; Singer Literary Agency Inc., Evelyn; Slopen Literary Agency, Beverley; Spectrum Literary Agency; Spitzer Literary Agency, Philip G.; Sternig & Byrne Literary Agency; Sunshine Literary Agency; Swayne Agency Literary Management & Consulting, Inc., The; Talbot Agency, The John; Teal Literary Agency, Patricia; Toad Hall, Inc.; Van der Leun & Associates; Vines Agency, Inc., The; Wald Associates, Inc., Mary Jack; Wallace Literary Agency, Inc.; Ware Literary Agency, John A.; Watkins Loomis Agency, Inc.; Watt & Associates, Sandra; Waxman Agency, Inc., Scott; Weiner Literary Agency, Cherry; West Coast Literary Associates; Wieser & Wieser, Inc.; Witherspoon & Associates, Inc.; Wright Representatives, Ann; Zachary Shuster Agency; Zeckendorf Assoc. Inc., Susan

Open to all Fiction Categories: Bernstein Literary Agency, Meredith; Brown Limited, Curtis; Bykofsky Associates, Inc., Sheree; Circle of Confusion Ltd.; Cohen Literary Agency Ltd., Hy; Congdon Associates,

Inc., Don; Curtis Associates, Inc., Richard; Fernandez Agent/Attorney, Justin E.; Goodman Associates; Hoffman Literary Agency, Berenice; Lazear Agency Incorporated; Madsen Agency, Robert; Moran Agency, Maureen; Ober Associates, Harold; Writers House

Picture Book: Books & Such; Brown Literary Agency, Inc., Andrea; Browne Ltd., Pema; Cohen, Inc. Literary Agency, Ruth; Dwyer & O'Grady, Inc.; Elek Associates, Peter; Ellenberg Literary Agency, Ethan; Finesse Literary Agency; Flannery Literary; Harris Literary Agency, Inc., The Joy; Hawkins & Associates, Inc., John; Heacock Literary Agency, Inc.; Kouts, Literary Agent, Barbara S.; Levine Literary Agency, Paul S.; Multimedia Product Development, Inc.; National Writers Literary Agency; Norma-Lewis Agency, The; Rubenstein Literary Agency, Inc., Pesha; Russell & Volkening; Scagnetti Talent & Literary Agency, Jack; Taylor, Literary Agent, Rebecca; Van der Leun & Associates; Wald Associates, Inc., Mary Jack; Wecksler-Incomco; Wonderland Press, Inc., The; Writers House

Psychic/Supernatural: Allen Literary Agency, Linda; Allred and Allred Literary Agents; Appleseeds Management; Authors & Artists Group, Inc.; Barrett Books Inc., Loretta; Bleecker Street Associates; Bookmark Literary Agency; Brandt & Brandt Literary Agents Inc.; Browne Ltd., Pema; Buck Agency, Howard; Cadden, Fuller & Burkhalter LLP; Collin Literary Agent, Frances; Doyen Literary Services, Inc.; Elmo Agency Inc., Ann; Finesse Literary Agency; Fleury Agency, B.R.; Grace Literary Agency, Carroll; Greenburger Associates, Inc., Sanford J.; Harris Literary Agency, Inc., The Joy; Hawkins & Associates, Inc., John; Henshaw Group, Richard; Infinity Management International; J de S Associates Inc.; Jabber-wocky Literary Agency; JLA Literary Agency; Kleinman, Esq. of Graybill & English L.L.C., Jeffrey M.; Larsen/Elizabeth Pomada Literary Agents, Michael; Levine Literary Agency, Paul S.; Lincoln Literary Agency, Ray; Literary Group, The; Maass Literary Agency, Donald; Marshall Agency, The Evan; McGrath, Helen; Mura Enterprises, Inc., Dee; Naggar Literary Agency, Jean V.; Northwest Literary Services; Para-view, Inc.; Pelter, Rodney; Perkins, Rubie & Associates; Pevner, Inc., Stephen; Rhodes Literary Agency, Jodie; Rowland Agency, The Damaris; Rubenstein Literary Agency, Inc., Pesha; Sedgeband Literary Asso-ciates; Simenauer Literary Agency, Jacqueline; Sternig & Byrne Literary Agency; Sunshine Literary Agency; Van der Leun & Associates; Vines Agency, Inc., The; Weiner Literary Agency, Cherry

Regional: Allen Literary Agency, Linda; Allred and Allred Literary Agents; Baldi Literary Agency, Ma-laga; Bova Literary Agency, The Barbara; Brandt & Brandt Literary Agents Inc.; Buck Agency, Howard; C G & W Associates; Cohen Agency, The; Collin Literary Agent, Frances; Dawson Associates, Liza; Elmo Agency Inc., Ann; Fleury Agency, B.R.; Gibson Agency, The Sebastian; Greenburger Associates, Inc., Sanford J.; Greene, Literary Agent, Randall Elisha; Harris Literary Agency, Inc., The Joy; Hawkins & Associates, Inc., John; Jabberwocky Literary Agency; JLA Literary Agency; Kleinman, Esq. of Graybill & English L.L.C., Jeffrey M.; Knight Agency, The; Koster Literary Agency, LLC, Elaine; Larkin, Sabra Elliott; Levine Literary Agency, Paul S.; Lincoln Literary Agency, Ray; Manus & Associates Literary Agency; Mura Enterprises, Inc., Dee; Nazor Literary Agency, Karen; Paraview, Inc.; Pelter, Rodney; Rhodes Literary Agency, Jodie; Shepard Agency, The; Singer Literary Agency Inc., Evelyn; Stauffer Asso-ciates, Nancy; Van der Leun & Associates; Vines Agency, Inc., The; Watt & Associates, Sandra; West Coast Literary Associates

Religious/Inspirational: Alive Communications, Inc.; Allred and Allred Literary Agents; Amber Liter-ary; Authors & Artists Group, Inc.; Barrett Books Inc., Loretta; BigScore Productions Inc.; Books & Such; Browne Ltd., Pema; Buck Agency, Howard; Cadden, Fuller & Burkhalter LLP; Charisma Communications, Ltd.; Crawford Literary Agency; Finesse Literary Agency; Harris Literary Agency, Inc., The Joy; Hawkins & Associates, Inc., John; J de S Associates Inc.; JLA Literary Agency; Joy Literary Agency; Knight Agency, The; Larsen/Elizabeth Pomada Literary Agents, Michael; Levine Literary Agency, Paul S.; Mar-shall Agency, The Evan; Multimedia Product Development, Inc.; Pelter, Rodney; Seymour Agency, The; Sternig & Byrne Literary Agency; Sunshine Literary Agency; United Tribes; Van der Leun & Associates; Watt & Associates, Sandra; Waxman Agency, Inc., Scott

Romance: Allen, Literary Agent, James; Allred and Allred Literary Agents; Amber Literary; Amsterdam Agency, Marcia; Authentic Creations Literary Agency; Barrett Books Inc., Loretta; Bernstein & Associates, Inc., Pam; Bleecker Street Associates; Books & Such; Bova Literary Agency, The Barbara; Brandt & Brandt Literary Agents Inc.; Browne Ltd., Pema; Buck Agency, Howard; C G & W Associates; Carvainis Agency, Inc., Maria; Cohen Agency, The; Cohen, Inc. Literary Agency, Ruth; Collin Literary Agent, Frances; Diamond Literary Agency, Inc.; Ellenberg Literary Agency, Ethan; Elmo Agency Inc., Ann; Finesse Literary Agency; Flaherty, Literary Agent, Joyce A.; Fleury Agency, B.R.; Fogelman Literary Agency, The; Gibson Agency, The Sebastian; Gislason Agency, The; Grace Literary Agency, Carroll; Greene, Literary Agent, Randall Elisha; Grosvenor Literary Agency, The; Harris Literary Agency, Inc., The Joy; Herner Rights Agency, Susan; Hogenson Agency, Barbara; Hopkins Literary Associates; JLA Literary Agency; Kern Literary Agency, Natasha; Kidde, Hoyt & Picard; Knight Agency, The; Larkin, Sabra Elliott; Larsen/Elizabeth Pomada Literary Agents, Michael; Levine Literary Agency, Paul S.; Lincoln

Literary Agency, Ray; Literary Group, The; Lowenstein Associates, Inc.; Maass Literary Agency, Donald; Marshall Agency, The Evan; McGrath, Helen; McHugh Literary Agency; Multimedia Product Development, Inc.; Mura Enterprises, Inc., Dee; Norma-Lewis Agency, The; Northwest Literary Services; Paraview, Inc.; Pinder Lane & Garon-Brooke Associates, Ltd.; Pine Associates, Inc, Arthur; Rhodes Literary Agency, Jodie; Rotrosen Agency LLC, Jane; Rowland Agency, The Damaris; Rubenstein Literary Agency, Inc., Pesha; Sage Acre Marketing & Publishing Solutions; Scagnetti Talent & Literary Agency, Jack; Sedgeband Literary Associates; Seligman, Literary Agent, Lynn; Seymour Agency, The; Simenauer Literary Agency, Jacqueline; Sunshine Literary Agency; Taylor, Literary Agent, Rebecca; Teal Literary Agency, Patricia; Toad Hall, Inc.; Travis Literary Agency, Susan; Van der Leun & Associates; Vines Agency, Inc., The; Waxman Agency, Inc., Scott; Weiner Literary Agency, Cherry; West Coast Literary Associates; Wieser & Wieser, Inc.; Wright Representatives, Ann; Zachary Shuster Agency

Science Fiction: Allen, Literary Agent, James; Allred and Allred Literary Agents; Amber Literary; Amsterdam Agency, Marcia; Appleseeds Management; Bova Literary Agency, The Barbara; Brandt & Brandt Literary Agents Inc.; Browne Ltd., Pema; Cohen Agency, The; Collin Literary Agent, Frances; Communications and Entertainment, Inc.; Core Creations, Inc.; Ellenberg Literary Agency, Ethan; Finesse Literary Agency; Fleury Agency, B.R.; Gibson Agency, The Sebastian; Gislason Agency, The; Halsey North, Reese; Harris Literary Agency; Hawkins & Associates, Inc., John; Henshaw Group, Richard; Herner Rights Agency, Susan; Infinity Management International; Jabberwocky Literary Agency; JLA Literary Agency; Kidd Agency, Inc., Virginia; Kleinman, Esq. of Graybill & English L.L.C., Jeffrey M.; Kraas Agency, Irene; Lawyer's Literary Agency, Inc.; Lewis & Company, Karen; Maass Literary Agency, Donald; Marshall Agency, The Evan; McGrath, Helen; Mura Enterprises, Inc., Dee; National Writers Literary Agency; Northwest Literary Services; Perkins, Rubie & Associates; Pinder Lane & Garon-Brooke Associates, Ltd.; Protter Literary Agent, Susan Ann; Renaissance Literary Agency; Rhodes Literary Agency, Jodie; Sedgeband Literary Associates; Seligman, Literary Agent, Lynn; Spectrum Literary Agency; Sternig & Byrne Literary Agency; Sunshine Literary Agency; Toad Hall, Inc.; Vines Agency, Inc., The; Weiner Literary Agency, Cherry; West Coast Literary Associates

Sports: Allred and Allred Literary Agents; Authentic Creations Literary Agency; Authors Alliance, Inc.; Barrett Books Inc., Loretta; Brandt & Brandt Literary Agents Inc.; Buck Agency, Howard; Charisma Communications, Ltd.; DHS Literary, Inc.; Donovan Literary, Jim; Ducas, Robert; Everitt Literary Agency, Inc., Charles; Finesse Literary Agency; Fleury Agency, B.R.; Gibson Agency, The Sebastian; Greenburger Associates, Inc., Sanford J.; Greene, Arthur B.; Harris Literary Agency, Inc., The Joy; Hawkins & Associates, Inc., John; Henshaw Group, Richard; Infinity Management International; Jabberwocky Literary Agency; JCA Literary Agency, Inc.; JLA Literary Agency; Lasher Agency, The Maureen; Levine Literary Agency, Paul S.; Lincoln Literary Agency, Ray; Literary Group, The; Multimedia Product Development, Inc.; Mura Enterprises, Inc., Dee; National Writers Literary Agency; Pelter, Rodney; Rhodes Literary Agency, Jodie; Robbins Literary Agency, BJ; Russell & Volkening; Scagnetti Talent & Literary Agency, Jack; Shepard Agency, The; Spitzer Literary Agency, Philip G.; Van der Leun & Associates; Vines Agency, Inc., The; Waxman Agency, Inc., Scott; Wright Representatives, Ann

Thriller/Espionage: Acacia House Publishing Services Ltd.; Agents Inc. for Medical and Mental Health Professionals; Alive Communications, Inc.; Allen Literary Agency, Linda; Allred and Allred Literary Agents; Amber Literary; Amsterdam Agency, Marcia; Authentic Creations Literary Agency; Authors Alliance, Inc.; Authors & Artists Group, Inc.; Baldi Literary Agency, Malaga; Barrett Books Inc., Loretta; Bedford Book Works, Inc., The; Bernstein & Associates, Inc., Pam; Bleecker Street Associates; Boates Literary Agency, Reid; Bova Literary Agency, The Barbara; Brandt & Brandt Literary Agents Inc.; Browne Ltd., Pema; Buck Agency, Howard; C G & W Associates; Carvainis Agency, Inc., Maria; Communications and Entertainment, Inc.; Connor Literary Agency; Crawford Literary Agency; Darhansoff & Verrill Literary Agents; Dawson Associates, Liza; DH Literary, Inc.; DHS Literary, Inc.; Diamond Literary Agency, Inc.; Dijkstra Literary Agency, Sandra; Donovan Literary, Jim; Ducas, Robert; Dystel Literary Management, Jane; Ellenberg Literary Agency, Ethan; Elmo Agency Inc., Ann; ES Talent Agency; Farber Literary Agency Inc.; Finesse Literary Agency; Flaherty, Literary Agent, Joyce A.; Fleury Agency, B.R.; Freymann Literary Agency, Sarah Jane; Gibson Agency, The Sebastian; Goldfarb & Associates; Grace Literary Agency, Carroll; Greenburger Associates, Inc., Sanford J.; Greene, Arthur B.; Greene, Literary Agent, Randall Elisha; Grosvenor Literary Agency, The; Halsey North, Reese; Harris Literary Agency; Harris Literary Agency, Inc., The Joy; Hawkins & Associates, Inc., John; Henshaw Group, Richard; Herner Rights Agency, Susan; Hogenson Agency, Barbara; Infinity Management International; Jabberwocky Literary Agency; JCA Literary Agency, Inc.; JLA Literary Agency; Joy Literary Agency; Kidde, Hoyt & Picard; Kleinman, Esq. of Graybill & English L.L.C., Jeffrey M.; Klinger, Inc., Harvey; Koster Literary Agency, LLC, Elaine; Kraas Agency, Irene; Lampack Agency, Inc., Peter; Larkin, Sabra Elliott; Lasher Agency, The Maureen; Lawyer's Literary Agency, Inc.; Levine Literary Agency, Inc., Ellen; Levine Literary Agency, Paul S.; Lewis & Company, Karen; Lincoln Literary Agency, Ray; Lindstrom Literary Group; Literary

Group, The; Love Literary Agency, Nancy; Lowenstein Associates, Inc.; Lukeman Literary Management Ltd.; Maass Literary Agency, Donald; Maccoby Literary Agency, Gina; Manus & Associates Literary Agency; Marshall Agency, The Evan; McBride Literary Agency, Margret; McGrath, Helen; McHugh Literary Agency; Multimedia Product Development, Inc.; Mura Enterprises, Inc., Dee; Naggar Literary Agency, Jean V.; Norma-Lewis Agency, The; Northwest Literary Services; Otitis Media; Paraview, Inc.; Pelter, Rodney; Perkins, Rubie & Associates; Pevner, Inc., Stephen; Pine Associates, Inc, Arthur; Protter Literary Agent, Susan Ann; Quicksilver Books-Literary Agents; Rees Literary Agency, Helen; Reichstein Literary Agency, The Naomi; Renaissance Literary Agency; Rhodes Literary Agency, Jodie; Robbins Literary Agency, BJ; Rotrosen Agency LLC, Jane; Russell & Volkening; Sanders Literary Agency, Victoria; Scagnetti Talent & Literary Agency, Jack; Shepard Agency, The; Simenauer Literary Agency, Jacqueline; Singer Literary Agency Inc., Evelyn; Spitzer Literary Agency, Philip G.; Sternig & Byrne Literary Agency; Straus Agency, Inc., Robin; Sunshine Literary Agency; Swayne Agency Literary Management & Consulting, Inc., The; Van der Leun & Associates; Vines Agency, Inc., The; Wald Associates, Inc., Mary Jack; Ware Literary Agency, John A.; Watt & Associates, Sandra; Weiner Literary Agency, Cherry; West Coast Literary Associates; Wieser & Wieser, Inc.; Witherspoon & Associates, Inc.; Wonderland Press, Inc., The; Wright Representatives, Ann; Zachary Shuster Agency; Zeckendorf Assoc. Inc., Susan

Westerns/Frontier: Alive Communications, Inc.; Allred and Allred Literary Agents; Amber Literary; Amsterdam Agency, Marcia; Brandt & Brandt Literary Agents Inc.; Buck Agency, Howard; DHS Literary, Inc.; Donovan Literary, Jim; Finesse Literary Agency; Fleury Agency, B.R.; Grace Literary Agency, Carroll; Hawkins & Associates, Inc., John; J de S Associates Inc.; JCA Literary Agency, Inc.; Joy Literary Agency; Kern Literary Agency, Natasha; Levine Literary Agency, Paul S.; Literary Group, The; Marshall Agency, The Evan; McBride Literary Agency, Margret; Mura Enterprises, Inc., Dee; Norma-Lewis Agency, The; Northwest Literary Services; Pelter, Rodney; Rhodes Literary Agency, Jodie; Scagnetti Talent & Literary Agency, Jack; Seymour Agency, The; Van der Leun & Associates; Vines Agency, Inc., The; Weiner Literary Agency, Cherry; West Coast Literary Associates; Wright Representatives, Ann

Young Adult: Alive Communications, Inc.; Allen, Literary Agent, James; Allred and Allred Literary Agents; Amber Literary; Amsterdam Agency, Marcia; Bookmark Literary Agency; Books & Such; Brandt & Brandt Literary Agents Inc.; Brown Literary Agency, Inc., Andrea; Browne Ltd., Pema; Carvainis Agency, Inc., Maria; Cohen, Inc. Literary Agency, Ruth; Dwyer & O'Grady, Inc.; Ellenberg Literary Agency, Ethan; Elmo Agency Inc., Ann; ES Talent Agency; Farber Literary Agency Inc.; Finesse Literary Agency; Fitzgerald Literary Management; Flannery Literary; Fleury Agency, B.R.; Harris Literary Agency, Inc., The Joy; Henshaw Group, Richard; J de S Associates Inc.; Joy Literary Agency; Kidd Agency, Inc., Virginia; Kirchoff/Wohlberg, Inc., Authors' Representation Division; Kouts, Literary Agent, Barbara S.; Kraas Agency, Irene; Levine Literary Agency, Paul S.; Lincoln Literary Agency, Ray; Literary Group, The; Maccoby Literary Agency, Gina; Mura Enterprises, Inc., Dee; National Writers Literary Agency; Norma-Lewis Agency, The; Rhodes Literary Agency, Jodie; Russell & Volkening; Schiavone Literary Agency, Inc.; Schulman, A Literary Agency, Susan; Sternig & Byrne Literary Agency; Sunshine Literary Agency; Taylor, Literary Agent, Rebecca; Tiersten Literary Agency, Irene; Tobias—A Literary Agency for Children's Books, Ann; Van der Leun & Associates; Wald Associates, Inc., Mary Jack; Writers House; Zachary Shuster Agency

NONFEE-CHARGING LITERARY AGENTS/NONFICTION

Agriculture/Horticulture: Amster Literary Enterprises, Betsy; Baldi Literary Agency, Malaga; Brandt & Brandt Literary Agents Inc.; Buck Agency, Howard; Casselman Literary Agency, Martha; Ellison Inc., Nicholas; Everitt Literary Agency, Inc., Charles; Fleury Agency, B.R.; ForthWrite Literary Agency; Fredericks Literary Agency, Inc., Jeanne; Gartenberg, Literary Agent, Max; Goodman-Andrew-Agency, Inc.; Greene, Literary Agent, Randall Elisha; Hawkins & Associates, Inc., John; Kleinman, Esq. of Graybill & English L.L.C., Jeffrey M.; Larkin, Sabra Elliott; Lieberman Associates, Robert; Lincoln Literary Agency, Ray; Multimedia Product Development, Inc.; Mura Enterprises, Inc., Dee; Northwest Literary Services; Parks Agency, The Richard; Schlessinger Agency, Blanche; Shepard Agency, The; Travis Literary Agency, Susan; Watt & Associates, Sandra

Animals: Acacia House Publishing Services Ltd.; Baldi Literary Agency, Malaga; Balkin Agency, Inc.; Bent, Literary Agent, Jenny; Bial Agency, Daniel; Bleecker Street Associates; Boates Literary Agency, Reid; Book Deals, Inc.; Boston Literary Group, The; Brandt & Brandt Literary Agents Inc.; Buck Agency, Howard; Castiglia Literary Agency; Cornfield Literary Agency, Robert; DH Literary, Inc.; Ducas, Robert; Dystel Literary Management, Jane; Ellison Inc., Nicholas; Everitt Literary Agency, Inc., Charles; Finesse Literary Agency; Flaherty, Literary Agent, Joyce A.; Fleury Agency, B.R.; Fredericks Literary Agency, Inc., Jeanne; Freymann Literary Agency, Sarah Jane; Gartenberg, Literary Agent, Max; Gibson Agency, The Sebastian; Gislason Agency, The; Greene, Arthur B.; Grosvenor Literary Agency, The; Hawkins &

Associates, Inc., John; Henshaw Group, Richard; JCA Literary Agency, Inc.; Kern Literary Agency, Natasha; Kleinman, Esq. of Graybill & English L.L.C., Jeffrey M.; Larkin, Sabra Elliott; Lasher Agency, The Maureen; Levant & Wales, Literary Agency, Inc.; Levine Communications, Inc., James; Lincoln Literary Agency, Ray; Literary Group, The; Love Literary Agency, Nancy; Lowenstein Associates, Inc.; Lukeman Literary Management Ltd.; Marshall Agency, The Evan; McHugh Literary Agency; Multimedia Product Development, Inc.; Mura Enterprises, Inc., Dee; National Writers Literary Agency; New Century Literary Agency; Nine Muses and Apollo; Northwest Literary Services; Parks Agency, The Richard; Reichstein Literary Agency, The Naomi; Rein Books, Inc., Jody; Rhodes Literary Agency, Jodie; Roghaar Literary Agency, Inc., Linda; Rosenkranz Literary Agency, Rita; Rowland Agency, The Damaris; Schiavone Literary Agency, Inc.; Shepard Agency, The; Stauffer Associates, Nancy; Straus Agency, Inc., Robin; Teal Literary Agency, Patricia; Toad Hall, Inc.; Ware Literary Agency, John A.; Watt & Associates, Sandra; Writers House; Zachary Shuster Agency

Anthropology/Archaeology: Allen Literary Agency, Linda; Allred and Allred Literary Agents; Altair Literary Agency; Amber Literary; Authentic Creations Literary Agency; Baldi Literary Agency, Malaga; Balkin Agency, Inc.; Bent, Literary Agent, Jenny; Bial Agency, Daniel; Bleecker Street Associates; Boates Literary Agency, Reid; Borchardt Inc., Georges; Boston Literary Group, The; Brandt & Brandt Literary Agents Inc.; Buck Agency, Howard; Casselman Literary Agency, Martha; Castiglia Literary Agency; Collin Literary Agent, Frances; Coover Agency, The Doe; Cornfield Literary Agency, Robert; Darhansoff & Verrill Literary Agents; DH Literary, Inc.; Dijkstra Literary Agency, Sandra; Dystel Literary Management, Jane; Educational Design Services, Inc.; Elek Associates, Peter; Ellison Inc., Nicholas; Elmo Agency Inc., Ann; Everitt Literary Agency, Inc., Charles; Fleury Agency, B.R.; Fredericks Literary Agency, Inc., Jeanne; Freymann Literary Agency, Sarah Jane; Fullerton Associates, Sheryl B.; Gibson Agency, The Sebastian; Goodman-Andrew-Agency, Inc.; Grosvenor Literary Agency, The; Hawkins & Associates, Inc., John; Heacock Literary Agency, Inc.; Herner Rights Agency, Susan; Hochmann Books, John L.; James Peter Associates, Inc.; JCA Literary Agency, Inc.; Kellock Company, Inc., The; Kern Literary Agency, Natasha; Kleinman, Esq. of Graybill & English L.L.C., Jeffrey M.; Lampack Agency, Inc., Peter; Larkin, Sabra Elliott; Larsen/Elizabeth Pomada Literary Agents, Michael; Lasher Agency, The Maureen; Levine Literary Agency, Inc., Ellen; Lieberman Associates, Robert; Lincoln Literary Agency, Ray; Literary Group, The; Lowenstein Associates, Inc.; Lukeman Literary Management Ltd.; Mann Agency, Carol; McHugh Literary Agency; Morrison, Inc., Henry; Multimedia Product Development, Inc.; Mura Enterprises, Inc., Dee; Otitis Media; Parks Agency, The Richard; Quicksilver Books-Literary Agents; Reichstein Literary Agency, The Naomi; Rhodes Literary Agency, Jodie; Roghaar Literary Agency, Inc., Linda; Rosenkranz Literary Agency, Rita; Ross Literary Agency, The Gail; Russell & Volkening; Sage Acre Marketing & Publishing Solutions; Schiavone Literary Agency, Inc.; Schulman, A Literary Agency, Susan; Seligman, Literary Agent, Lynn; Singer Literary Agency Inc., Evelyn; Slopen Literary Agency, Beverley; Straus Agency, Inc., Robin; Toad Hall, Inc.; United Tribes; Wallace Literary Agency, Inc.; Ware Literary Agency, John A.; Watt & Associates, Sandra; Witherspoon & Associates, Inc.

Art/Architecture/Design: Allen Literary Agency, Linda; Allred and Allred Literary Agents; Altair Literary Agency; Amber Literary; Authors & Artists Group, Inc.; Baldi Literary Agency, Malaga; Bent, Literary Agent, Jenny; Boates Literary Agency, Reid; Boston Literary Group, The; Brandt & Brandt Literary Agents Inc.; Brown Associates Inc., Marie; Buck Agency, Howard; Cornfield Literary Agency, Robert; Ellison Inc., Nicholas; Everitt Literary Agency, Inc., Charles; Finesse Literary Agency; Fleury Agency, B.R.; ForthWrite Literary Agency; Fredericks Literary Agency, Inc., Jeanne; Freymann Literary Agency, Sarah Jane; Gartenberg, Literary Agent, Max; Goodman-Andrew-Agency, Inc.; Grace Literary Agency, Carroll; Grosvenor Literary Agency, The; Hawkins & Associates, Inc., John; Heacock Literary Agency, Inc.; Hochmann Books, John L.; Hogenson Agency, Barbara; James Peter Associates, Inc.; JCA Literary Agency, Inc.; Kellock Company, Inc., The; Kidde, Hoyt & Picard; Kleinman, Esq. of Graybill & English L.L.C., Jeffrey M.; Lampack Agency, Inc., Peter; Larkin, Sabra Elliott; Larsen/Elizabeth Pomada Literary Agents, Michael; Lasher Agency, The Maureen; Levine Communications, Inc., James; Levine Literary Agency, Paul S.; Lieberman Associates, Robert; Lincoln Literary Agency, Ray; Lukeman Literary Management Ltd.; Mann Agency, Carol; Millard Literary Agency, Martha; Nathan, Ruth; Norma-Lewis Agency, The; Parks Agency, The Richard; Perkins, Rubie & Associates; Reichstein Literary Agency, The Naomi; Rosenkranz Literary Agency, Rita; Russell & Volkening; Sage Acre Marketing & Publishing Solutions; Seligman, Literary Agent, Lynn; Seymour Agency, The; Straus Agency, Inc., Robin; United Tribes; Watkins Loomis Agency, Inc.; Watt & Associates, Sandra; Wecksler-Incomco; Weingel-Fidel Agency, The; Wonderland Press, Inc., The; Writers House; Zeckendorf Assoc. Inc., Susan

Biography/Autobiography: Acacia House Publishing Services Ltd.; Alive Communications, Inc.; Allen Literary Agency, Linda; Allred and Allred Literary Agents; Altair Literary Agency; Amber Literary; Amster Literary Enterprises, Betsy; Andrews & Associates Inc., Bart; Authentic Creations Literary Agency; Authors Alliance, Inc.; Authors & Artists Group, Inc.; Baldi Literary Agency, Malaga; Balkin Agency, Inc.;

Bedford Book Works, Inc., The; Bent, Literary Agent, Jenny; Bial Agency, Daniel; Bleecker Street Associates; Boates Literary Agency, Reid; Book Deals, Inc.; Borchardt Inc., Georges; Boston Literary Group, The; Bova Literary Agency, The Barbara; Brandt & Brandt Literary Agents Inc.; Brown Associates Inc., Marie; Buck Agency, Howard; Bykofsky Associates, Inc., Sheree; C G & W Associates; Carvainis Agency, Inc., Maria; Casselman Literary Agency, Martha; Castiglia Literary Agency; Charisma Communications, Ltd.; Clausen, Mays & Tahan, LLC; Collin Literary Agent, Frances; Coover Agency, The Doe; Cornfield Literary Agency, Robert; Crawford Literary Agency; Cypher, The Cypher Agency, James R.; Darhansoff & Verrill Literary Agents; Daves Agency, Joan; Dawson Associates, Liza; DH Literary, Inc.; DHS Literary, Inc.; Dijkstra Literary Agency, Sandra; Donovan Literary, Jim; Ducas, Robert; Dystel Literary Management, Jane; Ellenberg Literary Agency, Ethan; Elmo Agency Inc., Ann; Evans Inc., Mary; Everitt Literary Agency, Inc., Charles; Feigen/Parrent Literary Management; Finesse Literary Agency; Fleury Agency, B.R.; Fogelman Literary Agency, The; ForthWrite Literary Agency; Franklin Associates, Ltd., Lynn C.; Fredericks Literary Agency, Inc., Jeanne; Freymann Literary Agency, Sarah Jane; Gartenberg, Literary Agent, Max; Gibson Agency, The Sebastian; Gislason Agency, The; Goodman-Andrew-Agency, Inc.; Grace Literary Agency, Carroll; Greene, Literary Agent, Randall Elisha; Grosvenor Literary Agency, The; Halsey North, Reese; Harris Literary Agency; Hawkins & Associates, Inc., John; Heacock Literary Agency, Inc.; Henshaw Group, Richard; Herner Rights Agency, Susan; Hill Associates, Frederick; Hochmann Books, John L.; Hogenson Agency, Barbara; J de S Associates Inc.; Jabberwocky Literary Agency; James Peter Associates, Inc.; JCA Literary Agency, Inc.; JLA Literary Agency; Joy Literary Agency; Kellock Company, Inc., The; Kern Literary Agency, Natasha; Ketz Agency, Louise B.; Kidde, Hoyt & Picard; Kleinman, Esq. of Graybill & English L.L.C., Jeffrey M.; Klinger, Inc., Harvey; Knight Agency, The; Koster Literary Agency, LLC, Elaine; Kouts, Literary Agent, Barbara S.; Lampack Agency, Inc., Peter; Larkin, Sabra Elliott; Larsen/Elizabeth Pomada Literary Agents, Michael; Lasher Agency, The Maureen; Lawyer's Literary Agency, Inc.; Levant & Wales, Literary Agency, Inc.; Levine Communications, Inc., James; Levine Literary Agency, Inc., Ellen; Levine Literary Agency, Paul S.; Lincoln Literary Agency, Ray; Lindstrom Literary Group; Lipkind Agency, Wendy; Literary and Creative Artists, Inc.; Literary Group, The; Love Literary Agency, Nancy; Lowenstein Associates, Inc.; Lukeman Literary Management Ltd.; Maccoby Literary Agency, Gina; Mann Agency, Carol; Manus & Associates Literary Agency; March Tenth, Inc.; Marshall Agency, The Evan; McBride Literary Agency, Margret; McCauley, Gerard; McGrath, Helen; McHugh Literary Agency; Michaels Literary Agency, Inc., Doris S.; Millard Literary Agency, Martha; Morrison, Inc., Henry; Multimedia Product Development, Inc.; Mura Enterprises, Inc., Dee; Naggar Literary Agency, Jean V.; Nathan, Ruth; National Writers Literary Agency; Nazor Literary Agency, Karen; New Century Literary Agency; New England Publishing Associates, Inc.; Nine Muses and Apollo; Norma-Lewis Agency, The; Northwest Literary Services; Otitis Media; Parks Agency, The Richard; Pevner, Inc., Stephen; Pinder Lane & Garon-Brooke Associates, Ltd.; Protter Literary Agent, Susan Ann; Quicksilver Books-Literary Agents; Raymond, Literary Agent, Charlotte Cecil; Rees Literary Agency, Helen; Reichstein Literary Agency, The Naomi; Renaissance Literary Agency; Rhodes Literary Agency, Jodie; Rinaldi Literary Agency, Angela; Rittenberg Literary Agency, Inc., Ann; Robbins Literary Agency, BJ; Robbins Office, Inc., The; Roghaar Literary Agency, Inc., Linda; Rosenkranz Literary Agency, Rita; Ross Literary Agency, The Gail; Rotrosen Agency LLC, Jane; Russell & Volkening; Sage Acre Marketing & Publishing Solutions; Sanders Literary Agency, Victoria; Scagnetti Talent & Literary Agency, Jack; Schiavone Literary Agency, Inc.; Schlessinger Agency, Blanche; Schulman, A Literary Agency, Susan; Sebastian Literary Agency; Sedgeband Literary Associates; Seligman, Literary Agent, Lynn; Shepard Agency, The; Singer Literary Agency Inc., Evelyn; Skolnick Literary Agency, Irene; Slopen Literary Agency, Beverley; Spieler Agency, The; Spitzer Literary Agency, Philip G.; Stauffer Associates, Nancy; Sternig & Byrne Literary Agency; Straus Agency, Inc., Robin; Sunshine Literary Agency; Teal Literary Agency, Patricia; 2M Communications Ltd.; United Tribes; Valcourt Agency, Inc., The Richard R.; Vines Agency, Inc., The; Wald Associates, Inc., Mary Jack; Wallace Literary Agency, Inc.; Ware Literary Agency, John A.; Watkins Loomis Agency, Inc.; Waxman Agency, Inc., Scott; Wecksler-Incomco; Weingel-Fidel Agency, The; West Coast Literary Associates; Witherspoon & Associates, Inc.; Wonderland Press, Inc., The; Writers House; Zachary Shuster Agency; Zeckendorf Assoc. Inc., Susan

Business: Alive Communications, Inc.; Allen Literary Agency, Linda; Altair Literary Agency; Amster Literary Enterprises, Betsy; Authors Alliance, Inc.; Authors & Artists Group, Inc.; Baldi Literary Agency, Malaga; Bedford Book Works, Inc., The; Bial Agency, Daniel; Bleecker Street Associates; Boates Literary Agency, Reid; Book Deals, Inc.; Boston Literary Group, The; Bova Literary Agency, The Barbara; Brandt & Brandt Literary Agents Inc.; Brown Associates Inc., Marie; Browne Ltd., Pema; Buck Agency, Howard; Bykofsky Associates, Inc., Sheree; Carvainis Agency, Inc., Maria; Castiglia Literary Agency; Connor Literary Agency; Coover Agency, The Doe; Cypher, The Cypher Agency, James R.; Dawson Associates, Liza; DHS Literary, Inc.; Diamond Literary Agency, Inc.; Dijkstra Literary Agency, Sandra; Donovan Literary, Jim; Ducas, Robert; Dystel Literary Management, Jane; Educational Design Services, Inc.; Ellenberg Literary Agency, Ethan; Ellison Inc., Nicholas; Elmo Agency Inc., Ann; Everitt Literary Agency, Inc., Charles; Feigen/Parrent Literary Management; Finesse Literary Agency; Fleury Agency, B.R.; Fogelman

Literary Agency, The; ForthWrite Literary Agency; Fredericks Literary Agency, Inc., Jeanne; Freymann Literary Agency, Sarah Jane; Fullerton Associates, Sheryl B.; Gibson Agency, The Sebastian; Goodman-Andrew-Agency, Inc.; Greene, Literary Agent, Randall Elisha; Grosvenor Literary Agency, The; Hawkins & Associates, Inc., John; Heacock Literary Agency, Inc.; Henshaw Group, Richard; Herman Agency LLC, The Jeff; Herner Rights Agency, Susan; J de S Associates Inc.; Jabberwocky Literary Agency; James Peter Associates, Inc.; JCA Literary Agency, Inc.; JLA Literary Agency; Kellock Company, Inc., The; Kern Literary Agency, Natasha; Ketz Agency, Louise B.; Kleinman, Esq. of Graybill & English L.L.C., Jeffrey M.; Knight Agency, The; Konner Literary Agency, Linda; Koster Literary Agency, LLC, Elaine; Lampack Agency, Inc., Peter; Larkin, Sabra Elliott; Larsen/Elizabeth Pomada Literary Agents, Michael; Lasher Agency, The Maureen; Levant & Wales, Literary Agency, Inc.; Levine Communications, Inc., James; Levine Literary Agency, Paul S.; Lieberman Associates, Robert; Lincoln Literary Agency, Ray; Literary and Creative Artists, Inc.; Literary Group, The; Lowenstein Associates, Inc.; Lukeman Literary Management Ltd.; Mann Agency, Carol; Manus & Associates Literary Agency; Marshall Agency, The Evan; McBride Literary Agency, Margret; McGrath, Helen; McHugh Literary Agency; Michaels Literary Agency, Inc., Doris S.; Millard Literary Agency, Martha; Multimedia Product Development, Inc.; Mura Enterprises, Inc., Dee; Nazor Literary Agency, Karen; New Century Literary Agency; New England Publishing Associates, Inc.; Nine Muses and Apollo; Parks Agency, The Richard; Paton Literary Agency, Kathi J.; Pine Associates, Inc, Arthur; Quicksilver Books-Literary Agents; Rees Literary Agency, Helen; Reichstein Literary Agency, The Naomi; Rein Books, Inc., Jody; Rhodes Literary Agency, Jodie; Rinaldi Literary Agency, Angela; Rosenkranz Literary Agency, Rita; Ross Literary Agency, The Gail; Roth, Literary Representation, Carol Susan; Rotrosen Agency LLC, Jane; Russell & Volkening; Sage Acre Marketing & Publishing Solutions; Schlessinger Agency, Blanche; Sebastian Literary Agency; Seligman, Literary Agent, Lynn; Shepard Agency, The; Shepard Agency, The Robert E.; Singer Literary Agency Inc., Evelyn; Slopen Literary Agency, Beverley; Snell Literary Agency, Michael; Spieler Agency, The; Spitzer Literary Agency, Philip G.; Sunshine Literary Agency; Swayne Agency Literary Management & Consulting, Inc., The; Toad Hall, Inc.; Travis Literary Agency, Susan; United Tribes; Vines Agency, Inc., The; Waxman Agency, Inc., Scott; Wecksler-Incomco; Wieser & Wieser, Inc.; Witherspoon & Associates, Inc.; Wonderland Press, Inc., The; Writers House; Zachary Shuster Agency

Child Guidance/Parenting: Alive Communications, Inc.; Allen Literary Agency, Linda; Altair Literary Agency; Amber Literary; Amster Literary Enterprises, Betsy; Amsterdam Agency, Marcia; Authentic Creations Literary Agency; Authors Alliance, Inc.; Authors & Artists Group, Inc.; Bent, Literary Agent, Jenny; Bernstein & Associates, Inc., Pam; Bial Agency, Daniel; Bleecker Street Associates; Boates Literary Agency, Reid; Books & Such; Boston Literary Group, The; Brandt & Brandt Literary Agents Inc.; Browne Ltd., Pema; Buck Agency, Howard; Bykofsky Associates, Inc., Sheree; Castiglia Literary Agency; Cohen Agency, The; Connor Literary Agency; Coover Agency, The Doe; DH Literary, Inc.; DHS Literary, Inc.; Dijkstra Literary Agency, Sandra; Donovan Literary, Jim; Dystel Literary Management, Jane; Educational Design Services, Inc.; Elek Associates, Peter; Ellenberg Literary Agency, Ethan; Ellison Inc., Nicholas; Elmo Agency Inc., Ann; Everitt Literary Agency, Inc., Charles; Farber Literary Agency Inc.; Finesse Literary Agency; Flaherty, Literary Agent, Joyce A.; Flannery Literary; Fleury Agency, B.R.; Fogelman Literary Agency, The; ForthWrite Literary Agency; Fredericks Literary Agency, Inc., Jeanne; Freymann Literary Agency, Sarah Jane; Gartenberg, Literary Agent, Max; Goodman-Andrew-Agency, Inc.; Grosvenor Literary Agency, The; Hawkins & Associates, Inc., John; Henshaw Group, Richard; Herner Rights Agency, Susan; James Peter Associates, Inc.; JCA Literary Agency, Inc.; Kellock Company, Inc., The; Kern Literary Agency, Natasha; Kleinman, Esq. of Graybill & English L.L.C., Jeffrey M.; Knight Agency, The; Konner Literary Agency, Linda; Koster Literary Agency, LLC, Elaine; Kouts, Literary Agent, Barbara S.; Larsen/Elizabeth Pomada Literary Agents, Michael; Lasher Agency, The Maureen; Levine Communications, Inc., James; Levine Literary Agency, Paul S.; Lincoln Literary Agency, Ray; Literary Group, The; Love Literary Agency, Nancy; Lowenstein Associates, Inc.; Lukeman Literary Management Ltd.; Mann Agency, Carol; Manus & Associates Literary Agency; Marshall Agency, The Evan; McBride Literary Agency, Margret; McHugh Literary Agency; Millard Literary Agency, Martha; Multimedia Product Development, Inc.; Mura Enterprises, Inc., Dee; Naggar Literary Agency, Jean V.; National Writers Literary Agency; Nazor Literary Agency, Karen; New Century Literary Agency; New England Publishing Associates, Inc.; Norma-Lewis Agency, The; Northwest Literary Services; Parks Agency, The Richard; Paton Literary Agency, Kathi J.; Pinder Lane & Garon-Brooke Associates, Ltd.; Quicksilver Books-Literary Agents; Reichstein Literary Agency, The Naomi; Rein Books, Inc., Jody; Rhodes Literary Agency, Jodie; Rinaldi Literary Agency, Angela; Robbins Literary Agency, BJ; Rosenkranz Literary Agency, Rita; Rotrosen Agency LLC, Jane; Rubenstein Literary Agency, Inc., Pesha; Sage Acre Marketing & Publishing Solutions; Schiavone Literary Agency, Inc.; Schulman, A Literary Agency, Susan; Sebastian Literary Agency; Seligman, Literary Agent, Lynn; Shepard Agency, The; Simenauer Literary Agency, Jacqueline; Singer Literary Agency Inc., Evelyn; Slopen Literary Agency, Beverley; Spieler Agency, The; Straus Agency, Inc., Robin; Sunshine Literary Agency; Teal Literary Agency, Patricia; Toad Hall, Inc.; Travis Literary Agency, Susan; 2M Communications Ltd.; United Tribes; Writers House; Zeckendorf Assoc. Inc., Susan

Computers/Electronics: Allen Literary Agency, Linda; Amber Literary; Authors Alliance, Inc.; Authors & Artists Group, Inc.; Bleecker Street Associates; Buck Agency, Howard; DHS Literary, Inc.; Ellison Inc., Nicholas; Elmo Agency Inc., Ann; Evans Inc., Mary; Finesse Literary Agency; ForthWrite Literary Agency; Henshaw Group, Richard; Herman Agency LLC, The Jeff; JCA Literary Agency, Inc.; Kleinman, Esq. of Graybill & English L.L.C., Jeffrey M.; Knight Agency, The; Levine Communications, Inc., James; Levine Literary Agency, Paul S.; Lieberman Associates, Robert; Manus & Associates Literary Agency; Mura Enterprises, Inc., Dee; Nazor Literary Agency, Karen; Reichstein Literary Agency, The Naomi; Rhodes Literary Agency, Jodie; Rosenkranz Literary Agency, Rita; Shepard Agency, The; Swayne Agency Literary Management & Consulting, Inc., The

Cooking/Food/Nutrition: Agents Inc. for Medical and Mental Health Professionals; Allred and Allred Literary Agents; Authors Alliance, Inc.; Authors & Artists Group, Inc.; Baldi Literary Agency, Malaga; Bernstein & Associates, Inc., Pam; Bial Agency, Daniel; Bleecker Street Associates; Book Deals, Inc.; Bova Literary Agency, The Barbara; Brandt & Brandt Literary Agents Inc.; Browne Ltd., Pema; Bykofsky Associates, Inc., Sheree; Casselman Literary Agency, Martha; Castiglia Literary Agency; Clausen, Mays & Tahan, LLC; Connor Literary Agency; Coover Agency, The Doe; Cornfield Literary Agency, Robert; DHS Literary, Inc.; Dijkstra Literary Agency, Sandra; Dystel Literary Management, Jane; Ellenberg Literary Agency, Ethan; Ellison Inc., Nicholas; Elmo Agency Inc., Ann; Farber Literary Agency Inc.; Finesse Literary Agency; Flaherty, Literary Agent, Joyce A.; Fleury Agency, B.R.; ForthWrite Literary Agency; Fredericks Literary Agency, Inc., Jeanne; Freymann Literary Agency, Sarah Jane; Gibson Agency, The Sebastian; Goodman-Andrew-Agency, Inc.; Grace Literary Agency, Carroll; Hawkins & Associates, Inc., John; Henshaw Group, Richard; Herner Rights Agency, Susan; Hill Associates, Frederick; Hochmann Books, John L.; Hogenson Agency, Barbara; Jabberwocky Literary Agency; JLA Literary Agency; Joy Literary Agency; Kleinman, Esq. of Graybill & English L.L.C., Jeffrey M.; Klinger, Inc., Harvey; Knight Agency, The; Konner Literary Agency, Linda; Koster Literary Agency, LLC, Elaine; Larkin, Sabra Elliott; Larsen/Elizabeth Pomada Literary Agents, Michael; Lasher Agency, The Maureen; Lescher & Lescher Ltd.; Levine Communications, Inc., James; Levine Literary Agency, Paul S.; Lincoln Literary Agency, Ray; Literary and Creative Artists, Inc.; Literary Group, The; Love Literary Agency, Nancy; Lukeman Literary Management Ltd.; Marshall Agency, The Evan; McBride Literary Agency, Margret; McHugh Literary Agency; Millard Literary Agency, Martha; Multimedia Product Development, Inc.; New Century Literary Agency; Norma-Lewis Agency, The; Northwest Literary Services; Parks Agency, The Richard; Quicksilver Books-Literary Agents; Reichstein Literary Agency, The Naomi; Rhodes Literary Agency, Jodie; Rinaldi Literary Agency, Angela; Robbins Literary Agency, BJ; Rosenkranz Literary Agency, Rita; Ross Literary Agency, The Gail; Rotrosen Agency LLC, Jane; Rowland Agency, The Damaris; Russell & Volkening; Scagnetti Talent & Literary Agency, Jack; Schlessinger Agency, Blanche; Seligman, Literary Agent, Lynn; Shepard Agency, The; Simenauer Literary Agency, Jacqueline; Slopen Literary Agency, Beverley; Spieler Agency, The; Straus Agency, Inc., Robin; Taylor, Literary Agent, Rebecca; Toad Hall, Inc.; Travis Literary Agency, Susan; United Tribes; Van der Leun & Associates; Wieser & Wieser, Inc.; Writers House

Crafts/Hobbies: Allred and Allred Literary Agents; Authentic Creations Literary Agency; Authors Alliance, Inc.; Authors & Artists Group, Inc.; Brandt & Brandt Literary Agents Inc.; Buck Agency, Howard; Connor Literary Agency; Ellison Inc., Nicholas; Elmo Agency Inc., Ann; Finesse Literary Agency; Flaherty, Literary Agent, Joyce A.; ForthWrite Literary Agency; Fredericks Literary Agency, Inc., Jeanne; Grace Literary Agency, Carroll; Hawkins & Associates, Inc., John; Kellock Company, Inc., The; Kleinman, Esq. of Graybill & English L.L.C., Jeffrey M.; Levine Literary Agency, Paul S.; Lincoln Literary Agency, Ray; Literary Group, The; Lowenstein Associates, Inc.; Marshall Agency, The Evan; Multimedia Product Development, Inc.; Norma-Lewis Agency, The; Parks Agency, The Richard; Reichstein Literary Agency, The Naomi; Rhodes Literary Agency, Jodie; Rosenkranz Literary Agency, Rita; Shepard Agency, The; Toad Hall, Inc.; Watt & Associates, Sandra

Current Affairs: Allred and Allred Literary Agents; Amber Literary; Authentic Creations Literary Agency; Authors Alliance, Inc.; Authors & Artists Group, Inc.; Baldi Literary Agency, Malaga; Balkin Agency, Inc.; Bedford Book Works, Inc., The; Bernstein & Associates, Inc., Pam; Bial Agency, Daniel; Bleecker Street Associates; Boates Literary Agency, Reid; Book Deals, Inc.; Borchardt Inc., Georges; Boston Literary Group, The; Brandt & Brandt Literary Agents Inc.; Buck Agency, Howard; Bykofsky Associates, Inc., Sheree; C G & W Associates; Castiglia Literary Agency; Charisma Communications, Ltd.; Connor Literary Agency; Cypher, The Cypher Agency, James R.; Darhansoff & Verrill Literary Agents; DH Literary, Inc.; DHS Literary, Inc.; Dijkstra Literary Agency, Sandra; Donovan Literary, Jim; Ducas, Robert; Dystel Literary Management, Jane; Educational Design Services, Inc.; Ellenberg Literary Agency, Ethan; Ellison Inc., Nicholas; Elmo Agency Inc., Ann; Evans Inc., Mary; Everitt Literary Agency, Inc., Charles; Feigen/Parrent Literary Management; Fogelman Literary Agency, The; Franklin Associates, Ltd., Lynn C.; Fredericks Literary Agency, Inc., Jeanne; Freymann Literary Agency, Sarah Jane; Fullerton

Associates, Sheryl B.; Gartenberg, Literary Agent, Max; Gibson Agency, The Sebastian; Goodman-Andrew-Agency, Inc.; Greene, Literary Agent, Randall Elisha; Grosvenor Literary Agency, The; Halsey North, Reese; Hawkins & Associates, Inc., John; Henshaw Group, Richard; Herner Rights Agency, Susan; Hill Associates, Frederick; Hochmann Books, John L.; J de S Associates Inc.; Jabberwocky Literary Agency; James Peter Associates, Inc.; JCA Literary Agency, Inc.; JLA Literary Agency; Kellock Company, Inc., The; Kern Literary Agency, Natasha; Ketz Agency, Louise B.; Kidde, Hoyt & Picard; Kleinman, Esq. of Graybill & English L.L.C., Jeffrey M.; Knight Agency, The; Koster Literary Agency, LLC, Elaine; Kouts, Literary Agent, Barbara S.; Lampack Agency, Inc., Peter; Larkin, Sabra Elliott; Larsen/Elizabeth Pomada Literary Agents, Michael; Lasher Agency, The Maureen; Levant & Wales, Literary Agency, Inc.; Levine Literary Agency, Inc., Ellen; Levine Literary Agency, Paul S.; Lincoln Literary Agency, Ray; Lindstrom Literary Group; Lipkind Agency, Wendy; Literary Group, The; Love Literary Agency, Nancy; Lowenstein Associates, Inc.; Lukeman Literary Management Ltd.; Maccoby Literary Agency, Gina; Mann Agency, Carol; Manus & Associates Literary Agency; March Tenth, Inc.; Marshall Agency, The Evan; McBride Literary Agency, Margret; McCauley, Gerard; McGrath, Helen; McHugh Literary Agency; Michaels Literary Agency, Inc., Doris S.; Millard Literary Agency, Martha; Multimedia Product Development, Inc.; Mura Enterprises, Inc., Dee; Naggar Literary Agency, Jean V.; Nazor Literary Agency, Karen; New Century Literary Agency; Nine Muses and Apollo; Norma-Lewis Agency, The; Parks Agency, The Richard; Perkins, Rubie & Associates; Pine Associates, Inc, Arthur; Quicksilver Books-Literary Agents; Raymond, Literary Agent, Charlotte Cecil; Rees Literary Agency, Helen; Reichstein Literary Agency, The Naomi; Rein Books, Inc., Jody; Rhodes Literary Agency, Jodie; Rinaldi Literary Agency, Angela; Robbins Literary Agency, BJ; Rosenkranz Literary Agency, Rita; Rotrosen Agency LLC, Jane; Russell & Volkening; Sage Acre Marketing & Publishing Solutions; Sanders Literary Agency, Victoria; Scagnetti Talent & Literary Agency, Jack; Schiavone Literary Agency, Inc.; Schulman, A Literary Agency, Susan; Sebastian Literary Agency; Seligman, Literary Agent, Lynn; Shepard Agency, The; Shepard Agency, The Robert E.; Simenauer Literary Agency, Jacqueline; Singer Literary Agency Inc., Evelyn; Skolnick Literary Agency, Irene; Slopen Literary Agency, Beverley; Spieler Agency, The; Spitzer Literary Agency, Philip G.; Stauffer Associates, Nancy; Straus Agency, Inc., Robin; Swayne Agency Literary Management & Consulting, Inc., The; United Tribes; Valcourt Agency, Inc., The Richard R.; Van der Leun & Associates; Vines Agency, Inc., The; Wald Associates, Inc., Mary Jack; Wallace Literary Agency, Inc.; Ware Literary Agency, John A.; Watkins Loomis Agency, Inc.; Watt & Associates, Sandra; Wecksler-Incomco; West Coast Literary Associates; Wieser & Wieser, Inc.; Witherspoon & Associates, Inc.; Zachary Shuster Agency

Education: Allred and Allred Literary Agents; Amber Literary; Authors & Artists Group, Inc.; Boston Literary Group, The; Buck Agency, Howard; Cohen Agency, The; Dystel Literary Management, Jane; Elmo Agency Inc., Ann; Everitt Literary Agency, Inc., Charles; Finesse Literary Agency; Fleury Agency, B.R.; Fogelman Literary Agency, The; Goodman-Andrew-Agency, Inc.; Grace Literary Agency, Carroll; JLA Literary Agency; Joy Literary Agency; Kellock Company, Inc., The; Kern Literary Agency, Natasha; Kleinman, Esq. of Graybill & English L.L.C., Jeffrey M.; Larkin, Sabra Elliott; Levant & Wales, Literary Agency, Inc.; Levine Literary Agency, Paul S.; Lieberman Associates, Robert; Literary Group, The; Lowenstein Associates, Inc.; Millard Literary Agency, Martha; Mura Enterprises, Inc., Dee; National Writers Literary Agency; New Century Literary Agency; Reichstein Literary Agency, The Naomi; Rhodes Literary Agency, Jodie; Robbins Literary Agency, BJ; Roghaar Literary Agency, Inc., Linda; Ross Literary Agency, The Gail; Russell & Volkening; Sage Acre Marketing & Publishing Solutions; Schiavone Literary Agency, Inc.; Schulman, A Literary Agency, Susan; Seligman, Literary Agent, Lynn; Simenauer Literary Agency, Jacqueline; United Tribes

Ethnic/Cultural Interests: Allen Literary Agency, Linda; Allred and Allred Literary Agents; Altair Literary Agency; Amster Literary Enterprises, Betsy; Authors & Artists Group, Inc.; Baldi Literary Agency, Malaga; Bent, Literary Agent, Jenny; Bial Agency, Daniel; Bleecker Street Associates; Boates Literary Agency, Reid; Book Deals, Inc.; Boston Literary Group, The; Brandt & Brandt Literary Agents Inc.; Brown Associates Inc., Marie; Browne Ltd., Pema; Buck Agency, Howard; Bykofsky Associates, Inc., Sheree; C G & W Associates; Castiglia Literary Agency; Cohen Agency, The; Cohen, Inc. Literary Agency, Ruth; Connor Literary Agency; Coover Agency, The Doe; Cypher, The Cypher Agency, James R.; DH Literary, Inc.; DHS Literary, Inc.; Dijkstra Literary Agency, Sandra; Dystel Literary Management, Jane; Educational Design Services, Inc.; Ellison Inc., Nicholas; Everitt Literary Agency, Inc., Charles; Finesse Literary Agency; Fogelman Literary Agency, The; Freymann Literary Agency, Sarah Jane; Fullerton Associates, Sheryl B.; Goodman-Andrew-Agency, Inc.; Greene, Literary Agent, Randall Elisha; Hawkins & Associates, Inc., John; Herner Rights Agency, Susan; J de S Associates Inc.; James Peter Associates, Inc.; JCA Literary Agency, Inc.; Kellock Company, Inc., The; Kern Literary Agency, Natasha; Kidde, Hoyt & Picard; Kleinman, Esq. of Graybill & English L.L.C., Jeffrey M.; Knight Agency, The; Koster Literary Agency, LLC, Elaine; Kouts, Literary Agent, Barbara S.; Larkin, Sabra Elliott; Larsen/Elizabeth Pomada Literary Agents, Michael; Lasher Agency, The Maureen; Levant & Wales, Literary Agency, Inc.; Levine Literary Agency, Paul S.; Lewis & Company, Karen; Lincoln Literary Agency, Ray; Lindstrom Literary Group; Literary

Group, The; Love Literary Agency, Nancy; Lowenstein Associates, Inc.; Maccoby Literary Agency, Gina; Mann Agency, Carol; Manus & Associates Literary Agency; McBride Literary Agency, Margret; Michaels Literary Agency, Inc., Doris S.; Millard Literary Agency, Martha; Multimedia Product Development, Inc.; Mura Enterprises, Inc., Dee; Nazor Literary Agency, Karen; New Century Literary Agency; Nine Muses and Apollo; Norma-Lewis Agency, The; Northwest Literary Services; Parks Agency, The Richard; Perkins, Rubie & Associates; Pevner, Inc., Stephen; Quicksilver Books-Literary Agents; Raymond, Literary Agent, Charlotte Cecil; Reichstein Literary Agency, The Naomi; Rein Books, Inc., Jody; Rhodes Literary Agency, Jodie; Robbins Literary Agency, BJ; Rosenkranz Literary Agency, Rita; Ross Literary Agency, The Gail; Russell & Volkening; Sage Acre Marketing & Publishing Solutions; Sanders Literary Agency, Victoria; Schiavone Literary Agency, Inc.; Schulman, A Literary Agency, Susan; Sebastian Literary Agency; Sedgeband Literary Associates; Seligman, Literary Agent, Lynn; Shepard Agency, The Robert E.; Singer Literary Agency Inc., Evelyn; Spieler Agency, The; Spitzer Literary Agency, Philip G.; Stauffer Associates, Nancy; Straus Agency, Inc., Robin; Sunshine Literary Agency; Swayne Agency Literary Management & Consulting, Inc., The; Travis Literary Agency, Susan; 2M Communications Ltd.; United Tribes; Van der Leun & Associates; Vines Agency, Inc., The; Wald Associates, Inc., Mary Jack; Watkins Loomis Agency, Inc.; Waxman Agency, Inc., Scott; West Coast Literary Associates; Witherspoon & Associates, Inc.; Wonderland Press, Inc., The

Gay/Lesbian Issues: Allen Literary Agency, Linda; Altair Literary Agency; Authors & Artists Group, Inc.; Baldi Literary Agency, Malaga; Bent, Literary Agent, Jenny; Bial Agency, Daniel; Bleecker Street Associates; Boston Literary Group, The; Brandt & Brandt Literary Agents Inc.; Browne Ltd., Pema; Buck Agency, Howard; Bykofsky Associates, Inc., Sheree; Core Creations, Inc.; Cypher, The Cypher Agency, James R.; Daves Agency, Joan; DHS Literary, Inc.; Ducas, Robert; Dystel Literary Management, Jane; Evans Inc., Mary; Feigen/Parent Literary Management; Finesse Literary Agency; Freymann Literary Agency, Sarah Jane; Fullerton Associates, Sheryl B.; Goodman-Andrew-Agency, Inc.; Hawkins & Associates, Inc., John; Henshaw Group, Richard; Herner Rights Agency, Susan; Hochmann Books, John L.; Jabberwocky Literary Agency; James Peter Associates, Inc.; JCA Literary Agency, Inc.; Kidde, Hoyt & Picard; Kleinman, Esq. of Graybill & English L.L.C., Jeffrey M.; Konner Literary Agency, Linda; Koster Literary Agency, LLC, Elaine; Larsen/Elizabeth Pomada Literary Agents, Michael; Levant & Wales, Literary Agency, Inc.; Levine Communications, Inc., James; Levine Literary Agency, Paul S.; Lewis & Company, Karen; Lincoln Literary Agency, Ray; Literary Group, The; Lowenstein Associates, Inc.; McBride Literary Agency, Margret; Mura Enterprises, Inc., Dee; Parks Agency, The Richard; Perkins, Rubie & Associates; Pevner, Inc., Stephen; Pinder Lane & Garon-Brooke Associates, Ltd.; Reichstein Literary Agency, The Naomi; Rhodes Literary Agency, Jodie; Robbins Literary Agency, BJ; Rosenkranz Literary Agency, Rita; Ross Literary Agency, The Gail; Russell & Volkening; Sage Acre Marketing & Publishing Solutions; Sanders Literary Agency, Victoria; Schiavone Literary Agency, Inc.; Schulman, A Literary Agency, Susan; Shepard Agency, The Robert E.; Spieler Agency, The; Swayne Agency Literary Management & Consulting, Inc., The; 2M Communications Ltd.; United Tribes; Watkins Loomis Agency, Inc.; Witherspoon & Associates, Inc.; Wonderland Press, Inc., The; Zachary Shuster Agency

Government/Politics/Law: Agents Inc. for Medical and Mental Health Professionals; Allen Literary Agency, Linda; Altair Literary Agency; Amber Literary; Authors Alliance, Inc.; Baldi Literary Agency, Malaga; Bial Agency, Daniel; Black Literary Agency, David; Bleecker Street Associates; Boates Literary Agency, Reid; Bookmark Literary Agency; Boston Literary Group, The; Brandt & Brandt Literary Agents Inc.; Buck Agency, Howard; Charisma Communications, Ltd.; Cohen Agency, The; Connor Literary Agency; Cypher, The Cypher Agency, James R.; DH Literary, Inc.; Dijkstra Literary Agency, Sandra; Ducas, Robert; Dystel Literary Management, Jane; Educational Design Services, Inc.; Ellison Inc., Nicholas; Evans Inc., Mary; Everitt Literary Agency, Inc., Charles; Feigen/Parent Literary Management; Finesse Literary Agency; Fogelman Literary Agency, The; Gibson Agency, The Sebastian; Gislason Agency, The; Goodman-Andrew-Agency, Inc.; Greene, Literary Agent, Randall Elisha; Grosvenor Literary Agency, The; Hawkins & Associates, Inc., John; Henshaw Group, Richard; Herman Agency LLC, The Jeff; Herner Rights Agency, Susan; Hill Associates, Frederick; Hochmann Books, John L.; J de S Associates Inc.; Jabberwocky Literary Agency; James Peter Associates, Inc.; JCA Literary Agency, Inc.; JLA Literary Agency; Kellock Company, Inc., The; Kleinman, Esq. of Graybill & English L.L.C., Jeffrey M.; Lampack Agency, Inc., Peter; Larkin, Sabra Elliott; Larsen/Elizabeth Pomada Literary Agents, Michael; Lasher Agency, The Maureen; Lawyer's Literary Agency, Inc.; Levine Literary Agency, Paul S.; Lincoln Literary Agency, Ray; Literary and Creative Artists; Literary Group, The; Love Literary Agency, Nancy; Lowenstein Associates, Inc.; Mann Agency, Carol; Marshall Agency, The Evan; McBride Literary Agency, Margret; Morrison, Inc., Henry; Mura Enterprises, Inc., Dee; Naggar Literary Agency, Jean V.; National Writers Literary Agency; Nazor Literary Agency, Karen; New Century Literary Agency; New England Publishing Associates, Inc.; Norma-Lewis Agency, The; Parks Agency, The Richard; Rees Literary Agency, Helen; Reichstein Literary Agency, The Naomi; Rein Books, Inc., Jody; Rhodes Literary Agency, Jodie; Robbins Literary Agency, BJ; Robbins Office, Inc., The; Rosenkranz Literary Agency, Rita; Ross Literary

Agency, The Gail; Russell & Volkening; Sage Acre Marketing & Publishing Solutions; Sanders Literary Agency, Victoria; Schiavone Literary Agency, Inc.; Schulman, A Literary Agency, Susan; Sebastian Literary Agency; Seligman, Literary Agent, Lynn; Shepard Agency, The; Shepard Agency, The Robert E.; Singer Literary Agency Inc., Evelyn; Snell Literary Agency, Michael; Spieler Agency, The; Spitzer Literary Agency, Philip G.; Straus Agency, Inc., Robin; United Tribes; Valcourt Agency, Inc., The Richard R.; Ware Literary Agency, John A.; West Coast Literary Associates; Witherspoon & Associates, Inc.; Zachary Shuster Agency

Health/Medicine: Agents Inc. for Medical and Mental Health Professionals; Allred and Allred Literary Agents; Altair Literary Agency; Amster Literary Enterprises, Betsy; Authors Alliance, Inc.; Authors & Artists Group, Inc.; Baldi Literary Agency, Malaga; Balkin Agency, Inc.; Bedford Book Works, Inc., The; Bent, Literary Agent, Jenny; Bernstein & Associates, Inc., Pam; Bleecker Street Associates; Boates Literary Agency, Reid; Book Deals, Inc.; Boston Literary Group, The; Brandt & Brandt Literary Agents Inc.; Browne Ltd., Pema; Buck Agency, Howard; Bykofsky Associates, Inc., Sheree; Carvainis Agency, Inc., Maria; Casselman Literary Agency, Martha; Castiglia Literary Agency; Clausen, Mays & Tahan, LLC; Collin Literary Agent, Frances; Connor Literary Agency; Coover Agency, The Doe; Cypher, The Cypher Agency, James R.; Darhansoff & Verrill Literary Agents; Dawson Associates, Liza; DH Literary, Inc.; Diamond Literary Agency, Inc.; Dijkstra Literary Agency, Sandra; Donovan Literary, Jim; Ducas, Robert; Dystel Literary Management, Jane; Ellenberg Literary Agency, Ethan; Ellison Inc., Nicholas; Elmo Agency Inc., Ann; Everitt Literary Agency, Inc., Charles; Feigen/Parrent Literary Management; Finesse Literary Agency; Flaherty, Literary Agent, Joyce A.; Fleury Agency, B.R.; Fogelman Literary Agency, The; Forth-Write Literary Agency; Franklin Associates, Ltd., Lynn C.; Fredericks Literary Agency, Inc., Jeanne; Freymann Literary Agency, Sarah Jane; Gartenberg, Literary Agent, Max; Gibson Agency, The Sebastian; Gislason Agency, The; Goodman-Andrew-Agency, Inc.; Grace Literary Agency, Carroll; Greene, Literary Agent, Randall Elisha; Grosvenor Literary Agency, The; Harris Literary Agency; Hawkins & Associates, Inc., John; Heacock Literary Agency, Inc.; Henshaw Group, Richard; Herman Agency LLC, The Jeff; Herner Rights Agency, Susan; Hochmann Books, John L.; J de S Associates Inc.; Jabberwocky Literary Agency; James Peter Associates, Inc.; JCA Literary Agency, Inc.; JLA Literary Agency; Joy Literary Agency; Kellock Company, Inc., The; Kern Literary Agency, Natasha; Kleinman, Esq. of Graybill & English L.L.C., Jeffrey M.; Klinger, Inc., Harvey; Knight Agency, The; Konner Literary Agency, Linda; Koster Literary Agency, LLC, Elaine; Kouts, Literary Agent, Barbara S.; Lampack Agency, Inc., Peter; Larkin, Sabra Elliott; Larsen/Elizabeth Pomada Literary Agents, Michael; Lasher Agency, The Maureen; Levant & Wales, Literary Agency, Inc.; Levine Communications, Inc., James; Levine Literary Agency, Inc., Ellen; Levine Literary Agency, Paul S.; Lieberman Associates, Robert; Lincoln Literary Agency, Ray; Lipkind Agency, Wendy; Literary and Creative Artists, Inc.; Literary Group, The; Love Literary Agency, Nancy; Lowenstein Associates, Inc.; Lukeman Literary Management Ltd.; Mann Agency, Carol; Manus & Associates Literary Agency; March Tenth, Inc.; Marshall Agency, The Evan; McBride Literary Agency, Margret; McGrath, Helen; McHugh Literary Agency; Michaels Literary Agency, Inc., Doris S.; Millard Literary Agency, Martha; Multimedia Product Development, Inc.; Mura Enterprises, Inc., Dee; Naggar Literary Agency, Jean V.; New England Publishing Associates, Inc.; Nine Muses and Apollo; Norma-Lewis Agency, The; Otitis Media; Parks Agency, The Richard; Pinder Lane & Garon-Brooke Associates, Ltd.; Pine Associates, Inc, Arthur; Protter Literary Agent, Susan Ann; Quicksilver Books-Literary Agents; Rees Literary Agency, Helen; Reichstein Literary Agency, The Naomi; Rein Books, Inc., Jody; Rhodes Literary Agency, Jodie; Rinaldi Literary Agency, Angela; Robbins Literary Agency, BJ; Rosenkranz Literary Agency, Rita; Ross Literary Agency, The Gail; Roth, Literary Representation, Carol Susan; Rotrosen Agency LLC, Jane; Rowland Agency, The Damaris; Russell & Volkening; Sage Acre Marketing & Publishing Solutions; Scagnetti Talent & Literary Agency, Jack; Schiavone Literary Agency, Inc.; Schlessinger Agency, Blanche; Schulman, A Literary Agency, Susan; Sebastian Literary Agency; Seligman, Literary Agent, Lynn; Shepard Agency, The; Simenauer Literary Agency, Jacqueline; Singer Literary Agency Inc., Evelyn; Snell Literary Agency, Michael; Spitzer Literary Agency, Philip G.; Straus Agency, Inc., Robin; Sunshine Literary Agency; Teal Literary Agency, Patricia; Toad Hall, Inc.; Travis Literary Agency, Susan; 2M Communications Ltd.; United Tribes; Ware Literary Agency, John A.; Waxman Agency, Inc., Scott; Wieser & Wieser, Inc.; Witherspoon & Associates, Inc.; Wonderland Press, Inc., The; Writers House; Zachary Shuster Agency; Zeckendorf Assoc. Inc., Susan

History: Allen Literary Agency, Linda; Allen, Literary Agent, James; Allred and Allred Literary Agents; Altair Literary Agency; Amber Literary; Amster Literary Enterprises, Betsy; Authentic Creations Literary Agency; Authors Alliance, Inc.; Authors & Artists Group, Inc.; Baldi Literary Agency, Malaga; Balkin Agency, Inc.; Bedford Book Works, Inc., The; Bent, Literary Agent, Jenny; Bial Agency, Daniel; Bleecker Street Associates; Boates Literary Agency, Reid; Book Deals, Inc.; Borchardt Inc., Georges; Boston Literary Group, The; Brandt & Brandt Literary Agents Inc.; Brown Associates Inc., Marie; Buck Agency, Howard; Bykofsky Associates, Inc., Sheree; Castiglia Literary Agency; Clausen, Mays & Tahan, LLC; Collin Literary Agent, Frances; Communications and Entertainment, Inc.; Coover Agency, The Doe; Cornfield Literary

Agency, Robert; Cypher, The Cypher Agency, James R.; Darhansoff & Verrill Literary Agents; Dawson Associates, Liza; DH Literary, Inc.; Dijkstra Literary Agency, Sandra; Donovan Literary, Jim; Ducas, Robert; Dystel Literary Management, Jane; Educational Design Services, Inc.; Ellenberg Literary Agency, Ethan; Ellison Inc., Nicholas; Elmo Agency Inc., Ann; Evans Inc., Mary; Everitt Literary Agency, Inc., Charles; Finesse Literary Agency; Fleury Agency, B.R.; ForthWrite Literary Agency; Franklin Associates, Ltd., Lynn C.; Fredericks Literary Agency, Inc., Jeanne; Freymann Literary Agency, Sarah Jane; Gartenberg, Literary Agent, Max; Gibson Agency, The Sebastian; Goodman-Andrew-Agency, Inc.; Grace Literary Agency, Carroll; Greene, Literary Agent, Randall Elisha; Grosvenor Literary Agency, The; Halsey North, Reese; Hawkins & Associates, Inc., John; Heacock Literary Agency, Inc.; Herman Agency LLC, The Jeff; Herner Rights Agency, Susan; Hochmann Books, John L.; Hogenson Agency, Barbara; J de S Associates Inc.; Jabberwocky Literary Agency; James Peter Associates, Inc.; JCA Literary Agency, Inc.; JLA Literary Agency; Kellock Company, Inc., The; Ketz Agency, Louise B.; Kidde, Hoyt & Picard; Kleinman, Esq. of Graybill & English L.L.C., Jeffrey M.; Knight Agency, The; Koster Literary Agency, LLC, Elaine; Kouts, Literary Agent, Barbara S.; Lampack Agency, Inc., Peter; Larkin, Sabra Elliott; Larsen/Elizabeth Pomada Literary Agents, Michael; Lasher Agency, The Maureen; Levine Literary Agency, Inc., Ellen; Levine Literary Agency, Paul S.; Lincoln Literary Agency, Ray; Lindstrom Literary Group; Lipkind Agency, Wendy; Literary Group, The; Love Literary Agency, Nancy; Lowenstein Associates, Inc.; Maccoby Literary Agency, Gina; Mann Agency, Carol; March Tenth, Inc.; Marshall Agency, The Evan; McBride Literary Agency, Margret; McCauley, Gerard; McGrath, Helen; McHugh Literary Agency; Michaels Literary Agency, Inc., Doris S.; Millard Literary Agency, Martha; Morrison, Inc., Henry; Mura Enterprises, Inc., Dee; Naggar Literary Agency, Jean V.; Nazor Literary Agency, Karen; New Century Literary Agency; New England Publishing Associates, Inc.; Norma-Lewis Agency, The; Otitis Media; Parks Agency, The Richard; Pevner, Inc., Stephen; Pinder Lane & Garon-Brooke Associates, Ltd.; Quicksilver Books-Literary Agents; Raymond, Literary Agent, Charlotte Cecil; Rees Literary Agency, Helen; Reichstein Literary Agency, The Naomi; Rein Books, Inc., Jody; Renaissance Literary Agency; Rhodes Literary Agency, Jodie; Rittenberg Literary Agency, Inc., Ann; Roghaar Literary Agency, Inc., Linda; Rosenkranz Literary Agency, Rita; Russell & Volkening; Sage Acre Marketing & Publishing Solutions; Sanders Literary Agency, Victoria; Schiavone Literary Agency, Inc.; Schulman, A Literary Agency, Susan; Sedgeband Literary Associates; Seligman, Literary Agent, Lynn; Shepard Agency, The; Shepard Agency, The Robert E.; Spieler Agency, The; Spitzer Literary Agency, Philip G.; Straus Agency, Inc., Robin; United Tribes; Valcourt Agency, Inc., The Richard R.; Van der Leun & Associates; Vines Agency, Inc., The; Wald Associates, Inc., Mary Jack; Wallace Literary Agency, Inc.; Ware Literary Agency, John A.; Watkins Loomis Agency, Inc.; Waxman Agency, Inc., Scott; Wecksler-Incomco; West Coast Literary Associates; Wieser & Wieser, Inc.; Witherspoon & Associates, Inc.; Wonderland Press, Inc., The; Writers House; Zachary Shuster Agency; Zeckendorf Assoc. Inc., Susan

How-to: Alive Communications, Inc.; Allred and Allred Literary Agents; Altair Literary Agency; Amber Literary; Amster Literary Enterprises, Betsy; Authentic Creations Literary Agency; Authors Alliance, Inc.; Authors & Artists Group, Inc.; Balkin Agency, Inc.; Bedford Book Works, Inc., The; Bernstein & Associates, Inc., Pam; Bial Agency, Daniel; Bleecker Street Associates; Boston Literary Group, The; Bova Literary Agency, The Barbara; Browne Ltd., Pema; Buck Agency, Howard; Bykofsky Associates, Inc., Sheree; Clausen, Mays & Tahan, LLC; Connor Literary Agency; Core Creations, Inc.; Crawford Literary Agency; Cypher, The Cypher Agency, James R.; Dawson Associates, Liza; DH Literary, Inc.; Elmo Agency Inc., Ann; Feigen/Parrent Literary Management; Finesse Literary Agency; Flaherty, Literary Agent, Joyce A.; Fleury Agency, B.R.; Fredericks Literary Agency, Inc., Jeanne; Fullerton Associates, Sheryl B.; Goodman-Andrew-Agency, Inc.; Grace Literary Agency, Carroll; Grosvenor Literary Agency, The; Harris Literary Agency; Heacock Literary Agency, Inc.; Henshaw Group, Richard; Herman Agency LLC, The Jeff; Herner Rights Agency, Susan; JLA Literary Agency; Joy Literary Agency; Kellock Company, Inc., The; Kleinman, Esq. of Graybill & English L.L.C., Jeffrey M.; Knight Agency, The; Konner Literary Agency, Linda; Koster Literary Agency, LLC, Elaine; Larkin, Sabra Elliott; Larsen/Elizabeth Pomada Literary Agents, Michael; Lasher Agency, The Maureen; Levine Literary Agency, Paul S.; Literary and Creative Artists, Inc.; Literary Group, The; Love Literary Agency, Nancy; Lowenstein Associates, Inc.; Manus & Associates Literary Agency; Marshall Agency, The Evan; McBride Literary Agency, Margret; McGrath, Helen; McHugh Literary Agency; Michaels Literary Agency, Inc., Doris S.; Millard Literary Agency, Martha; Multimedia Product Development, Inc.; Mura Enterprises, Inc., Dee; National Writers Literary Agency; Nazor Literary Agency, Karen; New Century Literary Agency; Northwest Literary Services; Parks Agency, The Richard; Paton Literary Agency, Kathi J.; Quicksilver Books-Literary Agents; Reichstein Literary Agency, The Naomi; Rein Books, Inc., Jody; Rhodes Literary Agency, Jodie; Robbins Literary Agency, BJ; Rosenkranz Literary Agency, Rita; Rotrosen Agency LLC, Jane; Scagnetti Talent & Literary Agency, Jack; Schiavone Literary Agency, Inc.; Schlessinger Agency, Blanche; Schulman, A Literary Agency, Susan; Seligman, Literary Agent, Lynn; Simenauer Literary Agency, Jacqueline; Singer Literary Agency Inc., Evelyn; Swayne Agency Literary Management & Consulting, Inc., The; Teal Literary Agency, Patricia; Toad Hall,

Inc.; Travis Literary Agency, Susan; United Tribes; Vines Agency, Inc., The; Watt & Associates, Sandra; Wonderland Press, Inc., The; Zachary Shuster Agency

Humor: Allred and Allred Literary Agents; Amber Literary; Amsterdam Agency, Marcia; Authors & Artists Group, Inc.; Bedford Book Works, Inc., The; Bial Agency, Daniel; Bleecker Street Associates; Books & Such; Buck Agency, Howard; Bykofsky Associates, Inc., Sheree; Clausen, Mays & Tahan, LLC; Connor Literary Agency; Core Creations, Inc.; Dystel Literary Management, Jane; Finesse Literary Agency; Harris Literary Agency; Henshaw Group, Richard; Hogenson Agency, Barbara; Jabberwocky Literary Agency; JLA Literary Agency; Kellock Company, Inc., The; Kleinman, Esq. of Graybill & English L.L.C., Jeffrey M.; Larsen/Elizabeth Pomada Literary Agents, Michael; Levine Literary Agency, Paul S.; Literary Group, The; Lowenstein Associates, Inc.; March Tenth, Inc.; Marshall Agency, The Evan; Multimedia Product Development, Inc.; Mura Enterprises, Inc., Dee; New Century Literary Agency; Otitis Media; Parks Agency, The Richard; Pevner, Inc., Stephen; Rein Books, Inc., Jody; Robbins Literary Agency, BJ; Rosenkranz Literary Agency, Rita; Ross Literary Agency, The Gail; Rotrosen Agency LLC, Jane; Sanders Literary Agency, Victoria; Schiavone Literary Agency, Inc.; Seligman, Literary Agent, Lynn; Vines Agency, Inc., The; Watt & Associates, Sandra

Interior Design/Decorating: Allred and Allred Literary Agents; Amber Literary; Authors & Artists Group, Inc.; Baldi Literary Agency, Malaga; Brandt & Brandt Literary Agents Inc.; Buck Agency, Howard; Connor Literary Agency; Ellison Inc., Nicholas; Finesse Literary Agency; Fleury Agency, B.R.; ForthWrite Literary Agency; Fredericks Literary Agency, Inc., Jeanne; Freymann Literary Agency, Sarah Jane; Grace Literary Agency, Carroll; Hawkins & Associates, Inc., John; Hogenson Agency, Barbara; Kellock Company, Inc., The; Kleinman, Esq. of Graybill & English L.L.C., Jeffrey M.; Larkin, Sabra Elliott; Larsen/Elizabeth Pomada Literary Agents, Michael; Levine Literary Agency, Paul S.; Lincoln Literary Agency, Ray; Marshall Agency, The Evan; Reichstein Literary Agency, The Naomi; Rosenkranz Literary Agency, Rita; Seligman, Literary Agent, Lynn; Shepard Agency, The; Wonderland Press, Inc., The; Writers House

Juvenile Nonfiction: Allred and Allred Literary Agents; Amber Literary; Bleecker Street Associates; Books & Such; Brandt & Brandt Literary Agents Inc.; Brown Associates Inc., Marie; Brown Literary Agency, Inc., Andrea; Browne Ltd., Pema; Cohen, Inc. Literary Agency, Ruth; Dwyer & O'Grady, Inc.; Educational Design Services, Inc.; Elek Associates, Peter; Ellenberg Literary Agency, Ethan; Elmo Agency Inc., Ann; Finesse Literary Agency; Flannery Literary; Fleury Agency, B.R.; ForthWrite Literary Agency; Hawkins & Associates, Inc., John; Henshaw Group, Richard; Joy Literary Agency; Kirchoff/Wohlberg, Inc., Authors' Representation Division; Kouts, Literary Agent, Barbara S.; Lewis & Company, Karen; Lincoln Literary Agency, Ray; Literary Group, The; Maccoby Literary Agency, Gina; Millard Literary Agency, Martha; Morrison, Inc., Henry; Multimedia Product Development, Inc.; Mura Enterprises, Inc., Dee; Naggar Literary Agency, Jean V.; National Writers Literary Agency; New Century Literary Agency; Norma-Lewis Agency, The; Rhodes Literary Agency, Jodie; Rubenstein Literary Agency, Inc., Pesha; Russell & Volkening; Schiavone Literary Agency, Inc.; Schulman, A Literary Agency, Susan; Seymour Agency, The; Shepard Agency, The; Singer Literary Agency Inc., Evelyn; Sternig & Byrne Literary Agency; Sunshine Literary Agency; Targ Literary Agency, Inc., Roslyn; Taylor, Literary Agent, Rebecca; Tiersten Literary Agency, Irene; Tobias—A Literary Agency for Children's Books, Ann; Treimel New York, S©ott; Wald Associates, Inc., Mary Jack; Wecksler-Incomco; Writers House; Zachary Shuster Agency

Language/Literature/Criticism: Acacia House Publishing Services Ltd.; Allred and Allred Literary Agents; Authors Alliance, Inc.; Baldi Literary Agency, Malaga; Balkin Agency, Inc.; Bent, Literary Agent, Jenny; Bial Agency, Daniel; Boates Literary Agency, Reid; Brandt & Brandt Literary Agents Inc.; Buck Agency, Howard; Castiglia Literary Agency; Cohen Agency, The; Connor Literary Agency; Coover Agency, The Doe; Cornfield Literary Agency, Robert; Cypher, The Cypher Agency, James R.; Darhansoff & Verrill Literary Agents; DH Literary, Inc.; Dijkstra Literary Agency, Sandra; Educational Design Services, Inc.; Ellison Inc., Nicholas; Finesse Literary Agency; Goodman-Andrew-Agency, Inc.; Grosvenor Literary Agency, The; Halsey North, Reese; Hawkins & Associates, Inc., John; Heacock Literary Agency, Inc.; Herner Rights Agency, Susan; Hill Associates, Frederick; Jabberwocky Literary Agency; James Peter Associates, Inc.; JCA Literary Agency, Inc.; Kidde, Hoyt & Picard; Kleinman, Esq. of Graybill & English L.L.C., Jeffrey M.; Larkin, Sabra Elliott; Larsen/Elizabeth Pomada Literary Agents, Michael; Levant & Wales, Literary Agency, Inc.; Levine Literary Agency, Paul S.; Lincoln Literary Agency, Ray; Literary Group, The; Lowenstein Associates, Inc.; Lukeman Literary Management Ltd.; March Tenth, Inc.; Marshall Agency, The Evan; New Century Literary Agency; New England Publishing Associates, Inc.; Nine Muses and Apollo; Parks Agency, The Richard; Pevner, Inc., Stephen; Quicksilver Books-Literary Agents; Reichstein Literary Agency, The Naomi; Rhodes Literary Agency, Jodie; Robbins Office, Inc., The; Rosenkranz Literary Agency, Rita; Russell & Volkening; Sage Acre Marketing & Publishing Solutions; Sanders Literary Agency, Victoria; Schiavone Literary Agency, Inc.; Seligman, Literary Agent, Lynn; Shepard Agency, The; Spitzer Literary Agency, Philip G.; Straus Agency, Inc., Robin; United Tribes; Van der Leun & Associates; Wald Associates, Inc., Mary Jack; Wallace Literary Agency, Inc.; Ware Literary Agency,

John A.; Watt & Associates, Sandra; West Coast Literary Associates; Wonderland Press, Inc., The; Zachary Shuster Agency

Memoirs: Acacia House Publishing Services Ltd.; Authors Alliance, Inc.; Authors & Artists Group, Inc.; Baldi Literary Agency, Malaga; Bial Agency, Daniel; Bleecker Street Associates; Borchardt Inc., Georges; Carvainis Agency, Inc., Maria; Clausen, Mays & Tahan, LLC; Coover Agency, The Doe; Cypher, The Cypher Agency, James R.; Dawson Associates, Liza; Ducas, Robert; Everitt Literary Agency, Inc., Charles; Feigen/Parrent Literary Management; Finesse Literary Agency; Flaherty, Literary Agent, Joyce A.; Franklin Associates, Ltd., Lynn C.; Halsey North, Reese; James Peter Associates, Inc.; JCA Literary Agency, Inc.; JLA Literary Agency; Kidde, Hoyt & Picard; Kleinman, Esq. of Graybill & English L.L.C., Jeffrey M.; Larsen/Elizabeth Pomada Literary Agents, Michael; Levant & Wales, Literary Agency, Inc.; Levine Literary Agency, Inc., Ellen; Levine Literary Agency, Paul S.; Lieberman Associates, Robert; Lindstrom Literary Group; Literary and Creative Artists, Inc.; Literary Group, The; Love Literary Agency, Nancy; Lowenstein Associates, Inc.; Manus & Associates Literary Agency; Millard Literary Agency, Martha; Multimedia Product Development, Inc.; Mura Enterprises, Inc., Dee; Naggar Literary Agency, Jean V.; New Century Literary Agency; Northwest Literary Services; Parks Agency, The Richard; Pevner, Inc., Stephen; Pinder Lane & Garon-Brooke Associates, Ltd.; Protter Literary Agent, Susan Ann; Quicksilver Books-Literary Agents; Rhodes Literary Agency, Jodie; Rittenberg Literary Agency, Inc., Ann; Robbins Literary Agency, BJ; Robbins Office, Inc., The; Schlessinger Agency, Blanche; Spieler Agency, The; 2M Communications Ltd.; United Tribes; Valcourt Agency, Inc., The Richard R.; Van der Leun & Associates; Vines Agency, Inc., The; Watt & Associates, Sandra; Weingel-Fidel Agency, The; Witherspoon & Associates, Inc.; Zachary Shuster Agency; Zeckendorf Assoc. Inc., Susan

Military/War: Acacia House Publishing Services Ltd.; Allred and Allred Literary Agents; Amber Literary; Authors Alliance, Inc.; Bial Agency, Daniel; Bleecker Street Associates; Bookmark Literary Agency; Boston Literary Group, The; Brandt & Brandt Literary Agents Inc.; Browne Ltd., Pema; Buck Agency, Howard; Charisma Communications, Ltd.; Dijkstra Literary Agency, Sandra; Donovan Literary, Jim; Ducas, Robert; Dystel Literary Management, Jane; Educational Design Services, Inc.; Ellison Inc., Nicholas; Everitt Literary Agency, Inc., Charles; Finesse Literary Agency; Gartenberg, Literary Agent, Max; Gibson Agency, The Sebastian; Grosvenor Literary Agency, The; Hawkins & Associates, Inc., John; Henshaw Group, Richard; Hochmann Books, John L.; J de S Associates Inc.; Jabberwocky Literary Agency; James Peter Associates, Inc.; JCA Literary Agency, Inc.; Kellock Company, Inc., The; Ketz Agency, Louise B.; Levine Literary Agency, Paul S.; Literary Group, The; Lukeman Literary Management Ltd.; Marshall Agency, The Evan; McCauley, Gerard; McGrath, Helen; McHugh Literary Agency; Mura Enterprises, Inc., Dee; New Century Literary Agency; New England Publishing Associates, Inc.; Otitis Media; Parks Agency, The Richard; Pinder Lane & Garon-Brooke Associates, Ltd.; Rhodes Literary Agency, Jodie; Rosenkranz Literary Agency, Rita; Russell & Volkening; Scagnetti Talent & Literary Agency, Jack; Schiavone Literary Agency, Inc.; Spitzer Literary Agency, Philip G.; Sunshine Literary Agency; Valcourt Agency, Inc., The Richard R.; Vines Agency, Inc., The; Writers House

Money/Finance/Economics: Altair Literary Agency; Amster Literary Enterprises, Betsy; Authors Alliance, Inc.; Authors & Artists Group, Inc.; Baldi Literary Agency, Malaga; Bedford Book Works, Inc., The; Bial Agency, Daniel; Bleecker Street Associates; Book Deals, Inc.; Boston Literary Group, The; Bova Literary Agency, The Barbara; Brandt & Brandt Literary Agents Inc.; Brown Associates Inc., Marie; Browne Ltd., Pema; Buck Agency, Howard; Castiglia Literary Agency; Clausen, Mays & Tahan, LLC; Connor Literary Agency; Coover Agency, The Doe; Cypher, The Cypher Agency, James R.; DH Literary, Inc.; Diamond Literary Agency, Inc.; Dijkstra Literary Agency, Sandra; Donovan Literary, Jim; Ducas, Robert; Dystel Literary Management, Jane; Educational Design Services, Inc.; Ellison Inc., Nicholas; Elmo Agency Inc., Ann; Everitt Literary Agency, Inc., Charles; Feigen/Parrent Literary Management; Finesse Literary Agency; Fleury Agency, B.R.; ForthWrite Literary Agency; Fredericks Literary Agency, Inc., Jeanne; Gartenberg, Literary Agent, Max; Grosvenor Literary Agency, The; Hawkins & Associates, Inc., John; Henshaw Group, Richard; Jabberwocky Literary Agency; James Peter Associates, Inc.; JCA Literary Agency, Inc.; JLA Literary Agency; Kellock Company, Inc., The; Ketz Agency, Louise B.; Kleinman, Esq. of Graybill & English L.L.C., Jeffrey M.; Knight Agency, The; Konner Literary Agency, Linda; Koster Literary Agency, LLC, Elaine; Lampack Agency, Inc., Peter; Larkin, Sabra Elliott; Larsen/Elizabeth Pomada Literary Agents, Michael; Levine Communications, Inc., James; Levine Literary Agency, Paul S.; Lieberman Associates, Robert; Lincoln Literary Agency, Ray; Literary Group, The; Lowenstein Associates, Inc.; Lukeman Literary Management Ltd.; Mann Agency, Carol; Manus & Associates Literary Agency; Marshall Agency, The Evan; McBride Literary Agency, Margret; Michaels Literary Agency, Inc., Doris S.; Millard Literary Agency, Martha; Multimedia Product Development, Inc.; Mura Enterprises, Inc., Dee; New Century Literary Agency; New England Publishing Associates, Inc.; Parks Agency, The Richard; Pine Associates, Inc, Arthur; Rees Literary Agency, Helen; Reichstein Literary Agency, The Naomi; Rhodes Literary Agency, Jodie; Rinaldi Literary Agency, Angela; Rosenkranz Literary Agency, Rita; Ross Literary

Agency, The Gail; Rotrosen Agency LLC, Jane; Russell & Volkening; Sage Acre Marketing & Publishing Solutions; Schulman, A Literary Agency, Susan; Sebastian Literary Agency; Seligman, Literary Agent, Lynn; Shepard Agency, The; Shepard Agency, The Robert E.; Simenauer Literary Agency, Jacqueline; Singer Literary Agency Inc., Evelyn; Spieler Agency, The; Sunshine Literary Agency; United Tribes; Vines Agency, Inc., The; Waxman Agency, Inc., Scott; Wieser & Wieser, Inc.; Witherspoon & Associates, Inc.; Writers House; Zachary Shuster Agency

Music/Dance/Theater/Film: Acacia House Publishing Services Ltd.; Allen Literary Agency, Linda; Allred and Allred Literary Agents; Altair Literary Agency; Amber Literary; Andrews & Associates Inc., Bart; Appleseeds Management; Authors Alliance, Inc.; Authors & Artists Group, Inc.; Baldi Literary Agency, Malaga; Balkin Agency, Inc.; Bial Agency, Daniel; Boston Literary Group, The; Brandt & Brandt Literary Agents Inc.; Brown Associates Inc., Marie; Buck Agency, Howard; Bykofsky Associates, Inc., Sheree; Cohen Agency, The; Communications and Entertainment, Inc.; Cornfield Literary Agency, Robert; Cypher, The Cypher Agency, James R.; Donovan Literary, Jim; Ellison Inc., Nicholas; Farber Literary Agency Inc.; Feigen/Parrent Literary Management; Fleury Agency, B.R.; Gartenberg, Literary Agent, Max; Gibson Agency, The Sebastian; Goodman-Andrew-Agency, Inc.; Greene, Arthur B.; Grosvenor Literary Agency, The; Hawkins & Associates, Inc., John; Heacock Literary Agency, Inc.; Henshaw Group, Richard; Hochmann Books, John L.; Hogenson Agency, Barbara; Jabberwocky Literary Agency; James Peter Associates, Inc.; JCA Literary Agency, Inc.; JLA Literary Agency; Kellock Company, Inc., The; Kleinman, Esq. of Graybill & English L.L.C., Jeffrey M.; Knight Agency, The; Kouts, Literary Agent, Barbara S.; Lampack Agency, Inc., Peter; Larkin, Sabra Elliott; Larsen/Elizabeth Pomada Literary Agents, Michael; Levine Literary Agency, Paul S.; Lieberman Associates, Robert; Lincoln Literary Agency, Ray; Literary Group, The; Lowenstein Associates, Inc.; Lukeman Literary Management Ltd.; March Tenth, Inc.; Marshall Agency, The Evan; McBride Literary Agency, Margret; Michaels Literary Agency, Inc., Doris S.; Millard Literary Agency, Martha; Nathan, Ruth; Nazor Literary Agency, Karen; New Century Literary Agency; Norma-Lewis Agency, The; Otitis Media; Parks Agency, The Richard; Perkins, Rubie & Associates; Pevner, Inc., Stephen; Pinder Lane & Garon-Brooke Associates, Ltd.; Reichstein Literary Agency, The Naomi; Rein Books, Inc., Jody; Renaissance Literary Agency; Rhodes Literary Agency, Jodie; Robbins Literary Agency, BJ; Rosenkranz Literary Agency, Rita; Russell & Volkening; Sanders Literary Agency, Victoria; Scagnetti Talent & Literary Agency, Jack; Schulman, A Literary Agency, Susan; Seligman, Literary Agent, Lynn; Shepard Agency, The; Spitzer Literary Agency, Philip G.; Straus Agency, Inc., Robin; 2M Communications Ltd.; United Tribes; Wald Associates, Inc., Mary Jack; Ware Literary Agency, John A.; Wecksler-Incomco; Weingel-Fidel Agency, The; West Coast Literary Associates; Witherspoon & Associates, Inc.; Writers House; Zachary Shuster Agency; Zeckendorf Assoc. Inc., Susan

Nature/Environment: Acacia House Publishing Services Ltd.; Allen Literary Agency, Linda; Altair Literary Agency; Authors Alliance, Inc.; Authors & Artists Group, Inc.; Baldi Literary Agency, Malaga; Balkin Agency, Inc.; Bial Agency, Daniel; Bleecker Street Associates; Boates Literary Agency, Reid; Boston Literary Group, The; Brandt & Brandt Literary Agents Inc.; Browne Ltd., Pema; Buck Agency, Howard; Castiglia Literary Agency; Collin Literary Agent, Frances; Coover Agency, The Doe; Cypher, The Cypher Agency, James R.; Darhansoff & Verrill Literary Agents; DH Literary, Inc.; Dijkstra Literary Agency, Sandra; Donovan Literary, Jim; Ducas, Robert; Elek Associates, Peter; Ellison Inc., Nicholas; Evans Inc., Mary; Everitt Literary Agency, Inc., Charles; Finesse Literary Agency; Flaherty, Literary Agent, Joyce A.; Fleury Agency, B.R.; ForthWrite Literary Agency; Fredericks Literary Agency, Inc., Jeanne; Freymann Literary Agency, Sarah Jane; Gartenberg, Literary Agent, Max; Gibson Agency, The Sebastian; Goodman-Andrew-Agency, Inc.; Grosvenor Literary Agency, The; Hawkins & Associates, Inc., John; Heacock Literary Agency, Inc.; Henshaw Group, Richard; Herner Rights Agency, Susan; Jabberwocky Literary Agency; JCA Literary Agency, Inc.; Joy Literary Agency; Kellock Company, Inc., The; Kern Literary Agency, Natasha; Kleinman, Esq. of Graybill & English L.L.C., Jeffrey M.; Koster Literary Agency, LLC, Elaine; Kouts, Literary Agent, Barbara S.; Larkin, Sabra Elliott; Larsen/Elizabeth Pomada Literary Agents, Michael; Lasher Agency, The Maureen; Levant & Wales, Literary Agency, Inc.; Levine Communications, Inc., James; Levine Literary Agency, Paul S.; Lieberman Associates, Robert; Lincoln Literary Agency, Ray; Literary Group, The; Love Literary Agency, Nancy; Lowenstein Associates, Inc.; Lukeman Literary Management Ltd.; Manus & Associates Literary Agency; Marshall Agency, The Evan; McHugh Literary Agency; Michaels Literary Agency, Inc., Doris S.; Multimedia Product Development, Inc.; Mura Enterprises, Inc., Dee; Nazor Literary Agency, Karen; New Century Literary Agency; New England Publishing Associates, Inc.; Norma-Lewis Agency, The; Northwest Literary Services; Parks Agency, The Richard; Paton Literary Agency, Kathi J.; Quicksilver Books-Literary Agents; Raymond, Literary Agent, Charlotte Cecil; Reichstein Literary Agency, The Naomi; Rein Books, Inc., Jody; Rhodes Literary Agency, Jodie; Robbins Literary Agency, BJ; Roghaar Literary Agency, Inc., Linda; Rosenkranz Literary Agency, Rita; Ross Literary Agency, The Gail; Rotrosen Agency LLC, Jane; Rowland Agency, The Damaris; Russell & Volkening; Schiavone Literary Agency, Inc.; Schulman, A Literary Agency, Susan; Seligman, Literary Agent, Lynn; Shepard Agency, The; Singer Literary Agency Inc., Evelyn; Spitzer

Literary Agency, Philip G.; Straus Agency, Inc., Robin; Toad Hall, Inc.; Travis Literary Agency, Susan; United Tribes; Vines Agency, Inc., The; Wald Associates, Inc., Mary Jack; Ware Literary Agency, John A.; Watkins Loomis Agency, Inc.; Watt & Associates, Sandra; Wecksler-Incomco; West Coast Literary Associates; Wieser & Wieser, Inc.; Writers House

New Age/Metaphysics: Allred and Allred Literary Agents; Altair Literary Agency; Authors Alliance, Inc.; Authors & Artists Group, Inc.; Bent, Literary Agent, Jenny; Bial Agency, Daniel; Bleecker Street Associates; Browne Ltd., Pema; Buck Agency, Howard; Castiglia Literary Agency; Dystel Literary Management, Jane; Ellenberg Literary Agency, Ethan; Ellison Inc., Nicholas; Finesse Literary Agency; Fleury Agency, B.R.; Franklin Associates, Ltd., Lynn C.; Fullerton Associates, Sheryl B.; Grosvenor Literary Agency, The; Hawkins & Associates, Inc., John; Heacock Literary Agency, Inc.; Henshaw Group, Richard; Herner Rights Agency, Susan; J de S Associates Inc.; JCA Literary Agency, Inc.; JLA Literary Agency; Kern Literary Agency, Natasha; Koster Literary Agency, LLC, Elaine; Larsen/Elizabeth Pomada Literary Agents, Michael; Levant & Wales, Literary Agency, Inc.; Levine Communications, Inc., James; Levine Literary Agency, Paul S.; Lewis & Company, Karen; Literary Group, The; Love Literary Agency, Nancy; Lowenstein Associates, Inc.; Lukeman Literary Management Ltd.; Marshall Agency, The Evan; Millard Literary Agency, Martha; Naggar Literary Agency, Jean V.; Northwest Literary Services; Pevner, Inc., Stephen; Quicksilver Books-Literary Agents; Rhodes Literary Agency, Jodie; Rosenkranz Literary Agency, Rita; Roth, Literary Representation, Carol Susan; Rowland Agency, The Damaris; Schulman, A Literary Agency, Susan; Simenauer Literary Agency, Jacqueline; Sunshine Literary Agency; Toad Hall, Inc.; Vines Agency, Inc., The; Watt & Associates, Sandra

Open to all Nonfiction Categories: Barrett Books Inc., Loretta; Bernstein Literary Agency, Meredith; Brown Limited, Curtis; Circle of Confusion Ltd.; Cohen Literary Agency Ltd., Hy; Congdon Associates, Inc., Don; Curtis Associates, Inc., Richard; Doyen Literary Services, Inc.; Fernandez Agent/Attorney, Justin E.; Fleming Agency, Peter; Ghosts & Collaborators International; Goldfarb & Associates; Goodman Associates; Greenburger Associates, Inc., Sanford J.; Hoffman Literary Agency, Berenice; Lake Agency, The Candace; Lazear Agency Incorporated; Levant & Wales, Literary Agency, Inc.; Madsen Agency, Robert; Ober Associates, Harold; Paraview, Inc.; Pelter, Rodney; Sandum & Associates; Snell Literary Agency, Michael; Talbot Agency, The John

Photography: Allred and Allred Literary Agents; Altair Literary Agency; Authors & Artists Group, Inc.; Baldi Literary Agency, Malaga; Boston Literary Group, The; Buck Agency, Howard; Connor Literary Agency; Ellison Inc., Nicholas; Finesse Literary Agency; Fleury Agency, B.R.; ForthWrite Literary Agency; Fredericks Literary Agency, Inc., Jeanne; Gibson Agency, The Sebastian; Grace Literary Agency, Carroll; Grosvenor Literary Agency, The; Hawkins & Associates, Inc., John; Hogenson Agency, Barbara; JCA Literary Agency, Inc.; Kellock Company, Inc., The; Kleinman, Esq. of Graybill & English L.L.C., Jeffrey M.; Larkin, Sabra Elliott; Larsen/Elizabeth Pomada Literary Agents, Michael; Levine Literary Agency, Paul S.; Lukeman Literary Management Ltd.; Millard Literary Agency, Martha; Nazor Literary Agency, Karen; Norma-Lewis Agency, The; Otitis Media; Pevner, Inc., Stephen; Rosenkranz Literary Agency, Rita; Russell & Volkening; Seligman, Literary Agent, Lynn; Vines Agency, Inc., The; Wald Associates, Inc., Mary Jack; Wecksler-Incomco; Wonderland Press, Inc., The

Popular Culture: Allen Literary Agency, Linda; Allred and Allred Literary Agents; Altair Literary Agency; Amster Literary Enterprises, Betsy; Amsterdam Agency, Marcia; Authors & Artists Group, Inc.; Balkin Agency, Inc.; Bedford Book Works, Inc., The; Bent, Literary Agent, Jenny; Bernstein & Associates, Inc., Pam; Bial Agency, Daniel; Bleecker Street Associates; Book Deals, Inc.; Boston Literary Group, The; Browne Ltd., Pema; Buck Agency, Howard; Bykofsky Associates, Inc., Sheree; Connor Literary Agency; Cypher, The Cypher Agency, James R.; Daves Agency, Joan; DH Literary, Inc.; DHS Literary, Inc.; Donovan Literary, Jim; Dystel Literary Management, Jane; Elek Associates, Peter; Ellenberg Literary Agency, Ethan; Elmo Agency Inc., Ann; Evans Inc., Mary; Finesse Literary Agency; Flaherty, Literary Agent, Joyce A.; Fogelman Literary Agency, The; Fullerton Associates, Sheryl B.; Gibson Agency, The Sebastian; Goodman-Andrew-Agency, Inc.; Grosvenor Literary Agency, The; Halsey North, Reese; Heacock Literary Agency, Inc.; Henshaw Group, Richard; Herner Rights Agency, Susan; Hogenson Agency, Barbara; Jabberwocky Literary Agency; James Peter Associates, Inc.; JCA Literary Agency, Inc.; JLA Literary Agency; Kellock Company, Inc., The; Kern Literary Agency, Natasha; Kidde, Hoyt & Picard; Kleinman, Esq. of Graybill & English L.L.C., Jeffrey M.; Knight Agency, The; Konner Literary Agency, Linda; Koster Literary Agency, LLC, Elaine; Lampack Agency, Inc., Peter; Larkin, Sabra Elliott; Larsen/Elizabeth Pomada Literary Agents, Michael; Lasher Agency, The Maureen; Levant & Wales, Literary Agency, Inc.; Levine Literary Agency, Inc., Ellen; Levine Literary Agency, Paul S.; Lindstrom Literary Group; Literary Group, The; Love Literary Agency, Nancy; Lowenstein Associates, Inc.; Lukeman Literary Management Ltd.; Maccoby Literary Agency, Gina; Manus & Associates Literary Agency; March Tenth, Inc.; McBride Literary Agency, Margret; Millard Literary Agency, Martha; Multimedia Product Development, Inc.; National Writers Literary Agency; Nazor Literary Agency, Karen; New Century Literary Agency; Norma-

Lewis Agency, The; Parks Agency, The Richard; Perkins, Rubie & Associates; Pevner, Inc., Stephen; Quicksilver Books-Literary Agents; Reichstein Literary Agency, The Naomi; Rein Books, Inc., Jody; Rhodes Literary Agency, Jodie; Rinaldi Literary Agency, Angela; Robbins Literary Agency, BJ; Roghaar Literary Agency, Inc., Linda; Rosenkranz Literary Agency, Rita; Rotrosen Agency LLC, Jane; Russell & Volkening; Sage Acre Marketing & Publishing Solutions; Sanders Literary Agency, Victoria; Schiavone Literary Agency, Inc.; Schulman, A Literary Agency, Susan; Seligman, Literary Agent, Lynn; Shepard Agency, The Robert E.; Simenauer Literary Agency, Jacqueline; Spitzer Literary Agency, Philip G.; Stauffer Associates, Nancy; Sternig & Byrne Literary Agency; Straus Agency, Inc., Robin; Swayne Agency Literary Management & Consulting, Inc., The; Toad Hall, Inc.; Travis Literary Agency, Susan; United Tribes; Vines Agency, Inc., The; Ware Literary Agency, John A.; Watkins Loomis Agency, Inc.; Watt & Associates, Sandra; Waxman Agency, Inc., Scott; Wonderland Press, Inc., The

Psychology: Agents Inc. for Medical and Mental Health Professionals; Allen Literary Agency, Linda; Allred and Allred Literary Agents; Altair Literary Agency; Amber Literary; Amster Literary Enterprises, Betsy; Authors Alliance, Inc.; Authors & Artists Group, Inc.; Baldi Literary Agency, Malaga; Bedford Book Works, Inc., The; Bent, Literary Agent, Jenny; Bernstein & Associates, Inc., Pam; Bial Agency, Daniel; Bleecker Street Associates; Boates Literary Agency, Reid; Book Deals, Inc.; Boston Literary Group, The; Brandt & Brandt Literary Agents Inc.; Brown Associates Inc., Marie; Browne Ltd., Pema; Buck Agency, Howard; Bykofsky Associates, Inc., Sheree; Cadden, Fuller & Burkhalter LLP; Castiglia Literary Agency; Clausen, Mays & Tahan, LLC; Coover Agency, The Doe; Core Creations, Inc.; Cypher, The Cypher Agency, James R.; Dawson Associates, Liza; DH Literary, Inc.; Diamond Literary Agency, Inc.; Dijkstra Literary Agency, Sandra; Dystel Literary Management, Jane; Ellenberg Literary Agency, Ethan; Ellison Inc., Nicholas; Elmo Agency Inc., Ann; Farber Literary Agency Inc.; Feigen/Parrent Literary Management; Finesse Literary Agency; Flaherty, Literary Agent, Joyce A.; Fleury Agency, B.R.; Fogelman Literary Agency, The; ForthWrite Literary Agency; Franklin Associates, Ltd., Lynn C.; Fredericks Literary Agency, Inc., Jeanne; Freymann Literary Agency, Sarah Jane; Fullerton Associates, Sheryl B.; Gartenberg, Literary Agent, Max; Gibson Agency, The Sebastian; Gislason Agency, The; Goodman-Andrew-Agency, Inc.; Greene, Literary Agent, Randall Elisha; Grosvenor Literary Agency, The; Hawkins & Associates, Inc., John; Heacock Literary Agency, Inc.; Henshaw Group, Richard; Herman Agency LLC, The Jeff; Herner Rights Agency, Susan; James Peter Associates, Inc.; JCA Literary Agency, Inc.; JLA Literary Agency; Kellock Company, Inc., The; Kern Literary Agency, Natasha; Kidde, Hoyt & Picard; Kleinman, Esq. of Graybill & English L.L.C., Jeffrey M.; Klinger, Inc., Harvey; Knight Agency, The; Konner Literary Agency, Linda; Koster Literary Agency, LLC, Elaine; Kouts, Literary Agent, Barbara S.; Larkin, Sabra Elliott; Larsen/Elizabeth Pomada Literary Agents, Michael; Lasher Agency, The Maureen; Levant & Wales, Literary Agency, Inc.; Levine Communications, Inc., James; Levine Literary Agency, Inc., Ellen; Levine Literary Agency, Paul S.; Lieberman Associates, Robert; Lincoln Literary Agency, Ray; Lindstrom Literary Group; Literary Group, The; Love Literary Agency, Nancy; Lowenstein Associates, Inc.; Lukeman Literary Management Ltd.; Mann Agency, Carol; Manus & Associates Literary Agency; Marshall Agency, The Evan; McBride Literary Agency, Margret; McGrath, Helen; Millard Literary Agency, Martha; Multimedia Product Development, Inc.; Naggar Literary Agency, Jean V.; New Century Literary Agency; New England Publishing Associates, Inc.; Nine Muses and Apollo; Parks Agency, The Richard; Paton Literary Agency, Kathi J.; Pinder Lane & Garon-Brooke Associates, Ltd.; Pine Associates, Inc, Arthur; Protter Literary Agent, Susan Ann; Quicksilver Books-Literary Agents; Raymond, Literary Agent, Charlotte Cecil; Reichstein Literary Agency, The Naomi; Rein Books, Inc., Jody; Rhodes Literary Agency, Jodie; Rinaldi Literary Agency, Angela; Robbins Literary Agency, BJ; Rosenkranz Literary Agency, Rita; Ross Literary Agency, The Gail; Rotrosen Agency LLC, Jane; Russell & Volkening; Sage Acre Marketing & Publishing Solutions; Sanders Literary Agency, Victoria; Schiavone Literary Agency, Inc.; Schulman, A Literary Agency, Susan; Sebastian Literary Agency; Seligman, Literary Agent, Lynn; Shepard Agency, The; Simenauer Literary Agency, Jacqueline; Singer Literary Agency Inc., Evelyn; Slopen Literary Agency, Beverley; Snell Literary Agency, Michael; Spitzer Literary Agency, Philip G.; Straus Agency, Inc., Robin; Sunshine Literary Agency; Teal Literary Agency, Patricia; Travis Literary Agency, Susan; United Tribes; Vines Agency, Inc., The; Ware Literary Agency, John A.; Watt & Associates, Sandra; Weingel-Fidel Agency, The; West Coast Literary Associates; Wieser & Wieser, Inc.; Wonderland Press, Inc., The; Writers House; Zachary Shuster Agency; Zeckendorf Assoc. Inc., Susan

Religious/Inspirational: Alive Communications, Inc.; Allred and Allred Literary Agents; Altair Literary Agency; Amber Literary; Authors Alliance, Inc.; Authors & Artists Group, Inc.; Bent, Literary Agent, Jenny; Bernstein & Associates, Inc., Pam; Bial Agency, Daniel; BigScore Productions Inc.; Bleecker Street Associates; Books & Such; Boston Literary Group, The; Brown Associates Inc., Marie; Browne Ltd., Pema; Buck Agency, Howard; Bykofsky Associates, Inc., Sheree; Cadden, Fuller & Burkhalter LLP; Castiglia Literary Agency; Clausen, Mays & Tahan, LLC; Crawford Literary Agency; Dystel Literary Management, Jane; Ellenberg Literary Agency, Ethan; Ellison Inc., Nicholas; Finesse Literary Agency; ForthWrite Literary Agency; Franklin Associates, Ltd., Lynn C.; Freymann Literary Agency, Sarah Jane;

Gislason Agency, The; Grosvenor Literary Agency, The; Heacock Literary Agency, Inc.; Herner Rights Agency, Susan; JLA Literary Agency; Joy Literary Agency; Kellock Company, Inc., The; Knight Agency, The; Larkin, Sabra Elliott; Larsen/Elizabeth Pomada Literary Agents, Michael; Levine Communications, Inc., James; Levine Literary Agency, Paul S.; Literary Group, The; Lowenstein Associates, Inc.; Lukeman Literary Management Ltd.; Marshall Agency, The Evan; McBride Literary Agency, Margret; Multimedia Product Development, Inc.; Naggar Literary Agency, Jean V.; Nine Muses and Apollo; Pevner, Inc., Stephen; Quicksilver Books-Literary Agents; Rein Books, Inc., Jody; Rhodes Literary Agency, Jodie; Roghaar Literary Agency, Inc., Linda; Rosenkranz Literary Agency, Rita; Ross Literary Agency, The Gail; Roth, Literary Representation, Carol Susan; Rowland Agency, The Damaris; Schulman, A Literary Agency, Susan; Seymour Agency, The; Shepard Agency, The; Simenauer Literary Agency, Jacqueline; Singer Literary Agency Inc., Evelyn; Sunshine Literary Agency; Toad Hall, Inc.; Vines Agency, Inc., The; Watt & Associates, Sandra; Waxman Agency, Inc., Scott

Science/Technology: Agents Inc. for Medical and Mental Health Professionals; Allred and Allred Literary Agents; Altair Literary Agency; Authentic Creations Literary Agency; Authors & Artists Group, Inc.; Baldi Literary Agency, Malaga; Balkin Agency, Inc.; Bedford Book Works, Inc., The; Bent, Literary Agent, Jenny; Bial Agency, Daniel; Bleecker Street Associates; Boates Literary Agency, Reid; Book Deals, Inc.; Boston Literary Group, The; Brandt & Brandt Literary Agents Inc.; Cadden, Fuller & Burkhalter LLP; Carvainis Agency, Inc., Maria; Castiglia Literary Agency; Cypher, The Cypher Agency, James R.; Darhansoff & Verrill Literary Agents; DH Literary, Inc.; Dijkstra Literary Agency, Sandra; Ducas, Robert; Dystel Literary Management, Jane; Educational Design Services, Inc.; Elek Associates, Peter; Ellenberg Literary Agency, Ethan; Ellison Inc., Nicholas; Evans Inc., Mary; Everitt Literary Agency, Inc., Charles; Finesse Literary Agency; Fleury Agency, B.R.; ForthWrite Literary Agency; Fredericks Literary Agency, Inc., Jeanne; Gartenberg, Literary Agent, Max; Gibson Agency, The Sebastian; Grosvenor Literary Agency, The; Harris Literary Agency; Hawkins & Associates, Inc., John; Heacock Literary Agency, Inc.; Henshaw Group, Richard; Herner Rights Agency, Susan; Jabberwocky Literary Agency; JCA Literary Agency, Inc.; JLA Literary Agency; Kern Literary Agency, Natasha; Ketz Agency, Louise B.; Kleinman, Esq. of Graybill & English L.L.C., Jeffrey M.; Klinger, Inc., Harvey; Larkin, Sabra Elliott; Larsen/Elizabeth Pomada Literary Agents, Michael; Lasher Agency, The Maureen; Levant & Wales, Literary Agency, Inc.; Levine Communications, Inc., James; Levine Literary Agency, Inc., Ellen; Levine Literary Agency, Paul S.; Lieberman Associates, Robert; Lincoln Literary Agency, Ray; Lindstrom Literary Group; Lipkind Agency, Wendy; Literary Group, The; Love Literary Agency, Nancy; Lowenstein Associates, Inc.; Manus & Associates Literary Agency; Marshall Agency, The Evan; McBride Literary Agency, Margret; McHugh Literary Agency; Multimedia Product Development, Inc.; Mura Enterprises, Inc., Dee; National Writers Literary Agency; Nazor Literary Agency, Karen; New England Publishing Associates, Inc.; Parks Agency, The Richard; Perkins, Rubie & Associates; Pevner, Inc., Stephen; Protter Literary Agent, Susan Ann; Quicksilver Books-Literary Agents; Reichstein Literary Agency, The Naomi; Rein Books, Inc., Jody; Rhodes Literary Agency, Jodie; Rosenkranz Literary Agency, Rita; Ross Literary Agency, The Gail; Russell & Volkening; Schiavone Literary Agency, Inc.; Seligman, Literary Agent, Lynn; Shepard Agency, The Robert E.; Singer Literary Agency Inc., Evelyn; Snell Literary Agency, Michael; Straus Agency, Inc., Robin; United Tribes; Vines Agency, Inc., The; Ware Literary Agency, John A.; Watkins Loomis Agency, Inc.; Weingel-Fidel Agency, The; Witherspoon & Associates, Inc.; Writers House; Zachary Shuster Agency; Zeckendorf Assoc. Inc., Susan

Self-Help/Personal Improvement: Agents Inc. for Medical and Mental Health Professionals; Alive Communications, Inc.; Allred and Allred Literary Agents; Altair Literary Agency; Amster Literary Enterprises, Betsy; Amsterdam Agency, Marcia; Authentic Creations Literary Agency; Authors Alliance, Inc.; Authors & Artists Group, Inc.; Bent, Literary Agent, Jenny; Bernstein & Associates, Inc., Pam; Bial Agency, Daniel; BigScore Productions Inc.; Bleecker Street Associates; Boates Literary Agency, Reid; Book Deals, Inc.; Books & Such; Boston Literary Group, The; Bova Literary Agency, The Barbara; Brandt & Brandt Literary Agents Inc.; Brown Associates Inc., Marie; Browne Ltd., Pema; Bykofsky Associates, Inc., Sheree; Cadden, Fuller & Burkhalter LLP; Castiglia Literary Agency; Client First—A/K/A Leo P. Haffey Agency; Connor Literary Agency; Crawford Literary Agency; Cypher, The Cypher Agency, James R.; Dawson Associates, Liza; DH Literary, Inc.; Diamond Literary Agency, Inc.; Dijkstra Literary Agency, Sandra; Ellenberg Literary Agency, Ethan; Elmo Agency Inc., Ann; Feigen/Parrent Literary Management; Finesse Literary Agency; Flaherty, Literary Agent, Joyce A.; Fleury Agency, B.R.; Franklin Associates, Ltd., Lynn C.; Fredericks Literary Agency, Inc., Jeanne; Freymann Literary Agency, Sarah Jane; Fullerton Associates, Sheryl B.; Gartenberg, Literary Agent, Max; Gislason Agency, The; Goodman-Andrew-Agency, Inc.; Grosvenor Literary Agency, The; Harris Literary Agency; Hawkins & Associates, Inc., John; Heacock Literary Agency, Inc.; Henshaw Group, Richard; Herman Agency LLC, The Jeff; Herner Rights Agency, Susan; J de S Associates Inc.; James Peter Associates, Inc.; JLA Literary Agency; Joy Literary Agency; Kellock Company, Inc., The; Kern Literary Agency, Natasha; Kidde, Hoyt & Picard; Kleinman, Esq. of Graybill & English L.L.C., Jeffrey M.; Klinger, Inc., Harvey; Knight Agency, The; Konner Literary

Agency, Linda; Koster Literary Agency, LLC, Elaine; Kouts, Literary Agent, Barbara S.; Larkin, Sabra Elliott; Larsen/Elizabeth Pomada Literary Agents, Michael; Lasher Agency, The Maureen; Levant & Wales, Literary Agency, Inc.; Levine Communications, Inc., James; Levine Literary Agency, Paul S.; Lewis & Company, Karen; Lincoln Literary Agency, Ray; Literary and Creative Artists, Inc.; Literary Group, The; Love Literary Agency, Nancy; Lowenstein Associates, Inc.; Lukeman Literary Management Ltd.; Mann Agency, Carol; Manus & Associates Literary Agency; Marshall Agency, The Evan; McBride Literary Agency, Margret; McGrath, Helen; McHugh Literary Agency; Michaels Literary Agency, Inc., Doris S.; Millard Literary Agency, Martha; Multimedia Product Development, Inc.; Mura Enterprises, Inc., Dee; Naggar Literary Agency, Jean V.; New Century Literary Agency; New England Publishing Associates, Inc.; Norma-Lewis Agency, The; Northwest Literary Services; Parks Agency, The Richard; Pinder Lane & Garon-Brooke Associates, Ltd.; Pine Associates, Inc, Arthur; Quicksilver Books-Literary Agents; Reichstein Literary Agency, The Naomi; Rein Books, Inc., Jody; Rhodes Literary Agency, Jodie; Rinaldi Literary Agency, Angela; Robbins Literary Agency, BJ; Roghaar Literary Agency, Inc., Linda; Rosenkranz Literary Agency, Rita; Ross Literary Agency, The Gail; Roth, Literary Representation, Carol Susan; Rotrosen Agency LLC, Jane; Scagnetti Talent & Literary Agency, Jack; Schiavone Literary Agency, Inc.; Schlessinger Agency, Blanche; Schulman, A Literary Agency, Susan; Sebastian Literary Agency; Seligman, Literary Agent, Lynn; Shepard Agency, The; Simenauer Literary Agency, Jacqueline; Singer Literary Agency Inc., Evelyn; Stauffer Associates, Nancy; Sunshine Literary Agency; Swayne Agency Literary Management & Consulting, Inc., The; Targ Literary Agency, Inc., Roslyn; Teal Literary Agency, Patricia; Toad Hall, Inc.; Travis Literary Agency, Susan; 2M Communications Ltd.; United Tribes; Vines Agency, Inc., The; Watt & Associates, Sandra; Waxman Agency, Inc., Scott; Weiner Literary Agency, Cherry; Witherspoon & Associates, Inc.; Wonderland Press, Inc., The; Writers House; Zachary Shuster Agency

Sociology: Agents Inc. for Medical and Mental Health Professionals; Allen Literary Agency, Linda; Allred and Allred Literary Agents; Altair Literary Agency; Amber Literary; Amster Literary Enterprises, Betsy; Authors & Artists Group, Inc.; Baldi Literary Agency, Malaga; Balkin Agency, Inc.; Bernstein & Associates, Inc., Pam; Bial Agency, Daniel; Bleecker Street Associates; Boston Literary Group, The; Bova Literary Agency, The Barbara; Brandt & Brandt Literary Agents Inc.; Buck Agency, Howard; Castiglia Literary Agency; Coover Agency, The Doe; Cypher, The Cypher Agency, James R.; Dawson Associates, Liza; Dijkstra Literary Agency, Sandra; Educational Design Services, Inc.; Ellison Inc., Nicholas; Everitt Literary Agency, Inc., Charles; Finesse Literary Agency; Flaherty, Literary Agent, Joyce A.; Fleury Agency, B.R.; ForthWrite Literary Agency; Fullerton Associates, Sheryl B.; Gibson Agency, The Sebastian; Gislason Agency, The; Goodman-Andrew-Agency, Inc.; Grosvenor Literary Agency, The; Hawkins & Associates, Inc., John; Heacock Literary Agency, Inc.; Henshaw Group, Richard; Herner Rights Agency, Susan; Hochmann Books, John L.; J de S Associates Inc.; Jabberwocky Literary Agency; JCA Literary Agency, Inc.; Joy Literary Agency; Kellock Company, Inc., The; Kidde, Hoyt & Picard; Kleinman, Esq. of Graybill & English L.L.C., Jeffrey M.; Larsen/Elizabeth Pomada Literary Agents, Michael; Lasher Agency, The Maureen; Levine Communications, Inc., James; Levine Literary Agency, Paul S.; Lieberman Associates, Robert; Lincoln Literary Agency, Ray; Lipkind Agency, Wendy; Literary Group, The; Love Literary Agency, Nancy; Lowenstein Associates, Inc.; Mann Agency, Carol; McBride Literary Agency, Margret; Multimedia Product Development, Inc.; Mura Enterprises, Inc., Dee; Naggar Literary Agency, Jean V.; Nazor Literary Agency, Karen; New Century Literary Agency; New England Publishing Associates, Inc.; Parks Agency, The Richard; Pevner, Inc., Stephen; Quicksilver Books-Literary Agents; Raymond, Literary Agent, Charlotte Cecil; Reichstein Literary Agency, The Naomi; Rein Books, Inc., Jody; Rinaldi Literary Agency, Angela; Rittenberg Literary Agency, Inc., Ann; Robbins Literary Agency, BJ; Ross Literary Agency, The Gail; Russell & Volkening; Sage Acre Marketing & Publishing Solutions; Schiavone Literary Agency, Inc.; Schulman, A Literary Agency, Susan; Sebastian Literary Agency; Seligman, Literary Agent, Lynn; Shepard Agency, The; Shepard Agency, The Robert E.; Slopen Literary Agency, Beverley; Spieler Agency, The; Spitzer Literary Agency, Philip G.; Straus Agency, Inc., Robin; United Tribes; Vines Agency, Inc., The; Wald Associates, Inc., Mary Jack; Weiner Literary Agency, Cherry; Weingel-Fidel Agency, The; Zeckendorf Assoc. Inc., Susan

Sports: Agents Inc. for Medical and Mental Health Professionals; Alive Communications, Inc.; Allred and Allred Literary Agents; Altair Literary Agency; Authentic Creations Literary Agency; Authors Alliance, Inc.; Authors & Artists Group, Inc.; Bedford Book Works, Inc., The; Bial Agency, Daniel; Black Literary Agency, David; Bleecker Street Associates; Boates Literary Agency, Reid; Brandt & Brandt Literary Agents Inc.; Browne Ltd., Pema; Buck Agency, Howard; Connor Literary Agency; Cypher, The Cypher Agency, James R.; DHS Literary, Inc.; Dijkstra Literary Agency, Sandra; Donovan Literary, Jim; Ducas, Robert; Everitt Literary Agency, Inc., Charles; Finesse Literary Agency; Fogelman Literary Agency, The; Fredericks Literary Agency, Inc., Jeanne; Gartenberg, Literary Agent, Max; Gibson Agency, The Sebastian; Goodman-Andrew-Agency, Inc.; Greene, Arthur B.; Hawkins & Associates, Inc., John; Henshaw Group, Richard; J de S Associates Inc.; Jabberwocky Literary Agency; JCA Literary Agency, Inc.; JLA Literary Agency; Kellock Company, Inc., The; Ketz Agency, Louise B.; Klinger, Inc., Harvey; Knight Agency,

The; Larsen/Elizabeth Pomada Literary Agents, Michael; Lasher Agency, The Maureen; Levine Communications, Inc., James; Levine Literary Agency, Paul S.; Lincoln Literary Agency, Ray; Literary Group, The; Lowenstein Associates, Inc.; McBride Literary Agency, Margret; McCauley, Gerard; McGrath, Helen; Michaels Literary Agency, Inc., Doris S.; Multimedia Product Development, Inc.; Mura Enterprises, Inc., Dee; National Writers Literary Agency; Nazor Literary Agency, Karen; New Century Literary Agency; Northwest Literary Services; Quicksilver Books-Literary Agents; Reichstein Literary Agency, The Naomi; Rhodes Literary Agency, Jodie; Robbins Literary Agency, BJ; Rosenkranz Literary Agency, Rita; Ross Literary Agency, The Gail; Rotrosen Agency LLC, Jane; Russell & Volkening; Scagnetti Talent & Literary Agency, Jack; Shepard Agency, The; Shepard Agency, The Robert E.; Spitzer Literary Agency, Philip G.; Vines Agency, Inc., The; Ware Literary Agency, John A.; Watt & Associates, Sandra; Waxman Agency, Inc., Scott; Wieser & Wieser, Inc.; Zachary Shuster Agency

Translations: Balkin Agency, Inc.; Daves Agency, Joan; Ellison Inc., Nicholas; Grosvenor Literary Agency, The; J de S Associates Inc.; JCA Literary Agency, Inc.; JLA Literary Agency; Kleinman, Esq. of Graybill & English L.L.C., Jeffrey M.; Lukeman Literary Management Ltd.; Northwest Literary Services; Sanders Literary Agency, Victoria; Schulman, A Literary Agency, Susan; Seligman, Literary Agent, Lynn; United Tribes; Vines Agency, Inc., The; Wald Associates, Inc., Mary Jack; Watkins Loomis Agency, Inc.

Travel: Acacia House Publishing Services Ltd.; Baldi Literary Agency, Malaga; Balkin Agency, Inc.; Bial Agency, Daniel; Borchardt Inc., Georges; Buck Agency, Howard; Coover Agency, The Doe; Cypher, The Cypher Agency, James R.; Ducas, Robert; Flaherty, Literary Agent, Joyce A.; Franklin Associates, Ltd., Lynn C.; Gibson Agency, The Sebastian; Hawkins & Associates, Inc., John; James Peter Associates, Inc.; Larsen/Elizabeth Pomada Literary Agents, Michael; Love Literary Agency, Nancy; Lowenstein Associates, Inc.; Multimedia Product Development, Inc.; Mura Enterprises, Inc., Dee; Naggar Literary Agency, Jean V.; National Writers Literary Agency; Nazor Literary Agency, Karen; Northwest Literary Services; Parks Agency, The Richard; Pevner, Inc., Stephen; Rittenberg Literary Agency, Inc., Ann; Simenauer Literary Agency, Jacqueline; Spieler Agency, The; 2M Communications Ltd.; Van der Leun & Associates; Vines Agency, Inc., The; Ware Literary Agency, John A.; Watt & Associates, Sandra; Weingel-Fidel Agency, The; Witherspoon & Associates, Inc.

True Crime/Investigative: Allen, Literary Agent, James; Allred and Allred Literary Agents; Amber Literary; Appleseeds Management; Authentic Creations Literary Agency; Authors Alliance, Inc.; Authors & Artists Group, Inc.; Baldi Literary Agency, Malaga; Balkin Agency, Inc.; Bernstein & Associates, Inc., Pam; Bial Agency, Daniel; Bleecker Street Associates; Boates Literary Agency, Reid; Bookmark Literary Agency; Boston Literary Group, The; Bova Literary Agency, The Barbara; Brandt & Brandt Literary Agents Inc.; Browne Ltd., Pema; Buck Agency, Howard; Bykofsky Associates, Inc., Sheree; Charisma Communications, Ltd.; Clausen, Mays & Tahan, LLC; Collin Literary Agent, Frances; Connor Literary Agency; Coover Agency, The Doe; Core Creations, Inc.; Cypher, The Cypher Agency, James R.; DH Literary, Inc.; DHS Literary, Inc.; Dijkstra Literary Agency, Sandra; Donovan Literary, Jim; Ducas, Robert; Dystel Literary Management, Jane; Elek Associates, Peter; Ellenberg Literary Agency, Ethan; Ellison Inc., Nicholas; Elmo Agency Inc., Ann; Everitt Literary Agency, Inc., Charles; Finesse Literary Agency; Fleury Agency, B.R.; Fogelman Literary Agency, The; Gartenberg, Literary Agent, Max; Gibson Agency, The Sebastian; Goodman-Andrew-Agency, Inc.; Grace Literary Agency, Carroll; Greene, Literary Agent, Randall Elisha; Grosvenor Literary Agency, The; Halsey North, Reese; Henshaw Group, Richard; Herner Rights Agency, Susan; Jabberwocky Literary Agency; JCA Literary Agency, Inc.; JLA Literary Agency; Kleinman, Esq. of Graybill & English L.L.C., Jeffrey M.; Klinger, Inc., Harvey; Knight Agency, The; Lampack Agency, Inc., Peter; Larkin, Sabra Elliott; Larsen/Elizabeth Pomada Literary Agents, Michael; Lasher Agency, The Maureen; Lawyer's Literary Agency, Inc.; Levine Literary Agency, Paul S.; Literary Group, The; Love Literary Agency, Nancy; Lowenstein Associates, Inc.; Lukeman Literary Management Ltd.; Marshall Agency, The Evan; McBride Literary Agency, Margret; McHugh Literary Agency; Millard Literary Agency, Martha; Multimedia Product Development, Inc.; Mura Enterprises, Inc., Dee; New Century Literary Agency; New England Publishing Associates, Inc.; Norma-Lewis Agency, The; Northwest Literary Services; Otitis Media; Pinder Lane & Garon-Brooke Associates, Ltd.; Quicksilver Books-Literary Agents; Real Criminals; Reichstein Literary Agency, The Naomi; Renaissance Literary Agency; Rhodes Literary Agency, Jodie; Rinaldi Literary Agency, Angela; Robbins Literary Agency, BJ; Robbins Office, Inc., The; Ross Literary Agency, The Gail; Rotrosen Agency LLC, Jane; Russell & Volkening; Sage Acre Marketing & Publishing Solutions; Scagnetti Talent & Literary Agency, Jack; Schiavone Literary Agency, Inc.; Schlessinger Agency, Blanche; Schulman, A Literary Agency, Susan; Sedgeband Literary Associates; Seligman, Literary Agent, Lynn; Simenauer Literary Agency, Jacqueline; Slopen Literary Agency, Beverley; Spitzer Literary Agency, Philip G.; Teal Literary Agency, Patricia; Vines Agency, Inc., The; Wald Associates, Inc., Mary Jack; Ware Literary Agency, John A.; Watkins Loomis Agency, Inc.; Watt & Associates, Sandra; Weingel-Fidel Agency, The; West Coast Literary Associates; Wieser & Wieser, Inc.; Witherspoon & Associates, Inc.; Writers House; Zachary Shuster Agency; Zeckendorf Assoc. Inc., Susan

Women's Issues/Women's Studies: Alive Communications, Inc.; Allen Literary Agency, Linda; Allred and Allred Literary Agents; Altair Literary Agency; Amber Literary; Amster Literary Enterprises, Betsy; Authentic Creations Literary Agency; Authors & Artists Group, Inc.; Baldi Literary Agency, Malaga; Bent, Literary Agent, Jenny; Bernstein & Associates, Inc., Pam; Bial Agency, Daniel; Bleecker Street Associates; Boates Literary Agency, Reid; Books & Such; Borchardt Inc., Georges; Boston Literary Group, The; Bova Literary Agency, The Barbara; Brandt & Brandt Literary Agents Inc.; Brown Associates Inc., Marie; Browne Ltd., Pema; Buck Agency, Howard; Bykofsky Associates, Inc., Sheree; C G & W Associates; Carvainis Agency, Inc., Maria; Casselman Literary Agency, Martha; Castiglia Literary Agency; Clausen, Mays & Tahan, LLC; Cohen Agency, The; Cohen, Inc. Literary Agency, Ruth; Connor Literary Agency; Coover Agency, The Doe; Crawford Literary Agency; Cypher, The Cypher Agency, James R.; Daves Agency, Joan; Dawson Associates, Liza; DH Literary, Inc.; Dijkstra Literary Agency, Sandra; Dystel Literary Management, Jane; Educational Design Services, Inc.; Ellison Inc., Nicholas; Elmo Agency Inc., Ann; Feigen/Parrent Literary Management; Finesse Literary Agency; Flaherty, Literary Agent, Joyce A.; Fogelman Literary Agency, The; ForthWrite Literary Agency; Fredericks Literary Agency, Inc., Jeanne; Freymann Literary Agency, Sarah Jane; Fullerton Associates, Sheryl B.; Gartenberg, Literary Agent, Max; Gibson Agency, The Sebastian; Goodman-Andrew-Agency, Inc.; Grace Literary Agency, Carroll; Grosvenor Literary Agency, The; Halsey North, Reese; Hawkins & Associates, Inc., John; Heacock Literary Agency, Inc.; Henshaw Group, Richard; Herner Rights Agency, Susan; Hill Associates, Frederick; Jabberwocky Literary Agency; James Peter Associates, Inc.; JCA Literary Agency, Inc.; Joy Literary Agency; Kellock Company, Inc., The; Kern Literary Agency, Natasha; Kidde, Hoyt & Picard; Kirkland Literary Agency, The; Kleinman, Esq. of Graybill & English L.L.C., Jeffrey M.; Klinger, Inc., Harvey; Knight Agency, The; Konner Literary Agency, Linda; Koster Literary Agency, LLC, Elaine; Kouts, Literary Agent, Barbara S.; Lampack Agency, Inc., Peter; Larkin, Sabra Elliott; Larsen/Elizabeth Pomada Literary Agents, Michael; Lasher Agency, The Maureen; Levant & Wales, Literary Agency, Inc.; Levine Communications, Inc., James; Levine Literary Agency, Inc., Ellen; Levine Literary Agency, Paul S.; Lewis & Company, Karen; Lincoln Literary Agency, Ray; Lipkind Agency, Wendy; Literary Group, The; Love Literary Agency, Nancy; Lowenstein Associates, Inc.; Lukeman Literary Management Ltd.; Maccoby Literary Agency, Gina; Mann Agency, Carol; Manus & Associates Literary Agency; Marshall Agency, The Evan; McBride Literary Agency, Margret; McGrath, Helen; Michaels Literary Agency, Inc., Doris S.; Millard Literary Agency, Martha; Multimedia Product Development, Inc.; Mura Enterprises, Inc., Dee; Naggar Literary Agency, Jean V.; Nazor Literary Agency, Karen; New Century Literary Agency; New England Publishing Associates, Inc.; Nine Muses and Apollo; Norma-Lewis Agency, The; Northwest Literary Services; Parks Agency, The Richard; Paton Literary Agency, Kathi J.; Quicksilver Books-Literary Agents; Rees Literary Agency, Helen; Reichstein Literary Agency, The Naomi; Rein Books, Inc., Jody; Rhodes Literary Agency, Jodie; Rinaldi Literary Agency, Angela; Rittenberg Literary Agency, Inc., Ann; Robbins Literary Agency, BJ; Roghaar Literary Agency, Inc., Linda; Rosenkranz Literary Agency, Rita; Rotrosen Agency LLC, Jane; Rowland Agency, The Damaris; Russell & Volkening; Sage Acre Marketing & Publishing Solutions; Sanders Literary Agency, Victoria; Scagnetti Talent & Literary Agency, Jack; Schulman, A Literary Agency, Susan; Sebastian Literary Agency; Seligman, Literary Agent, Lynn; Shepard Agency, The; Shepard Agency, The Robert E.; Simenauer Literary Agency, Jacqueline; Singer Literary Agency Inc., Evelyn; Slopen Literary Agency, Beverley; Snell Literary Agency, Michael; Spieler Agency, The; Straus Agency, Inc., Robin; Swayne Agency Literary Management & Consulting, Inc., The; Taylor, Literary Agent, Rebecca; Teal Literary Agency, Patricia; Travis Literary Agency, Susan; 2M Communications Ltd.; United Tribes; Vines Agency, Inc., The; Ware Literary Agency, John A.; Watkins Loomis Agency, Inc.; Watt & Associates, Sandra; Weingel-Fidel Agency, The; West Coast Literary Associates; Witherspoon & Associates, Inc.; Writers House; Zachary Shuster Agency; Zeckendorf Assoc. Inc., Susan

Literary Agents: Fee-charging

This section contains literary agencies that charge a fee to writers in addition to taking a commission on sales. Several agencies charge fees only under certain circumstances, generally for previously unpublished writers. These agencies are indicated by a briefcase $\$$ symbol. Most agencies will consider you unpublished if you have subsidy publishing, local or small press publication credits only; check with a prospective agency before sending material to see if you fit its definition of published.

Agents who charge one-time marketing fees in excess of $100 are also included in this section. Those who charge less than $100 and do not charge for other services appear in the Literary Agents: Nonfee-charging section. Some agents in this section also charge for office expenses such as photocopying, foreign postage, long distance phone calls or express mail services. Often your agent will deduct such expenses from the advance or royalties. Make sure you have a clear understanding of what these expenses are before signing any agency agreement.

For a detailed explanation of the agency listings and for more information on approaching agents, read Quick Start Guide to Using Your *Guide to Literary Agents* on page 2 and Finding the Right Agent: What Every Writer Needs to Know on page 16. When reading through this section, keep in mind the following information specific to the fee-charging listings:

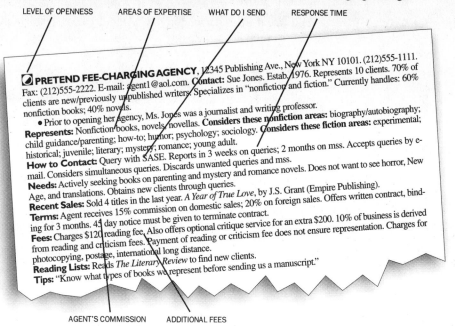

LEVEL OF OPENNESS AREAS OF EXPERTISE WHAT DO I SEND RESPONSE TIME

PRETEND FEE-CHARGING AGENCY, 12345 Publishing Ave., New York NY 10101. (212)555-1111. Fax: (212)555-2222. E-mail: agent1@aol.com. **Contact:** Sue Jones. Estab. 1976. Represents 10 clients. 70% of clients are new/previously unpublished writers. Specializes in "nonfiction and fiction." Currently handles: 60% nonfiction books; 40% novels.
• Prior to opening her agency, Ms. Jones was a journalist and writing professor.
Represents: Nonfiction books, novels, novellas. **Considers these nonfiction areas:** biography/autobiography; child guidance/parenting; how-to; humor; psychology; sociology. **Considers these fiction areas:** experimental; historical; juvenile; literary; mystery; romance; young adult.
How to Contact: Query with SASE. Reports in 3 weeks on queries; 2 months on mss. Accepts queries by e-mail. Considers simultaneous queries and mss. Discards unwanted queries and mss.
Needs: Actively seeking books on parenting and mystery and romance novels. Does not want to see horror, New Age, and translations. Obtains new clients through queries.
Recent Sales: Sold 4 titles in the last year. *A Year of True Love,* by J.S. Grant (Empire Publishing).
Terms: Agent receives 15% commission on domestic sales; 20% on foreign sales. Offers written contract, binding for 3 months. 45 day notice must be given to terminate contract.
Fees: Charges $120 reading fee. Also offers optional critique service for an extra $200. 10% of business is derived from reading and criticism fees. Payment of reading or criticism fee does not ensure representation. Charges for photocopying, postage, international long distance.
Reading Lists: Reads *The Literary Review* to find new clients.
Tips: "Know what types of books we represent before sending us a manuscript."

AGENT'S COMMISSION ADDITIONAL FEES

QUICK REFERENCE ICONS

At the beginning of some listings, you will find one or more of the following symbols for quick identification of features particular to that listing.

N: Agency new to this edition.

✔ Change in address, contact information or phone number from last year's edition.

⑤ Agents who charge fees to previously unpublished writers only.

♦ Canadian agency.

OPENNESS

Each agency has an icon indicating its openness to submissions. Before contacting any agency, check the listing to make sure it is open to new clients.

○ Newer agency actively seeking clients.

◐ Agency seeking both new and established writers.

◑ Agency prefers to work with established writers, mostly obtains new clients through referrals.

◎ Agency handling only certain types of work or work by writers under certain circumstances.

⊘ Agency not currently seeking new clients. We include these agencies to let you know they are currently not open to new clients. *Unless you have a strong recommendation from someone well respected in the field, our advice is to avoid approaching these agents.*

SUBHEADS

Each listing is broken down into subheads to make locating specific information easier. In the first section, you'll find contact information for each agency, including the agency's address, phone number, e-mail and website address. Also provided here is information on an agency's size, its willingness to work with new or previously unpublished writers, and its areas of specialization.

Member Agents: To help you locate the best person for your writing, agencies with more than one agent list member names and its individual specialties.

Represents: Only query agents who represent the type of material you write. Here agencies specify what nonfiction and fiction subjects they consider. To help narrow your search, check the **Agents Specialties Index** immediately after the fee-charging listings.

How to Contact: Most agents prefer initially to receive a query letter briefly describing your work. (See Queries That Made It Happen on page 35.) Some agents ask for an outline and a number of sample chapters, but send these only if requested to do so. Agents also indicate if they accept queries by fax or e-mail, and if they are receptive to simultaneous submissions.

Needs: Here agents list what areas they are currently seeking as well as subjects they do *not* wish to receive. Also listed is the agent's preferred way of meeting new clients.

Recent Sales: Agents provide specific titles they've sold to give a sense of the types of material they represent. Looking at the publisher of those titles also can tell you the caliber of publishing contacts the agent has developed. Just having an agent is not enough—you want an agent who can sell your work.

Terms: The sales commissions are the same as those taken by nonfee-charging agents: 10 to 15 percent for domestic sales, 20 to 25 percent for foreign or dramatic sales, with the difference going to the co-agent. Also listed are details about contracts.

Fees: On top of their commission, agents in this section charge writers various fees. Often, payment of reading or critique fees does not ensure representation. In order to understand what services are provided for the different fees and to learn the issues surrounding fee-charging agents, read the Reading Fees and Critique Services section below, and Understanding Fees— What Writers Must Know on page 15. Also listed here are any additional office expenses.

Writers' Conferences: Here agents list the writers' conferences they attend to discover new talent. For more information about a specific conference, check the Writers' Conferences section starting on page 292.

Reading List: Learn what magazines and journals agents read to discover potential clients.

Tips: Agents offer advice for writers and additional instructions about submitting to their agency.

SPECIAL INDEXES AND ADDITIONAL HELP

This book contains several indexes to facilitate your search for an agent. Use the indexes to help narrow your list of possible agents to query.

Additional Fee-charging Agents: Many literary agents are also interested in scripts; many script agents will also consider book manuscripts. Fee-charging script agents who primarily sell scripts but also handle at least 10 to 15 percent book manuscripts appear among the listings in this section, with the contact information, breakdown of work currently handled and a note to check the full listing in the script section. Fee-charging script agencies that sell scripts and less than 10 to 15 percent book manuscripts appear at the end of this section on page 224. Complete listings for these agents also appear in the Script Agents section.

Agents Specialties Index: Immediately following this section of listings is an index which organizes agencies according to the subjects they are interested in receiving. This index should help you compose a list of agents specializing in your areas. Cross-referencing categories and concentrating on agents interested in two or more aspects of your manuscript might increase your chances of success. Agencies open to all nonfiction or fiction topics are grouped under the subject heading "open."

Agents Index: Often you will read about an agent who is an employee of a larger agency and you may not be able to locate her business phone or address. Starting on page 341 is a list of agents' names in alphabetical order along with the name of the agency they work for. Find the name of the person you would like to contact and then check the agency listing.

Geographic Index: For writers looking for an agent close to home, this index lists agents state-by-state.

Agencies Indexed by Openness to Submissions: This index lists agencies according to their receptivity to new clients.

Listing Index: This index lists all agencies and conferences listed in the book.

READING FEES AND CRITIQUE SERVICES

The issue of reading fees is as controversial for literary agents as for those looking for representation. While some agents dismiss the concept as inherently unethical and a scam, others see merit in the system, provided an author goes into it with his eyes open. Some writers spend hundreds of dollars for an "evaluation" that consists of a poorly written critique full of boiler-plate language that says little, if anything, about their individual work. Others have received the helpful feedback they needed to get their manuscript in shape and have gone on to publish their work successfully.

Since January 1, 1996, however, all members of the AAR have been prohibited from directly charging reading fees. Until that time some members were allowed to continue to charge fees, provided they adhered to guidelines designed to protect the client. A copy of the AAR's Canon of Ethics may be obtained for $7 and a 55¢ SAE. The address is listed in Professional Organizations toward the end of the book.

Be wary of an agent who recommends a specific book doctor. While the relationship may be that the agent trusts that professional editor's work, it is too hard to tell if there are other reasons the agent is working with him (like the agent is receiving a kickback for the referral). As with the AAR, the Writers Guild of America, which franchises literary agencies dealing largely in scripts, prohibits their signatories from such recommendations simply because it is open to abuse.

Researching agents

In discussing consideration of a fee-charging agent, we must underscore the importance of research. Don't be bowled over by an impressive brochure or an authoritative manner. At the same time, overly aggressive skepticism may kill your chances with a legitimate agent. Business-like, professional behavior will help you gather the material you need to make an informed decision.

- **Ask questions about the fees.** Obtain a fee schedule, making sure you understand what the fees cover and what to expect for your money.
- **Request a sample critique.** Looking at what the agent has done for another person's manuscript is the best way to decide if the critique is worth the price. Are the suggestions helpful and specific? Do they offer advice you couldn't get elsewhere, such as in writing groups, conferences and seminars, or reference books?
- **Ask for recent sales an agent has made.** Many agents have a pre-printed list of sales they can send you. If there haven't been any sales made in the past two years, what is the agent living on? An agent's worth to you, initially, is who they know and work with. In the listings we provide information on the percentage of income an agency receives from commissions on sales and the percentage from reading or critique fees.
- **Verify a few of these sales.** To verify the publisher has a book by that title, check *Books in Print*. To verify the agent made the sale, call the contracts department of the publisher and ask who the agent of record is for a particular title.

Recently, there has been a trend among a few agents to recommend contracts with subsidy publishers that ask the writer to pay from $3,500 to $6,000 toward the cost of publication. These deals are open to writers directly, without the intermediating "assistance" of an agent. Your best defense is to carefully examine the list of an agent's recent sales and investigate some of the publishers. We chose not to include agents who work with subsidy publishers.

Don't hesitate to ask the questions that will help you decide. The more you know about an agent and her abilities, the fewer unpleasant surprises you'll receive.

Different types of fees

Fees range from one agency to another in nomenclature, price and purpose. Here are some of the more frequent services and their generally accepted definitions.

- **Reading fee.** This is charged for reading a manuscript (most agents do not charge to look at queries alone). Often the fee is paid to outside readers. It is generally a one-time, nonrefundable fee, but some agents will return the fee or credit it to your account if they decide to take you on as a client. Often an agent will offer to refund the fee upon sale of the book, but that isn't necessarily a sign of good faith. If the agency never markets your manuscript no sale would ever be made and the fee never refunded.
- **Evaluation fee.** Sometimes a reading fee includes a written evaluation, but many agents charge for this separately. An evaluation may be a one-paragraph report on the marketability of a manuscript or a several-page evaluation covering marketability along with flaws and strengths of the manuscript.
- **Marketing fees.** Usually a one-time charge to offset the costs of handling work, marketing fees cover a variety of expenses and may include initial reading or evaluation. Beware of agencies charging a monthly marketing fee; there is nothing to compel them to submit your work in a timely way if they are getting paid anyway.
- **Critiquing service.** Although "critique" and "evaluation" are sometimes used interchangeably, a critique is usually more extensive, with suggestions on ways to improve the manuscript. Many agents offer critiques as a separate service and have a standard fee scale, based on a per-page or word-length basis. Some agents charge fees based on the extent of the service required, ranging from overall review to line-by-line commentary.

- **Editing service.** While we do not list businesses whose primary source of income is from editing, we do list agencies who also offer this service. Many do not distinguish between critiques and edits, but we define editing services as critiques that include detailed suggestions on how to improve the work and reduce weaknesses. Editing services can be charged on similar bases as critiquing services.
- **Other services.** Depending on an agent's background and abilities, the agent may offer a variety of other services to writers including ghostwriting, typing, copyediting, proofreading, translating, book publicity and legal advice.

Be forwarned that payment of a critique or editing fee does not ensure an agent will take you on as a client. However, if you feel you need more than sales help and do not mind paying for an evaluation or critique from a professional, the agents listed in this section may interest you.

FEE-CHARGING AGENTS

$ Ⓐ **AEI/ATCHITY EDITORIAL/ENTERTAINMENT INTERNATIONAL, Literary Management & Motion Picture Production**, 9601 Wilshire Blvd., Box 1202, Beverly Hills CA 90210. (323)932-0407. Fax: (323)932-0321. E-mail: aeikja@lainet.com. Website: www.aeionline.com. **Contact:** Kenneth Atchity. Estab. 1996. Represents 50 clients. 75% of clients are new/previously unpublished writers. Specializes in novel film tie-ins. "We also specialize in taking successfully self-published books to the national market." Currently handles: 30% nonfiction books; 40% novels; 30% movie scripts.

● Prior to opening his agency, Dr. Atchity was a professor of comparative literature at Occidental College, a Fullbright Professor at University of Bologna, and an instructor from 1970-1987 at the UCLA writer's program. He is the author of 13 books and has produced 20 films for video, television and theater. He was also co-editor of *Dreamworks*, a quarterly devoted to the relationship between art and dreams.

Member Agents: Kenneth Atchity (President); Chi-Li Wong (Partner and Vice President of Development and Production); Vincent Atchity (Associate Manager, Executive Vice President of Writers Lifeline); Kendra Mitchell (associate manager); Margo Hamilton (associate manager); Vicki Preminger (associate manager); Elizabeth Fujiwara (Honolulu); Lenny Cavellero (Boston); Mai-Ding Wong (New York); Robbyn Leonard (San Francisco); Andrea McKeown (Vice President); David Angsten (Vice President Development); Julie Mooney (senior editor), Rosemary McKenna (Vice Presidents Research, AEI Reference).

Represents: Nonfiction books, novels, movie scripts, TV scripts. **Considers these nonfiction areas:** biography/autobiography; business; government/politics/law; money/finance/economics; New Age/metaphysics; popular culture; self-help/personal improvement; true crime/investigative; women's issues/women's studies. **Considers these fiction areas:** action/adventure; contemporary issues; erotica; historical; horror; literary; mainstream; mystery/suspense; romance; science fiction; thriller/espionage.

Also Handles: Feature film, TV MOW, no episodic. **Considers these script subject areas:** action/adventure; comedy; contemporary issues; detective/police/crime; erotica; horror; mainstream; mystery/suspense; psychic/supernatural; romantic comedy and drama; science fiction; teen; thriller.

How to Contact: Send query letter, including synopsis and first 50 pages/3 sample chapters, with SASE. "Nothing, including scripts, will be returned without the SASE. Please send a professional return envelope and sufficient postage. Make your cover letter to the point and focused, your synopsis compelling and dramatic." Accepts queries by fax and e-mail. Prefers to be only reader. For books, reports in 2 weeks on queries; 2 months on mss. For scripts, reports in 1 month on queries; 2 months on mss. Returns materials only with SASE.

Needs: No "episodic" scripts, treatments, or ideas; no "category" fiction of any kind. Nothing drug-related, fundamental religious. No poetry, children's books, "interior" confessional fiction or novelty books. "We are always looking for true, heroic, *contemporary* women's stories for both book and television. We have a fondness for thrillers (both screenplays and novels), romantic comedies, as well as for mainstream nonfiction appealing to everyone today. We rarely do 'small audience' books." Obtains new clients through referrals, directories.

Recent Sales: Sold 16 book titles and 7 script projects in the last year. *The Adams Financial and Accounting Dictionary*, by Howard Bonham (Adams); *I Don't Have To Make Everything All Better*, by Gary and Joy Lundberg (Viking); *A Midnight Carole*, by Patricia Davis (St. Martin's Press). *Movie script(s) optioned/sold: Life, or Somthing Like It* (New Regency); *Eulogy for Joseph Way* (Warner Brothers).

Terms: For books, agent receives 15% commission on domestic sales; 30% on foreign sales. Offers written contract, binding for 1 year, with 30 day cancellation clause. For scripts, agent receives 15% commission; (0% when produce).

Fees: No reading fee for nonfiction, screenplays and fiction by previously published writers. $35 processing fee for unsolicited fiction proposals from unpublished writers. $150 one-time advance against expenses, upon signing, for previously unpublished writers. Offers criticism service through "AEI Writers Lifeline," with fees ranging from $250-750. "We offer this service to writers requesting specific feedback for their careers or seeking to enter our Lifeline Program for one-on-one coaching. The Writers Lifeline Program offers proposal, rewriting and ghostwriting services." 10% of revenue is derived from reading fees or criticism service. Payment of criticism or reading fee does not ensure representation.

Tips: "Take writing seriously as a career, which requires disciplined time and full attention (as described in *The Mercury Transition* and *A Writer's Time* by Kenneth Atchity). Most submissions, whether fiction or nonfiction, are rejected because the writing is not at a commercially competitive dramatic level. Our favorite client is one who has the desire and talent to develop both a novel and a film career and who is determined to learn everything possible about the business of writing, publishing, and producing. Dream big. Risk it. Never give up. Go for it! The rewards in this career are as endless as your imagination, and the risks, though real, are not greater than the risk of suffocating on a more secure career path. Begin by learning all you can about the business of writing, publishing and producing, and recognizing that as far-off and exalted as they may seem, the folks in these professions are as human as anyone else. We're enthusiasts, like you. Make us enthused."

[$] [✏] THE AHEARN AGENCY, INC., 2021 Pine St., New Orleans LA 70118-5456. (504)861-8395. Fax: (504)866-6434. E-mail: pahearn@aol.com. **Contact:** Pamela G. Ahearn. Estab. 1992. Member of RWA. Represents 25 clients. 20% of clients are new/previously unpublished writers. Specializes in historical romance; also very interested in mysteries and suspense fiction. Currently handles: 15% nonfiction books; 85% novels.

● Prior to opening her agency, Ms. Ahearn was an agent for eight years and an editor with Bantam Books.

Represents: Nonfiction books, novels, short story collections (if stories previously published). **Considers these nonfiction areas:** animals; biography; business; child guidance/parenting; current affairs; ethnic/cultural interests; gay/lesbian issues; health/medicine; history; juvenile nonfiction; music/dance/theater/film; popular culture; self-help/personal improvement; true crime/investigative; women's issues/women's studies. **Considers these fiction areas:** action/adventure; contemporary issues; detective/police/crime; ethnic; family saga; fantasy; feminist; gay; glitz; historical; horror; humor/satire; juvenile; lesbian; literary; mainstream; mystery/suspense; psychic/supernatural; regional; romance (contemporary, gothic, historical, regency); science fiction; thriller/espionage; westerns/frontier.

How to Contact: Query with SASE. Reports in 1 month on queries; 10 weeks on mss.

Needs: Does not want to receive category romance. Obtains new clients "usually through listings such as this one and client recommendations. Sometimes at conferences."

Recent Sales: *The Concubine's Tattoo*, by Laura Joh Rowland (St. Martin's Press); *A Prince Among Men*, by Kate Moore (Avon Books); *In the Dark*, by Meagan McKinney (Kensington).

Terms: Agent receives 15% commission on domestic sales; 20% on foreign sales. Offers written contract, binding for 1 year; renewable by mutual consent.

Fees: "I charge a reading fee to previously unpublished authors, based on length of material. Fees range from $125-400 and are nonrefundable. When authors pay a reading fee, they receive a three- to five-page single-spaced critique of their work, addressing writing quality and marketability." Critiques written by Pamela G. Ahearn. Charges for photocopying. 10% of business derived from reading fees or criticism services. Payment of reading fee does not ensure representation.

Writers' Conferences: Midwest Writers Workshop, Moonlight & Magnolias, RWA National conference (Orlando); Virginia Romance Writers (Williamsburg, VA); Florida Romance Writers (Ft. Lauderdale, FL); Golden Triangle Writers Conference; Bouchercon (Monterey, November).

Tips: "Be professional! Always send in exactly what an agent/editor asks for, no more, no less. Keep query letters brief and to the point, giving your writing credentials and a very brief summary of your book. If one agent rejects you, keep trying—there are a lot of us out there!"

[✏] [◎] ALP ARTS CO., 221 Fox Rd., Suite 7, Golden CO 80403-8517. Phone/fax: (303)582-5189. E-mail: sffuller@alparts.com. **Contact:** Ms. Sandy Ferguson Fuller. Estab. 1994. Member of SCBWI. Represents 40 clients. 55% of clients are new/previously unpublished writers. "Specializes in children's books. Works with picture book authors and illustrators, also middle-grade and YA writers, nonfiction and fiction." Currently handles: 100% juvenile or young adult proposals.

● Prior to becoming an agent, Ms. Fuller worked for 25 years in all aspects of children's book publishing, including international work, editorial, sales, marketing, retailing, wholesale buying, consulting. She is also a published author/illustrator.

Member Agents: Sandy Ferguson Fuller, director; Lynn Volkens, administrative assistant.

Represents: Juvenile and young adult books, all types. **Considers juvenile nonfiction. Considers juvenile and young adult fiction, picture books.**

Also Handles: Scripts. "Will co-agent." **Considers these script areas:** juvenile (all); teen (all). Query with SASE. Reports in 3 weeks on queries; 2 months on mss.

How to Contact: Query with SASE. For picture books and easy readers send entire ms. Reports in 3 weeks on queries; 10 weeks on mss.

Needs: "Children's/YA—all books and related media products, including scripts and licensing programs." Does not want to receive any adult material. Obtains new clients from referrals, solicitation and at conferences.

Recent Sales: *Morning Dance*, by Hannert (Chronicle); *Geo Almanac*, by Siegel/McLoone (Blackbirch); *This Is the Sea That Feeds Us*, by Baldwin (Dawn). Other clients include Holly Huth, Kathy Johnson-Clarke, Pattie Schnetzler, Roberta Collier Morales, Frank Kramer, John Denver (Estate), Bonnie Turner, Hazel Krantz.

Terms: 10-15% commission on domestic sales. 20% illustration only. Offers written contract, with 30 day cancellation clause.

Fees: Basic consultation is $60/picture books, easy readers; $90 middle grade or young adult proposal. Contract custom to client's needs. Charges for postage, photocopying costs. Charges $25 fee/submission for nonpublished authors. Long-distance phone consultation at $60/hour plus phone bill. Consultation in person: $60/hour. Will prorate. Receipts supplied to client for all of the above. 30% of business derived from criticism fees.

Writers' Conferences: PPWC (Colorado Springs, CO, April); BEA (Chicago, June); SCBWI (October).

Reading List: Reads *Publishers Weekly*; *Booklist*; *Horn Book*; *SCBWI Bulletin*; *Children's Writer*; etc. to find new clients.

Tips: Agency representation is not for everyone. Some aspiring or published authors and/or illustrators have more confidence in their own abilities to target and market work. Others are 'territorial' or prefer to work directly with the publishers. The best agent/client relationships exist when complete trust is established prior to representation. I recommend at least one (or several) consultations via phone or in person with a prospective agent. References are important. Also, the author or illustrator should have a clear idea of the agent's role i.e., editorial/critiquing input, 'post-publication' responsibilities, exclusive or non-exclusive representation, fees, industry reputation, etc. Each author or illustrator should examine his or her objectives, talents, time constraints, and perhaps more important, personal rapport with an individual agent prior to representation."

AUTHOR AUTHOR LITERARY AGENCY LTD., P.O. Box 56534, Lougheed Mall R.P.O., Burnaby, British Columbia V3J 7W2 Canada. (604)415-0056. Fax: (604)415-0076. President: Joan Rickard. Associate Editor: Eileen McGaughey. **Contact:** Pat Litke. Estab. 1992. Member of Writers' Guild of Alberta, Federation of British Columbia Writers and CAA. Represents 20 clients. "Welcomes new writers." Currently handles: 20% nonfiction books; 5% scholarly books; 25% juvenile books; 45% novels; 5% short story collections.

Represents: Book-length fiction and nonfiction, adult and juvenile (of every genre except poetry, screenplays or magazine stories/articles).

How to Contact: "We prefer sample chapter submissions of about fifty consecutive pages, but writers may submit entire proposals. Due to publishers' constraints, book proposals should rarely exceed 100,000 words. Please ensure manuscripts are properly formatted: unbound; allow 1″ borders on all sides; double-space throughout manuscript (no extra double-spaces between paragraphs); indent paragraphs five character spaces; print size should provide about 250 words/page. No dot matrix. Include a brief synopsis of your proposal (*high impact*, as displayed on the back of books' covers), and your author's bio. Each may be shorter than, but not exceed, 100 words (double-space, indent paragraphs). For response to inquiries and/or return of submissions, writers must enclose self-addressed stamped envelopes *Note: stamps are not valid for mailing beyond a country's borders!* Send Canadian postage, IRCs, or certified check or international money order in Canadian currency. If you wish acknowledgment of your proposal's arrival, include SASE and pretyped letter or form." Accepts queries by fax. Considers simultaneous queries and submissions. Reports in about 1 month for queries; about 3 months for submissions. Returns materials only with SASE.

Recent Sales: *Wild Liard Waters*, by Ferdi Wenger (Caitlin); *Bull Rider*, by Floyd Cowan (Detselig); *Battling the Bulge*, by Roderick Dingwall, M.D. (Temeron Books).

Terms: Agent receives 15% commission on domestic (Canadian) sales; 20% on foreign (non-Canadian) sales. Offers written contract.

Fees: "No fee for authors book-published in the same genre as their current endeavors. Otherwise, to partially defray our time and disbursements in studying and responding to submissions, a nominal entry fee of US $75 per proposal is charged: certified checks or international (if non-Canadian) money orders only. If agency agrees to represent, no further fees are required. Charges for usual marketing disbursements only: photocopying of manuscripts, long-distance telephone/fax, and express of proposals to/from publishers. Long distance inquiries via phone or fax are returned collect. We do not utilize e-mail. Confers with and reports promptly to authors on marketing communications. Consulting fees to non-clients (e.g., marketing or contractual advice, etc.): $45/hr. Office hours: 9-5, Monday-Friday."

Tips: "Whether writing fiction or nonfiction, for adults or children, study your chosen genre thoroughly to learn style/technique and what publishers are contracting. Its a very fight, competitive market. Be professional with your presentation's appearance. Form *and* substance sell proposals. The initial impact sets the stage for agents and editors in anticipating the caliber of your literary ability. If undistracted by mechanical flaws, your audience may focus upon your proposal's content. For your guidance, our 22-page booklet, *"CRASH COURSE" for Proposals to Book and Magazine Publishers: Business Letters, Basic Punctuation/Information Guidelines & Manuscript Formatting*, is available for US $8.95 (includes postage/handling). Certified checks or international (if non-Canadian) money orders only."

THE AUTHOR'S AGENCY, P.O. Box 16590, Boise ID 83715-6590. (208)376-5477. E-mail: rjwinchell@aol.com. **Contact:** R.J. Winchell. Estab. 1995. Represents 40 clients. 35% of clients are new/previously unpublished writers. "We specialize in high concepts which have a dramatic impact." Currently handles: 50% nonfiction books; 50% novels.

● Prior to opening her agency, Ms. Winchell taught writing and wrote book reviews. Ms. Winchell is a summa

---

THE PUBLISHING FIELD is constantly changing! If you're still using this book and it is 2001 or later, buy the newest edition of *Guide to Literary Agents* at your favorite bookstore or order directly from Writer's Digest Books at (800)289-0963.

cum laude gradutate of Pacific Lutheran University and a nationally publisher writer.

Represents: Nonfiction books, novels, movie scripts, TV scripts. **Considers these nonfiction areas:** animals; anthropology/archaeology; biography/autobiography; business; child guidance/parenting; cooking/food/nutrition; crafts/hobbies; current affairs; education; ethnic/cultural interests; government/politics/law; health/medicine; history; how-to; humor; interior design/decorating; language/literature/criticism; memoirs; military/war; money/finance/economics; music/dance/theater/film; nature/environment; New Age/metaphysics; photography; popular culture; psychology; religious/inspirational; science/technology; self-help/personal improvement; sociology; sports; translations; travel; true crime/investigative; women's issues/women's studies. **Considers "any fiction supported by the author's endeavor to tell a story with excellent writing."**

Also Handles: Feature film, animation, TV MOW, miniseries, episodic drama, animation. Considers all script subject areas. "We represent very few scripts but we are open to them."

How to Contact: Query or send 3 chapters with SASE. Accepts queries by e-mail. "But, they must be to the point." **Considers simultaneous queries and submissions. Reports in 4-6 weeks. Returns materials only with SASE.**

Needs: Obtains new writers through "speaking engagements and referrals such as this book."

Recent Sales: *"What If Our World Is Their Heaven?" conversations with Philip K. Dick* (Overlook Press); Johnny Rutherford autobiography, by Johnny Rutherford with David Craft (Triumph Books).

Terms: Agent receives 15% commission on domestic sales; 15% on foreign sales. Offers written contract on project-by-project basis.

Fees: Charges for expenses (photocopying, etc.). 90% of business is derived from commissions on sales. "No reading fee, ever." Occasionally provides an editing service, charges $450 *minimum* for service. Editing service does not ensure representation.

Tips: "We obtain writers through speaking engagements, and referrals such as this book. We believe that writers make a valuable contribution to society. As such, we offer encouragement and support to writers, whether we represent them or not. Publishing continues to be competitive industry. Writers need not only talent, but patience with the process in order to see their work in print."

AUTHORS' MARKETING SERVICES LTD., 666 Spadina Ave., Suite 2508, Toronto, Ontario M5S 2H8 Canada. (416)463-7200. Fax: (416)920-5119. E-Mail: authors_lhoffman@compuserve.com. **Contact:** Larry Hoffman. Estab. 1978. Represents 17 clients. 25% of clients are new/previously unpublished writers. Specializes in thrillers, romance, parenting and self-help. Currently handles: 65% nonfiction books; 10% juvenile books; 20% novels; 5% other.

● Prior to opening his agency, Mr. Hoffman worked at Coles for five years and was director of marketing for the book store chain.

Member Agents: Sharon DeWinter (romance, women's fiction); Bok Busboom (adventure), Antonia Hoffman (fiction/romance).

Represents: Nonfiction books, novels. **Considers these nonfiction areas:** biography/autobiography; business; child guidance/parenting; cooking/food/nutrition; current affairs; education; health/medicine; history; how-to; military/war; money/finance/economics; nature/environment; popular culture; psychology; science/technology; self-help/personal improvement; sports; true crime/investigative. **Considers these fiction areas:** action/adventure; cartoon/comic; detective/police/crime; family saga; fantasy; historical; horror; humor/satire; literary; mainstream; mystery/suspense; psychic/supernatural; romance (contemporary, gothic, historical, regency); science fiction; thriller/espionage.

How to Contact: Query. Accepts queries by fax or e-mail. Considers simultaneous queries. Reports in 1 week on queries; 2 months on mss. Returns materials only with SASE.

Needs: Obtains new clients through recommendations from other writers and publishers, occasional solicitation.

Recent Sales: Sold 6 titles in the last year. *EDF for Windows*, by R. Lavers (Pearson Professional); *Firesale*, by L. Whittington (HarperCollins).

Terms: Agent receives 15% commission on domestic sales; 20% on foreign sales. Offers written contract, binding for 6-9 months to complete first sale.

Fees: Charges $395 reading fee. "A reading/evaluation fee of $395 applies only to unpublished authors, and the fee must accompany the completed manuscript. Criticism service is included in the reading fee. The critique averages three to four pages in length, and discusses strengths and weaknesses of the execution, as well as advice aimed at eliminating weaknesses." 95% of business is derived from commissions on ms sales. Payment of criticism fee does not ensure representation.

Tips: "Never submit first drafts. Prepare the manuscript as cleanly and as perfectly, in the writer's opinion, as possible."

ELIZABETH H. BACKMAN, 86 Johnnycake Hollow Rd., Pine Plains NY 12567. (518)398-9344. Fax: (518)398-6368. **Contact:** Elizabeth H. Backman. Also: 60 Sutton Place S., New York NY 10022. **Contact:** Louise Gault. Estab 1981. Represents 50 clients. Specializes in nonfiction, women's interest and positive motivation. Currently handles: 33-60% nonfiction books; 40% fiction.

Represents: Considers these nonfiction areas: biography/memoirs; business; child guidance/parenting; cooking/food/nutrition; sports; current affairs; dance; ethnic/cultural interests; government/politics/law; health/medicine; history; photography; pop science; psychology; inspirational; self-help/personal improvement; sports; women's issues/women's studies. **Considers these fiction areas:** ethnic; fantasy; historical; mystery/suspense; regional; science fiction; thriller/espionage; men's adventure and suspense; women's contemporary fiction.

How to Contact: Query with sample ms and SASE. Reports in 3 weeks on queries; 6 weeks on mss.

Recent Sales: *Stress for Success*, by James Loehr; *Digital Hood & Other Stories*, by Peter Rondinone (Picador).

Terms: Agent receives 15% commission on domestic sales; commission between 10-20% on foreign sales. Offers written contract on request, binding for 1-3 years.

Fees: Charges $50 reading fee for proposal/3 sample chapters, $100 for complete ms. Offers criticism service. Charges for photocopying, postage, telephone, fax, typing, editing, special services.

Writers' Conference: International Women's Writing Guild conferences.

Tips: Obtains new clients through referrals from other editors. "I help writers prepare their proposals so they can get best possible deal with publisher. May not be the highest advance but best overall deal."

◙ JOSEPH A. BARANSKI LITERARY AGENCY, 214 North 2100 Rd., Lecompton KS 66050. (785)887-6010. Fax: (785)887-6263. **Contact:** D.A. Baranski. Estab. 1975. Represents over 50 clients. "We handle both film and publishing clients." Currently handles 25% nonfiction books; 15% movie scripts; 50% novels; 5% TV scripts; 2% syndicated material; 2% textbooks; 1% stage plays.

• Prior to becoming an agent, Mr. Baranski was a lawyer.

How to Contact: Query. Reports in 2 weeks on queries.

Needs: Obtains new clients through recommendations from others. "We are not openly soliciting new material at this time. Looking to add only two or three clients in the coming year."

Recent Sales: Prefers not to share information on specific sales.

Terms: Agent receives 10% commission on domestic sales; 20% on foreign sales. Offers written contract, binding for 1 year with options. 30 days notice must be given to terminate contract.

Fees: "95% of our new clients come through a recommendation. For potential clients who insist on our firm reading their unsolicited material our fee is $150."

Tips: "Be careful. The sharks are always cruising."

✔ ◙ ◎ THE BRINKE LITERARY AGENCY, 29851 Malibu Rancho Rd., Agoura CA 91301. (818)706-8533. **Contact:** Jude Stone. Estab. 1988. Represents 15 clients. Specialty is New Age—inspirational, spiritual. "Also, novels that are of a high level and for a higher purpose." Currently handles: 40% nonfiction books; 60% novels.

Member Agents: Allan Silberhartz (law, reader, advisor); Roger Engel (reader).

Represents: Considers these nonfiction areas: animals; anthropology/archaeology; biography/autobiography; meditation; history; New Age/metaphysics; religious/inspirational; self-help/personal improvement. **Considers these fiction areas:** action/adventure; fantasy; mystery/suspense; psychic/supernatural; religious/inspirational; romance (contemporary); science fiction; thriller/espionage; New Age.

How to Contact: Query with SASE.

Needs: Actively seeking "manuscripts that raise consciousness." Does not want to receive cookbooks or business books. Obtains new clients through recommendations from others, queries, mail.

Recent Sales: *Soul Psychology: Keys to Ascension*, by Dr. Joshua David Stone (Ballantine); *Invocations to the Light*, by Wistancia (Blue Dolphin).

Terms: Agent receives 15% commissions on domestic sales; 20% on foreign sales. Offers written contract, binding for 1 year.

Fees: Charges $125 reading fee for novel ms, $100 for screenplays. No charges for office expenses.

Writers' Conferences: Santa Barbara Writers Conference; BEA (Chicago, June).

Tips: Offers complete critique/evaluation or a contract.

Ⓝ ◌ ◙ ◎ JIM BUCHAN LITERARY SERVICE, 1422 Longleaf Ct., Matthews NC 28104. (704)708-8151. Fax: (704)708-8155. E-mail: buchanj@aol.com. Website: www.crosslinknet.org. **Contact:** Jim Buchan. Estab. 1998. Represents 10 clients. 90% of clients are new/unpublished writers. Specializes in books for the Christian market, but covers a variety of genres: fiction, nonfiction, children's books, science fiction, devotional materials, etc. Currently handles: 60% nonfiction books, 20% juvenile books, 10% novels, 10% textbooks.

• Prior to becoming an agent, Mr. Buchan was an attorney, a pastor and an editor at *Ministries Today* magazine.

Represents: Nonfiction books, juvenile books, novels. **Considers these nonfiction areas:** biography/autobiography; business; child guidance/parenting; cooking/food/nutrition; current affairs; government/politics/law; health/medicine; history; how-to; humor; music/dance/theater film; religious/inspirational; self-help/personal improvement; sports; leadership topics. **Considers these fiction areas:** action/adventure; cartoon/comic; family saga; fantasy; historical; humor/satire; juvenile; mystery; picture book; religious/inspirational; science fiction; sports; thriller/espionage; young adult.

How to Contact: Send entire ms or outline/proposal. Accepts queries by fax and e-mail. Considers simultaneous queries and submissions. Reports in 2 months. Returns material only with SASE.

Needs: Obtains new clients through recommendations from other authors and at conferences.

Recent Sales: Sold 1 title in the last year. Prefers not to share information on specific sales.

Terms: Agent receives 20% commission on domestic sales; 25% on foreign sales. Offers written contract, binding for 9 months. 1 month notice must be given to terminate contract.

CHECK THE AGENT SPECIALTIES INDEX to find agents who are interested in your specific nonfiction or fiction subject area.

Fees: Charges $75 for ms evaluation, "refundable if I agree to represent the author. Fee applies to all authors." Charges $75 critique fee. Critique deals with writing style, marketability, etc. and is done by Jim Buchan. Charges for postage, photocopying and other directly related expenses. 5% of business is derived from reading fees or criticism service. Payment of reading or critique fees does not ensure representation.

Tips: "We have provided free initial phone consultation for many first-time authors."

⊞ 🖫 ⊘ CAMBRIDGE LITERARY ASSOCIATES, 150 Merrimac St., Newburyport MA 01950. (978)499-0374. Fax: (978)499-0374. E-mail: mrmv@aol.com. Website: members.aol.com/mrmv/index.html. **Contact:** Michael R. Valentino. Estab. 1995. Represents 100 clients. 70% of clients are new/unpublished writers. Specializes in high profile stories, but has experience in a number of genres. Currently handles: 30% nonfiction books; 5% juvenile books; 5% story collections; 60% novels.

Member Agents: Ralph Valentino (screenplays).

Represents: Nonfiction books, scholarly books, novels. **Considers these nonfiction areas:** animals; anthropology/archaeology; biography/autobiography; business; child guidance/parenting; computers/electronics; cooking/food/nutrition; crafts/hobbies; current affairs; education; government/politics/law; health/medicine; history; how-to; humor; memoirs; military/war; money/finance/economics; music/dance/theater/film; nature/environment; popular culture; religious/inspirational; science/technology; self-help/personal improvement; sports; true crime/investigative; women's issues/women's studies. **Considers these fiction areas:** action/adventure; detective/police/crime; experimental; fantasy; historical; mainstream; mystery; regional; romance; religious/inspirational; science fiction; sports; thriller/espionage; westerns/frontier; young adult.

Also Handles: Movie scripts. **Considers these script subject areas:** action/adventure; comedy; detective/police/crime; family saga; historical; mainstream; mystery/suspense; religious/inspirational; romantic comedy; romantic drama; science fiction; thriller/espionage; western/frontier.

How to Contact: Query with SASE. Accepts queries by e-mail. Considers simultaneous queries. Reports in 1 week on queries; 6 weeks on mss.

Needs: Actively seeking self-help, psychology, mystery/suspense. Does not want to receive New Age, experimental, poetry. Obtains new clients through referrals from clients and listings in directories.

Recent Sales: Sold 8 book titles and 1 script project in the last year. *Broken Promises/Mended Hearts*, by Dr. Joel Block (NTC/Contemporary); *Cutter's Island*, by Vincent Panella (Academy Chicago Publishing); *Self-Defense For Women*, by Elizabeth Pennell (Adams Media Publishing); *Walt: Backstage Adventures with Disney*, by Charles Shaws (Adams Media Publishing). ***Movie/TV MOW scripts optioned:*** *Rogue Husband*, by Judy Singer (Blatt/Danielson Productions). Other clients include Joe Sorrentino, Paul Lazarus, Anne Abernathy Roth, Ewonda White.

Terms: Agent receives 15% commission on domestic sales; 20% on foreign sales. Offers written contract, binding for 6 months with an option to renew. 30 days notice must be given to terminate contract.

Fees: Criticism service. Charges $1/page. Most critiques written by Mike Valentino. 30% of business is derived from criticism service. Payment of criticism does not ensure representation. Charges marketing fee for novels if author wants agency to pitch both print and film rights. Waived for print rights only Charge is $30/month for 6 months maximum.

Writers' Conferences: Sleuthfest Mystery Writer's Conference (Ft. Lauderdale FL, March).

⊘ THE CATALOG™ LITERARY AGENCY, P.O. Box 2964, Vancouver WA 98668-2964. Phone/fax: (360)694-8531. **Contact:** Douglas Storey. Estab. 1986. Represents 70 clients. 50% of clients are new/previously unpublished writers. Specializes in business, health, psychology, money, science, how-to, self-help, technology, parenting, women's interest. Currently handles: 50% nonfiction books; 20% juvenile books; 30% novels.

● Prior to opening his agency, Mr. Storey was a business planner—"especially for new products." He has Masters degrees in both business and science.

Represents: Nonfiction books, textbooks, juvenile books, novels. **Considers these nonfiction areas:** agriculture/horticulture; animals; anthropology/archaeology; business; child guidance/parenting; computers/electronics; cooking/food/nutrition; crafts/hobbies; current affairs; education; ethnic/cultural interests; government/politics/law; health/medicine; how-to; juvenile nonfiction; military/war; money/finance/economics; nature/environment; photography; popular culture; psychology; science/technology; self-help/personal improvement; sociology; sports; women's issues/women's studies. **Considers these fiction areas:** action/adventure; family saga; horror; juvenile; mainstream; romance; science fiction; thriller/espionage; young adult.

How to Contact: Query. Accepts queries by fax; no e-mail queries. Considers simultaneous queries and submissions. Reports in 2 weeks on queries; 3 weeks on mss. Returns materials only with SASE.

Needs: Does not want to receive poetry, short stories or religious works.

Recent Sales: Sold 2 titles in the last year. *The Simplified Classroom Aquarium*, by Ed Stansbury (Charles C. Thomas, Publisher); *Seven Story Tower*, by Hoffman (Plenum Publishing). Clients include Martin Pall, Ken Boggs, Ken Hutchins and Bruce Dierenfield.

Terms: Agent receives 15% on domestic sales; 20% on foreign sales. Offers written contract, binding for about 9 months.

Fees: Does not charge a reading fee. Charges an upfront handling fee from $85-250 that covers photocopying, telephone and postage expense.

🖫 ♥ COLLIER ASSOCIATES, P.O. Box 20149, W. Palm Beach FL 33416-1361. (561)697-3541. Fax: (561)478-4316. **Contact:** Dianna Collier. Estab. 1976. Member of MWA. Represents over 200 clients. 20% of clients are new/

previously unpublished writers. Specializes in "adult fiction and nonfiction books directed at general audience, and novelization rights to screenplays under contract to producers only. This is a small agency that rarely takes on new clients because of the many authors it represents already." Currently handles: 50% nonfiction books; 50% novels.
Member Agents: Dianna Collier (food, history, self help, women's issues, most fiction, especially mystery, romance); Bill Vassilopoulos (financial, biography, autobiography, most fiction especially mystery).
Represents: Nonfiction, novels. **Considers these nonfiction areas:** biography/autobiography of well-known people; exposés; business and investment books for general audience; cooking/food/nutrition (by prominent people/chefs); crafts/hobbies; popular works of political subjects and history; popular reference; how-to; self-help/personal improvement; true crime/investigative; women's issues/women's studies. **Considers these fiction areas:** action/adventure; detective/police/crime; historical; mainstream; mystery/suspense; romance (contemporary, historical); thriller/espionage. "We do not handle textbooks, plays, screenplays, children's books, novelties, cartoon books, Star Trek novels, books of trivia, newspaper columns, articles, short stories, novellas, pamphlets nor pornography."
How to Contact: Query with SASE. Reports in 2 months on queries; 4 months "or longer" on mss. Rejection may be much quicker.
Needs: Obtains new clients through recommendations from others.
Recent Sales: Prefers not to share information on specific sales.
Terms: Agent receives 15% commission on domestic sales; 20% on foreign sales and dramatic rights. Offers written contract.
Fees: Charges $75 reading fee for unpublished trade book authors. "Reserves the right to charge a reading fee on manuscripts submitted by unpublished authors." Charges for mailing expenses, photocopying and express mail, "if requested, with author's consent, and for copies of author's published books used for rights sales."
Writers' Conferences: BEA (Los Angeles, April); Florida Mystery Writers (Ft. Lauderdale, March); Key West Mystery Weekend (September).
Reading Lists: Reads *Business Week, Publishers Weekly, New York Times, Palm Beach Post, Food & Wine, Cooking Light, Travel & Leisure* and others to find new clients. "An article may spark an idea for a new project or may find a writer for an existing project."
Tips: "ALWAYS submit query first with description and biographical information. No telephone calls or unsolicited mss, please! For fiction, query first with outline, first three chapters or 50 pages. If you want material returned, send check or money order for exact amount of postage with word count and submission history. Same for nonfiction, though chapter selection can be random; include audience and how project is different from competition. Manuscript should be 12 point typeface, double-spaced, one and one-half-inch margins, edited and clean!"

N ◯ **⊘** **CREATIVE LITERARY AGENCY,** P.O. Box 506, Birmingham MI 48009-0506. (248)932-0441. **Contact:** Michele Rooney. Represents 10 clients. 40% of clients are new/previously unpublished writers. Currently handles: 10% nonfiction books; 20% juvenile books, 5% scholarly books; 50% novels; 5% syndicated material; 5% textbooks; 5% poetry.
• Prior to opening her agency, Ms. Rooney received a degree in journalism, worked as a newspaper reporter and editor and was a book editor and editing consultant.
Represents: Nonfiction books, juvenile books, scholarly books, novels, textbooks, poetry books, short story collections.
Considers these nonfiction areas: animals; art/architecture/design; biography/autobiography; business; child guidance/parenting; computers/electronics; cooking/food/nutrition; crafts/hobbies; current affairs; education; government/politics/law; health/medicine; history; how-to; humor; interior design/decorating; juvenile nonfiction; language/literature/criticism; memoirs; money/finance/economics; music/dance/theater/film; nature/environment; New Age/metaphysics; photography; popular culture; psychology; religious/inspirational; science/technology; self-help/personal improvement; sociology; sports; true crime/investigative; women's studies; travel. **Considers these fiction areas:** action/adventure; contemporary issues; detective/police/crime; family saga; fantasy; feminist; glitz; historical; horror; humor/satire; juvenile; literary; mainstream; mystery; psychic/supernatural; regional; romance; religious/inspirational; science fiction; sports; thriller/espionage; westerns/frontier; young adult.
How to Contact: Query with SASE. Does not accept queries by fax or e-mail. Considers simultaneous queries. Reports in 2 weeks on queries; 6 weeks on mss. Returns materials only with SASE.
Needs: Actively seeking travel books, cookbooks, fiction from promising new authors. Does not want to receive TV or movie scripts. Obtains new clients through conferences, recommendations and query letters.
Recent Sales: New agency with no reported sales. Clients include Jennie Martin.
Terms: Agent receives 10% commission on domestic sales; 15% on foreign sales. Offers written contract, binding for 60 days.
Fees: Charges $145 reading fee, includes evaluation/critique. Reading fee is refunded upon author's first sale. 12% of business is derived from criticism fees. Charges $25/month marketing fee.
Writer's Conferences: Michigan Writers Conference (Troy MI, August 2000).
Tips: "Always write with the reader in mind. Don't be afraid to buck convention and follow your own muse. Your unique writing voice and personal style should shine through in your work."

⊘ **◎** **BONNIE R. CROWN INTERNATIONAL LITERATURE AND ARTS AGENCY,** 50 E. Tenth St., New York NY 10003-6221. (212)475-1999. **Contact:** Bonnie Crown. Estab. 1976. Member of Association of Asian Studies. Represents 5 clients. Specializes in Asian cross-cultural and translations of Asian literary works, American writers influenced by one or more Asian cultures. Currently handles: 10% scholarly books; 90% fiction.

● Prior to opening her agency, Ms. Crown was director of the Asian Literature Program, The Asia Society.

Represents: Nonfiction books, novels, short story collections (if first published in literary magazines). **Considers these nonfiction areas:** translations of Asian works in humanities. **Considers these fiction areas:** ethnic; experimental; family saga; historical; humor/satire; literary (influenced by Asia).

How to Contact: Query with SASE. Does not accept queries by fax or e-mail. Considers simultaneous queries and submissions. Reports in 2 weeks on queries; 2-4 weeks on mss. Returns materials only with SASE.

Needs: Actively seeking "fiction of literary merit." Does not want to receive "any work that contains violence, rape or drugs." Obtains new clients through "referrals from other authors and listings in reference works. If interested in agency representation, send brief query with SASE."

Recent Sales: "No recent sales of new work. A variety of rights sold from previously published works." Clients include William J. Higginson, Linda Ty-Casper, Harold Wright, B.J. Chenayil, Chee-Hahn Hang.

Terms: Agent receives 15% commission on domestic sales; 20% on foreign sales.

Fees: Charges for processing submission of ms, usually $25-50.

Reading Lists: Reads "various literary journals" to find new clients. Looks for "a distinctive style, a connection with Asian culture."

◢ CS INTERNATIONAL LITERARY AGENCY, 43 W. 39th St., New York NY 10018-3811. (212)921-1610. E-mail: csliterary@aol.com. **Contact:** Cynthia Neesemann. Estab. 1996. Represents 25 clients. Specializes in full-length fiction, nonfiction and screenplays (no pornography). "We prefer feature film scripts. Clients think we give very good critiques." Currently handles: 33% nonfiction books; 33% movie and TV scripts; 33% novels.

● Prior to opening her agency, Ms. Neesemann worked with another literary agency and also as a real estate broker—residential and commercial—and a foreign correspondent.

Represents: Nonfiction books, juvenile books, novels. **Considers all nonfiction areas. Considers all fiction areas.** "Must see queries to decide on subjects."

Also Handles: Feature film, TV MOW, sitcom, animation, documentary. **Considers these script areas:** action/adventure; cartoon/animation; comedy; contemporary issues; detective/police/crime; ethnic; family saga; fantasy; feminist; historical; juvenile; mainstream; mystery/suspense; psychic/supernatural; religious/inspirational; romance (comedy, drama); science fiction; sports; teen; thriller; westerns/frontier. "Must see queries to decide on all subjects."

How to Contact: Query. Accepts queries by e-mail. Considers simultaneous queries. Reports in 1-2 weeks on queries; 2-3 weeks on mss. Returns materials only with SASE.

Needs: Obtains new clients through recommendations, solicitation and at conferences.

Recent Sales: Prefers not to share information on specific sales.

Terms: Agent receives 15% commission on domestic sales; variable percentage on foreign sales. Sometimes offers written contract.

Fees: Charges reading fee for unestablished writers. Offers criticism service for varied fees. Fee depends upon length of manuscript. Average fee is $75 for each 100 pages submitted (partial mss considered). "I usually read and write critiques of one or two pages in length. Fee for average length screenplay is $75." Critique may be done through a written letter or through a phone conversation. Payment of critique fee does not ensure representation. Charges for marketing, office expenses, long distance phone calls, postage and photocopying depending on amount of work involved.

Tips: "Professional but friendly, we are interested in helping beginning writers to improve their writing skills and style with suggestions for better plotting and structure where needed. Manuscript analysis and evaluation of nonfiction, fiction, screennplays, and plays as well as research available for a reasonable fee."

Ⓝ ◢ ◎ THE WILSON DEVEREUX COMPANY, P.O. Box 3517, 915 Bay Ridge Ave. Annapolis MD 21403. (410)263-0880. Fax: (410)263-1479. E-mail: bdb4@wildev.com. Website: www.wildev.com. **Contact:** B.D. Barker. Represents 25 clients. 10% of clients are new/unpublished writers. Specializes in popular trade science books and the "For Dummies" line published by IDG Books Worldwide. Currently handles: 95% nonfiction books, 5% scholarly books.

● Prior to becoming an agent, B.D. Barker was a senior financial professional.

Represents: Nonfiction books. **Considers these nonfiction areas:** biography/autobiography; how-to; science/technology.

How to Contact: Query with SASE. Accepts queries by e-mail. Considers simultaneous queries. Reports in 1 week on queries; 6 weeks on mss. Returns materials only with SASE. "Rapid response to queries by e-mail."

Needs: Actively seeking science writers, proposals for trade science books, "For Dummies" proposals in math, science, history, hobbies. Does not want to receive fiction, religious material or children's books. Obtains new clients through referrals (from current clients), website, conferences.

Recent Sales: Prefers not to share information on specific sales.

Terms: Agent receives 15% commission on domestic sales; 15% on foreign sales. Offers written contract.

IF YOU'RE LOOKING for a particular agent, check the Agents Index to find at which agency the agent works. Then check the listing for that agency in the appropriate section.

Fees: Charges for direct expenses with a limit of $500.

☑ ◐ **THE DICKENS GROUP**, 3024 Madelle Ave., Louisville KY 40206. (502)897-6740. Fax: (502)894-9815. E-mail: sami@thedickens.win.net. Website: www.dickensliteraryagency.com. **Contact:** Ann Bloch. Estab. 1991. Currently handles: 50% nonfiction books; 50% novels.
- Prior to becoming agents, Dr. Solinger (president of Dickens) was a professor of pediatric cardiology; Ms. Hughes (vice president) was a professional screenwriter and editor. Ted Solinger (computer/electronic, fiction and nonfiction, sports, physical fitness).

Member Agents: Bob Solinger (literary and contemporary American fiction); (Ms.) Sam Hughes (top-list nonfiction, commercial and literary fiction).

Represents: Nonfiction books, novels. **Considers these nonfiction areas:** biography/autobiography; business; computers/electronics; cooking/food/nutrition; current affairs; government/politics/law; health/medicine; history; popular culture; science/technology; true crime/investigative. **Considers these fiction areas:** ethnic; literary; mainstream; mystery/suspense; thriller/espionage.

How to Contact: Query with SASE. *No unsolicited material.*

Needs: Actively seeking biographers, journalists, investigative reporters—"professionals writing fiction and nonfiction in their specialties." Does not want to receive poetry, essays, short stories, juvenile.

Recent Sales: *Stars that Shine*, by Julie Clay (Simon & Schuster); *Brenda*, by Brenda Lee, et al (Hyperion); *Murcheston: The Wolf's Tale*, by David Holland (TOR); *The Peace Corps*, by Dillon Banerjee (Ten Speed).

Terms: Agent receives 15% commission on domestic sales; 20% on foreign sales. Offers written contract "only if requested by author."

Fees: Charges $20 reading fee for unpublished writers.

Tips: "Write a good concise, nonhyped query letter; include a paragraph about yourself."

◐ **FENTON ENTERTAINMENT GROUP, INC.**, (formerly Law Offices of Robert L. Fenton PC), 31800 Northwestern Hwy., #390, Farmington Hills MI 48334. (248)855-8780. Fax: (248)855-3302. **Contact:** Robert L. Fenton, president. Estab. 1960. Signatory of SAG. Represents 40 clients. 25% of clients are new/previously unpublished writers. Currently handles: 25% nonfiction books; 10% scholarly books; 10% textbooks; 12% juvenile books; 35% novels; 2% short story collections; 5% movie scripts.
- Mr. Fenton has been an entertainment attorney for over 25 years, was a producer at 20th Century Fox and Universal Studios for several years and is a bestselling author.

Member Agents: Robert L. Fenton.

Represents: Nonfiction books, novels, short story collections, syndicated material. **Considers these nonfiction areas:** biography/autobiography; business; child guidance/parenting; computers/electronics; current affairs; government/politics/law; health/medicine; military/war; money/finance/economics; music/dance/theater/film; religious/inspirational; science/technology; self-help/personal improvement; sports; true crime/investigative; women's issues/women's studies. **Considers these fiction areas:** action/adventure; contemporary issues; detective/police/crime; ethnic; glitz; historical; humor/satire; mainstream; mystery/suspense; romance; science fiction; sports; thriller/espionage; westerns/frontier.

Also Handles: Feature film; TV MOW, episodic drama, syndicated material. **Considers these script areas:** action/adventure; comedy; detective/police/crime; family saga; glitz; mainstream; mystery/suspense; romantic comedy/drama; science fiction; sports; thriller/espionage; western/frontier.

How to Contact: Query with SASE. Send 3-4 sample chapters (approximately 75 pages). Accepts queries by fax. Prefers to be only reader. Reports in 1 month on queries; 2 months on mss. Discards unwanted queries and mss.

Needs: Obtains new clients through recommendations from others, individual inquiry.

Recent Sales: *Destination Mars*, by David Tyson (Sterling); *McClennan Legacy*, by Lee Ann Dougherty (Sterling). *TV scripts sold:* *Woman on the Ledge*, by Hal Sitowitz (Robert Fenton, producer, NBC); *Double Standard* (Robert Fenton, producer, NBC).

Terms: Agent receives 15% on domestic sales. Offers written contract, binding for 1 year.

Fees: Charges reading fee of $350. "To waive reading fee, author must have been published at least 3 times by a mainline New York publishing house." Critique service: $350. Charges for office expenses, postage, photocopying, etc. 25% of business is derived from reading fees or critique service. Payment of critique fee does not ensure representation.

◐ **FORT ROSS INC. RUSSIAN-AMERICAN PUBLISHING PROJECTS**, 269 W. 259 St., Riverdale NY 10471-1921. (718)884-1042. Fax: (718)884-3373. E-mail: ftross@ix.netcom.com. **Contact:** Dr. Vladimir P. Kartsev. Estab. 1992. Represents about 100 clients. 2% of clients are new/previously unpublished writers. Specializes in selling rights for Russian books and illustrations (covers) to American publishers and vice versa; also Russian-English and English-Russian translations. Currently handles: 50% nonfiction books; 10% juvenile books; 4% movie scripts; 2% short story collections; 30% novels; 2% novellas; 2% poetry.

Member Agents: Ms. Olga Borodyanskaya (fiction, nonfiction); Ms. Svetlana Kolmanovskaya (nonfiction); Mr. Konsrantin Paltchikov (romance, science fiction, fantasy, thriller).

Represents: Nonfiction books, juvenile books, novels. **Considers these nonfiction areas:** biography/autobiography; history; memoirs; music/dance/theater/film; psychology; self-help/personal improvement; true crime/investigative. **Considers these fiction areas:** action/adventure; cartoon/comic; detective/police/crime; erotica; fantasy; horror; mystery/suspense; romance (contemporary, gothic, historical, regency); science fiction; thriller/espionage; young adult.

How to Contact: Send published book or galleys. Accepts queries by fax or e-mail. Considers simultaneous queries and submissions. Returns materials only with SASE.

Needs: Actively seeking adventure,fiction, mystery, romance, science fiction, thriller and from established authors and illustrators for Russian market." Obtains new clients through recommendations from others.

Recent Sales: Sold 20 titles. *My Struggle*, by Vladimir Zhirinovsky (Barricade, NY); *The Racing Hearts*, by Patricia Hagan (AST, Russia).

Terms: Agent receives 10% commission on domestic sales; 20% on foreign sales. Offers written contract, binding for 1 year with 2 month cancellation clause.

Tips: "Authors and book illustrators (especially cover art) are welcome for the following genres: romance, fantasy, science fiction, mystery and adventure."

FRAN LITERARY AGENCY, 7235 Split Creek, San Antonio TX 78238-3627. (210)684-1659. **Contacts:** Fran Rathmann, Kathy Kenney. Estab. 1993. Signatory of WGA and member of ASCAP. Represents 33 clients. 60% of clients are new/previously unpublished writers. "Very interested in Star Trek novels/teleplays. If you write for *Star Trek*, plese follow the Pocket books guidelines on the Internet." Currently handles: 25% nonfiction books; 15% juvenile books; 30% novels; 5% novellas; 5% poetry books; 20% teleplays/screenplays.

Represents: Nonfiction and fiction. **Considers these nonfiction areas:** agriculture/horticulture; animals; anthropology/archaeology; art/architecture/design; biography/autobiography; business; child guidance/parenting; cooking/food/nutrition; crafts/hobbies; current affairs; education; ethnic/cultural interests; government/politics/law; health/medicine; history; how-to; humor; interior design/decorating; juvenile nonfiction; memoirs; music/dance/theater/film; military/war; nature/environment; religious/inspirational; self-help/personal improvement; sports; true crime/investigative; women's issues/women's studies. **Considers these fiction areas:** action/adventure; cartoon/comic; contemporary issues; detective/police/crime; family saga; fantasy; glitz; historical; horror; humor/satire; juvenile; literary; mainstream; mystery/suspense; picture book; regional; religious/inspirational; romance (gothic, regency); science fiction; sports; thriller/espionage; westerns/frontier; young adult.

Also Handles: Feature film, documentary, animation, TV MOW, sitcom, miniseries, syndicated material, animation, episodic drama. **Considers these script subject areas:** action/adventure; cartoon/animation; comedy; contemporary issues; detective/police/crime; ethnic; family saga; fantasy; historical; horror; humor; juvenile; mainstream; mystery/suspense; religious/inspirational; romantic comedy and drama; science fiction; sports; teen; thriller; westerns/frontier.

How to Contact: For books, send entire ms with SASE. For scripts, please query before sending ms. Reports in 2 weeks on queries; 2 months on mss. "Please send SASE or Box!"

Needs: Obtains clients through referrals, yellow pages.

Recent Sales: Sold 14 titles and 3 script projects in the last year. *Empire*, by Frederick Wilkins (Avalon); *Hecho En Mexico*, by Francisca Consejal (Scholastic); *The River Otter and the Sea Otter*, by Fran Rathmann (Little, Brown). *TV scripts optioned/sold*: *Hecho En Mexico*, by Francisca Consejal (FR Productions); *Timothy*, by Daniel Greene (Jerry Entertainment).

Terms: Agent receives 15% commission on domestic sales; 20% on foreign sales and performance sales. Needs "letter of agreement," usually binding for 2 years.

Fees: Charges $25 processing fee, credit after sale. Written criticism service $150, average 4 pages. "Critique includes corrections/comments/suggestions on mechanics, grammar, punctuation, plot, characterization, dialogue, marketability, etc." 90% of business is derived from commissions on mss sales; 10% from criticism services. Payment of fee does not ensure representation.

Writers' Conferences: SAWG (San Antonio, spring).

GEM LITERARY SERVICES, 4717 Poe Rd., Medina OH 44256-9745. E-mail: gemlit@earthlink.net. Website: www.gembooks.com. **Contact:** Darla Pfenninger. Estab. 1992. Member of ABA, Sisters in Crime. Represents 49 clients. 70% of clients are new/previously unpublished writers. Currently handles: 10% nonfiction books; 25% juvenile books; 65% novels.

Member Agents: Darla Pfenninger (nonfiction, science fiction, horror, New Age); Laura Weber (mystery, Christian, all others).

Represents: Nonfiction books, scholarly books, textbooks, juvenile books, novels. **Considers these nonfiction areas:** biography/autobiography; business; child guidance/parenting; computers/electronics; cooking/food/nutrition; current affairs; gay/lesbian issues; government/politics/law; how-to; humor; juvenile nonfiction; money/finance/economics; music/dance/theater/film; New Age/metaphysics; religious/inspirational; science/technology; self-help/personal improvement; true crime/investigative; women's issues/women's studies. **Considers these fiction areas:** action/adventure; detective/police/crime; family saga; fantasy; feminist; historical; horror; humor/satire; juvenile; literary; mainstream; mystery; picture book; psychic/supernatural; regional; romance (gothic, historical); science fiction; thriller/espionage; westerns/frontier; young adult.

How to Contact: Send outline/proposal with SASE for response. Accepts queries by e-mail. Considers simultaneous queries and submissions. Reports in 2 weeks on queries; 1 month on mss. Returns materials only with SASE.

Recent Sales: Sold 3 titles in the last year. *101 Golf Drills*, by Glen Berggoetz (Sportsmasters); *Devil's Moon*, by Robert Clark (Books in Motion).

Terms: Agent receives 15% commission on domestic sales; 20% on foreign sales. Offers written contract, binding for 6 months, with 30 day cancellation clause.

Fees: Charges $75-175 for office expenses, refunded upon sale of property.

Writer's Conference: Midwest Writers Conference (Canton OH, September/October), ABA, Ohio Writer.
Reading List: Reads *Publishers Weekly*; *Poets & Writers*; *The Writer*; *Writer's Journal* to find new clients. Looks for "writers who are serious about their writing and the amount of work that it takes to become successful."
Tips: Obtains new clients through recommendations and solicitations. "Looking for well-thought-out plots, not run-of-the-mill story lines."

✔ ⊘ **GLADDEN UNLIMITED**, 3808 Georgia St., #212, San Diego CA 92106. **Contact:** Carolan Gladden. Estab. 1987. Represents 30 clients. 95% of clients are new/previously unpublished writers. Currently handles: 5% nonfiction; 95% novels.
● Prior to becoming an agent Ms. Gladden worked as an editor, writer, and real estate and advertising agency representative.
Represents: Novels, nonfiction. **Considers these nonfiction areas:** celebrity biography; business; how-to; self-help; true crime/investigative. **Considers these fiction areas:** action/adventure; detective/police/crime; ethnic; glitz; horror; thriller. "No romance, mystery, short fiction or children's."
How to Contact: Query only with synopsis by mail. Reports in 2 weeks on queries; 2 months on mss.
Needs: Does not want to receive romance, mystery, children's or short fiction.
Recent Sales: Prefers not to share information on specific sales.
Terms: Agent receives 10% commission on domestic sales; 20% on foreign sales.
Fees: Does not charge a reading fee. Charges evaluation fee. Marketability evaluation: $100 (manuscript to 400 pages.) $200 (over 400 pages.) "Offers six to eight pages of diagnosis and specific recommendations to turn the project into a saleable commodity. Also includes a copy of the book 'Be a Successful Writer.' Dedicated to helping new authors achieve publication."

⊘ ◎ **THE CHARLOTTE GUSAY LITERARY AGENCY**, 10532 Blythe, Los Angeles CA 90064-3312. (310)559-0831. E-mail: gusay1@aol.com. **Contact:** Charlotte Gusay. Estab. 1988. Member of Authors Guild and PEN, signatory of WGA. Represents 30 clients. 50% of clients are new/previously unpublished writers. Specializes in fiction, nonfiction, children's (multicultural, nonsexist), children's illustrators, screenplays, books to film.
● Prior to opening her agency, Ms. Gusay was a vice president for an audiocassette producer and also a bookstore owner.
Represents: Nonfiction books, scholarly books, juvenile books, travel books, novels. **Considers all nonfiction areas and most fiction areas.** No romance, short stories, science fiction or horror.
Also Handles: Feature film. **Considers these script subject areas:** action/adventure; comedy; detective/police/crime; ethnic; experimental; family saga; feminist; gay/lesbian; historical; humor; mainstream; mystery/suspense; romantic (comedy, drama); sports; thriller; western/frontier.
How to Contact: Query with SASE. "SASE always required for response. Queries only, *no* unsolicited manuscripts. Initial query should be 1- to 2-page synopsis with SASE." Reports in 4-6 weeks on queries; 6-10 weeks on mss; 10 weeks on scripts.
Needs: Actively seeking "the next *English Patient*." Does not want to receive poetry, science fiction, horror. Usually obtains new clients through referrals and queries.
Recent Sales: *Bye-Bye*, by Jane Ransom (Pocket Books/Simon & Schuster); *Loteria and Other Stories*, by Ruben Mendoza (St. Martin's Press); *Ten Pearls of Wisdom*, by Eleanor Jacobs (Kadansha).
Terms: Agent receives 15% commission on domestic sales; 10% on dramatic sales; 25% on foreign sales. Offers written contract, binding for "usually 1 year." Charges for out-of-pocket expenses such as long distance phone calls, fax, express mail, postage, etc.
Fees: Charges $35 processing fee to read first 3 chapters of ms.
Writers' Conferences: Writers Connection (San Jose, CA); Scriptwriters Connection (Studio City, CA); National Women's Book Association (Los Angeles), California Writers Conference (Monterey, CA).
Tips: "Please be professional."

⑤ ⊘ ◎ **ANDREW HAMILTON'S LITERARY AGENCY**, P.O. Box 604118, Cleveland OH 44104-0118. (216)881-1032. E-mail: agent22@writeme.com. Website: members.aol.com/clevetown/prof/. **Contact:** Andrew Hamilton. Estab. 1991. Represents 15 clients. 60% of clients are new/previously unpublished writers. Specializes in African-American fiction and nonfiction. Currently handles: 50% nonfiction books; 7% scholarly books; 3% juvenile books; 40% novels.
● Prior to opening his agency, Mr. Hamilton served as editor at several legal publications.
Member Agent: Andrew Hamilton (music, business, self-help, how-to, sports).
Represents: Nonfiction books, novels. **Considers these nonfiction areas:** animals; biography/autobiography; business; child guidance/parenting; cooking/food/nutrition; current affairs; government/politics/law; health/medicine; history; money/finance/economics; psychology; self-help/personal improvement; sociology; sports; true crime/investigative; women's issues/women's studies; minority concerns; pop music. **Considers these fiction areas:** action/adventure; confessional; contemporary issues; detective/police/crime; erotica; ethnic; family saga; humor/satire; mystery/suspense; psychic/supernatural; romance (contemporary); sports; thriller/espionage; westerns/frontier; young adult.
How to Contact: Send entire ms. Accepts queries by e-mail. Considers simultaneous queries and submissions. Reports in 1 week on queries; 3 weeks on mss. Returns materials only with SASE.

Needs: Actively seeking good nonfiction books. Does not want to receive poetry. Obtains new clients through recommendations.

Recent Sales: Sold 2 titles in the last year. *Outcast . . .*, by Michael Hobbs (Middle Passage Press); *My Journey*, by Victor Yee (Shin Publishing); *Til Death*, Viranda Sladdy (Notthills Publications).

Terms: Agent receives 15% commission on domestic sales; 20% on foreign sales. Offers written contract.

Fees: "Reading fees are for new authors and are nonrefundable. My reading fee is $50 for 60,000 words or less; $100 for manuscripts over 60,000 words; $150 for ms up to 150,000 words; and $250 for ms over $150,000. I charge a one time marketing fee of $250 for manuscripts." 30% of business is derived from reading fees or criticism services.

Tips: "Be patient: the wheels turn slowly in the publishing world."

N **$** **◓** **HARTLINE LITERARY AGENCY**, 123 Queenston Dr., Pittsburgh PA 15235-5429. (412)829-2495 or 2483. Fax: (412)829-2450. E-mail: jachart@aol.com. Website: www.hartlinemarketing.com/. **Contact:** Joyce A. Hart. Estab. 1990. Represents 7 clients. 30% of clients are new/previously unpublished writers. Specializes in the Christian bookseller market. Currently handles: 40% nonfiction books; 60% novels.

Member Agents: Joyce A. Hart (adult/fiction); Mary Busha (adult/fiction).

Represents: Nonfiction books, novels. **Considers these nonfiction subject areas:** business; child guidance/parenting; cooking/food/nutrition; money/finance/economics; religious/inspirational; self-help/personal improvement; women's issues. **Considers these fiction subject areas:** action/adventure; contemporary issues; family saga; historical; literary; mystery (amateur sleuth, cozy); regional; religious/inspirational; romance (contemporary, gothic, historical, regency); thriller/espionage.

How to Contact: Send outline and 3 sample chapters. Accepts queries by fax or e-mail. Considers simultaneous queries and submissions. Reports in 1 month on queries; 2 months on mss. Returns materials only with SASE.

Needs: Actively seeking adult fiction, self-help, nutritional books, devotional, business. Does not want to receive science fiction, erotica, gay and lesbian fantasy, horror, etc. Obtains new writers through recommendations from others.

Recent Sales: Sold 5 titles in the last year. *Men Are Clams, Women are Crow Bars*, by Dr. David Clarke (Promise Press); *Celebrate Kids!*, by Angie Peters (Concordia); *Winning the Parenting War*, by Dr. David Clarke (Promise Press).

Terms: Agent receives 15% commission on domestic sales. Offers written contract.

Fees: Offers criticism service to freelance editor for first-time writers. 10% of business is derived from criticism service. Charges $20-25/hour. Payment of criticism fee does not ensure representation. Charges for photocopying and postage.

☑ **◓** **THE EDDY HOWARD AGENCY**, % 732 Coral Ave., Lakewood NJ 08701. (732)942-1023. **Contact:** Eddy Howard Pevovar, N.D., Ph.D. Estab. 1986. Signatory of WGA. Represents 20 clients. 10% of clients are new/previously unpublished writers. Specializes in film, sitcom and literary. Currently handles: 5% nonfiction books; 5% scholarly books; 5% juvenile books; 5% novels; 30% movie scripts; 30% TV scripts; 10% stage plays; 5% short story collections; 1% syndicated material; 4% other.

• See the expanded listing for this agency in Script Agents.

◐ **INDEPENDENT PUBLISHING AGENCY: A LITERARY AND ENTERTAINMENT AGENCY**, P.O. Box 176, Southport CT 06490-0176. Phone/fax: (203)332-7629. E-mail: henryberry@aol.com. **Contact:** Henry Berry. Estab. 1990. Represents 40 clients. 50% of clients are new/previously unpublished writers. Especially interested in topical nonfiction (historical, political, social topics, cultural studies, health, business) and literary and genre fiction. Currently handles: 70% nonfiction books; 10% juvenile books; 20% novels and short story collections.

• Prior to opening his agency, Mr. Berry was a book reviewer, writing instructor and publishing consultant. Mr. Cherici has more than 10 years experience as an independent publisher, publishing consultant and agent.

Represents: Nonfiction books, juvenile books, novels, short story collections. **Considers these nonfiction areas:** anthropology/archaeology; art/architecture/design; biography/autobiography; business; child guidance/parenting; cooking/food/nutrition; crafts/hobbies; current affairs; ethnic/cultural interests; government/politics/law; history; juvenile nonfiction; language/literature/criticism; military/war; money/finance/economics; music/dance/theater/film; nature/environment; photography; popular culture; psychology; religious; science/technology; self-help/personal improvement; sociology; sports; true crime/investigative; women's issues/women's studies. **Considers these fiction areas:** action/adventure; cartoon/comic; confessional; contemporary issues; crime; erotica; ethnic; experimental; fantasy; feminist; historical; humor/satire; juvenile; literary; mainstream; mystery/suspense; picture book; psychic/supernatural; thriller/espionage; young adult.

Also Handles: Now accepting screenplays. "In response to interest from individuals in the film business, Mr. Berry has expanded the scope of the Independent Publishing Agency to handle manuscripts, screenplays, and books that may be of interest to such individuals for film development. In expanding the agency, Mr. Berry has entered into an association with Peter Cherici."

How to Contact: Send synopsis/outline plus 2 sample chapters. Reports in 2 weeks on queries; 6 weeks on mss.

Needs: Usually obtains new clients through referrals from clients, notices in writer's publications.

Recent Sales: Recent sales available upon request by prospective clients.

Terms: Agent receives 15% commission on domestic sales; 20% on foreign sales and film rights with co-agent involved. Offers "agreement that spells out author-agent relationship."

Fees: No fee for queries with sample chapters; $250 reading fee for evaluation/critique of complete ms. Offers criticism service if requested. Written critique averages 3 pages—includes critique of the material, suggestions on how to make it marketable and advice on marketing it. Charges $25/month for clients for marketing costs. 10% of business is derived from criticism services.

Tips: Looks for "proposal or chapters professionally presented, with clarification of the distinctiveness of the project and grasp of intended readership."

◯ CAROLYN JENKS AGENCY, 24 Concord Ave., Suite 412, Cambridge MA 02138. (617)354-5099. E-mail: carojenks@aol.com. **Contact:** Carolyn Jenks. Re-estab. 1990. Signatory of WGA. 40% of clients are new/previously unpublished writers. Specializes in "development of promising authors." Currently handles: 20% nonfiction books; 75% novels; 5% movie scripts. Co-agents for TV in Los Angeles.

• Prior to opening her agency, Ms. Jenks was a managing editor, editor, journalist, actress and producer.

Represents: Fiction and nonfiction books. **Considers these nonfiction areas:** animals; biography/autobiography; business; ethnic/cultural interests; gay/lesbian issues; health/medicine; history; language/literature/criticism; theater/film; nature/environment; metaphysics; religious/inspirational; science/technology; sociology; translations; women's issues/women's studies. **Considers these fiction areas:** contemporary issues; ethnic; feminist; gay; historical; lesbian; literary; mainstream; mystery/suspense; psychic/supernatural; religious/inspirational; romance (contemporary, historical); thriller/espionage; westerns.

Also Handles: Feature film, TV MOW. **Considers these script subject areas:** comedy; contemporary issues; historical; mainstream; mystery; romantic comedy and drama; thriller; westerns/frontier.

How to Contact: Query with bio and SASE. Accepts queries by e-mail; does not accept faxed queries. Considers simultaneous queries and submissions. Reports in 2 weeks on queries; 6 weeks on mss. Returns materials only with SASE.

Needs: Actively seeking "exceptionally talented writers committed to work that makes a contribution to the state of the culture." Does not want to receive gratuitous violence; drugs scenes that are a cliché; war stories unless they transcend; sagas, or clichéd coming of age stories." Interested in building international stable of authors based in USA, London, Paris, Bangkok."

Recent Sales: Sold 1 book title in the last year. *The Red Tent*, by Anita Diamant (St. Martin's Press); *The War of Maps*, by Tom Foley (Forge).

Terms: Agent receives 15% commission on domestic sales; 10% on film and TV. Offers written contract.

Fees: Charges reading fee to non-WGA members on a sliding scale. 120,000 words $200; screenplay $175. WGA members exempted. Payment of reading fee does not ensure representation or include criticism. 10% of business is derived from reading fees. Charges for photocopying.

Tips: "Query first in writing with SASE or to carojenks@aol.com. Do not send samples of writing by e-mail."

◯ JOHNSON WARREN LITERARY AGENCY, 115 W. California Blvd., Suite 173, Pasadena CA 91105. (626)583-8750. Fax: (909)624-3930. E-mail: jwla@aol.com. **Contact:** Billie Johnson. Signatory of WGA. Represents 25 clients. 95% of clients are new/unpublished writers. Currently represents 30% movie scripts; 50% novels; 5% TV scripts; 15% nonfiction books.

• Prior to becoming an agent, Billie Johnson worked 25 years in accounting and project management.

Represents: Feature film, TV MOW. **Considers these script subject areas:** action/adventure; contemporary issues; detective/police/crime; mainstream; mystery/suspense; romance (comedy, drama); thriller/espionage.

How to Contact: Query. Reports in 1-4 weeks on queries; 2-4 months on mss.

Needs: Actively seeking nonfiction projects. Does not want to receive science fiction, horror, children's, religious material. Obtains new clients through solicitations via reference books and internet registry.

Recent Sales: Sold 7 projects in the last year. Prefers not to share information on specific sales.

Terms: Agent receives 15% commission on domestic sales; 20% on foreign sales; 10% on scripts. Offers written contract. 30 days notice must be given to terminate contract.

Fees: Offers criticism service. 10% of business is derived from criticism service. Payment of criticism fees does not ensure representation. Charges for actual costs reimbursements.

Writer's Conferences: Romance Writers of America National Conference (Anaheim); Bouchercon (Philadelphia); Sisters in Crime (L.A.).

Tips: "This agency is open to new writers and enjoys a teamwork approach to projects. JWLA has an on-staff promotions director to bolster publicity efforts."

✓ $ ◯ LITERARY GROUP WEST, 746 W. Shaw, Suite 127, Clovis CA 93612. (209)297-9409. Fax: (209)225-5606. **Contact:** Ray Johnson or Alyssa Williams. Estab. 1993. Represents 6 clients. 50% of clients are new/previously unpublished writers. Specializes in novels. Currently handles: 20% nonfiction books; 70% novels; 10% novellas.

Member Agents: B.N. Johnson, Ph.D. (English literature).

Represents: Nonfiction books, novels. **Considers these nonfiction areas:** current affairs; ethnic/cultural interests;

TO FIND AN AGENT near you, check the Geographic Index.

military/war; true crime/investigative. **Considers these fiction areas:** action/adventure; detective/police/crimes; historical; mainstream; thriller/espionage.

How to Contact: Query with SASE. Reports in 1 week on queries; 1 months on mss. Does not want to receive unsolicited mss.

Needs: Obtains new clients through queries and referrals.

Recent Sales: Prefers not to share information on specific sales.

Terms: Agent receives 15% commission on domestic sales; 20% on foreign sales. Offers written contract.

Fees: Charges expense fees to unpublished authors. Deducts expenses from sales of published authors.

Writers' Conferences: Fresno County Writers Conference.

Tips: "Query first with strong letter. Please send SASE with query letter."

◯ **MAGNETIC MANAGEMENT**, 415 Roosevelt Ave., Lehigh FL 33972-4402. (941)369-6488. **Contact:** Steven Dameron. Estab. 1996. Represents 5 clients. 100% of clients are new/unpublished writers. Specializes in new authors with passion and drive; fiction and screenplays. Currently handles: 10% juvenile books; 50% movie scripts; 30% novels; 10% TV scripts.

• Prior to opening his agency, Mr. Dameron was a talent manager and acting instructor.

Represents: Juvenile books, movie scripts, novels, TV scripts. **Considers these nonfiction areas:** biography/autobiography. No nonfiction unless Christian biography. **Considers these fiction areas:** action/adventure; contemporary issues; detective/police/crime; fantasy; glitz; horror; humor/satire; juvenile; literary; mainstream; mystery/suspense; religious/inspirational; romance (contemporary); science fiction; thriller/espionage; young adult.

Also Handles: Feature film. **Considers these script areas:** action/adventure; comedy. "Correct format, not too talkie and fast pace."

How to Contact: Query with SASE. Considers simultaneous queries. Reports in 1 week on queries; 3 weeks on mss. Returns materials only with SASE.

Needs: Actively seeking mystery/suspense novels, mainstream, screenplays (action and comedy with low to medium budgets). Usually obtains new clients through solicitation.

Recent Sales: Sold 1 book title and 3 script projects in the last year. *Star Quality* (Morris Publishing); *Movie scripts optioned/sold: The Last Laugh*, by S. Thomas (Sez Who Productions).

Terms: Agent receives 10% commission on domestic sales; 20% on foreign sales. Offers written contract, binding for 1 year. 30 days notice must be given to terminate contract.

Fees: Charges $40 reading fee, makes minor notes on ms. Also charges some clients $1/page for editing of manuscript. Payment of fee does not ensure representation. "Writers usually get form letters when they are rejected therefore they're left *in the dark*. With me they will know *why* they are being returned. (I hate the word rejected)."

Tips: "Don't let rejection discourage you. What one agent thinks is trash could be considered a treasure to another. I give everyone a chance. Don't give up! Good work always finds a home! We have a select client list and offer personal replies to all authors. No form letters here! We really care about authors and their work."

▓◯ **VIRGINIA C. McKINLEY, LITERARY AGENCY**, EFLS, 545 Eighth Ave., Box 046, Suite 401, New York NY 10018. (212)330-0685. **Contact:** Virginia C. McKinley. Estab. 1992. 100% of clients are new/previously unpublished writers. Specializes in religious material, self-help and textbooks. Currently handles: 30% nonfiction books; 20% juvenile books; 40% novels; 10% poetry books.

Member Agent: Virginia C. McKinley (religious books, biography/autobiography, fiction).

Represents: Nonfiction books, movie scripts, TV scripts. **Considers these nonfiction areas:** animals; biography/autobiography; business; child guidance/parenting; ethnic/cultural interests; health/medicine; money/finance/economics; theater/film; psychology; religious/inspirational; self-help/personal improvement; sociology; sports; women's issues/women's studies. **Considers these fiction areas:** contemporary issues; ethnic; family saga; feminist; humor/satire; literary; religous/inspiration.

Also Handles: Feature film, miniseries. **Considers these script subject areas:** comedy; contemporary issues; ethnic; family saga; humor; juvenile; mainstream; religious/inspirational; romantic comedy; science fiction; sports.

How to Contact: Query with entire ms or 3 sample chapters. Prefers to be only reader. Reports in 4-6 weeks on queries; 1 month on mss. Returns materials only with SASE.

Needs: Obtains new clients through solicitation.

Recent Sales: Prefers not to share information on specific sales.

Terms: Agent receives 15% commission on domestic sales; 20% on foreign sales. Offers written contract.

Fees: Criticism service: $125 for 3-page critique. Payment of criticism fee does not ensure representation.

Tips: "No multiple submissions. We feel a dynamic relationship between author and agent is essential. SASE must be included with ms or 3 chapters; also query. Will work with writer to develop his full potential."

✓ 💲 ◯ **McLEAN LITERARY ASSOCIATES**, (formerly Hutton-McLean Literary Associates), 2205 157th Lane SW, Tenino WA 98589-9490. (360)264-5129. Fax: (360)264-5159. E-mail: mcleanlit@thurston.com. Website: www.mcleanlit.com. **Contact:** Donna McLean Nixon. Also: 55449 Riviera, La Quinta CA 92253. (760)771-BOOK. **Contact:** Nan deBrandt. Estab. 1984. Represents 65 clients. 85% of clients are new/previously unpublished writers. Currently handles: 40% nonfiction books; 10% children's books; 30% fiction; 20% religious/inspirational/metaphysics/philosophy.

• Prior to opening her agency, Ms. McLean specialized in starting up small businesses and/or increasing profits.

Member Agents: Nan deBrandt; Donna McLean.

Represents: Fiction and nonfiction books, juvenile books, short story collections. **Considers these nonfiction areas:** health/medicine; how-to; self help; psychology; new thought; critical thinking; scholarly; biography/autobiography; religious. **Considers these fiction areas:** juvenile; gay; romance; mystery.

How to Contact: Query first with SASE. "To receive brochure send SASE or visit website: www.mcleanlit.com."

Needs: Does not want to receive poetry. Obtains new clients through recommendations from others and personal contacts at literary functions.

Recent Sales: *Gems of the Seven Color Rays*, by Stuber (Llewellyn); *Secrets for Dealing with Teenagers*, by Hanks (HCI).

Terms: Agent receives 15% on domestic sales; 20% on foreign sales.

Fees: Charges a reading fee of $100 for children's, $250 for fiction, $250 for nonfiction. "No editing required for authors who've been published in the same genre in the prior few years by a major house. Other writers are charged an evaluation fee and is refundable from commissions. For nonfiction, we completely edit the proposal/outline and sample chapter; for fiction and children's, we need the entire manuscript. Editing includes book formats, questions, comments, suggestions for expansion, cutting and pasting, etc." Also offers other services: proofreading, rewriting, proposal development. 20% of business is derived from reading or criticism fees.

Writers' Conferences: BEA (Chicago, June); Frankfurt Book Fair (Germany, October); Pacific Northwest Writer's (Washington, July).

Tips: "Study and make your proposal as perfect and professional as you possibly can."

✓ 💲 💿 **MEWS BOOKS LTD.**, 20 Bluewater Hill, Westport CT 06880. (203)227-1836. Fax: (203)227-1144. E-mail: mewsbooks@aol.com. **Contact:** Sidney B. Kramer. Estab. 1972. Represents 35 clients. Prefers to work with published/established authors; works with small number of new/unpublished authors "producing professional work." Specializes in juvenile (preschool through young adult), cookery, self-help, adult nonfiction and fiction, parenting, technical and medical and electronic publishing. Currently handles: 20% nonfiction books; 10% novels; 20% juvenile books; 10% electronic; 40% miscellaneous.

Member Agent: Fran Pollak (assistant).

Represents: Nonfiction books, novels, juvenile books, character merchandising and video and TV use of illustrated published books.

How to Contact: Query with précis, outline, character description, a few pages of sample writing and author's bio. Does not accept queries by fax or e-mail. Considers simultaneous queries. Returns materials only with SASE.

Recent Sales: Sold 10 titles in the last year. *Jane Butel's Quick and Easy Southwestern Cookbook*, by Jane Butel (Harmony Books); *Modern Radar Transmitters*, by J.M. Kawecki (Prentice Hall).

Terms: Agent receives 15% commission on domestic sales; 20% on foreign sales.

Fees: Does not charge a reading fee. "If material is accepted, agency asks for $350 circulation fee (4-5 publishers), which will be applied against commissions (waived for published authors)." Charges for photocopying, postage expenses, telephone calls and other direct costs.

Tips: "Principle agent is an attorney and former publisher. Offers consultation service through which writers can get advice on a contract or on publishing problems."

🅽 💟 ◎ **THE MUMFORD LITERARY AGENCY, INC.**, P.O. Box 770909, Houston TX 77215-0909. (713)974-4473. Fax: (713)785-9640. E-mail: ronmumford@aol.com. **Contact:** Ron Mumford. Estab. 1997. Represents 50 clients. 50% of clients are new/unpublished writers. Handles a wide variety of material. Specializes in religious titles. Currently handles: 60% nonfiction books; 2% juvenile books; 1% movie scripts; 1% scholarly books; 35% novels; 1% novellas..

 • Prior to opening his agency, Mr. Mumford was a writer for newspapers and magazines, and a licensed financial consultant.

Represents: Nonfiction books, juvenile books, movie scripts, novels, novellas. **Considers these nonfiction areas:** biography/autobiography; business; child guidance/parenting; computers/electronics; cooking/food/nutrition; crafts/hobbies; education; ethnic/cultural interests; government/politics/law; history; how-to; humor; military/war; money/finance/economics; music/dance/theater/film; nature/environment; religious/inspirational; self-help/personal improvement; sports; true crime/investigative; women's issues/women's studies. **Considers these fiction areas:** action/adventure; ethnic; family saga; fantasy; feminist; historical; horror; humor/satire; juvenile; literary; mystery (amateur sleuth, hardboiled detective); picture book; regional; religious/inspirational; romance (contemporary, historical, regency); science fiction; suspense; thriller/espionage.

How to Contact: Query or send outline/proposal with SASE. Reports in 1 month on queries; 6 weeks on mss. Does not accept queries by e-mail or fax.

Needs: Actively seeking published authors. Does not want to receive any sacreligious material, unedited or unformatted material. Obtains new clients through queries and recommendations from others.

Recent Sales: Sold 10 titles in the last year. *This Is Christmas*, by Donna Cooner, Ed.D. (Waterbrook Press); *The Sisters Series (New Beginnings)*, by Debra White Smith (Harvest House); *Secrets Employers Fear You'll Know*, by Greg Shelton (M. Evans & Co.); *Hunkered Down*, by Sterling Rogers (Jona Books). Other clients include Greg Shelton, Debra White Smith, Donna Cooner, Myra Barnes, Howard Bushart, Joe Tidwell III, C.R. Cooper, Miriam Minger.

Terms: Agent receives 15% commission on domestic sales; 20% on foreign sales. Offers written contract, binding for 1 year. 1 month notice must be given to terminate contract.

Fees: Charges $500 one time fee to cover marketing fee, office expenses, postage, photocopying. May refer to editor, receives no money for referral.
Writer's Conferences: Christian Book Association (Orlando FL, July 99).
Tips: "Use a third party editor before submission unless you are a published author."

✓ ⬛ **BK NELSON LITERARY AGENCY & LECTURE BUREAU**, 84 Woodland Rd., Pleasantville NY 10570-1322. (914)741-1322. Fax: (914)741-1324. Also: 139 S. Beverly Dr., Suite 323, Beverly Hills CA 90212. (310)858-7006. Fax: (310)858-7967. E-mail: bknelson4@cs.com. Website: www.bknelson.com. **Contact:** B.K. Nelson, John Benson, Chip Ashbach or Erv Rosenfeld. Estab. 1980. Member of NACA, Authors Guild, NAFE, ABA, AAUW, WGA. Represents 62 clients. 40% of clients are new/previously unpublished writers. Specializes in business, self-help, how-to, novels, screenplays, biographies. Currently handles: 30% nonfiction books; 5% CD-ROM/electronic products; 30% novels; 20% movie scripts; 10% TV scripts; 10% stage plays.
• Prior to opening her agency, Ms. Nelson worked for Eastman and Dasilva, a law firm specializing in entertainment law, and at American Play Company, a literary agency.
Member Agents: B.K. Nelson (business books, self help); John Benson (Director of Lecture Bureau, sports); Erv Rosenfeld (TV scripts); Chip Ashbach (novels); Jean Rejaunier (biography, theatrical).
Represents: Nonfiction books, CD-ROM/electronic products, business books, novels, plays and screenplays. **Considers these nonfiction areas:** anthropology/archaeology; art/architecture/design; biography/autobiography; business; child guidance/parenting; computers/electronics; cooking/food/nutrition; crafts/hobbies; current affairs; education; ethnic/cultural interests; government/politics/law; health/medicine; history; how-to; language/literature/criticism; memoirs; military/war; money/finance/economics; music/dance/theater/film; nature/environment; popular culture; psychology; religious/inspirational; science/technology; self-help/personal improvement; sociology; sports; travel; true crime/investigative; women's issues/women's studies. **Considers these fiction areas:** action/adventure; cartoon/comic; contemporary issues; detective/police/crime; family saga; fantasy; feminist; glitz; historical; horror; literary; mainstream; mystery/suspense; psychic/supernatural; romance (contemporary, historical); science fiction; sports; thriller/espionage; westerns/frontier.
Also Handles: Feature film, documentary, animation, TV MOW, episodic drama, sitcom, variety show, miniseries, animation, stage plays. **Considers these script subject areas:** action/adventure; cartoon; comedy; contemporary issues; detective/police/crime; family saga; fantasy; historical; horror; mainstream; psychic/supernatural; romantic comedy and drama; thriller; westerns/frontier.
How to Contact: Query with SASE. Reports in 2 weeks on queries; 1 month on ms.
Needs: Actively seeking screenplays. Does not want to receive unsolicited material. Obtains new clients through referrals and reputation with editors.
Recent Sales: Sold 40 titles in the last year. *How to, I do,* by Christine Cudance and Holly Lefevre; *Oktoberfest: Cooking with Beer,* by Armand Vanderstigchel. Other clients include Arthur Pell, Robert W. Bly, Antony Mora, Leon Katz, Ph.D., Professor Emeritus Drama Yale, Anne Marie Baugh, Lilly Walters, Branden Ward, Paula Moulton, Bill Green, Jason and Edith Marks.
Terms: Agent receives 20% on domestic sales; 25% on foreign sales. Offers written contract, exclusive for 8-12 months.
Fees: Charges $450 reading fee for mss; $250 for screenplays; $4/page for proposals. "It is not refundable. We usually charge for the first reading only. The reason for charging in addition to time/expense is to determine if the writer is saleable and thus a potential client." Offers editorial services ranging from book query critiques for $50 to ghost writing a corporate book for $100,000. "After sale, charge any expenses over $50 for FedEx, long distance, travel or luncheons. We always discuss deducting expenses with author before deducting."
Recent Sales: *Plays optioned for off-Broadway: Gianni Schicchi,* by John Morogiello; *Obediently Yours, Orson Welles,* by Richard France; *TV scripts optioned/sold: American Harvest,* by Brandon Ward (starring Johnny Depp); *Nellie Bly,* by Jason Marks (Brandon Ward for TNT).
Tips: "We handle the business aspect of the literary and lecture fields. We handle careers as well as individual book projects. If the author has the ability to write and we are harmonious, success is certain to follow with us handling the selling/business."

💲 ⬛ **PELHAM LITERARY AGENCY**, 2290 E. Fremont Ave., Suite C, Littleton CO 80122. (303)347-0623. **Contact:** Howard Pelham. Estab. 1994. Represents 10 clients. 50% of clients are new/previously unpublished writers. Specializes in genre fiction. Currently handles: 20% nonfiction books; 80% novels.
• Prior to opening his agency, Mr. Pelham worked as a writer and college professor.
Member Agents: Howard Pelham, Jim Meals.
Represents: Novels, short story collections. **Considers these fiction areas:** action/adventure; detective/police/crime; fantasy; horror; literary; mainstream; romance (contemporary, gothic, historical); science fiction; sports; thriller/espionage; westerns/frontier.
How to Contact: Send outline and sample chapters or query with description of novel or manuscript. Considers simultaneous queries and submissions. Reports in 3 weeks on queries; 2 months on mss. Returns materials only with SASE.
Needs: Actively seeking all adult genre fiction. Does not want to receive movie scripts, children's mss, young adult fiction.
Recent Sales: Sold 2 titles in the last year. *The Passenger,* by Patrick A. Davis (Putnam); *Blowout,* by Robert Howarth (Intermedia).

Terms: Agent receives 15% commission on domestic sales; 20% on foreign sales. Offers written contract, with 30 day cancellation clause.

Fees: Charges $95 reading fee to unpublished writers. Offers criticism service. 90% of business is derived from commissions on sales.

Writers' Conferences: Rocky Mountain Book Fair.

Tips: "Most of my clients have been from recommendation by other writers. Submit the most manuscript possible."

✓ ⬦ PELHAM-HEUISLER LITERARY AGENCY, 2496 N. Palo Santo Dr., Tucson AZ 85745-1082. E-mail: heuisler@flash.net. Represents 24 clients. 80% of clients are new/unpublished writers. Specializes in "bringing the work of unpublished authors up to marketing standards." Currently handles: 30% nonfiction books; 10% juvenile books; 60% novels.

● Prior to opening their agency, William Heuisler was in law enforcement and a writer.

Member Agents: William Heuisler (fiction, how-to, nonfiction).

Represents: Nonfiction books, novels. **Considers these nonfiction areas:** anthropology/archaeology; art/architecture/ design; biography/autobiography; current affairs; government/politics/law; history; how-to; humor; language/literature/ criticism; military/war; religious/inspirational; self-help/personal improvement; true crime/investigative. **Considers all fiction areas.**

How to Contact: Query with SASE. Accepts queries by e-mail. Considers simultaneous queries and submissions. Reports in 2 weeks on queries; 2 months on mss. Returns materials only with SASE.

Needs: Actively seeking publishable writers. Obtains new clients through publications like the *Guide to Literary Agents*.

Recent Sales: Sold 2 titles in the last year. *The General*, by Patrick Davis (G.P. Putnam's Sons); *Blowout*, by Robert Howarth (Intermedia).

Terms: Agent receives 15% commission on domestic sales. Offers written contract. 30 days notice must be given to terminate contract.

Fees: Charges $2/1,000 words for new writers. Fee refundable upon sale. The fee for criticism is the reading fee. "We give a thorough, critique to each writer whose manuscript we read (at least five pages of detailed observation and criticism)." 40% of business is derived from reading fees or criticism service. Payment of criticism or reading fee(s) does not ensure representation.

✓ $ ⬦ WILLIAM PELL AGENCY, 5 Canterbury Mews, Southampton NY 11968 (516)287-6778. Fax: (516)287-4992. **Contact:** William Pell. Estab. 1990. Represents 26 clients. 85% of clients are new/previously unpublished writers.

● Prior to becoming an agent, Ms. Kelly served as an editor for 3 London publishers.

Member Agent: Susan Kelly, associate editor/novels.

Represents: Novels. **Considers biography/autobiography; action/adventure, detective/police/crime, thriller/espionage.**

How to Contact: Query with first 2 chapters. Reports in 1 month on queries; 3 months on mss.

Recent Sales: Sold 3 titles in the last year. *Mind-Set*, by Paul Dostor (Penguin USA); *Endangered Beasties*, by Derek Pell (Dover); *Grown Men*, by S. Mawe (Avon).

Terms: Agent receives 15% commission on domestic sales; 20% on foreign sales. Offers written contract, binding for 2 years.

Fees: Charges $100-500 reading fee for new writers. 10% of business is derived from reading fees or criticism services. Payment of criticism fees does not ensure representation.

⬦ PMA LITERARY AND FILM MANAGEMENT, INC., 132 W. 22nd St., 12th Floor, New York NY 10011-1817. (212)929-1222. Fax: (212)206-0238. E-mail: pmalitfilm@aol.com. Website: www.pmalitfilm.com. **Contact:** Peter Miller, president. Estab. 1975. Represents 80 clients. 50% of clients are new/unpublished writers. Specializes in commercial fiction and nonfiction, thrillers, true crime and "fiction with *real* motion picture and television potential." Currently handles: 50% fiction; 25% nonfiction; 25% screenplays.

● 1997 marks Mr. Miller's 25th anniversary as an agent.

Member Agents: Delin Cormeny, vice president; Peter Miller, president (fiction, nonfiction and motion picture properties); Steven Schattenberg, director of development (screenplays); Dan Calvisi, development associate.

Represents: Fiction, nonfiction, film scripts. **Considers these nonfiction areas:** animals; biography/autobiography; business; child guidance/parenting; cooking/food/nutrition; crafts/hobbies; current affairs; ethnic/cultural interests; government/politics/law; history; how-to; humor; juvenile nonfiction; money/finance/economics; music/dance/theater/film;

FOR EXPLANATIONS OF THESE SYMBOLS,
SEE THE INSIDE FRONT AND BACK COVERS OF THIS BOOK

photography; popular culture; travel; true crime/investigative; women's issues/women's studies. **Considers these fiction areas:** action/adventure; contemporary issues; detective/police/crime; ethnic; family saga; gay; historical; humor/satire; lesbian; literary; mainstream; mystery/suspense; romance (historical); science fiction; thriller/espionage; westerns/frontier.

Also Handles: Feature film, TV MOW, miniseries. **Considers these script areas:** action/adventure; comedy; contemporary issues; detective/police/crime; family saga; historical; mainstream; mystery/suspense; psychic/supernatural; romantic comedy; romantic drama; science fiction; thriller; westerns/frontier.

How to Contact: Query with outline and/or sample chapters. Accepts queries by fax or e-mail. Prefers to be only reader. Writer's guidelines for $5 \times 8\frac{1}{2}$ SASE with 2 first-class stamps. Reports in 3 weeks on queries; 6-8 weeks on ms. Submissions and queries without SASE will not be returned. Returns materials only with SASE.

Needs: Actively seeking professional journalists, first-time novelists, ethnic and female writers. *No unsolicited mss.*

Recent Sales: Sold 25 titles and 5 script projects in the last year. *Chocolate for a Woman's Heart*, by Kay Allenbaugh (Simon & Schuster); *Untitled*, by Nancy Taylor Rosenberg (Hyperion); *Rage Factor*, by Chris Rogers (Bantam). Other clients include Jay Bonansinga, Vincent Bugliosi, John Glatt, Michael Eberhardt, Kay Allenbaugh, Susan Wright, Ted Sennett, Nancy Taylor Rosenberg, Chris Rogers, James Dallesandro.

Terms: Agent receives 15% commission on domestic sales; 20-25% on foreign sales.

Fees: Does not charge a reading fee. Offers sub-contracted criticism service. "Fee varies on the length of the manuscript from $150-500. Publishing professionals/critics are employed by PMA to write five- to eight-page reports." Charges for photocopying.

Writers' Conferences: Romance Writer's Conference (Chicago, October); North Carolina Writers Network Conference (Wilmington, November); Charleston Writers Conference (March).

⬤ PUDDINGSTONE LITERARY AGENCY, Affiliate of SBC Enterprises Inc., 11 Mabro Dr., Denville NJ 07834-9607. (201)366-3622. **Contact:** Alec Bernard or Eugenia Cohen. Estab. 1972. Represents 25 clients. 80% of clients are new/previously unpublished writers. Currently handles: 10% nonfiction books; 70% novels; 20% movie scripts.

● Prior to becoming a agent, Mr. Bernard was a motion picture/television story editor and an executive managing editor for a major publishing house.

Represents: Nonfiction books, novels, movie scripts. **Considers these nonfiction areas:** business; how-to; language/literature/criticism; military/war; true crime/investigative. **Considers these fiction areas:** action/adventure; detective/police/crime; horror; science fiction; thriller/espionage.

How to Contact: Query first with SASE including $1 cash processing fee, "which controls the volume and eliminates dilettantism among the submissions." Reports immediately on queries; 1 month on mss "that are requested by us."

Needs: Obtains new clients through referrals and listings.

Recent Sales: Sold 2 titles in the last year. *The Action-Step Plan to Owning And Operating A Small Business*, by E. Toncré (Prentice-Hall).

Terms: Agent receives 10-15% sliding scale (decreasing) on domestic sales; 20% on foreign sales. Offers written contract, binding for 1 year with renewals.

Fees: Charges reading fee for unsolicited mss over 20 pages. Negotiated fees for market analysis available. Charges for photocopying for foreign sales.

💲 ⬤ DIANE RAINTREE LITERARY AGENCY, (formerly Diane Raintree Agency), 360 W. 21st St., New York NY 10011-3305. (212)242-2387. **Contact:** Diane Raintree. Estab. 1977. Represents 6-8 clients. Specializes in novels, film and TV scripts, memoirs, plays, poetry and children's books.

● Prior to opening her agency, Ms. Raintree was a a senior editor for Dial Press, copyeditor and proofreader for Zebra Books and Charter Books, and a reader for Avon Books.

Represents: Considers most fiction areas.

Also Handles: Feature film: TV MOW, sitcom. **Considers these script areas:** action/adventure; comedy; contemporary issues; detective/police/crime; ethnic; family saga; historical; juvenile; mainstream; mystery/suspense; psychic/supernatural; romance (romantic comedy, romantic drama); science fiction; teen; thriller/suspense.

How to Contact: Phone first. Send entire script if requested with SASE. Reports in 1 week on queries; 1-3 months on mss.

Recent Sales: Prefers not to share information on specific sales.

Terms: Agent receives 10% on domestic sales. "Writer should engage an entertainment lawyer for negotiations of film and TV option and contract."

Fees: May charge reading fee. "Amount varies from year to year."

🎬 ◐ JANIS RENAUD, LITERARY AGENT, Dept. 341, 20465 Douglas Crescent, Langley, British Columbia V3A 4B6 Canada. E-mail: jrliterary25@hotmail.com. Website: www.3.bc.sympatico.ca/literary1/literary1.html. **Contact:** Janis Renaud. Estab. 1998. Specializes in "seeking and nurturing new writers and helping them to reach their full potential by offering personalized care and service."

● Prior to opening her agency, Ms. Renaud worked as an independent television producer, casting director and writer (MOWs, documentary).

Represents: Nonfiction books, juvenile books, scholarly books, novels, textbooks, novellas, short story collections. **Considers these nonfiction areas:** agriculture/horticulture; animals; anthropology/archaeology; art/architecture/design; biography/autobiography; business; child guidance/parenting; cooking/food/nutrition; crafts/hobbies; current affairs;

education; ethnic/cultural interests; government/politics/law; health/medicine; history; how-to; humor; interior design/decorating; juvenile nonfiction; language/literature/criticism; money/finance/economics; music/dance/theater/film; nature/environment; New Age/metaphysics; popular culture; psychology; religious/inspirational; science/technology; self-help/personal improvement; sociology; sports; true crime/ investigative; women's issues/women's studies. **Considers these fiction areas:** cartoon/comic; confessional; contemporary issues; ethnic; experimental; family saga; glitz; historical; horror; humor/satire; juvenile; literary; mainstream; mystery (amateur sleuth); suspense; psychic/supernatural; regional; religious/inspirational; romance (contemporary, gothic, historical, regency); science fiction; sports; thriller/espionage; young adult.

How to Contact: Query with SASE (writers outside Canada must include IRCs). "Fiction should include a short synopsis, chapter outline, first chapter, and approximate word count. A half page bio is also helpful. Nonfiction should include a chapter outline, author credentials, research done, meaning, audience, competition, and how you think your book is different. Approximate word count." Accepts queries by e-mail, "maximum of one page. No attachments." Considers simultaneous queries and submissions. *No telephone or faxed queries, please.* Reports in 1 month on queries. Returns materials only with SASE.

Needs: Actively seeking all genres and writers willing to work hard at their craft. The following are of particular interest: literary fiction, women's issues, mystery, suspense, thrillers, true crime, young adult, romance, health, parapsychology, show business and how-to books. Not interested in any graphic violence or pornographic material, poetry, anthologies, westerns, science fiction, adventure or erotica.

Recent Sales: Prefers not to share information on specific sales.

Needs: Obtains new clients through advertising, referrals and conferences.

Terms: Agent receives 15% commission on domestic sales; 20% on foreign sales. Offers written contract, binding for 1 year, with renewals. Book by book basis. 60 days written notice must be given to terminate contract.

Fees: Charges one-time flat marketing fee to defer costs. Cost is $225, minimum of 5-6 targeted publishers.

Writers' Conferences: Writer's World (British Columbia, fall).

N $ ○ ⊘ SCHERF, INC. LITERARY MANAGEMENT, P.O. Box 80180, Las Vegas NV 89180-0180. (702)243-4895. Fax: (702)243-7460. E-mail: ds@scherf.com. Website: www.scherf.com. **Contact:** Mr. Dietmar Scherf. Estab. 1999. Specializes in discovering new authors, especially in the highly competitive fiction market. "As much as possible, we want to give every new author with a fresh voice a chance to find a publisher for their work. And we manage literary properties for established writers." Currently handles: 20% nonfiction books; 75% novels; 5% novellas.

• Prior to opening his agency, Mr. Scherf wrote several nonfiction books, and has been a publisher and editor since 1983.

Member Agents: Dietmar Scherf (fiction); Gail Kirby (fiction/nonfiction).

Represents: Nonfiction, novels, novellas. **Considers these nonfiction areas:** business; how-to; money/finance/economics; popular culture; psychology; religious/inspirational; self-help/personal improvement; true crime/investigative. **Considers these fiction areas:** action/adventure; literary; mainstream; mystery; religious/inspirational; thriller/espionage.

How to Contact: Query with SASE. Does not accept queries by fax or e-mail. Considers simultaneous queries and submissions. Reports in 2 months on queries; 3 months on mss. Returns materials only with SASE.

Needs: Actively seeking well-written contemporary fiction with broad commercial appeal. Does not want to receive gay, lesbian, erotica, or anything with foul language. Obtains new clients through recommendations from others, writing contests, unsolicited queries.

Recent Sales: New agency with no recorded sales.

Terms: Agent receives 10-15% commission on domestic sales; 15-20% on foreign sales (depending if new or established author). Offers written contract, binding on a case by case basis. 24 hour notice must be given to terminate contract, if no sales are pending.

Fees: Charges processing fee for new writers. Charges for postage, photocopying. May refer new writers to editing service. 0% of business is derived from referrals.

Tips: "Write the best manuscript, and polish it to the max. Write a story that you love and are enthusiastic about. Learn good writing skills through books, seminars/courses, etc., especially regarding characterization, dialogue, plot etc. in respect to novels. Know your competition well, and read books from authors that may fall into your category. In nonfiction, do the best research on your subject and be different than your competition with a new approach."

✓ ⊘ SLC ENTERPRISES, 852 Highland Place, Highland Park IL 60035. (847)432-7553. Fax: (847)432-7554. **Contact:** Ms. Carole Golin. Estab. 1985. Represents 30 clients. 50% of clients are new/previously unpublished writers. Currently handles: 75% nonfiction books; 5% juvenile books; 20% novels.

Member Agent: Stephen Cogil (sports).

Represents: Nonfiction books, juvenile books, novels, short story collections. **Considers these nonfiction areas:**

VISIT THE WRITER'S DIGEST WEBSITE at www.writersdigest.com for hot new markets, daily market updates, writers' guidelines and much more.

biography/autobiography, business, cooking/food/nutrition; current affairs; history; memoirs; sports; women's issues/women's studies; Holocaust studies. **Considers these fiction areas:** detective/police/crime; feminist; historical; juvenile; literary; picture book; regional; sports; young adult.

How to Contact: Query with outline/proposal. Accepts queries by fax. Prefers to be only reader. Reports in 2 weeks on queries; 1 months on mss. Returns materials only with SASE.

Recent Sales: Sold 5 titles in the last year. *The Raiders—A History*, by John Lombardo (Contemporary).

Terms: Agent receives 15% commission on domestic sales. Offers written contract, binding for 9 months.

Fees: Charges $150 reading fee for entire adult ms; $75-150 for children's ms, depending on length and number of stories. Reading fee includes overall critique plus specifics. No line editing for grammar etc. Charges no other fees. 20% of business is derived from reading and criticism fees.

MICHAEL STEINBERG LITERARY AGENCY, P.O. Box 274, Glencoe IL 60022. (847)835-8881. **Contact:** Michael Steinberg. Estab. 1980. Represents 27 clients. 5% of clients are new/previously unpublished writers. Specializes in business and general nonfiction, mysteries, science fiction. Currently handles: 75% nonfiction books; 25% novels.

Represents: Nonfiction books, novels. **Considers these nonfiction areas:** biography; business; computers; law; history; how-to; money/finance/economics; self-help/personal improvement. **Considers these fiction areas:** action/adventure; contemporary issues; detective/police/crime; erotica; mainstream; mystery/suspense; science fiction; thriller/espionage.

How to Contact: Query for guidelines with SASE. *No unsolicited mss.* Considers simultaneous queries and submissions. Reports in 2 weeks on queries; 6 weeks on mss. Returns materials only with SASE.

Needs: Obtains new clients through unsolicited inquiries and referrals from editors and authors.

Recent Sales: Sold 4 titles in the last year. *Guide to Investing, 3rd ed.*, by Michael Steinberg (Prentice-Hall); *Surviving the Millenium Crash*, by Jake Bernstein (Prentice-Hall).

Terms: Agent receives 15% on domestic sales; 15-20% on foreign sales. Offers written contract, which is binding, "but at will."

Fees: Charges $75 reading fee for outline and chapters 1-3; $200 for a full ms to 100,000 words. Criticism included in reading fee. Charges actual phone and postage, which is billed back quarterly. 5% of business derived from reading fees or criticism services.

Writers' Conferences: BEA (Chicago).

Tips: "We do not solicit new clients. Do not send generically addressed, photocopied query letters."

GLORIA STERN AGENCY, 12535 Chandler Blvd., #3, North Hollywood CA 91607-1934. Phone/fax: (818)508-6296. E-mail: cywrite@juno.com. Website: www.geocities.com/Athens/1980writers.html. **Contact:** Gloria Stern. Estab. 1984. Member of IWOSC, SCW. Represents 14 clients. 80% of clients are new/unpublished writers. Specializes in consultation, writer's services (ghost writing, editing, critiquing, etc.) and electronic media consultation, design. Currently handles: 79% fiction; 19% nonfiction books; 8% movie scripts; 2% reality based, CDs.

• This agency is not affiliated with the Gloria Stern Literary Agency in Texas. Prior to becoming an agent, Ms. Stern was a film editor/researcher.

Member Agent: Gloria Stern (fiction, screenplays, electronic/interactive media).

Represents: Novels, short story collections. **Considers these nonfiction areas:** biography/autobiography; business; child guidance/parenting; computers/electronics; cooking; current affairs; education; ethnic/cultural interests; gay/lesbian issues; health/medicine; how-to; language/literature/criticism; money/finance/economics; music/dance/theater/film; New Age/metaphysical; popular culture; psychology (pop); self-help/personal improvement; sociology; true crime/investigative; women's issues/women's studies. **Considers these fiction areas:** action/adventure; contemporary issues; detective/police/crime; erotica; fantasy; feminist; glitz; horror; literary; mainstream; romance (contemporary, gothic, historical, regency); science fiction; thriller/espionage; western/frontier.

Also Handles: Feature film, TV MOW. **Considers these script subject areas:** action/adventure; comedy; contemporary issues; detective/police/crime; erotica; ethnic; family saga; fantasy; feminist; gay; glitz; historical; horror; juvenile; mainstream; mystery/suspense; psychic/supernatural; romantic comedy; romantic drama; science fiction; sports; thriller; westerns/frontier.

How to Contact: Query with short bio, credits, synopsis, genre. Prefers to be only reader. Reports in 1 month on queries; 6 weeks on mss. Returns materials only with SASE.

Needs: Actively seeking electronic projects. Does not want to receive "gratuitous violence; non-professional 'true stories.' " Obtains new clients from listing books, classes, lectures, listings, word of mouth and online column.

Recent Sales: Sold 2 titles in the last year. Prefers not to share information on specific sales.

Terms: Agent receives 12% commission on domestic sales; 20% on foreign sales. Offers written contract, binding for 1 year.

Fees: Charges reading fee, by project (by arrangement), $45/hour for unpublished writers. Criticism service: $45/hour. Critiques are "detailed analysis of all salient points regarding such elements as structure, style, pace, development, publisher's point of view and suggestions for rewrites if needed." Charges for long-distance, photocopying and postage. 38% of income derived from commission from sales, 29% from reading fees, 26% from correspondence students, 7% from teaching. Payment of criticism fee does not ensure representation.

Writers' Conferences: BEA (Chicago, June); Show Biz Expo (Los Angeles, May); SigGraph (Los Angeles, August).

Tips: "To a writer interested in representation: Be sure that you have researched your field and are aware of current publishing demands. Writing is the only field in which all the best is readily available to the beginning writer. Network, take classes, persevere and most of all, write, write and rewrite."

[N:] [$] [◑] MARIANNE STRONG LITERARY AGENCY, 65 E. 96th St., New York NY 10128. (212)249-1000. Fax: (212)831-3241. **Contact:** Marianne Strong. Estab. 1978. Represents 15 clients. Specializes in biographies. Currently handles: 80% nonfiction books; 5% scholarly books; 5% novels; 10% TV scripts.
Member Agent: Mai D. Wong.
Represents: Nonfiction books, novels, TV scripts, syndicated material. **Considers these nonfiction areas:** art/architecture/design; biography/autobiography; business; child guidance/parenting; cooking/food/nutrition; current affairs; education; health/medicine; history; how-to; interior design/decorating; juvenile nonfiction; military/war; money/finance/economics; religious/inspirational; self-help/personal improvement; true crime; women's issues/women's studies. **Considers these fiction areas:** action/adventure; contemporary issues; detective/police/crime; family saga; glitz; historical; literary; mainstream; religious/inspirational; romance (contemporary, gothic, historical, regency); thriller/espionage; western/frontier.
How to Contact: Send complete outline plus 4-6 sample chapters. Reports "fairly soon" on queries; 2 months on mss.
Needs: Obtains new clients through recommendations from others.
Recent Sales: Prefers not to share information on specific sales.
Terms: Agent receives 15% commission on domestic sales; 20% on foreign sales. Offers written contract, binding for the life of book or play.
Fees: Charges a reading fee for unpublished writers only, "refundable when manuscript sold." Offers criticism service. "If using outside freelance writers and editors, entire fee goes to them. Critiques prepared by freelance writers and editors who receive entire fee." Charges for long distance calls for established clients.
Tips: "Submit a totally professional proposal with a story line that elucidates the story from A to Z plus several perfectly typed or word processed chapters. No disks, please. Also include background information on the author, especially literary or journalistic references."

[◐] DAWSON TAYLOR LITERARY AGENCY, 4722 Holly Lake Dr., Lake Worth FL 33463-5372. (561)965-4150. Fax: (561)641-9765. **Contact:** Dawson Taylor, Attorney at Law. Estab. 1974. Represents 34 clients. 80% of clients are new/previously unpublished writers. Specializes in nonfiction, fiction, sports, military history. Currently handles: 80% nonfiction; 5% scholarly books; 15% novels.
  ● Prior to opening his agency, Mr. Taylor served as book editor at the *National Enquirer* from 1976-1983, and book editor at the *Globe* from 1984-1991.
Represents: Nonfiction books, textbooks, scholarly books, novels. **Considers all nonfiction areas.** Specializes in nonfiction on sports, especially golf. **Considers these fiction areas:** detective/police/crime; mystery/suspense; thriller/espionage.
How to Contact: Query with outline. Does not accept queries by fax. Prefers to be the only reader. Reports in 5 days on queries; 10 days on mss. Returns materials only with SASE.
Needs: Obtains new clients through "recommendations from publishers and authors who are presently in my stable."
Recent Sales: Sold 5 titles in the last year. *Life & Times of Jack Nicklaus* (Sleeping Bear); *Picture Perfect Golf* (NTC Contemporary).
Terms: Agent receives 15% or 20% commission "depending upon editorial help." Offers written contract, indefinite, but cancellable on 60 days notice by either party.
Fees: "Reading fees are subject to negotiation, usually $100 for normal length manuscript, more for lengthy ones. Reading fee includes critique and sample editing. Criticism service subject to negotiation, from $100. Critiques are on style and content, include editing of manuscript, and are written by myself." 10% of business is derived from reading fees or criticism services. Payment of reading or criticism fee does not ensure representation.

[$] [◐] JEANNE TOOMEY ASSOCIATES, 95 Belden St., Falls Village CT 06031-1113. (860)824-0831/5469. Fax: (860)824-5460. **Contact:** Jeanne Toomey, president. Assistant: Peter Terranova. Estab. 1985. Represents 10 clients. 50% of clients are new/previously unpublished writers. Specializes in "nonfiction; biographies of famous men and women; history with a flair—murder and detection. We look for local history books—travel guides, as well as religion, crime and media subjects—as of special interest to us. No children's books, no poetry, no Harlequin-type romances." Currently handles: 45% nonfiction books; 20% novels; 35% movie scripts.
  ● Prior to opening her agency, Ms. Toomey was a newspaper reporter—"worked all over the country for AP, NY Journal-American, Brooklyn Daily Eagle, Orlando Sentinel, Stamford Advocate, Asbury Park Press, News Tribune (Woodbridge, NJ)."
Member Agents: Peter Terranova (religion, epigraphy); Jeanne Toomey (crime, media, nature, animals).
Represents: Nonfiction books, novels, short story collections, movie scripts. **Considers these nonfiction areas:** agriculture/horticulture; animals; anthropology/archaeology; art/architecture/design; biography/autobiography; government/politics/law; history; interior design/decorating; money/finance/economics; nature/environment; true crime/investigative. **Considers these fiction areas:** detective/police/crime; psychic/supernatural; thriller/espionage.
How to Contact: Send outline plus 3 sample chapters. "Query first, please!" Accepts queries by fax. Considers simultaneous queries. Reports in 1 month. Returns materials only with SASE.

Needs: Actively seeking already published authors. Does not want to receive poetry, children's books, Harlequin type romance, science fiction or sports.

Recent Sales: Sold 2 book titles in the last year. *Beyond the Brooklyn Bridge*, by Bernice Carton (Sunstone Press).

Terms: Agent receives 15% commission on domestic sales; 10% on foreign sales.

Fees: Charges $100 reading fee for unpublished authors; no fee for published authors. "The $100 covers marketing fee, office expenses, postage, photocopying. We absorb those costs in the case of published authors."

Writers' Conferences: Mystery Weekend (Mohawk, NY).

✔ Ⓞ **PHYLLIS TORNETTA AGENCY**, 4 Kettle Lane, Mashpee MA 02649. (508)529-8821. **Contact:** Phyllis Tornetta, president. Estab. 1979. Represents 22 clients. 35% of clients are new/unpublished writers. Specializes in romance, contemporary. Currently handles: 100% novels.

Represents: Novels and juvenile.

How to Contact: Query with outline and SASE. No unsolicited mss. Reports in 1 month.

Recent Sales: No sales reported in last year. Prior sales: *Heart of the Wolf*, by Sally Dawson (Leisure); *Jennie's Castle*, by Elizabeth Sinclair (Silhouette).

Terms: Agent receives 15% commission on domestic sales and 20% on foreign sales.

Fees: Charges a $100 reading fee for full mss.

💲 Ⓞ **A TOTAL ACTING EXPERIENCE**, Dept. N.W., 20501 Ventura Blvd., Suite 399, Woodland Hills CA 91364-2348. (818)340-9249. **Contact:** Dan A. Bellacicco. Estab. 1984. Signatory of WGA, SAG, AFTRA. Represents 30 clients. 50% of clients are new/previously unpublished writers. Specializes in "quality instead of quantity." Currently handles: 5% nonfiction books; 5% juvenile books; 10% novels; 5% novellas; 5% short story collections; 50% movie scripts; 10% TV scripts; 5% stage plays; 5% how-to books and videos.

 • See the expanded listing for this agency in Script Agents.

Ⓝ 💲 Ⓞ **VISIONS PRESS**, P.O. Box 4904, Valley Village CA 91617-0904. (805)722-8241. **Contact:** Allen Brown. Estab. 1991. "We prefer to support writers who incorporate African-American issues in the storyline. We handle adult romance novels and consciousness-raising pieces." Currently handles: 50% novels; 50% newspaper columns and magazine features.

Represents: Novels, newspaper columns and magazine features. **Considers these magazine areas:** ethnic/cultural interests; gay/lesbian issues; religious/inspirational; self-help/personal improvement; women's issues/women's studies. **Considers these fiction areas:** confessional; contemporary issues; erotica; ethnic; gay; lesbian; mainstream; romance (contemporary); young adult.

How to Contact: Send outline and 2 sample chapters and author bio. Reports in 2 weeks on queries; 1 month on mss.

Needs: Obtains new clients through recommendations from others and through inquiries.

Recent Sales: Available upon request.

Terms: Agent receives 10% commission on domestic sales; 15% on foreign sales. Offers written contract, specific length of time depends on type of work—novel newspaper column or magazine feature.

Fees: Charges reading fee. Fees are based on length of manuscript ($100 for up to 300 pages; $150 for any length thereafter)." Offers critique service. "Same as for the reading fee. Both the reading fee and the critique fee entitle the author to a critique of his/her work by one of our editors. We are interested in everyone who has a desire to be published . . . to hopefully realize their dream. To that end, we provide very honest and practical advice on what needs to be done to correct a manuscript." Additional fees "will be negotiated with the author on a project by project basis. Often there is a one-time fee charged that covers all office expenses associated with the marketing of a manuscript." 10% of business is derived from reading fees or critique services. Payment of critique fee does not ensure representation.

Writers' Conferences: "We do not usually attend writing conferences. Most of our contacts are made through associations with groups such as NAACP, Rainbow Coalition, Urban League and other such groups that promote consciousness-raising activities by African-Americans. We look for talent among African-American scholars and African-American 'common folk' who can usually be found sharing their opinions and visions at an issues-related conference and town hall type meeting."

Tips: "We believe the greatest story ever told has yet to be written! For that reason we encourage every writer to uninhibitedly pursue his/her dream of becoming published. A no from us should simply be viewed as a temporary setback that can be overcome by another attempt to meet our high expectations. Discouraged, frustrated and demoralized are words we have deleted from our version of the dictionary. An aspiring writer must have the courage to press on and believe in his/her talent."

TO RECEIVE REGULAR TIPS AND UPDATES about writing and Writer's Digest publications via e-mail, send an e-mail with "SUBSCRIBE NEWSLETTER" in the body of the message to "newsletter-request@writersdigest.com."

N $ ☻ WINDFALL MANAGEMENT, 4084 Mandeville Canyon Rd., Los Angeles CA 90049-1032. (310)471-6317. Fax: (310)471-4577. E-mail: windfall@deltanet.com. **Contact:** Jeanne Field. Represents 20 clients. Windfall is a management company representing writers and books to the film and television industry. "We are especially interested in mainstream and independent film writers or playwrights." Currently handles: 20% novels; 50% movie scripts; 25% TV scripts; 5% stage plays.
  • See the expanded listing for this agency in Script Agents.

$ ◎ WOLCOTT LITERARY AGENCY, P.O. Box 7493, Shawnee Mission KS 66207-7493. (913)327-1440. E-mail: nordwolc@oz.sunflower.org. Website: oz.sunflower.org/~nordwolc. **Contact:** Chris Wolcott. Estab. 1996. Member of Kansas City Professional Writer's Group. Represents over 10 clients. 90% of clients are new/previously unpublished writers. Specializes in mass-market genre fiction, science fiction, fantasy, horror, romance, erotica, etc. Currently handles: 10% movie scripts, 90% novels.
Represents: Novels, novellas, short story collections. **Considers these fiction areas:** action/adventure; detective/police/crime; erotica; experimental; fantasy; historical; horror; humor/satire; literary; mainstream; memoirs; mystery/suspense; psychic/supernatural; romance (gothic, historical); science fiction; thriller/espionage; westerns/frontier; young adult.
Also Handles: Movie scripts. **Considers these script subject areas:** documentary screenplays only.
How to Contact: Query with short explanation of storyline and SASE. "We accept e-mail queries for faster responses." Considers simultaneous queries and submissions. Reports in 3 weeks on queries; 7 weeks on mss; 1-5 days on e-mail queries. Returns materials only with SASE.
Needs: Actively seeking wide spectrum of fiction and pertinent nonfiction. Does not want to receive poetry. Obtains new clients through recommendations from others, conferences, unsolicited queries and from their Website at oz.sunflower.org/~nordwolc.
Recent Sales: Sold 3 titles in the last year. *The Final Beat*, by B. Driscol (EMB); *Security Row*, by Frank Sonny (Lombard). Other clients include Tom Walsh, Mike Gallagher and John Altman.
Terms: Agent receives 10% commission on domestic sales; 20% on foreign sales. Offers written contract, binding for 1 year, with a 30 day termination clause.
Fees: Reading fee: $150 for outline and full ms to 100,000 words; $50 for short stories to 10,000 words. Fee is for new/previously unpublished writers only, includes a critique of all works they agree to review. Criticism service: all works reviewed receive a detailed critique. The critiques, written by the agents, focus on story flow, content and format, not necessarily punctuation and grammar, and advise as to the proper format for submissions. Charges for postage on submissions to publishers. "There are no hidden fees." 10% of business is derived from reading fees or criticism service.
Reading List: Reads *Publishers Weekly* to find new clients. Looks for "freshness and, most importantly, marketability."
Tips: "We form a strategy to help new authors get their name into the market so approaching the larger houses is made easier. We want you to succeed. It all starts with a simple query letter. Drop us a line, we'd like to hear from you."

✓ ◎ THE WRITE THERAPIST, 2000 N. Ivar, Suite 3, Hollywood CA 90068. (213)465-2630. E-mail: gorma333 @excite.com. **Contact:** Shyama Ross. Estab. 1980. Represents 6 clients. 90% of clients are new/previously unpublished writers. Currently handles: 40% nonfiction; 60% fiction (novels).
  • Prior to becoming an agent, Ms. Ross was a book editor for 20 years.
Represents: Considers contemporary fiction and nonfiction including: pop psychology, philosophy, mysticism, Eastern religion, self-help, business, health, commerical novels.
Needs: Actively seeking "quality contemporary fiction and all nonfiction." Does not want to receive "science fiction, fantasy, horror, erotic or sexist material." Obtains new clients through recommendations from others, solicitation and seminars.
Recent Sales: Prefers not to share information on specific sales.
Terms: Agent receives 15% commission on domestic sales; 20% on foreign sales.
Fees: Does not charge a reading fee. Charges $125 critique fee for mss up to 300 pages, $15 each additional 60 pages. "Critique fees are 100% refundable if a sale is made." Critique consists of "detailed analysis of manuscript in terms of structure, style, characterizations, etc. and marketing potential, plus free guidesheets for fiction or nonfiction." Charges $100 one-time marketing fee. 50% of business is derived from commission on ms sales; 50% is derived from criticism and editing services. Payment of a criticism fee does not ensure agency representation. Offers editing on potentially publishable mss.
Reading Lists: Reads *Publishers Weekly*, *Writer's Digest* and *Hollywood Reporter* to find new clients. Looks for "a unique voice/story."
Tips: "We aggressively seek film rights/sales on all novels."

✓ ☻ KAREN GANTZ ZAHLER LITERARY AGENCY, 860 Fifth Ave., 8th Floor, New York NY 10021.
Contact: Karen Gantz Zahler. Estab. 1990. Represents 40 clients. Specializes in nonfiction, cookbooks. Currently handles: 70% nonfiction books; 20% novels; 10% movie scripts.
  • Ms. Gantz is also an entertainment lawyer.
Represents: Nonfiction books, novels, movie scripts. **Considers all nonfiction and fiction areas;** "anything great."
How to Contact: Prefers to obtain new clients through recommendations. Query with SASE. Reports in 2 months.
Recent Sales: *Lifting the Fog of War*, by Admiral Bill Owens (Farrar, Straus & Giroux); *Testing 1, 2, 3*, by Stanley Kaplan (Carol Publishing).

Terms: Agent receives 15% commission on domestic sales; 20% commission on foreign sales. Offers written contract, binding for 1 year. Also offers a ms analysis service for $450.

Writers' Conferences: BEA.

Tips: "I'm a literary property lawyer and provide excellent negotiating services and exploitation of subsidiary rights. I take on one or two unsolicited clients annually."

⬤ BARBARA J. ZITWER AGENCY, 525 West End Ave. #1114, New York NY 10024. (212)501-8426. Fax: (212)501-8462. E-mail: bjzitwerag@aol.com. **Contact:** Barbara J. Zitwer. Estab. 1994. Represents 30 clients. 99% of clients are new/previously unpublished writers. Specializes in literary-commercial fiction, nonfiction, pop culture, selling film rights to clients' work. Currently handles: 35% nonfiction books, 65% novels.

  • Prior to opening her agency, Ms. Zitwer was an international foreign publishing scout for Franklin & Seigal Associates, film producer.

Represents: Nonfiction books, novels. **Considers these nonfiction areas:** biography/autobiography; current affairs; ethnic/cultural interests; gay/lesbian issues; humor; language/literature/criticism; memoirs; music/dance/theater/film; nature/environment; New Age/metaphysics; popular culture; psychology; self-help/personal improvement; true crime/investigative. **Considers these fiction areas:** detective/police/crime; ethnic; gay; glitz; humor/satire; literary; mainstream; mystery/suspense; thriller/espionage.

How to Contact: Send outline and 3 sample chapters with SASE. Prefers to be only reader. Reports in 2 weeks on queries; 4-6 weeks on mss. Returns materials only with SASE.

Needs: Actively seeking "commercial fiction—very strong literary fiction and pop-culture nonfiction—unusual memoirs and works that can be sold for film and TV. I am aggressively selling a lot of movie and TV rights in Hollywood." Does not want to receive "cookbooks, science books, business books, serious academic books, children's or young adults books, illustrated books or graphic novels unless they are humor books with illustrations." Usually obtains clients through recommendations from other clients and editors.

Recent Sales: *Anonymous Rex*, by Eric Garcia (Random House); *Walk of Fame*, by Sharon Krum (Quartet Books); as literary agent for the Estate of Timothy Leary, sold *Smart Loving* (Thunder's Mouth Press).

Terms: Agent receives 15% commission on domestic sales; 25% on foreign sales. Offers a written contract, binding for 6 months. Charges for postage, photocopying, long distance calls, legal fees for movie contracts. Usually obtains clients through recommendations from other clients and editors.

Fees: Charges reading fee of $595 for unsolicited mss and/or mss whose authors wish to have a written critique and editorial suggestions. "All manuscripts which I read on a paid basis are considered for representation, but representation is not guaranteed." $595 fee is for mss of 400 pgs. For mss over 400 pgs., additional fee of $50 per 100 pgs. "Many authors have requested editorial critiques and feedback and therefore I decided to start a reading service. In today's highly competitive market where editors no longer edit and want extremely polished books, I can provide an experienced and professional service to the first time writer or a more experienced writer who is having problems with his/her book. Having a critique by an agent is most productive because the agent is the person who knows what the publisher wants and what shape a book needs to be in in order to be submitted." I do not charge a reading fee for work I solicit and request to read.

Writers' Conferences: Marymount Manhattan Writer's Conference (New York, May).

Tips: "1. Check your agent's reputation with editors and publishers. 2. Try to meet your potential agent. 3. Make sure you and the agent have the same goals. 4. Make sure you are given very specific updates on submissions and rejection letters. 5. Educate yourself—you need to be a part of your business too."

Additional Fee-charging Agents

The following fee-charging agencies have indicated they are *primarily* interested in handling the work of scriptwriters. However, they also handle less than 10-15 percent book manuscripts. After reading the listing (you can find the page number in the Listings Index), send a query to obtain more information on their needs and manuscript submissions policies.

Agape Productions
Camejo & Assoc., Suzanna
Gelff Agency, The Laya

Agents Specialties Index: Fee-charging

The subject index is divided into fiction and nonfiction subject categories for Fee-charging Literary Agents. To find an agent interested in the type of manuscript you've written, see the appropriate sections under subject headings that best describe your work. Check the Listings Index for the page number of the agent's listing or refer to the section of Fee-charging Literary Agents preceding this index. Agents who are open to most fiction, nonfiction or script subjects appear under the "Open to all Categories" heading.

FEE-CHARGING LITERARY AGENTS/FICTION

Action/Adventure: AEI/Atchity Editorial/Entertainment International; Ahearn Agency, Inc., The; Authors' Marketing Services Ltd.; Brinke Literary Agency, The; Buchan Literary Service, Jim; Cambridge Literary Associates; Catalog Literary Agency, The; Collier Associates; Creative Literary Agency; Fenton Entertainment Group, Inc.; Fort Ross Inc. Russian-American Publishing Projects; Fran Literary Agency; GEM Literary Services; Gladden Unlimited; Gusay Literary Agency, The Charlotte; Hamilton's Literary Agency, Andrew; Hartline Literary Agency; Independent Publishing Agency: A Literary and Entertainment Agency; Literary Group West; Magnetic Management; Mumford Literary Agency, Inc., The; Pelham Literary Agency; Pell Agency, William; PMA Literary and Film Management, Inc.; Puddingstone Literary Agency; Scherf, Inc. Literary Management; Steinberg Literary Agency, Michael; Stern Agency, Gloria; Strong Literary Agency, Marianne; Windfall Management; Wolcott Literary Agency

Cartoon/Comic: Authors' Marketing Services Ltd.; Buchan Literary Service, Jim; Fort Ross Inc. Russian-American Publishing Projects; Fran Literary Agency; Gusay Literary Agency, The Charlotte; Howard Agency, The Eddy; Independent Publishing Agency: A Literary and Entertainment Agency; Renaud, Literary Agent, Janis

Confessional: Gusay Literary Agency, The Charlotte; Hamilton's Literary Agency, Andrew; Independent Publishing Agency: A Literary and Entertainment Agency; Renaud, Literary Agent, Janis; Visions Press; Windfall Management

Contemporary Issues: AEI/Atchity Editorial/Entertainment International; Ahearn Agency, Inc., The; Creative Literary Agency; Fenton Entertainment Group, Inc.; Fran Literary Agency; Gusay Literary Agency, The Charlotte; Hamilton's Literary Agency, Andrew; Hartline Literary Agency; Howard Agency, The Eddy; Independent Publishing Agency: A Literary and Entertainment Agency; Jenks Agency, Carolyn; Magnetic Management; McKinley, Literary Agency, Virginia C.; PMA Literary and Film Management, Inc.; Renaud, Literary Agent, Janis; Steinberg Literary Agency, Michael; Stern Agency, Gloria; Strong Literary Agency, Marianne; Tornetta Agency, Phyllis; Visions Press; Windfall Management

Detective/Police/Crime: Ahearn Agency, Inc., The; Authors' Marketing Services Ltd.; Cambridge Literary Associates; Collier Associates; Creative Literary Agency; Fenton Entertainment Group, Inc.; Fort Ross Inc. Russian-American Publishing Projects; Fran Literary Agency; GEM Literary Services; Gladden Unlimited; Gusay Literary Agency, The Charlotte; Hamilton's Literary Agency, Andrew; Independent Publishing Agency: A Literary and Entertainment Agency; Literary Group West; Magnetic Management; Pelham Literary Agency; Pell Agency, William; PMA Literary and Film Management, Inc.; Puddingstone Literary Agency; SLC Enterprises; Steinberg Literary Agency, Michael; Stern Agency, Gloria; Strong Literary Agency, Marianne; Taylor Literary Agency, Dawson; Toomey Associates, Jeanne; Windfall Management; Wolcott Literary Agency; Zitwer Agency, Barbara J.

Erotica: AEI/Atchity Editorial/Entertainment International; Fort Ross Inc. Russian-American Publishing Projects; Gusay Literary Agency, The Charlotte; Hamilton's Literary Agency, Andrew; Independent Publishing Agency: A Literary and Entertainment Agency; Steinberg Literary Agency, Michael; Stern Agency, Gloria; Visions Press; Wolcott Literary Agency

Ethnic: Ahearn Agency, Inc., The; Backman, Elizabeth H.; Crown International Literature and Arts Agency, Bonnie R.; Dickens Group, The; Fenton Entertainment Group, Inc.; Gladden Unlimited; Gusay Literary Agency, The Charlotte; Hamilton's Literary Agency, Andrew; Independent Publishing Agency: A Literary and Entertainment Agency; Jenks Agency, Carolyn; McKinley, Literary Agency, Virginia C.; Mumford Literary Agency, Inc., The; PMA Literary and Film Management, Inc.; Renaud, Literary Agent, Janis; Visions Press; Zitwer Agency, Barbara J.

Experimental: Crown International Literature and Arts Agency, Bonnie R.; Gusay Literary Agency, The Charlotte; Independent Publishing Agency: A Literary and Entertainment Agency; Renaud, Literary Agent, Janis; Wolcott Literary Agency

Family Saga: Ahearn Agency, Inc., The; Authors' Marketing Services Ltd.; Buchan Literary Service, Jim; Catalog Literary Agency, The; Creative Literary Agency; Crown International Literature and Arts Agency, Bonnie R.; Fran Literary Agency; GEM Literary Services; Gusay Literary Agency, The Charlotte; Hamilton's Literary Agency, Andrew; Hartline Literary Agency; Howard Agency, The Eddy; Jenks Agency, Carolyn; McKinley, Literary Agency, Virginia C.; Mumford Literary Agency, Inc., The; PMA Literary and Film Management, Inc.; Renaud, Literary Agent, Janis; Strong Literary Agency, Marianne; Windfall Management

Fantasy: Ahearn Agency, Inc., The; Authors' Marketing Services Ltd.; Brinke Literary Agency, The; Buchan Literary Service, Jim; Cambridge Literary Associates; Creative Literary Agency; Fort Ross Inc. Russian-American Publishing Projects; Fran Literary Agency; GEM Literary Services; Gusay Literary Agency, The Charlotte; Howard Agency, The Eddy; Independent Publishing Agency: A Literary and Entertainment Agency; Magnetic Management; Mumford Literary Agency, Inc., The; Pelham Literary Agency; Stern Agency, Gloria; Windfall Management; Wolcott Literary Agency

Feminist: Ahearn Agency, Inc., The; Creative Literary Agency; GEM Literary Services; Gusay Literary Agency, The Charlotte; Independent Publishing Agency: A Literary and Entertainment Agency; Jenks Agency, Carolyn; McKinley, Literary Agency, Virginia C.; Mumford Literary Agency, Inc., The; SLC Enterprises; Stern Agency, Gloria; Windfall Management; Ahearn Agency, Inc., The

Gay: Gusay Literary Agency, The Charlotte; Jenks Agency, Carolyn; McLean Literary Agency; PMA Literary and Film Management, Inc.; Visions Press; Windfall Management; Zitwer Agency, Barbara J.

Glitz: Ahearn Agency, Inc., The; Creative Literary Agency; Fenton Entertainment Group, Inc.; Fran Literary Agency; Gladden Unlimited; Gusay Literary Agency, The Charlotte; Magnetic Management; Renaud, Literary Agent, Janis; Stern Agency, Gloria; Strong Literary Agency, Marianne; Zitwer Agency, Barbara

Historical: AEI/Atchity Editorial/Entertainment International; Ahearn Agency, Inc., The; Authors' Marketing Services Ltd.; Backman, Elizabeth H.; Buchan Literary Service, Jim; Cambridge Literary Associates; Collier Associates; Creative Literary Agency; Crown International Literature and Arts Agency, Bonnie R.; Fenton Entertainment Group, Inc.; Fran Literary Agency; GEM Literary Services; Gusay Literary Agency, The Charlotte; Hartline Literary Agency; Howard Agency, The Eddy; Independent Publishing Agency: A Literary and Entertainment Agency; Jenks Agency, Carolyn; Literary Group West; Mumford Literary Agency, Inc., The; PMA Literary and Film Management, Inc.; Renaud, Literary Agent, Janis; SLC Enterprises; Strong Literary Agency, Marianne; Windfall Management; Wolcott Literary Agency

Horror: AEI/Atchity Editorial/Entertainment International; Ahearn Agency, Inc., The; Authors' Marketing Services Ltd.; Catalog Literary Agency, The; Creative Literary Agency; Fort Ross Inc. Russian-American Publishing Projects; Fran Literary Agency; GEM Literary Services; Gladden Unlimited; Magnetic Management; Mumford Literary Agency, Inc., The; Pelham Literary Agency; Puddingstone Literary Agency; Renaud, Literary Agent, Janis; Stern Agency, Gloria; Wolcott Literary Agency

Humor/Satire: Ahearn Agency, Inc., The; Authors' Marketing Services Ltd.; Buchan Literary Service, Jim; Creative Literary Agency; Crown International Literature and Arts Agency, Bonnie R.; Fenton Entertainment Group, Inc.; Fran Literary Agency; GEM Literary Services; Gusay Literary Agency, The Charlotte; Hamilton's Literary Agency, Andrew; Howard Agency, The Eddy; Independent Publishing Agency: A Literary and Entertainment Agency; Magnetic Management; McKinley, Literary Agency, Virginia C.; Pell Agency, William; PMA Literary and Film Management, Inc.; Renaud, Literary Agent, Janis; Windfall Management; Wolcott Literary Agency; Zitwer Agency, Barbara J.

Juvenile: Ahearn Agency, Inc., The; Alp Arts Co.; Author Author Literary Agency Ltd.; Buchan Literary Service, Jim; Catalog Literary Agency, The; Creative Literary Agency; Fran Literary Agency; GEM Literary Services; Gusay Literary Agency, The Charlotte; Howard Agency, The Eddy; Independent Publishing Agency: A Literary and Entertainment Agency; Magnetic Management; McLean Literary Agency; Mews Books Ltd.; Mumford Literary Agency, Inc., The; Renaud, Literary Agent, Janis; SLC Enterprises; Windfall Management

Lesbian: Ahearn Agency, Inc., The; Gusay Literary Agency, The Charlotte; Jenks Agency, Carolyn; PMA Literary and Film Management, Inc.; Visions Press

Literary: AEI/Atchity Editorial/Entertainment International; Ahearn Agency, Inc., The; Authors' Marketing Services Ltd.; Creative Literary Agency; Crown International Literature and Arts Agency, Bonnie R.; Dickens Group, The; Fran Literary Agency; GEM Literary Services; Gusay Literary Agency, The Charlotte; Hartline Literary Agency; Howard Agency, The Eddy; Independent Publishing Agency: A Literary and Entertainment Agency; Jenks Agency, Carolyn; Magnetic Management; McKinley, Literary Agency, Virginia C.; Mumford Literary Agency, Inc., The; Pelham Literary Agency; PMA Literary and Film Management, Inc.; Renaud, Literary Agent, Janis; Scherf, Inc. Literary Management; SLC Enterprises; Stern Agency, Gloria; Strong Literary Agency, Marianne; Windfall Management; Wolcott Literary Agency; Zitwer Agency, Barbara J.

Mainstream: AEI/Atchity Editorial/Entertainment International; Ahearn Agency, Inc., The; Authors' Marketing Services Ltd.; Cambridge Literary Associates; Catalog Literary Agency, The; Collier Associates; Creative Literary Agency; Dickens Group, The; Fenton Entertainment Group, Inc.; Fran Literary Agency; GEM Literary Services; Gusay Literary Agency, The Charlotte; Howard Agency, The Eddy; Independent Publishing Agency: A Literary and Entertainment Agency; Jenks Agency, Carolyn; Literary Group West; Magnetic Management; Pelham Literary Agency; PMA Literary and Film Management, Inc.; Renaud, Literary Agent, Janis; Scherf, Inc. Literary Management; Steinberg Literary Agency, Michael; Stern Agency, Gloria; Strong Literary Agency, Marianne; Visions Press; Windfall Management; Wolcott Literary Agency; Write Therapist, The; Zitwer Agency, Barbara J.

Mystery/Suspense: AEI/Atchity Editorial/Entertainment International; Ahearn Agency, Inc., The; Authors' Marketing Services Ltd.; Backman, Elizabeth H.; Brinke Literary Agency, The; Buchan Literary Service, Jim; Cambridge Literary Associates; Collier Associates; Creative Literary Agency; Dickens Group, The; Fenton Entertainment Group, Inc.; Fort Ross Inc. Russian-American Publishing Projects; Fran Literary Agency; GEM Literary Services; Gusay Literary Agency, The Charlotte; Hamilton's Literary Agency, Andrew; Hartline Literary Agency; Independent Publishing Agency: A Literary and Entertainment Agency; Jenks Agency, Carolyn; Magnetic Management; McLean Literary Agency; Mumford Literary Agency, Inc., The; PMA Literary and Film Management, Inc.; Renaud, Literary Agent, Janis; Scherf, Inc. Literary Management; Steinberg Literary Agency, Michael; Taylor Literary Agency, Dawson; Windfall Management; Wolcott Literary Agency; Zitwer Agency, Barbara J.

Open to all Fiction Categories: Author Author Literary Agency Ltd.; Author's Agency, The; CS International Literary Agency; Pelham-Heuisler Literary Agency; Raintree Literary Agency, Diane; Total Acting Experience, A; Zahler Literary Agency, Karen Gantz

Picture Book: Alp Arts Co.; Buchan Literary Service, Jim; Fran Literary Agency; GEM Literary Services; Gusay Literary Agency, The Charlotte; Howard Agency, The Eddy; Independent Publishing Agency: A Literary and Entertainment Agency; Mumford Literary Agency, Inc., The; SLC Enterprises

Psychic/Supernatural: Ahearn Agency, Inc., The; Authors' Marketing Services Ltd.; Brinke Literary Agency, The; Creative Literary Agency; GEM Literary Services; Gusay Literary Agency, The Charlotte; Hamilton's Literary Agency, Andrew; Independent Publishing Agency: A Literary and Entertainment Agency; Jenks Agency, Carolyn; Renaud, Literary Agent, Janis; Toomey Associates, Jeanne; Wolcott Literary Agency

Regional: Ahearn Agency, Inc., The; Backman, Elizabeth H.; Cambridge Literary Associates; Creative Literary Agency; Fran Literary Agency; GEM Literary Services; Gusay Literary Agency, The Charlotte; Hartline Literary Agency; Howard Agency, The Eddy; Mumford Literary Agency, Inc., The; Renaud, Literary Agent, Janis; SLC Enterprises

Religious/Inspirational: Brinke Literary Agency, The; Buchan Literary Service, Jim; Cambridge Literary Associates; Creative Literary Agency; Fran Literary Agency; Gusay Literary Agency, The Charlotte; Hartline Literary Agency; Jenks Agency, Carolyn; Magnetic Management; McKinley, Literary Agency, Virginia C.; Renaud, Literary Agent, Janis; Scherf, Inc. Literary Management; Strong Literary Agency, Marianne

Romance: AEI/Atchity Editorial/Entertainment International; Ahearn Agency, Inc., The; Authors' Marketing Services Ltd.; Brinke Literary Agency, The; Cambridge Literary Associates; Catalog Literary Agency, The; Collier Associates; Creative Literary Agency; Fenton Entertainment Group, Inc.; Fort Ross Inc. Russian-American Publishing Projects; Fran Literary Agency; GEM Literary Services; Hamilton's Literary Agency, Andrew; Hartline Literary Agency; Jenks Agency, Carolyn; Magnetic Management; McLean Literary Agency; Mumford Literary Agency, Inc., The; Pelham Literary Agency; PMA Literary and Film Management, Inc.; Renaud, Literary Agent, Janis; Stern Agency, Gloria; Strong Literary Agency, Marianne; Tornetta Agency, Phyllis; Visions Press; Windfall Management; Wolcott Literary Agency

Science Fiction: AEI/Atchity Editorial/Entertainment International; Ahearn Agency, Inc., The; Authors' Marketing Services Ltd.; Backman, Elizabeth H.; Brinke Literary Agency, The; Buchan Literary Service, Jim; Cambridge Literary Associates; Catalog Literary Agency, The; Creative Literary Agency; Fenton Entertainment Group, Inc.; Fort Ross Inc. Russian-American Publishing Projects; Fran Literary Agency; GEM Literary Services; Magnetic Management; Mumford Literary Agency, Inc., The; Pelham Literary Agency; PMA Literary and Film Management, Inc.; Puddingstone Literary Agency; Renaud, Literary Agent, Janis; Steinberg Literary Agency, Michael; Stern Agency, Gloria; Windfall Management; Wolcott Literary Agency

Sports: Backman, Elizabeth H.; Buchan Literary Service, Jim; Cambridge Literary Associates; Creative Literary Agency; Fenton Entertainment Group, Inc.; Fran Literary Agency; Gusay Literary Agency, The Charlotte; Hamilton's Literary Agency, Andrew; Howard Agency, The Eddy; Pelham Literary Agency; Renaud, Literary Agent, Janis; SLC Enterprises; Windfall Management

Thriller/Espionage: AEI/Atchity Editorial/Entertainment International; Ahearn Agency, Inc., The; Authors' Marketing Services Ltd.; Backman, Elizabeth H.; Brinke Literary Agency, The; Buchan Literary Service, Jim; Cambridge Literary Associates; Catalog Literary Agency, The; Collier Associates; Creative Literary Agency; Dickens Group, The; Fenton Entertainment Group, Inc.; Fort Ross Inc. Russian-American Publishing Projects; Fran Literary Agency; GEM Literary Services; Gladden Unlimited; Gusay Literary Agency, The Charlotte; Hamilton's Literary Agency, Andrew; Hartline Literary Agency; Independent Publishing Agency: A Literary and Entertainment Agency; Jenks Agency, Carolyn; Literary Group West; Magnetic Management; Mumford Literary Agency, Inc., The; Pelham Literary Agency; Pell Agency, William; PMA Literary and Film Management, Inc.; Puddingstone Literary Agency; Renaud, Literary Agent, Janis; Scherf, Inc. Literary Management; Steinberg Literary Agency, Michael; Stern Agency, Gloria; Strong Literary Agency, Marianne; Taylor Literary Agency, Dawson; Toomey Associates, Jeanne; Windfall Management; Wolcott Literary Agency; Zitwer Agency, Barbara J.

Westerns/Frontier: Ahearn Agency, Inc., The; Cambridge Literary Associates; Creative Literary Agency; Fenton Entertainment Group, Inc.; Fran Literary Agency; GEM Literary Services; Gusay Literary Agency, The Charlotte; Hamilton's Literary Agency, Andrew; Jenks Agency, Carolyn; Pelham Literary Agency; PMA Literary and Film Management, Inc.; Stern Agency, Gloria; Strong Literary Agency, Marianne; Windfall Management; Wolcott Literary Agency

Young Adult: Alp Arts Co.; Buchan Literary Service, Jim; Cambridge Literary Associates; Catalog Literary Agency, The; Creative Literary Agency; Fort Ross Inc. Russian-American Publishing Projects; Fran Literary Agency; GEM Literary Services; Gusay Literary Agency, The Charlotte; Hamilton's Literary Agency, Andrew; Independent Publishing Agency: A Literary and Entertainment Agency; Magnetic Management; Renaud, Literary Agent, Janis; SLC Enterprises; Visions Press; Windfall Management; Wolcott Literary Agency

FEE-CHARGING LITERARY AGENTS/NONFICTION

Agriculture/Horticulture: Catalog Literary Agency, The; Fran Literary Agency; Renaud, Literary Agent, Janis; Toomey Associates, Jeanne

Animals: Ahearn Agency, Inc., The; Author's Agency, The; Brinke Literary Agency, The; Cambridge Literary Associates; Catalog Literary Agency, The; Creative Literary Agency; Fran Literary Agency; Hamilton's Literary Agency, Andrew; Jenks Agency, Carolyn; McKinley, Literary Agency, Virginia C.; PMA Literary and Film Management, Inc.; Renaud, Literary Agent, Janis; Toomey Associates, Jeanne; Total Acting Experience, A; Windfall Management

Anthropology: Author's Agency, The; Brinke Literary Agency, The; Cambridge Literary Associates; Catalog Literary Agency, The; Fran Literary Agency; Independent Publishing Agency: A Literary and Entertainment Agency; Pelham-Heuisler Literary Agency; Renaud, Literary Agent, Janis; Toomey Associates, Jeanne

Art/Architecture/Design: Creative Literary Agency; Fran Literary Agency; Independent Publishing Agency: A Literary and Entertainment Agency; Pelham-Heuisler Literary Agency; Renaud, Literary Agent, Janis; Strong Literary Agency, Marianne; Toomey Associates, Jeanne; Total Acting Experience, A

Biography/Autobiography: AEI/Atchity Editorial/Entertainment International; Ahearn Agency, Inc., The; Author's Agency, The; Authors' Marketing Services Ltd.; Backman, Elizabeth H.; Brinke Literary Agency, The; Buchan Literary Service, Jim; Cambridge Literary Associates; Collier Associates; Creative Literary Agency; Devereux Company, The Wilson; Dickens Group, The; Fenton Entertainment Group, Inc.; Fort Ross Inc. Russian-American Publishing Projects; Fran Literary Agency; GEM Literary Services; Gladden Unlimited; Hamilton's Literary Agency, Andrew; Howard Agency, The Eddy; Independent Publishing Agency: A Literary and Entertainment Agency; Jenks Agency, Carolyn; Magnetic Management; McKinley, Literary Agency, Virginia C.; McLean Literary Agency; Mumford Literary Agency, Inc., The; Pelham-Heuisler Literary Agency; Pell Agency, William; PMA Literary and Film Management, Inc.; Renaud, Literary Agent, Janis; SLC Enterprises; Steinberg Literary Agency, Michael; Stern Agency, Gloria; Strong Literary Agency, Marianne; Toomey Associates, Jeanne; Total Acting Experience, A; Windfall Management; Zitwer Agency, Barbara J.

Business: AEI/Atchity Editorial/Entertainment International; Ahearn Agency, Inc., The; Author's Agency, The; Authors' Marketing Services Ltd.; Backman, Elizabeth H.; Buchan Literary Service, Jim; Cambridge Literary Associates; Catalog Literary Agency, The; Collier Associates; Creative Literary Agency; Dickens Group, The; Fenton Entertainment Group, Inc.; Fran Literary Agency; GEM Literary Services; Gladden Unlimited; Hamilton's Literary Agency, Andrew; Hartline Literary Agency; Howard Agency, The Eddy; Independent Publishing Agency: A Literary and Entertainment Agency; Jenks Agency, Carolyn; McKinley, Literary Agency, Virginia C.; Mumford Literary Agency, Inc., The; Puddingstone Literary Agency; Renaud, Literary Agent, Janis; Scherf, Inc. Literary Management; SLC Enterprises; Steinberg Literary Agency, Michael; Stern Agency, Gloria; Strong Literary Agency, Marianne; Total Acting Experience, A

Child Guidance/Parenting: Ahearn Agency, Inc., The; Author's Agency, The; Authors' Marketing Services Ltd.; Backman, Elizabeth H.; Buchan Literary Service, Jim; Cambridge Literary Associates; Catalog Literary Agency, The; Creative Literary Agency; Fenton Entertainment Group, Inc.; Fran Literary Agency; GEM Literary Services; Hamilton's Literary Agency, Andrew; Hartline Literary Agency; Howard Agency, The Eddy; Independent Publishing Agency: A Literary and Entertainment Agency; McKinley, Literary Agency, Virginia C.; Mumford Literary Agency, Inc., The; PMA Literary and Film Management, Inc.; Renaud, Literary Agent, Janis; Stern Agency, Gloria; Strong Literary Agency, Marianne; Total Acting Experience, A

Computers/Electronics: Cambridge Literary Associates; Catalog Literary Agency, The; Creative Literary Agency; Dickens Group, The; Fenton Entertainment Group, Inc.; GEM Literary Services; Howard Agency, The Eddy; Mumford Literary Agency, Inc., The; Steinberg Literary Agency, Michael; Stern Agency, Gloria; Total Acting Experience, A

Cooking/Food/Nutrition: Author's Agency, The; Authors' Marketing Services Ltd.; Backman, Elizabeth H.; Buchan Literary Service, Jim; Cambridge Literary Associates; Catalog Literary Agency, The; Collier Associates; Creative Literary Agency; Dickens Group, The; Fran Literary Agency; GEM Literary Services; Hamilton's Literary Agency, Andrew; Hartline Literary Agency; Independent Publishing Agency: A Literary and Entertainment Agency; Mews Books Ltd.; Mumford Literary Agency, Inc., The; PMA Literary and Film Management, Inc.; Renaud, Literary Agent, Janis; SLC Enterprises; Stern Agency, Gloria; Strong Literary Agency, Marianne; Total Acting Experience, A

Crafts/Hobbies: Author's Agency, The; Cambridge Literary Associates; Catalog Literary Agency, The; Collier Associates; Creative Literary Agency; Fran Literary Agency; Independent Publishing Agency: A Literary and Entertainment Agency; Mumford Literary Agency, Inc., The; PMA Literary and Film Management, Inc.; Renaud, Literary Agent, Janis; Total Acting Experience, A

Current Affairs: Ahearn Agency, Inc., The; Author's Agency, The; Authors' Marketing Services Ltd.; Backman, Elizabeth H.; Buchan Literary Service, Jim; Cambridge Literary Associates; Catalog Literary Agency, The; Creative Literary Agency; Dickens Group, The; Fenton Entertainment Group, Inc.; Fran Literary Agency; GEM Literary Services; Hamilton's Literary Agency, Andrew; Independent Publishing Agency: A Literary and Entertainment Agency; Literary Group West; Pelham-Heuisler Literary Agency; PMA Literary and Film Management, Inc.; Renaud, Literary Agent, Janis; SLC Enterprises; Stern Agency, Gloria; Strong Literary Agency, Marianne; Total Acting Experience, A; Zitwer Agency, Barbara J.

Education: Author's Agency, The; Authors' Marketing Services Ltd.; Cambridge Literary Associates; Catalog Literary Agency, The; Creative Literary Agency; Fran Literary Agency; Mumford Literary Agency,

Inc., The; Renaud, Literary Agent, Janis; Stern Agency, Gloria; Strong Literary Agency, Marianne; Total Acting Experience, A

Ethnic/Cultural Interests: Ahearn Agency, Inc., The; Author's Agency, The; Backman, Elizabeth H.; Catalog Literary Agency, The; Fran Literary Agency; Independent Publishing Agency: A Literary and Entertainment Agency; Jenks Agency, Carolyn; Literary Group West; McKinley, Literary Agency, Virginia C.; Mumford Literary Agency, Inc., The; PMA Literary and Film Management, Inc.; Renaud, Literary Agent, Janis; Stern Agency, Gloria; Total Acting Experience, A; Visions Press; Zitwer Agency, Barbara J.

Gay/Lesbian Issues: Ahearn Agency, Inc., The; GEM Literary Services; Jenks Agency, Carolyn; Stern Agency, Gloria; Visions Press; Zitwer Agency, Barbara J.

Government/Politics/Law: AEI/Atchity Editorial/Entertainment International; Author's Agency, The; Backman, Elizabeth H.; Buchan Literary Service, Jim; Cambridge Literary Associates; Catalog Literary Agency, The; Creative Literary Agency; Dickens Group, The; Fenton Entertainment Group, Inc.; Fran Literary Agency; GEM Literary Services; Hamilton's Literary Agency, Andrew; Howard Agency, The Eddy; Independent Publishing Agency: A Literary and Entertainment Agency; Mumford Literary Agency, Inc., The; Pelham-Heuisler Literary Agency; PMA Literary and Film Management, Inc.; Renaud, Literary Agent, Janis; Steinberg Literary Agency, Michael; Toomey Associates, Jeanne; Total Acting Experience

Health/Medicine: Ahearn Agency, Inc., The; Author's Agency, The; Authors' Marketing Services Ltd.; Backman, Elizabeth H.; Buchan Literary Service, Jim; Cambridge Literary Associates; Catalog Literary Agency, The; Creative Literary Agency; Dickens Group, The; Fenton Entertainment Group, Inc.; Fran Literary Agency; Hamilton's Literary Agency, Andrew; Jenks Agency, Carolyn; McKinley, Literary Agency, Virginia C.; McLean Literary Agency; Mews Books Ltd.; Renaud, Literary Agent, Janis; Stern Agency, Gloria; Strong Literary Agency, Marianne; Total Acting Experience, A

History: Ahearn Agency, Inc., The; Author's Agency, The; Authors' Marketing Services Ltd.; Backman, Elizabeth H.; Brinke Literary Agency, The; Buchan Literary Service, Jim; Cambridge Literary Associates; Collier Associates; Creative Literary Agency; Dickens Group, The; Fort Ross Inc. Russian-American Publishing Projects; Fran Literary Agency; Hamilton's Literary Agency, Andrew; Howard Agency, The Eddy; Independent Publishing Agency: A Literary and Entertainment Agency; Jenks Agency, Carolyn; Mumford Literary Agency, Inc., The; Pelham-Heuisler Literary Agency; PMA Literary and Film Management, Inc.; Renaud, Literary Agent, Janis; SLC Enterprises; Steinberg Literary Agency, Michael; Strong Literary Agency, Marianne; Toomey Associates, Jeanne; Total Acting Experience, A; Windfall Management

How-to: Author's Agency, The; Authors' Marketing Services Ltd.; Buchan Literary Service, Jim; Cambridge Literary Associates; Catalog Literary Agency, The; Collier Associates; Creative Literary Agency; Devereux Company, The Wilson; Fran Literary Agency; GEM Literary Services; Howard Agency, The Eddy; McLean Literary Agency; Mumford Literary Agency, Inc., The; Pelham-Heuisler Literary Agency; PMA Literary and Film Management, Inc.; Puddingstone Literary Agency; Renaud, Literary Agent, Janis; Scherf, Inc. Literary Management; Steinberg Literary Agency, Michael; Stern Agency, Gloria; Strong Literary Agency, Marianne; Total Acting Experience, A

Humor: Author's Agency, The; Buchan Literary Service, Jim; Cambridge Literary Associates; Creative Literary Agency; Fran Literary Agency; GEM Literary Services; Mumford Literary Agency, Inc., The; Pelham-Heuisler Literary Agency; PMA Literary and Film Management, Inc.; Renaud, Literary Agent, Janis; Total Acting Experience, A; Zitwer Agency, Barbara J.

Interior Design/Decorating: Author's Agency, The; Creative Literary Agency; Fran Literary Agency; Renaud, Literary Agent, Janis; Strong Literary Agency, Marianne; Toomey Associates, Jeanne

Juvenile: Ahearn Agency, Inc., The; Alp Arts Co.; Author Author Literary Agency Ltd.; Catalog Literary Agency, The; Creative Literary Agency; Fran Literary Agency; GEM Literary Services; Independent Publishing Agency: A Literary and Entertainment Agency; McLean Literary Agency; Mews Books Ltd.; PMA Literary and Film Management, Inc.; Renaud, Literary Agent, Janis; Strong Literary Agency, Marianne; Total Acting Experience, A; Windfall Management

Language/Literature/Criticism: Author's Agency, The; Creative Literary Agency; Howard Agency, The Eddy; Independent Publishing Agency: A Literary and Entertainment Agency; Jenks Agency, Carolyn; Pelham-Heuisler Literary Agency; Puddingstone Literary Agency; Renaud, Literary Agent, Janis; Stern Agency, Gloria; Total Acting Experience, A; Zitwer Agency, Barbara J.

Memoirs: Author's Agency, The; Cambridge Literary Associates; Creative Literary Agency; Fort Ross Inc. Russian-American Publishing Projects; Fran Literary Agency; SLC Enterprises; Windfall Management; Zitwer Agency, Barbara J.

Military/War: Author's Agency, The; Authors' Marketing Services Ltd.; Cambridge Literary Associates; Catalog Literary Agency, The; Fenton Entertainment Group, Inc.; Fran Literary Agency; Independent Publishing Agency: A Literary and Entertainment Agency; Literary Group West; Mumford Literary Agency, Inc., The; Pelham-Heuisler Literary Agency; Puddingstone Literary Agency; Strong Literary Agency, Marianne; Total Acting Experience, A

Money/Finance/Economics: AEI/Atchity Editorial/Entertainment International; Author's Agency, The; Authors' Marketing Services Ltd.; Cambridge Literary Associates; Catalog Literary Agency, The; Creative Literary Agency; Fenton Entertainment Group, Inc.; GEM Literary Services; Hamilton's Literary Agency, Andrew; Hartline Literary Agency; Independent Publishing Agency: A Literary and Entertainment Agency; McKinley, Literary Agency, Virginia C.; Mumford Literary Agency, Inc., The; PMA Literary and Film Management, Inc.; Renaud, Literary Agent, Janis; Scherf, Inc. Literary Management; Steinberg Literary Agency, Michael; Stern Agency, Gloria; Strong Literary Agency, Marianne; Toomey Associates, Jeanne; Total Acting Experience, A

Music/Dance/Theater/Film: Ahearn Agency, Inc., The; Author's Agency, The; Backman, Elizabeth H.; Buchan Literary Service, Jim; Cambridge Literary Associates; Creative Literary Agency; Fenton Entertainment Group, Inc.; Fort Ross Inc. Russian-American Publishing Projects; Fran Literary Agency; GEM Literary Services; Hamilton's Literary Agency, Andrew; Independent Publishing Agency: A Literary and Entertainment Agency; Jenks Agency, Carolyn; McKinley, Literary Agency, Virginia C.; Mumford Literary Agency, Inc., The; PMA Literary and Film Management, Inc.; Renaud, Literary Agent, Janis; Stern Agency, Gloria; Total Acting Experience, A; Zitwer Agency, Barbara J.

Nature/Environment: Author's Agency, The; Authors' Marketing Services Ltd.; Cambridge Literary Associates; Catalog Literary Agency, The; Creative Literary Agency; Fran Literary Agency; Independent Publishing Agency: A Literary and Entertainment Agency; Jenks Agency, Carolyn; Mumford Literary Agency, Inc., The; Renaud, Literary Agent, Janis; Toomey Associates, Jeanne; Total Acting Experience, A; Zitwer Agency, Barbara J.

New Age/Metaphysics: AEI/Atchity Editorial/Entertainment International; Author's Agency, The; Brinke Literary Agency, The; Creative Literary Agency; GEM Literary Services; Jenks Agency, Carolyn; Renaud, Literary Agent, Janis; Stern Agency, Gloria; Total Acting Experience, A; Zitwer Agency, Barbara

Open to all Nonfiction Categories: Author Author Literary Agency Ltd.; CS International Literary Agency; Gusay Literary Agency, The Charlotte; Write Therapist, The; Zahler Literary Agency, Karen Gantz

Photography: Author's Agency, The; Backman, Elizabeth H.; Catalog Literary Agency, The; Creative Literary Agency; Independent Publishing Agency: A Literary and Entertainment Agency; PMA Literary and Film Management, Inc.; Total Acting Experience, A

Popular Culture: AEI/Atchity Editorial/Entertainment International; Ahearn Agency, Inc., The; Author's Agency, The; Authors' Marketing Services Ltd.; Cambridge Literary Associates; Catalog Literary Agency, The; Creative Literary Agency; Dickens Group, The; Independent Publishing Agency: A Literary and Entertainment Agency; PMA Literary and Film Management, Inc.; Renaud, Literary Agent, Janis; Scherf, Inc. Literary Management; Stern Agency, Gloria; Total Acting Experience, A; Zitwer Agency, Barbara J.

Psychology: Author's Agency, The; Authors' Marketing Services Ltd.; Backman, Elizabeth H.; Catalog Literary Agency, The; Creative Literary Agency; Fort Ross Inc. Russian-American Publishing Projects; Hamilton's Literary Agency, Andrew; Independent Publishing Agency: A Literary and Entertainment Agency; McKinley, Literary Agency, Virginia C.; McLean Literary Agency; Renaud, Literary Agent, Janis; Scherf, Inc. Literary Management; Stern Agency, Gloria; Total Acting Experience, A; Zitwer Agency, Barbara J.

Religious/Inspirational: Author's Agency, The; Backman, Elizabeth H.; Brinke Literary Agency, The; Buchan Literary Service, Jim; Cambridge Literary Associates; Creative Literary Agency; Fenton Entertainment Group, Inc.; Fran Literary Agency; GEM Literary Services; Hartline Literary Agency; Independent Publishing Agency: A Literary and Entertainment Agency; Jenks Agency, Carolyn; McKinley, Literary Agency, Virginia C.; McLean Literary Agency; Mumford Literary Agency, Inc., The; Pelham-Heuisler Literary Agency; Renaud, Literary Agent, Janis; Scherf, Inc. Literary Management; Strong Literary Agency, Marianne; Total Acting Experience, A; Visions Press

Science/Technology: Author's Agency, The; Authors' Marketing Services Ltd.; Backman, Elizabeth H.; Cambridge Literary Associates; Catalog Literary Agency, The; Creative Literary Agency; Devereux Company, The Wilson; Dickens Group, The; Fenton Entertainment Group, Inc.; GEM Literary Services; Independent Publishing Agency: A Literary and Entertainment Agency; Jenks Agency, Carolyn; Mews Books Ltd.; Renaud, Literary Agent, Janis; Total Acting Experience, A

Self-Help/Personal Improvement: AEI/Atchity Editorial/Entertainment International; Ahearn Agency, Inc., The; Author's Agency, The; Authors' Marketing Services Ltd.; Backman, Elizabeth H.; Brinke Literary Agency, The; Buchan Literary Service, Jim; Cambridge Literary Associates; Catalog Literary Agency, The; Collier Associates; Creative Literary Agency; Fenton Entertainment Group, Inc.; Fort Ross Inc. Russian-American Publishing Projects; Fran Literary Agency; GEM Literary Services; Gladden Unlimited; Hamilton's Literary Agency, Andrew; Hartline Literary Agency; Independent Publishing Agency: A Literary and Entertainment Agency; McKinley, Literary Agency, Virginia C.; McLean Literary Agency; Mews Books Ltd.; Mumford Literary Agency, Inc., The; Pelham-Heuisler Literary Agency; Renaud, Literary Agent, Janis; Scherf, Inc. Literary Management; Steinberg Literary Agency, Michael; Stern Agency, Gloria; Strong Literary Agency, Marianne; Total Acting Experience, A; Visions Press; Zitwer Agency, Barbara J.

Sociology: Author's Agency, The; Catalog Literary Agency, The; Creative Literary Agency; Hamilton's Literary Agency, Andrew; Howard Agency, The Eddy; Independent Publishing Agency: A Literary and Entertainment Agency; Jenks Agency, Carolyn; McKinley, Literary Agency, Virginia C.; Renaud, Literary Agent, Janis; Stern Agency, Gloria; Total Acting Experience, A

Sports: Author's Agency, The; Authors' Marketing Services Ltd.; Backman, Elizabeth H.; Buchan Literary Service, Jim; Cambridge Literary Associates; Catalog Literary Agency, The; Creative Literary Agency; Fenton Entertainment Group, Inc.; Hamilton's Literary Agency, Andrew; Independent Publishing Agency: A Literary and Entertainment Agency; McKinley, Literary Agency, Virginia C.; Mumford Literary Agency, Inc., The; Renaud, Literary Agent, Janis; SLC Enterprises; Taylor Literary Agency, Dawson; Total Acting Experience, A

Translations: Author's Agency, The; Crown International Literature and Arts Agency, Bonnie R.; Jenks Agency, Carolyn; Total Acting Experience, A

Travel: Author's Agency, The; Creative Literary Agency; PMA Literary and Film Management, Inc.

True Crime/Investigative: AEI/Atchity Editorial/Entertainment International; Ahearn Agency, Inc., The; Author's Agency, The; Authors' Marketing Services Ltd.; Cambridge Literary Associates; Collier Associates; Creative Literary Agency; Dickens Group, The; Fenton Entertainment Group, Inc.; Fort Ross Inc. Russian-American Publishing Projects; GEM Literary Services; Gladden Unlimited; Hamilton's Literary Agency, Andrew; Independent Publishing Agency: A Literary and Entertainment Agency; Literary Group West; Mumford Literary Agency, Inc., The; Pelham-Heuisler Literary Agency; PMA Literary and Film Management, Inc.; Puddingstone Literary Agency; Renaud, Literary Agent, Janis; Scherf, Inc. Literary Management; Stern Agency, Gloria; Strong Literary Agency, Marianne; Toomey Associates, Jeanne; Total Acting Experience, A; Zitwer Agency, Barbara J.

Women's Issues/Women's Studies: AEI/Atchity Editorial/Entertainment International; Ahearn Agency, Inc., The; Author's Agency, The; Backman, Elizabeth H.; Cambridge Literary Associates; Catalog Literary Agency, The; Collier Associates; Creative Literary Agency; Fenton Entertainment Group, Inc.; GEM Literary Services; Hamilton's Literary Agency, Andrew; Hartline Literary Agency; Independent Publishing Agency: A Literary and Entertainment Agency; Jenks Agency, Carolyn; McKinley, Literary Agency, Virginia C.; Mumford Literary Agency, Inc., The; PMA Literary and Film Management, Inc.; Renaud, Literary Agent, Janis; SLC Enterprises; Stern Agency, Gloria; Strong Literary Agency, Marianne; Total Acting Experience, A; Visions Press

Script Agents

Making it as a screenwriter takes time. For starters, a good script takes time. It takes time to write. It takes time to rewrite. It takes time to write the four or five scripts that precede the really great one. The learning curve from one script to the next is tremendous, and you'll probably have a drawer full of work before you're ready to approach an agent. Your talent has to show on the page, and the page has to excite people.

Once you have a script that says what you want it to say, that is the best idea you've ever had, expressed in the best way you know, put it aside. And get on with the next "best idea you've ever had." Practice and hone your skills until you are ready to enter the race. The more horses you enter, the better your chances to win, place or show.

You'll need both confidence and insecurity at the same time. Confidence to enter the business at all. For a 22-week season, a half-hour sitcom buys 2 freelance scripts. There are less than 300 television movies and less than 100 big screen feature films produced each year. Nevertheless, in recent years the number of cable channels buying original movies has grown, independent film houses have sprouted up all over the country, and more studios are buying direct to video scripts—all of which offer a wide range of opportunities for emerging scriptwriters. If you're good, and you persevere, you will find work. Believe in yourself and your talent, because if you don't, no one else will.

Use your insecurity to spur you and your work on to become better. Accept that, at the beginning, you know little. Then go out and learn. Read all the books you can find on scriptwriting, from format to dramatic structure. Learn the formulas, but don't become formulaic. Observe the rules, but don't be predictable. Absorb what you learn, and make it your own.

And finally, you'll need a good agent. In this book we call agents handling screenplays or teleplays script agents, but in true West Coast parlance they are literary agents, since they represent writers as opposed to actors or musicians. Most studios, networks and production companies will return unsolicited manuscripts unopened for legal protection. An agent has the entree to get your script on the desk of a story analyst or development executive.

The ideal agent understands what a writer writes, is able to explain it to others, and has credibility with individuals who are in a position to make decisions. An agent sends out material, advises what direction a career should take and makes the financial arrangements. And how do you get a good agent? By going back to the beginning—great scripts.

THE SPEC SCRIPT

There are two sides to an agent's representation of a scriptwriter: finding work on an existing project and selling original scripts. Most writers break in with scripts written on "spec," that is, on speculation without a specific sale in mind. A spec script is a calling card that demonstrates skills, and gets your name and abilities before influential people. Movie spec scripts are always original, not for a sequel. Spec scripts for TV are always based on existing TV shows, not for an original concept.

More often than not, a spec script will not be made. An original movie spec can either be "optioned" or "bought" outright, with the intention of making a movie, or it can attract rewrite work on a script for an existing project. For TV, on the basis of the spec script, a writer can be invited in to pitch five or six ideas to the producers. If an idea is bought, the writer is paid to flesh out the story to an outline. If that is acceptable, the writer can be commissioned to write the script. At that point the inhouse writing staff comes in, and in a lot of cases, rewrites the script. But it's a sale, and the writer receives the residuals every time that episode is shown anywhere in the world. The goal is to sell enough scripts so you are invited to join the writing staff.

What makes a good spec script? Good writing for a start. Write every single day. Talk to as many people you can find who are different from you. Take an acting class to help you really hear dialogue. Take a directing class to see how movies are put together. If you are just getting started, working as an assistant to an established screenwriter can be beneficial. You get excellent experience, and as your name becomes attached to scripts, you'll have more assets to bring with you as you start to approach agents.

Learn the correct dramatic structure, and internalize those rules. Then throw them away and write intuitively. The three-act structure is basic and crucial to any dramatic presentation. Act 1—get your hero up a tree. Act 2—throw rock at him. Act 3—get him down. Some books will tell you that certain events have to happen by a certain page. What they're describing is not a template, but a rhythm. Good scriptwriting is good storytelling.

Spec scripts for movies

If you're writing for movies, explore the different genres until you find one you feel comfortable writing. Read and study scripts for movies you admire to find out what makes them work. Choose a premise for yourself, not "the market." What is it you care most about? What is it you know the most about? Write it. Know your characters and what they want. Know what the movie is about, and build a rising level of tension that draws the reader in and makes her care about what happens.

For feature films, you'll need two or three spec scripts, and perhaps a few long-form scripts (miniseries, movies of the week or episodics) as well. Your scripts should depict a layered story with characters who feel real, each interaction presenting another facet of their personalities.

Spec scripts for TV

If you want to write for TV, watch a lot of it. Tape several episodes of a show, and analyze them. Where do the jokes fall? Where do the plot points come? How is the story laid out? Read scripts of a show to find out what professional writers do that works. (Script City, (800)676-2522, and Book City, (800)4-CINEMA, have thousands of movie and TV scripts for sale.)

Your spec script will demonstrate your knowledge of the format and ability to create believable dialogue. Choosing a show you like with characters you're drawn to is important. Current hot shows for writers include *Ally McBeal*, *Everybody Loves Raymond*, *Law and Order*, *Dharma & Greg* and *Just Shoot Me*. Newer shows may also be good bets, such as *Felicity* and *Will & Grace*. If a show has been on three or more years, a lot of story lines have already been done, either on camera or in spec scripts. Your spec should be for today's hits, not yesterday's.

The previous year saw a surge in popularity of television shows where the cast is predominantly composed of teenagers. Shows like *Buffy the Vampire Slayer* and *Dawson's Creek* appealed so strongly to both adult and teen audiences that almost every network raced to add similar shows to their fall lineup. Animated sitcoms like *The Simpsons*, which are aimed at adult audiences, are also growing in popularity.

You probably already want to write for a specific program. Paradoxically, to be considered for that show your agent will submit a spec script for a different show, because—to protect themselves from lawsuits—producers do not read scripts written for their characters. So pick a show similar in tone and theme to the show you really want to write for. If you want to write for *Friends*, submit a spec script for *Suddenly Susan*. The hour-long dramatic shows are more individual in nature. You practically would have had to attend med school to write for *ER*, but *Law and Order* and *NYPD Blue* have a number of things in common that would make them good specs for one another. Half-hour shows generally have a writing staff and only occasionally buy freelance scripts. Hour-long shows are more likely to pick up scripts written by freelancers.

In writing a spec script, you're not just writing an episode. You're writing an *Emmy-winning* episode. You are not on staff yet; you have plenty of time. Make this the episode the staff writers wish they had written. But at the same time, certain conventions must be observed. The regular characters always have the most interesting story line. Involve all the characters in the episode. Don't introduce important new characters.

SELLING YOURSELF TO THE SALESPEOPLE

Scriptwriting is an art and craft. Marketing your work is salesmanship, and it's a very competitive world. Read the trades, attend seminars, stay on top of the news. Make opportunities for yourself.

But at the same time, your writing side always has to be working, producing pages for the selling side to hawk. First you sell yourself to an agent. Then the agent sells herself to you. If you both feel the relationship is mutually beneficial, the agent starts selling you to others.

All agents are open to third-party recommendations, referrals from a person whose opinion is trusted. To that end, you can pursue development people, producers' assistants, anyone who will read your script. Mail room employees at the bigger agencies are agents in training. They're looking for the next great script that will earn them a raise and a promotion to the next rung.

The most common path, however, is through a query letter. In one page you identify yourself, what your script is about and why you're contacting this particular agent. Show that you've done some research, and make the agent inclined to read your script. Find a connection to the agent like "we both attended the same college," or mention recent sales you know through your reading the agent has made. Give a three- or four-line synopsis of your screenplay, with some specific plot elements, not just a generic premise. You can use comparisons as shorthand. *Men in Black* could be described as "*Ghostbusters* meets *Alien*" and lets the reader into the story quickly, through something she's familiar with already. Be sure to include your name, return address and telephone number in your letter, as well as a SASE. If the response is positive, the agent probably will want to contact you by phone to let you know of her interest, but she will need the SASE to send you a release form that must accompany your script.

Your query might not be read by the agent but by an assistant. That's okay. There are few professional secretaries in Hollywood, and assistants are looking for material that will earn them the step up they've been working for.

To be taken seriously, your script must be presented professionally. Few agents have the time to develop talent. A less than professional script will be read only once. If it's not ready to be seen, you may have burned that bridge. Putting the cart before the horse, or the agent before the script, will not get you to where you want to go.

Read everything you can about scripting and the industry. As in all business ventures, you must educate yourself about the market to succeed. There are a vast number of books to read. Samuel French Bookstores [(323)876-0570] offers an extensive catalog of books for scriptwriters. *From Script to Screen*, by Linda Seger and Edward Jay Whetmore, J. Michael Straczynski's *The Complete Book of Scriptwriting* and Richard Walter's *Screenwriting* are highly recommended books on the art of scriptwriting. Study the correct format for your type of script. Cole and Haag's *Complete Guide to Standard Script Formats* is a good source for the various formats. Newsletters such as *Hollywood Scriptwriter* are good sources of information. Trade publications such as *The Hollywood Reporter*, *Premiere*, *Variety* and *Written By* are invaluable as well. A number of smaller magazines have sprung up in the last few years, including *Script Magazine* and *New York Screenwriter*. See the Books & Publications of Interest section for more information.

When Should a Screenwriter Get an Agent?

BY CHARLES DEEMER

Beginning screenwriters invariably worry about getting an agent too early in their development. Not only are there important skills to learn before an agent is necessary (including marketing skills) but too-early contact with important agencies can prematurely—and permanently—close doors that might open a few years down the road. It's crucial that young screenwriters jump through the career hoops in the proper order.

Even before learning the craft, you must know what you are getting into. Screenwriting is unlike any other form of writing in several important ways.

For example, perhaps in no other writing field are language skills less important. A mediocre writer who masters the special craft of filmic storytelling will be more successful than a brilliant writer with mediocre storytelling skills. Screenwriting requires writing with great economy, and a screenplay is more a blueprint for a movie than a literary document to be read. Writers in love with language may be discouraged by how irrelevant their rhetorical skills can be in this world.

Screenwriting is also more collaborative than other forms of writing. The goal of a screenwriter is to sell a script so it may become a movie, and the first step of this process is to put the screenplay into development. What this really means is that the writer, who created the story, no longer determines what happens. The vision of a producer, director or actor becomes much more important. The writer is reduced to a hired hand, making changes dictated by others.

In this context, the contrast between playwriting and screenwriting is striking. Whereas a playwright forever owns his material and changes in a script cannot be made without the writer's permission, a screenwriter relinquishes ownership once the contract is signed. This reality is hard for many writers to accept, and such writers should not pursue a career in screenwriting.

LEARN THE CRAFT

For those who can accept these first two obstacles, learning craft is the highest priority. There are many ways to do this, from reading books and taking classes to studying scripts and videos of movies. The following essential skills must be mastered:

Format

Screenplays are written in a special format which has evolved in such a way that the writer no longer "calls the shots" of the camera. This format must be followed.

Language

Screenplays are written in sparse, compressed prose with little rhetorical dressing or complexity (even something as common as a complex sentence is rare in a tight screenplay). There is

---

CHARLES DEEMER *is the author of* Screenwright: The Craft of Screenwriting *(Xlibris Corporation) and* Seven Come Eleven: Stories and Plays, 1969-1999 *(Writers Club Press). Over three dozen of his plays have been produced and six of his screenplays optioned. He teaches undergraduate and graduate screenwriting courses at Portland State University and since 1994 has been the webmaster of the Screenwriters and Playwrights Home Page at www.screenwright.com.*

so much "white space" on the page that the compressed language of a 100-page screenplay would become only 25 or 30 pages of prose. Think of a screenplay as a 30-page novel, in which only the essentials of the story are written.

Plot

Screenplay stories have a clear main character or hero who has a clear goal with clear obstacles standing in the way of reaching it. Most complexity and subtlety in a film come from the filmmaker and visual effects, not from the writer and story effects. In screenwriting, simplicity is a virtue.

Structure

Screenplay stories have a very clear beginning, middle and end, or what is called "classic three-act structure." There are almost no exceptions to this structure in the Hollywood film industry (including independent films), no matter what genre of story is being told. *Titanic, Dead Poet's Society, True Lies, Carrie, North By Northwest, Bird Cage, E.T.* and even *My Dinner with Andre* all have classic three-act structure.

Pace

Screenplay narrative is driven by a strong sense of "what happens next." Dramatic movement in a screenplay is constant and intense no matter what kind of story is being told, or whether physical or psychological action drives the narrative. There should be no lapses in story interest, no time for the audience to run out for popcorn.

Timing

Scenes in a screenplay are short and efficient. Every scene over a page in length must be defended. There are no wasted moments in a screenplay.

BEFORE YOU CONTACT AN AGENT

Once the craft of screenwriting is mastered, there are three steps to take before seeking an agent: entering contests, querying independent producers without an agent and deciding whether or not to move to Southern California.

Contests

Several contests have become important clearing houses for discovering new screenwriting talent. The two most important of these contests are the Nicholl Screenwriting Fellowship and the Austin Heart of Film Screenwriting Contest. The serious young screenwriter should enter each annually. Many other contests are out there—the list growing almost monthly—but none have the prestige and practical advantages of these two. Even reaching the quarter-finals in the Nicholl or Austin will open doors to agents and producers. However, be forewarned that about 5,000 people a year enter these contests, and that number keeps growing. (For information on Nicholl, go to www.oscars.org/academy/nichollindex.html; for Austin, call (800)310-3378.)

Independent producers

Many independent producers will accept "queries" from unagented screenwriters. A query is a short letter—never over a page—in which you "pitch" your story and briefly summarize what credentials you may have. If producers are interested, they will request a script. If a producer becomes interested enough to want to "option" your screenplay, you then have leverage with which to seek an agent. (An option gives the producer temporary legal ownership of the script during a time period, usually a year, in which to try to finance the movie. In the past, scripts were optioned for ten percent of the purchase price, but a trend distressing to writers has been the appearance of the "free option," which speaks to the crowded "buyers' market" business climate in Hollywood.)

Several tools are helpful in this self-marketing process. The most important is the *Hollywood Creative Directory* (*HCD*), which is available in print three times a year or online (updated weekly at www.hcdonline.com). This directory contains virtually every production company in the movie business, and there are hundreds of them. Facing the *HCD* can be overwhelming, so you need a strategy. I suggest this one, which requires a connection to the Internet. If you don't have one, get one—it will save you hours of research.

First, make a list of movies meeting the following criterion: "The producers of such-and-such would do a really good job on my script." Try to think of as many movies as you can.

Take this list to the Internet Movie Database (www.imdb.com), and look up each one in turn. Go to the movie credits, and write down all of the producers and production companies listed, especially the smaller companies you've never heard of (as opposed to Warner Bros. or Columbia) who probably originated the project. These unknown companies are the ones most receptive to beginning screenwriters.

Next take this information to the online *HCD*, and look up each production company and producer. If you find an e-mail address, use it; if not, use the postal address. If you use the latter, look for the name of the person with "development" after his title, and direct the letter there. If sending an e-mail, put "Pitch" in the subject line, and it will be directed to the right person.

E-mail or postage-mail your *brief* query letter. Any good screenwriting book will have examples of these. I suggest you do something else before sending out your queries: get your own 800 number. This is not expensive, and having your own 800 number will invite producers, who live on the phone (but who do *not* like unsolicited phone calls!), to respond to you.

Once you've exhausted your list of producers and companies, go back to the *HCD* and contact anyone who looks appropriate (that is, they don't specialize in genre movies inappropriate for your script). Self-marketing is a numbers game. Several hundred query letters may be sent out before interest is obtained. Nevertheless, a ten percent response rate (one of ten requesting a script) is good.

Moving to Los Angeles

As you market your script, give serious thought to your goals as a screenwriter. There are two basic kinds of screenwriters: those who live in Los Angeles and are full-time writers, making most of their money on assignments; and everyone else. The latter, wherever they live (usually out of Los Angeles), write what are called "spec scripts," which are scripts written "on speculation" and marketed after they are written. These writers usually support themselves with other work, such as teaching or other kinds of writing.

All established, full-time screenwriters, on the other hand, get paid first and write second. They take assignments but also pitch their own ideas, seldom writing anything they don't first get paid to write.

If you want to join the ranks of the mainstream, you must live in Los Angeles. Period. It's where meetings are held and decisions are made; it's where networking happens and assignments are taken. If this is your goal, then you must decide how to survive in Los Angeles while paying your professional dues there.

If you don't want to live in Los Angeles, then accept the fact that your screenwriting will be part time; you still must make a living.

As you market your script yourself, you immediately begin another. A serious screenwriter always has a new script in the works. There are no exceptions to this drive.

APPROACHING AGENTS

Finally, once you have producer interest in a script or have placed well in a contest, it is time to approach agents. If you live in Los Angeles, agents will be delighted to see a local return address on your query letter and will be more curious to meet you. They may even invite you to their office for a meeting.

At any rate, only query agents on the Writers Guild of America-signatory list (available at www.wga.org). Agents on this list agree to abide by certain standards and rules set by the Writers Guild of America, the screenwriters' union. For example, these agents don't charge reading fees to Guild members—and if you find an agent who charges fees, run. Once you sell a script, you'll be required to join the union yourself.

Anyone who knows a working screenwriter will hear horror stories. They are true. This field is neither nice nor respectful to writers. That is why most career screenwriters graduate to directing, where they have more artistic control, and from there to producing, where they control the purse strings and, therefore, everything.

But this information should not surprise you once you think about it. Can you name a screenwriter who isn't also a director? On the other hand, can you name a director of stage plays? In theater, the playwright is the artist; in film, the director is the artist.

Despite these challenges and unpleasantries, many of us have screenwriting in our blood. If you do as well, welcome to the strangest, most frustrating arena a writer can find. Despite everything, you're going to love what you do.

Script Agents 101: What Do They Do and How Do You Get One?

BY NEILL D. HICKS

There are three people who may be able to help you get your screenplay read by the right producer: a literary agent, an entertainment attorney and a personal manager.

Contrary to popular belief, you do not have to have an agent to get your script read. But it helps. At best, an agent is your mentor and guide through the maze of Hollywood. At worst, an agent is a necessary evil. Let's clear up a few misconceptions about what an agent is and is not.

- **An agent is not an employment office.** True, the agent's job is to get you work, but you can't expect the agent to keep you employed steadily. The agent functions as a kind of broker, matching writers with available projects and scripts with interested producers. An agent can only go so far in introducing you or your material to prospective buyers—but no one can sell a production company something they don't want. Even the word "sell" is probably misapplied to an agent because that makes it seem that selling scripts is no different from selling encyclopedias or ironing boards. The fact is agents are not so much sales people as they are advisors to both client and customer. If the customer (i.e., the producer) wants to buy, the agent can match the producer with a client. If the customer is not inclined to buy, there's not much the agent can do. The truth is that perhaps one out of ten jobs you get as a writer will come as a direct result of the agent's efforts. Instead, *you* are the person who will sell. You have to make the contacts and network with industry people, then the agent can follow up to negotiate your contract.

- **An agent is not your mother.** It's not your agent's job to comfort you when you're feeling blue or talk you through your down periods. The agent won't lift your spirits by telling you how fantastic you are, and there will almost never be cookies and milk waiting for you after a hard day at the keyboard. The agent is a businessperson in a hard-nosed and sometimes brutal industry. The agent needs for you to be an adult, not a deadweight.

- **An agent is not a banker.** If your financial life is in a mess, don't expect the agent to bail you out or even to get you that "one little job" so you can pay the rent. There are, of course, stories of those big-hearted agents who kept their clients' careers going by loaning them money and allowing them to live in the guest house until they hit the big time. Don't count on it. It's up to you to take care of your own economic well being.

- **Agents are in business for themselves.** They have mortgages and car payments and kids in private school and office staffs to support. An agent gets ten percent of the clients' fees for writing—but ten percent of the *working* clients' fees. If an agent has, let's say, 50 writers in the stable, at least half of those must be getting paid at any given time in order for the agent to make a living. The hard business truth is that it really doesn't make any

NEILL D. HICKS *is a screenwriter specializing in thriller and action-adventure films and long-form television. His screenwriting credits include* Rumble in the Bronx, First Strike, Dead Reckoning *and* Don't Talk to Strangers. *He is also a Senior Instructor in the UCLA Extension Writers' Program. This article is excerpted with permission from Michael Wiese Productions, from* Screenwriting 101: The Essential Craft of Feature Film Writing *(ISBN: 0-941188-72-9), published September 1999, $16.95, www.mwp.com, (800)833-5738.*

difference to the agent whether the ten percent comes from you or the next writer on the list, as long as the agent can meet the monthly expenses.

- **An agent is your team member.** You have to trust the agent and the agent has to trust you, or you're both going to sink. Certainly an agent must like your work and believe in your abilities. But at the same time, you must have some faith in the agent's instincts. The agent is, after all, supposed to have an ear to the ground and should know what producers are looking for. If your agent says a particular piece of your material isn't going to sell in the current market, you need to listen. Rather than jumping immediately on the defensive and refusing to make any changes, try to work out with your agent some kind of adjustment to make the material marketable. Keep in mind that agents only make money if you make money, so they're just as eager as you are to make a sale.

- **The agent is the business half of your partnership.** In contract negotiations, the agent can keep you, the creative person, at a comfortable distance from the producer so that you're not faced with making both creative and financial decisions. As a writer you want to be cooperative and give the production company what it needs to make a successful movie. But you need to limit that cooperation to the artistic arena or you might very well find yourself working for free. When the producer wants you to do an extra rewrite, or maybe another script on the side, you can always say the magic words, "Talk to my agent."

- **The agent supplies validity.** An agent's submission of a script to a producer testifies that the material is worthy of consideration. The producer is far more likely to read a script sent in by an agent than one that comes in over the transom. In fact, most production companies simply do not accept unsolicited material They will often return the envelope unopened. This is in part because of the fear of lawsuits over copyright infringement, but it is also because the producers don't have time to read material that hasn't been screened by someone who believes it's right for them. Of course, you may meet a producer at a party or live next door or be recommended by someone the producer trusts, and therefore get the script to the company without an agent. But most of the time an agent is a necessary channel of communication from writer to producer.

AGENTS

The best way to go about getting an agent as a beginning screenwriter is to be recommended by a producer or by one of the agent's clients who has read your work and is willing to vouch for you. Even if you know someone who has an agent, however, asking a friend to testify on your behalf is not as simple as it sounds. No matter how it may appear to you, your friend probably isn't that secure about his relationship with producers and agents. It's a funny business that way, but everyone is always a little uncertain about his standing, so introducing a prospective client to an agent is risky. If you're a fabulous writer, your friend may be diminishing his own ranking with the agency; and if you're not such a good writer, the agent is going to have doubts about your friend's judgment.

Your first step in getting your own agent, then, is to consult the list of *Franchised Agencies* published by the Writers Guild. These are agencies that have agreed to abide by the Writers Guild Manager Basic Agreement (MBA) in their negotiations with signatory producers. Some of the agents on the list are huge mega-agencies like William Morris or Creative Artists Agency or International Creative Management, but most are medium to small agents. New writers have virtually no chance of being represented by the mega-agencies who specialize in taking on clients *after* they have become a success. They package writers and directors and stars together to make movies—and all the elements of the package are represented by the same agency so the commissions are multiplied accordingly.

Among the medium and small agencies, some have reputations for dealing primarily in television, others in feature films, and some even in particular areas like television sitcoms or animation. You need to make yourself known to these agents so they can decide if they want to represent you.

Of course, the worst possible way to make yourself known is to send them an unsolicited script. Chances are you won't get a reply of any kind, and your script will find an instant home in the dumpster outside the agent's office. If you have no screenwriting credits and no one to introduce you, there's only one way to approach an agent—a query letter. Like a résumé that gets you the job interview, a query letter is your best sales tool for attracting an agent.

Query letter checklist

Write a query letter to an agency requesting that they read your sample screenplay. Keep the letter as short and easy to read as possible.

☑ In the first paragraph, interest the agent in your story by providing a hook, a provocative statement about your story or an intriguing question about the main character. Give the agent a *very brief* summary of the premise of the story, such as, "a story about a young man who almost starts World War III by tapping into the national defense computer with his home PC."

☑ In the second paragraph, give the agent a little background about yourself. If you're a published writer in some other area such as journalism, be sure to say so, without necessarily giving a complete list of your credits. If you're a professional or expert in some field, be sure to mention that.

☑ Ask the agency if it would be interested in reading your screenplay and offer to express mail it. You may also want to include a self-addressed, stamped postcard with the simple statement, "Yes, I am interested in reading your screenplay _____." typed neatly on the back.

If an agent does respond favorably to your query, send the script immediately with a polite cover letter. Then wait. Six to eight weeks is not an unreasonable amount of time to wait for a reply. If you have not heard from the agent in two months, you may want to send another polite reminder note or telephone call. If you still don't hear, assume that the agent is not interested in handling your material.

Of course you can send query letters to several agents at the same time, but avoid blanketing the whole list. Stick to two or three for the first time out, and if you don't receive a response from them, then go to the next two or three on your list. And remember—spelling, punctuation and neatness do count! Give the agent the most professional picture of yourself that you possibly can.

One more word before we leave the subject of agents. No legitimate agent will ask you for a "reader's fee" or any money up front in order to consider your material. If you do get such a request, run as fast as possible in the opposite direction.

ENTERTAINMENT ATTORNEYS

Even if you have a very good agent, there's another member you want on your team, an *entertainment attorney*. Some entertainment attorneys are willing to function like agents, that is, sending out material and negotiating deals, but for the most part a good entertainment attorney is the most useful in reviewing contracts for you. The agent negotiates the deal, sometimes in highly pressured situations, and hammers out the general outlines of the understanding you have with the producer. The producer will then have the legal staff or business affairs department draw up a contract for you to sign. Most agents are not lawyers, and though they may be very familiar with contract language, they generally have neither the time nor the temperament to look over the fine points of legal rhetoric. An attorney familiar with entertainment law can potentially save you thousands of dollars and untold anguish down the road by reviewing your contract now before you sign it. Most of these attorneys will work on a commission basis or an hourly fee of two to three hundred dollars. Be sure you have a clear agreement before your attorney begins work, but never hesitate to have any contract reviewed. The entertainment attorney's counsel is worth whatever the cost may be.

PERSONAL MANAGERS

One other member you may have on your screenplay sales team is a *personal manager*. Unlike agents, personal managers are not regulated by the Writers Guild, and while they technically cannot solicit work for a writer nor negotiate a contract, they can be useful in shaping the writer's career. Most managers take a 15 percent cut of the writer's fees and provide services such as publicity, press releases and general promotion for their clients. Actors have used personal managers for years, but writers have only recently started using them. Most writers find that the combination of an agent and a personal manager is overkill, and the relationship between the manager and agent can be one of conflict, leaving the writer trying to please two masters. Still, personal managers tend to be easier to come by than agents, and if you don't have an agent yet, a personal manager may be able to open some doors that you cannot open by yourself. Remember, though, that managers, like agents, only make money if their clients make money, so you're still going to have to do the lion's share of the hustling yourself.

Working with Script Agents: What You Should Expect

BY DAVID TROTTIER

As you might guess, there are many advantages to acquiring an agent. Agents save you time. They know the territory and how to negotiate a deal. Because agents are expected by the industry to screen writers, the fact that you have one greatly multiplies your chances of finding work. Best of all, agents don't cost anything until they sell your script. Some large agencies, such as ICM and CAA, package scripts; that is, they add talent or a director to generate a studio deal. They are generally more difficult to break into than small agencies. Although a small agency may be a better choice for the novice, you want whomever you can get!

You may have heard how difficult it is to get read. First of all, it is true that agents will seldom read your script, but their assistants will *if* the agent is properly approached.

First, secure a list of approved agencies from the Writers Guild. Their list is coded so that you can select the agencies that are accepting submissions. Keep in mind that the Guild lists agencies, but not individual agents. For this, you may need to go to a directory, like this one or the agent's directory put out by Hollywood Creative Directories.

Study the various agency lists and directories you have acquired. If you are using a directory, you will single out the literary agent that is farthest down the list in a given agency. As a last resort, call specific agencies and ask, "Who handles new writers?" If you admire an established writer, you may contact the WGA for the name of his or her agent.

The point is to get the name of *individual* agents. You will *not* send them your script. You will instead send a query letter to about five agents at a time. Mailing to five agents at a time enables you to evaluate their responses and improve your query before you contact more agents. You will only contact one agent per agency.

WORKING WITH AN AGENT

Let's assume you have queried several agencies, and one has requested your script. You mail your script to the agent with a cover letter. She loves your script and calls.

When an agent calls, she shows her interest by asking the magic question: "What else have you done?" Hopefully, you have written a second dynamite script and have other ideas to talk about. Most likely this agent will want to meet you personally. There are a few issues that you and your agent will want to settle at this meeting.

One is the contract. The agent gets ten percent. No reputable agent charges a reading fee. Be wary of requests for cash or for referrals to specific script consultants. However, an agent may legitimately ask you to cover the cost of photocopying your script.

In Writers Guild-signatory contract, there is a 90-day clause: If the agent has not found you work in 90 days, you can terminate the contract. Before you do, however, remember that selling a script takes time. Many agents will not tender a contract until an offer is made by a producer for your script or services. If your agent is a WGA-signatory, then this is usually not a problem— the eventual contract will be WGA-approved.

DAVID TROTTIER *is a consultant, writer, producer and screenwriting teacher. This article is an excerpt reprinted from The Screenwriter's Bible—3rd E. by David Trottier, published by Silman-James Press.*

Your agent will want to discuss your career. What do you want to write? Are any genres of particular interest to you? Do you want to write for television? Are you willing to travel to Los Angeles for necessary meetings? Are there certain things you are unwilling to write (such as stories that demean women)? Be careful not to sound too picky about what you'll write.

While in Hollywood, choose your battles carefully. Many are not worth fighting; some are.

If you have several scripts, and an agent doesn't like one of them, ask for a release so you can go out and sell it yourself. If you feel uneasy about a particular agent, ask him to tell you about his current clients and recent sales. You'll get an idea of his ability.

Always remember, the agent's primary motivation is money, not helping writers with passion (although that can be a secondary motivation). The agent has 20 to 30 other clients, most of whom can bring in a higher commission than you. The agent represents you because he sees bigger sales down the road and believes you can write the material his contacts want.

Therefore, communicate to the agent your desire for a writing career, your willingness to work hard, and to accept writing assignments and development deals. Keep in mind, though, screenwriters rarely get assignments for adaptations and rewrites unless they've had a big sale.

In addition to commitment, your agent wants to see in you an ability to perform as a writer and as a *pitcher*—how well you present yourself and your ideas.

Most agents work on a weekly cycle. Each Monday, they set out to sell one or two scripts by Friday. They're also hoping to secure writing assignments for their clients. In fact, they'll often meet with their producer contacts to match their writers to the producers' project ideas. If an agent loves your script and sees that it is similar to some producer's goal, they'll have it delivered to that producer. Often, that results in a meeting that you attend with the producer, which (the agent hopes) results in a development deal.

Although agents are not writing coaches, they will prepare you for meetings and advise you on the ebb and flow of market tides.

There are four kinds of situations that an agent can arrange

1. **The outright sale of your spec script**. Your agent will suggest a strategy for selling your script. She will want to generate heat and solicit the interest of more than one buyer in your script. This can result in an auction. This is the stuff dreams are made of. You will be paid six figures or higher plus receive a bonus of a like amount or even greater amount *if* the screenplay is actually produced. There are also residuals on video cassettes. It will all be spelled out in your book-length contract.

2. **A literary purchase and option agreement, commonly called an** *option*: Here the buyer is not quite so enthusiastic or simply doesn't want to put a lot of money into the script immediately. In either case, the producer buys an option to the rights for a short period of time (six months to a year) for a small "down payment" of anywhere from zero to $20,000. During that *option period*, the producer uses the script to attract talent and/or money. At the end of the option period, the producer will either pay the purchase price or pass. In the case of a pass, you keep any option money originally given to you, plus the rights to the script revert to you.

3. **A development deal**. Here, the agent uses your script as a lure to arrange a meeting or pitching session with a producer where you pitch *your* ideas—this can result in a development deal or sale (if the story you pitch is already scripted).

4. **An audition**. The fourth and most likely scenario is your sample script secures you an audition meeting for an open writing assignment, such as a development deal to execute the producer's idea into a script. In the case of episodic television, you will be paid to write a couple of episodes plus get residuals if the show goes into syndication.

Once the agent negotiates a deal and conditions are met, the check is sent to the agent, from which he pays you your 90 percent.

Shakespeare in Love's Marc Norman on Life As a Writer in Hollywood

BY MEGAN NORRIS

Marc Norman knows Hollywood from every angle. He's lived in Los Angeles his entire life. He worked his way up from humble beginnings as a studio mail boy and along the way has written successful television scripts, screenplays, a musical and three novels. On March 21, 1999, Norman achieved his greatest career success to date. He won two Academy Awards for writing and producing the romantic comedy *Shakespeare in Love*. The film, which he co-wrote with Tom Stoppard, won seven Oscars, including Best Picture.

Marc Norman

Several agents have helped Norman navigate the rough waters of Hollywood since his start in the business. His relationship with agents began with Adams, Ray and Rosenberg, an agency no longer in existence. He is currently with Dave Wirtschafter of International Creative Management (ICM), one of the entertainment industry's top agencies.

Have you always known you wanted to be in the movie/television business?

Not at all. I went to Berkeley in the 1960s, and my ambition was to stay there the rest of my life. The only practical way to do that is by getting on the faculty. I had a bachelor's in English, and I went on to study for my master's. I was going to get my Ph.D. in English and teach because that would keep me in this world I liked. While studying for my master's, I began to fall out of love with the notion of teaching. It threw me for a loop because I didn't have a plan B. I thought, well, I like movies, though it seemed shallow to base a career decision on that thought. On the other hand, I wasn't married and didn't have any children. I was as free as I was ever going to be.

What was your first step towards getting involved in the movie business?

People who aren't from Los Angeles think everybody here is connected to the movie business, and that's not true. It's a very small business, and most people in Los Angeles have no more to do with it than people in Cincinnati. My family didn't have any connections. I didn't have an Uncle John who was a producer, so I basically had to walk in the gate and apply for a job. The only job I could get was as a mail boy.

You've written three novels, the first of which was published in 1972. Is that how you first started writing?

No, I started writing for television. After a couple of years, I began writing movies. I wrote my first novel, *Bike Riding in Los Angeles*, when I just wanted to write something on my own. I

MEGAN NORRIS *is a senior, with a major in journalism, at Miami University in Oxford and a freelancer for Writer's Digest Books.*

found a cheap way to print my book—it cost me $600. I gave it away to my friends. When that was done, I was broke. I decided the best thing to do for myself was write the most commercial screenplay I could and try to sell it. That was a movie called *Oklahoma Crude*.

Somebody from Columbia Pictures, the company that made the movie, came to me and said, "I have ties to the New York book business, and we have a new idea. We want to publish a novel in advance of the movie. Would you like to write a novel of *Oklahoma Crude*?" I said sure, so I went to Italy with my family, and *Oklahoma Crude* was written in Florence in between changing diapers. The novel was published by Dutton, by an editor named Hal Charlotte—a wonderful man. He said, "I love your manuscript; have you written any other prose?" I said, "Well, I've written this novel I never show to anybody." I sent him *Bike Riding in Los Angeles*, and he published it. So within the course of a year and a half, I went from a person who thought he could never be a novelist, to somebody who published two.

Why didn't writing for television appeal to you?

Episodic television is the same day-to-day. Characters can't learn from one week to the next. It's a given of television that the main actors have to stay the same. That seemed artificial and not very rewarding to me.

Your first film credit was for *Oklahoma Crude*. What is required to get a credit on a film?

It's determined by rules set by the Writers Guild of America, which is the writers' trade union. Basically, you have to pass certain criteria. You have to either write the original screenplay or be hired to rewrite the screenplay.

Do you think your career has benefited by your membership in the Writers Guild of America?

The WGA is a policing organization. It sets rules not only for writers but also for how writers are handled financially and structurally by their employers. The employers have to sign off on contracts in order to employ Writers Guild writers. Most importantly, the Writers Guild controls workplace conditions. In essence, membership is mandatory. I don't know many screenwriters who are not in the WGA and who don't want to be.

How did you get the idea for *Shakespeare in Love*?

I'm happy to say the initial idea came from one of my kids. I have two sons, Alex and Zack. Growing up in the family of a freelance writer, they determined early on that it was good for them to come up with ideas for their dad. Zack took an Elizabethan history course in college, and one day he called me from school and said, "Okay, here it is. Shakespeare starting out in the Elizabethan theater." I knew it was a fantastic idea—there had never been anything like it. It was a chance to take something obscure and make it prominent.

How did *Shakespeare in Love* evolve from that point?

I played around with the idea for a couple of years, but I wasn't getting anywhere with it. I couldn't figure out how to tell Shakespeare's story. Then one day I realized I had been staring at my solution for two years. Shakespeare was a screenwriter. Shakespeare was me, in essence, or somebody like me. He writes for a living and wants to do something better than what he's done before. That was the first idea. The second idea was, what play does he write? *Romeo and Juliet* was an obvious choice for a lot of reasons. Everybody knows it so you can show pieces of it in the movie without presenting the entire play. People could argue that before *Romeo*, Shakespeare's not Shakespeare. *Romeo* is his first amazing play. The question became, "What happened to him during the writing of *Romeo*?" And, of course, in Hollywood tradition, he meets a girl. The third leg of the concept is the girl can't be in the theater, so she's got to be a boy.

What were some of the problems you encountered when trying to get this film onto the screen?

It became a financial problem. The film was almost made in 1992 with Julia Roberts. We were in England in preproduction about a month away from starting to shoot, and it collapsed. There were an awful lot of bills that had to be paid by anyone else who wanted to make this movie. It wasn't until Miramax took a chance and paid the debt that the movie got made.

You worked with Tom Stoppard for *Shakespeare in Love* but got sole credit for *Oklahoma Crude*. How would you compare working as a team to working alone?

It depends on the situation. Tom brought things to the script I never thought of. As for *Oklahoma Crude*, I knew the world portrayed in that movie better than anybody else, and I don't think anybody could have improved it. Writers in Hollywood can't afford to be too tied to presenting their unique view of the world—that's something you do in a novel. It's not useful to act like a novelist when you're a screenwriter.

How was your agent, Dave Wirtschafter at ICM, involved during the development of the film?

My agent is very important. He is both an advisor and a partner. There were times when he would give me advice on what I wanted to do and how I wanted to do it. And there were times when he would say, "Don't do that. I veto that." His job is to help me negotiate something that is a minefield. There were times when I could have stepped on something and blown myself up. By blowing myself up, I mean either killing the chance of the movie to get made or killing the chance of remaining connected to the movie. I look back at what I did for *Shakespeare in Love* as successfully making it through a minefield.

You won several awards for the screenplay of *Shakespeare in Love*, the Writers Guild Award, the Golden Globes and, of course, the Academy Award. How do you think these awards changed your relationship with your agent and with the world of Hollywood itself?

I'm grateful for the awards, and I'll tell you how I use them. When I feel I've done a lousy day's work and I'm kicking myself for being a talentless poser, I can look at those awards and say, "I did something good once." In terms of altering the relationship with my agent, it hasn't because he shares in the awards. When his clients get awards and recognition or their movies make a lot of money, his position improves.

Was Dave Wirtschafter your first agent?

No, I've had about four or five.

Why did you originally decide to get an agent?

In this business you need an agent for a couple of reasons. First, he has access to markets and people you don't. Secondly, he is another opinion—I respect his judgment. He also has access to more experienced people in his company who he can turn to for help. The movie business can be baffling and absurd, and an agent can help you understand it.

How did you get your first agent?

I fell into the best situation for somebody starting out. Adams, Ray and Rosenberg had just hired a new agent, Bob Wunsch, who was anxious to establish himself by bringing new clients to the agency. I had an original screenplay, and he liked it.

Are there any benefits to being with a well-known agency such as ICM?

You can argue both sides. You'd be surprised by how many prominent actors, writers and directors are with agents that essentially have a couple clients and work out of a small office. By being at a bigger agency, I get more information. There are more people reporting to my agent.

Is it necessary for a writer to have an agent to sell his script?

It is in the movie business. It's really a legal issue. Studios and producers don't want to read scripts that are not submitted through an agent or a lawyer because of liability issues. They're concerned because if they read a script and refuse it, then five years later make a movie that's similar, the writer could say, "You copied my idea. I'm suing you." By submitting through an agent or a lawyer, there's a record of submissions on paper. As far as I know, the only people in this business who will read scripts that are not represented by agents, are agents.

What are some of the biggest mistakes a beginning writer makes when trying to find an agent?

The biggest mistake a young writer could make would be mistrusting his own gut instinct and common sense, and making choices on the basis of fantasies. Well, this guy is so and so's agent, and that'll do me a lot of good cause so and so's famous. As opposed to I trust this person, this person seems honest. The best judgment is to pick somebody not because of where he works or who he represents but for his the sense of honesty and decency.

If a writer wants to be in the movie business, does he need to live in Los Angeles?

Theoretically, you can live anywhere in the world and work in this town, especially in this electronic age. Practically speaking, it doesn't work that way. The attitude of people who work in this town is, if you don't live here and share the pain, you're an outsider. For writers, as well as anybody else in the business, you've got to come here and live the life. There are guys in Chicago, Atlanta and New York who've had successful film writing careers, but it's not easy.

Now that you have your Academy Award, what else do you want?

I want to write better. That's what I've always been interested in. I see myself as a long distance runner who goes out to the track every morning and runs by himself with a stopwatch in his hand. After five or six miles, when he crosses the finish line, he looks down at his watch. If he's gone a second faster, he smiles. He's had a good day. I just keep on trying to go a second faster.

Script Agents: Nonfee-charging & Fee-charging

This section contains agents who sell feature film scripts, television scripts and theatrical stage plays. The listings in this section differ slightly from those in the literary agent sections. Nonfee-charging and fee-charging agencies are listed together. Fee-charging agents are indicated by a clapper $ symbol. A breakdown of the types of scripts each agency handles is included in the listing.

Many of the script agents listed here are signatories to the Writers Guild of America Artists' Manager Basic Agreement. They have paid a membership fee and agreed to abide by the WGA's standard code of behavior. Agents who are WGA signatories are not permitted to charge a reading fee to WGA members, but are allowed to do so to nonmembers. They are permitted to charge for critiques and other services, but they may not refer you to a particular script doctor. Enforcement is uneven, however. Although a signatory can, theoretically, be stripped of its signatory status, this rarely happens.

It's a good idea to register your script before sending it out, and the WGA offers a registration service to members and nonmembers alike. Membership in the WGA is earned through the accumulation of professional credits and carries a number of significant benefits. Write the Guild for more information on specific agencies, script registration and membership requirements.

For a detailed explanation of the agency listings and for more information on approaching agents, read Quick Start Guide to Using Your *Guide to Literary Agents* on page 2 and Finding the Right Agent: What Every Writer Needs to Know on page 16. When reading through this section, keep in mind the following information specific to the script agent listings:

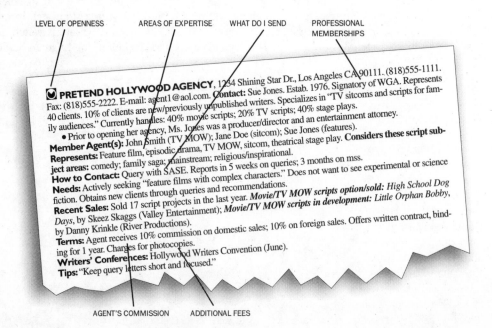

LEVEL OF OPENNESS   AREAS OF EXPERTISE   WHAT DO I SEND   PROFESSIONAL MEMBERSHIPS

PRETEND HOLLYWOOD AGENCY, 1234 Shining Star Dr., Los Angeles CA 90111. (818)555-1111. Fax: (818)555-2222. E-mail: agent1@aol.com. **Contact:** Sue Jones. Estab. 1976. Signatory of WGA. Represents 40 clients. 10% of clients are new/previously unpublished writers. Specializes in "TV sitcoms and scripts for family audiences." Currently handles: 40% movie scripts; 20% TV scripts; 40% stage plays.
• Prior to opening her agency, Ms. Jones was a producer/director and an entertainment attorney.
Member Agent(s): John Smith (TV MOW); Jane Doe (sitcom); Sue Jones (features).
Represents: Feature film, episodic drama, TV MOW, sitcom, theatrical stage play. **Considers these script subject areas:** comedy; family saga; mainstream; religious/inspirational.
How to Contact: Query with SASE. Reports in 5 weeks on queries; 3 months on mss. Does not want to see experimental or science fiction. Obtains new clients through queries and recommendations.
Needs: Actively seeking "feature films with complex characters."
Recent Sales: Sold 17 script projects in the last year. *Movie/TV MOW scripts option/sold:* High School Dog Days, by Skeez Skaggs (Valley Entertainment); *Movie/TV MOW scripts in development:* Little Orphan Bobby, by Danny Krinkle (River Productions).
Terms: Agent receives 10% commission on domestic sales; 10% on foreign sales. Offers written contract, binding for 1 year. Charges for photocopies.
Writers' Conferences: Hollywood Writers Convention (June).
Tips: "Keep query letters short and focused."

AGENT'S COMMISSION   ADDITIONAL FEES

QUICK REFERENCE ICONS

At the beginning of some listings, you will find one or more of the following symbols for quick identification of features particular to that listing.

> ⒩ Agency new to this edition.
>
> ☑ Change in address, contact information or phone number from last year's edition.
>
> ⓢ Fee-charging script agent.
>
> ⚏ Canadian agency.

OPENNESS

Each agency has an icon indicating its openness to submissions. Before contacting any agency, check the listing to make sure it is open to new clients.

> ◖ Newer agency actively seeking clients.
>
> ◕ Agency seeking both new and established writers.
>
> ◕ Agency prefers to work with established writers, mostly obtains new clients through referrals.
>
> ◎ Agency handling only certain types of work or work by writers under certain circumstances.
>
> ⊘ Agency not currently seeking new clients. We include these agencies to let you know they are currently not open to new clients. *Unless you have a strong recommendation from someone well respected in the field, our advice is to avoid approaching these agents.*

SUBHEADS

Each listing is broken down into subheads to make locating specific information easier. In the first section, you'll find contact information for each agency. You'll also learn if the agent is a WGA signatory or a member of any other professional organizations. Further information is provided which indicates an agency's size, its willingness to work with a new or previously unpublished writer, and its areas of specialization.

Member Agents: Agencies comprised of more than one agent list member agents and their individual specialties to help you determine the most appropriate person for your query letter.

Represents: Make sure you query only agents who represent the type of material you write. To help you narrow your search, we've included an **Agents Specialties Index** and a **Script Agents Format Index** immediately after the script agent listings.

How to Contact: Most agents open to submissions prefer initially to receive a query letter briefly describing your work. Script agents usually discard material sent without a SASE. Here agents also indicate if they accept queries by fax or e-mail, and if they consider simultaneous submissions.

Needs: Here agents list what areas they are currently seeking as well as subjects they do *not* wish to receive. Also listed is the agent's preferred way of meeting new clients.

Recent Sales: Reflecting the different ways scriptwriters work, agents list scripts optioned or sold and scripting assignments procured for clients. The film industry is very secretive about sales, but you may be able to get a list of clients or other references upon request.

Terms: Most agents' commissions range from 10 to 15 percent, and WGA signatories may not earn over 10 percent from WGA members.

Fees: Agencies who charge some type of fee (for reading, critiques, consultations, promotion, marketing, etc.) are indicated with a clapper (ⓢ) symbol by their name. Also listed here are additional office fees.

Writers' Conferences: For screenwriters unable to move to Los Angeles, writers' conferences provide another venue for meeting agents. For more information about a specific conference, check the Writers' Conferences section starting on page 292.

Tips: Agents offer advice and additional instructions for writers looking for representation.

SPECIAL INDEXES AND ADDITIONAL HELP

This book contains several indexes to help facilitate your search for an agent. Use the indexes to help narrow your list of possible agents to query.

Additional Script Agents: Many script agents are also interested in book manuscripts; many literary agents will also consider scripts. Agents who primarily sell books but also handle at least 10 to 15 percent scripts appear among the listings in this section, with the contact information, breakdown of work currently handled and a note to check the full listing in either the Nonfee-charging or Fee-charging sections. Those literary agents who sell mostly books and less than 10 to 15 percent scripts appear in a list at the end of this section on page 282. Complete listings for these agents also appear in either the Nonfee-charging or Fee-charging sections.

Agents Specialties Index: Immediately following this section of listings is an index divided into various subject areas specific to scripts, such as mystery, romantic comedy and teen. This index should help you compose a list of agents specializing in your areas. Cross-referencing categories and concentrating on agents interested in two or more aspects of your manuscript might increase your chances of success. Agencies open to all categories are grouped under the subject heading "open."

Script Agents Format Index: Following the **Agents Specialties Index** is an index organizing agents according to the script types they consider: such as TV movie of the week (MOW), sitcom or episodic drama.

Agents Index: Often you will read about an agent who is an employee of a larger agency and you may not be able to locate her business phone or address. Starting on page 341, is a list of agents' names in alphabetical order along with the name of the agency they work for. Find the name of the person you would like to contact and then check the agency listing.

Geographic Index: For writers looking for an agent close to home, this index lists agents state-by-state.

Agencies Indexed by Openness to Submissions: This index lists agencies according to their receptivity to new clients.

Listing Index: This index lists all agencies and conferences listed in the book.

SCRIPT AGENTS

☑ ◑ **ABOVE THE LINE AGENCY**, 9200 Sunset Blvd., #804, Los Angeles CA 90069. (310)859-6115. Fax: (310)859-6119. **Contact:** Bruce Bartlett. Owner: Rima Bauer Greer. Estab. 1994. Signatory of WGA. Represents 20 clients. 5% of clients are new/previously unpublished writers. Currently handles: 2½% juvenile books; 5% novels; 90% movie scripts; 2½% TV scripts.
  • Prior to starting her own agency, Ms. Greer served as president with Writers & Artists Agency.
Represents: Feature film, TV MOW, animation.
How to Contact: Query with SASE. Reports in 1 month on queries.
Recent Sales: *Movie scripts sold:* 2000, by Andrea Davis (Fox); *Rain in Spain*, by Frank Cappello (Universal); *Here & Now*, by Ryan Rowe (Columbia). *Scripting assignments: Mephisto in Onyx*, by Greg Widen (Miramax); *Prometheus Project*, by Engelbach and Wolff (Fox).
Terms: Agent receives 10% commission on domestic sales; 10% on foreign sales.

☒ ◑ **ACME TALENT & LITERARY**, 6310 San Vicente Blvd., #520, Los Angeles CA 90048. (323)954-2263. Fax: (323)954-2262. **Contact:** Lisa Lindo Lieblein. Estab. 1993. Signatory of WGA. Represents 12 clients. Specializes in "feature films, completed specs or pitches by established produced writers and new writers (no TV)." Currently handles: 100% movie scripts.
Member Agents: Lisa Lindo Lieblein (feature film specs); "also nine additional agents handling talent in Los Angeles, and two talent agents in New York."
Represents: Feature film. **Considers all script subject areas.** "Prefer high concept."
How to Contact: Query with SASE. Accepts queries by fax. Considers simultaneous queries. Reports in 1 week on queries; 3 months on mss. Returns unwanted materials only with SASE.
Needs: Actively seeking great feature scripts. Does not want to receive unsolicited material. Obtains new clients through recommendations from others.
Recent Sales: Sold 10 projects in the last year. Prefers not to share information on specicfic sales.

Terms: Agent receives 10% commission on domestic sales; 10% on foreign sales. Offers written contract, binding for 1 year.

Tips: "We are very hands on, work developmentally with specs in progress. Individual attention due to low number of clients. All sales have been major 6-7 figures."

☒ ◑ AEI/ATCHITY EDITORIAL/ENTERTAINMENT INTERNATIONAL, Literary Management & Motion Picture Production, 9601 Wilshire Blvd., Box 1202, Beverly Hills CA 90210. (323)932-0407. Fax: (323)932-0321. E-mail: aeikja@lainet.com. Website: www.aeionline.com. **Contact:** Kenneth Atchity. Estab. 1996. Represents 50 clients. 75% of clients are new/previously unpublished writers. Specializes in novel-film tie-ins. "We also specialize in taking successfully self-published books to the national market." Currently handles: 30% nonfiction books; 40% novels; 30% movie scripts.
  • See the expanded listing for this agency in Literary Agents: Fee-charging.

☑ ☒ ◑ AGAPÉ PRODUCTIONS, P.O. Box 147, Flat Rock IN 47234-0147. (812)587-5654. Fax: (812)587-0024. **Contact:** Terry Porter. Administrative Assistant: David Ruiz. Estab. 1990. Signatory of WGA. Works with Indiana Film Commission. Member of BOD Christian Film and TV Commission. Represents 55 clients. 30% of clients are new/previously unpublished writers. Specializes in movie scripts, TV scripts, packaging deals. Currently handles: 2% juvenile books; 4% novels; 70% movie scripts; 10% TV scripts; 2% stage plays; 6% syndicated material; 4% animation.
  • Prior to becoming an agent, Mr. Porter was a concert promoter and music agent. He also owns www.flatrock-records.com. (national independent label).

Member Agents: (Mr.) Terry D. Porter.

Represents: Feature film, animation, stage plays, miniseries, documentary, episodic drama, TV MOW, sitcom. **Considers these script subject areas:** action/adventure; biography/autobiography; cartoon/animation; family saga; comedy; historical, juvenile, mainstream, science fiction; romantic comedy, romantic drama, thriller/espionage; true crime/investigative; westerns/frontier.

Also Handles: Novels, syndicated material, animation/cartoon.

How to Contact: Query with SASE. Send outline/proposal. Reports in 2 weeks on queries; 1 month on mss.

Needs: Actively seeking "motion picture scripts (true stories, history, any genre manuscripts)." Does not want to receive "unsolicited materials. Send query letter first." Obtains new clients through solicitation, at conferences.

Recent Sales: *Movie/TV MOW in development: Brainfry*, by Brian Benson (Paramount Special Effects); *Cherokee Rose*, by William Hodges (Warner Brothers); *Primeval*, by James Greenway (John Preverall). *Scripting Assignments: Hitler's Revenge* (novel to script), by Roy Gass. Other clients include Jane Kirkpatrick, William Hodges, Mike Logue, Bruce Clark, Lee Martin and Brad Catherman.

Terms: Agent receives 10% commission on domestic sales; 15% on foreign sales. Offers written contract, binding for 1 year.

Fees: Charges reading fee: $30 for MP/TV scripts, $50 for novels. Offers criticism service at same rates. "Critiques written by agent and professional readers I employ." 25% of business is derived from reading or criticism fees. Charges $100/quarter for all office expenses except photocopying. Will provide binders if necessary.

Writers' Conferences: ELF Literary Conference (Pigeon Forge, TN); Austin Film Fest.

Tips: "We have numerous contacts within entertainment industry that allow production companies and film executive (director of development) to review/consider purchasing or optioning material. Publishing company contacts are very good."

☑ ◑ THE AGENCY, 1800 Avenue of the Stars, Suite 1114, Los Angeles CA 90067-4206. (310)551-3000. **Contact:** Nick Mechanic. Estab. 1984. Signatory of WGA. Represents 300 clients. No new/previously unpublished writers. Specializes in TV and motion pictures. Currently handles: 45% movie scripts; 45% TV scripts; 10% syndicated material.

Represents: Feature film, animation; TV MOW, miniseries, episodic drama, sitcom, animation. **Considers these script subject areas:** action/adventure; cartoon/animation; comedy; contemporary issues; detective/police/crime; ethnic; family saga; fantasy; historical; horror; juvenile; mainstream; military/war; mystery/suspense; psychic/supernatural; romantic comedy and drama; science fiction; teen; thriller; westerns/frontier; women's issues.

How to Contact: Query with SASE. Reports in 2 weeks on queries.

Needs: Obtains new clients through recommendations from others.

Recent Sales: Prefers not to share information on specific sales.

Terms: Agent receives 10% commission on domestic sales; 10% on foreign sales. Offers written contract, binding for 2 years.

◑ ALLRED AND ALLRED, LITERARY AGENTS, (formerly All-Star Talent Agency), 7834 Alabama Ave., Canoga Park CA 91304-4905. (818)346-4313. **Contact:** Robert Allred. Estab. 1991. Represents 5 clients. 100% of clients are new/previously unpublished writers. Specializes in books. Currently handles: books, movie scripts, TV scripts.
  • See the expanded listing for this agency in Literary Agents: Nonfee-charging.

◑ MICHAEL AMATO AGENCY, ,1650 Broadway, Suite 307, New York NY 10019. (212)247-4456 or 4457. **Contact:** Michael Amato. Estab. 1970. Member of SAG, AFTRA. Represents 6 clients. 2% of clients are new/previously unpublished writers.

Represents: Feature film, documentary, animation, TV MOW, miniseries, episodic drama. **Considers action/adventure stories only.**
How to Contact: Query with SASE.. Reports within a month on queries. Does not return scripts.
Needs: Obtains new clients through recommendations.
Recent Sales: Prefers not to share information on specific sales.

 **MARCIA AMSTERDAM AGENCY**, 41 W. 82nd St., New York NY 10024-5613. (212)873-4945. **Contact:** Marcia Amsterdam. Estab. 1970. Signatory of WGA. Currently handles: 15% nonfiction books; 70% novels; 10% movie scripts; 5% TV scripts.
   • See the expanded listing for this agency in Literary Agents: Nonfee-charging.

AUTHORS ALLIANCE INC., 25 Claremont Ave., Suite 3C, New York NY 10027. Phone/fax: (212)662-9788. E-mail: camp544@aol.com. **Contact:** Chris Cane. Represents 25 clients. 10% of clients are new/previously unpublished writers. Specializes in "biographies, especially of historical figures and big name celebrities." Currently hands: 40% nonfiction books, 30% movie scripts, 30% novels.
   • See the expanded listing for this agency in Literary Agents: Nonfee-charging.

BASKOW AGENCY, 2948 E. Russell Rd., Las Vegas NV 89120. (702)733-7818. Fax: (702)733-2052. **Contact:** Jaki Baskow. Estab. 1976. Represents 8 clients. 40% of clients are new/previously unpublished writers. Currently handles: 20% movie scripts; 70% TV scripts; 5% novels; 5% nonfiction books.
Member Agents: Crivolus Sarulus (scripts); Jaki Baskou.
Represents: Feature film, episodic drama, TV movie of the week, sitcom, documentary, variety show, miniseries. **Considers these script subject areas:** action/adventure; comedy; contemporary issues; family saga; glitz; biography/autobiography; mystery/suspense; religious/inspirational; romance (comedy, drama); science fiction (juvenile only); thriller/espionage.
How to Contact: Send outline/proposal and treatments. Reports in 1 month.
Needs: Actively seeking unique scripts/all American true stories, kids projects and movie of the weeks. Does not want to receive heavy violence. Obtains new clients through recommendations.
Recent Sales: Sold 3 projects in the last year. *Movie/TV MOW scripts: Malpractice*, by Larry Leirketen (Blakely); *Angel of Death* (CBS). Other clients include Cheryl Anderson, Camisole Prods, Michael Store.
Terms: Agent receives 10% commission on domestic sales; 10% on foreign sales. Offers written contract.

THE BENNETT AGENCY, 150 S. Barrington Ave., Suite #1, Los Angeles CA 90049. (310)471-2251. Fax: (310)471-2254. **Contact:** Carole Bennett. Estab. 1984. Signatory of WGA, DGA. Represents 15 clients. 2% of clients are new/previously unpublished writers. Specializes in TV sitcom. Currently handles: 5% movie scripts; 95% TV scripts.
Member Agents: Carole Bennett (owner); Tanna Herr (features).
Represents: Feature film, sitcom. **Considers these script subject areas:** comedy; family saga; mainstream.
How to Contact: Query with SASE. Reports in 2 months on queries if SASE included. Accepts queries by fax. Considers simultaneous queries. Returns materials only with SASE.
Needs: Obtains new clients through recommendations from others.
Recent Sales: *Scripting assignments:* "Most of our clients are on staff on such half-hour sitcoms as *Friends* and *Dharma & Greg*."
Terms: Agent receives 10% commission on domestic sales. Offers written contract.

BERMAN BOALS AND FLYNN INC., 208 W. 30th St., #401, New York NY 10001. (212)868-1068. **Contact:** Judy Boals or Jim Flynn. Estab. 1972. Member of AAR, Signatory of WGA. Represents about 35 clients. Specializes in dramatic writing for stage, film, TV.
Represents: Feature film, TV scripts, stage plays.
How to Contact: Query with SASE.
Needs: Obtains new clients through recommendations from others.
Recent Sales: Prefers not to share information on specific sales.
Terms: Agent receives 10% commission.

THE BOHRMAN AGENCY, 8899 Beverly Blvd., Suite 811, Los Angeles CA 90048. (310)550-5444; Fax: (310)550-5445. **Contact:** Michael Hruska, Caren Bohrman or Glen Neumann. Signatory of WGA.

FOR EXPLANATIONS OF THESE SYMBOLS,
SEE THE INSIDE FRONT AND BACK COVERS OF THIS BOOK

Represents: Feature film, TV scripts, theatrical stage play. **Considers all script subject areas.**
How to Contact: Query with SASE. If interested, reports in 2 weeks. Does not read unsolicited mss.
Needs: Obtains clients by referral only.
Recent Sales: Prefers not to share information on specific sales.

◑ **ALAN BRODIE REPRESENTATION**, (incorporating Michael Imison Playwrights Ltd.), 211 Piccadilly, London W1V 9LD England. 0171-917-2871. Fax: 0171-917-2872. E-mail: alanbrodie@aol.com. **Contact:** Alan Brodie or Sarah McNair. Member of PMA. 10% of clients are new/previously unpublished writers. Specializes in stage, film and television.
   • North American writers should send SAE with IRCs for response, available at most post offices.
Needs: No unsolicited mss. Obtains new clients through personal recommendation.
Recent Sales: Prefers not to share information on specific sales.
Terms: Agent receives 10-15% commission on sales. Charges for photocopying.
Tips: "Biographical details can be helpful. Generally only playwrights whose work has been performed will be considered."

◑ **BRUCE BROWN AGENCY**, 1033 Gayley Ave., Suite 207, Los Angeles CA 90024-3417. (310)208-1835. Fax: (310)208-2485. **Contact:** Bruce Brown. Estab. 1993. Signatory of WGA. Represents 40 clients. 5% of clients are new/unpublished writers. Specializes in situation comedy and drama (television series); writers and directors; TV longform, features, cable, soap operas, animation.
Member Agents: Jennifer Good.
Represents: Feature film, episodic drama, soap opera, TV MOW, sitcom, animation. **Considers all script areas.**
How to Contact: Query with SASE.
Needs: Obtains new clients through recommendations from studios, networks, other clients.
Recent Sales: Prefers not to share information on specific sales.
Terms: Agent receives 10% commission on domestic sales. Offers written contract, binding for 2 years.

◐ **CURTIS BROWN LTD.**, 10 Astor Place, New York NY 10003-6935. (212)473-5400. Member of AAR; signatory of WGA. **Contact:** Perry Knowlton, chairman; Timothy Knowlton, CEO; Peter L. Ginsberg, president. Queries to Blake Peterson.
   • See the expanded listing for this agency in Literary Agents: Nonfee-charging.

☑ ⑤ ◐ **KELVIN C. BULGER AND ASSOCIATES**, 11 E. Adams St., Suite 604, Chicago IL 60603. (312)692-1002. E-mail: kcbwoi@aol.com. **Contact:** Kelvin C. Bulger. Estab. 1992. Signatory of WGA. Represents 25 clients. 90% of clients are new/previously unpublished writers. Currently handles: 75% movie scripts; 25% TV scripts.
Represents: Feature film, documentary, TV MOW, syndicated material. **Considers these script subject areas:** action/adventure; cartoon/animation; comedy; contemporary issues; ethnic; family saga; religious/inspirational.
How to Contact: Query with SASE. Reports in 3 weeks on queries; 2 months on mss. "If material is to be returned, writer must enclose SASE."
Needs: Obtains new clients through solicitations and recommendations.
Recent Sales: Optioned 1 script project in the last year. *Renaissance* (short story), by Byron Tate (optioned—True Life Publishing).
Terms: Agent receives 10% commission on domestic sales; 10% on foreign sales. Offers written contract, binding for 6 months-1 year.
Fees: Charges $50 nonrefundable reading fee. Payment of fee does not ensure representation. Charges clients for postage.
Tips: "Proofread before submitting to agent. We only reply to letter of inquiries if SASE is enclosed."

⑤ ◐ ◎ **BUSCHER CONSULTANTS**, 452 Edgewood Rd., Venice FL 34293. (941)408-9113. Fax: (941)493-7223. E-mail: buschern@aol.com. Website: www.BuscherConsultants.com. **Contact:** Nancy Buscher. Estab. 1995. Signatory of WGA. Represents 30 clients. 98% of clients are new/unpublished writers. Specializes in scripts for family audiences. Currently handles: 98% movie scripts; 2% TV Features. "We occasionally match novelists with screenwriters."
   • Prior to becoming an agent, Ms. Buscher was a scriptwriter and worked in advertising.
Represents: Feature film, TV MOW, animation. **Considers "any genre that fits our criteria—family audiences."**
How to Contact: Send SASE for guidelines. Does not want to receive anything without an SASE for return or response.
Needs: Obtains new clients through solicitation.
Recent Sales: Prefers not to share information on specific sales.
Terms: Agent receives 10% commission on domestic sales; negotiable on foreign sales. Offers written contract, binding for 2 years. "We request four clean (of typos, etc.) scripts up front to get us started."
Fees: Charges reading fee of $20/script.

☑ ⑤ ◎ **SUZANNA CAMEJO & ASSOC.**, 3000 W. Olympic Blvd., Santa Monica CA 90404. (310)449-4064. Fax: (310)449-4026. E-mail: scamejo@earthlink.net. **Contact:** Elizabeth Harris. Estab. 1992. Represents 5 clients. 30%

of clients are new/previously unpublished writers. Specializes in environmental issues, animal rights, women's stories, art-oriented, children/family; no action/adventure or violence. Currently handles: 80% movie scripts; 5% novels; 10% TV scripts; 5% life stories.

Member Agents: Suzanna Camejo (issue oriented); Elizabeth Harris (creative associate).

Represents: Feature film, novels, TV scripts, life stories. **Considers these script areas:** contemporary issues; ethnic; family saga; feminist; historical; romantic comedy; romantic drama; science fiction; thriller; environmental.

Also Handles: Considers these nonfiction areas: animals; nature/environment; women's issues/women's studies. Considers these fiction areas: ethnic; family saga; romance (comedy); environmental; animal.

How to Contact: Send outline/proposal and completed scripts (no treatments). Accepts queries by fax. Does not accept e-mail queries. Considers simultaneous queries. Reports in 1 month on mss. Returns materials only with SASE.

Recent Sales: *Primal Scream*, by John Shirley (Showtime); *The Christmas Project*, by Joe Hindy (Ganesha Partners).

Needs: Obtains new clients through recommendations from others and queries.

Terms: Agent receives 10% commission on domestic sales; 10% on foreign sales. Offers written contract, binding for 1 year, with 3 weeks cancellation clause.

Fees: Charges $20 reading fee (per script or ms). Criticism service: $20 (per script or ms). Critiques of storyline, subplot, backstory, pace, characterization, dialogue, marketability, commerciality by professional readers. Charges postage for returned scripts.

Writers' Conferences: Cannes Film Festival (France, May); Telluride Film Festival (Colorado, September); Sundance Film Festival (Utah, January); AFM (Los Angeles, February).

Tips: "If the feature script is well written (three acts, backstory, subplot), with good characters and dialogue, the material is moving, funny or deals with important issues and is nonviolent (no war stories, please), we will read it and represent it."

◎ THE MARSHALL CAMERON AGENCY, 19667 NE 20th Lane, Lawtey FL 32058. Phone/fax: (904)964-7013. E-mail: marshall_cameron@hotmail.com. **Contact:** Margo Prescott. Estab. 1986. Signatory of WGA. Specializes in feature films. Currently handles: 100% movie scripts.

Member Agents: Margo Prescott; Ashton Prescott; John Nicholas (New York co-agent).

Represents: Feature film. **Considers these script subject areas:** action/adventure; comedy; detective/police/crime; drama (contemporary); mainstream; thriller/espionage.

How to Contact: Query by letter with SASE or by e-mail. No phone queries. Accepts queries by e-mail. Considers simultaneous queries. Reports in 1 week on queries; 1-2 months on mss. Returns materials only with SASE.

Recent Sales: Prefers not to share information on specific sales.

Terms: Agent receives 10% commission on domestic sales; 20% on foreign sales. Offers written contract, binding for 1 year.

Tips: "Often professionals in film will recommend us to clients. We also actively solicit material. Always enclose SASE with your query."

◎ CEDAR GROVE AGENCY ENTERTAINMENT, P.O. Box 1692, Issaquah WA 98027-0068. (425)837-1687. Fax: (425)391-7907. E-mail: cedargroveagency@juno.com. Website: freeyellow.com/members/cedargrove/index.html. **Contact:** Amy Taylor or Samantha Powers. Estab. 1995. Member of Cinema Seattle. Represents 7 clients. 100% of clients are new/unpublished writers. Currently handles: 90% movie scripts; 10% TV scripts.

• Prior to becoming agents, Ms. Taylor worked for the stock brokerage firm, Morgan Stanley Dean Witter; Ms. Powers was a customer service/office manager. Cedar Grove Agency Entertainment was formed in the Pacific Northwest to take advantage of the rich and diverse culture as well as the many writers that reside there.

Member Agents: Amy Taylor (Executive Vice President-Motion Picture Division); Samantha Powers (Story Editor).

Represents: Feature film, TV MOW, sitcom. **Considers these script subject areas:** action/adventure; comedy; detective/police/crime; family saga; biography/autobiography; juvenile; mystery/suspense; romance (comedy); science fiction; sports; thriller/espionage; western/frontier.

How to Contact: Query with 1 page synopsis and SASE. "E-mail okay." Reports in 10 days on queries; 6-8 weeks on mss. *"Please! No phone calls!"*

Needs: Does not want to receive period pieces or horror genres. Prefer no children script dealing with illness, or scripts with excessive substance abuse. Obtains new clients through referrals and website.

Recent Sales: Prefers not to share information on specific sales.

Terms: Agent receives 10% commission on domestic sales. Offers written contract, binding for 6-12 months. 30 day notice must be given to terminate contract.

Tips: "We focus on finding that rare gem, the undiscovered, multi-talented writer, no matter where they live. Write, write, write! Find time everyday to write. Network with other writers when possible, and write what you know. Learn the craft through books. Read scripts of your favorite movies. Enjoy what you write!"

ℕ ◎ CHADWICK & GROS LITERARY AGENCY, Lessman@screenplay Pkwy. 671, Baton Rouge LA 70806-5426. (225)338-9861. Fax: (225)338-0279. E-mail: agentap@email.com. Website: colorpro.com/chadwick-gros/. **Contact:** Anna Piazza, director. Estab. 1998. Represents 20 clients. 95% of clients are new/unpublished writers. Currently handles: 90% movie scripts; 10% TV MOW, scripts.

• Prior to becoming an agent, Ms. Piazza was a talent scout for Rinehart & Associates.

Member Agents: Tony Seigan (overseas officer); Dinah Van Sandt (associate director, Texas office); Theron T. Jacks (business advisor).

Represents: Feature film, episodic drama, soap opera, TV MOW, sitcom, documentary, variety show, miniseries, animation. **Considers all script subject areas.**

How to Contact: E-mail for guidelines. "Study our website thoroughly before querying via e-mail." Accepts queries by fax and e-mail. Considers simultaneous queries. Returns materials only with SASE.

Needs: Actively seeking "good attitudes; tough-minded, sure-footed, determined amateurs." Obtains new clients through website and listings in directories.

Recent Sales: Because this agency is new, they have no recorded sales.

Terms: Agent receives 10% commission on domestic sales; 15% on foreign sales. Offers written contract, binding for 1-2 years. 6 months notice must be given to terminate contract.

Tips: "Be most businesslike when you tap on an agency's door. Agencies are business offices and every exchange costs money, time, effort, grief or joy."

✔️ ◎ **CHARISMA COMMUNICATIONS, LTD.**, 250 W. 54th St., Suite 807 New York NY 10019. (212)832-3020. Fax: (212)867-6906. **Contact:** James W. Grau. Estab. 1972. Represents 10 clients. 20% of clients are new/previously unpublished writers. Specializes in organized crime, Indian casinos, FBI, CIA, secret service, NSA, corporate and private security, casino gaming, KGB. Currently handles: 50% nonfiction books; 20% movie scripts; 20% TV scripts; 10% other.

• See the expanded listing for this agency in Literary Agents: Nonfee-charging.

◓ **CINEMA TALENT INTERNATIONAL**, 8033 Sunset Blvd., PMB Suite 808, West Hollywood CA 90046. (213)656-1937. **Contact:** Marie Heckler. Estab. 1976. Represents approximately 23 clients. 3% of clients are new/previously unpublished writers. Currently handles: 1% nonfiction books; 1% novels; 95% movie scripts; 3% TV scripts.

Member Agents: George Kriton; George N. Rumanes; Maria Heckler (motion pictures); Nicholas Athans (motion pictures).

Represents: Feature film, TV scripts

Also Handles: Nonfiction books; novels.

How to Contact: Query with outline/proposal plus 2 sample chapters and SASE. Reports in 4-5 weeks on queries and mss.

Needs: Obtains new clients through recommendations from others.

Recent Sales: Prefers not to share information on specific sales.

Terms: Agent receives 10% on domestic sales; 20% on foreign sales. Offers written contract, binding for 2 years.

◓ **CIRCLE OF CONFUSION LTD.**, 666 Fifth Ave., Suite 303, New York NY 10103. (212)969-0653. Fax: (718)997-0521. E-mail: circleltd@aol.com. **Contact:** Rajeev K. Agarwal, Lawrence Mattis. Estab. 1990. Signatory of WGA. Represents 25 clients. 60% of clients are new/previously unpublished writers. Specializes in screenplays for film and TV. Currently handles: 5% novels; 5% novellas; 90% movie scripts.

Member Agents: Rajeev Agarwal; Lawrence Mattis; Annmarie Negretti; John Sherman.

Represents: Feature film. **Considers all script subject areas.**

Also Handles: Nonfiction books, novels, novellas, short story collections. **Considers all nonfiction and fiction areas.**

How to Contact: Query with SASE. Reports in 1 month on queries; 2 months on mss.

Needs: Obtains new clients through queries, recommendations and writing contests.

Recent Sales: *Movie/TV MOW scripts optioned/sold:* The Matrix, by Wachowski Brothers (Warner Brothers); *Ghosts of October*, by Chabot/Peterka (Dreamworks); *Blood of the Gods*, by Jaswinski (Warner Brothers); *Droid*, by Massa (Warner Brothers).

Terms: Agent receives 10% commission on domestic sales; 10% on foreign sales. Offers written contract, binding for 1 year.

Tips: "We look for screenplays and other material for film and television."

◓ **CLIENT FIRST—A/K/A LEO P. HAFFEY AGENCY**, P.O. Box 128049, Nashville TN 37212-8049. (615)463-2388. E-mail: c1@nashville.net. Website: www.c-1st.com or www.nashville.net/~c1. **Contact:** Robin Swensen. Estab. 1990. Signatory of WGA. Represents 21 clients. 25% of clients are new/previously unpublished writers. Specializes in movie scripts and novels for sale to motion picture industry. Currently handles: 40% novels; 60% movie scripts.

Member Agent: Leo Haffey (attorney/agent to the motion picture industry).

Represents: Feature film, animation. **Considers these script subject areas:** action/adventure; cartoon; animation;

THE PUBLISHING FIELD is constantly changing! If you're still using this book and it is 2001 or later, buy the newest edition of *Guide to Literary Agents* at your favorite bookstore or order directly from Writer's Digest Books at (800)289-0963.

comedy; contemporary issues; detective/police/crime; family saga; historical; mystery/suspense; romance (contemporary, historical); science fiction; sports; thriller/espionage; westerns/frontier.

Also Handles: Novels, novellas, short story collections and self-help books.

How to Contact: Query with SASE. Accepts queries by e-mail. Considers simultaneous queries. Reports in 1 week on queries; 2 months on mss. Returns materials only with SASE.

Needs: Obtains new clients through referrals.

Recent Sales: Prefers not to share information on specific sales.

Terms: Offers written contract, binding for a negotiable length of time.

Tips: "The motion picture business is a numbers game like any other. The more you write the better your chances of success. Please send a SASE along with your query letter."

◎ COMMUNICATIONS AND ENTERTAINMENT, INC., 2851 South Ocean Blvd. #5K, Boca Raton FL 33432-8407. (561)391-9575. Fax: (561)391-7922. **Contact:** James L. Bearden. Estab. 1989. Represents 10 clients. 50% of clients are new/previously unpublished writers. Specializes in TV, film and print media. Currently handles: 5% juvenile books; 40% movie scripts; 10% novels; 40% TV scripts.

• Prior to opening his agency, Mr. Bearden worked as a producer/director and an entertainment attorney.

Member Agents: James Bearden (TV/film); Roslyn Ray (literary).

Represents: Movie scripts, TV scripts, syndicated material.

Also Handles: Considers these nonfiction areas: history; music/dance/theater/film. **Considers these fiction areas:** action/adventure; cartoon/comic; contemporary issues; fantasy; historical; science fiction; thriller/espionage.

How to Contact: For scripts, query with SASE. For books, query with outline/proposal or send entire ms with SASE. Reports in 1 month on queries; 3 months on mss.

Needs: Actively seeking "synopsis, treatment or summary." Does not want to receive "scripts/screenplays unless requested." Obtains new clients through referrals and recommendations.

Recent Sales: Prefers not to share information on specific sales.

Terms: Agent receives 10% commission on domestic sales; 5% on foreign sales. Offers written contract, varies with project.

Tips: "Be patient."

🅽 ◎ COMMUNICATIONS MANAGEMENT ASSOCIATES, 1129 Sixth Ave., #1, Rockford IL 61104-3147. (815)964-1335. Fax: (815)964-3061. **Contact:** Thomas R. Lee. Estab. 1989. Represents 30 clients. 50% of clients are new/previously unpublished writers. Specializes in research, editing and financing. Currently handles: 10% novels; 80% movie scripts; 5% TV scripts; 5% nonfiction.

Represents: Feature film; TV MOW; animation; documentary; miniseries. **Considers these fiction areas:** action/adventure; biography/autobiography; cartoon/animation; comedy; contemporary issues; detective/police/crime; erotica; fantasy; historical; horror; juvenile; mainstream; psychic/supernatural; religious; romantic comedy; romantic drama; science fiction; teen; thriller/espionage; western/frontier.

Also Handles: Novels, short story collections, nonfiction books, juvenile books, scholarly books, novellas, poetry books. **Considers these fiction areas:** action/adventure; contemporary issues; detective/police/crime; erotica; fantasy; historical; horror; juvenile; mainstream; mystery/suspense; picture book; romance (historical, regency); science fiction; thriller/espionage; westerns/frontier; young adult.

How to Contact: Query with outline/proposal, 3 sample chapters and a release. Include SASE. Accepts queries by fax and e-mail. Considers simultaneous queries and submissions. Reports on queries "if interested." Discards unwanted queries/mss.

Needs: Obtains new clients through referrals only.

Recent Sales: Prefers not to share information. Send query for list of credits.

Terms: Agent receives 10% commission on domestic sales; 15% on foreign sales. Offers written contract binding for 2-4 months with 60-day cancellation clause. Charges for postage, photocopying and office expenses.

Writers' Conferences: BEA.

Tips: "Don't let greed or fame-seeking, of anything, but a sincere love or writing push you into this business."

🅂 ◯ CS INTERNATIONAL LITERARY AGENCY, 43 W. 39th St., New York NY 10018-3811. (212)921-1610. **Contact:** Cynthia Neesemann. Estab. 1996. Represents 25 clients. Specializes in full-length fiction, nonfiction and screenplays (no pornography). Currently handles: 33% nonfiction books; 33% movie and TV scripts; 33% novel.

• See the expanded listing for this agency in Literary Agents: Fee-charging.

◎ DADE/SCHULTZ ASSOCIATES, 12302 Sarah St., Studio City CA 91604. (818)760-3100. Fax: (818)760-1395. **Contact:** R. Ernest Dade. Represents 10 clients.

Represents: Feature film. **Considers all script subject areas.**

How to Contact: Query with brief synopsis and SASE. Reports in 1 week if interested.

Recent Sales: Prefers not to share information on specific sales.

Terms: Agent receives 10% commissions on domestic sales; 10% on foreign sales.

◎ DOUROUX & CO., 445 S. Beverly Dr., Suite 310, Beverly Hills CA 90212-4401. (310)552-0900. Fax: (310)552-0920. E-mail: douroux@relaypoint.net. Website: www.relaypoint.net/~douroux. **Contact:** Michael E. Douroux. Estab.

1985. Signatory of WGA, member of DGA. 20% of clients are new/previously unpublished writers. Currently handles: 50% movie scripts; 50% TV scripts.
Member Agents: Michael E. Douroux (chairman/CEO).
Represents: Movie scripts, feature film, TV scripts, TV MOW, episodic drama, sitcom, animation. **Considers these script subject areas:** action/adventure; comedy; detective/police/crime; family saga; fantasy; historical; mainstream; mystery/suspense; romantic comedy and drama; science fiction; thriller/espionage; westerns/frontier.
How to Contact: Query with SASE.
Recent Sales: Prefers not to share information on specific sales.
Terms: Agent receives 10% commission. Offers written contract, binding for 2 years. Charges for photocopying only.

◎ DRAMATIC PUBLISHING, 311 Washington St., Woodstock IL 60098. (815)338-7170. Fax: (815)338-8981. E-mail: plays@dramaticpublishing.com. Website: www.dramaticpublishing.com. **Contact:** Linda Habjan. Estab. 1885. Specializes in a full range of stage plays, musicals, adaptations and instructional books about theater. Currently handles: 2% textbooks; 98% stage plays.
Represents: Stage plays.
How to Contact: Query with SASE. Reports in 4-6 months.
Recent Sales: Prefers not to share information on specific sales.

◢ EPSTEIN-WYCKOFF AND ASSOCIATES, 280 S. Beverly Dr., #400, Beverly Hills CA 90212-3904. (310)278-7222. Fax: (310)278-4640. **Contact:** Karin Wakefield. Estab. 1993. Signatory of WGA. Represents 15 clients. Specializes in features, TV, books and stage plays. Currently handles: 1% nonfiction books; 1% novels; 60% movie scripts; 30% TV scripts; 2% stage plays.
Member Agents: Karin Wakefield (literary); Craig Wyckoff (talent); Gary Epstein (talent).
Represents: Feature film, TV MOW, miniseries, episodic drama, sitcom, animation, soap opera, stage plays. **Considers these script subject areas:** action/adventure; comedy; contemporary issues; detective/police/crime; erotica; family saga; feminist; gay/lesbian; historical; juvenile; mainstream; mystery/suspense; romantic comedy and drama; teen; thriller.
Also Handles: Nonfiction books, novels.
How to Contact: Query with SASE. Reports in 2 weeks on queries; 1 month on mss, if solicited.
Needs: Obtains new clients through recommendations, queries.
Recent Sales: Prefers not to share information on specific sales.
Terms: Agent receives 15% commission on domestic sales of books, 10% on scripts; 20% on foreign sales. Offers written contract, binding for 1 year. Charges for photocopying.
Writers' Conferences: Book Expo America.

✔ ◢ ES TALENT AGENCY, 777 Davis St., San Francisco CA 94111. (415)543-6575. Fax: (415)543-6534. **Contact:** Ed Silver. Estab. 1995. Signatory of WGA. Represents 50-75 clients. 70% of clients are new/previously unpublished writers. Specializes in theatrical screenplays, MOW and miniseries. Currently handles: 50% nonfiction books; 25% movie scripts; 25% novels.
  • Prior to opening his agency, Mr. Silver was an entertainment business manager.
Member Agent: Ed Silver.
Represents: Feature film, TV MOW. **Considers general nonfiction areas. Considers these script areas:** action/adventure; comedy; contemporary issues; detective/police/crime; erotica; ethnic; experimental; family saga; mainstream; mystery/suspense; romantic drama; sports; thriller.
Also Handles: Nonfiction, fiction. **Considers these fiction areas:** action/adventure; contemporary issues; detective/police/crime; erotica; experimental; historical; humor/satire; literary; mainstream; mystery/suspense; thriller/espionage; young adult.
How to Contact: Query with SASE. Accepts queries by fax. Considers simultaneous queries. Reports in 3-4 weeks. Returns materials only with SASE.
Needs: Actively seeking "anything good and original." Obtains new clients through recommendations and queries from WGA agency list.
Recent Sales: Sold 4 book titles and 2 script options in the last year. *Books: Sacred Remedies*, by Mel Ash (Prentice Hall); *Cannabible*, by Jason King (Ten-Speed); *Big Book of Humorous Games*, by Don T. Amblin (McGraw-Hill); *Movie/TV MOW scripts optioned/sold:Scouts Honor*, by Curtis Lim (Kwacizer).
Terms: Agent receives 10% commission on script sales; 15-20% on novels; 20% on foreign sales. Offers written contract with 30 day cancellation clause. Charges for postage and photocopying.

💲 ◢ ESQ. MANAGEMENT, P.O. Box 16194, Beverly Hills CA 90209-2194 (310)252-9879. **Contact:** Patricia E. Lee, Esq. Estab. 1996. Member of Motion Picture Editors Guild. Represents 2 clients. 0% of clients are new/unpublished writers. Specializes in representing people who are working professionals in more than one area. Currently handles: 100% movie scripts.
  • Prior to opening her agency, Ms. Lee was a film editor.
Represents: Feature film, TV MOW, sitcom, animation, miniseries. **Considers these script subject areas:** action/adventure; cartoon/animation; comedy; contemporary issues; detective/police/crime; erotica; ethnic; fantasy; feminist; gay/lesbian; historical; horror; biography/autobiography; juvenile; mystery/suspense; psychic/supernatural; religious/inspirational; romance (comedy, drama); science fiction; teen; thriller/espionage; western/frontier.

How to Contact: Query with 1-page synopsis. Include SASE. Considers simultaneous queries and submissions. Discards unwanted queries; returns mss.

Needs: Actively seeking writers who have been optioned and/or have made at least one sale previously. Obtains new clients through listings in agents/managers directories; print ads; referrals.

Recent Sales: Prefers not to share information on specific sales.

Terms: Agent receives 9% commission on domestic sales; 9% on foreign sales. Offers written contract, binding for 2 years. "During the two-year period, contract can only be terminated under certain specified circumstances."

Fees: "No reading fee unless material submitted for our critiquing/proofreading service. Criticism services: "Rates vary from $150-450 depending on length of report." 10% of business is derived from criticism fees. Payment of criticism fee does not ensure representation. Charges $30/month for postage, photocopying, etc.

Tips: "Make sure you've got a good query letter. Enclose a résumé or a bio."

⊘ FEIGEN/PARENT LITERARY MANAGEMENT, 10158 Hollow Glen Circle, Bel Air CA 90077-2112. (310)271-0606. Fax: (310)274-0503. E-mail: 104063.3247@compuserve.com. **Contact:** Brenda Feigen, Joanne Parrent. Estab. 1995. Member of PEN USA West, Authors Guild, and LA County Bar Association. Represents 35-40 clients. 20-30% of clients are new/previously unpublished writers. Currently handles: 40% nonfiction books; 25% movie scripts; 30% novels; 5% TV scripts.

  • See the expanded listing for this agency in Literary Agents: Nonfee-charging.

✓ ⊘ FILMWRITERS LITERARY AGENCY, 4932 Long Sahdow Dr., Midlothian VA 23112. (804)744-1718. **Contact:** Helene Wagner. Signatory of WGA.

  • Prior to opening her agency, Ms. Wagner was director of the Virginia Screenwriters' Forum for 7 years and taught college level screenwriting classes. "As a writer myself, I have won or been a finalist in most major screenwriting competitions throughout the country and have a number of my screenplays optioned. Through the years I have enjoyed helping and working with other writers. Some have gone on to have their movies made, optioned their work and won national contests."

Represents: Feature film, TV MOW, miniseries. **Considers these script subject areas:** action/adventure; comedy; contemporary issues; detective/police/crime; historical; horror; juvenile; mystery/suspense; psychic/supernatural; romantic comedy; romantic drama; teen; thriller/espionage.

How to Contact: Query plus 1- to 4-page synopsis and SASE. "No phone calls or unsolicited scripts will be accepted." Considers simultaneous queries. Reports in 1-2 weeks on queries; up to a month on mss. Returns unwanted material only with SASE or discards.

Needs: Actively seeking "original and intelligent writing; professional in caliber, correctly formatted and crafted with strong characters and storytelling." Does not want to receive "clones of last year's big movies. Somebody's first screenplay that's filled with 'talking heads,' camera directions, real life 'chit-chat' that doesn't belong in a movie, or a story with no conflict or drama in it." Obtains new clients through recommendations from others and solicitation.

Recent Sales: Sold 2 script projects in the last year. *Movie/TV MOW script(s) optioned/sold: Between Heaven & Hell*, by Charles Deemer (Never a Dull Moment Productions).

Terms: Agent receives 10% commission on domestic sales; 10% on foreign sales. Offers written contract. The writer supplies photocopying and postage. Once a writer sells, the agency will supply photocopying and postage.

Tips: "Professional writers wait until they have at least four drafts done before they send out their work because they know it takes that much hard work to make a story and characters work. Show me something I haven't seen before with characters that I care about, that jump off the page. I not only look at writer's work, I look at the writer's talent. If I believe in a writer, even though a piece may not sell, I'll stay with the writer and help nurture that talent which a lot of the big agencies won't do."

⊘ FIRST LOOK TALENT AND LITERARY AGENCY, 264 S. La Cienega, Suite 1068, Beverly Hills CA 90211. (310)967-5761. Also: 511 Avenue of the Americas, Suite 3000, New York NY 10011. (212)216-9522. E-mail: firstlookla@firstlookagency.com or firstlookny@firstlookagency.com. Website: www.firstlookagency.com. **Contact:** Burt Avalone. Estab. 1997. Represents 18 clients. 30% of clients are new/unpublished writers. Currently handles: 70% movie scripts; 5% stage plays; 25% TV scripts.

  • Prior to becoming agents, Burt Avalone and Ken Richards were agents at other agencies. Harry Nolan was vice president of development for a major production company.

Member Agents: Burt Avalone (NY, all literary); Ken Richards (LA, features, TV); Harry Nolan (LA, Features, TV); Julie Stein (LA, TV MOW).

Represents: Feature film, TV MOW, TV scripts, stage plays, "anything that screams movie." **Considers these script subject areas:** action/adventure, cartoon/animation, comedy, contemporary issues, family saga, fantasy, historical, horror, juvenile, mainstream, military/war, mystery/suspense, psychic/supernatural, romance, science fiction, sports, teen, thriller/espionage, westerns/frontier.

IF YOU'RE LOOKING for a particular agent, check the Agents Index to find at which agency the agent works. Then check the listing for that agency in the appropriate section.

How to Contact: Query or electronic query via website. Reports in 10 days on queries; 1 months on mss.
Needs: Actively seeking fresh, new ideas. Obtains new clients through referrals.
Recent Sales: Sold 6 projects in the last year. Prefers not to share information on specific sales.
Terms: Agent receives 10% commission on domestic sales; 10% on foreign sales. Offers written contract, binding for 1 year.
Tips: "We're willing to consider ideas for features and TV that haven't been scripted yet. If we're excited about the idea, we'll help with its development. We've even made the pitching easier for completed scripts or script ideas via the easy-to-follow instructions on our website. Don't spend six months or more of your life writing something you're not excited about. For better or worse, Hollywood responds more quickly to a great idea with mediocre execution than the other way around."

FITZGERALD LITERARY MANAGEMENT, 84 Monte Alto Rd., Santa Fe NM 87505. Phone/fax: (505)466-1186. **Contact:** Lisa FitzGerald. Estab. 1994. Represents 12 clients. 75% of clients are new/unpublished writers. Represents screenwriters and film rights to novels. Currently represents: 75% movie scripts; 15% film rights to novels; 5% TV scripts; 5% film rights to stage plays.
  • Prior to opening her agency, Ms. FitzGerald headed development at Universal Studios for Bruce Evans and Raynold Gideon, Oscar-nominated writer-producers. She also served as Executive Story Analyst at CBS, and held positions at Curtis Brown Agency in New York and Adams, Ray & Rosenberg Talent Agency in Los Angeles.
Represents: Feature film, TV MOW. **Considers these script subject areas:** action/adventure; comedy; contemporary issues; detective/police/crime; erotica; ethnic; family saga; fantasy; historical; horror; biography/autobiography; juvenile; mainstream; mystery/suspense; psychic/supernatural; romance (comedy, drama); science fiction; sports; teen; thriller/espionage; western/frontier. "Any subject, if the query sounds of interest."
Also Handles: Novels. **Considers these fiction areas:** children's books, young adult novels and mainstream novels with film potential.
How to Contact: Query with 1 page synopsis and SASE. Prefers to be only reader. "Will not respond if no SASE included. No faxed queries, please." Reports in 2 weeks on queries; 4-6 weeks on mss. Returns materials only with SASE.
Needs: Actively seeking mainstream feature film scripts. Does not want to receive true stories. Obtains new clients through referrals from other clients or business contacts, writers conferences, screenplay contests, queries.
Recent Sales: Sold 7 book titles and 5 script projects in the last year. Prefers not to share information on specific sales.
Terms: Agent receives 10-15% commission on domestic sales. Offers written contract, binding for 1-2 years. Charges for photocopying and postage.
Tips: "Know your craft. Read produced screenplays. Enter screenplay contests. Educate yourself on the business in general (read *The Hollywood Reporter* or *Daily Variety*). Learn how to pitch. Keep writing and don't be afraid to get your work out there."

B.R. FLEURY AGENCY, P.O. Box 149352, Orlando FL 32814-9352. (407)895-8494. Fax: (407)898-3923. E-mail: brfleuryagency@juno.com. **Contact:** Blanche or Margaret. Estab. 1994. Signatory of WGA. Currently handles: 70% books; 30% scripts.
Represents: Feature film, TV MOW. **Considers these script subject areas:** action/adventure; comedy; detective/police/crime; family saga; historical; horror; mainstream; mystery/suspense; psychic/supernatural; romantic comedy and drama; thriller.
Also Handles: Nonfiction books, novels. **Considers these nonfiction areas:** agriculture/horticulture; animals; anthropology/archaeology; art/architecture/design; biography; business; child guidance/parenting; cooking/food/nutrition; education; health/medicine; how-to; humor; interior design/decorating; juvenile; money/finance/economics; film; nature/environment; New Age/metaphysics; photography; psychology; science/technology; self-help/personal improvement; sociology; true crime/investigative. **Considers these fiction areas:** action; detective/police/crime; ethnic; experimental; family saga; fantasy; historical; horror; humor/satire; literary; mainstream; mystery/suspense; psychic/supernatural; regional; romance (contemporary, gothic, historical, regency); science fiction; sports; thriller/espionage; westerns/frontier; young adult.
How to Contact: Query with SASE or call for information. Accepts queries by fax and e-mail, "2 pages maximum." Prefers to be the only reader. Reports immediately on queries; 3 months for mss.
Needs: Obtains new clients through referrals and listings.
Recent Sales: Prefers not to share information on specific sales.
Terms: Receives commission according to WGA guidelines. Agent receives 15% commission on domestic sales. Offers written contract, binding as per contract. Charges for business expenses directly related to work represented.
Tips: "Be creative."

FRAN LITERARY AGENCY, 7235 Split Creek, San Antonio TX 78238-3627. (210)684-1569. **Contact:** Fran Rathmann, Kathy Kenney. Estab. 1993. Signatory of WGA, member of ASCAP. Represents 33 clients. 60% of clients are new/previously unpublished writers. "Very interested in Star Trek novels/screenplays." Currently handles: 25% nonfiction books; 15% juvenile books; 30% novels; 5% novellas; 5% poetry books; 20% teleplays/screenplays.
  • See the expanded listing for this agency in Literary Agents: Fee-charging.

⊘ THE BARRY FREED CO., 2040 Ave. of the Stars, #400, Los Angeles CA 90067. (310)277-1260. Fax: (310)277-3865. E-mail: blfreed@aol.com. **Contact:** Barry Freed. Signatory of WGA. Represents 15 clients. 95% of clients are new/unpublished writers. Currently represents: 100% movie scripts.
   • Prior to opening his agency, Mr. Freed worked for ICM.
Represents: Feature film, TV MOW. **Considers these script subject areas:** action/adventure; comedy; contemporary issues; detective/police/crime; ethnic; family saga; horror; mainstream; mystery/suspense; science fiction; sports; teen; thriller/espionage.
How to Contact: Query with SASE. Reports immediately on queries; in 3 moths on mss.
Needs: Actively seeking adult drama, comedy, romantic comedy, science fiction. Does not want to receive period, westerns. Obtains new clients through recommendations from others.
Recent Sales: Prefers not to share information on specific sales.
Terms: Offers written contract binding for 2 years.
Tips: "Our clients are a highly qualified small roster of writers who write comedy, action adventure/thrillers, adult drama, romantic comedy."

⊙ ROBERT A. FREEDMAN DRAMATIC AGENCY, INC., 1501 Broadway, Suite 2310, New York NY 10036. (212)840-5760. **Contact:** Robert A. Freedman, president; Selma Luttinger, vice president; Marta Prueger, associate. Estab. 1928. Member of AAR, signatory of WGA. Prefers to work with established authors; works with a small number of new authors. Specializes in plays, movie scripts and TV scripts.
   • Robert Freedman has served as vice president of the dramatic division of AAR.
Represents: Movie scripts, TV scripts, stage plays.
How to Contact: Query with SASE. No unsolicited mss. Usually reports in 2 weeks on queries; 3 months on mss.
Recent Sales: "We will speak directly with any prospective client concerning sales that are relevant to his/her specific script."
Terms: Agent receives 10% on dramatic sales; "and, as is customary, 20% on amateur rights." Charges for photocopying.

⊙ SAMUEL FRENCH, INC., 45 W. 25th St., New York NY 10010-2751. (212)206-8990. Fax: (212)206-1429. **Contact:** William Talbot and Lawrence Harbison, editors. Estab. 1830. Member of AAR. Represents plays which it publishes for production rights.
Member Agents: Pam Newton; Brad Lohrenze.
Represents: Theatrical stage play, musicals, variety show. **Considers these script subject areas:** comedy; contemporary issues; detective/police/crime; ethnic; experimental; fantasy; horror; mystery/suspense; religious/inspirational; thriller.
How to Contact: Query or send entire ms. Replies "immediately" on queries; decision in 2-8 months regarding publication. "Enclose SASE."
Recent Sales: Prefers not to share information on specific sales.
Terms: Agent usually receives 10% professional production royalties; variable amateur production royalties.

⊠ ⊙ THE GAGE GROUP, 9255 Sunset Blvd., Suite 515, Los Angeles CA 90069. (310)859-8777. Fax: (310)859-8166. Estab. 1976. Signatory of WGA. Represents 27 clients.
Represents: Movies scripts, feature film, TV scripts, theatrical stage play. **Considers all script subject areas.**
How to Contact: Query with SASE. Reports in 2-4 weeks on queries and mss.
Recent Sales: Prefers not to share information on specific sales.
Terms: Agent receives 10% commission on domestic sales; 10% commission on foreign sales.

⊘ $ THE LAYA GELFF AGENCY, 16133 Ventura Blvd., Suite 700, Encino CA 91436. (818)996-3100. Estab. 1985. Signatory of WGA. Represents many clients. Specializes in TV and film scripts; WGA members preferred. "Also represents writers to publishers." Currently handles: 40% movie scripts; 40% TV scripts; 20% book mss.
Represents: Feature film, TV scripts.
How to Contact: Query with SASE. Reports in 2 weeks on queries; 1 month on mss. "Must have SASE for reply."
Needs: Obtains new clients through recommendations from others.
Recent Sales: Prefers not to share information on specific sales.
Terms: Agent receives 10% commission on domestic sales; 10% on foreign sales. Offers standard WGA contract.
Fees: Charges reading fee for book representation only.

⊘ THE SEBASTIAN GIBSON AGENCY, P.O. Box 13350, Palm Desert CA 92255-3350. (760)837-3726. Fax: (619)322-3857. **Contact:** Sebastian Gibson. Estab. 1995. Member of the California Bar Association, Nevada Bar Association. 100% of clients are new/previously unpublished writers. Specializes in fiction.
   • See the expanded listing for this agency in Literary Agents: Nonfee-Charging.

⊘ GRAHAM AGENCY, 311 W. 43rd St., New York NY 10036. (212)489-7730. **Contact:** Earl Graham, owner. Estab. 1971. Represents 40 clients. 30% of clients are new/unproduced writers. Specializes in playwrights and screenwriters only. Currently handles: movie scripts, stage plays.
Represents: Theatrical stage play, feature film. No one-acts, no material for children.

How to Contact: Query with SASE. "We consider on the basis of the letters of inquiry." Writers *must* query before sending any material for consideration. Reports in 3 months on queries; 6 weeks on mss.

Needs: "We're interested in commercial material of quality." Obtains new clients through queries and referrals.

Recent Sales: Prefers not to share information on specific sales.

Terms: Agent receives 10% commission.

Tips: "Write a concise, intelligent letter giving the gist of what you are offering."

ⓜ ARTHUR B. GREENE, 101 Park Ave., 26th Floor, New York NY 10178. (212)661-8200. Fax: (212)370-7884. **Contact:** Arthur Greene. Estab. 1980. Represents 20 clients. 10% of clients are new/previously unpublished writers. Specializes in movies, TV and fiction. Currently handles: 25% novels; 10% novellas; 10% short story collections; 25% movie scripts; 10% TV scripts; 10% stage plays; 10% other.

Represents: Feature film, TV MOW, stage play. **Considers these script subject areas:** action/adventure; detective/police/crime; horror; mystery/suspense.

Also Handles: Novels. **Considers these nonfiction areas:** animals; music/dance/theater/film; sports. **Considers these fiction areas:** action/adventure; detective/police/crime; horror; mystery/suspense; sports; thriller/espionage.

How to Contact: Query with SASE. Reports in 2 weeks on queries. No written contract, 30 day cancellation clause. 100% of business is derived from commissions on sales.

Needs: Obtains new clients through recommendations from others.

Recent Sales: Prefers not to share information on specific sales.

Terms: Agent receives 10% commission on domestic sales; 20% on foreign sales.

✓ ⓜ CAROLYN HODGES AGENCY, 1980 Glenwood Dr., Boulder CO 80304-2329. (303)443-4636. Fax: (303)443-4636. E-mail: hodgesc@earthlink.net. **Contact:** Carolyn Hodges. Estab. 1989. Signatory of WGA. Represents 15 clients. 90% of clients are new/previously unpublished writers. Represents only screenwriters for film and TV MOW. Currently handles: 15% movie scripts; 45% TV scripts.

● Prior to opening her agency, Ms. Hodges was a freelance writer and founded the Writers in the Rockies Screenwriting Conference.

Represents: Movie scripts, feature film, TV scripts, TV MOW. **Considers these script subject areas:** action/adventure; comedy; contemporary issues; erotica; experimental; horror; mainstream; mystery/suspense; psychic/supernatural; romance (comedy, drama).

How to Contact: Query with 1-page synopsis and SASE. Accepts queries by fax or e-mail. Considers simultaneous queries and submissions. Reports in 1 week on queries; 10 weeks on mss. "Please, no queries by phone." Returns materials only with SASE.

Needs: Obtains new clients by referral only.

Recent Sales: Sold 3 projects in the last year. *Fantasy Land*, by Robert Lilly (Gallus Enterprises); *Ribit*, by Janie Norris (K. Peterson); *Two Hour Layover*, by Steven Blake (River Road Enterprises).

Terms: Agent receives 10% on domestic sales; foreign sales "depend on each individual negotiation." Offers written contract, standard WGA. No charge for criticism. "I always try to offer concrete feedback, even when rejecting a piece of material." Charges for postage. "Sometimes we request reimbursement for long-distance phone and fax charges."

Writers' Conferences: Director and founder of Writers in the Rockies Film Screenwriting Conference (Boulder CO, August).

Tips: "Become proficient at your craft. Attend all workshops accessible to you. READ all the books applicable to your area of interest. READ as many 'produced' screenplays as possible. Live a full, vital and rewarding life so your writing will have something to say. Get involved in a writer's support group. Network with other writers. Receive 'critiques' from your peers and consider merit of suggestions. Don't be afraid to re-examine your perspective."

ⓜ BARBARA HOGENSON AGENCY, 165 West End Ave., Suite 19-C, New York NY 10023. (212)874-8084. Fax: (212)362-3011. **Contact:** Barbara Hogenson. Estab. 1994. Member of AAR, signatory of WGA. Represents 60 clients. 5% of clients are new/previously unpublished writers. Currently handles: 35% nonfiction books; 15% novels; 15% movie scripts; 35% stage plays.

● Prior to opening her own agency, Ms. Hogenson was with the prestigious Lucy Kroll Agency for 10 years.

Represents: Feature film, soap opera, theatrical stage play, TV MOW, sitcom.

Also Handles: Nonfiction books, novels. **Considers these nonfiction areas:** art/architecture/design; biography/autobiography; cooking/food/nutrition; history; humor; interior design/decorating; music/dance/theater/film; photography; popular culture. **Considers these fiction areas:** action/adventure; contemporary issues; detective/police/crime; ethnic; historical; humor/satire; literary; mainstream; mystery/suspense; romance (contemporary); thriller/espionage.

How to Contact: Query with outline and SASE. No unsolicited mss. Reports in 1 month.

Needs: Obtains new clients strictly by referral.

Terms: Agent receives 10% on film and TV sales; 15% commission on domestic sales of books; 20% on foreign sales of books. Offers written contract. 100% of business derived from commissions on sales.

Recent Sales: *Sweet Chaos*, by Carol Brightman; *Cordelia Underwood*, by Van Reid (Viking/Penguin); *South Mountain Road*, by Hesper Anderson (Simon & Schuster). *Movie/TV MOW scripts optioned/sold: Woman Wanted*, by Joanna Glass (Phoenician Entertainment).

✓ 💲 ☑ **THE EDDY HOWARD AGENCY**, % 732 Coral Ave., Lakewood NJ 08701. (732)942-1023. **Contact:** Eddy Howard Pevovar, N.D., Ph.D. Estab. 1986. Signatory of WGA. Member of Author's Guild. Represents 20 clients. 10% of clients are new/previously unpublished writers. Specializes in film, sitcom and literary. Currently handles: 5% nonfiction books; 5% scholarly books; 5% juvenile books; 5% novels; 30% movie scripts; 30% TV scripts; 10%•stage plays; 5% short story collections; 1% syndicated material; 4% other.
Member Agents: Eddy Howard Pevovar, N.D., Ph.D. (agency executive).
Represents: Feature film, documentary, animation, TV MOW, miniseries, episodic drama, sitcom, variety show, animation, soap opera, educational, stage plays. **Considers these script subject areas:** cartoon/animation; comedy; contemporary issues; erotica; family saga; historical; juvenile; mainstream; teen; western/frontier.
Also Handles: Nonfiction books, scholarly books, textbooks, juvenile books, novels, novellas, short story collections, syndicated material. **Considers these nonfiction areas:** biography/autobiography; business; child guidance/parenting; computers/electronics; government/politics/law; history; how-to; language/literature/criticism; sociology. **Considers these fiction areas:** cartoon/comic; contemporary issues; family saga; historical; fantasy; humor/satire; juvenile; literary; mainstream; picture book; regional; sports.
How to Contact: Query with outline and letter—include phone number. Include SASE. Prefers to be only reader. Reports in 5 days on queries; up to 1 month on mss. Returns materials only with SASE.
Needs: Obtains new clients through recommendations from others and by submissions.
Recent Sales: Sold 4 book titles and 1 script project in the last year. Prefers not to share information on specific sales.
Terms: Agent receives 10% commission on domestic sales; 15% on foreign sales. Offers written contract.
Fees: No reading fees. Offers criticism service: corrective—style, grammar, punctuation, spelling, format. Technical critical evaluation with fee (saleability, timeliness, accuracy).
Writers' Conferences: Instructor—Writers Workshops at Brookdale College; Community Education Division.
Tips: "I was rejected 12 times before I ever had my first book published and I was rejected 34 times before my first magazine article was published. Stick to what you believe in. . . . Don't give up! Never give up! Take constructive criticism for whatever it's worth and keep yourself focused. Each rejection a beginner receives is one step closer to the grand finale—acceptance. It's sometimes good to get your manuscript peer reviewed. I think it's a great idea to hire an editor and have them correct your manuscript if you're a new author, or if you've written something technical or even historical. I personally use media services for my work. This is one way to obtain objective analysis of your work, and see what others think about it. Remember, if it weren't for new writers . . . there'd be *no* writers."

◑ 📷 **HUDSON AGENCY**, 3 Travis Lane, Montrose NY 10548. (914)737-1475. Fax: (914)736-3064. E-mail: hudagency@juno.com. **Contact:** Susan or Pat Giordano. Estab. 1994. Signatory of WGA. Represents 30 clients. 50% of clients are new/previously unpublished writers. Specializes in feature film and TV. Also specializes in animation writers. Currently handles: 50% movie scripts; 50% TV scripts and TV animation.
Member Agents: Sue Giordano (TV animation); Pat Giordano (MOW, features); Cheri Santone (features and animation); Sunny Gross (Canada contact).
Represents: Feature film, documentary, animation, TV MOW, miniseries, sitcom; PG or PG-13 only. **Considers these script subject areas:** action/adventure; cartoon/animation; comedy; contemporary issues; detective/police/crime; family saga; fantasy; juvenile; mystery/suspense; romantic comedy and drama; teen; westerns/frontier.
How to Contact: Send outline and sample pages with SASE. Accepts queries by fax or e-mail. Reports in 1 week on queries; 3 weeks on mss. Returns material only with SASE.
Needs: Actively seeking "writers with television and screenwriting education or workshops under their belts." Does not want to receive "R-rated material, no occult, no one that hasn't taken at least one screenwriting workshop." Obtains new clients through recommendations from others and listing on WGA agency list.
Recent Sales: Prefers not to share information on specific sales. "See website."
Terms: Agent receives 10% commission on domestic sales; 10% on foreign sales.
Tips: "Yes, we may be small, but we work very hard for our clients. Any script we are representing gets excellent exposure to producers. Our network has over 1,000 contacts in the business and growing rapidly. We are GOOD salespeople. Ultimately it all depends on the quality of the writing and the market for the subject matter. Do not query unless you have taken at least one screenwriting course and read all of Syd Field's books."

🅽 ☑ **INFINITY MANAGEMENT INTERNATIONAL**, 425 N. Robertson Blvd., Los Angeles CA 90048. (310)276-9321. Fax: (310)276-1706. **Contact:** Jon Karas. Estab. 1990. Member of Conference of Personal Managers. Represents 75 clients. 10% of clients are new/unpublished writers. Currently handles: 5% nonfiction books; 15% novels; 60% movie scripts; 20% TV scripts.
 • Prior to becoming an agent, Mr. Karas was an attorney in New York and an agent at William Morris in Beverly Hills CA.
Member Agents: Jon M. Karas (film , TV); Traci Ching (film, TV); David Posner (film, TV, books); Larry Collins (film, TV, books).
Represents: Feature film, episodic drama, sitcom, miniseries. **Considers these script subject areas:** action/adventure; comedy; detective/police/crime; erotica; fantasy; horror; mainstream; mystery/suspense; psychic/supernatural; romantic comedy; romantic drama; science fiction; sports; teen; thriller/espionage.
Also Handles: Novels. **Considers these fiction areas:** action/adventure; detective/police/crime; erotica; fantasy; horror; mystery; psychic/supernatural; science fiction; sports; thriller/espionage.

insider report

From fiction to screenplays: how agents help careers grow

"Beware of the wise who are young and gifted," wrote novelist Russell Banks. "They quickly become irreplaceable." The particular wise man Banks had in mind when he penned this phrase was a Princeton graduate from West Virginia, Pinckney Benedict. Benedict's first collection of short stories, *Town Smokes*, had just been published to rave reviews, and many like Banks thought of him as nothing less than a short fiction prodigy. Now, over ten years later, Pinckney Benedict has proven Banks nothing less than a prophet.

In an effort to diversify his skills as a writer, Benedict has made a major contribution to almost every publishing niche worth inhabiting, including screenwriting. To date Benedict has published a second book of short stories, *The Wrecking Yard*, a

Pickney Benedict

novel, *Dogs of God*, and countless interviews, book reviews, and nonfiction articles with magazines like *Bomb* and *Esquire*. And with the release of his feature film *Four Days* starring Colm Meaney, William Forsythe and Lolita Davidovich, Benedict made a serious leap and proved himself an "irreplaceable" screenwriter as well.

But Benedict is quick to admit that no matter how wise or talented one may be, it is imperative that a writer have a trustworthy agent, especially when the author splits his time between fiction and screenwriting. "It leads to all kinds of weirdness," says Benedict. "For instance, right now I am working on the screenplay of my first novel, *Dogs of God*. When a writer gets paid to have his book optioned the standard agenting rate is 15 percent. But the agenting rate for working on a screenplay is ten percent. When you do both, things get confusing. You have to have an agent you can trust to work out all the details. I don't have time because I'm writing. The checks come in, and I would never know if I am getting what I deserve. I am lucky because I have my agent, David Black, of the David Black Literary Agency—it's just inconceivable that he would ever hurt me."

How did you meet your agent?

Right before I went to graduate school at the University of Iowa, one of my short stories won the *Chicago Tribune*'s Nelson Algren Award. David called me—I think he makes a habit of calling people who win to ask if they need representation. At the time I didn't think I needed an agent. I am shy about the business end of writing, and I had talked to my teacher at Princeton, Joyce Carol Oates. She told me she had written three books before getting an agent. My first book of short stories, *Town Smokes*, had just been accepted by Ontario Review Press, and I didn't feel like I had anything to offer an agent. I didn't even know if I'd be able to write anything else. But David kept at me.

Photo by Richard Boyd

How is using an agent for a book different from using one for film?
Worlds apart. In fact, David's agency doesn't handle film at all. David has a co-agent in Los Angeles do the film work—Lucy Stille from Paradigm handled the film sub rights when my novel was optioned.

How did you get involved with the movie *Four Days*?
A creative team from Toronto, Greg Dummett and Curtis Wehrfritz, had acquired the rights to *Four Days*, a novel by Canadian author John Buell. The director had read my novel *Dogs of God*, and thought I might be good for the script. We spent some time kicking around ideas for how the adaptation should go. At first the idea was to shoot a low-budget 15-minute vignette and use that to try and raise money. I went home and wrote a 20-page script. When Greg and Curtis read it, they changed their minds about the vignette and decided to raise money for the entire feature. They gave me feedback, and I went to work on the whole screenplay.

That's when I got back in touch with my agents. Lucy Stille had a problem in that she was used to working on film rights for literary works—not screenplays. I was worried because when it came to movies I was a total neophyte. Because I was new, I didn't want an ironclad contract. I pleaded with David's assistant Susan Raihofer to help with the negotiations. We cobbled together a very loose contract, where I got paid a percentage of the movie's total budget. That's good because Greg and Curtis ended up raising more money for shooting than they thought they would. A contract like that is great incentive for the writer to do as good a job as possible, because much of a movie's funding is based on the quality of the script.

You said you were also working on a screenplay of your own novel. How's that going? Is the contract similar?
Not really. I did a lot of free revision on *Four Days*. The *Dogs of God* project is more structured. This time the company that optioned the novel had a specific idea about what they wanted in the script. Actually, I am the second guy to work on the project. They asked me to work on it originally, but at the time I didn't know anything about writing for film, so they got someone else. Later they called to ask questions about the book. I told them I was working on *Four Days* and would be interested in giving *Dogs of God* a shot, too.

One of the things I like about screenwriting is that I get paid for every revision. In fiction, revision comes with the territory. You expect your editor to ask for changes and you pretty much have to make them. In film, the contracts usually specify the terms of revision. If the producers want an extensive rewrite in *x* number of weeks, the contracts stipulate how much the author gets paid for that service.

Did the David Black Literary Agency help you with that contract as well?
Yes, but it's a sensitive situation. Because of my other projects, it's been five years since my last novel. David is a literary agent, and every word I put into a screenplay is a word I'm not putting into a book. He wants me to work on my fiction, even though he is understanding of my need to work on other projects. I've promised him a new novel by the fall. But I know of a few people whose agents aren't so understanding. I have one friend who had to cut her literary agent out of her film deals altogether.

> **Would you advise a person just starting out to get two agents, one for each field?**
> I am cautious. I've never gone outside my family of agents, and I don't want to. But I might advise someone interested primarily in film to get two agents. Like I said, the business is very different—worlds apart.
>   —*Brad Vice*

How to Contact: Query with SASE. Accepts queries by fax. *No unsolicited mss.* Prefers to be the only reader. Reports in 10 days on queries; 1 month on mss. Returns materials only with SASE.
Needs: Actively seeking established film and TV writers, and novelists. Obtains new clients through referrals from industry professionals.
Recent Sales: Sold 25 script projects in the last year. *Movie/TV MOW script(s) optioned/sold: Evolution*, by Don Jakoby (Ivan Reitman); *Kill Van Full*, by Richard Regen (Sounenfeld). *Movie/TV MOW scripts in development: Live by the Sword*, by Steve Molton (Showtime Miniseries); *Boom.* by Joel Silverman (Fried Films). Other clients include Sheldon Lettich, Jamie Mayer, Mike Bouifer, Judy and Sandy Berg, Yule Caise, Loren-Paul Caplin, Paul Duran, John Penney, Brian Lane, George Ferris.
Terms: Agent receives 15% commission on domestic sales; 25% on foreign sales. Offers written contract. Twenty days notice must be given to terminate contract.
Writers' Conferences: Maui Writer's Conference (HI, September).
Tips: "We have excellent long-term personal relationships in the film and television production communities, close ties with publishers and New York book agents. We provide hands-on involvement with development of material."

INTERNATIONAL CREATIVE MANAGEMENT, 8942 Wilshire Blvd., Beverly Hills CA 90211. (310)550-4000. Fax: (310)550-4100. East Coast office: 40 W. 57th St., New York NY 10019. (212)556-5600. Fax: (212)556-5665. Signatory of WGA, member of AAR.
  • See expanded listing for this agency in Literary Agents: Nonfee-charging.

INTERNATIONAL LEONARDS CORP., 3612 N. Washington Blvd., Indianapolis IN 46205-3534. (317)926-7566. **Contact:** David Leonards. Estab. 1972. Signatory of WGA. Currently handles: 50% movie scripts; 50% TV scripts.
Represents: Feature film, animation, TV MOW, sitcom, variety show. **Considers these script subject areas:** action/adventure; cartoon/animation; comedy; contemporary issues; detective/police/crime; horror; mystery/suspense; romantic comedy; science fiction; sports; thriller.
How to Contact: Query with SASE. Prefers to be only reader. Reports in 1 month on queries; 6 months on mss. Returns materials only with SASE.
Needs: Obtains new clients through recommendations and queries.
Recent Sales: Prefers not to share information on specific sales.
Terms: Agent receives 10% commission on domestic sales; 10% on foreign sales. Offers written contract, following "WGA standard," which "varies."

JLA LITERARY AGENCY, 5704 Gist Ave., Baltimore MD 21215-3508. (410)578-0468. Fax: (410)578-0237. E-mail: jlaagency@aol.com. **Contact:** Jeffrey O'Bomeghie. Estab. 1999. Represents 12 clients. 60% of clients are new/previously unpublished writers. Specializes in literary fiction and nonfiction. "We are especially interested in mainstream works." Currently handles: 40% nonfiction books; 40% novels; 20% movie scripts.
  • See the expanded listing for this agency in Literary Agents: Nonfee-charging.

JOHNSON WARREN LITERARY AGENCY, 115 W. California Blvd., Suite 173, Pasadena CA 91105. (626)583-8750. Fax: (909)624-3930. E-mail: jwa@aol.com. **Contact:** Billie Johnson. Signatory of WGA. Represents 25 clients. 95% of clients are new/unpublished writers. This agency is open to new writers and enjoys a teamwork approach to projects. JWLA has an on-staff promotions director to bolster publicity efforts. Currently handles: 30% movie scripts; 50% novels; 5% TV scripts; 15% nonfiction books.
  • See the expanded listing for this agency in the Literary Agents: Fee-charging.

LESLIE KALLEN AGENCY, 15303 Ventura Blvd., Sherman Oaks CA 91403. (818)906-2785. Fax: (818)906-8931. Website: www.lesliekallen.com. **Contact:** J.R. Gowan. Estab. 1988. Signatory of WGA, DGA. Specializes in feature films and MOWs.
Represents: Feature film, TV MOW.
How to Contact: Query with SASE. "No phone inquiries for representation."
Recent Sales: Prefers not to share information on specific sales.
Terms: Agent receives 10% commission on domestic sales.

Tips: "Write a two- to three-paragraph query that makes an agent excited to read the material."

CHARLENE KAY AGENCY, 901 Beaudry St., Suite 6, St. Jean/Richelieu, Quebec J3A 1C6 Canada. (450)348-5296. **Contact:** Louise Meyers, director of development. Estab. 1992. Signatory of WGA; member of BMI. 100% of clients are new/previously unpublished writers. Specializes in teleplays and screenplays. "No novels, books or manuscripts." Currently handles: 25% TV scripts; 50% TV spec scripts; 25% movie scripts.
  • Prior to opening her agency, Ms. Kay was a scriptwriter.
Represents: Feature film, animation, TV MOW, episodic drama, sitcom, and spec scripts for existing TV series. **Considers these script subject areas:** action/adventure; fantasy; psychic/supernatural; romantic comedy; romantic drama; science fiction; biography/autobiography; family saga. No thrillers. "We seek stories that are out of the ordinary, something we don't see too often. A *well-written* and *well-constructed* script is important."
How to Contact: Query with outline/proposal by mail only. No phone calls. Include SASE (or SASE with IRC outside Canada). "No reply without SASE." Reports in 1 month on queries. Reports in 8-10 weeks on mss. Returns materials only with SASE.
Needs: Does not want to receive "thrillers or barbaric and erotic films."
Recent Sales: Prefers not to share information on specific sales.
Terms: Agent receives 10% commission on domestic sales; 10% on foreign sales. Offers written contract, binding for 1 year. Returns Canadian scripts if SASE provided; returns scripts from US if 15 IRCs are included with an envelope.
Tips: "This agency is listed on the WGA lists and query letters arrive by the dozens every week. As our present clients understand, success comes with patience. A sale rarely happens overnight, especially when you are dealing with totally unknown writers. We are not impressed by the credentials of a writer, amateur or professional or by his or her pitching techniques, but by his or her story ideas and ability to build a well-crafted script."

TYLER KJAR AGENCY, 5116 Lankershim Blvd., North Hollywood CA 91601. (818)760-0321. Fax: (818)760-0642. **Contact:** Tyler Kjar. Estab. 1974. Signatory of WGA. 10% of clients are new/previously unpublished writers. Currently handles: 50% movie scripts; 50% TV scripts.
Represents: Movie scripts, feature film, TV scripts, TV MOW, miniseries, sitcom, stage plays. **Considers these script subject areas:** action/adventure; family saga; horror; romantic comedy and drama; science fiction; teen; American period pieces (nonwestern); children/8 + with positive roles (no drugs, blood, guns, relating in today's society).
How to Contact: Query with SASE; do not send outline or script. Reports in 2 weeks on queries; 6 weeks on mss.
Needs: Actively seeking youth-oriented screenplays with positive emphasis on personal exchange; no guns or drugs. Obtains new clients from recommendations.
Recent Sales: Prefers not to share information on specific sales.
Fees: Charges reading fee. Criticism service: $100. Critiques done by Tyler Kjar.
Tips: "Most scripts are poorly written, with incorrect format, too much description, subject matter usually borrowed from films they have seen. Must follow established format."

PAUL KOHNER, INC., 9300 Wilshire Blvd., Suite 555, Beverly Hills CA 90212-3211. (310)550-1060. **Contact:** Stephen Moore. Estab. 1938. Member of ATA, signatory of WGA. Represents 150 clients. 10% of clients are new/ previously unpublished writers. Specializes in film and TV rights sales and representation of film and TV writers.
Represents: Film/TV rights to published books; feature film, documentary, animation, TV MOW, miniseries, episodic drama, sitcom, variety show, animation; soap opera, stage plays. **Considers these script subject areas:** action/adventure; comedy; detective/police/crime; family saga; historical; mainstream; mystery/suspense; romantic comedy and drama.
Recent Sales: Prefers not to share information.
Terms: Agent receives 10% commission on domestic sales; 10% on foreign sales. Offers written contract, binding for 1-3 years. "We charge for copying manuscripts or scripts for submission unless a sufficient quantity is supplied by the author. All unsolicited material is automatically discarded unread."

THE CANDACE LAKE AGENCY, 9200 Sunset Blvd., Suite 820, Los Angeles CA 90069. (310)247-2115. Fax: (310)247-2116. E-mail: clagency@earthlink.net. **Contact:** Ryan Lewis. Estab. 1977. Signatory of WGA, member of DGA. 50% of clients are new/previously unpublished writers. Specializes in screenplay and teleplay writers. Currently handles: 20% novels; 40% movie scripts; 40% TV scripts.
Member Agents: Candace Lake (president/agent); Carolyn Finger (agent); Ryan Lewis (assistant).
Represents: Feature film, TV MOW, episodic drama, sitcom. **Considers all script subject areas.** Query with SASE. No unsolicited material. Reports in 1 month on queries; 3 months on scripts.
Also Handles: Novels. **Considers all fiction types.**
How to Contact: Query with SASE. Accepts queries by fax. Considers simultaneous queries. Returns materials only with SASE or else discards. Reports in 1 month on queries; 3 months on mss.
Needs: No unsolicited material. Obtains new clients through referrals.
Recent Sales: Prefers not to share information on specific sales.
Terms: Agent receives 10% commission on domestic sales; 10% on foreign sales. Offers written contract, binding for 2 years. Charges for photocopying. 100% of business is derived from commissions on sales.

LARCHMONT LITERARY AGENCY, 444 N. Larchmont Blvd., Suite 200, Los Angeles CA 90004. (323)856-3070. Fax: (323)856-3071. E-mail: agent@larchmontlit.com. **Contact:** Joel Millner. Estab. 1998. Signatory

of WGA, member of DGA. Specializes in feature writers and feature writer/directors. "We maintain a small, highly selective client list and offer a long-term career management style of agenting that larger agencies can't provide." Currently handles: 5% novels, 90% movie scripts, 5% cable or TV films.
   ● Prior to becomning an agent, Mr. Millner attended NYU Film School and participated in The William Morris agent training program.
Represents: Movie scripts, feature film, novels. **Considers these script subject areas:** action/adventure; biography/ autobiography; cartoon/animation; comedy; contemporary issues; detective/police/crime; family saga; fantasy; historical; horror; mainstream; mystery/suspense; psychic/supernatural; romantic comedy; romantic drama; science fiction; sports; thriller/espionage; western/frontier.
Also Handles: Considers these fiction areas: action/adventure; cartoon/comic; contemporary issues; detective/police crime; family saga; fantasy; historical; horror; humor/satire; juvenile; literary; mainstream; mystery; psychic/supernatural; romance; science fiction; sports; thriller/espionage; westerns/frontier.
How to Contact: Query with SASE. Accepts queries by e-mail. Prefers to be the only reader. Reports in 2 weeks. *No unsolicited scripts.* Discards unwanted queries and mss.
Needs: Actively seeking spec feature scripts or established feature writers. Obtains new clients through recommendations from current clients, producers, studio execs, and university writing programs, national writing contests.
Recent Sales: Prefers not to share information on specific sales.
Terms: Agent receives 10% commission on domestic sales. No written contract.
Writers' Conferences: NYU Film School (Los Angeles, June 1999).
Tips: "Please do not send a script until it is in its best possible draft."

$ **Ø** **LEGACIES**, 501 Woodstork Circle, Bradenton FL 34209-7393. (941)792-9159. Fax: (941)795-0552. **Contact:** Mary Ann Amato, executive director. Estab. 1993. Signatory of WGA, member of Florida Motion Picture & Television Association, Board of Talent Agents, Dept. of Professional Regulations License No. TA 0000404. 50% of clients are new/previously unpublished writers. Specializes in screenplays. Currently handles: 10% fiction books; 80% screeplays; 10% stage plays.
Represents: Feature film, TV MOW. **Considers these script subject areas:** comedy; contemporary issues; family saga; feminist; historical.
How to Contact: Query, then send entire ms. Enclose SASE. Does not accept e-mail or phone queries. Reports in 2 weeks on queries; 6 weeks on mss.
Recent Sales: *Movie optioned/sold*: *Journey from the Jacarandas*, by Patricia A. Friedberg; *Progress of the Sun*, by Patricia A. Friedberg.
Terms: Agent receives 15% commission on domestic sales; 20% on foreign sales (WGA percentages on member sales). Offers written contract.
Fees: Offers criticism service: $100 for scripts, slightly higher for novels. Critique includes "in-depth recommendations for rewrites." Payment of criticism fees does not ensure representation. Charges for "upfront charge to cover cost of phone, fax, postal and delivery expenses."
Tips: "New writers should purchase script writing computer programs, or read and apply screenplay format before submitting."

N **Ø** **PAUL S. LEVINE LITERARY AGENCY**, 1054 Superba Ave., Venice CA 90291-3940. (310)450-6711. Fax: (310)450-0181. E-mail: pslevine@ix.netcom.com. **Contact:** Paul S. Levine. Estab. 1996. Member of the Attorney-State Bar of California. Represents over 100 clients. 75% of clients are new/unpublished writers. Currently handles: 30% nonfiction books; 30% novels; 10% movie scripts; 30% TV scripts.
   ● See the expanded listing for this agency in Literary Agents: Nonfee-charging.

Ø **ROBERT MADSEN AGENCY**, 1331 E. 34th St., Suite #1, Oakland CA 94602-1032. (510)223-2090. Agent: Robert Madsen. Senior Editor: Kim Van Nguyen. Estab. 1992. Represents 5 clients. 100% of clients are new/previously unpublished writers. Currently handles: 25% nonfiction books; 25% fiction books; 25% movie scripts; 25% TV scripts.
   ● See the expanded listing for this agency in Literary Agents: Nonfee-charging.

$ **◯** **MAGNETIC MANAGEMENT**, 415 Roosevelt Ave., Lehigh FL 33972-4402. (941)369-6488. **Contact:** Steven Dameron. Estab. 1996. Represents 5 clients. 100% of clients are new/unpublished writers. Specializes in new authors with passion and drive; fiction and screenplays. Currently handles: 10% juvenile books; 50% movie scripts; 30% novels; 10% TV scripts.
   ● See the expanded listing for this agency in Literary Agents: Fee-charging.

◔ **MAJOR CLIENTS AGENCY**, 345 N. Maple Dr., #395, Beverly Hills CA 90210. (310)205-5000. (310)205-5099. **Contact:** Donna Williams Fontno. Estab. 1985. Signatory of WGA. Represents 200 clients. 0% of clients are new/previously unpublished writers. Specializes in TV writers, creators, directors and film writers/directors. Currently handles: 30% movie scripts; 70% TV scripts.
Represents: Movie scripts, feature films, TV scripts, TV MOW, sitcom. **Considers these script subject areas:** detective/police/crime; erotica; family saga; horror; mainstream; mystery/suspense; sports; thriller/espionage.
How to Contact: Send outline/proposal. Include SASE. Reports in 2 weeks on queries; 1 month on scripts.
Recent Sales: Prefers not to share information on specific sales.

Terms: Agent receives 10% commission on domestic sales; 10% on foreign sales. Offers written contract.

N O O THE STUART M. MILLER CO., 11684 Ventura Blvd., #225, Studio City CA 91604-2699. (818)506-6067. Fax: (818)506-4079. E-mail: smmco@aol.com. **Contact:** Stuart Miller. Estab. 1977. Signatory of WGA, member of DGA. Currently handles: 40% multimedia; 10% novels; 50% movie scripts.
Represents: Movie scripts. **Considers these script subject areas:** action/adventure; biography/autobiography; cartoon/animation; comedy; contemporary issues; detective/police/crime; family saga; historical; mainstream; multimedia; mystery/suspense; romantic comedy; romantic drama; science fiction; sports; teen; thriller/espionage.
Also Handles: Nonfiction books, novels. **Considers these nonfiction areas:** biography/autobiography; computers/electronics; current affairs; government/politics/law; health/medicine; history; how-to; memoirs; military/war; self-help/personal improvement; true crime/investigative. **Considers these fiction areas:** action/adventure; contemporary issues; detective/police/crime; historical; literary; mainstream; mystery; science fiction; sports; thriller/espionage.
How to Contact: Query with SASE, include outline/proposal. Accepts queries by fax and e-mail. Considers simultaneous queries. Reports in 3 days on queries; 6 weeks on mss. Returns material only with SASE.
Recent Sales: Prefers not to share information on specific sales.
Terms: Agent receives 10% commission on domestic sales; 15-20% on foreign sales. Offers written contract, binding for 2 years. Follows WGA standards for contract termination.
Tips: "Always include SASE, e-mail address or fax number with query letters. Make it easy to respond."

☑ O O MOMENTUM MARKETING, 1112 E. Laguna Dr., Tempe AZ 85282-5516. (480)777-0957. E-mail: klepage@concentric.net. **Contact:** Kerry LePage. Estab. 1995. Signatory of WGA. Represents 11 clients. 80% of clients are new/unpublished writers. Represents Arizona-based writers only. Currently represents: 75% movie scripts; 25% TV scripts.
• Prior to opening her agency, Ms. LePage was a marketing consultant, writer and actress.
Represents: Feature film, episodic drama, TV MOW, sitcom. **Considers these script subject areas:** action/adventure; cartoon/animation; comedy; contemporary/issues; detective/police/crime; ethnic; experimental; family saga; fantasy; feminist; gay/lesbian; historical; horror; biography/autobiography; juvenile; mainstream; mystery/suspense; psychic/supernatural; religious/inspirational; romance (comedy, drama); science fiction; sports; teen; thriller/espionage; western/frontier.
How to Contact: Send 1-page outline, 5-7 sample pages and SASE. Accepts queries by e-mail. Considers simultaneous queries and submissions. Reports in 4-6 weeks on queries; 3 months on mss. Returns unwanted queries/mss only with SASE.
Needs: Actively seeking Arizona-based writers; projects that could be produced in Arizona; excellent writing. Obtains new clients through word of mouth, WGA agency list, queries and by phone.
Recent Sales: Prefers not to share information on specific sales.
Terms: Agent receives 10% commission on domestic sales; 10% on foreign sales. Offers written contract, binding for 1 year. 10 day written notice will be given to terminate contract. Charges for postage, long distance—no more than $50/writer will be charged without their prior approval.
Tips: "We keep our client list small in order to provide personal attention to writer's career. Strong network of contacts in Arizona and Los Angeles. Make sure script is properly formatted, no misspellings, appropriate length. Be open to constructive criticism and believe in yourself."

O MONTEIRO ROSE AGENCY, 17514 Ventura Blvd., #205, Encino CA 91316. (818)501-1177. Fax: (818)501-1194. E-mail: monrose@ix.netcom.com. Website: www.monteiro-rose.com. **Contact:** Milissa Brockish. Estab. 1987. Signatory of WGA. Represents over 50 clients. Specializes in scripts for animation, TV and film. Currently handles: 40% movie scripts; 20% TV scripts; 40% animation.
Member Agents: Candace Monteiro (literary); Fredda Rose (literary); Milissa Brockish (literary); Jason Dravis (literary).
Represents: Feature film, animation, TV MOW, episodic drama. **Considers these script subjects:** action/adventure; cartoon/animation; comedy; contemporary issues; detective/police/crime; ethnic; family saga; historical; juvenile; mainstream; mystery/suspense; psychic/supernatural; romantic comedy and drama; science fiction; teen; thriller.
How to Contact: Query with SASE. Accepts queries by fax, "but cannot guarantee reply without SASE." Reports in 1 week on queries; 2 months on mss. Returns materials only with SASE.
Needs: Obtains new clients through recommendations from others in the entertainment business and query letters.
Recent Sales: Prefers not to share information on specific sales.
Terms: Agent receives 10% commission on domestic sales. Offers standard WGA 2 year contract, with 90-day cancellation clause. Charges for photocopying.
Tips: "It does no good to call and try to speak to an agent before they have read your material, unless referred by

ALWAYS INCLUDE a self-addressed, stamped envelope (SASE) for reply or return of your query or manuscript.

someone we know. The best and only way, if you're a new writer, is to send a query letter with a SASE. If agents are interested, they will request to read it. Also enclose a SASE with the script if you want it back."

[N] [$] [☑] MONTGOMERY-WEST LITERARY AGENCY, 7450 Butler Hills Dr., Salt Lake City UT 84121-5008. Fax:(801)943-3044. **Contact:** Carole Western. Estab. 1989. Represents 50 clients. 80% of clients are new/previously unpublished writers. Specializes in movie and TV scripts. Currently handles: 10% novels; 90% movie scripts.
   ● Prior to opening her agency, Ms. Western was a creative writing teacher, holding a Royal Society Arts degree from London University in English Literature, and interned in two talent literary agencies. She's also a published author.
Member Agents: Carole Western (movie and TV scripts); Nancy Gummery (novel, consultant and editor); Mary Barnes (novels, nonfiction).
Represents: Movie scripts, feature film, TV scripts, TV MOW. **Considers these script subject areas:** action/adventure; comedy; detective/police/crime; family saga; feminist; glitz; juvenile; mainstream; mystery/suspense; romantic comedy; romantic drama; science fiction; teen; thriller/espionage.
Also Handles: Novels.
How to Contact: Query with outline, 26 pages, a $25 critique fee and SASE. Reports in 2 months on queries; 10 weeks on mss.
Needs: Actively seeking screenplays and novels. Does not want to receive fantasy or animation.
Recent Sales: Sold 10 projects in the last year. *Movie/TV MOW scripts optioned/sold: Hack*, by Brian Bruns (Incline Productions); *Illumination*, by Judy Daggy (Incline Productions); *Movie/TV MOW scripts in development: The Beautiful Ones*, by Maurice Billington (Atlantic Film); *A Window In Time*, by David Trottier (Hill/Field Enterprises); *Scripting assignments: Backstage Pass*, by Joel Sousa (Shooting Star Pics).
Terms: Agent receives 10% commission on movie scripts; 15% on foreign sales; 15% on networking sales with other agencies. Charges for telephone, fax, postage, photocopies and all other office expenses.
Fees: Charges $25 critique fee for first 26 pages. No additional fee if remainder is requested. 5% of business is derived from reading or criticism fees.
Writers' Conferences: Attends 3 workshops a year; WGA West Conference.
Tips: "Send in only the finest product you can and keep synopses and treatments brief and to the point. Have patience and be aware of the enormous competition in the writing field."

[☑] DEE MURA ENTERPRISES, INC., 269 W. Shore Dr., Massapequa NY 11758-8225. (516)795-1616. Fax: (516)795-8757. E-mail: samurai5@ix.netcom.com. **Contact:** Dee Mura, Ken Nyquist. Estab. 1987. Signatory of WGA. 50% of clients are new/previously published writers. "We work on everything, but are especially interested in literary fiction and commercial fiction, in true life stories, true crime, women's stories and issues and unique nonfiction." Currently handles: 25% nonfiction books; 10% scholarly books; 15% juvenile books; 25% novels; 25% movie scripts.
   ● See the expanded listing for this agency in Literary Agents: Nonfee-charging.

[☑] FIFI OSCARD AGENCY INC., 24 W. 40th St., New York NY 10018. (212)764-1100. **Contact:** Ivy Fischer Stone, Literary Department. Estab. 1956. Member of AAR, signatory of WGA. Represents 108 clients. 5% of clients are new/unpublished writers. "Writer must have published articles or books in major markets or have screen credits if movie scripts, etc." Specializes in literary novels, commercial novels, mysteries and nonfiction, especially celebrity biographies and autobiographies. Currently handles: 40% nonfiction books; 40% novels; 5% movie scripts; 10% stage plays; 5% TV scripts.
   ● See the expanded listing for this agency in Literary Agents: Nonfee-charging.

[☑] DOROTHY PALMER, 235 W. 56 St., New York NY 10019. Phone/fax: (212)765-4280 (press *51 for fax). Estab. 1990. Signatory of WGA. Represents 12 clients. Works with published writers only. Specializes in screenplays, TV. Currently handles: 70% movie scripts, 30% TV scripts.
   ● In addition to being a literary agent, Ms. Palmer has worked as a talent agent for 27 years.
Represents: Feature film, TV MOW, episodic drama, sitcom, miniseries. **Considers these script subject areas:** action/adventure; comedy; contemporary issues; detective/police/crime; family saga; feminist; mainstream; mystery/suspense; romantic comedy; romantic drama; thriller/espionage.
How to Contact: Query with SASE. "Published writers *only*." Prefers to be only reader. Returns materials only with SASE.
Needs: Actively seeking successful, published writers (screenplays only). Does not want to receive work from new or unpublished writers. Obtains new clients through recommendations from others.
Recent Sales: Prefers not to share information on specific sales.
Terms: Agent receives 10% commission on domestic sales; 10% on foreign sales. Offers written contract, binding for 1 year.
Tips: "Do *not* telephone. When I find a script that interests me, I call the writer. Calls to me are a turn-off because they cut into my reading time."

[☑] PANDA TALENT, 3721 Hoen Ave., Santa Rosa CA 95405. (707)576-0711. Fax: (707)544-2765. **Contact:** Audrey Grace. Estab. 1977. Signatory of WGA, SAG, AFTRA, Equity. Represents 10 clients. 80% of clients are new/previously unpublished writers. Currently handles: 5% novels; 40% TV scripts; 50% movie scripts; 5% stage plays.

Story Readers: Steven Grace (science fiction/war/action); Vicki Lima (mysteries/romance); Cleo West (western/true stories).
Represents: Feature film, TV MOW, episodic drama, sitcom. **Considers these script subject areas:** action/adventure; animals; comedy; detective/police/crime; ethnic; family saga; military/war; mystery/suspense; romantic comedy and drama; science fiction; true crime/investigative; westerns/frontier.
How to Contact: Query with treatment. Reports in 3 weeks on queries; 2 months on mss. Must include SASE.
Recent Sales: Prefers not to share information on specific sales.
Terms: Agent receives 10% commission on domestic sales; 10% on foreign sales.

⚫ BARRY PERELMAN AGENCY, 9200 Sunset Blvd., #1201, Los Angeles CA 90069. (310)274-5999. Fax: (310)274-6445. **Contact:** Chris Robert. Estab. 1982. Signatory of WGA, DGA. Represents 40 clients. 15% of clients are new/previously unpublished writers. Specializes in motion pictures/packaging. Currently handles: 99% movie scripts; 1% stage plays.
Member Agents: Barry Perelman (motion picture/packaging/below-the-line); Chris Robert (motion picture).
Represents: Movie scripts. **Considers these script areas:** action/adventure; biography/autobiography; contemporary issues; detective/police/crime; historical; horror; mystery/suspense; romance; science fiction; thriller/espionage.
How to Contact: Send outline/proposal with query. Include SASE. Reports in 1 month.
Needs: Obtains new clients through recommendations and query letters.
Recent Sales: Prefers not to share information on specific sales.
Terms: Agent receives 10% commission on domestic sales; 10% on foreign sales. Offers written contract, binding for 1-2 years. Charges for postage and photocopying.

✅ ⚫ STEPHEN PEVNER, INC., 248 W. 73rd St., 2nd Floor, New York NY 10023. (212)496-0474. Also: 450 N. Rossmore Ave., Los Angeles CA 90004. (323)464-5546. Fax: (323)464-5588. E-mail: spevner@aol.com. **Contact:** Stephen Pevner. Estab. 1991. Member of AAR. Represents under 50 clients. 50% of clients are new/previously unpublished writers. Specializes in motion pictures, novels, humor, pop culture, urban fiction, independent filmmakers. Currently handles: 25% nonfiction books; 25% novels; TV scripts; stage plays.
 • Mr. Pevner represents a number of substantial independent writer/directors. See the expanded listing for this agency in Literary Agents: Nonfee-charging.

⚫ A PICTURE OF YOU, 1176 Elizabeth Dr., Hamilton OH 45013-3507. Phone/fax: (513)863-1108. E-mail: apoy1@aol.com. **Contact:** Lenny Minelli. Estab. 1993. Signatory of WGA. Represents 40 clients. 50% of clients are new/previously unpublished writers. Specializes in screenplays and TV scripts. Currently handles: 80% movie scripts; 10% TV scripts; 10% syndicated material.
 • Prior to opening his agency, Mr. Minelli was an actor/producer for 10 years. Also owned and directed a talent agency and represented actors and actresses from around the world.
Represents: Feature film, animation, miniseries, documentary, TV MOW, sitcom, episodic drama, syndicated material. **Considers all script subject areas.**
Also Handles: Nonfiction books, novels, novellas, short story collections. **Considers these nonfiction areas:** gay/lesbian issues; history; juvenile nonfiction; music/dance/theatre/film; religious/inspirational; self-help/personal. **Considers these fiction areas:** action/adventure; detective/police/crime; erotica; ethnic; family saga; fantasy; gay/lesbian; glitz; historical; horror; literary; mainstream; mystery/suspense; religious; romance (contemporary, gothic, historical); thriller/espionage; westerns/frontier; young adult.
How to Contact: Query with SASE first. Reports in 3 weeks on queries; 1 month on scripts.
Needs: Obtains new clients through recommendations and queries.
Recent Sales: *Movie/TV MOW scripts optioned/sold:* Stranglehold, by L.I. Isgro; *Bodyslams in the Boardroom*, by Gary M. Cappetta; *Scripting assignments:* The Governor, by Gary M. Cappetta.
Terms: Agent receives 10% commission on domestic sales; 15% on foreign sales. Offers written contract, binding for 1 year, with 90 day cancellation clause. Charges for postage/express mail and long distance calls. 100% of business is derived from commissions on sales.
Tips: "Make sure that the script is the best it can be before seeking an agent."

ℕ ⚫ PINKHAM LITERARY AGENCY, 418 Main St., Amesbury MA 01913. (978)388-4210. Fax: (978)388-4221. E-mail: jnoblepink@aol.com. Website: www.pinkhamliterary.com. **Contact:** Joan Noble Pinkham. Estab. 1996. Specializes in novels, how-tos, mysteries, screenplays. Currently handles: 30% movie scripts; 10% nonfiction books; 60% novels.
 • Prior to opening her agency, Ms. Pinkham was a published author, ghost writer, public relations executive and broadcaster. She also wrote for TV in London and Boston. In addition, Ms. Pinkham owns Sea & Coast Films.
Member Agents: Edward P. Mannix (contract law, entertainment); Catherine Joyce (business, marketing).
Represents: Feature film, TV movie of the week, novels, mysteries. **Considers these script subject areas:** action/adventure; comedy; detective/police/crime; historical; mystery/suspense; psychic/supernatural; thriller/espionage.
How to Contact: Query with SASE. Accepts queries by e-mail. Prefers to be only reader. Returns materials only with SASE or discards. Reports immediately on queries; 1 month on mss.
Needs: Actively seeking new writers. Does not want to receive horror, children's or stage plays. Obtains new clients through recommendations, conferences and website.

Recent Sales: Prefers not to share information on specific sales.

Terms: Agent receives 15% commission on domestic sales; 20% on foreign sales. Offers written contract, binding for 1 year. 90 days notice must be given to terminate contract.

Fees: Charges reading fee of $1/page to new writers only. Does not charge a reading fee to WGA members. Offers criticism service. Criticism service: "$400 and up for several detailed pages." Editing fee: $400 and up. Charges $50, reserved in client's name, for expenses. "Any expenses are deducted as they occur or are billed to us, postage, phone calls, copies, etc."

Tips: "We work with our writers in development and consult on marketing. We are all writers; also winners of national awards. We are developing new writers. This area of Massachusetts is host to many talented writers and artists, as well as craftsmen. We are taking our time with these people—knowing the time and patience it takes. We regularly do business in Hollywood and are listed in *Hollywood Agents & Managers Directory*, *Writer's Guide to Hollywood* and *Kempers-London*."

$ PMA LITERARY AND FILM MANAGEMENT, INC., 132 W. 22nd St., 12th Floor, New York NY 10011-1817. (212)929-1222. Fax: (212)206-0238. E-mail: pmalitfilm@aol.com. Website: www.pmalitfilm.com. President: Peter Miller. Estab. 1975. Represents 80 clients. 50% of clients are new/unpublished writers. Specializes in commercial fiction and nonfiction, thrillers, true crime and "fiction with *real* motion picture and television potential." Currently handles: 50% fiction; 25% nonfiction; 25% screenplays.

   • See the expanded listing for this agency in Literary Agents: Fee-charging.

✓ PREFERRED ARTISTS TALENT AGENCY, (formerly HWA Talent Reps), 16633 Ventura Blvd., Suite 1421, Encino CA 91436. (818)990-0305. Fax: (818)990-2736. **Contact:** Kimber Wheeler. Estab. 1985. Signatory of WGA. 90% of clients are new/previously unpublished writers. Currently handles: 90% movie scripts, 10% novels.

Represents: Movie scripts, novels. **Considers these script areas:** action/adventure; biography/autobiography; cartoon/comic; comedy; contemporary issues; detective/police/crime; ethnic; family saga; fantasy; feminist; gay; horror; lesbian; mystery/suspense; psychic/supernatural; romance; science fiction; sports; thriller/espionage.

How to Contact: Query with outline/proposal and SASE.

Recent Sales: Prefers not to share information on specific sales.

Terms: Agent receives 10% commission on domestic sales. Offers written contract, binding for 1 year. WGA rules on termination apply.

Tips: "A good query letter is important. Use any relationship you have in the business to get your material read."

✓ THE QUILLCO AGENCY, 3104 W. Cumberland Court, Westlake Village CA 91362. (805)495-8436. Fax: (805)297-4469. **Contact:** Sandy Mackey (owner). Estab. 1993. Signatory of WGA. Represents 70 clients.

Represents: Feature film, documentary, animation, TV MOW. No Vietnam, Mob, women-bashing, or exploitation films.

How to Contact: Not accepting query letters at this time. Prefers to be only reader. Returns materials only with SASE.

Recent Sales: Prefers not to share information on specific sales.

Terms: Agent receives 10% commission on domestic sales; 10% on foreign sales.

N DAN REDLER ENTERTAINMENT, 18730 Hatteras St., #8, Tarzana CA 91356 (818)776-0938. Fax: (818)705-6870. **Contact:** Dan Redler. Represents 10 clients. Currently handles: 100% movie scripts.

   • Prior to opening his management company, Mr. Redler was a production executive.

Represents: Movie scripts, feature film. **Considers these script subject areas:** action/adventure; biography/autobiography; comedy; contemporary issues; detective/police/crime; ethnic; family saga; fantasy; feminist; historical; horror; juvenile; mainstream; mystery/suspense; psychic/supernatural; romantic comedy; romantic drama; science fiction; sports; teen; thriller/espionage.

How to Contact: Query with SASE. Accepts queries by fax. Prefers to be only reader. Reports in 2 weeks on queries; 1 month on mss. Returns materials only with SASE.

Needs: Actively seeking mainstream and contemporary scripts. Does not want to receive small noncommercial stories.

Recent Sales: Prefers not to share information on specific sales.

Terms: Agent receives 10% commission on domestic sales; 10% on foreign sales and subagent fees. Offers written contract, binding for 2 years. Writer must supply all copies of scripts.

Tips: "We offer personal service, indepth career guidance, and aggressive sales efforts."

REDWOOD EMPIRE AGENCY, P.O. Box 1946, Guerneville CA 95446-1146. (707)869-1146. E-mail: redemp@sonic.net. **Contact:** Jim Sorrells or Rodney Shull. Estab. 1992. Represents 10 clients. 90% of clients are new/previously unpublished writers. Specializes in screenplays, big screen or TV. Currently handles: 100% movie scripts.

VISIT THE WRITER'S DIGEST WEBSITE at www.writersdigest.com for hot new markets, daily market updates, writers' guidelines and much more.

Represents: Feature film, animation (movie), TV MOW. **Considers these script subject areas:** comedy; contemporary issues; erotica; family saga; feminist; gay; mainstream; mystery/suspense; romantic comedy; romantic drama; thriller.
How to Contact: Query with 1 page synopsis with SASE. Reports in 1 week on queries; 1 month on mss.
Needs: Obtains new clients through word of mouth, letter in *Hollywood Scriptwriter*.
Recent Sales: Prefers not to share information on specific sales.
Terms: Agent receives 10% commission on domestic sales; 10% on foreign sales. Offers criticism service: structure, characterization, dialogue, format style. No fee for criticism service.
Tips: "Most interested in ordinary people confronting real-life situations."

◐ **RENAISSANCE LITERARY AGENCY**, (formerly Renaissance—H.N. Swanson), 9220 Sunset Blvd., Suite 302, Los Angeles CA 90069. (310)858-5365. **Contact:** Joel Gotler. Member of SAG, AFTRA, DGA. Represents 250 clients. 10% of clients are new/previously unpublished writers. Specializes in selling movies and TV rights from books. Currently handles: 90% novels; 10% movie and TV scripts..
   • See the expanded listing for this agency in Literary Agents: Nonfee-charging.

✻ 💲 ○ **JANIS RENAUD, LITERARY AGENT**, Dept. 341, 20465 Douglas Crescent, Langley, British Columbia V3A 4B6 Canada. E-mail: jrliterary25@hotmail.com. Website: www.3.bc.sympatico.ca/literary1/literary1.html. **Contact:** Janis Renaud. Estab. 1998. Specializes in "seeking and nurturing new writers, helping them to reach their full potential by offering personalized care and service."
   • See expanded listing for this agency in the Literary Agents: Fee-charging.

✓ ◐ **ROBINSON TALENT AND LITERARY MANAGEMENT**, (formerly Robinson Talent and Literary Agency), 1101 S. Robertson Blvd., Suite 21, Los Angeles CA 90035. (310)278-0801. Fax: (310)278-0807. **Contact:** Margaretrose Robinson. Estab. 1992. Franchised by DGA/SAG. Represents 150 clients. 10% of screenwriting clients are new/previously unpublished writers; all are WGA members. "We represent screenwriters, playwrights, novelists and producers, directors." Currently handles: 15% novels; 40% movie scripts; 40% TV scripts; 5% stage plays.
   • Prior to becoming an agent, Ms. Robinson worked as a designer.
Member Agents: Margaretrose Robinson (adaptation of books and plays for development as features or TV MOW); Kevin Douglas (scripts for film and TV).
Represents: Feature film, documentary, TV MOW, miniseries, episodic drama, variety show, stage play, CD-ROM. **Considers these script subject areas:** action/adventure; cartoon/animation; comedy; contemporary issues; detective/police/crime; erotica; ethnic; experimental; family saga; fantasy; mainstream; mystery/suspense; psychic/supernatural; religious/inspirational; romantic comedy and drama; science fiction; sports; teen; thriller; western/frontier.
How to Contact: Send outline/proposal, synopsis or log line with SASE.
Needs: Obtains new clients only through referral.
Recent Sales: Prefers not to share information on specific sales. Clients include Steve Edelman, Merryln Hammond and Michael Hennessey.
Terms: Agent receives 10% commission on domestic sales; 10% on foreign sales. Offers written contract, binding for 2 years minimum. Charges for photocopying, messenger, Federal Express and postage when required.
Tips: "We are a talent agency specializing in the copyright business. Fifty percent of our clients generate copyright—screenwriters, playwrights and novelists. Fifty percent of our clients service copyright—producers, directors and cinematographers. We represent only produced, published and/or WGA writers who are eligible for staff TV positions as well as novelists and playwrights whose works may be adapted for film on television."

💲 ◐ **JACK SCAGNETTI TALENT & LITERARY AGENCY**, 5118 Vineland Ave., #102, North Hollywood CA 91601. (818)762-3871. **Contact:** Jack Scagnetti. Estab. 1974. Signatory of WGA, member of Academy of Television Arts and Sciences. Represents 50 clients. 50% of clients are new/previously unpublished writers. Specializes in film books with many photographs. Currently handles: 20% nonfiction books; 70% movie scripts; 10% TV scripts.
   • Prior to opening his agency, Mr. Scagnetti wrote nonfiction books and magazine articles on movie stars, sports and health subjects and was a magazine and newspaper editor.
Member Agents: Janet Brown, Karen Gesner (books); Carolyn Carpenter (scripts).
Represents: Feature film, miniseries, episodic drama, animation (movie), TV MOW, sitcom. **Considers these script subject areas:** action/adventure; comedy; detective/police/crime; family saga; historical; horror; mainstream; mystery/suspense; romantic comedy and drama; sports; thriller.
Also Handles: Nonfiction, novels. **Considers these nonfiction areas:** biography/autobiography; cooking/food/nutrition; health; current affairs; how-to; military/war; music/dance/theater/film; self-help/personal; sports; true crime/investigative; women's issues/women's studies. **Considers these fiction areas:** action/adventure; contemporary issues; detective/police/crime; family saga; historical; mainstream; mystery/suspense; picture book; romance (contemporary); sports; thriller/espionage; westerns/frontier.
How to Contact: Query with outline/proposal and SASE. Considers simultaneous queries. Reports in 1 month on queries; 2 months on mss. Returns materials only with SASE.
Needs: Actively seeking books and screenplays. Does not want to receive TV scripts for existing shows. Obtains new clients through "referrals by others and query letters sent to us."
Recent Sales: *Movie/TV MOW scripts optioned/sold: Hidden Casualties* by Sandra Warren (Skylark Films); *Kastner's*

Cutthroats (44 Blue Prod.). **Movie/TV MOW scripts in development:** *Pain,* by Charles Pickett (feature, Concorde-New Horizons).

Terms: Agent receives 15% commission on domestic sales; 15% on foreign sales. Offers written contract, binding for 6 months-1 year. Charges for postage and photocopies.

Fees: Offers criticism service. "Fee depends upon condition of original copy and number of pages."

Tips: "Write a good synopsis, short and to the point and include marketing data for the book."

N ⊙ ◎ SUSAN SCHULMAN, A LITERARY AGENCY, 454 W. 44th St., New York NY 10036-5205. (212)713-1633/4/5. Fax: (212)586-8830. E-mail: schulman@aol.com. President: Susan Schulman. Estab. 1979. Member of AAR, Dramatists Guild, Women's Media Group, signatory of WGA. 10-15% of clients are new/unpublished writers. Prefers to work with published/established authors; works with a small number of new/unpublished authors. Specializes in self-help, New Age, spirituality and books for, by and about women's issues including family, careers, health and spiritual development. "And, most importantly, we love working with writers." Currently handles: 70% nonfiction books; 20% novels; 10% stage plays.

 • See the expanded listing for this agency in Literary Agents: Nonfee-charging.

⊙ SHAPIRO-LICHTMAN-STEIN, (formerly Shapiro-Lichtman), Shapiro-Lichtman Building, 8827 Beverly Blvd., Los Angeles CA 90048. Fax: (310)859-7153. **Contact:** Martin Shapiro. Estab. 1969. Signatory of WGA. 10% of clients are new/previously unpublished writers.

Represents: Feature film, miniseries, variety show, soap opera, episodic drama, animation (movie), theatrical stage play, TV MOW, sitcom, animation (TV). **Considers these script areas:** action/adventure; cartoon/animation; comedy; contemporary issues; detective/police/crime; ethnic; family saga; historical; horror; mainstream; mystery/suspense; romance (comedy, drama); science fiction; teen; thriller; westerns/frontier.

Also Handles: Nonfiction books, novels, novellas. **Considers all nonfiction areas. Considers all fiction areas.**

How to Contact: Query with SASE. Accepts queries by fax. Considers simultaneous queries. Reports in 10 days on queries. Returns materials only with SASE.

Needs: Obtains new clients through recommendations from others.

Recent Sales: Prefers not to share information on specific sales.

Terms: Agent receives 10% commission on domestic sales; 20% on foreign sales. Offers written contract, binding for 2 years.

☑ ⊙ KEN SHERMAN & ASSOCIATES, 9507 Santa Monica Blvd. Beverly Hills CA 90210. (310)273-3840. Fax: (310)271-2875. **Contact:** Greg Minattan. Estab. 1989. Member of DGA, BAFTA, PEN Int'l, signatory of WGA. Represents approx. 50 clients. 10% of clients are new/previously unpublished writers. Specializes in solid writers for film, TV, books and rights to books for film and TV. Currently handles: nonfiction books, juvenile books, novels, movie scripts, TV scripts.

 • Prior to opening his agency, Mr. Sherman was with the William Morris Agency, The Lantz Office and Paul Kohner, Inc.

Represents: Nonfiction, fiction, movie scripts, TV scripts, film and television rights to books. **Considers all script subjects, nonfiction and fiction areas.**

How to Contact: *Contact by referral only please.* Reports in approximately 1 month on mss.

Recent Sales: Sold over 25 projects in the last year. *Priscilla Salyers Story,* by Andrea Baynes (ABC); *Toys of Glass,* by Martin Booth (ABC/Saban Ent.). *Brazil,* by John Updike (film rights to Glaucia Carmagos); *Fifth Sacred Thing,* by Starhawk (Bantam); *Questions From Dad,* by Dwight Twilly (Tuttle); *Snow Falling on Cedars,* by David Guterson (Universal Pictures).

Needs: Obtains new clients through recommendations only.

Terms: Agent receives 15% commission on domestic book sales, 10% for WGA projects. Offers written contract only. Charges for office expenses, postage, photocopying, negotiable expenses.

Writers' Conferences: Maui; Squaw Valley; Santa Barbara; Sante Fe.

⊙ SILVER SCREEN PLACEMENTS, 602 65th St., Downers Grove IL 60516-3020. (630)963-2124. Fax: (630)963-1998. E-mail: levin29@idt.net. **Contact:** William Levin. Estab. 1991. Signatory of WGA. Represents 11 clients. 100% of clients are new/previously unpublished writers. Currently handles: 10% juvenile books, 10% novels, 80% movie scripts.

 • Prior to opening his agency, Mr. Levin did product placement for motion pictures/TV.

Represents: Movie scripts, feature film. **Considers these script subject areas:** action/adventure; comedy; contemporary issues; detective/police/crime; family saga; fantasy; historical; juvenile; mainstream; mystery/suspense; science fiction; thriller/espionage; young adult.

Also Handles: Juvenile books, novels. **Considers these nonfiction areas:** education; juvenile nonfiction; language/literature/criticism. **Consider these fiction areas:** action/adventure; contemporary issues; detective/police/crime; family saga; historical; humor/satire; juvenile; mainstream; mystery/suspense; science fiction; thriller/espionage; young adult.

How to Contact: Brief query with outline/proposal and SASE. Reports in 2 weeks on queries; 6-8 weeks on mss.

Needs: Actively seeking "screenplays for young adults, 17-30." Does not want to receive "horror/religious/X-rated." Obtains new clients through recommendations from other parties, as well as being listed with WGA and *Guide to Literary Agents.*

Recent Sales: Sold 3 projects plus 2 options in the last year. Prefers not to share information on specific sales. Clients include Jean Hurley, Charles Geier, Robert Smola, Sherri Fullmer, Michael Jeffries and Yair Packer.
Terms: Agent receives 10% commission on screenplay/teleplay sales; 15% on foreign and printed media sales. Offers written contract, binding for 2 years. May make referrals to freelance editors. Use of editors does not ensure representation. 0% of business is derived from referrals to editing service.
Tips: "Advise against 'cutsie' inquiry letters."

N ⊘ SISTER MANIA PRODUCTIONS, INC., 916 Penn St., Brackenridge PA 15014. (412)226-2964. Website: www.sistermania.com. **Contact:** Literary Department. Estab. 1978. Signatory of WGA. Represents 12 clients. 20% of clients are new/previously unpublished writers. "We also package, develop and produce." Currently handles: 80% movie scripts, 10% TV scripts, 10% syndicated material.
Represents: Feature film, TV scripts, syndicated material. **Considers these script subject areas:** action/adventure; comedy; detective/police/crime; experimental; family saga; horror; romance; thriller/espionage; true crime/investigative.
Also Handles: Nonfiction books, juvenile books, scholarly books, novels. **Considers these nonfiction areas:** biography/autobiography; business; computers/electronics; history; humor; juvenile nonfiction; military/war; money/finance/economics; music/dance/theater/film; New Age metaphysics; science/technology; self-help/personal improvement; women's issues/women's studies. **Considers these fiction areas:** action/adventure; contemporary issues; detective/police/crime; ethnic; family saga; fantasy; historical; horror; humor/satire; juvenile; literary; mainstream; mystery/suspense; picture book; romance (contemporary); science fiction; thriller/espionage.
How to Contact: Query with SASE. Prefers to be only reader. Reports up to 1 month on queries; 1-2 months on mss. Returns materials only with SASE.
Needs: Usually obtains new clients through "very creative query with project creative and executive appeal in maintaining integrity through quality products."
Recent Sales: *Movie/TV MOW scripts optioned/sold: The Pope,* by Sam Walker and Darleen Pusey; *Happytime Manor,* by Gordon Webb; *Movie/TV MOW scripts in development: Accidentally On Purpose* and *Mind Fodder. Scripting assignments:* biography on Bonnie Consolo.
Terms: Offers written contract. Offers criticism service, no fees for clients.

◑ SOLOWAY GRANT KOPALOFF & ASSOCIATES, 6399 Wilshire Blvd., Los Angeles CA 90048. (213)782-1854. Fax: (213)782-1877. E-mail: sgkassoc@pacbell.net. **Contact:** Don Kopaloff. Estab. 1976. Member of AFF, DGA, signatory of WGA.
Member Agents: Arnold Soloway, Susan Grant, Don Kopaloff, Michelle Wallerstein.
Represents: Movie scripts, TV scripts. **Considers all script subject areas.**
How to Contact: Query with SASE. Reports in 1 month if interested. After query letter is accepted, writer must sign release. *Not accepting unsolicited mss.*
Recent Sales: Prefers not to share information on specific sales.
Terms: Agent receives 10% commission on domestic sales; 10% commission on foreign sales.

⊘ CAMILLE SORICE AGENCY, 13412 Moorpark St., #C, Sherman Oaks CA 91423. (818)995-1775. **Contact:** Camille Sorice. Estab. 1988. Signatory of WGA.
Represents: Feature film. **Considers these script subject areas:** action/adventure; comedy; detective/police/crime; family saga; historical; mystery/suspense; romantic comedy and drama; westerns/frontier.
How to Contact: Send query letter with synopsis. Include SASE. Reports in 6 weeks on mss.
Recent Sales: Prefers not to share information on specific sales.
Tips: "No calls. Query letters accepted."

⊘ STANTON & ASSOCIATES LITERARY AGENCY, 4413 Clemson Dr., Garland TX 75042-5246. (972)276-5427. Fax: (972)276-5426. E-mail: preston8@onramp.net. Website: rampages.onramp.net/~preston8. **Contact:** Henry Stanton, Harry Preston. Estab. 1990. Signatory of WGA. Represents 36 clients. 90% of clients are new screenwriters. Specializes in screenplays. Currently handles: 50% movie scripts; 40% TV scripts; 10% books.
   • Prior to joining the agency, Mr. Preston was with the MGM script department and an author and screenwriter for 40 years.
Represents: Feature film, TV MOW. **Considers these script subject areas:** action/adventure; comedy; romantic comedy; romantic drama; thriller.
How to Contact: Query with SASE. Accepts queries by fax or e-mail. Considers simultaneous queries and submissions. Reports in 1 week on queries; 1 month on screenplays (review). Returns materials only with SASE.

TO RECEIVE REGULAR TIPS AND UPDATES about writing and Writer's Digest publications via e-mail, send an e-mail with "SUBSCRIBE NEWSLETTER" in the body of the message to "newsletter-request@writersdigest.com."

Needs: Does not want to see science fiction, fantasy or horror. Obtains new clients through WGA listing, *Hollywood Scriptwriter*, word of mouth (in Dallas).
Recent Sales: *A Tale Worth Telling* (*The Life of Saint Patrick*), (Angelic Entertainment); *Chipita* (uprize Productions); *Today I Will Nourish My Inner Martyr* (Prima Press); *Barbara Jordan, The Biography* (Golden Touch Press).
Terms: Agent receives 15% commission on domestic sales. Offers written contract, binding for 2 years on individual screenplays. Returns scripts with reader's comments.
Tips: "We have writers available to edit or ghostwrite screenplays and books. Fees vary dependent on the writer. All writers should always please enclose a SASE with any queries."

STONE MANNERS AGENCY, 8436 W. Third St., Suite 740, Los Angeles CA 90048. (323)655-1313. **Contact:** Tim Stone. Estab. 1982. Signatory of WGA. Represents 135 clients.
Represents: Movie scripts, TV scripts. **Considers all script subject areas.**
How to Contact: *Not considering scripts at this time.*
Recent Sales: Prefers not to share information on specific sales.
Terms: Agent receives 10% commission on domestic sales; 10% commission on foreign sales.

SUITE A MANAGEMENT, 1101 S. Robertson Blvd., Suite 210, Los Angeles CA 90035. (310)278-0801. Fax: (310)278-0807. E-mail: suit-a@juno.com. Website: www.suite-a-management.com. **Contact:** Lloyd D. Robinson. Estab. 1996. Represents 50 clients. 15% of clients are new/unpublished writers. Representing writers, producers and directors of Movies of the Week for Network and Cable, Features with Budgets under 10Mil and Pilots/Series. Included among clients are a large percentage of novelists whose work is available for adaptation to screen and television. Currently handles: 40% movie scripts; 20% novels; 10% animation; 15% TV scripts; 10% stage plays; 5% multimedia.
   • Prior to becoming an agent, Mr. Robinson owned Lenhoff/Robinson Talent & Literary Agency, Inc. for over 5 years.
Represents: Feature film, theatrical stage play, TV MOW, animation. **Considers "all areas within the current mainstream for film and television."** Also handles Internet interactive segmented movies.
How to Contact: Fax one page bio (educational/credits), including title, WGA registration number, 2 sentence log line and 1 paragraph synopsis. Accepts queries by fax or e-mail. Consider simultaneous queries. Reports in 10 days on fax queries. Returns unwanted qureies and mss.
Needs: Actively seeking "Writers with produced credits." Obtains new clients through recommendations from existing client base as well as new writers from various conferences.
Recent Sales: Sold 1 book title and 2 script projects in the last year. *Books: Nobody Drowns in Mineral Lake*, by Michael Druxman (Center Press); *Movie TV/MOW scripts optioned sold: Bridge of Dragons*, starring Dolph Lundgreen; *Cold Harvest*, starring Gary Daniels.
Terms: Agent receives 10% commission on domestic sales; 10% on foreign sales. Offers written contract, binding for 1 year. 3 month notice will be given to terminate contract. Charges for overnight mail, printing and duplication charges. All charges require "prior approval" by writer.
Writers' Conferences: Sherwood Oaks College (Hollywood); Infotainment Annual (Black Talent News) (Los Angeles, April); Writers Connection (Los Angeles, August).

SYDRA TECHNIQUES CORP., 481 Eighth Ave. E 24, New York NY 10001. (212)631-0009. Fax: (212)631-0715. E-mail: sbuck@virtualnews.com. **Contact:** Sid Buck. Estab. 1988. Signatory of WGA. Represents 30 clients. 80% of clients are new/unpublished writers. Currently handles: 30% movie scripts; 10% novels; 30% TV scripts; 10% nonfiction books; 10% stage plays; 10% multimedia.
   • Prior to opening his agency, Mr. Buck was an artist's agent.
Represents: Feature film, TV MOW, sitcom, animation. **Considers these script subject areas:** action/adventure; cartoon/animation; comedy; contemporary issues; detective/police/crime; family saga; biography/autobiography; mainstream; mystery/suspense; science fiction; sports.
How to Contact: Send outline/proposal with SASE. Reports in 1 month.
Needs: "We are open." Obtains new clients through recommendations.
Recent Sales: Prefers not to share information on specific sales.
Terms: Agent receives 10% commission on domestic sales; 15% on foreign sales. Offers written contract, binding for 2 years. 120 day notice must be given to terminate contract.

TALENT SOURCE, 107 E. Hall St., P.O. Box 14120, Savannah GA 31416-1120. (912)232-9390. Fax: (912)232-8213. E-mail: mshortt@ix.netcom.com. Website: www.talentsource.com. **Contact:** Michael L. Shortt. Estab. 1991. Signatory of WGA. 35% of clients are new/previously unpublished writers. Currently handles: 75% movie scripts; 25% TV scripts.
   • Prior to becoming an agent, Mr. Shortt was a television program producer.
Represents: Feature film, episodic drama, TV MOW, sitcom. **Considers these script areas:** comedy; contemporary issues; detective/police/crime; erotica; family saga; horror; juvenile; mainstream; mystery/ suspense; romance (comedy, drama); teen. Also handles CD-Roms, direct videos.
How to Contact: Send outline with character breakdown. Include SASE. Reports in 10 weeks on queries.
Needs: Actively seeking "character-driven stories (e.g., *Sling Blade*, *Sex Lies & Videotape*)." Does not want to receive "big budget special effects science fiction." Obtains new clients through word of mouth.

Recent Sales: Prefers not to share information on specific sales.

Terms: Agent receives 10% commission on domestic sales; 15% on foreign sales. Offers written contract.

✔ ◑ **THE TANTLEFF OFFICE**, 375 Greenwich St., Suite 603, New York NY 10013. (212)941-3939. Fax: (212)941-3948. **Contact:** Jack Tantleff, president. Estab. 1986. Signatory of WGA, member of AAR. Specializes in theater, film, TV.

Member Agents: Jack Tantleff (theater); Charmaine Ferenczi (theater); Jill Bock (TV and film); John Santoianni (TV, film, theater); Bill Timms (talent); Amy Mazur (talent).

Represents: Feature film, soap opera, episodic drama, theatrical stage play, sitcom, animation (TV), musicals. **Considers these script subject areas:** comedy; contemporary issues; mainstream; mystery/suspense; romantic comedy; romantic drama.

How to Contact: Query with outline. Include SASE. Accepts queries by fax. Returns material only with SASE.

Recent Sales: Prefers not to share information on specific sales.

Terms: Agent receives 10% commission on domestic sales; 10% on dramatic sales; 10% on foreign sales.

✔ ◑ ◎ **TOAD HALL, INC.**, RR2, Box 16B, Laceyville PA 18623. (717)869-2942. Fax: (717)869-1031. E-mail: toadhallco@aol.com. Website: www.toadhallinc.com. **Contact:** Sharon Jarvis, Anne Pinzow. Estab. 1982. Member of AAR. Represents 35 clients. 10% of clients are new/previously unpublished writers. Specializes in popular nonfiction, some category fiction. Prefers New Age, paranormal, unusual but popular approaches. Currently handles: 50% nonfiction books; 40% novels; 5% movie scripts; 5% ancillary projects.

   • See the expanded listing for this agency in Literary Agents: Nonfee-charging.

⑤ ◑ **JEANNE TOOMEY ASSOCIATES**, 95 Belden St., Falls Village CT 06031-1113. (860)824-0831/5469. Fax: (860)824-5460. President: Jeanne Toomey. Assistant: Peter Terranova. Estab. 1985. Represents 10 clients. 50% of clients are new/previously unpublished writers. Currently handles: 45% nonfiction books; 20% novels; 35% movie scripts.

   • See the expanded listing for this agency in Literary Agents: Fee-charging.

⑤ ◑ **A TOTAL ACTING EXPERIENCE**, Dept. N.W., 20501 Ventura Blvd., Suite 399, Woodland Hills CA 91364-2348. (818)340-9249. **Contact:** Dan A. Bellacicco. Estab. 1984. Signatory of WGA, SAG, AFTRA. Represents 30 clients. 50% of clients are new/previously unpublished writers. Specializes in "quality instead of quantity." Currently handles: 5% nonfiction books; 5% juvenile books; 10% novels; 5% novellas; 5% short story collections; 50% movie scripts; 5% stage plays; 10% TV scripts; 5% how-to books and videos.

   • Prior to becoming an agent, Mr. Bellacicco worked in public relations, consulting, production and as a photo journalist.

Represents: Feature film, documentary, TV MOW, episodic drama, sitcom, variety show, soap opera, animation), stage plays, syndicated material, how-to books, videos. "No heavy drugs." **Considers these script subject areas:** action/adventure; cartoon/animation; comedy; contemporary issues; detective/police/crime; erotica; ethnic; experimental; family saga; fantasy; historical; horror; juvenile; mainstream; mystery/suspense; psychic/supernatural; religious/inspirational; romantic comedy and drama; science fiction; sports; teen; thriller; westerns/frontier.

Also Handles: Nonfiction books, textbooks, juvenile books, novels, novellas, short story collections, poetry books. **Considers these nonfiction areas:** animals; art/architecture/design; biography/autobiography; business; child guidance/parenting; computers/electronics; cooking/food/nutrition; crafts/hobbies; current affairs; education; ethnic/cultural interests; government/politics/law; health/medicine; history; how-to; humor; juvenile nonfiction; language/literature/criticism; military/war; money/finance/economics; music/dance/theater/film; nature/environment; New Age/metaphysics; photography; popular culture; psychology; religious/inspirational; science/technology; self-help/personal improvement; sociology; sports; translations; true crime/investigative; women's issues/women's studies; "any well-written work!" **Considers these fiction areas:** action/adventure; cartoon/comic; confessional; contemporary issues; detective/police/crime; erotica; ethnic; experimental; family saga; fantasy; glitz; historical; horror; humor/satire; juvenile; literary; mainstream; mystery/suspense; picture book; psychic/supernatural; regional; religious/inspirational; romance (contemporary, gothic, historical, regency); science fiction; sports; thriller/espionage; westerns/frontier; young adult.

How to Contact: Query with outline and 3 sample chapters. Include SASE. Prefers to be only reader. Reports in 3 months on mss. "We will respond *only* if interested; material will *not* be returned. Please include your e-mail address and release form with photo I.D." Discards unwanted queries/mss.

Needs: Obtains new clients through mail and conferences.

Recent Sales: Prefers not to share information on specific sales.

Terms: Agent receives 10% on domestic sales; 10% on foreign sales. Offers written contract, binding for 2 years or more.

Fees: Offers criticism service (for our clients only at no charge.) 60% of business is derived from commission on ms sales.

Tips: "We seek new sincere, quality writers for a long-term relationship. We would love to see film, television, and stage material that remains relevant and provocative 20 years from today; dialogue that is fresh and unpredictable; story and characters that are enlightening, humorous, witty, creative, inspiring, and, most of all, entertaining. Please keep in mind quality not quantity. Your characters must be well delineated and fully developed with high contrast. Respond only if you appreciate our old-fashioned agency nurturing, strong guidance, and in return: your honesty, loyalty and a quality commitment."

[N] [O] [Ø] **VEGAS LITERARY AGENCY**, P.O. Box 1172, Hollywood CA 90078. (310)712-3483. **Contact:** Tom Kenway. Estab. 1999. Represents 15 clients. 100% of clients are new/previously unpublished writers. Specializes in high-concept science fiction screenplays. Currently handles: 80% movie scripts; 20% TV scripts.
   • Prior to becoming an agent, Mr. Delaney was a consultant to screenwriters, providing them with critiques and marketing services. This agency is headquartered in Sark, U.K.
Member Agents: Tom Kenway (TV scripts); John Delaney, CEO (movie scripts, books).
Represents: Movie scripts, feature film, episodic drama, soap opera, TV scripts, TV MOW, sitcom, documentary, syndicated material, miniseries, animation. **Considers all script subject areas.**
Also Handles: Nonfiction books, scholarly books, textbooks, short story collections. **Considers all nonfiction areas. Considers all fiction areas.**
How to Contact: Query with SASE or send outline/proposal and 5 sample chapters. Does not accept queries by fax or e-mail. Considers simultaneous queries and submissions. Reports in 2 weeks on queries; 1 month on mss. Returns materials only with SASE.
Needs: Actively seeking screenplay writers with high quality scripts. Does not want to receive low quality scripts. Obtains new clients through referrals from industry people.
Recent Sales: New agency with no recorded sales.
Terms: Agent receives 15% commission on domestic sales; 20% on foreign sales. Offers written contract, binding for 1 year. "Contract is irrevocably binding by our agency. Contract must be renewed by client after each year." Charges for delivery service, photocopies. Offers free criticism service. 0% of business is derived from criticism fees.
Tips: "Send us professional scripts with a short cover letter. We are only interested in clients with very good etiquette; talk to us nicely, and we'll talk to you nicely. If you can't do that, then don't contact us."

[N] [O] **VISIONARY ENTERTAINMENT**, 8265 Sunset Blvd., #102, Los Angeles CA 90046. (323)848-9538. Fax: (323)848-8614. E-mail: shawnhopkins@earthlink.net. **Contact:** Shawn Hopkins. Represents 50 clients. 20% of clients are new/unpublished writers. "We are a talent and literary management company. Our literary division specializes in developing and producing scripts with our clients." Currently handles: 75% movie scripts; 25% TV scripts.
   • Prior to becoming an agent, Ms. Hopkins was a studio executive. Visionary Entertainment formerly focused representing talent and has recently started representing writers as well.
Member Agents: Tom Parziale (actors and writers); Ed Goldstone (actors and nonfiction writers); Brian Alexander (actors, novelists and playwrights).
Represents: Movie scripts, feature film, episodic drama, novels, TV scripts, sitcom. **Considers all script subject areas.** Also interested in video games and original online programing.
Also Handles: Considers all fiction areas.
How to Contact: Send outline/proposal. Include SASE. Accepts queries by fax and e-mail. Considers simultaneous queries. Reports in 1 month on queries. Discards unwanted queries and mss.
Needs: Actively seeking fresh ideas and good writers. Does not want to receive clichéd ideas. Obtains new clients through recommendations from others.
Recent Sales: Sold 4 projects in the last year. *Movie/TV MOW script(s) optioned/sold: The Fighting Temptations*, by Elizabeth Hunter (MTV Films Paramount); *Ship of Ghouls*, by Jeff Walch (Bandeira/Dreamworks); *Never Been Kissed*, by Scott Murphy (Kushner-Locke); *How to Lose a Man in Ten Days*, by Michelle Alexander (Paramount).
Terms: Agent receives 15% commission on domestic sales. Offers written contract, binding for 2 years. 60 day notice must be given to terminate contract.
Tips: "Write well, and don't use cliché themes or characters."

[O] **WARDLOW AND ASSOCIATES**, 1501 Main St., Suite 204, Venice CA 90291. (310)452-1292. Fax: (310)452-9002. E-mail: wardlowas@aol.com. **Contact:** David Wardlow. Estab. 1980. Signatory of WGA. Represents 30 clients. 5% of clients are new/previously unpublished writers. Currently handles: 50% movie scripts; 50% TV scripts.
Member Agents: David Wardlow (literary, packaging); Jeff Ordway (literary).
Represents: Feature film, TV MOW, miniseries, episodic drama, sitcom. **Considers all script subject areas**, particularly: action/adventure; contemporary issues; detective/police/crime; family saga; fantasy; gay; horror; humor; mainstream; mystery/suspense; romance; science fiction; thriller; western/frontier.
How to Contact: Query with SASE. Accepts queries by fax or e-mail. Considers simultaneous queries. Replies only to queries which they are interested in unless accompanied by SASE. Will not read unsolicited screenplays/manuscripts. Returns unwanted materials only with SASE.
Needs: Obtains new clients through recommendations from others and solicitation. Does not want to receive "new sitcom/drama series ideas from beginning writers."

FOR INFORMATION ON THE CONFERENCES agents attend, refer to the conference section in this book.

Recent Sales: Prefers not to share information on specific sales.
Terms: Agent receives 10% commission on domestic sales; 10% on foreign sales. Offers written contract, binding for 1 year.

N ◐ DONNA WAUHOB AGENCY, 3135 Industrial Rd., #204, Las Vegas NV 89109-1122. (702)733-1017. Fax: (702)733-1215. E-mail: dwauhob@wizard.com. **Contact:** Donna Wauhob. Represents 7 clients. Currently handles: 10 juvenile books; 50% movie scripts; 40% TV scripts.
   • Prior to opening her agency, Ms. Wauhob was a model, secretary, and an AF of M agent since 1968.
Represents: Movie scripts, feature film, episodic drama, soap opera, TV scripts, TV MOW, sitcom, theatrical stage play, variety show, poetry books, short story collections, miniseries, animation. **Considers these script subject areas:** action/adventure; cartoon/animation; comedy; detective/police/crime; family saga; juvenile; romantic comedy; romantic drama; teen; thriller/espionage; western/frontier.
Also Handles: Nonfiction books, juvenile books, novels. **Considers these nonfiction areas:** animals; child guidance/parenting; cooking/food/nutrition.
How to Contact: Send entire ms. Include SASE. Accepts queries by fax and e-mail. Considers simultaneous queries and submissions. Reports in 1 month.
Needs: Actively seeking film and TV scripts, juvenile, teen action, cartoon, comedy, family.
Recent Sales: This is a new agency with no recorded sales.
Terms: Agent receives 10% commission on domestic and foreign sales. Offers written contract. 6 months notice must be given to terminate contract.

◐ PEREGRINE WHITTLESEY AGENCY, 345 E. 80 St., New York NY 10021. (212)737-0153. Fax: (212)734-5176. **Contact:** Peregrine Whittlesey. Estab. 1986. Signatory of WGA. Represents 30 clients. 50% of clients are new/previously unpublished writers. Specializes in playwrights who also write for screen and TV. Currently handles: 20% movie scripts, 80% stage plays.
Represents: Feature film, stage plays.
How to Contact: Query with SASE. Reports in 1 week on queries; 1 month on mss.
Needs: Obtains new clients through recommendations from others.
Recent Sales: *The Stick Wife* and *0 Pioneers!*, by Darrah Cloud (Dramatic Publishing); *Alabama Rain*, by Heather McCutchen (Dramatic Publishing).
Terms: Agent receives 10% commission on domestic sales; 15% on foreign sales. Offers written contract, binding for 2 years.

N $ ◐ WINDFALL MANAGEMENT, 4084 Mandeville Canyon Rd., Los Angeles CA 90049-1032. (310)471-6317. Fax: (310)471-4577. E-mail: windfall@deltanet.com. **Contact:** Jeanne Field. Represents 20 clients. Windfall is a management company representing writers and books to the film and television industry. "We are especially interested in mainstream and independent film writers or playwrights." Currently handles: 20% novels; 50% movie scripts; 25% TV scripts; 5% stage plays.
   • Prior to becoming an agent, Ms. Field was a producer in the film and television business.
Represents: Movie scripts, TV scripts, TV MOW, theatrical stage play, documentary, miniseries. **Considers these script subject areas:** action/adventure; biography/autobiography; comedy; contemporary issues; detective/police/crime; experimental; family saga; fantasy; feminist; gay/lesbian; historical; juvenile; mainstream; multimedia; mystery/suspense; romantic comedy; romantic drama; science fiction; sports; teen; thriller/espionage; western/frontier.
Also Handles: Nonfiction books, juvenile books, novels, novellas. **Considers these nonfiction areas:** animals, biography/autobiography; history; juvenile nonfiction; memoirs. **Considers these fiction areas:** action/adventure; confessional; contemporary issues; detective/police/crime; family saga; fantasy; feminist; gay/lesbian; historical; humor/satire; juvenile; literary; mainstream; mystery; romance; science fiction; sports; thriller/espionage; westerns/frontier; young adult.
How to Contact: Query with SASE. Accepts queries by e-mail. Considers simultaneous queries. Reports in 2 weeks on queries. Discards unwanted queries and mss.
Needs: Actively seeking "well-written material that can be attractive to the entertainment industry." Obtains new clients through recommendations and referrals.
Recent Sales: Sold 5 book titles and 10 script projects in the last year. *The Animal Factory*, by Edward Bunker (No Exit Press); *Cold Caller*, by Jason Starr (Norton); *Nothing Personal*, by Jason Starr (No Exit Press); *Little Boy Blue*, by Edward Bunker (St. Martin's Press). *Movie/TV MOW scripts optioned:* The Devil In Me, by Beaty Reynolds (Daly-Harris Productions); *Just Another Dead Man*, by John Binder (Pressman Co.). Other clients include Joshua Binder, Randall Sullivan, Leon Martell, Stephanie Waxman, Nell Cox, Dani Minnick, Benjie Aeronson, Jon Klein, Charles Oyamo Gordon.
Terms: Agent receives 10% commission on domestic sales. Offers written contract, binding for 1 year. 60 day notice must be given to terminate contract.
Fees: Charges a maximum of $150/year on copying, postage, for new clients who are unproved only.
Tips: "Live in either New York of Los Angeles. A writer must be available for meetings."

✓ ◐ THE WRIGHT CONCEPT, 1612 W. Olive Ave., Suite 205, Burbank CA 91506. (818)954-8943. Fax: (818)954-9370. E-mail: mrwright@www.wrightconcept.com. Website: www.wrightconcept.com. **Contact:** Marcie

Get the 2001 EDITION

at this year's price!

Completely Updated Each Year

The most current source of literary & script agents avail.

Guide to Literary Agents

500+ AGENTS WHO SELL WHAT YOU WRITE

550 agencies
80 new listings
500+ phone numbers
220 e-mail addresses & websites
105 subject categories
120+ conferences

FROM THE PUBLISHERS OF WRITER'S MARKET

You already know an agent can be the key to selling your work. But, how do you know when you're ready to sign on with one? And, how do you select an agent that's right for you? To make such crucial decisions you need the most up-to-date information on the agents out there and what they can offer you. That's exactly what you'll find in *Guide to Literary Agents*.

Through this special offer, you can get a jump on next year today! If you order now, you'll get the *2001 Guide to Literary Agents* at the 2000 price—just $21.99—no matter how much the regular price may increase!

2001 Guide to Literary Agents will be published and ready for shipment in January 2001.

More books to help you write & sell your work

☐ **Yes!** I want the most current edition of *Guide to Literary Agents*. Please send me the 2001 edition at the 2000 price—$21.99. (NOTE: *2001 Guide to Literary Agents* will be ready for shipment in January 2001.) #10684

Additional books from the back of this card:

Book	Price
#	$
#	$
#	$
#	$
Subtotal	$

*Add $3.50 postage and handling for one book; $1.50 for each additional book.

Postage & Handling	$

Payment must accompany order. Ohioans add 6% sales tax. Canadians add 7% GST.

Total	$

VISA/MasterCard orders call TOLL FREE 1-800-289-0963 or FAX 1-888-590-4082

☐ Payment enclosed $_____ (or)

Charge my: ☐ Visa ☐ MasterCard Exp._____

Account #_____

Signature_____

Name_____

Address_____

City_____

State/Prov._____ Zip/PC _____

30-Day Money Back Guarantee on every book you buy!

6582

Mail to: Writer's Digest Books • 1507 Dana Avenue • Cincinnati, OH 45207

Write Better & Sell More
with help from these Writer's Digest Books!

The Insider's Guide to Getting an Agent
Lori Perkins
Getting an agent is sometimes crucial to getting published. But, how do you locate the one that's right for you? This New York literary agent offers advice, sample queries and proposals that provide the guidance you need to find an agent that suits your needs.
#10630/$16.99/240p/pb

Formatting & Submitting Your Manuscript
Writer's Market Library
Learn how to prepare and present your novels, personal essays, articles and proposals, screenplays and scripts, short stories, poetry, children's books, greeting cards, and more. Successful agents and editors share their formatting do's and don'ts using dozens of visual samples.
#10618/$18.99/208p/pb

Your Novel Proposal: From Creation to Contract
Blythe Camenson & Marshall J. Cook
The only guide of its kind covering everything from the query letter to the book deal! Drawing on the experience of authors, editors and agents, this book provides the essential details needed to get published in today's rapidly changing fiction industry.
#10628/$18.99/256p/hc

I'd Rather Be Writing
Marcia Golub
Part information, part inspiration, this guide gives you the help you need to find more time to pursue the writing hobby or career you love. Learn how to balance parenthood and the need for uninterrupted writing time, find techniques for seeing ideas through to finished stories, and find tips for keeping journals, notes and more.
#10629/$18.99/256p/pb

Facts in a Flash: A Research Guide for Writers
Ellen Metter
Take the frustration out of your research projects with this mix of humor, data and savvy research techniques—from cruising the stacks to surfing the net.
#10632/$24.99/432p/hc

The Writer's Guide to Character Traits
Dr. Linda Edelstein
Create original, complex characters using a variety of personality traits found in this handy guide. Dozens of personality types are profiled including business tycoons, psychopaths, addicts, serial killers, over-achievers, philanthropists and more.
#10631/$18.99/288p/hc

Books are available at your local bookstore, or directly from the publisher using the order card on the reverse.

Wright. Estab. 1985. Signatory of WGA, DGA. Specializes in TV comedy writers and feature comedy writers. Currently handles: 50% movie scripts; 50% TV scripts.

Member Agents: Marcie Wright (TV/movie).

Represents: Feature film, TV MOW, episodic drama, sitcom, variety show, animation, syndicated material. **Considers these script subject areas:** action/adventure, teen; thriller. Also handles CD-Rom games.

How to Contact: Query with SASE. Reports in 2 weeks.

Needs: Obtains new clients through recommendations and queries.

Recent Sales: *Movie/TV MOW script(s) optioned/sold: Mickey Blue Eyes* (Castlerock); *The Pentagon Wars* (HBO); *Shot Through the Heart* (HBO).

Terms: Agent receives 10% commission on sales. Offers written contract, binding for 1 year, with 90 day cancellation clause. 100% of business is derived from commissions on sales.

Writers' Conferences: Speaks at UCLA 3-4 times a year; Southwest Writers Workshop (Albuquerque, August); *Fade-In Magazine* Oscar Conference (Los Angeles, May); *Fade-In Magazine* Top 100 People in Hollywood (Los Angeles, August); University of Georgia's Harriett Austin Writers Conference; Houston Film Festival.

◖ ANN WRIGHT REPRESENTATIVES, 165 W. 46th St., Suite 1105, New York NY 10036-2501. (212)764-6770. Fax: (212)764-5125. **Contact:** Dan Wright. Estab. 1961. Signatory of WGA. Represents 23 clients. 30% of clients are new/unpublished writers. Prefers to work with published/established authors; works with a small number of new/unpublished authors. "Eager to work with any author with material that we can effectively market in the motion picture business worldwide." Specializes in "books or screenplays with strong motion picture potential." Currently handles: 50% novels; 40% movie scripts; 10% TV scripts.

- Prior to becoming an agent, Mr. Wright was a writer, producer and production manager for film and television (alumni of CBS Television).

Represents: Feature film, TV MOW, episodic drama, sitcom. **Considers these script subject areas:** action/adventure; comedy; detective/police/crime; gay; historical; horror; lesbian; mainstream; mystery/suspense; psychic/supernatural; romantic comedy and drama; sports; thriller; westerns/frontier.

Also Handles: Novels. **Considers these fiction areas:** action/adventure; detective/police/crime; feminist; gay/lesbian; humor/satire; literary; mainstream; mystery/suspense; romance (contemporary, historical, regency); sports; thriller/espionage; westerns/frontier.

How to Contact: Query with outline and SASE. Does not read unsolicited mss. Reports in 3 weeks on queries; 4 months on mss. "All work must be sent with a SASE to ensure its return."

Needs: Actively seeking "strong competitive novelists and screen writers." Does not want to receive "fantasy or science fiction projects at this time." Obtains new clients through recommendations from others.

Recent Sales: Sold 7 projects in the last year. Prefers not to share information on specific sales.

Terms: Agent receives 10% commission on domestic sales; 10% on dramatic sales; 15-20% on foreign sales; 20% on packaging. Offers written contract, binding for 2 years. Critiques only works of signed clients. Charges for photocopying expenses.

Tips: "Send a letter with SASE. Something about the work, something about the writer."

☑ ◖ WRITERS & ARTISTS AGENCY, (formerly Writers & Artists), 19 W. 44th St., Suite 1000, New York NY 10036. (212)391-1112. Fax: (212)575-6397. **Contact:** William Craver, Nicole Graham, Jeff Berger. Estab. 1970. Member of AAR, signatory of WGA. Represents 100 clients. West Coast location: 8383 Wilshire Blvd., Suite 550, Los Angeles CA 90211. (323)866-0900. Fax: (323)659-1985.

Represents: Movie scripts, feature film, TV scripts, TV MOW, miniseries, episodic drama, stage plays. **Considers all script subject areas.**

How to Contact: Query with brief description of project, bio and SASE. Reports in 1 month on queries only when accompanied by SASE. No unsolicited mss accepted.

Recent Sales: Prefers not to share specific information on specific sales.

Additional Script Agents

The following agencies have indicated they are *primarily* interested in handling book manuscripts, but also handle less than 10-15 percent scripts. After reading the listing (you can find the page number in the Listings Index), send a query to obtain more information on their needs and manuscript submissions policies.

Appleseeds Management
Baranski Literary Agency, Joseph A.
Browne Ltd., Pema
Cambridge Literary Associates
Fenton Entertainment Group, Inc.
Flannery Literary
Fogelman Literary Agency, The
Fort Ross Inc. Russian-American
   Publishing Projects
Gusay Literary Agency, The
   Charlotte

Independent Publishing Agency: A
   Literary and Entertainment
   Agency
Jenks Agency, Carolyn
Lawyer's Literary Agency, Inc.
Lazear Agency Incorporated
Literary and Creative Artists, Inc.
McKinley, Literary Agency,
   Virginia C.
Morrison, Inc., Henry
Multimedia Product Development

Mumford Literary Agency, Inc., The
National Writers Literary Agency
Puddingstone Literary Agency
Raintree Literary Agency, Diane
Stern Agency, Gloria
Strong Literary Agency, Marianne
Vines Agency, Inc., The
Wolcott Literary Agency
Zachary Shuster Agency

Agents Specialties Index: Script

This subject index is divided into script subject categories. To find an agent interested in the type of screenplay you've written, see the appropriate sections under subject headings that best describe your work. Check the Listings Index for the page number of the agent's listing or refer to the section of Script Agents preceding this index. Agents who are open to most script subject areas appear under the "Open to all Categories" heading.

Action/Adventure: AEI/Atchity Editorial/Entertainment International; Agapé Productions; Agency, The; Amato Agency, Michael; Baskow Agency; Brown Ltd., Curtis; Bulger and Associates, Kelvin C.; Cameron Agency, The Marshall; Cedar Grove Agency Entertainment; Client First—A/K/A Leo P. Haffey Agency; Communications Management Associates; CS International Literary Agency; Douroux & Co.; Epstein-Wyckoff and Associates; ES Talent Agency; Esq. Management; Feigen/Parrent Literary Management; Filmwriters Literary Agency; First Look Talent and Literary Agency; FitzGerald Literary Management; Fleury Agency, B.R.; Fran Literary Agency; Freed Co., The Barry; Greene, Arthur B.; Hodges Agency, Carolyn; Hudson Agency; Infinity Management International; International Leonards Corp.; JLA Literary Agency; Johnson Warren Literary Agency; Kay Agency, Charlene; Kjar Agency, Tyler; Kohner, Inc., Paul; Larchmont Literary Agency; Levine Literary Agency, Paul S.; Magnetic Management; Miller Co., The Stuart M.; Momentum Marketing; Monteiro Rose Agency; Montgomery-West Literary Agency; Mura Enterprises, Inc., Dee; Palmer, Dorothy; Panda Talent; Perelman Agency, Barry; Pinkham Literary Agency; Preferred Artists Talent Agency; Redler Entertainment, Dan; Renaissance Literary Agency; Robinson Talent and Literary Management; Scagnetti Talent & Literary Agency, Jack; Shapiro-Lichtman-Stein; Silver Screen Placements; Sister Mania Productions, Inc.; Sorice Agency, Camille; Stanton & Associates Literary Agency; Sydra Technique Corp.; Toad Hall, Inc.; Total Acting Experience, A; Wardlow and Associates; Wauhob Agency, Donna; Windfall Management; Wright Concept, The; Wright Representatives, Ann

Animation: Above the Line Agency; Agapé Productions; Agency, The; Allred and Allred, Literary Agents; Amato Agency, Michael; Brown Agency, Bruce; Buscher Consultants; Chadwick & Gros Literary Agency; Client First—A/K/A Leo P. Haffey Agency; Communications Management Associates; CS International Literary Agency; Douroux & Co.; Epstein-Wyckoff and Associates; Esq. Management; Fran Literary Agency; Howard Agency, The Eddy; Hudson Agency; International Leonards Corp.; Kay Agency, Charlene; Kohner, Inc., Paul; Levine Literary Agency, Paul S.; Monteiro Rose Agency; Mura Enterprises, Inc., Dee; Panda Talent; Pevner, Inc., Stephen; Picture of You, A; Quillco Agency, The; Redwood Empire Agency; Robinson Talent and Literary Management; Scagnetti Talent & Literary Agency, Jack; Shapiro-Lichtman-Stein; Suite A Management; Sydra Technique Corp.; Tantleff Office, The; Total Acting Experience, A; Vegas Literary Agency; Wauhob Agency, Donna; Wright Concept, The

Biography/Autobiography: Agapé Productions; Baskow Agency; Cedar Grove Agency Entertainment; Communications Management Associates; Esq. Management; FitzGerald Literary Management; Kay Agency, Charlene; Larchmont Literary Agency; Levine Literary Agency, Paul S.; Miller Co., The Stuart M.; Momentum Marketing; Perelman Agency, Barry; Preferred Artists Talent Agency; Redler Entertainment, Dan; Sydra Technique Corp.; Windfall Management

Cartoon/Animation: Agapé Productions; Agency, The; Bulger and Associates, Kelvin C.; Client First—A/K/A Leo P. Haffey Agency; Communications Management Associates; CS International Literary Agency; Esq. Management; First Look Talent and Literary Agency; Fran Literary Agency; Howard Agency, The Eddy; Hudson Agency; International Leonards Corp.; Larchmont Literary Agency; Levine Literary Agency, Paul S.; Miller Co., The Stuart M.; Momentum Marketing; Monteiro Rose Agency; Mura Enterprises, Inc., Dee; Preferred Artists Talent Agency; Renaissance Literary Agency; Robinson Talent and Literary Management; Shapiro-Lichtman-Stein; Sydra Technique Corp.; Total Acting Experience, A; Wauhob Agency, Donna

Comedy: AEI/Atchity Editorial/Entertainment International; Agapé Productions; Agency, The; Amsterdam Agency, Marcia; Baskow Agency; Bennett Agency, The; Brown Ltd., Curtis; Bulger and Associates, Kelvin C.; Cameron Agency, The Marshall; Cedar Grove Agency Entertainment; Client First—A/K/A Leo

P. Haffey Agency; Communications Management Associates; CS International Literary Agency; Douroux & Co.; Epstein-Wyckoff and Associates; ES Talent Agency; Esq. Management; Feigen/Parrent Literary Management; Filmwriters Literary Agency; First Look Talent and Literary Agency; FitzGerald Literary Management; Fleury Agency, B.R.; Fran Literary Agency; Freed Co., The Barry; French, Inc., Samuel; Hodges Agency, Carolyn; Howard Agency, The Eddy; Hudson Agency; Infinity Management International; International Leonards Corp.; Kohner, Inc., Paul; Larchmont Literary Agency; Legacies; Levine Literary Agency, Paul S.; Magnetic Management; Miller Co., The Stuart M.; Momentum Marketing; Monteiro Rose Agency; Montgomery-West Literary Agency; Mura Enterprises, Inc., Dee; Palmer, Dorothy; Panda Talent; Pevner, Inc., Stephen; Pinkham Literary Agency; Preferred Artists Talent Agency; Redler Entertainment, Dan; Redwood Empire Agency; Renaissance Literary Agency; Robinson Talent and Literary Management; Scagnetti Talent & Literary Agency, Jack; Schulman, A Literary Agency, Susan; Shapiro-Lichtman-Stein; Silver Screen Placements; Sister Mania Productions, Inc.; Sorice Agency, Camille; Stanton & Associates Literary Agency; Sydra Technique Corp.; Talent Source; Tantleff Office, The; Toad Hall, Inc.; Total Acting Experience, A; Wauhob Agency, Donna; Windfall Management; Wright Representatives, Ann

Contemporary Issues: AEI/Atchity Editorial/Entertainment International; Agency, The; Baskow Agency; Client First—A/K/A Leo P. Haffey Agency; Communications Management Associates; CS International Literary Agency; Epstein-Wyckoff and Associates; ES Talent Agency; Esq. Management; Feigen/Parrent Literary Management; Filmwriters Literary Agency; First Look Talent and Literary Agency; FitzGerald Literary Management; Fran Literary Agency; Freed Co., The Barry; French, Inc., Samuel; Hodges Agency, Carolyn; Hudson Agency; International Leonards Corp.; JLA Literary Agency; Johnson Warren Literary Agency; Larchmont Literary Agency; Legacies; Levine Literary Agency, Paul S.; Miller Co., The Stuart M.; Momentum Marketing; Monteiro Rose Agency; Mura Enterprises, Inc., Dee; Palmer, Dorothy; Perelman Agency, Barry; Preferred Artists Talent Agency; Redler Entertainment, Dan; Redwood Empire Agency; Renaissance Literary Agency; Robinson Talent and Literary Management; Scagnetti Talent & Literary Agency, Jack; Schulman, A Literary Agency, Susan; Shapiro-Lichtman-Stein; Silver Screen Placements; Sydra Technique Corp.; Talent Source; Tantleff Office, The; Toad Hall, Inc.; Total Acting Experience, A; Wardlow and Associates; Windfall Management

Detective/Police/Crime: AEI/Atchity Editorial/Entertainment International; Agency, The; Brown Ltd., Curtis; Cameron Agency, The Marshall; Cedar Grove Agency Entertainment; Client First—A/K/A Leo P. Haffey Agency; Communications Management Associates; CS International Literary Agency; Douroux & Co.; Epstein-Wyckoff and Associates; ES Talent Agency; Esq. Management; Filmwriters Literary Agency; FitzGerald Literary Management; Fleury Agency, B.R.; Fran Literary Agency; Freed Co., The Barry; French, Inc., Samuel; Greene, Arthur B.; Hudson Agency; Infinity Management International; International Leonards Corp.; JLA Literary Agency; Johnson Warren Literary Agency; Kohner, Inc., Paul; Larchmont Literary Agency; Levine Literary Agency, Paul S.; Major Clients Agency; Miller Co., The Stuart M.; Momentum Marketing; Monteiro Rose Agency; Montgomery-West Literary Agency; Mura Enterprises, Inc., Dee; Palmer, Dorothy; Panda Talent; Perelman Agency, Barry; Pevner, Inc., Stephen; Pinkham Literary Agency; Preferred Artists Talent Agency; Redler Entertainment, Dan; Renaissance Literary Agency; Robinson Talent and Literary Management; Scagnetti Talent & Literary Agency, Jack; Schulman, A Literary Agency, Susan; Shapiro-Lichtman-Stein; Silver Screen Placements; Sister Mania Productions, Inc.; Sorice Agency, Camille; Sydra Technique Corp.; Talent Source; Toad Hall, Inc.; Total Acting Experience, A; Wardlow and Associates; Wauhob Agency, Donna; Windfall Management; Wright Representatives, Ann

Erotica: AEI/Atchity Editorial/Entertainment International; Communications Management Associates; Epstein-Wyckoff and Associates; ES Talent Agency; Esq. Management; FitzGerald Literary Management; Hodges Agency, Carolyn; Howard Agency, The Eddy; Infinity Management International; Levine Literary Agency, Paul S.; Major Clients Agency; Redwood Empire Agency; Renaissance Literary Agency; Robinson Talent and Literary Management; Talent Source; Total Acting Experience, A

Ethnic: Agency, The; Brown Ltd., Curtis; Bulger and Associates, Kelvin C.; Camejo & Assoc., Suzanna; CS International Literary Agency; ES Talent Agency; Esq. Management; FitzGerald Literary Management; Fran Literary Agency; Freed Co., The Barry; French, Inc., Samuel; JLA Literary Agency; Levine Literary Agency, Paul S.; Momentum Marketing; Monteiro Rose Agency; Panda Talent; Preferred Artists Talent Agency; Redler Entertainment, Dan; Renaissance Literary Agency; Robinson Talent and Literary Management; Shapiro-Lichtman-Stein; Toad Hall, Inc.; Total Acting Experience, A

Experimental: ES Talent Agency; French, Inc., Samuel; Hodges Agency, Carolyn; Levine Literary Agency, Paul S.; Momentum Marketing; Renaissance Literary Agency; Robinson Talent and Literary Management; Sister Mania Productions, Inc.; Total Acting Experience, A; Windfall Management

Family Saga: Agapé Productions; Agency, The; Baskow Agency; Bennett Agency, The; Bulger and Associates, Kelvin C.; Camejo & Assoc., Suzanna; Cedar Grove Agency Entertainment; Client First—A/

K/A Leo P. Haffey Agency; CS International Literary Agency; Douroux & Co.; Epstein-Wyckoff and Associates; ES Talent Agency; Feigen/Parent Literary Management; First Look Talent and Literary Agency; FitzGerald Literary Management; Fleury Agency, B.R.; Fran Literary Agency; Freed Co., The Barry; Howard Agency, The Eddy; Hudson Agency; Kay Agency, Charlene; Kjar Agency, Tyler; Kohner, Inc., Paul; Larchmont Literary Agency; Legacies; Levine Literary Agency, Paul S.; Major Clients Agency; Miller Co., The Stuart M.; Momentum Marketing; Monteiro Rose Agency; Montgomery-West Literary Agency; Mura Enterprises, Inc., Dee; Palmer, Dorothy; Panda Talent; Preferred Artists Talent Agency; Redler Entertainment, Dan; Redwood Empire Agency; Renaissance Literary Agency; Robinson Talent and Literary Management; Scagnetti Talent & Literary Agency, Jack; Shapiro-Lichtman-Stein; Silver Screen Placements; Sister Mania Productions, Inc.; Sorice Agency, Camille; Sydra Technique Corp.; Talent Source; Toad Hall, Inc.; Total Acting Experience, A; Wardlow and Associates; Wauhob Agency, Donna; Windfall Management

Fantasy: Agency, The; Communications Management Associates; CS International Literary Agency; Douroux & Co.; Esq. Management; First Look Talent and Literary Agency; FitzGerald Literary Management; Fran Literary Agency; French, Inc., Samuel; Hudson Agency; Infinity Management International; Kay Agency, Charlene; Larchmont Literary Agency; Levine Literary Agency, Paul S.; Momentum Marketing; Mura Enterprises, Inc., Dee; Palmer, Dorothy; Preferred Artists Talent Agency; Redler Entertainment, Dan; Renaissance Literary Agency; Robinson Talent and Literary Management; Silver Screen Placements; Toad Hall, Inc.; Total Acting Experience, A; Wardlow and Associates; Windfall Management

Feminist: Brown Ltd., Curtis; Camejo & Assoc., Suzanna; CS International Literary Agency; Epstein-Wyckoff and Associates; Esq. Management; Feigen/Parent Literary Management; Legacies; Levine Literary Agency, Paul S.; Momentum Marketing; Montgomery-West Literary Agency; Mura Enterprises, Inc., Dee; Preferred Artists Talent Agency; Redler Entertainment, Dan; Redwood Empire Agency; Renaissance Literary Agency; Schulman, A Literary Agency, Susan; Toad Hall, Inc.; Windfall Management

Gay/Lesbian: Brown Ltd., Curtis; Epstein-Wyckoff and Associates; Esq. Management; Feigen/Parent Literary Management; Levine Literary Agency, Paul S.; Momentum Marketing; Mura Enterprises, Inc., Dee; Pevner, Inc., Stephen; Preferred Artists Talent Agency; Redwood Empire Agency; Renaissance Literary Agency; Wardlow and Associates; Windfall Management; Wright Representatives, Ann; Baskow Agency; Levine Literary Agency, Paul S.; Montgomery-West Literary Agency; Mura Enterprises, Inc., Dee; Pevner, Inc., Stephen

Historical: Agapé Productions; Agency, The; Brown Ltd., Curtis; Camejo & Assoc., Suzanna; Client First—A/K/A Leo P. Haffey Agency; Communications Management Associates; CS International Literary Agency; Douroux & Co.; Epstein-Wyckoff and Associates; Esq. Management; Filmwriters Literary Agency; First Look Talent and Literary Agency; FitzGerald Literary Management; Fleury Agency, B.R.; Fran Literary Agency; Howard Agency, The Eddy; Kohner, Inc., Paul; Larchmont Literary Agency; Legacies; Levine Literary Agency, Paul S.; Miller Co., The Stuart M.; Momentum Marketing; Monteiro Rose Agency; Mura Enterprises, Inc., Dee; Perelman Agency, Barry; Pinkham Literary Agency; Redler Entertainment, Dan; Renaissance Literary Agency; Scagnetti Talent & Literary Agency, Jack; Schulman, A Literary Agency, Susan; Shapiro-Lichtman-Stein; Silver Screen Placements; Sorice Agency, Camille; Toad Hall, Inc.; Total Acting Experience, A; Windfall Management; Wright Representatives, Ann

Horror: AEI/Atchity Editorial/Entertainment International; Agency, The; Brown Ltd., Curtis; Esq. Management; Filmwriters Literary Agency; First Look Talent and Literary Agency; FitzGerald Literary Management; Fleury Agency, B.R.; Fran Literary Agency; Freed Co., The Barry; French, Inc., Samuel; Greene, Arthur B.; Hodges Agency, Carolyn; Infinity Management International; International Leonards Corp.; JLA Literary Agency; Kjar Agency, Tyler; Larchmont Literary Agency; Levine Literary Agency, Paul S.; Major Clients Agency; Momentum Marketing; Mura Enterprises, Inc., Dee; Perelman Agency, Barry; Pevner, Inc., Stephen; Preferred Artists Talent Agency; Redler Entertainment, Dan; Renaissance Literary Agency; Scagnetti Talent & Literary Agency, Jack; Shapiro-Lichtman-Stein; Sister Mania Productions, Inc.; Talent Source; Toad Hall, Inc.; Total Acting Experience, A; Wardlow and Associates; Wright Representatives, Ann

Juvenile: Agapé Productions; Agency, The; Cedar Grove Agency Entertainment; Communications Management Associates; CS International Literary Agency; Epstein-Wyckoff and Associates; Esq. Management; First Look Talent and Literary Agency; FitzGerald Literary Management; Fran Literary Agency; Howard Agency, The Eddy; Hudson Agency; Levine Literary Agency, Paul S.; Momentum Marketing; Monteiro Rose Agency; Montgomery-West Literary Agency; Mura Enterprises, Inc., Dee; Redler Entertainment, Dan; Renaissance Literary Agency; Silver Screen Placements; Talent Source; Toad Hall, Inc.; Total Acting Experience, A; Wauhob Agency, Donna; Windfall Management

Mainstream: AEI/Atchity Editorial/Entertainment International; Agapé Productions; Agency, The; Amsterdam Agency, Marcia; Bennett Agency, The; Brown Ltd., Curtis; Cameron Agency, The Marshall; Communications Management Associates; CS International Literary Agency; Douroux & Co.; Epstein-Wyckoff and Associates; ES Talent Agency; First Look Talent and Literary Agency; FitzGerald Literary Management; Fleury Agency, B.R.; Fran Literary Agency; Freed Co., The Barry; Hodges Agency, Carolyn; Howard Agency, The Eddy; Infinity Management International; JLA Literary Agency; Johnson Warren Literary Agency; Kohner, Inc., Paul; Larchmont Literary Agency; Levine Literary Agency, Paul S.; Major Clients Agency; Miller Co., The Stuart M.; Momentum Marketing; Monteiro Rose Agency; Montgomery-West Literary Agency; Mura Enterprises, Inc., Dee; Palmer, Dorothy; Pevner, Inc., Stephen; Redler Entertainment, Dan; Redwood Empire Agency; Renaissance Literary Agency; Robinson Talent and Literary Management; Scagnetti Talent & Literary Agency, Jack; Schulman, A Literary Agency, Susan; Shapiro-Lichtman-Stein; Silver Screen Placements; Sydra Technique Corp.; Talent Source; Tantleff Office, The; Toad Hall, Inc.; Total Acting Experience, A; Wardlow and Associates; Windfall Management; Wright Representatives, Ann

Multimedia: Levine Literary Agency, Paul S.; Miller Co., The Stuart M.; Suite A Management; Sydra Technique Corp.; Talent Source; Visionary Entertainment; Windfall Management

Mystery/Suspense: AEI/Atchity Editorial/Entertainment International; Agency, The; Amsterdam Agency, Marcia; Baskow Agency; Brown Ltd., Curtis; Cedar Grove Agency Entertainment; Client First—A/K/A Leo P. Haffey Agency; CS International Literary Agency; Douroux & Co.; Epstein-Wyckoff and Associates; ES Talent Agency; Esq. Management; Filmwriters Literary Agency; First Look Talent and Literary Agency; FitzGerald Literary Management; Fleury Agency, B.R.; Fran Literary Agency; Freed Co., The Barry; French, Inc., Samuel; Greene, Arthur B.; Hodges Agency, Carolyn; Hudson Agency; Infinity Management International; International Leonards Corp.; JLA Literary Agency; Johnson Warren Literary Agency; Kohner, Inc., Paul; Larchmont Literary Agency; Levine Literary Agency, Paul S.; Major Clients Agency; Miller Co., The Stuart M.; Momentum Marketing; Monteiro Rose Agency; Montgomery-West Literary Agency; Mura Enterprises, Inc., Dee; Palmer, Dorothy; Panda Talent; Perelman Agency, Barry; Pinkham Literary Agency; Preferred Artists Talent Agency; Redler Entertainment, Dan; Redwood Empire Agency; Renaissance Literary Agency; Robinson Talent and Literary Management; Scagnetti Talent & Literary Agency, Jack; Schulman, A Literary Agency, Susan; Shapiro-Lichtman-Stein; Silver Screen Placements; Sorice Agency, Camille; Sydra Technique Corp.; Talent Source; Tantleff Office, The; Toad Hall, Inc.; Total Acting Experience, A; Wardlow and Associates; Windfall Management; Wright Representatives, Ann

Open to all Categories: Acme Talent & Literary; Allred and Allred, Literary Agents; Bohrman Agency, The; Brown Agency, Bruce; Chadwick & Gros Literary Agency; Circle of Confusion Ltd.; Dade/Schultz Associates; Gage Group, The; Lake Agency, The Candace; Madsen Agency, Robert; Picture of You, A; Sherman & Associates, Ken; Soloway Grant Kopaloff & Associates; Stone Manners Agency; Suite A Management; Vegas Literary Agency; Visionary Entertainment; Wardlow and Associates; Writers & Artists Agency

Psychic/Supernatural: AEI/Atchity Editorial/Entertainment International; Agency, The; Brown Ltd., Curtis; Communications Management Associates; CS International Literary Agency; Esq. Management; Filmwriters Literary Agency; First Look Talent and Literary Agency; FitzGerald Literary Management; Fleury Agency, B.R.; Hodges Agency, Carolyn; Infinity Management International; Kay Agency, Charlene; Larchmont Literary Agency; Levine Literary Agency, Paul S.; Momentum Marketing; Monteiro Rose Agency; Mura Enterprises, Inc., Dee; Pinkham Literary Agency; Preferred Artists Talent Agency; Redler Entertainment, Dan; Renaissance Literary Agency; Robinson Talent and Literary Management; Schulman, A Literary Agency, Susan; Total Acting Experience, A; Wright Representatives, Ann

Regional: Bulger and Associates, Kelvin C.; Esq. Management; Momentum Marketing

Religious/Inspirational: Baskow Agency; Communications Management Associates; CS International Literary Agency; Esq. Management; Fran Literary Agency; French, Inc., Samuel; Levine Literary Agency, Paul S.; Momentum Marketing; Mura Enterprises, Inc., Dee; Renaissance Literary Agency; Robinson Talent and Literary Management; Schulman, A Literary Agency, Susan; Total Acting Experience, A

Romance: Amsterdam Agency, Marcia; Brown Ltd., Curtis; Cedar Grove Agency Entertainment; Client First—A/K/A Leo P. Haffey Agency; First Look Talent and Literary Agency; Johnson Warren Literary Agency; Palmer, Dorothy; Panda Talent; Perelman Agency, Barry; Preferred Artists Talent Agency; Sister Mania Productions, Inc.; Wardlow and Associates

Romantic Comedy: AEI/Atchity Editorial/Entertainment International; Agapé Productions; Agency, The; Amsterdam Agency, Marcia; Baskow Agency; Brown Ltd., Curtis; Camejo & Assoc., Suzanna;

Cedar Grove Agency Entertainment; Communications Management Associates; CS International Literary Agency; Douroux & Co.; Epstein-Wyckoff and Associates; ES Talent Agency; Esq. Management; Filmwriters Literary Agency; FitzGerald Literary Management; Fleury Agency, B.R.; Fran Literary Agency; Hodges Agency, Carolyn; Hudson Agency; Infinity Management International; International Leonards Corp.; JLA Literary Agency; Johnson Warren Literary Agency; Kay Agency, Charlene; Kjar Agency, Tyler; Kohner, Inc., Paul; Larchmont Literary Agency; Levine Literary Agency, Paul S.; Miller Co., The Stuart M.; Momentum Marketing; Monteiro Rose Agency; Montgomery-West Literary Agency; Mura Enterprises, Inc., Dee; Palmer, Dorothy; Panda Talent; Pevner, Inc., Stephen; Redler Entertainment, Dan; Redwood Empire Agency; Renaissance Literary Agency; Robinson Talent and Literary Management; Scagnetti Talent & Literary Agency, Jack; Shapiro-Lichtman-Stein; Sorice Agency, Camille; Stanton & Associates Literary Agency; Talent Source; Tantleff Office, The; Toad Hall, Inc.; Total Acting Experience, A; Wauhob Agency, Donna; Windfall Management; Wright Representatives, Ann

Romantic Drama: AEI/Atchity Editorial/Entertainment International; Agapé Productions; Agency, The; Amsterdam Agency, Marcia; Baskow Agency; Brown Ltd., Curtis; Camejo & Assoc., Suzanna; Communications Management Associates; CS International Literary Agency; Douroux & Co.; Epstein-Wyckoff and Associates; ES Talent Agency; Esq. Management; Filmwriters Literary Agency; FitzGerald Literary Management; Fleury Agency, B.R.; Fran Literary Agency; Hodges Agency, Carolyn; Hudson Agency; Infinity Management International; JLA Literary Agency; Johnson Warren Literary Agency; Kay Agency, Charlene; Kjar Agency, Tyler; Kohner, Inc., Paul; Larchmont Literary Agency; Levine Literary Agency, Paul S.; Miller Co., The Stuart M.; Momentum Marketing; Monteiro Rose Agency; Montgomery-West Literary Agency; Mura Enterprises, Inc., Dee; Palmer, Dorothy; Panda Talent; Pevner, Inc., Stephen; Redler Entertainment, Dan; Redwood Empire Agency; Renaissance Literary Agency; Robinson Talent and Literary Management; Scagnetti Talent & Literary Agency, Jack; Shapiro-Lichtman-Stein; Sorice Agency, Camille; Stanton & Associates Literary Agency; Talent Source; Tantleff Office, The; Total Acting Experience, A; Wauhob Agency, Donna; Windfall Management; Wright Representatives, Ann

Science Fiction: AEI/Atchity Editorial/Entertainment International; Agapé Productions; Agency, The; Baskow Agency; Camejo & Assoc., Suzanna; Cedar Grove Agency Entertainment; Client First—A/K/A Leo P. Haffey Agency; Communications Management Associates; CS International Literary Agency; Douroux & Co.; Esq. Management; First Look Talent and Literary Agency; FitzGerald Literary Management; Fran Literary Agency; Freed Co., The Barry; Infinity Management International; International Leonards Corp.; JLA Literary Agency; Kay Agency, Charlene; Kjar Agency, Tyler; Larchmont Literary Agency; Levine Literary Agency, Paul S.; Miller Co., The Stuart M.; Momentum Marketing; Monteiro Rose Agency; Montgomery-West Literary Agency; Mura Enterprises, Inc., Dee; Panda Talent; Perelman Agency, Barry; Preferred Artists Talent Agency; Redler Entertainment, Dan; Renaissance Literary Agency; Robinson Talent and Literary Management; Shapiro-Lichtman-Stein; Silver Screen Placements; Sydra Technique Corp.; Toad Hall, Inc.; Total Acting Experience, A; Wardlow and Associates; Windfall Management

Sports: Cedar Grove Agency Entertainment; Client First—A/K/A Leo P. Haffey Agency; CS International Literary Agency; ES Talent Agency; First Look Talent and Literary Agency; Fran Literary Agency; Freed Co., The Barry; Infinity Management International; International Leonards Corp.; Larchmont Literary Agency; Levine Literary Agency, Paul S.; Major Clients Agency; Miller Co., The Stuart M.; Momentum Marketing; Mura Enterprises, Inc., Dee; Preferred Artists Talent Agency; Redler Entertainment, Dan; Renaissance Literary Agency; Robinson Talent and Literary Management; Scagnetti Talent & Literary Agency, Jack; Sydra Technique Corp.; Total Acting Experience, A; Windfall Management; Wright Representatives, Ann

Teen: AEI/Atchity Editorial/Entertainment International; Agency, The; Communications Management Associates; CS International Literary Agency; Epstein-Wyckoff and Associates; Esq. Management; Filmwriters Literary Agency; First Look Talent and Literary Agency; FitzGerald Literary Management; Fran Literary Agency; Freed Co., The Barry; Howard Agency, The Eddy; Hudson Agency; Infinity Management International; Kjar Agency, Tyler; Levine Literary Agency, Paul S.; Miller Co., The Stuart M.; Momentum Marketing; Monteiro Rose Agency; Montgomery-West Literary Agency; Mura Enterprises, Inc., Dee; Pevner, Inc., Stephen; Redler Entertainment, Dan; Renaissance Literary Agency; Robinson Talent and Literary Management; Schulman, A Literary Agency, Susan; Shapiro-Lichtman-Stein; Talent Source; Total Acting Experience, A; Wauhob Agency, Donna; Windfall Management; Wright Concept, The

Thriller/Espionage: AEI/Atchity Editorial/Entertainment International; Agapé Productions; Agency, The; Baskow Agency; Brown Ltd., Curtis; Camejo & Assoc., Suzanna; Cameron Agency, The Marshall; Cedar Grove Agency Entertainment; Client First—A/K/A Leo P. Haffey Agency; Communications Management Associates; CS International Literary Agency; Douroux & Co.; Epstein-Wyckoff and Associates; ES Talent Agency; Esq. Management; Feigen/Parrent Literary Management; Filmwriters Literary Agency; First Look Talent and Literary Agency; FitzGerald Literary Management; Fleury Agency, B.R.; Fran

Literary Agency; Freed Co., The Barry; French, Inc., Samuel; Infinity Management International; International Leonards Corp.; JLA Literary Agency; Johnson Warren Literary Agency; Larchmont Literary Agency; Levine Literary Agency, Paul S.; Major Clients Agency; Miller Co., The Stuart M.; Momentum Marketing; Monteiro Rose Agency; Montgomery-West Literary Agency; Mura Enterprises, Inc., Dee; Palmer, Dorothy; Perelman Agency, Barry; Pinkham Literary Agency; Preferred Artists Talent Agency; Redler Entertainment, Dan; Redwood Empire Agency; Renaissance Literary Agency; Robinson Talent and Literary Management; Scagnetti Talent & Literary Agency, Jack; Shapiro-Lichtman-Stein; Silver Screen Placements; Sister Mania Productions, Inc.; Stanton & Associates Literary Agency; Total Acting Experience, A; Wardlow and Associates; Wauhob Agency, Donna; Windfall Management; Wright Concept, The; Wright Representatives, Ann

Westerns/Frontier: Agapé Productions; Agency, The; Brown Ltd., Curtis; Cedar Grove Agency Entertainment; Client First—A/K/A Leo P. Haffey Agency; Communications Management Associates; CS International Literary Agency; Douroux & Co.; Esq. Management; First Look Talent and Literary Agency; FitzGerald Literary Management; Fran Literary Agency; Howard Agency, The Eddy; Hudson Agency; Larchmont Literary Agency; Levine Literary Agency, Paul S.; Momentum Marketing; Mura Enterprises, Inc., Dee; Panda Talent; Renaissance Literary Agency; Robinson Talent and Literary Management; Shapiro-Lichtman-Stein; Sorice Agency, Camille; Total Acting Experience, A; Wardlow and Associates; Wauhob Agency, Donna; Windfall Management; Wright Representatives, Ann

Script Agents/Format Index

This index will help you determine agencies interested in handling scripts for particular types of movies or TV programs. These formats are delineated into ten categories; animation; documentary; episodic drama; feature film; miniseries; movie of the week (MOW); sitcom; soap opera; stage play; variety show. Once you find the agency you're interested in, refer to the Listing Index for the page number.

Animation: Above the Line Agency; Agapé Productions; Agency, The; Allred and Allred, Literary Agents; Amato Agency, Michael; Brown Agency, Bruce; Buscher Consultants; Chadwick & Gros Literary Agency; Client First—A/K/A Leo P. Haffey Agency; Communications Management Associates; CS International Literary Agency; Douroux & Co.; Epstein-Wyckoff and Associates; Esq. Management; Fran Literary Agency; Howard Agency, The Eddy; Hudson Agency; International Leonards Corp.; Kay Agency, Charlene; Kohner, Inc., Paul; Levine Literary Agency, Paul S.; Monteiro Rose Agency; Mura Enterprises, Inc., Dee; Panda Talent; Pevner, Inc., Stephen; Picture of You, A; Quillco Agency, The; Redwood Empire Agency; Robinson Talent and Literary Management; Scagnetti Talent & Literary Agency, Jack; Shapiro-Lichtman-Stein; Suite A Management; Sydra Technique Corp.; Tantleff Office, The; Vegas Literary Agency; Wauhob Agency, Donna; Wright Concept, The

Documentary: Agapé Productions; Allred and Allred, Literary Agents; Amato Agency, Michael; Baskow Agency; Bulger And Associates, Kelvin C.; Chadwick & Gros Literary Agency; Charisma Communications, Ltd.; Communications Management Associates; CS International Literary Agency; Fran Literary Agency; Howard Agency, The Eddy; Hudson Agency; Kohner, Inc., Paul; Levine Literary Agency, Paul S.; Mura Enterprises, Inc., Dee; Pevner, Inc., Stephen; Picture of You, A; Quillco Agency, The; Robinson Talent and Literary Management; Vegas Literary Agency; Windfall Management

Episodic Drama: Agapé Productions; Agency, The; Allred and Allred, Literary Agents; Amato Agency, Michael; Baskow Agency; Brown Agency, Bruce; Chadwick & Gros Literary Agency; Douroux & Co.; Epstein-Wyckoff and Associates; Fran Literary Agency; Howard Agency, The Eddy; Infinity Management International; Kay Agency, Charlene; Kohner, Inc., Paul; Lake Agency, The Candace; Levine Literary Agency, Paul S.; Momentum Marketing; Monteiro Rose Agency; Mura Enterprises, Inc., Dee; Palmer, Dorothy; Panda Talent; Pevner, Inc., Stephen; Picture of You, A; Robinson Talent and Literary Management; Scagnetti Talent & Literary Agency, Jack; Shapiro-Lichtman-Stein; Talent Source; Tantleff Office, The; Toad Hall, Inc.; Vegas Literary Agency; Wardlow and Associates; Wauhob Agency, Donna; Wright Concept, The; Wright Representatives, Ann; Writers & Artists Agency

Feature Film: Above the Line Agency; Acme Talent & Literary; AEI/Atchity Editorial/Entertainment International; Agapé Productions; Agency, The; Allred and Allred, Literary Agents; Amato Agency, Michael; Amsterdam Agency, Marcia; Baskow Agency; Bennett Agency, The; Berman Boals and Flynn Inc.; Bohrman Agency, The; Brown Agency, Bruce; Bulger And Associates, Kelvin C.; Buscher Consultants; Camejo & Assoc., Suzanna; Cameron Agency, The Marshall; Cedar Grove Agency Entertainment; Chadwick & Gros Literary Agency; Charisma Communications, Ltd.; Cinema Talent International; Circle of Confusion Ltd.; Client First—A/K/A Leo P. Haffey Agency; Communications Management Associates; CS International Literary Agency; Dade/Schultz Associates; Douroux & Co.; Epstein-Wyckoff and Associates; ES Talent Agency; Esq. Management; Feigen/Parrent Literary Management; Filmwriters Literary Agency; First Look Talent and Literary Agency; FitzGerald Literary Management; Fleury Agency, B.R.; Fran Literary Agency; Freed Co., The Barry; Gage Group, The; Gelff Agency, The Laya; Graham Agency; Greene, Arthur B.; Hodges Agency, Carolyn; Hogenson Agency, Barbara; Howard Agency, The Eddy; Hudson Agency; Infinity Management International; International Leonards Corp.; Johnson Warren Literary Agency; Kallen Agency, Leslie; Kay Agency, Charlene; Kjar Agency, Tyler; Kohner, Inc., Paul; Lake Agency, The Candace; Larchmont Literary Agency; Legacies; Levine Literary Agency, Paul S.; Madsen Agency, Robert; Magnetic Management; Major Clients Agency; Momentum Marketing; Monteiro Rose Agency; Montgomery-West Literary Agency; Mura Enterprises, Inc., Dee; Oscard Agency, Inc., Fifi; Palmer, Dorothy; Panda Talent; Pevner, Inc., Stephen; Picture of You, A; Pinkham Literary Agency; PMA Literary and Film Management, Inc.; Quillco Agency, The; Redwood Empire Agency; Renaissance Literary

Agency; Robinson Talent and Literary Management; Scagnetti Talent & Literary Agency, Jack; Schulman, A Literary Agency, Susan; Shapiro-Lichtman-Stein; Silver Screen Placements; Sister Mania Productions, Inc.; Sorice Agency, Camille; Stanton & Associates Literary Agency; Suite A Management; Sydra Technique Corp.; Talent Source; Tantleff Office, The; Toad Hall, Inc.; Vegas Literary Agency; Wardlow and Associates; Wauhob Agency, Donna; Whittlesey Agency, Peregrine; Wright Concept, The; Wright Representatives, Ann; Writers & Artists Agency

Miniseries: Agapé Productions; Agency, The; Amato Agency, Michael; Baskow Agency; Chadwick & Gros Literary Agency; Charisma Communications, Ltd.; Communications Management Associates; Epstein-Wyckoff and Associates; Esq. Management; Filmwriters Literary Agency; Fran Literary Agency; Howard Agency, The Eddy; Hudson Agency; Infinity Management International; Kjar Agency, Tyler; Kohner, Inc., Paul; Levine Literary Agency, Paul S.; Mura Enterprises, Inc., Dee; Palmer, Dorothy; Pevner, Inc., Stephen; Picture of You, A; PMA Literary and Film Management, Inc.; Robinson Talent and Literary Management; Scagnetti Talent & Literary Agency, Jack; Shapiro-Lichtman-Stein; Vegas Literary Agency; Wardlow and Associates; Wauhob Agency, Donna; Windfall Management; Writers & Artists Agency

Movie of the Week: Above the Line Agency; AEI/Atchity Editorial/Entertainment International; Agapé Productions; Agency, The; Allred and Allred, Literary Agents; Amato Agency, Michael; Amsterdam Agency, Marcia; Baskow Agency; Brown Agency, Bruce; Bulger and Associates, Kelvin C.; Buscher Consultants; Cedar Grove Agency Entertainment; Chadwick & Gros Literary Agency; Charisma Communications, Ltd.; Communications Management Associates; CS International Literary Agency; Douroux & Co.; Epstein-Wyckoff and Associates; ES Talent Agency; Esq. Management; Feigen/Parrent Literary Management; Filmwriters Literary Agency; First Look Talent and Literary Agency; FitzGerald Literary Management; Fleury Agency, B.R.; Fran Literary Agency; Freed Co., The Barry; Greene, Arthur B.; Hodges Agency, Carolyn; Hogenson Agency, Barbara; Howard Agency, The Eddy; Hudson Agency; International Leonards Corp.; Johnson Warren Literary Agency; Kallen Agency, Leslie; Kay Agency, Charlene; Kjar Agency, Tyler; Kohner, Inc., Paul; Lake Agency, The Candace; Legacies; Levine Literary Agency, Paul S.; Major Clients Agency; Momentum Marketing; Monteiro Rose Agency; Montgomery-West Literary Agency; Mura Enterprises, Inc., Dee; Palmer, Dorothy; Panda Talent; Pevner, Inc., Stephen; Picture of You, A; Pinkham Literary Agency; PMA Literary and Film Management, Inc.; Quillco Agency, The; Redwood Empire Agency; Robinson Talent and Literary Management; Scagnetti Talent & Literary Agency, Jack; Shapiro-Lichtman-Stein; Stanton & Associates Literary Agency; Suite A Management; Sydra Technique Corp.; Talent Source; Toad Hall, Inc.; Vegas Literary Agency; Wardlow and Associates; Wauhob Agency, Donna; Windfall Management; Wright Concept, The; Wright Representatives, Ann; Writers & Artists Agency

Sitcom: Agapé Productions; Agency, The; Allred and Allred, Literary Agents; Amsterdam Agency, Marcia; Baskow Agency; Bennett Agency, The; Brown Agency, Bruce; Cedar Grove Agency Entertainment; Chadwick & Gros Literary Agency; CS International Literary Agency; Douroux & Co.; Epstein-Wyckoff and Associates; Esq. Management; Fran Literary Agency; Hogenson Agency, Barbara; Howard Agency, The Eddy; Hudson Agency; Infinity Management International; International Leonards Corp.; Kay Agency, Charlene; Kjar Agency, Tyler; Kohner, Inc., Paul; Lake Agency, The Candace; Levine Literary Agency, Paul S.; Major Clients Agency; Momentum Marketing; Mura Enterprises, Inc., Dee; Palmer, Dorothy; Panda Talent; Picture of You, A; Scagnetti Talent & Literary Agency, Jack; Shapiro-Lichtman-Stein; Sydra Technique Corp.; Talent Source; Tantleff Office, The; Vegas Literary Agency; Wardlow and Associates; Wauhob Agency, Donna; Wright Concept, The; Wright Representatives, Ann

Soap Opera: Allred and Allred, Literary Agents; Brown Agency, Bruce; Chadwick & Gros Literary Agency; Epstein-Wyckoff and Associates; Hogenson Agency, Barbara; Howard Agency, The Eddy; Kohner, Inc., Paul; Shapiro-Lichtman-Stein; Tantleff Office, The; Vegas Literary Agency; Wauhob Agency, Donna

Theatrical Stage Play: Agapé Productions; Allred and Allred, Literary Agents; Berman Boals and Flynn Inc.; Bohrman Agency, The; Brodie Representation, Alan; Dramatic Publishing; Epstein-Wyckoff and Associates; First Look Talent and Literary Agency; Freedman Dramatic Agency, Inc., Robert A.; French, Inc., Samuel; Graham Agency; Greene, Arthur B.; Hogenson Agency, Barbara; Howard Agency, The Eddy; Kjar Agency, Tyler; Kohner, Inc., Paul; Madsen Agency, Robert; Oscard Agency, Inc., Fifi; Pevner, Inc., Stephen; Robinson Talent and Literary Management; Schulman, A Literary Agency, Susan; Shapiro-Lichtman-Stein; Suite A Management; Tantleff Office, The; Total Acting Experience, A; Wauhob Agency, Donna; Whittlesey Agency, Peregrine; Windfall Management; Writers & Artists Agency

Theatrical Stage Play: Agapé Productions; Allred and Allred, Literary Agents; Berman Boals and Flynn Inc.; Bohrman Agency, The; Brodie Representation, Alan; Dramatic Publishing; Epstein-Wyckoff and Associates; First Look Talent and Literary Agency; Freedman Dramatic Agency, Inc., Robert A.; French,

Writers' Conferences: Venues for Meeting Literary Agents

To a novice writer, agents might seem like alien beings from on high, passing god-like judgments in total anonymity, with little or no explanation about why a manuscript is lacking and what can be done to fix it. An isolated writer sending out work for agents' consideration can feel frustration at the lack of communication, anger or depression from impersonal rejection, and confusion about what to do next. If only you could talk with agents, you reason, and explain your book, any agent would jump at the chance to represent it!

That may be. And attending a conference that includes agents gives you the opportunity to listen and learn more about what agents do, as well as talk with them about your work. Even agents view conferences as advantageous events. Agent Ethan Ellenberg says, "Writers' conferences represent a unique opportunity to see and hear an agent, giving you a far deeper exposure to their interests, personality and abilities than any research you could do. As an agent, I find it very useful to meet with current and prospective clients who've already been published. At a conference, we can have a full discussion. For the unpublished writer, it's much trickier because few agents really want to read anything during a conference. Nevertheless, it is possible to pitch a project and catch an agent's eye." Meredith Bernstein, of the Meredith Bernstein Literary Agency, adds, "The advantages of attending writers' conferences are numerous. First of all, you get to meet a number of new faces and voices while simultaneously being your own public relations firm. The one-on-one meetings are a chance to get up-close and personal with people you may want to represent. In general, the networking opportunities are terrific—and like everything else in life: showing up counts!"

Ideally, a conference should include a panel or two with a number of agents because you get a variety of views about agenting from those who do it. You also will be able to see how agents differ from one another, that not all agents are alike, that some are more personable, more trustworthy, or simply look like they might click better with you than others. When only one agent attends a conference there's a tendency for every writer at that conference—especially if they meet with the agent or hear one of his lectures—to think, "Ah, this is the agent I've been looking for!" When you get a larger sampling of agents, though, you get a wider, more eclectic group from which to choose.

Besides including panels of agents discussing what representation means and how to go about securing it, many of these gatherings also include time, either scheduled or impromptu, to meet briefly with an agent to discuss your work.

You may interest agents by meeting them in person and discussing your work. If they're impressed, they will invite you to submit a query, a proposal, a few sample chapters, or possibly the entire manuscript. Some conferences even arrange for agents to review manuscripts in advance and schedule one-on-one sessions where you can receive specific feedback/advice on your work. Ask writers who attend conferences and they'll tell you that at the very least you'll walk away with more knowledge than you came with. At the very best, you'll receive an invitation to send a suitable agent your material. Then it's up to your writing.

FINDING A CONFERENCE

Many writers try to make it to at least one conference a year, but cost and location can count as much as subject matter or other considerations, when determining which conference to attend.

There are conferences in almost every state and province that will answer your needs for information about writing, and offer you a way to connect with a community of other writers. Such connections can help you not only learn about the pros and cons of different agents writers have worked with, but they also can provide you a renewed sense of purpose and direction in your own writing.

When reading through this section, keep in mind the following information to help you pick the best conference for your needs:

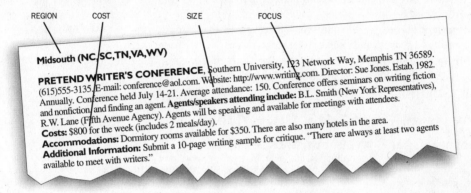

REGION COST SIZE FOCUS

Midsouth (NC, SC, TN, VA, WV)
PRETEND WRITER'S CONFERENCE, Southern University, 123 Network Way, Memphis TN 36589. (615)555-3135. E-mail: conference@aol.com. Website: http://www.writing.com. Director: Sue Jones. Estab. 1982. Annually. Conference held July 14-21. Average attendance: 150. Conference offers seminars on writing fiction and nonfiction, and finding an agent. **Agents/speakers attending include:** B.L. Smith (New York Representatives), R.W. Lane (Fifth Avenue Agency). Agents will be speaking and available for meetings with attendees. **Costs:** $800 for the week (includes 2 meals/day). **Accommodations:** Dormitory rooms available for $350. There are also many hotels in the area. **Additional Information:** Submit a 10-page writing sample for critique. "There are always at least two agents available to meet with writers."

REGIONS

To make it easier for you to find a conference close to home—or to find one in an exotic locale to fit into your vacation plans—we've separated this section into geographical regions. The regions are as follows:

Northeast (pages 294-300): Connecticut, Maine, Massachusetts, New Hampshire, New York, Rhode Island, Vermont.
Midatlantic (pages 300-301): Washington DC, Delaware, Maryland, New Jersey, Pennsylvania.
Midsouth (pages 301-303): North Carolina, South Carolina, Tennessee, Virginia, West Virginia.
Southeast (pages 303-305): Alabama, Arkansas, Florida, Georgia, Louisiana, Mississippi, Puerto Rico.
Midwest (pages 305-307): Illinois, Indiana, Kentucky, Michigan, Ohio.
North Central (pages 307-308): Iowa, Minnesota, Nebraska, North Dakota, South Dakota, Wisconsin.
South Central (pages 308-311): Colorado, Kansas, Missouri, New Mexico, Oklahoma, Texas.
West (pages 311-313): Arizona, California, Hawaii, Nevada, Utah.
Northwest (pages 313-314): Alaska, Idaho, Montana, Oregon, Washington, Wyoming.
Canada (pages 314-315).

QUICK REFERENCE ICONS

At the beginning of some listings, you will find one or more of the following symbols for quick identification of features particular to that listing.

- **N** Conference new to this edition.
- ✔ Change in address, contact information, phone number or e-mail address from last year's edition.
- Canadian conference.

SUBHEADS

Each listing is divided into subheads to make locating specific information easier. In the first section, you'll find contact information for each conference. Also given are conference dates, plus its specific focus and size. If a conference is small, you may receive more individual attention from speakers. If it is large, there may be a greater number and variety of agents in attendance. Finally, names of agents who will be speaking or have spoken in the past are listed along with details about their availability during the conference.

Costs: Looking at the price of seminars, plus room and board, may help writers on a tight budget narrow their choices.

Accommodations: Here conferences list overnight accommodation and travel information. Often conferences held in hotels will reserve rooms at a discount price.

Additional Information: A range of features are given here, including information on contests, individual meetings, and brochure availability.

Northeast (CT, MA, ME, NH, NY, RI, VT)

☑ **BREAD LOAF WRITERS' CONFERENCE**, Middlebury College, Middlebury VT 05753. (802)443-5286. Fax: (802)443-2087. E-mail: blwc@middlebury.edu. Website: www.middlebury.edu/~blwc. Administrative Coordinator: Carol Knauss. Estab. 1926. Annual. Conference held in late August. Conference duration: 11 days. Average attendance: 230. For fiction, nonfiction and poetry. Held at the summer campus in Ripton, Vermont (belongs to Middlebury College).
Costs: $1,730 (includes room/board) (1999).
Accommodations: Accommodations are at Ripton. Onsite accommodations $605 (1999).

N **FEMINIST WOMEN'S WRITING WORKSHOPS, INC.**, P.O. Box 6583, Ithaca NY 14851. Directors: Kit Wainer and Margo Gumosky. Estab. 1975. Workshop held every summer. Workshop duration: 8 days. Average attendance: 30-45 women writers. "Workshops provide a women-centered community for writers of all levels and genres. Workshops are held on the campuses of Hobart/William Smith Colleges in Geneva, NY. Geneva is approximately midway between Rochester and Syracuse. College facilities such as pool, tennis courts and library are available. FWWW invites all interests. **Previous agents/speakers have included:** Dorothy Allison, National Book Award Finalist for *Bastard Out of Carolina*; Ruth Stone, author of *Second-Hand Coat*, *Who Is The Widow's Muse?* and *Simplicity*; and Alexis DeVeaux, poet, playwright, essayist and fiction writer.
Costs: $550 for tuition, room, board.
Accommodations: Private room and 3 meals included in fee.
Additional Information: "Writers may submit manuscripts up to 10 pages with application." Brochures/guidelines available for SASE.

☑ **HIGHLIGHTS FOUNDATION WRITERS WORKSHOP AT CHAUTAUQUA**, Dept. NM, 814 Court St., Honesdale PA 18431. (570)253-1192. Fax: (570)253-0179. Executive Director: Kent Brown. Estab. 1985. Annual. Workshop held July 15-22, 2000. Average attendance: 100. "Writer workshops geared toward those who write for children—beginner, intermediate, advanced levels. Small group workshops, one-to-one interaction between faculty and participants plus panel sessions, lectures and large group meetings. Workshop site is the picturesque community of Chautauqua, New York." Classes offered include Children's Interests, Writing Dialogue, Outline for the Novel, Conflict and Developing Plot. **Previous agents/speakers have included:** Eve Bunting, James Cross Giblin, Walter Dean Myers, Jane Yolen, Patricia Gauch, Jerry Spinelli and Ed Young.
Accommodations: "We coordinate ground transportation to and from airports, trains and bus stations in the Erie, PA and Jamestown/Buffalo, NY area. We also coordinate accommodations for conference attendees."
Additional Information: "We offer the opportunity for attendees to submit a manuscript for review at the conference." Workshop brochures/guidelines are available after January for SASE. Inquiries by fax OK.

☑ **HOFSTRA UNIVERSITY SUMMER WRITERS' CONFERENCE**, 250 Hofstra University, UCCE, Hempstead NY 11549-1090. (516)463-5016. Fax: (516)463-4833. E-mail: dcekah@hofstra.edu. Website: www.hofstra.edu (includes dates, faculty, general description, tuition). Director, Liberal Arts Studies: Kenneth Henwood. Estab. 1972. Annual (every summer, starting week after July 4). Conference to be held July 12 to July 23, 1999. Average attendance: 50. Conference offers workshops in short fiction, nonfiction, poetry, juvenile fiction, stage/screenwriting and, on occasion, one other genre such as detective fiction or science fiction. Site is the university campus, a suburban setting, 25 miles from NYC. Guest speakers are not yet known. "We have had the likes of Oscar Hijuelos, Robert Olen Butler, Hilma and Meg Wolitzer, Budd Schulberg and Cynthia Ozick."
Costs: Non-credit (2 meals, no room): approximately $375 per workshop. Credit: Approximately $1,000/workshop (2 credits) and $2,000/workshop (4 credits), graduate and undergraduate.

Get the Most from a Conference

Squeeze the most out of a conference by getting organized and staying involved. Follow these steps to ensure a worthwhile event.

Before you go:
• **Become familiar with all the pre-conference literature,** particularly the agenda. Study the maps of the area, especially the locations of the rooms in which your meetings/events are scheduled.
• **Make a list of three to five objectives you'd like to obtain,** e.g., whom you want to meet, what you want to learn more about, what you want to improve on, how many new markets you want to find.

At the conference:
• **Budget your time,** Label a map so you know ahead of time where, when and how to get to each session. Note what you want to do most. Then, schedule time with agents and editors for critique sessions.
• **Don't be afraid to explore new areas.** You are there to learn. Pick one or two sessions you wouldn't typically attend. This is an education; keep your mind open to new ideas and advice.
• **Allow time for mingling.** Some of the best information is given after the session. Find out "frank truths" and inside scoops. Asking people what they've learned at the conference will trigger a conversation that may branch into areas you want to know more about but won't hear from the speakers.
• **Learn about agents, editors and new markets.** Which are more open to new writers? Find a new contact in your area for future support.
• **Collect everything:** guidelines, sample issues, promotional fliers and especially business cards. Make notes about the personalities of the people you meet to remind you later who to contact and who to avoid.
• **Find inspiration for future projects.** While you're away from home, people-watch, take a walk, a bike ride or drive. You may even want to take pictures to enhance your memory.

After the conference:
• **Evaluate.** Write down the answers to these questions: Would I attend again? What were the pluses and minuses, e.g., speakers, location, food, topics, cost, lodging? What do I want to remember for next year? What should I try to do next time? Who would I like to meet?
• **Write a thank-you letter** to an agent or editor who has been particularly helpful. They'll remember you when you later submit.

Accommodations: Free bus operates between Hempstead Train Station and campus for those commuting from NYC. Dormitory rooms are available for approximately $350 for the 2 week conference. Those who request area hotels will receive a list. Hotels are approximately $75 and above/night.

Additional Information: "All workshops include critiquing. Each participant is given one-on-one time of a half hour with workshop leader. Only credit students must submit manuscripts when registering. We submit work to the Shaw Guides Contest and other Writer's Conferences and Retreats contests when appropriate."

IWWG MEET THE AUTHORS, AGENTS AND EDITORS: THE BIG APPLE WORKSHOPS, % International Women's Writing Guild, P.O. Box 810, Gracie Station, New York NY 10028-0082. (212)737-7536. Fax: (212)737-9469. E-mail: iwwg@iwwg.com. Website: www.iwwg.com. Executive Director: Hannelore Hahn. Estab. 1980. 19th

Biannual. 1999 workshops held April 15-16, 2000 and October 21-22, 2000. Average attendance: 200. Workshops to promote creative writing and professional success. Site: City Athletic Club of New York, mid-town New York City. Sunday afternoon openhouse with agents and editors. **Previous agents/speakers have included:** Meredith Bernstein and Jean V. Naggar.
Costs: $100 for members for the weekend; $120 for nonmembers for the weekend.
Accommodations: Information on transportation arrangements and overnight accommodations made available.
Additional Information: Workshop brochures/guidelines are available for SASE. Inquires by fax and e-mail OK. "Many contacts have been made between agents and authors over the years."

IWWG SUMMER CONFERENCE, % International Women's Writing Guild, P.O. Box 810, Gracie Station, New York NY 10028-0082. (212)737-7536. Fax: (212)737-9469. E-mail: iwwg@iwwg.com. Website: www.iwwg.com. Executive Director: Hannelore Hahn. Estab. 1977. 23rd Annual. Conference held from August 12-19, 2000. Average attendance: 500, including international attendees. Conference to promote writing in all genres, personal growth and professional success. Conference is held "on the tranquil campus of Skidmore College in Saratoga Springs, NY, where the serene Hudson Valley meets the North Country of the Adirondacks." Sixty-five different workshops are offered everyday. Theme: "Writing Towards Personal and Professional Growth."
Costs: $825 for week-long program with room and board. $400 for week-long program for commuters.
Accommodations: Transportation by air to Albany, New York, or Amtrak train available from New York City. Conference attendees stay on campus.
Additional Information: Features "lots of critiquing sessions and contacts with literary agents." Conference brochures/guidelines available for SASE. Inquires by fax and e-mail OK.

N: MARYMOUNT MANHATTAN COLLEGE'S WRITER'S CONFERENCE, 221 E. 71st St., New York NY 10021-4597. (212)734-4419. Fax: (212)734-3140. **Contact:** Conference Director. Estab. 1992. Annually. Conference held July 16. Conference duration: 1 day. Average attendance: 200. Fiction, nonfiction, memoir, playwriting and scriptwriting. Held at the writing center at Marymount Manhattan College. Panels include "How to Publicize and Market Your Work," "Writing For a Second Income," "Writing for the Women's Market," and more. **Agents/speakers attending include:** Clair Gerus (Clair Gerus Literary Agency); Nancy Love (Nancy Love Literary Agency); Ruth Nathan (Ruth Nathan Literary Agency; George Borchardt (George Borchardt Literary Agency); Linda Konner (Linda Konner Literary Agency); Rhoda Weyr (Rhoda Weyr Literary Agency); Jeff Herman (Jeff Herman Literary Agency); Molly Friederich (Aaron Priest Literary Agency); Loretta Barrett (Virginia Barber Literary Agency); Geri Thoma (Elaine Markson Literary Agency). Agents will be speaking.
Costs: $145 (includes lunch).
Additional Information: Brochures available for SASE. Inquiries by fax OK.

NEW ENGLAND SCREENWRITERS CONFERENCE, P.O. Box 6705, Providence RI 02940. (401)751-9300. Fax:(401)751-0121. E-mail: rphkmh@aol.com. Website: www.communitywriters.org. **Contact:** Robert Hofmann. Estab. 1996. Annually. Conference held early August. Conference duration: 3 days. Average attendance: 200. Conference concentrates on screenwriting. Held in hotel and university facilities in Providence, RI. Panels focus on aspects of marketing work and access to markets. **Previous speakers have included:** David Bartis (senior vice president of NBC), Ann Marie Gillen (CEO of Revelations Entertainment) and Paul Mason (senior vice president of Viacom).
Costs: $195 to $395, "depending on the track they take."
Accommodations: "Conference discounts are available for meals, lodging and travel." Information on overnight accommodation, including a list of area hotels, is posted on the website.
Additional Information: Offers onsite mentoring with submission prior to conference. Also offers a screenplay competition. Deadline in May. Send SASE for additional contest information (ATTN: Competition Director). Brochures available via SASE, fax or e-mail. "The host city of Providence, RI, was listed as a 'Renaissance City' by USA Today and is home to leading arts schools and an Ivy League university."

N: NEW ENGLAND WRITERS CONFERENCE, Box 483, Windsor VT 05089-0483. (802)674-2315. Fax: (802)674-5503. E-mail: newvtpoet@aol.com. Website: www.hometown.aol.com/newvtpoet/myhomepage/profile/html. **Contact:** Dr. Frank and Susan Anthony, co-directors. Estab. 1986. Annually. Conference held July 22, 2000. Conference duration: 1 day. Average attendance: 120. Held at The Grace-Outreach building 1 mile from Dartmouth campus. 2000 theme "Writing Without Walls." Panels of interest: "Agents," children's publishing, fiction and poetry. **Previous agents/speakers have included:** Upton Brady (Brady Literary Management); Christine Japely, editor (*Curious Rooms*); Anna Panunto , poetry reviewer (*Poets Podium*); John Kenneth Galbraith, keynote. Agents will be speaking and available for meetings with attendees.
Costs: $10 (includes workshop sessions, open readings, light refreshments, writer's panels and door prizes).
Accommodations: "Hotel list can be made available. There are many in the area."
Additional Information: "This, our twelfth conference, continues our attempt to have a truly affordable writers conference that has as much as most 3-4 day events." Brochures available for SASE or on website. Inquiries by e-mail and fax OK.

N: THE PERSPECTIVES IN CHILDREN'S LITERATURE CONFERENCE, 226 Furcolo Hall, School of Education, U-Mass, Amherst MA 01003-3035. E-mail: childlit@educ.umass.edu. **Contact:** Sanah Cisse and Stacy Frazer,

Meeting agents at conferences: how to get your foot in the door

"I just sold a book from that conference," says literary agent Meredith Bernstein referring to the annual International Women's Writing Guild's Big Apple: Meet the Agents conference. "It's a first novel by Sharon Wyse called *The Box Children*, and I absolutely flipped for it. I sent it out to a large selection of publishers, and in a little over a month and a half we had a deal with Riverhead Books."

Throughout her 18 years running the Meredith Bernstein Literary Agency, she has found attending writers' conferences a valuable way to discover potential clients. Besides the IWWG conference, Bernstein frequents conferences across the country, including the Golden Triangle Writers Guild in Beaumont, Texas, the Pacific Northwest Writers Conference in Seattle, Washington, and the Surrey Writers Conference in British Columbia. Not only does she share insights into her job as an agent and the publishing industry, but she often meets one-on-one with new writers. For any budding author, conferences provide a unique opportunity to network with agents like Bernstein.

Meredith Bernstein

With a client list that includes several Edgar winners, Agatha winner Nancy Pickard, NOW President Patricia Ireland, and Dennis Conner, author of *The America's Cup*, Bernstein says her start in the agency business was "kind of a fluke. I wanted to be a writer when I was growing up. And I actually wrote a full-length novel when I was 12—I thought I was Anne Frank reincarnated." Nevertheless, she avoided finding a job in publishing. "I thought publishing was dark and dreary. I started out being things like a story editor and a freelance reader, then worked as a scout for a feature film producer. One day I called up a literary agency and said, 'What's new?' The woman who worked for the agency said, 'I'm getting married. Do you want my job?' So, I was hired by Henry Morrison. I worked for him for five years, then left to open my own agency."

Almost as serendipitous as her introduction to the agenting world is the story of how she met her first client—and made her first sale. After being with Morrison only three months, a friend asked Bernstein to accompany her to a conference held by the IWWG. "I was full of vim and vigor, telling everybody at the conference I was an agent," says Bernstein. "I convinced the woman running the conference that I should speak on agenting—all my three months worth of knowledge. There was a woman there, Christina Baldwin, who described a book she had written, and I thought she was also Anne Frank reincarnated. I asked if I could read her book, and I fell in love with it. I only knew one publisher—a client of Henry's—so I pitched the book to him. He called me the next day, saying he wanted to buy it." That book, *One to One, Self-Understanding Through Journal Writing* (M. Evans and Co., Inc.), is still in print over 20 years later.

Since her first sale, Bernstein has continued to search conferences for new clients, claiming, "They have paid off for me." Nevertheless, the number of writers she meets forces her to be discerning about whom she chooses to represent. "At this stage in the game, I'm interested in writers who are committed to their work, have some knowledge about the publishing industry, are focused, have a clear idea of what they want to do and where they want to go with their work, and who are passionate about what they are doing."

In order to impress an agent, it's important for a writer to prepare for a conference. "Do your homework," advises Bernstein. "If you know who's going to be there, check out the books and magazines that talk about these people. Decide who is a good person to spend your time talking to." A common mistake, she says, is when writers approach agents who are inappropriate for their manuscripts. "If people line up to talk to me about military history, my eyes are going to glaze over. I'm not the right agent for that subject, and if they don't know that, they should."

Before speaking to Bernstein at a conference, a writer should know that her agency represents an even split of fiction and nonfiction. "The fiction has traditionally been a lot of romance—everything from the real category stuff to the single-title romance—and a lot of mysteries," she says. "I'm open to—and now selling—commercial and literary fiction, but it has to have a very strong voice. Commercial fiction should have characters you can't get out of your mind and a story that makes you want to turn the page. I'm also interested in thrillers and suspense, but not horror or science fiction. For nonfiction, I do absolutely everything across the board. I like narrative nonfiction, memoirs, parenting, health, spiritual, pet books, women's issues, humor, sports, business, you name it."

Bernstein is extremely honest with the writers she meets to avoid being swamped with submissions after a conference. "I don't want to encourage people to send me things I'm not interested in because I'm too far along in my career. I don't want to waste my time looking at things just to be nice. It's not fruitful for them and it's not fruitful for me." There are, of course, exceptions, "Sometimes I'll look at something because a person touches me in a particular way."

Writers who do make a strong impression on Bernstein should contact her after the conference through a one-page query letter with an enclosed self-addressed, stamped envelope. Because of the number of people she meets at conferences, be sure to mention that she showed interest in your manuscript. "If you talk to 60 people for 5 minutes at a time, it's hard to remember each one." Nevertheless, she admits, "If the person says, 'I'm sitting with a deal from a publisher. Would you handle it?' I might remember that."

For writers who aren't able to attended conferences, Bernstein is always open to receiving written queries. Still, she believes an important part of her job is meeting with writers and dispelling their fears about agents. "Being a presence at conferences gives writers the opportunity to see who you are. A lot of writers have a picture of agents as these people who live in an ivory tower or who are unapproachable. I like to show up at a conference and make people feel like of course they can write to me. But the most important thing is for them to realize that we are approachable."

—*Donya Dickerson*

coordinators. Estab. 1970. Annually. Conference held April 8, 2000. Conference duration: 1 day. Average attendance: 500. Conference focuses on various aspects of children's writing and illustration. Held at the University of Massachusetts School of Management. **Agents/speakers attending include:** Stephanie Owen-Lurie, Norma Simon, Barry Moser, Nancy Hope Wilson, James Ransome, Pat Mora. Agents will be speaking and available for meetings with attendees.
Costs: $50-55 (includes light breakfast, lunch, freebies, snacks). For an additional fee, attendees can earn academic credit.
Additional Information: "During lunch authors, writers, editors are assigned to a table giving participants an opportunity to converse, share experiences." Brochures available for SASE. Inquiries by e-mail and fax OK.

N: PUBLISH & PROSPER IN 2000, ASJA 1501 Broadway, Suite 302, New York NY 10036. (212)997-0947. Fax: (212)768-7414. E-mail: staff@asja.org. Website: www.asja.org. **Contact:** Alexandra Owens, executive director. Estab. 1971. Annually. Conference held in spring. Conference duration: 1 day. Average attendance: 500. Nonfiction. Held at a hotel in New York. For 1999 panels included "Freelancing for Magazines," "Techniques For Narrative Nonfiction," "Carving a Niche."
Costs: $195 (includes lunch).
Accommodations: "The hotel holding our conference always blocks out discounted rooms for attendees."
Additional Information: Brochures available in March. Inquiries by e-mail and fax OK.

☑ SOCIETY OF CHILDREN'S BOOK WRITERS & ILLUSTRATORS CONFERENCE/HOFSTRA CHILDREN'S LITERATURE CONFERENCE, Hofstra University, University College of Continuing Education, Republic Hall, Hempstead NY 11549-1022. (516)463-5016. Fax: (516)463-4833. E-mail: DCEKAH@Hofstra.edu. **Contact:** Kenneth Henwood. Estab. 1985. Annual. Conference to be held April 15, 2000. Average attendance: 150. Conference to encourage good writing for children. "Purpose is to bring together various professional groups—writers, illustrators, librarians, teachers—who are interested in writing for children. Each year we organize the program around a theme. Last year it was "Using Those 26 Letters." The conference takes place at the Student Center Building of Hofstra University, located in Hempstead, Long Island. "We have two general sessions, an editorial panel and five break-out groups held in rooms in the Center or nearby classrooms." **Previous agents/speakers have included:** Paula Danziger and Ann M. Martin, and 2 children's book editors critiqued randomly selected first-manuscript pages submitted by registrants.
Cost: $60 (previous year) for SCBWI members; $65 for nonmembers. Lunch included.
Additional Information: Special interest groups are offered in Submission Procedures, Fiction, Nonfiction, Writing Picture Books and Illustrating Picture Books.

☑ STATE OF MAINE WRITERS' CONFERENCE, 18 Hill Rd., Belmont MA 02478-4303. Co-chairs: June A. Knowles and Mary E. Pitts. Estab. 1941. Annual. Conference held August 15-18, 1999. Conference duration: 4 days. Average attendance: 50. "We try to present a balanced as well as eclectic conference. In addition to time and attention given to poetry, we also have children's literature, mystery writing, travel, novels/fiction, nonfiction, and other issues of interest to writers. Our speakers are publishers, editors, writers and other professionals. Our concentration is, by intention, a general view of writing to publish. We are located in Ocean Park, a small seashore village 14 miles south of Portland. Ours is a summer assembly center with many buildings from the Victorian Age. The conference meets in Porter Hall, one of the assembly buildings which is listed on the National Register of Historic Places. **Previous agents/speakers have included:** Lewis Turco, Amy MacDonald, Wesley McNair, Jeffrey Aronson, John N. Cole, Betsy Sholl, John Tagliabue, Christopher Keane and many others. We usually have about 10 guest presenters a year." Agents will be speaking, leading workshops and available for meetings with attendees.
Costs: $90 includes the conference banquet; if registering after August 10, $100. There is a reduced fee, $45, for students ages 21 and under. The fee does not include housing or meals which must be arranged separately by the conferees.
Accommodations: An accommodations list is available. "We are in a summer resort area and motels, guest houses and restaurants abound."
Additional Information: "We have about 9 contests on various genres. An announcement is available in the spring. The prizes, all modest, are awarded at the end of the conference and only to those who are registered." Send SASE for program available in May.

TEA WITH ELEANOR ROOSEVELT, International Women's Writing Guild, P.O. Box 810, Gracie Station, New York NY 10028-0082. (212)737-7536. Fax: (212)737-9469. E-mail: iwwg@iwwg.com. Website: www.IWWG.com. Executive Director: Hannelore Hahn. Estab. 1980. Annual conference held March 25, 2000. Average attendance: 50. Held at the Eleanor Roosevelt Center at Val-Kill in Hyde Park, NY. Two hours from New York City in the Hudson Valley.
Costs: $65 with lunch included.
Additional Information: Brochure/guidelines available for SASE. Inquiries by e-mail and fax OK.

VASSAR COLLEGE CHILDREN'S BOOK INSTITUTE OF PUBLISHING AND WRITING, (formerly Vassar College Institute of Publishing and Writing: Children's Books in the Marketplace), Vassar College, Box 300, Poughkeepsie NY 12604-0009. (914)437-5903. Fax: (914)437-7209. E-mail: mabruno@vassar.edu. Website: www.vassar.edu. Associate Director of College Relations: Maryann Bruno. Estab. 1983. Annual. Conference held mid-June. Conference

duration: 1 week. Average attendance: 30. Writing and publishing children's fiction and nonfiction. The conference is held at Vassar College, a 1,000-acre campus located in the mid-Hudson valley. The campus is self-contained, with residence halls, dining facilities, and classroom and meeting facilities. Vassar is located 90 miles north of New York City, and is accessible by car, train and air. Participants have use of Vassar's athletic facilities, including swimming, squash, tennis and jogging. Vassar is known for the beauty of its campus. The Institute is directed by author/editor Jean Marzollo and features top working professionals from the field of publishing. Agents will be speaking.
Costs: $900, includes full tuition, room and three meals a day.
Accommodations: Special conference attendee accommodations are in campus residence halls.
Additional Information: Writers may submit a 10-page sample of their writing for critique, which occurs during the week of the conference. Artists' portfolios are reviewed individually. Conference brochures/guidelines are available upon request. Inquiries by e-mail OK.

WESLEYAN WRITERS CONFERENCE, Wesleyan University, Middletown CT 06459. (860)685-3604. Fax: (860)347-3996. E-mail: agreene@wesleyan.edu. Website: www.wesleyan.edu/writing/conferen.html. Director: Anne Greene. Estab. 1956. Annual. Conference held the last week in June. Average attendance: 100. For fiction techniques, novel, short story, poetry, screenwriting, nonfiction, literary journalism, memoir. The conference is held on the campus of Wesleyan University, in the hills overlooking the Connecticut River. Meals and lodging are provided on campus. Features readings of new fiction, guest lectures on a range of topics including publishing and daily seminars. "Both new and experienced writers are welcome."
Costs: In 1999, day rate $680 (including meals); boarding students' rate $795 (including meals and room for 5 nights).
Accommodations: "Participants can fly to Hartford or take Amtrak to Meriden, CT. We are happy to help participants make travel arrangements." Overnight participants stay on campus.
Additional Information: Manuscript critiques are available as part of the program but are not required. Participants may attend seminars in several different genres. Scholarships and teaching fellowships are available, including the Jakobson awards for new writers and the Jon Davidoff Scholarships for journalists. Inquiries by e-mail and fax OK.

☑ **WRITERS RETREAT WORKSHOP**, % Write It/Sell It, P.O. Box 139, South Lancaster MA 01561-0139. Phone/fax: (978)368-0287 and (918)583-1471. E-mail: wrwwisi@aol.com. Website: www.Channel1.com/WISI. Director: Gail Provost Stockwell. Assistant Director: Lance Stockwell. Workshop Instructor, Carol Dougherty. Editor-in-Residence, Lorin Oberweger. Estab. 1987. May 26-June 4, 2000 workshop held at Marydale Retreat Center in Erlanger, KY (just south of Cincinnati, OH). Workshop duration: 10 days. Average attendance: 30. Focus on novels in progress. All genres. "The Writers Retreat Workshop is an intensive, personalized learning experience for small groups of serious-minded writers. Founded by the late Gary Provost, one of the country's leading writing instructors, and his wife Gail, an award-winning author, the WRW is a challenging and enriching adventure. The goal of the WRW staff is for students to leave with a clear understanding of the marketplace and how to craft their novels for publication. Through step-by-step classes, diagnostic sessions, editorial conferences, one-on-one brainstorming sessions with staff mentors, consultations with guests in residence (agents and editors), and informal 'shop talk' gatherings, in the heart of a supportive and spirited community of fellow writers, students make remarkable leaps in their storytelling, editing, and marketing skills."
Previous agents/speakers have included: Donald Maass (Donald Maass Literary Agency), Jim Hornfischer (The Literary Group, Int'l).
Costs: Costs (discount for past participants) $1,620 for 10 days which includes all food and lodging, tuition and private consultations. The Marydale Retreat Center is 5 miles from the Cincinnati airport and offers shuttle services.
Additional Information: Participants are selected based upon the appropriateness of this program for the applicant's specific writing project. Participants are asked to submit a brief overview before the workshop and are given assignments and ongoing feedback during the 10-day workshop. Brochures/guidelines are available for SASE, by calling (800)642-2494, or by e-mail request (wrwwisi@aol.com).

Midatlantic (DC, DE, MD, NJ, PA)

☑ **THE COLLEGE OF NEW JERSEY WRITERS' CONFERENCE**, English Dept., The College of New Jersey, P.O. Box 7718, Ewing NJ 08628-0718. (609)771-3254. Fax: (609)771-3345. E-mail: write@tcnj.edu. Director: Jean Hollander. Estab. 1980. Annual. Conference held April 4, 2000. Conference duration: 9 a.m. to 10 p.m. Average attendance: 600-1,000. "Conference concentrates on fiction (the largest number of participants), poetry, children's literature, play and screenwriting, magazine and newspaper journalism, overcoming writer's block, nonfiction and memoir writing. Conference is held at the student center at the college in two auditoriums and workshop rooms; also Kendall Theatre on campus." We focus on various genres: romance, detective, mystery, TV writing, etc. Topics have included "How to Get Happily Published," "How to Get an Agent" and "Earning a Living as a Writer." The conference usually presents twenty or so authors, editors and agents, plus two featured speakers. **Previous agents/speakers have included:** Arthur Miller, Saul Bellow, Toni Morrison, Joyce Carol Oates, Erica Jong and Alice Walker. Last year's evening presentation featured keynote speaker John Updike. Agents will be speaking and available for meetings with attendees.
Costs: General registration $45 for entire day, plus $8 for evening presentation. Lower rates for students.
Additional Information: Brochures/guidelines available.

N̄ MID-ATLANTIC MYSTERY BOOK FAIR & CONVENTION, Detecto Mysterioso Books at Society Hill Playhouse, 507 S. Eighth St., Philadelphia PA 19147-1325. (215)923-0211. Fax: (215)923-1789. E-mail: shp@erols.com. Website: www.erols.com/shp. **Contact:** Deen Kogan, chairperson. Estab. 1991. Annual. Convention held October 13-15, 2000. Average attendance: 450-500. Focus is on mystery, suspense, thriller, true crime novels. "an examination of the genre from many points of view." **Previous agents/speakers have included:** Lawrence Block, Jeremiah Healy, Neil Albert, Michael Connelly, Paul Levine, Eileen Dreyer, Earl Emerson, Wendy Hornsby. Agents will be speaking and available for informal meetings with attendees.
Costs: $125 registration fee.
Accommodations: Attendees must make their own transportation arrangements. Special room rate available at convention hotel.
Additional Information: "The Bookroom is a focal point of the convention. Twenty-five specialty dealers are expected to exhibit and collectables range from hot-off-the-press bestsellers to 1930's pulp; from fine editions to reading copies. Conference brochures/guidelines are available by mail or telephone. Inquiries by e-mail and fax OK."

N̄ NEW JERSEY ROMANCE WRITERS PUT YOUR HEART IN A BOOK CONFERENCE, P.O. Box 513, Plainsboro NJ 08536. (215)348-5948. E-mail: CBMATTERA@aol.com. Website: www.geocities.com/SoHo/Gallery/7019. President: Christine Bush Mattera. Estab. 1984. Annual. Conference held October 6-8, 2000. Average attendance: 400. Conference concentrating on romance fiction. "Workshops offered on various topics for all writers of romance, from beginner to multi-published." Held at the Doubletree Hotel in Somerset NJ. **Agents/speakers attending include:** Susan Wiggs, Jennifer Greene, Jennifer Crusie and Shirley Hailstock (authors); and Linda Hyatt and Deidre Knight (agents). Agents will be speaking and available for meetings with attendees.
Costs: $125 (New Jersey Romance Writers members) and $145 (nonmembers).
Accommodations: Special hotel rate available for conference attendees.
Additional Information: Sponsors Put Your Heart in a Book Contest for unpublished writers and the Golden Leaf Contest for published members of RWA. Conference brochures, guidelines and membership information are available for SASE. "Appointments offered for conference attendees, both published and unpublished, with editors and/or agents in the genre." New Atlantic Independent Booksellers Association promotion available for published conference attendees.

Midsouth (NC, SC, TN, VA, WV)

✓ AMERICAN CHRISTIAN WRITERS CONFERENCES, P.O. Box 110390, Nashville TN 37222-0390. (800)21-WRITE. E-mail: regaforder@aol.com. Website: www.ECPA.ORG/ACW (includes schedule). Director: Reg Forder. Estab. 1981. Annual. Conference duration: 2 days. Average attendance: 60. Fiction, nonfiction, scriptwriting. To promote all forms of Christian writing. Conferences held throughout the year in 36 US cities. Usually located at a major hotel chain like Holiday Inn.
Costs: Approximately $149 plus meals and accommodation.
Accommodations: Special rates available at host hotel.
Additional Information: Conference brochures/guidelines are available for SASE.

✓ HIGHLAND SUMMER CONFERENCE, Box 7014, Radford University, Radford VA 24142-7014. (540)831-5366. Fax: (540)831-5004. E-mail: gedwards@runet.edu. or jasbury@runet.edu. Website: www.runet.edu/~arsc. **Contact:** JoAnn Asbury. Chair, Appalachian Studies Program: Dr. Grace Toney Edwards. Estab. 1978. Annual. Conference held in mid-June. Conference duration: 12 days. Average attendance: 25. "The HSC features one (two weeks) or two (one week each) guest leaders each year. As a rule, our leaders are well-known writers who have connections, either thematic, or personal, or both, to the Appalachian region. The genre(s) of emphasis depends upon the workshop leader(s). In the past we have had as our leaders Robert Morgan, poet, essayist, fiction writer, teacher; Richard Hague, poet, essayist, author, teacher; Maggi Vaughn, Poet Laureate of Tennessee; and Betty Smith, author, musician, songsmith, among others. The Highland Summer Conference is held at Radford University, a school of about 9,000 students. Radford is in the Blue Ridge Mountains of southwest Virginia about 45 miles south of Roanoke, VA."
Costs: "Cost is based on current Radford tuition for 3 credit hours plus an additional conference fee. On-campus meals and housing are available at additional cost. In 1999, conference tuition was $433 for in-state undergraduates, $1,075 for out-of-state undergraduates, $475 for in-state graduates, $987 for out-of-state graduates."
Accommodations: "We do not have special rate arrangements with local hotels. We do offer accommodations on the Radford University Campus in a recently refurbished residence hall. (In 1998 cost was $19-28 per night.)"

THE PUBLISHING FIELD is constantly changing! If you're still using this book and it is 2001 or later, buy the newest edition of *Guide to Literary Agents* at your favorite bookstore or order directly from Writer's Digest Books at (800)289-0963.

Additional Information: "Conference leaders typically critique work done during the two-week conference, but do not ask to have any writing submitted prior to the conference beginning." Conference brochures/guidelines are available after February for SASE. Inquiries by e-mail and fax OK.

[N] **LOST STATE WRITERS CONFERENCE**, P.O. Box 1442, Greeneville TN 37744. (423)636-6738. E-mail: tamarac@xtn.net. Website: www.loststatewriters.xtn.net. **Contact:** Tamara Chapman, director. Estab. 1998. Annually. Conference held September 2000. Conference duration: 3 days. Average attendance: 300. Fiction, nonfiction, screenwriting, writing for children, poetry. Held at The General Morgan Inn & Conference Center, am historic hotel in Greeneville TN. Panels include fiction, nonfiction, and editor and agent panel, and a Southern writers panel. **Agents/speakers attending include:** representatives from William Morris, Virginia Barber, HarperCollins and Random House. Agents will be speaking and available for meetings with attendees.
Costs: $150 (includes all workshops and meals).
Accommodations: List of area hotels on website and brochure. Cost for on-site accommodations: $69.
Additional Information: Scholarships available. Brochures available for SASE. Inquiries by e-mail OK.

[✓] **NORTH CAROLINA WRITERS' NETWORK FALL CONFERENCE**, P.O. Box 954, Carrboro NC 27510-0954. (919)967-9540. Fax: (919)929-0535. E-mail: mail@ncwriters.org. Website: www.ncwriters.org. (features "history and information about the NC Writer's Network and our programs. Also has a links page to other writing-related websites.") Executive Director: Linda Hobson. Estab. 1985. Annual. "2000 Conference will be held in Fayetteville, NC, November 10-12, 2000." Average attendance: 450. "The conference is a weekend full of workshops, panels, readings and discussion groups. We try to have a variety of genres represented. In the past we have had fiction writers, poets, journalists, editors, children's writers, young adult writers, storytellers, playwrights, screenwriters, etc. We take the conference to a different location in North Carolina each year in order to best serve our entire state. We hold the conference at a conference center with hotel rooms available." **Previous agents/speakers have included:** Christy Fletcher (Carlisle & Co.); Neal Bascomb (Carlisle & Co.); Jennifer Robinson (PMA Literary & Film Agency). Agents will be speaking and available for meetings with attendees.
Costs: "Conference cost is approximately $175-190 and includes three meals."
Accommodations: "Special conference hotel rates are obtained, but the individual makes his/her own reservations. If requested, we will help the individual find a roommate."
Additional Information: Conference brochures/guidelines are available for 2 first-class stamps or on website. Inquiries by fax or e-mail OK.

[✓] **SEWANEE WRITERS' CONFERENCE**, 310 St. Luke's Hall, Sewanee TN 37383-1000. (931)598-1141. Fax: (931)598-1145. E-mail: cpeters@sewanee.edu. Website: www.sewanee.edu/writers_conference/home.html. (includes general conference information including schedule of events). Conference Director: Wyatt Prunty. Conference Coordinator: Cheri B. Peters. Estab. 1990. Annual. Conference held July 18-30, 2000. Conference duration: 12 days. Average attendance: 110. "We offer genre-based workshops (in fiction, poetry and playwriting), not theme-based workshops. The Sewanee Writers' Conference uses the facilities of the University of the South. Physically, the University is a collection of ivy-covered Gothic-style buildings, located on the Cumberland Plateau in mid-Tennessee. We allow invited editors, publishers and agents to structure their own presentations, but there is always opportunity for questions from the audience." The 1999 faculty included Ellen Douglas, Rachel Hadas, Barry Hannah, Robert Hass, Amy Hempel, John Hollander, Andrew Hudgins, Diane Johnson, Romulus Linney, Margot Livesey, Alice McDermott, Rick Moody, Marsha Norman and Padgett Powell.
Costs: Full conference fee in 1998 (tuition, board, basic room) was $1,200; a single room costs an additional $50.
Accommodations: Complimentary chartered bus service is available, on a limited basis, on the first and last days of the conference. Participants are housed in University dormitory rooms. Motel or B&B housing is available but not abundantly so. Dormitory housing costs are included in the full conference fee.
Additional Information: "We offer each participant (excluding auditors) the opportunity for a private manuscript conference with a member of the faculty. These manuscripts are due one month before the conference begins." Conference brochures/guidelines are available, "but no SASE is necessary. The conference has available a limited number of fellowships and scholarships; these are awarded on a competitive basis."

VIRGINIA ROMANCE WRITERS CONFERENCE: Step Back in Time, Romance, History, and Crime, Virginia Romance Writers, 13 Woodlawn Terrace, Fredericksburg VA 22405-3360. Fax: (540)371-3854. E-mail: spgreen man@aol.com. Website: www.Geocities.com/SoHo/museum/2164 (includes information about Virginia Romance Writers, authors, monthly meetings, workshops, conferences, contests). Conference Coordinator: Sandra Greeman. Conference held biennially. Next conference held March 23-25, 2001 in Williamsburg VA. Average attendance: 300. Offers workshops in basic and advanced writing, history and criminology. Also offers opportunities to meet with editors and agents, networking, book signing, Holt Medallion Awards Ceremony, special guest speakers, etc. **Previous agents/speakers have included:** Damaris Rowland (Damaris Rowland Agency), Louise Peters (Brock Gannon Literary Agency), Irene Goodman (Irene Goodman Literary Agency), Mary Sue and Michael Seymour (The Seymour Agency), Lynne Whitaker (Graybill & English), Caroline Tolley (Pocket Books/Prentice Hall), Kara Cesare (Bantam) and Martha Zinberg (Harlequin). Agents will be available for meetings with attendees. Write for additional information.

Southeast (AL, AR, FL, GA, LA, MS, Puerto Rico)

☑ **ARKANSAS WRITERS' CONFERENCE**, 6817 Gingerbread, Little Rock AR 72204. (501)565-8889. Fax: (501)565-7220. E-mail: pvining@aristotle.net. Counselor: Peggy Vining. Estab. 1944. Annual. Conference held June 1-3, 2000. Average attendance: 225. Fiction, nonfiction, scriptwriting and poetry. "We have a variety of subjects related to writing—we have some general sessions, some more specific, but try to vary each year's subjects."
Costs: Registration: $10; luncheon: $13; banquet: $14, contest entry $5.
Accommodations: "We meet at a Holiday Inn, select in Little Rock." Holiday Inn has a bus to and from airport. Rooms average $62.
Additional Information: "We have 36 contest categories. Some are open only to Arkansans, most are open to all writers. Our judges are not announced before conference but are qualified, many from out of state." Conference brochures are available for SASE after February 1. "We have had 226 attending from 12 states—over 3,000 contest entries from 43 states and New Zealand, Mexico and Canada. We have a get acquainted party Thursday evening for early arrivers."

☒ **FCRW ALL-DAY WORKSHOP**, P.O. Box 8604, Jacksonville FL 32239-8604. (352)687-3902. Fax: (352)687-8097. E-mail: esinclair1@aol.com. Website: www.angelfire.com/fl/romancewriting/. **Contact:** Laura Barone, president. Estab. 1994. Annually. Conference held spring. Conference duration: 1 day. May expand to include Friday night "night owl sessions." Average attendance: 75-100. Conference focuses on romance novel writing, but is open to the general public and covers all aspects of writing a fictional novel. Held at a Holiday Inn hotel. 1999 theme was *Elements of Best-Selling Novel*. **Agents/speakers attending include:** Pattie Steele-Perkins (Steele-Perkins Literary Agency). Agents will be speaking and available for meetings with attendees.
Costs: $55 (includes workshops, welcome packets, 1 raffle ticket, continental breakfast, full buffet lunch).
Accommodations: On-site accommodations with special rates available. In 1999, cost was $55 single or double per night.
Additional Information: "We raffle critiques by published authors." Brochures available 1 month before conference date for SASE. Inquiries by e-mail and fax OK.

☑ **FLORIDA FIRST COAST WRITERS' FESTIVAL**, 1012 W. State St., Room 1166, FCCJ Downtown Campus, Jacksonville FL 32202. (904)633-8243. Fax: (904)633-8435. E-mail: kclower@fccj.org. Website: astro.fccj.org/wf/ (includes festival workshop speakers, contest information). **Contacts:** Kathy Clower and Margo Martin. Estab. 1985. Annual. 2000 Festival: May 18-20. Average attendance: 300. All areas: mainstream plus genre. Fiction, nonfiction, scriptwriting, poetry, freelancing, etc. Offers seminars on narrative structure and plotting character development. Held at Sea Turtle Inn, Atlantic Beach, FL. **Previous agents/speakers have included:** Ricia Mainhardt (Ricia Mainhardt Agency), David Hendin (DH Literary, Inc.) and Charles Lenhoff. Agents will be speaking and available for meetings with attendees.
Costs: Maximum of $145 for 2 days, with 2 meals.
Accommodations: Sea Turtle Inn, (904)249-7402, has a special festival rate.
Additional Information: Conference brochures/guidelines are available for SASE. Sponsors a contest for short fiction, poetry and novels. Novel judges are David Poyer and Lenore Hart. Entry fees: $30, novels; $10, short fiction; $5, poetry. Deadline: November 1 in each year. "We offer one-on-one sessions for attendees to speak to selected writers, editors, etc., as time permits."

☑ **FLORIDA SUNCOAST WRITERS' CONFERENCE**, University of South Florida, Division of Lifelong Learning, 4202 E. Fowler Ave., MHH-116, Tampa FL 33620-6610. (813)974-2403. Fax: (813)974-5732. E-mail: kiersty @admin.usf.edu. Directors: Steve Rubin, Ed Hirshberg and Lagretta Lenkar. Estab. 1970. Annual. Held February 3-5. Conference duration: 3 days. Average attendance: 400. Conference covers poetry, short story, novel and nonfiction, including science fiction, detective, travel writing, drama, TV scripts, photojournalism and juvenile. "We do not focus on any one particular aspect of the writing profession but instead offer a variety of writing related topics. The conference is held on the picturesque university campus fronting the bay in St. Petersburg, Florida." Features panels with agents and editors. **Previous agents/speakers have included:** Lady P.D. James, Carolyn Forche, Marge Piercy, William Styron, John Updike, Joyce Carol Oates and David Guterson.
Costs: Call for information.
Accommodations: Special rates available at area motels. "All information is contained in our brochure."
Additional Information: Participants may submit work for critiquing. Extra fee charged for this service. Conference brochures/guidelines are available November 1999. Inquiries by e-mail and fax OK.

☒ **MOONLIGHT AND MAGNOLIAS WRITER'S CONFERENCE**, 826 Canterbury Rd., Gainesville GA 30501. E-mail: bcothran23@aol.com. Website: www.georgiaromancewriters.org. Estab. 1982. President, Georgia Romance Writers: Betty Cothran. 1998 Conference Chair: Rachelle Wadsworth. Conference held 3rd weekend in September. Average attendance: 300. "Conference focuses on writing women's fiction with emphasis on romance. 1999 conference included agents and editors from major publishing houses. Workshops included: beginning writer track, general interest topics, and professional issues for the published author, plus sessions for writing for alternative markets, young adult, inspirational, multicultural and Regency. Speakers included experts in law enforcement, screenwriting and research.

Literacy raffle and advertised speaker and GRW member autographing open to the public. Published authors make up 25-30% of attendees.

Costs: Hotel $79/day, single, double, triple, quad (1999). Conference: non GRW members $135 (early registration).

Additional Information: Maggie Awards for excellence are presented to unpublished writers. The Maggie Award for published writers is limited to Region 3 members of Romance Writers of America. Proposals per guidelines must be submitted in early June. Please check with president for new dates. Published authors judge first round, category editors judge finals. Guidelines available with SASE in February or on website. Brochure available for SASE in June. Send requests with SASE to Rachelle Wadsworth.

N NEW ORLEANS POPULAR FICTION CONFERENCE, P.O. Box 740113, New Orleans LA 70174-0113. (504)391-1320. E-mail: kathisn@aol.com. Website: www.sola.org. **Contact:** Kathleen Nance, co-chair. Estab. 1994. Annual. Conference held November 2000. Conference duration: 2 days. Average attendance: 135. Popular fiction. Held at hotel conference facilities in downtown New Orleans near the French Quarter. Panels include "Craft of Writing Workshop," "Creating Suspense," "Screenwriting." **Agents/speakers attending include:** Pam Ahearn, Irene Goodman, Rob Cohen. Agents will be speaking and available for meetings with attendees.

Costs: $155 for 2 days (includes 2 lunches, cocktail reception, handouts).

Accommodations: Limited on-site rooms available at $198/night. Other accommodations available.

Additional Information: Brochures available for SASE. Inquiries by e-mail OK.

N SOUTH FLORIDA WRITERS CONFERENCE, P.O. Box 570415, Miami FL 33257-0415. (305)275-8666. Fax: (305)285-0283. E-mail: mipress@aol.com. Website: www.writerssfl.com. **Contact:** Judi Welsh, conference director. Estab. 1997. Annually. Conference held March 3-5, 2000. Conference duration: 3 days. Average attendance: 100-150. Fiction, journalism, marketing, mystery, nonfiction, autobiography/memoir, playwriting, poetry, publishing, religion/self help, romance, screenwriting, travel, songwriting, memoirs, children's writing. Held at the University of Miami campus. Workshops include "Computer Technology for Writers," "Feature Writing," "How to Write & Publish a Book," "Contracts & Writers Rights," "Query & Submissions." **Agents/speakers attending include:** Barbara Parker (author, *Suspicion of Guilt*); Judith Ivory (author, *Beast*); Lester Goran (author, *Tales from the Irish Club*). Agents will be speaking and available for meetings with attendees.

Costs: $140 before December 1, $164 after December (includes open readings, reception, Saturday night banquet, Sunday brunch, source materials).

Accommodations: Discounted hotel rooms available near the conference.

Additional Information: Brochures available for SASE. Inquiries by e-mail and fax OK.

✓ SOUTHEASTERN WRITERS CONFERENCE, 114 Gould St., St. Simons Island GA 31522. (912)638-4781. E-mail: cappy4@technonet.com. President: Cappy Hall Rearick. Estab. 1975. Annual. Conference held June 18-24, 2000. Conference duration: 1 week. Average attendance: 100 (limited to 100 participants). Concentration is on fiction, poetry and juvenile—plus nonfiction, playwriting, storytelling and genre. Site is "St. Simons Island, GA. Conference held at Epworth-by-the-Sea Conference Center—tropical setting, beaches. Each year we offer market advice, agent updates. All our instructors are professional writers presently selling in New York." **Agents/speakers attending include:** Nancy Love (Nancy Love Agency), Andrea Schneeman (North-South Books). Agents will be speaking and available for meetings with attendees.

Costs: $270. Meals.and lodging are separate.

Accommodations: Information on overnight accommodations is made available. "On-site-facilities at a remarkably low cost. Facilities are motel style of excellent quality. Other hotels are available on the island."

Additional Information: "Three manuscripts of one chapter each are allowed in three different categories." Sponsors several contests, MANY cash prizes. Brochures are available March for SASE.

WORDS & MUSIC: A LITERARY FEAST IN NEW ORLEANS, (formerly New Orleans Writers' Conference), 632 Pirates Alley, New Orleans LA 70116. (504)586-1609. Fax: (504)522-9725. E-mail: faulkhouse@aol.com. Website: www.Wordsandmusic.org or members.aol.com/faulkhouse. Conference Director: Rosemary James DeSalvo. Estab. 1989. Annual. Conference held September 22-26, 2000. Conference duration: 5 days. Average attendance: 350-400. Presenters include authors, agents, editors and publishers. **Previous agents/speakers have included:** Deborah Grosvenor (Deborah Grosvenor Literary Agency); Vicky Bijur (Vicky Bijur Agency); and Mitch Douglas (International Creative Management). Agents will be speaking and available for meetings with attendees. Write for additional information.

✓ WRITING TODAY—BIRMINGHAM∗SOUTHERN COLLEGE, Box 549003, Birmingham AL 35254. (205)226-4921. Fax: (205)226-3072. E-mail: dcwilson@bsc.edu. Website: www.bsc.edu. Director of Special Events: Martha Ross. Estab. 1978. Annual. Conference held April 7-8, 2000. Average attendance: 400-500. "This is a two-day conference with approximately 18 workshops, lectures and readings. We try to offer workshops in short fiction, novels, poetry, children's literature, magazine writing, and general information of concern to aspiring writers such as publishing, agents, markets and research. The conference is sponsored by Birmingham-Southern College and is held on the campus in classrooms and lecture halls." **1999 speakers included:** Pat Conroy, Connie May Fowler, David Sedaris, Richard North Patterson.

Costs: $120 for both days. This includes lunches, reception and morning coffee and rolls.

Accommodations: Attendees must arrange own transporation. Local hotels and motels offer special rates, but participants must make their own reservations.

Additional Information: "We usually offer a critique for interested writers. We have had poetry and short story critiques. There is an additional charge for these critiques." Sponsors the Hackney Literary Competition Awards for poetry, short story and novels. Brochures available for SASE.

Midwest (IL, IN, KY, MI, OH)

N **ANTIOCH WRITERS' WORKSHOP**, P.O. Box 494, Yellow Springs OH 45387-0494. E-mail: info@antiochwr itersworkshop.com. Website: www.antiochwritersworkshop.com. Director: Gilah Rittenhouse. Estab. 1984. Annual. Conference held August 5-12, 2000. Average attendance: 80. Workshop concentration: poetry, nonfiction and fiction. Workshop located on Antioch College campus in the Village of Yellow Springs. **Speakers/agents in 1999 included:** Alison Lurie, Edward Hower, Julia B. Levine, Ruth L. Schwartz, Mary Quattlebuam, Clint McConn and Michel Marriot. Agents will be speaking and available for meetings with attendees.

Costs: Tuition is $475—lower for local and repeat—plus meals.

Accommodations: "We pick up attendees free at the airport." Accommodations made at dorms and area hotels. Cost is $16-26/night (for dorms).

Additional Information: Offers mss critique sessions. Conference brochures/guidelines are available after March 1998 for SASE.

THE COLUMBUS WRITERS CONFERENCE, P.O. Box 20548, Columbus OH 43220. (614)451-3075. Fax: (614)451-0174. E-mail: AngelaPL28@aol.com. Director: Angela Palazzolo. Estab. 1993. Annual. Conference held in September. Average attendance: 200. "The conference covers a wide variety of fiction and nonfiction topics. Writing topics have included novel, short story, children's, young adult, science fiction, fantasy, humor, mystery, playwriting, screenwriting, personal essay, travel, humor, cookbook, technical, query letter, corporate, educational and greeting cards. Other topics for writers: finding and working with an agent, targeting markets, research, time management, obtaining grants and writers' colonies." **Previous agents/speakers have included:** Lee K. Abbott, Lore Segal, Mike Harden, Oscar Collier, Maureen F. McHugh, Ralph Keyes, Stephanie S. Tolan, Bonnie Pryor, Dennis L. McKiernan, Karen Harper, Melvin Helitzer, Susan Porter, Les Roberts, Tracey E. Dils, J. Patrick Lewis and many other professionals in the writing field.

Costs: Early registration fee is $134 for full conference (includes Friday and Saturday sessions, Friday dinner program, and Saturday continental breakfast, lunch, and afternoon refreshments); otherwise, fee is $150. Early registration fee for Saturday only is $94; otherwise, fee is $110. Friday dinner program is $30.

Additional Information: Call, write, e-mail or send fax to obtain a conference brochure, available mid-summer.

✓ CHARLENE FARIS SEMINARS FOR BEGINNERS, 895 W. Oak St., Zionsville IN 46077-1208. Phone/fax: (317)873-0738. E-mail: photobee@iserve.net. Director: Charlene Faris. Estab. 1985. Held 2 times/year in the spring and summer near Indianapolis. Conference duration: 2 days. Average attendence: 10. Fiction, nonfiction and photography. Concentration on all areas of publishing and writing, particularly marketing and working with editors.

Costs: $200, tuition only; may attend only 1 day for $100.

Accommodations: Information on overnight accommodations available.

Additional Information: Guidelines available for SASE.

GREEN RIVER WRITERS NOVELS-IN-PROGRESS WORKSHOP, 11906 Locust Rd., Middletown KY 40243-1413. (502)245-4902. E-mail: mary_odell@ntr.net. Director: Mary E. O'Dell. Estab. 1991. Annual. Conference held March 12-19, 2000. Conference duration: 1 week. Average attendance: 55. Open to persons, college age and above, who have approximately 3 chapters (60 pages) or more of a novel. Mainstream and genre novels handled by individual instructors. Short fiction collections welcome. "Each novelist instructor works with a small group (5-7 people) for five days; then agents/editors are there for panels and appointments on the weekend." Site is The University of Louisville's Shelby Campus, suburban setting, graduate dorm housing (private rooms available with shared bath for each 2 rooms). "Meetings and classes held in nearby classroom building. Grounds available for walking, etc. Lovely setting, restaurants and shopping available nearby. Participants carpool to restaurants, etc. This year we are covering mystery, fantasy, mainstream/literary, suspense, historical."

VISIT THE WRITER'S DIGEST WEBSITE at www.writersdigest.com for hot new markets, daily market updates, writers' guidelines and much more.

Costs: Tuition—$375, housing $22 per night private, $18 shared. Does not include meals.
Accommodations: "We do meet participants' planes and see that participants without cars have transportation to meals, etc. If participants would rather stay in hotel, we will make that information available."
Additional Information: Participants send 60 pages/3 chapters with synopsis and $25 reading fee which applies to tuition. Deadline will be in late January. Conference brochures/guidelines are available for SASE.

☑ MIDLAND WRITERS CONFERENCE, Grace A. Dow Memorial Library, 1710 W. St. Andrews, Midland MI 48640-2698. (517)837-3442. Fax: (517)837-3468. E-mail: kred@vlc.lib.mi.us. Website: www.gracedowlibrary.org. Conference Chair: Katherine Redwine. Estab. 1980. Annual. Conference held June 10, 2000. Average attendance: 100. Fiction, nonfiction, children's and poetry. "The Conference is composed of a well-known keynote speaker and six workshops on a variety of subjects including poetry, children's writing, freelancing, agents, etc. The attendees are both published and unpublished authors. The Conference is held at the Grace A. Dow Memorial Library in the auditorium and conference rooms. Keynoters in the past have included Dave Barry, Pat Conroy, Kurt Vonnegut, Roger Ebert and Peggy Noonan." Agents will be speaking.
Costs: Adult - $60; students, senior citizens and handicapped—$50. A box lunch is available. Costs are approximate until plans for upcoming conference are finalized.
Accommodations: A list of area hotels is available.
Additional Information: Conference brochures/guidelines are mailed mid-April. Call or write to be put on mailing list. Inquiries by e-mail and fax OK.

MIDWEST WRITERS' CONFERENCE, 6000 Frank Ave. NW, Canton OH 44720-7599. (330)499-9600. Fax: (330)494-6121. E-mail: Druhe@Stark.Kent.Edu. Website: www.kent.state.edu. Conference Director: Debbie Ruhe. Estab. 1968. Annual. Conference held October 6 and 7, 2000. Conference duration: 2 days. Average attendance: 350. "The conference provides an atmosphere in which aspiring writers can meet with and learn from experienced and established writers through lectures, workshops, competitive contest, personal interviews and informal group discussions. The areas of concentration include fiction, nonfiction, juvenile literature and poetry. The Midwest Writers' Conference is held at Kent State University Stark Campus in Canton, Ohio." **Agents/speakers attending include:** Rita Dove, Jim Daniels, Steve Lane, Donna Downing, Tom Chierella, David Giffels, Mary Ann Weidt and Zee Edgell.
Costs: $95 includes Friday workshops, keynote address, Saturday workshops, box luncheon and manuscript entry fee (limited to two submissions); $70 for contest only (includes two manuscripts).
Accommodations: Arrangements are made with a local hotel which is near Kent Stark and offers a special reduced rate for conference attendees. Conferees must make their own reservations 3 weeks before the conference to be guaranteed this special conference rate.
Additional Information: Each manuscript entered in the contest will receive a critique. If the manuscript is selected for final judging, it will receive an additional critique from the final judge. Conference attendees are not required to submit manuscripts to the writing contest. Manuscript deadline is early August. For contest: A maximum of 1 entry for each category is permitted. Entries must be typed on 8½ × 11 paper, double-spaced. A separate page must accompany each entry bearing the author's name, address, phone, category and title of the work. Entries are not to exceed 3,000 words in length. Work must be original, unpublished and not a winner in any contest at the time of entry. Conference brochures and guidelines are available after June 2000 for SASE. Inquiries by e-mail and fax OK.

OAKLAND UNIVERSITY WRITERS' CONFERENCE, 231 Varner Hall, Rochester MI 48309-4401. (248)370-3125. Fax: (248)370-4280. E-mail: gjboddy@oakland.edu. Program Director: Gloria J. Boddy, program director. Estab. 1961. Annual. Conference held in October 13-14, 2000. Average attendance: 400. Held at Oakland University: Oakland Center: Vandenburg Hall and O'Dowd Hall. Each annual conference covers all aspects and types of writing in 36 concurrent workshops on Saturday. "It is a conference for beginning and established writers. It provides an opportunity to exchange ideas and perfect writing skills by meeting with agents, editors and successful writers." Major writers from various genres are speakers for the Saturday conference and luncheon program. Individual critiques and hands-on writing workshops are conducted Friday. Areas: nonfiction, young adult fiction, poetry, short fiction, chapbooks, magazine fiction, essay. Keynote speaker in 1999: Judith Guest, author of *Ordinary People*. **Previous agents/speakers have included:** Faye Bender, agent; Lyn Cryderman and Peter Blocksom, editors. Agents will be speaking and available for meetings with attendees.
Costs: 1999: Conference registration: $75; lunch, $12; individual ms, $48; writing workshop, $38.
Accommodations: Hotel list is available.
Additional Information: Conference brochure/guidelines available after September 1998 for SASE. Inquiries by e-mail and fax OK.

OF DARK & STORMY NIGHTS, Mystery Writers of America—Midwest Chapter, P.O. Box 1944, Muncie IN 47308-1944. (765)288-7402. E-mail: spurgeonmwa@juno.com. Workshop Director: W.W. Spurgeon. Estab. 1982. Annual. Workshop held June 10, 2000. Workshop duration: 1 day. Average attendance: 200. Fiction, nonfiction and scriptwriting. Dedicated to "writing *mystery* fiction and crime-related nonfiction. Workshops and panels presented on plotting, dialogue, promotion, writers' groups, dealing with agents, synopsis and manuscript presentation, plus various technical aspects of crime and mystery." Site is Holiday Inn, Rolling Meadows IL (suburban Chicago). **Previous agents/speakers have included:** Barbara Gislason and Andrew Zack, agents; Tom Clark, editor; Michael Black, Ann Blaine,

Barbara D'Amato, Sara Hoskinson Frommer, writers. "Our agents speak, do critiques and schmooze with those attending."
Costs: $125 for MWA members; $150 for non-members; $50 extra for ms critique.
Accommodations: Easily accessible by car or train (from Chicago) Holiday Inn, Rolling Meadows $89 per night plus tax; free airport bus (Chicago O'Hare) and previously arranged rides from train.
Additional Information: "We accept manuscripts for critique (first 30 pages maximum); $40 cost. Writers meet with critics during workshop for one-on-one discussions." Brochures available for SASE after February 1.

☑ **WRITERS' RETREAT WORKSHOP**, 2507 S. Boston Place, Tulsa OK 74114. Phone/fax: (918)583-1471. E-mail: wrwwisi@aol.com. Website: www.channel1.com/wisi. Director: Gail Provost Stockwell. Estab. 1987. Annual. Conference held May 26-June 4, 2000. Conference duration: 10 days. Average attendance: 30. Novels-in-progress, all genres. Held at Marydale Retreat Center in northern KY. "Teaches a proven step-by-step process for developing and completing a novel for publication, developed originally by the late Gary Provost. The practical application of lessons learned in classes, combined with continual private consultations with staff members, guarantees dramatic improvement in craft, writing technique and self-editing skills." **Agents/speakers attending include:** Donald Maass (Donald Maass Literary Agency), Elizabeth Lyon (author/editor). Agents will be speaking and available for meetings with attendees.
Costs: $1,620, new students; $1,460 returning students (includes lodging, meals, consultations and course materials.)
Accommodations: Marydale Retreat Center provides complimentary shuttle services between Cincinnati Airport and the center. "Varying agents/agencies have been represented over the years."

North Central (IA, MN, NE, ND, SD, WI)

☑ **GREAT LAKES WRITER'S WORKSHOP**, Alverno College, 3400 S. 43rd St., P.O. Box 343922, Milwaukee WI 53234-3922. (414)382-6176. Fax: (414)382-6332. Assistant Director: Cindy Jackson, Professional and Community Education. Estab. 1985. Annual. Workshop held June 18-19, 1999. Average attendance: 150. "Workshop focuses on a variety of subjects including fiction, writing for magazines, freelance writing, writing for children, poetry, marketing, etc. Participants may select individual workshops or opt to attend the entire weekend session. The workshop is held in Milwaukee, WI at Alverno College."
Costs: In 1999, cost was $80 for entire program.
Accommodations: Attendees must make their own travel arrangments. Accommodations are available on campus; rooms are in residence halls and are not air-conditioned. Cost in 1999 was $25 for single, $20 per person for double. There are also hotels in the surrounding area. Call (414)382-6040 for information regarding overnight accommodations.
Additional Information: "Some workshop instructors may provide critiques, but this changes depending upon the workshop and speaker. This would be indicated in the workshop brochure." Brochures are available for SASE after March. Inquiries by fax OK.

SINIPEE WRITERS' WORKSHOP, Loras College, 1450 Alta Vista, Dubuque IA 52004-0178. (319)588-7139. Fax: (319)588-7964. E-mail: lcrosset@loras.edu. Website: www.loras.edu. Director of Continuing Education: Linda Crossett. Director Emeritus: John Tigges. Estab. 1985. Annual conference held April 29, 2000. Average attendance: 50-75. To promote "primarily fiction although we do include a poet and a nonfiction writer on each program. The two mentioned areas are treated in such a way that fiction writers can learn new ways to expand their abilities and writing techniques." The workshop is held on the campus of Loras College in Dubuque. "This campus holds a unique atmosphere and everyone seems to love the relaxed and restful mood it inspires. This in turn carries over to the workshop, and friendships are made that last in addition to learning and experiencing what other writers have gone through to attain success in their chosen field." **Previous agents/speakers have included:** Christine DeSmet, screenwriter; Jerry Apps, fiction writer; Bill Pauley, poet; Dorothy Prell, publisher. New name for the Writing Prizes: The John Tigges Writing Prize for Short Fiction, Nonfiction and Poetry.
Costs: $60 early registration/$65 at the door. Includes all handouts, necessary materials for the workshop, coffee/snack break, lunch, drinks and snacks at autograph party following workshop.
Accommodations: Information is available for out-of-town participants, concerning motels, etc., even though the workshop is 1-day long.
Additional Information: Conference brochures/guidelines are available February/March 2000 for SASE. Limit 1,500 words (fiction and nonfiction), 40 lines (poetry). 1st prize in all 3 categories: $100 plus publication in an area newspaper or magazine; 2nd prize in both categories: $50; 3rd prize in both categories: $25. Written critique service available for contest entries, $15 extra.

UNIVERSITY OF WISCONSIN AT MADISON WRITERS INSTITUTE, 610 Langdon St., Madison WI 53703. (608)262-3447. Fax: (608)265-2475. Website: www.dcs.wisc.edu/lsa. Director: Christine DeSmet. Estab. 1990. Annual. Conference held August 3-4, 2000. Average attendance: 175. Conference held at University of Wisconsin at Madison. Themes: fiction and nonfiction. Guest speakers are published authors, editors and agents.
Costs: Approximately $185 for 2 days; critique fees.
Accommodations: Info on accommodations sent with registration confirmation. Critiques available. Conference brochures/guidelines are available for SASE.

☑ **WISCONSIN REGIONAL WRITERS' ASSOCIATION INC. CONFERENCES**, Wisconsin Regional Writers' Assn., 510 W. Sunset Ave., Appleton WI 54911-1139. (920)734-3724. E-mail: wrwa@lakefield.net. Website: www.inkwells.net/wrwa. President: Patricia Dunson Boverhuis. Estab. 1948. Conferences held in May and September. Conference duration: 1-2 days. Presenters include authors, agents, editors and publishers. Write for additional information.

South Central (CO, KS, MO, NM, OK, TX)

☑ **ASPEN SUMMER WORDS**, (formerly Aspen Writers' Conference), Aspen Writers' Foundation, Box 7726, Aspen CO 81612. (800)925-2526. Fax (970)920-5700. E-mail: aspenwrite@aol.com. Executive Director: Julie Comins. Estab. 1975. Annual. Conference held for 1 week during summer. Average attendance: 75. Retreat for fiction, poetry, nonfiction and children's literature. Festival includes readings, networking opportunities, talks with agents, editors and publishers. **1999 speakers have included:** Ron Carlson, fiction writer; Mary Crow, poet; Craig Nelson, agent; Pam Houston and other guest speakers.
Costs: $495/full tuition; $150/lecture pass (1998)
Accommodations Free shuttle to/from airport and around town. Information on overnight accommodations available. On-campus housing; (800) number for reservations. Rates for 1999: on-campus $55/night double; $110/night single; off-campus rates vary.
Additional Information: Manuscripts to be submitted for review by faculty prior to conference. Conference brochures are available for SASE.

☑ **AUSTIN WRITERS' LEAGUE WORKSHOPS/CONFERENCES/CLASSES**, 1501 W. Fifth St., Suite E-2, Austin TX 78703. (512)499-8914. Fax: (512)499-0441. E-mail: awl@writersleague.org. Website: www.writersleague.org. Executive Director: Jim Bob McMillan. Estab. 1982. Programs ongoing through the year. Duration: varies according to program. Average attendance from 15 to 200. To promote "all genres, fiction and nonfiction, poetry, writing for children, screenwriting, playwriting, legal and tax information for writers, also writing workshops for children and youth." Programs held at AWL Resource Center/Library, other sites in Austin and Texas. Topics include: finding and working with agents and publishers; writing and marketing short fiction; dialogue; characterization; voice; research; basic and advanced fiction writing/focus on the novel; business of writing; also workshops for genres. **Previous agents/speakers have included:** Dwight Swain, Natalie Goldberg, David Lindsey, Shelby Hearon, Gabriele Rico, Benjamin Saenz, Rosellen Brown, Sandra Scofield, Reginald Gibbons, Anne Lamott, Sterling Lord and Sue Grafton. In July the League holds its annual Agents! Agents! Agents! Conference provides writers with the opportunity to meet top agents from New York and the West Coast.
Costs: Varies from free to $185, depending on program. Most classes, $20-50; workshops $35-75; conferences: $125-185.
Accommodations: Special rates given at some hotels for program participants.
Additional Information: Critique sessions offered at some programs. Individual presenters determine critique requirements. Those requirements are then made available through Austin Writers' League office and in workshop promotion. Contests and awards programs are offered separately. Brochures/guidelines are available on request.

☑ **FRONTIERS IN WRITING**, P.O. Box 19303, Amarillo TX 79114. (806)354-2305. Fax: (806)354-2536. E-mail: cliff@nts-online.net. Website: www.divinejustice.com. Estab. 1980. Annual. Conference held June 2000. Duration: 1 day. Average attendance: 100. Nonfiction, poetry and fiction (including mystery, romance, science fiction and fantasy). **Agents/speakers for 1999 included:** Ann Crispin (science fiction), Don Maass (New York agent), Cherise Grant (Simon & Schuster editor), Melanie Rigney (Writer's Digest editor).
Costs: 1999 conference: $80 Members; $115 Non-members ($20 for membership). (Includes Friday night dinner, Saturday breakfast, lunch and beverages—lodging and transportation separate).
Accommodations: Special conference room rate.
Additional information: Further information available in brochure and on website. Sponsors a contest. Deadline: April 1, 2000. Guidelines available for SASE or on website. Writers may request information via fax. Brochures and guidelines available for SASE as of December 1999.

☒ **HEARTLAND WRITERS CONFERENCE**, P.O. Box 652. Kennett MO 63857. (573)297-3325. Fax: (573)297-3352. E-mail: hwg@heartlandwriters.org. Website: www.heartlandwriters.org. **Contact:** Pat Dunlap, attendee liaison. Estab. 1990. Biennial (even years). Conference held June 8-10, 2000. Conference duration: 3 days. Average attendance: 160. Popular fiction (all genres), nonfiction, children's, screenwriting, poetry. Held at the Best Western Coach House Inn in Sikeston MO. Panels for 1998 included "Finding the Time and Will to Write" and "Putting Reality into Your

Genre Fiction." **Previous agents/speakers attending include:** Alice Orr, Jennifer Jackson, Ricia Mainhardt, Christy Fletcher. Agents will be speaking and available for meetings with attendees.

Costs: In 1998: $175 for advance registration, $185 for general registration (includes lunch on Friday and Saturday, awards banquet Saturday, hospitality room and get-acquainted mixer Thursday night.

Accommodations: Blocks of rooms are available at special conference rate at conference venue and at two nearby motels. Cost: $45/night (1998 price).

Additional Information: Brochures available in January 2000. Inquiries by e-mail and fax OK.

☑ **HOUSTON WRITERS CONFERENCE**, P.O. Box 742683, Houston TX 77274-2683. (713)804-3281. E-mail: houwrites@aol.com. Website: www.houstonwrites.com. (includes information about the Houston Writers Conference and the Houston Writers League, which sponsors the conference). **Contact:** Ted Simmons. Estab. 1997. Annual. Conference held March 16-19, 2000. Conference duration: 2½ days. Average attendance: 250. For poetry, fiction, nonfiction, children's, mystery, romance, science fiction, screenwriting. **Previous agents/speakers have included:** Kimberley Cameron (Reece Halsey Agency); Denise Marcil (Denise Marcil Literary Agency); David Hale Smith (DHS Literary); Mitchell Waters (Curtis Brown, Ltd.); Marcie Wright (The Wright Concept). Agents will be speaking and available for meetings with attendees. Write for additional information or request via e-mail.

Costs: Early Bird Conference Registration is $225, and the deadline is December 1, 1999. December 2-February 1, 2000 registration is $240. After February 2, 2001, registration is $255. Houston Marriott Westside is hosting; room rate is $65 per night. Conference fee includes Thursday evening icebreaker/cocktail party, Friday and Saturday lunches, Saturday evening Awards banquet, and Sunday morning Agent/Editor Q&A Breakfast. Brochures available.

☑ **NATIONAL WRITERS ASSOCIATION FOUNDATION CONFERENCE**, 3140 S. Peoria, #295, Aurora CO 80014. (303)841-0246. Fax: (303)751-8593. E-mail address: sandywriter@aol.com. Website: www.nationalwriters.com. Executive Director: Sandy Whelchel. Estab. 1926. Annual. Conference held in Denver, CO. Conference held in June. Conference duration: 3 days. Average attendance: 200-300. General writing, marketing.

Costs: $200 (approx.).

Additional Information: Awards for previous contests will be presented at the conference. Conference brochures/ guidelines are available for SASE.

THE NEW LETTERS WEEKEND WRITERS CONFERENCE, University of Missouri-Kansas City, College of Arts and Sciences Continuing Ed. Division, 215 4825 Troost Bldg., 5100 Rockhill Rd., Kansas City MO 64110-2499. (816)235-2736. Fax: (816)235-5279. E-mail: mckinleym@umkc.edu. Estab. in the mid-70s as The Longboat Key Writers Conference. Annual. Runs during June. Conference duration is 3 days. Average attendance: 75. Nonfiction, scriptwriting. "The New Letters Weekend Writers Conference brings together talented writers in many genres for lectures, seminars, readings, workshops and individual conferences. The emphasis is on craft and the creative process in poetry, fiction, screenwriting, playwriting and journalism; but the program also deals with matters of psychology, publications and marketing. The conference is appropriate for both advanced and beginning writers. The conference meets at the beautiful Diastole conference center of The University of Missouri-Kansas City."

Costs: Several options are available. Participants may choose to attend as a non-credit student or they may attend for 1-3 hours of college credit from the University of Missouri-Kansas City. Conference registration includes continental breakfasts, Saturday dinner and Sunday lunch. For complete information, contact the University of Missouri-Kansas City.

Accommodations: Registrants are responsible for their own transportation, but information on area accommodations is made available.

Additional Information: Those registering for college credit are required to submit a ms in advance. Ms reading and critique is included in the credit fee. Those attending the conference for non-credit also have the option of having their ms critiqued for an additional fee. Conference brochures/guidelines are available for SASE after March. Inquiries by e-mail and fax OK.

:N: **PIKES PEAK WRITERS CONFERENCE**, 5550 North Union Blvd., Colorado Springs CO 80918. E-mail: ppwc@poboxes.com. Website: www.poboxes.com/ppwc. Estab. 1994. Annual. Conference held April 28-30, 2000; April 27-29, 2001. Conference duration: Friday 11:30 am to Sunday 2 pm. Average attendance: 350-400. Commercial fiction. Held at the Marriott Hotel. "Workshops, presentations and panels focus on writing and publishing genre fiction— romance, scifi and fantasy, suspense thrillers, action adventure, mysteries. **Agents/speakers attending include:** Mitchell Water (Curtis Brown); Lucienne Diver (Spectrum); Jean Price (Kirkland); Paul Levine; Joe Veltre (St. Martins); Jeannette Larson (Harcourt Brace Childrens); Michael Siedman (Walker Books); Laura Ann Gilman (Penguin ROC). Agents will be speaking and available for meetings with attendees.

TO RECEIVE REGULAR TIPS AND UPDATES about writing and Writer's Digest publications via e-mail, send an e-mail with "SUBSCRIBE NEWSLETTER" in the body of the message to "newsletter-request@writersdigest.com."

Costs: $230 (includes all meals).
Accommodations: Marriott Colorado Springs holds a block of rooms for conference attendees until March 30 at a special $73 rate (1-800-962-6982).
Additional Information: Readings with critique are available or Friday afternoon. Brochures available in October. Inquiries by e-mail OK.

✓ **ROCKY MOUNTAIN BOOK FESTIVAL**, 2123 Downing St., Denver CO 80211-5210. (303)839-8320. Fax: (303)839-8319. E-mail: ccftb_mm@compuserve.com. Website: www.aclin.org/~ccftb/. Executive Director: Christiane Citron. Estab. 1991. Annual. Festival held November 18-20. Festival duration: 3 days. Average attendance: 20,000. Festival promotes work published from all genres. Held at Denver Merchandise Mart in Denver. Offers a wide variety of panels. Approximately 200 authors are scheduled to speak each year. **Previous speakers have included:** Sherman Alexie, Dixie Carter, Dave Barry, Alice Walker, Dr. Andrew Weil and Jill Kerr Conway.
Costs: $4 adult; $2 child.
Additional Information: Please submit bio and publicity material for consideration.

ROCKY MOUNTAIN CHILDREN'S BOOK FESTIVAL, 2123 Downing St., Denver CO 80205-5210. (303)839-8320. Fax: (303)839-8319. E-mail: ccftb@compuserve.com. Program Coordinator: Anna Kaltenbach. Estab. 1996. Annual festival held last weekend in April. Festival duration: 2 days. Average attendance: 30,000. Festival promotes published work for and about children/families. Held at Denver Merchandise Mart. Approximately 100 authors speak annually. **Previous speakers have included:** Ann M. Martin, Sharon Creech, Laura Numeroff, Jean Craighead George, the Kratt Brothers and Bruce Lansky.
Costs: None.
Additional Information: Send SASE for brochure/guidelines. "For published authors of children's/family works only."

✓ **ROMANCE WRITERS OF AMERICA NATIONAL CONFERENCE**, 3707 FM 1960 West, Suite 555, Houston TX 77068. (281)440-6885, ext. 27. Fax: (281)440-7510. E-mail: info@rwanational.com. Website: www.rwanational.com. **Contact:** Chris McEachern, communications manager. Executive Director: Allison Kelley. Estab. 1981. Annual. Conference held in late July or early August. Average attendance: 1,500. Fiction writers, scriptwriters. Over 100 workshops on writing, researching and the business side of being a working writer. Publishing professionals attend and accept appointments. Keynote speaker is renowned romance writer. Conference will be held in Chicago, Illinois, in 1999 and Washington, DC in 2000.
Costs: $300.
Additional Information: Annual RITA awards are presented for romance authors. Annual Golden Heart awards are presented for unpublished writers. Conference brochures/guidelines are available for SASE.

🆕 **TAOS POETRY CIRCUS**, 5275 NDCBU, Taos NM 87571. (505)758-1800. E-mail: wpba@laplazz.org. Website: www.poetrycircus.org. **Contact:** Anne, director. Estab. 1982. Annually. Conference held June 2000. Conference duration: 9 days. Average attendance: 2,000. Poetry. Held near Taos NM.
Costs: $3-75 per event.
Accommodations: Special room rates are available from $55-65/double. Special rental car rates available with Enterprise.
Additional Information: Conference includes readings, slams, seminars, a performance and poetics workshop, and numerous free events, such as poetry video showing. Brochures available for SASE in March 2000. Inquiries by e-mail OK.

✓ **WRITER'S ROUNDTABLE CONFERENCE**, P.O. Box 461572, Garland TX 75046-1572. (972)495-7388, ext. 5, or (800)473-2538, ext. 5. Fax: (972)414-2839. E-mail: directors@wrc-online.com. Website: www.wrc-online.com. Executive Director: Deborah Morris. Estab. 1996. Annual. Conference held March 31-April 2, 2000. Conference duration: 1 weekend. Average attendance: 250 (limited, closes after 300). Fiction, nonfiction, screenwriting. "Writer's Roundtable Conference is geared toward professional (working) writers, and serious writers seeking to move toward full-time writing careers. The conference is multi-genre and includes TV-related writing as well as books and magazines. Both fiction and nonfiction are addressed." Held at the Renaissance Dallas North Hotel in Dallas, TX. Themes or panels of interest include "What Every Editor Looks For," "Writing for TV," "Be Your Own Publicist," "Toppling Genre Walls," "Avoiding Landmines in the Publishing Field," "Ghostwriting," "Writing for Children" and "The Art of Collaboration." **Agents/speakers will include:** Leyla Aker (Knopf), Bob Banner (TV producer/director), Diane Hess (Scholastic), Charles Rosenbaum (Broadman & Holman/Living Way), Donna Gould (N.Y. Publicist), Deborah Morris (author/producer), David H. Smith, Evan Fogelman and Jim Hornfischer (literary agents). Agents will be speaking and available for meetings with attendees.
Costs: Early Registration (through December 31, 1999): $195; Primary Registration (closes March 26, 2000): $275; Walk-Up Registration (subject to space availability): $325.
Accommodations: Registered attendees are eligible for discount rates from American Airlines, Avis Rental Cars, and the Renaissance Dallas North Hotel. Special room rates: $119 (single or double), $139 (triple), $159 (quad).
Additional Information: Registration includes complete set of conference audiotapes. Offers 15-minute one-on-one

consultations and "Pitch to the Pros" panels. Advance sign-up required. Brochures/guidelines available for SASE beginning August 15, 1999. Writers may request information via fax or e-mail.

☑ **WRITERS WORKSHOP IN SCIENCE FICTION**, English Department/University of Kansas, Lawrence KS 66045-2115. (785)864-3380. Fax: (785)864-4298. E-mail: jgunn@falcon.cc.ukans.edu. Website: falcon.cc.ukans.edu/~sfcenter/. Professor: James Gunn. Estab. 1985. Annual. Conference held July 3-16, 2000. Average attendance: 15. Conference for writing and marketing science fiction. "Housing is provided and classes meet in university housing on the University of Kansas campus. Workshop sessions operate informally in a lounge." 1999 guest writers: Frederick Pohl, Kij Johnson, John Ordover.
Costs: Tuition: $400. Housing and meals are additional.
Accommodations: Several airport shuttle services offer reasonable transportation from the Kansas City International Airport to Lawrence. During past conferences, students were housed in a student dormitory at $12.50/day double, $23.50/day single.
Additional Information: "Admission to the workshop is by submission of an acceptable story. Two additional stories should be submitted by the middle of June. These three stories are copied and distributed to other participants for critiquing and are the basis for the first week of the workshop; one story is rewritten for the second week." Brochures/guidelines are available for SASE. "The Writers Workshop in Science Fiction is intended for writers who have just started to sell their work or need that extra bit of understanding or skill to become a published writer."

NORMAN ZOLLINGER'S TAOS SCHOOL OF WRITING, P.O. Box 20496, Albuquerque NM 87154-0496. (505)294-4601. Fax: (505)294-7049. E-mail: spletzer@swcp.com. Website: www.us1.net/zollinger. Estab. 1993. Annual. 2000 conference held mid-July. Conference duration: 7 days. Average attendance: 50. Offers "small, intimate classes in fiction, nonfiction and screenwriting. Talks and panel discussions by noted authors, editors and agents." Held at Thunderbird Lodge in Taos Ski Valley, NM. "Somewhat rugged landscape, no elevators." **Previous agents/speakers have included:** Kathlee O'Neal Gear and W. Michael Gear (authors); and Irene Kraas (agent). Agents will be speaking and available for meetings with attendees.
Costs: $1,095 (includes double occupancy room, all meals and tuition). "Some single rooms at additional charge."
Accommodations: "Distraction-free rooms without telephones or televisions." For special transportation arrangements contact Kim Cox at International Tours of Albuquerque, (888)303-8687.
Additional Information: Submit 20 pages of ms, typed and double-spaced from the beginning of work in any of the following: novel excerpt (any genre, include 3-page synopsis), short story, feature article, or a portion of book-length nonfiction. For screenplays, submit first 30 pages typed in screenplay format. Write for brochure.

West (AZ, CA, HI, NV, UT)

N: DESERT DREAMS 2000, P.O. Box 1771, Chandler AZ 85244-1771. (480)491-0426. Fax: (480)917-1916. E-mail: drose60@aol.com. Website: members.aol.com/DROSE60. **Contact:** Allison Kinnaird, coordinator. Estab. 1986. Biannually. Conference held March 31-April 2, 2000. Conference duration: 3 days. Average attendance: 250. Fiction, screenwriting, research. Held at the Sheraton San Marcos Resort in Chandler AZ. **Agents/speakers attending include:** Steven Axelrod, Irene Goodman, Christopher Vogler, Jill Barnett, Susan Elizabeth Phillips, Debbie Macomber, Linda Lael Miller, Sandra Marton, and editors from Harlequin, Silhouette, Ballantine, Penguin. Agents will be speaking and available for meetings with attendees.
Costs: $180 for full conference (includes meals, seminars, appointments with editors and agents). $85 for Christopher Vogler only.
Accommodations: $125/night.
Additional Information: Synopsis review available for additional $20. Inquiries by e-mail and fax OK.

IWWG EARLY SPRING IN CALIFORNIA CONFERENCE, International Women's Writing Guild, P.O. Box 810, Gracie Station, New York NY 10028-0082. (212)737-7536. Fax: (212)737-9469. E-mail: iwwg@iwwg.com. Website: www.IWWG.com. Executive Director: Hannelore Hahn. Estab. 1982. Annual. Conference held March 10-12, 2000. Average attendance: 80. Conference to promote "creative writing, personal growth and empowerment." Site is a redwood forest mountain retreat in Santa Cruz, California.
Costs: $320 for weekend program with room and board, $150 for weekend program without room and board.
Accommodations: Accommodations are all at conference site.
Additional Information: Conference brochures/guidelines are available for SASE. Inquiries by e-mail and fax OK.

MAUI WRITERS CONFERENCE, P.O. Box 1118, Kihei HI 96753. (808)879-0061. Fax: (808)879-6233. E-mail: writers@maui.net. Website: www.mauiwriters.com (includes information covering all programs offered, writing competitions, presenters past and present, writers forum bulletin board, published attendees books, dates, price, hotel and travel information). Estab. 1993. Annual. Conference held the end of August (Labor Day weekend). Conference duration: 4 days. Conference site: Grand Wailea Resort. Average attendance: 800. For fiction, nonfiction, poetry, children's, young adult, horror, mystery, romance, science fiction, journalism, screenwriting. Editors and agents available for one-on-one consultations. **Previous speakers have included:** Ron Howard, David Guterson, Jack Canfield and Julie Garwood. Write or call for additional information.

Additional Information: "We offer a comprehensive view of the business of publishing, with over 2,000 consultation slots with industry agents, editors and screenwriting professionals as well as workshops and sessions covering writing instruction."

MOUNT HERMON CHRISTIAN WRITERS CONFERENCE, P.O. Box 413, Mount Hermon CA 95041-0413. (831)335-4466. Fax: (831)335-9218. E-mail: slist@mhcamps.org. Website: www.mounthermon.org. Director of Specialized Programs: David R. Talbott. Estab. 1970. Annual. Conference held Friday-Tuesday over Palm Sunday weekend, April 14-18, 2000. Average attendance: 250. "We are a broad-ranging conference for all areas of Christian writing, including fiction, children's, poetry, nonfiction, magazines, books, educational curriculum and radio and TV scriptwriting. This is a working, how-to conference, with many workshops within the conference involving on-site writing assignments. The conference is sponsored by and held at the 440-acre Mount Hermon Christian Conference Center near San Jose, California, in the heart of the coastal redwoods. Registrants stay in hotel-style accommodations, and full board is provided as part of conference fees. Meals are taken family style, with faculty joining registrants. The faculty/student ratio is about 1:6 or 7. The bulk of our faculty are editors and publisher representatives from major Christian publishing houses nationwide."

Costs: Registration fees include tuition, conference sessions, resource notebook, refreshment breaks, room and board and vary from $525 (economy) to $725 (deluxe), double occupancy (1999 fees).

Accommodations: Airport shuttles are available from the San Jose International Airport. Housing is not required of registrants, but about 95% of our registrants use Mount Hermon's own housing facilities (hotel style double-occupancy rooms). Meals with the conference are required and are included in all fees.

Additional Information: Registrants may submit 2 works for critique in advance of the conference, then have personal interviews with critiquers during the conference. No advance work is required however. Conference brochures/guidelines are available for SASE. Inquiries by e-mail and fax OK. "The residential nature of our conference makes this a unique setting for one-on-one interaction with faculty/staff. There is also a decided inspirational flavor to the conference, and general sessions with well-known speakers are a highlight."

NO CRIME UNPUBLISHED® MYSTERY WRITERS' CONFERENCE, Sisters in Crime/Los Angeles, P.O. Box 251646, Los Angeles CA 90025. (213)694-2972. Website: www.sistersincrimela.com. Conference Coordinator: Jamie Wallace. Estab. 1995. Annual. Conference held on June 6, 1999. Conference duration: 1 day. Average attendance: 200. Conference on mystery and crime writing. Usually held in hotel near Los Angeles airport. Two-track program: Craft and forensic sessions; keynote speaker, luncheon speaker, agent panel, book signings. In 1999: Earlene Fowler, keynote speaker; Patricia Schellerup and Billie Johnson, agents; authors, forensic experts.

Costs: $80 until May 1, 1999; $90 after May 1, 1999. Includes continental breakfast and lunch.

Accommodations: Airport shuttle to hotel. Optional overnight stay available. Hotel conference rate $99/night at the LAX Hilton. Arrangements made directly with hotel.

Additional Information: Conference brochure available for SASE.

PASADENA WRITERS' FORUM, P.C.C. Extended Learning Center, 1570 E. Colorado Blvd., Pasadena CA 91106-2003. (626)585-7608. Fax: (626)796-5204. E-mail: pcclearn@webcom.com. Coordinator: Meredith Brucker. Estab. 1954. Annual. Conference will be held March 4, 2000. Average attendance: 225. "For the novice as well as the professional writer in any field of interest: fiction or nonfiction, including scripts, children's, humor and poetry." Conference held on the campus of Pasadena City College. A panel discussion by agents, editors or authors is usually featured at the end of the day.

Costs: $100, including box lunch and coffee hour.

Additional Information: Brochure upon request, no SASE necessary. "Pasadena City College also periodically offers an eight-week class 'Writing for Publication'."

✓ **SDSU ANNUAL WRITER'S CONFERENCE**, San Diego State University, Extension Programs, 5250 Campanile Dr., Room 2503, San Diego CA 92182-1920. (858)484-8575. Fax: (858)538-6595. Website: www.writersconferences.com. Conference Director: Diane Dunaway. Conference held January 21-23, 2000. Average attendance: 400. For poetry, fiction, nonfiction, journalism, playwriting, screenplays, travel writing and children's. **Agents attending include:** Jillian Manus, Loretta Barrett and Peter Gethers. Offers opportunities to meet with editors and agents. Write for additional information or visit website.

✓ **SOCIETY OF CHILDREN'S BOOK WRITERS AND ILLUSTRATORS/NATIONAL CONFERENCE ON WRITING & ILLUSTRATING FOR CHILDREN**, 8271 Beverly Blvd., Los Angeles CA 90048-4515. (323)782-1010. Fax: (323)782-1892. E-mail: scbwi@juno.com. Website: www.scbwi.org. President: Stephen Mooser. Estab. 1972. Annual. Conference held in August. Conference duration: 4 days. Average attendance: 500. Writing and

---

CAN'T FIND A CONFERENCE? Conferences are listed by region. Check the introduction to this section for a list of regional categories.

illustrating for children. Site: Century Plaza Hotel in Los Angeles. **Previous agents/speakers have included:** Andrea Brown, Steven Malk, Scott Treimel (agents), Ashley Bryan, Bruce Coville, Karen Hesse, Harry Mazer, Lucia Monfried and Russell Freedman. Agents will be speaking and available for meetings with attendees.
Costs: $320 (members); $350 (late registration, members); $375 (nonmembers). Cost does not include hotel room.
Accommodations: Information on overnight accommodations made available. Conference rates at the hotel about $135/night.
Additional Information: Ms and illustration critiques are available. Conference brochures/guidelines are available (after June) with SASE.

N: TELEVISION WRITERS WORKSHOP, AF1, 2021 N. Western Ave., Los Angeles CA 90027. (323)856-7721. Fax: (323)856-7778. E-mail: jpetricca@afionline.org. Website: www.afionline.org. **Contact:** Joe Petriccia, associate director of workshops. Estab. 1986. Annually. Conference held fall 2000. Conference duration: 3 weeks. Average attendance: Up to 12 participants. Television writing, with an annual focus that changes each year (e.g. sitcom, MOW). Held at the American Film Institute Campus in Los Angeles. Past workshops were "Writing the Television Movie," "AFI/Sloan TV Writing Workshop—Writing One-Hour Dramas." Agents will be speaking.
Costs: $695 (includes staged readings, seminars with working writers/producers/directors and lunch and breakfast each day).
Additional Information: Brochures available for SASE. Inquiries by e-mail OK.

WRITERS CONNECTION SELLING TO HOLLYWOOD, P.O. Box 24770, San Jose CA 95154-4770. (408)445-3600. Fax: (408)445-3609. E-mail: info@sellingtohollywood.com. Website: www.sellingtohollywood.com. Directors: Steve and Meera Lester. Estab. 1988. Annual. Conference held in August in LA area. Conference duration: 3 days; August 2000. Average attendance: 275. "Conference targets scriptwriters and fiction writers, whose short stories, books, or scripts have strong cinematic potential, and who want to make valuable contacts in the film industry. Full conference registrants receive a private consultation with the film industry producer or professional of his/her choice who make up the faculty. Panels, workshops, 'Ask a Pro' discussion groups and networking sessions include over 50 agents, professional film and TV scriptwriters, and independent as well as studio and TV and feature film producers."
Costs: In 1999: full conference by July 15, $500; after July 15: $525. Includes some meals. Brochure available March 2000; phone, e-mail, fax or send written request.
Accommodations: $100/night (in LA) for private room; $50/shared room. Discount with designated conference airline.
Additional Information: "This is the premier screenwriting conference of its kind in the country, unique in its offering of an industry-wide perspective from pros working in all echelons of the film industry. Great for making contacts." Conference brochure/guidelines available March 2000; phone, e-mail, fax or send written request.

Northwest (AK, ID, MT, OR, WA, WY)

✓ CLARION WEST WRITERS' WORKSHOP, 340 15th Ave. E., Suite 350, Seattle WA 98112-5156. (206)322-9083. E-mail: kfishler@fishler.com. Website: www.sff.net.clarionwest/ (includes critiquing, workshopping, names, dates). **Contact:** Leslie Howle. Workshop held June 18-July 28, 2000. Workshop duration 6 weeks. Average attendance: 20. "Conference to prepare students for professional careers in science fiction and fantasy writing. Held at Seattle Central Community College on Seattle's Capitol Hill, an urban site close to restaurants and cafes, not too far from downtown." Deadline for applications: April 1. Agents will be speaking and available for meetings with attendees. Send SASE for more information.
Costs: Workshop: $1,400 ($100 discount if application received by March 1). Dormitory housing: $800, meals not included.
Accommodations: Students are strongly encouraged to stay on-site, in dormitory housing at Seattle University. Cost: $800, meals not included, for 6-week stay.
Additional Information: "This is a critique-based workshop. Students are encouraged to write a story a week; the critique of student material produced at the workshop forms the principal activity of the workshop. Students and instructors critique manuscripts as a group." Conference guidelines available for SASE. Limited scholarships are available, based on financial need. Students must submit 20-30 pages of ms to qualify for admission. Dormitory and classrooms are handicapped accessible.

N: WHIDBEY ISLAND WRITERS' CONFERENCE, 5456 Pleasant View Lane, Freeland WA 98249. (360)331-2739. E-mail: writers@whidbey.com. Website: www.whidbey.com/writers. **Contact:** Celeste Mergens, director. Annual. Conference held March 3-5, 2000. Conference duration: 3 days. Average attendance: 275 people. Fiction, nonfiction, screenwriting, writing for children and poetry. Conference held at conference hall, and break-out fireside chats in local homes near sea. Panels include: "Writing in a Bunny Eat Bunny World," "The Art of Revision." **Agents/speakers attending include:** Aaron Elkin (author), Sandra Martz (publisher), Susan Sloan (author), and more. Agents will be speaking and available for meetings with attendees.
Costs: $258 (includes workshops, events, 2 receptions and daily luncheons).
Accommodations: Information available for SASE. Shuttles to conference from airport will be arranged.

Additional Information: "If registrant desires an agent/editor consultation, you must submit the first five pages for a chapter book or youth novel or entire picture book idea with a written one-page synopsis." Brochures available for SASE. Inquiries by e-mail OK.

☑ WILLAMETTE WRITERS CONFERENCE, 9045 SW Barbur, Suite 5-A, Portland OR 97219. (503)452-1592. Fax: (503)452-0372. E-mail: wilwrite@teleport.com. Website: www.teleport.com/~wilwrite (includes meeting news; conference news; links to other sites). **Contact:** Bill Johnson. Estab. 1968. Annual. Conference held August 12-13. Average attendance: 320. "Willamette Writers is open to all writers, and we plan our conference accordingly. We offer workshops on all aspects of fiction, nonfiction, marketing, scriptwriting, the creative process, etc. Also we invite top notch inspirational speakers for key note addresses. Most often the conference is held on a local college campus which offers a scholarly atmosphere and allows us to keep conference prices down. Recent theme was 'Spotlight on Craft .' We always include at least one agent or editor panel and offer a variety of topics of interest to both fiction, screenwriters and nonfiction writers." **Previous agents/editors have included:** Faye Bender and Andrea Brown, literary agents; David Gassmand and Cindy Mintz, script agents; Airie Dekidiev and Michelle Howry, editors. Agents will be speaking and available for meetings with attendees.
Costs: Cost for full conference including meals is $210 members; $250 nonmembers.
Accomodations: If necessary, these can be made on an individual basis. Some years special rates are available.
Additional Information: Conference brochures/guidelines are available for catalog-size SASE.

YELLOW BAY WRITERS' WORKSHOP, Center for Continuing Education, University of Montana, Missoula MT 59812-1990. (406)243-2094. Fax: (406)243-2047. E-mail: hhi@selway.umt.edu. Website: www.umt.edu/ccesp/c&i/yellowba. **Contact:** Program Manager. Estab. 1988. Annual. Conference held mid August. Average attendance: 50-60. Includes four workshops: 2 fiction; 1 poetry; 1 creative nonfiction/personal essay. Conference "held at the University of Montana's Flathead Lake Biological Station, a research station with informal educational facilities and rustic cabin living. Located in northwestern Montana on Flathead Lake, the largest natural freshwater lake west of the Mississippi River. All faculty are requested to present a craft lecture—usually also have an editor leading a panel discussion." 1999 faculty included Pam Houston, Denis Johnson, Jane Miller and Fred Haefele.
Costs: In 1999, for all workshops, lodging (single occupancy) and meals $840; $815 with double occupancy; $495 for commuters.
Accommodations: Shuttle is available from Missoula to Yellow Bay for those flying to Montana. Cost of shuttle is $45.
Additional Information: Brochures/guidelines are available for SASE.

Canada

☑ 🍁 THE FESTIVAL OF THE WRITTEN ARTS, Box 2299, Sechelt, British Columbia V0N 3A0 Canada. (800)565-9631 or (604)885-9631. Fax: (604)885-3967. E-mail: written_arts@sunshine.net. Website: www.sunshine.net/rockwood. **Contact:** Gail Bull. Estab. 1983. Annual. Festival held: August 10-13. Average attendance: 3,500. To promote "all writing genres." Festival held at the Rockwood Centre. "The Centre overlooks the town of Sechelt on the Sunshine Coast. The lodge around which the Centre was organized was built in 1937 as a destination for holidayers arriving on the old Union Steamship Line; it has been preserved very much as it was in its heyday. A new twelve-bedroom annex was added in 1982, and in 1989 the Festival of the Written Arts constructed a 500-seat Pavilion for outdoor performances next to the annex. The festival does not have a theme. Instead, it showcases 20 or more Canadian writers in a wide variety of genres each year."
Costs: $12 per event or $150 for a four-day pass (Canadian funds.)
Accommodations: Lists of hotels and bed/breakfast available.
Additional Information: The festival runs contests during the 3½ days of the event. Prizes are books donated by publishers. Brochures/guidelines are available.

🅽 🍁 FESTIVAL OF WORDS, 88 Saskatchewan St. E., Moose Jaw, Saskatchewan S6H 0V4 Canada. (306)691-0557. Fax: (306)693-2994. E-mail: word.festival@sk.sympatico. Website: www3.sk.sympatico.ca/praifes. **Contact:** Gary Hyland, coordinator. Estab. 1997. Annually. Festival held July 28-30, 2000. Festival duration: 3 days. The festival celebrates the imaginative uses of language, and features fiction and nonfiction writers, screenwriters, poets, children's authors, songwriters, dramatists and film makers. Held at the Moose Jaw Public Library/Art Museum complex and in Crescent Park. **Previous agents/speakers have included:** Jane Urquhart, Susan Musgrave, M.T. Kelly, Terry Jordan, Sharon Butala, Steven Michael Berzensky, Dennis Cooley, Richard Stevenson, Don Kerr, Thelma Poirier, Ross King, David Richards, Helen Mouvre, Maryann Kovalski, Jo Bannatyne-Cugnet, Sue Bland, Jeanne de Moissac, Greg Button, Judith Silverthorne, Kit Pearson.
Costs: $95 for 1999 (includes 2 meals).
Accommodations: Motels, hotels, campgrounds, bed and breakfasts.
Additional Information: "Our festival is an ideal meeting ground for people who love words to meet and mingle, promote their books and meet their fans." Brochures available for SASE. Inquiries by e-mail and fax OK.

N̄ NATIONAL MUSEUM PUBLISHING SEMINAR, University of Chicago, 5835 S. Kimbark Ave., Chicago IL 60637. (773)702-1682. Fax: (773)702-6814. E-mail: s-medlock@uchicago.edu. **Contact:** Stephanie Medlock, director. Estab. 1988. Biannially. Conference held July 13-15, 2000. Conference duration: 3½ days. Average attendance: 250. Primarily nonfiction, writing and editing in museums. "Conference moves to a new city every time and is co-sponsored by the University and different museums. In 2000, the conference will take place in Ottawa and will be co-sponsored by the National Gallery Museum of Civilization." Themes or panels of interest include: "Writing for Children," "International Joint Ventures," and "Translations." Agents will be attending.
Costs: $360 (includes materials, two lunches, dinner and a reception).
Accomodations: "We have reserved rooms at the Chateau Laurier for $186 per night (Canadian dollars) and have discounted airfare with Air Canada."
Additional Information: Brochures available for SASE after January 1, 2000. Inquiries by fax and e-mail OK.

SAGE HILL WRITING EXPERIENCE, Box 1731, Saskatoon, Saskatchewan S7K 2Z4 Canada. Phone/fax: (306)652-7395. E-mail: sage.hill@sk.sympatico.ca. Website: www.lights.com/sagehill (features complete program, including application and scholarship information). Executive Director: Steven Ross Smith. Annual. Workshops held in August and October. Workshop duration 10-21 days. Attendance: limited to 40-50. "Sage Hill Writing Experience offers a special working and learning opportunity to writers at different stages of development. Top quality instruction, low instructor-student ratio and the beautiful Sage Hill settings offer conditions ideal for the pursuit of excellence in the arts of fiction, nonfiction, poetry and playwriting." The Sage Hill location features "individual accommodation, in-room writing area, lounges, meeting rooms, healthy meals, walking woods and vistas in several directions." Seven classes are held: Introduction to Writing Fiction & Poetry; Fiction Workshop; Writing Young Adult Fiction Workshop; Poetry Workshop; Poetry Colloquium; Fiction Colloquium; Playwriting Lab; Fall Poetry Colloquium. **1999 faculty included:** Don McKay, Elizabeth Philips, Dennis Cooley, Myrna Kostash, Dianne Warren and Robert Kroetsch.
Costs: $595 (Canadian) includes instruction, accommodation, meals and all facilities. Fall Poetry Colloquium: $875.
Accommodations: On-site individual accommodations located at Lumsden 45 kilometers outside Regina. Fall Colloquium is at Muenster, Saskatchewan, 150 kilometers east of Saskatoon.
Additional Information: For Introduction to Creative Writing: A five-page sample of your writing or a statement of your interest in creative writing; list of courses taken required. For workshop and colloquium program: A resume of your writing career and a 12-page sample of your work plus 5 pages of published work required. Application deadline is May 1. Guidelines are available for SASE. Inquiries by e-mail and fax OK. Scholarships and bursaries are available.

☑ ⚃ THE VANCOUVER INTERNATIONAL WRITERS FESTIVAL, 1398 Cartwright St., Vancouver, British Columbia V6H 3R8 Canada. (604)681-6330. Fax: (604)681-8400. E-mail: viwf@writersfest.bc.ca. Website: www.writersfest.bc.ca (includes information on festival). **Contact:** Dawn Brennan, general manager. Estab. 1988. Annual. Held October 18-22, 2000. Average attendance: 11,000. "This is a festival for readers and writers. The program of events is diverse and includes readings, panel discussions, seminars. Lots of opportunities to interact with the writers who attend." Held on Granville Island—in the heart of Vancouver. Two professional theaters are used as well as Performance Works (an open space). "We·try to avoid specific themes. Programming takes place between February and June each year and is by invitation." **In 1999, attending writers included:** Susan Faludi, Roddy Doyle, Timothy Findley and Isabel Allende.
Costs: Tickets are $6-20 (Canadian).
Accommodations: Local tourist info can be provided when necessary and requested.
Additional Information: Brochures/guidelines are available for SASE after August. Inquiries by e-mail and fax OK. "A reminder—this is a festival, a celebration, not a conference or workshop."

☑ ⚃ A WRITER'S W*O*R*L*D, Surrey Writers' Conference, 10707 146th St., Surrey, British Columbia V3R 1T5 Canada. (604)589-2221. Fax: (604)588-9286. E-mail: ikmason@bc.sympatico.ca. Website: www.vcn.bc.ca/swc/. Principal: Bonnie Deren. Estab. 1992. Annual. Conference held October 20-22, 2000. Conference duration: 3 days. Average attendance: 400. Conference for fiction (romance/science fiction/fantasy/mystery—changes focus depending upon speakers and publishers scheduled), nonfiction, scriptwriting and poetry. "For everyone from beginner to professional." Conference held at Sheraton Guildford. **Agent/speakers attending include:** Meredith Bernstein (Meredith Bernstein Literary Agency), Charlotte Gusay (Charlotte Gusay Literary Agency), Donald Maass (Donald Maass Literary Agency), Denise Marcil (Denise Marcil Literary Agency), Anne Sheldon and Michael Vidor (The Hardy Agency). Agents will be speaking and available for meetings with attendees.
Costs: $290 full conference.
Accommodations: On request will provide information on hotels and B&Bs. Conference rate: $109 (1999). Attendee must make own arrangements for hotel and transportation. For accomodations, call (800)661-2818.
Additional Information: Writer's contest entries must be submitted about 1 month early. Length: 1,000 words fiction, nonfiction, poetry, young writers (19 or less). Cash prizes awarded. Contest is judged by a qualified panel of writers and educators. Write, call or e-mail for additional information.

Resources
Professional Organizations

ORGANIZATIONS FOR AGENTS

ASSOCIATION OF AUTHORS' REPRESENTATIVES (AAR), P.O. Box 237201, Ansonia Station, New York NY 10023. Website: www.aar-online.org. A list of member agents is available for $7 and SAE with 2 first-class stamps.

ORGANIZATIONS FOR WRITERS

The following professional organizations publish newsletters and hold conferences and meetings at which they often share information on agents. Organizations with an asterisk (*) have members who are liaisons to the AAR

ACADEMY OF AMERICAN POETS, 584 Broadway, Suite 1208, New York NY 10012-3250. (212)274-0343. Website: www.poets.org.

AMERICAN MEDICAL WRITERS ASSOCIATION, 40 W. Gude Dr., Suite 101, Rockville MD 20850-1192. (301)493-0003. Website: www.amwa.org.

***AMERICAN SOCIETY OF JOURNALISTS & AUTHORS**, 1501 Broadway, Suite 302, New York NY 10036. (212)997-0947. Website: www.asja.org.

AMERICAN TRANSLATORS ASSOCIATION, 225 Reinekers Lane, Suite 590, Alexandria VA 22314. (703)683-6100. Website: www.atanet.org.

ASIAN AMERICAN WRITERS' WORKSHOP, 37 St. Mark's Place, New York NY 10003. (212)228-6718. Website: www.panix.com/~aaww/.

***ASSOCIATED WRITING PROGRAMS**, 4210 Roberts Rd., Fairfax VA 22030. (703)993-4301. Website: www.awpwriter.org.

***THE AUTHORS GUILD INC.**, 330 W. 42nd St., 29th Floor, New York NY 10036. (212)563-5904. Website: www.authorsguild.org.

THE AUTHORS LEAGUE OF AMERICA, INC., 330 W. 42nd St., New York NY 10036. (212)564-8350.

COUNCIL OF WRITERS ORGANIZATIONS, 12724 Sagamore Rd., Leawood KS 66209. (913)451-9023. Website: www.councilofwriters.com.

***THE DRAMATISTS GUILD**, 1501 Broadway, Suite 701, New York NY 11040. (212)398-9366.

EDUCATION WRITERS ASSOCIATION, 1331 H. St. NW, Suite 307, Washington DC 20005. (202)637-9700. Website: www.ewa.org.

***HORROR WRITERS ASSOCIATION**, S.P. Somtow, President, P.O. Box 50577, Palo Alto CA 94303. Website: www.horror.org.

INTERNATIONAL ASSOCIATION OF CRIME WRITERS INC., North American Branch, P.O. Box 8674, New York NY 10016. (212)243-8966.

INTERNATIONAL TELEVISION ASSOCIATION, 9202 N. Meridian St., Suite 200, Indianapolis IN 46260. (317)816-6269. Website: www.itva.org.

THE INTERNATIONAL WOMEN'S WRITING GUILD, P.O. Box 810, Gracie Station, New York NY 10028-0082. (212)737-7536. Website: www.iwwg.com. Provides a literary agent list to members and holds "Meet the Agents and Editors" in April and October.

***MYSTERY WRITERS OF AMERICA (MWA)**, 17 E. 47th St., 6th Floor, New York NY 10017. (212)888-8171. Website: www.mysterynet.com/mwa/.

NATIONAL ASSOCIATION OF SCIENCE WRITERS, Box 294, Greenlawn NY 11740. (516)757-5664. Website: www.nasw.org.

NATIONAL LEAGUE OF AMERICAN PEN WOMEN, 1300 17th St. NW, Washington DC 20036-1973. (202)785-1997. Website: www.members.aol.com/penwomen/.

NATIONAL WRITERS ASSOCIATION, 3140 S. Peoria, Suite 295, Aurora CO 80014. (303)841-0246. Website: www.nationalwriters.com. In addition to agent referrals, also operates an agency for members.

*NATIONAL WRITERS UNION, 113 University Place, 6th Floor, New York NY 10003-4527. (212)254-0279. Website: www.nwu.org. A trade union, this organization has an agent database available to members.

*PEN AMERICAN CENTER, 568 Broadway, New York NY 10012-3225. (212)334-1660. Website: www.pen.org.

*POETS & WRITERS, 72 Spring St., Suite 301, New York NY 10012. (212)226-3586. Website: www.pw.org. Operates an information line, taking calls from 11-3 EST Monday through Friday.

POETRY SOCIETY OF AMERICA, 15 Gramercy Park, New York NY 10003. (212)254-9628. Website: www.poetrysociety.org.

*ROMANCE WRITERS OF AMERICA, 3707 F.M. 1960 West, Suite 555, Houston TX 77068. (281)440-6885. Website: www.rwanational.com. Publishes an annual agent list for members for $10.

*SCIENCE FICTION AND FANTASY WRITERS OF AMERICA, P.O. Box 171, Unity ME 04988-0171. Website: www.sfwa.org.

SOCIETY OF AMERICAN BUSINESS EDITORS & WRITERS, University of Missouri, School of Journalism, 76 Gannett Hall, Columbia MO 65211. (573)882-7862. Website: www.sabew.org.

SOCIETY OF AMERICAN TRAVEL WRITERS, 4101 Lake Boone Trail, Suite 201, Raleigh NC 27607. (919)787-5181. Website: www.satw.org.

*SOCIETY OF CHILDREN'S BOOK WRITERS & ILLUSTRATORS, 8271 Beverly Blvd., Los Angeles CA 90048. (323)782-1010. Website: www.scbwi.org.

VOLUNTEER LAWYERS FOR THE ARTS, One E. 53rd St., 6th Floor, New York NY 10022. (212)319-2787. Website: www.artswire.org/artlaw/.

WASHINGTON INDEPENDENT WRITERS, 220 Woodward Bldg., 733 15th St. NW, Washington DC 20005. (202)347-4973. Website: www.washwriter.org/.

WESTERN WRITERS OF AMERICA, 1012 Fair St., Franklin TN 37064. (615)791-1444. Website: www.imt-.net/~gedison.

WRITERS CONNECTION, P.O. Box 24770, San Jose CA 95154-4770. (408)445-3600.

WRITERS GUILD OF ALBERTA, 3rd Floor, Percy Page Centre, 11759 Groat St., Edmonton, Alberta T5M 3K6 Canada. (780)422-8174. Website: writersguild.ab.ca.

*WRITERS GUILD OF AMERICA-EAST, 555 W. 57th St., New York NY 10019. (212)767-7800. Website: www.wgaeast.org/. Provides list of WGA signatory agents for $1.29.

WRITERS GUILD OF AMERICA-WEST, 7000 W. Third St., Los Angeles CA 90048. (310)550-1000. Website: www.wga.org. Provides a list of WGA signatory agents for $2.50 and SASE sent to Agency Department.

TABLE OF ACRONYMS

The organizations and their acronyms listed below are frequently referred to in the listings and are widely used in the industries of agenting and writing.

AAP	American Association of Publishers	NLAPW	National League of American Pen Women
AAR	Association of Authors' Representatives	NWA	National Writers Association
ABA	American Booksellers Association	OWAA	Outdoor Writers Association of America, Inc.
ABWA	Associated Business Writers of America	RWA	Romance Writers of America
AEB	Association of Editorial Businesses	SAG	Screen Actor's Guild
AFTRA	American Federation of TV and Radio Artists	SATW	Society of American Travel Writers
AGVA	American Guild of Variety Artists	SCBWI	Society of Children's Book Writers & Illustrators
AMWA	American Medical Writer's Association	SFRA	Science Fiction Research Association
ASJA	American Society of Journalists and Authors	SFWA	Science Fiction and Fantasy Writers of America
ATA	Association of Talent Agents	SPWA	South Plains Writing Association
AWA	Aviation/Space Writers Association	WGA	Writers Guild of America
		WIA	Women in the Arts Foundation, Inc.
CAA	Canadian Authors Association		
DGA	Director's Guild of America	WIF	Women in Film
GWAA	Garden Writers Association of America	WICI	Women in Communications, Inc.
		WIW	Washington Independent Writers
HWA	Horror Writers of America	WMG	Women's Media Group
IACP	International Association of Culinary Professionals	WNBA	Women's National Book Association
MOW	Movie of the Week	WRW	Washington Romance Writers (chapter of RWA)
MWA	Mystery Writers of America, Inc.		
NASW	National Association of Science Writers	WWA	Western Writers of America

Books & Publications of Interest

BOOKS

ADVENTURES IN THE SCREEN TRADE: A Personal View of Hollywood & Screenwriting, by William Goldman, published by Warner Books, 1271 Avenue of the Americas, New York NY 10020. (212)522-7200.

THE ART OF DRAMATIC WRITING, by Lajos Egri, published by Touchstone, a division of Simon & Schuster, 1230 Avenue of the Americas, New York NY 10020. (800)233-2348.

BE YOUR OWN LITERARY AGENT, by Martin Levin, published by Ten Speed Press, P.O. Box 7123, Berkeley CA 94707. (800)841-BOOK.

BUSINESS & LEGAL FORMS FOR AUTHORS AND SELF-PUBLISHERS, by Tad Crawford, published by Allworth Press, c/o Writer's Digest Books, 1507 Dana Ave., Cincinnati OH 45207. (800)289-0963. Website: www.writersdigest.com.

THE CAREER NOVELIST, by Donald Maass, published by Heinemann, 361 Hanover St., Portsmouth NH 03801-3912. (800)541-2086.

CHILDREN'S WRITER'S & ILLUSTRATOR'S MARKET, edited by Alice Pope, published by Writer's Digest Books, 1507 Dana Ave., Cincinnati OH 45207. (800)289-0963. Website: www.writersdigest.com.

THE COMPLETE BOOK OF SCRIPTWRITING, revised edition, by J. Michael Straczynski, published by Writer's Digest Books, 1507 Dana Ave., Cincinnati OH 45207. (800)289-0963. Website: www.writersdigest.com.

THE COMPLETE GUIDE TO STANDARD SCRIPT FORMATS: The Screenplay, by Hillis R. Cole and Judith H. Haag, published by CMC Publishing, 11642 Otsego St., N. Hollywood CA 91601. (818)980-9759.

THE COPYRIGHT HANDBOOK: How to Protect and Use Written Works, fifth edition, by Stephen Fishman, published by Nolo Press, 950 Parker St., Berkeley CA 94710. (800)992-6656. Website: www.nolo.com.

DRAMATISTS SOURCEBOOK, edited by Kathy Sova and Samantha Rachel Rabetz, published by Theatre Communications Group, Inc., 355 Lexington Ave., New York NY 10017-0217. (212)697-9387. Website: www.tcg.org.

EDITORS ON EDITING: What Writers Should Know About What Editors Do, edited by Gerald Gross, published by Grove-Atlantic, 841 Broadway, New York NY 10003-4793. (800)521-0178.

ELEMENTS OF STYLE FOR SCREENWRITERS: The Essential Manual for Writers of Screenplays, by Paul Argentini, published by Lone Eagle Publishing Company, 2337 Roscomare Rd., Suite 9, Los Angeles CA 90077-1851. (800)345-6257.

FOUR SCREENPLAYS: Studies in the American Screenplay, by Syd Field, published by Dell Publishing, 1540 Broadway, New York NY 10036-4094. (800)223-6834. Website: www.bdd.com.

FROM SCRIPT TO SCREEN: Collaborative Art of Filmmaking, by Linda Seger and Edward Jay Whetmore, published by Owl Books, Henry Holt & Co., Inc., 115 W. 18th St., New York NY 10011. (800)488-5233.

GETTING YOUR SCRIPT THROUGH THE HOLLYWOOD MAZE: An Insider's Guide, by Linda Stuart, published by Acrobat Books, P.O. Box 870, Venice CA 90294. (310)578-1055.

HOW TO BE YOUR OWN LITERARY AGENT, expanded revised edition, by Richard Curtis, published by Houghton Mifflin Company, 222 Berkeley St., Boston MA 02116. (800)225-3362. Website: www.hmco.com.

HOW TO FIND AND WORK WITH A LITERARY AGENT, audiotape, by Anita Diamant, published by Writer's AudioShop, 204 E. 35th St., Austin TX 78705.

HOW TO SELL YOUR SCREENPLAY: The Real Rules of Film & Television, by Carl Sautter, published by New Chapter Press, P.O. Box 383, Pound Ridge NY 10576. (914)742-9974.

HOW TO WRITE A BOOK PROPOSAL, revised edition, by Michael Larsen, published by Writer's Digest Books, 1507 Dana Ave., Cincinnati OH 45207. (800)289-0963. Website: www.writersdigest.com.

HOW TO WRITE A SELLING SCREENPLAY, by Christopher Keane, published by Bantam Doubleday Dell, 1540 Broadway, New York NY 10036. (800)223-6834.

HOW TO WRITE ATTENTION-GRABBING QUERY & COVER LETTERS, by John Wood, published by Writer's Digest Books, 1507 Dana Ave., Cincinnati OH 45207. (800)289-0963. Website: www.writersdigest. com.

HOW TO WRITE IRRESISTIBLE QUERY LETTERS, by Lisa Collier Cool, published by Writer's Digest Books, 1507 Dana Ave., Cincinnati OH 45207. (800)289-0963. Website: www.writersdigest.com.

INSIDER'S GUIDE TO GETTING PUBLISHED: Why They Always Reject Your Manuscript and What You Can Do About It, by John Boswell, published by Main Street Books, Bantam Doubleday Dell, 1540 Broadway, New York NY 10036-4094.

THE INSIDER'S GUIDE TO WRITING FOR SCREEN AND TELEVISION, by Ronald B. Tobias, published by Writer's Digest Books, 1507 Dana Ave., Cincinnati OH 45207. (800)289-0963. Website: www.writer sdigest.com.

KIRSCH'S HANDBOOK OF PUBLISHING LAW: For Authors, Publishers, Editors and Agents, by Jonathan Kirsch, published by Acrobat Books, P.O. Box 870, Venice CA 90294. (310)578-1055.

LITERARY AGENTS: A Writer's Introduction, by John F. Baker, published by Macmillan, 1633 Broadway, New York NY 10019-6785.

LITERARY AGENTS: The Essential Guide for Writers, by Debby Mayer, published by Penguin USA, 375 Hudson St., New York NY 10014-3657. (212)366-2000. Website: www.penguinputnam.com.

LITERARY AGENTS: What They Do, How They Do It, How to Find & Work with The Right One For You, by Michael Larsen, published by John Wiley & Sons, 605 Third Ave., New York NY 10158-0012. (212)850-6000. Website: www.wiley.com.

LITERARY MARKET PLACE (LMP), R.R. Bowker Company, 121 Chanlon Road, New Providence NJ 07974. (908)464-6800. Website: www.bowker.com.

MAKING A GOOD SCRIPT GREAT, second edition, by Dr. Linda Seger, published by Samuel French Trade, 7623 Sunset Blvd., Hollywood CA 90046. (212)206-8990.

MANUSCRIPT SUBMISSION, by Scott Edelstein, published by Writer's Digest Books, 1507 Dana Ave., Cincinnati OH 45207. (800)289-0963. Website: www.writersdigest.com.

MASTERING THE BUSINESS OF WRITING: A Leading Literary Agent Reveals the Secrets of Success, by Richard Curtis, published by Allworth Press, 10 E. 23rd St., Suite 210, New York NY 10010. (800)491-2808. Website: www.allworth.com.

THE NEW SCREENWRITER LOOKS AT THE NEW SCREENWRITER, by William Froug, published by Silman-James Press, 1181 Angelo Dr., Beverly Hills CA 90210.

NOVEL & SHORT STORY WRITER'S MARKET, edited by Barbara A. Kuroff, published by Writer's Digest Books, 1507 Dana Ave., Cincinnati OH 45207. (800)289-0963. Website: www.writersdigest.com.

OPENING THE DOORS TO HOLLYWOOD: How to Sell Your Idea, Story Book, Screenplay, by Carlos de Abreu & Howard J. Smith, published by Custos Morum Publishers, 433 N. Camden Dr., Suite 600, Beverly Hills CA 90210. (310)288-1910.

THE SCREENWRITER'S BIBLE: A Complete Guide to Writing, Formatting & Selling Your Script, by David Trottier, published by Silman-James Press, 3624 Shannon Rd., Los Angeles CA 90027. (323)661-9922.

SCREENWRITERS ON SCREENWRITING: The Best in the Business Discuss Their Craft, by Joel Engel, published by Hyperion, 114 Fifth Ave., New York NY 10011. (800)343-9204.

SCREENWRITING TRICKS OF THE TRADE, by William Froug, published by Silman-James Press, 3624 Shannon Rd. Los Angeles CA 90027. (323)661-9922.

SUCCESSFUL SCRIPTWRITING, by Jurgen Wolff and Kerry Cox, published by Writer's Digest Books, 1507 Dana Ave., Cincinnati OH 45207. (800)289-0963. Website: www.writersdigest.com.

TELEVISION & SCREEN WRITING: From Concept to Contract, by Richard A. Blum, published by Butterworth-Heinemann, 225 Wildwood Ave., Woburn MA 01801. (800)366-2665.

THE WHOLE PICTURE: Strategies for Screenwriting Success in the New Hollywood, by Richard Walter, published by Plume, an imprint of Penguin Putnam, 375 Hudson St., New York NY 10014-3657. (212)366-2000. Website: www.penguinputnam.com.

THE WRITER'S DIGEST GUIDE TO MANUSCRIPT FORMATS, by Dian Dincin Buchman and Seli Groves, published by Writer's Digest Books, 1507 Dana Ave., Cincinnati OH 45207. (800)289-0963. Website: www.writersdigest.com.

WRITER'S ESSENTIAL DESK REFERENCE, Second Edition, published by Writer's Digest Books, 1507 Dana Ave., Cincinnati OH 45207. (800)289-0963. Website: www.writersdigest.com.

WRITER'S GUIDE TO BOOK EDITORS, PUBLISHERS AND LITERARY AGENTS, by Jeff Herman, published by Prima Publishing, Box 1260, Rocklin CA 95677. (916)632-4400. Website: www.primapublishing. com.

THE WRITER'S GUIDE TO HOLLYWOOD PRODUCERS, DIRECTORS, & SCREENWRITER'S AGENTS, published by Prima Publishing, P.O. Box 1260, Rocklin CA 95677. (916)632-4400. Website: www.pri mapublishing.com.

THE WRITER'S LEGAL COMPANION, Third Edition, by Brad Bunnin and Peter Beren, published by Perseus Book Group, Addison Wesley, One Jacob Way, Reading MA 01867. (718)944-3700.

WRITER'S MARKET, edited by Kirsten Holm, published by Writer's Digest Books, 1507 Dana Ave., Cincinnati OH 45207. (800)289-0963. Website: www.writersdigest.com.

BOOKSTORES AND CATALOGS

BOOK CITY, 308 N. San Fernando Blvd., Burbank CA 91502, (818)848-4417, and 6627 Hollywood Blvd., Hollywood CA 90028. (323)466-2525. Website: www.hollywoodbookcity.com.

SAMUEL FRENCH THEATRE & FILM BOOKSHOPS, 7623 Sunset Blvd., Hollywood CA 90046. (323)876-0570 and 45 W. 25th St., Dept. W., New York NY 10010. (212)206-8990. Website: www.samuelfrench.c om.

SCRIPT CITY, 8033 Sunset Blvd., Suite 1500, Hollywood CA 90046. (800)676-2522. Website: www.scriptcity. net.

PUBLICATIONS

BOOK: The Magazine for the Reading Life, 4645 N. Rockwell St., Chicago IL 60625. (800)317-BOOK. Website: www.bookmagazine.com.

DAILY VARIETY, Daily Variety Ltd./Cahners Publishing Co., 5700 Wilshire Blvd., Suite 120, Los Angeles CA 90036. (312)649-5200.

EDITOR & PUBLISHER, The Editor & Publisher Co., Inc., 11 W. 19th St., New York NY 10011-4234. (212)675-4380. Website: www.mediainfo.com.

FICTION WRITER, 1507 Dana Ave., Cincinnati OH 45207. (800)888-6888. Website: www.writersdigest.com.

HOLLYWOOD AGENTS & MANAGERS DIRECTORY, published by Hollywood Creative Directory, 3000 Olympic Blvd., Suite 2525, Santa Monica CA 90404. (800)815-0503. Website: www.hcdonline.com.

HOLLYWOOD CREATIVE DIRECTORY, published by Hollywood Creative Directory, 3000 Olympic Blvd., Suite 2525, Santa Monica CA 90404. (800)815-0503. Website: www.hcdonline.com.

HOLLYWOOD REPORTER, 5055 Wilshire Blvd., Los Angeles CA 90036-4396. (213)525-2000. Website: www.hollywoodreporter.com.

HOLLYWOOD SCRIPTWRITER, P.O. Box 10277, Burbank CA 91510. (818)845-5525. Website: www.holly woodscriptwriter.com.

NEW YORK SCREENWRITER, published by the New York Screenwriter, 548 Eighth Ave., Suite 401, New York NY 10018. Website: www.nyscreenwriter.com.

POETS & WRITERS, 72 Spring St., 3rd Floor, New York NY 10012. (212)226-3586. Website: www.pw.org.

PREMIERE MAGAZINE, published by Hachette Filipacchi Magazines, 1633 Broadway, New York NY 10019. (800)289-2489. Website: premieremag.com.

PUBLISHERS WEEKLY, Bowker Magazine Group, 245 W. 17th St., New York NY 10011. (212)645-0067. Website: www.publishersweekly.com.

THE WRITER, 120 Boylston St., Boston MA 02116-4615. (617)423-3157.

WRITER'S DIGEST, 1507 Dana Ave., Cincinnati OH 45207. (800)888-6888. Website: www.writersdigest. com.

WRITTEN BY, The Journal of the Writers Guild of America, 7000 W. Third St., Los Angeles CA 90048. (888)WRITNBY. 974-8629. Website: www.wga.org/WrittenBY.

Websites of Interest

WRITING

Delphi Forums (www.delphi.com)
This site hosts forums on many topics including writing and publishing. Just type "writing" in the search bar, and you'll find pages where you can talk about your craft.

Zuzu's Petals Literary Resource (www.zuzu.com)
Contains 7,000 organized links to helpful resources for writers, artists, performers and researchers. Zuzu's Petals also publishes an electronic quarterly.

Writer's Exchange (writersexchange.about.com)
This site, hosted by writer Susan Molthrop, is a constantly updated resource devoted to the business of writing. Molthrop's goal is to include "everything I can discover to make your writing better, easier and more fun."

Inkspot (www.inkspot.com)
This site by the publishers of *Inklings*, a free biweekly newsletter for writers, includes market information, writing tips, interviews and networking opportunities.

AGENTS

Bagging the Right Literary Agent (www.romance-central.com/workshops/agent.htm)
This page includes an article by Rosalyn Alsobrook plus a quiz to help you rate potential agents.

LiteraryAgent.com (www.literaryagent.com)
A website devoted to helping authors and agents meet. Includes links to literary agents' homepages and articles as well as forums for writers.

WritersNet (www.writers.net)
This site includes a bulletin board where writers can discuss their experiences with agents. Also includes a searchable database of agents.

Agent Research and Evaluation (www.agentresearch.com)
This is the website of AR&E, a company that specializes in keeping tabs on literary agents. You can order their services here or check on a specific agent for free.

Writer Beware (www.sfwa.org/beware)
The Science Fiction Writers of America sponsor this page of warnings about agents and subsidy publishers.

SCREENWRITING

The Hollywood Reporter (www.hollywoodreporter.com)
Online version of print magazine for screenwriters. Get the buzz on the movie biz.

Daily Variety (nt.excite.com/142/variety)
This site archives the top stories from Daily Variety. Check here for the latest scoop on the movie and TV biz.

Samuel French, Inc. (www.samuelfrench.com/index.html)
This is the website of play publisher Samuel French that includes an index of authors and titles.

Screenwriter's Heaven (www.impactpc.freeserve.co.uk)
This is a page of links to many resources for screenwriters from workshops and competitions to scripts and software.

Done Deal (www.scriptsales.com)
The most useful features of this screenwriting site include descriptions of recently sold scripts, a list of script agents and a list of production companies.

MARKETING
BookTalk (www.booktalk.com)
This site "offers authors an opportunity to announce and market new releases to millions of viewers across the globe."

Authorlink (www.authorlink.com)
"The news, information and marketing community for editors, literary agents and writers." Showcases manuscripts of experienced and beginning writers.

BookWire (www.bookwire.com)
BookWire bills itself as the book industry's most comprehensive online information source. The site includes industry news, features, reviews, fiction, events, interviews and links to other book sites.

Writer's Digest (www.writersdigest.com)
This site includes information about writing books and magazines from Writer's Digest. It also has a huge, searchable database of writer's guidelines from thousands of publishers.

ORGANIZATIONS
The Association of Author's Representatives (www.bookwire.com/aar/)
This association page includes a list of member agents, their newsletter and their canon of ethics.

National Writer's Union (www.nwu.org/)
Site of the National Writer's Union—the trade union for freelance writers of all genres publishing in the U.S.

PEN American Center (www.pen.org)
Site of the organization of writers and editors that seek to defend the freedom of expression and promote contemporary literature.

Writer's Guild of America (www.wga.org)
The WGA site includes advice and information on the art and craft of professional screenwriting for film, television and interactive projects.

Glossary

Above the line. A budgetary term for movies and TV. The line refers to money budgeted for creative talent, such as actors, writers, directors and producers.

Advance. Money a publisher pays a writer prior to book publication, usually paid in installments, such as one-half upon signing the contract; one-half upon delivery of the complete, satisfactory manuscript. An advance is paid against the royalty money to be earned by the book. Agents take their percentage off the top of the advance as well as from the royalties earned.

Auction. Publishers sometimes bid for the acquisition of a book manuscript with excellent sales prospects. The bids are for the amount of the author's advance, guaranteed dollar amounts, advertising and promotional expenses, royalty percentage, etc.

Backlist. Those books still in print from previous years' publication.

Backstory. The history of what has happened before the action in your script takes place, affecting a character's current behavior.

Beat. Major plot points of a story.

Below the line. A budgetary term for movies and TV, referring to production costs, including production manager, cinematographer, editor and crew members such as gaffers, grips, set designers, make-up, etc.

Bible. The collected background information on all characters and storylines of all existing episodes, as well as projections of future plots.

Bio. Brief (usually one page) background information about an artist, writer or photographer. Includes work and educational experience.

Boilerplate. A standardized publishing contract. Most authors and agents make many changes on the boilerplate before accepting the contract.

Book club rights. Rights to sell a book through a book club.

Book packager. Draws elements of a book together, from the initial concept to writing and marketing strategies, then sells the book package to a book publisher and/or movie producer. Also known as book producer or book developer.

Business-size envelope. Also known as a #10 envelope.

Castable. A script with attractive roles for known actors.

Category fiction. A term used to include all various types of fiction. See *genre*.

Client. When referring to a literary or script agent, "client" is used to mean the writer whose work the agent is handling.

Clips. Writing samples, usually from newspapers or magazines, of your published work.

Commercial novels. Novels designed to appeal to a broad audience. These are often broken down into categories such as western, mystery and romance. See also *genre*.

Concept. A statement that summarizes a screenplay or teleplay—before the outline or treatment is written.

Contributor's copies. Copies of the author's book sent to the author. The number of contributor's copies is often negotiated in the publishing contract.

Co-agent. See *subagent*.

Co-publishing. Arrangement where author and publisher share publication costs and profits of a book. Also known as cooperative publishing.

Copyediting. Editing of a manuscript for writing style, grammar, punctuation and factual accuracy.

Copyright. A means to protect an author's work.

Cover letter. A brief descriptive letter sent with a manuscript submitted to an agent or publisher.

Coverage. A brief synopsis and analysis of a script, provided by a reader to a buyer considering purchasing the work.

Critiquing service. A service offered by some agents in which writers pay a fee for comments on the saleability or other qualities of their manuscript. Sometimes the critique includes suggestions on how to improve the work. Fees vary, as do the quality of the critiques. See also *editing service*.

Curriculum vitae. Short account of one's career or qualifications (i.e., résumé).

D person. Development person. Includes readers and story editors through creative executives who work in development and acquisition of properties for TV and movies.

Deal memo. The memorandum of agreement between a publisher and author that precedes the actual contract and includes important issues such as royalty, advance, rights, distribution and option clauses.

Development. The process where writers present ideas to producers overseeing the developing script through various stages to finished product.

Division. An unincorporated branch of a company.

Docudrama. A fictional film rendition of recent newsmaking events or people.

Editing service. A service offered by some agents in which writers pay a fee—either lump sum or per-page—to have their manuscript edited. The quality and extent of the editing varies from agency to agency. See also *critiquing service*.

Electronic rights. Secondary or subsidiary rights dealing with electronic/multimedia formats (e.g., CD-ROMs, electronic magazines).

Elements. Actors, directors and producers attached to a project to make an attractive package.

El-hi. Elementary to high school. A term used to indicate reading or interest level.

Episodic drama. Hour-long continuing TV show, often shown at 10 p.m.

Evaluation fees. Fees an agent may charge to evaluate material. The extent and quality of this evaluation varies, but comments usually concern the saleability of the manuscript.

Exclusive. Offering a manuscript, usually for a set period of time, to just one agent and guaranteeing that agent is the only one looking at the manuscript.

Film rights. May be sold or optioned by author to a person in the film industry, enabling the book to be made into a movie.

Floor bid. If a publisher is very interested in a manuscript he may offer to enter a floor bid when the book goes to auction. The publisher sits out of the auction, but agrees to take the book by topping the highest bid by an agreed-upon percentage (usually 10 percent).

Foreign rights. Translation or reprint rights to be sold abroad.

Foreign rights agent. An agent who handles selling the rights to a country other than that of the first book agent. Usually an additional percentage (about 5 percent) will be added on to the first book agent's commission to cover the foreign rights agent.

Genre. Refers to either a general classification of writing such as a novel, poem or short story or to the categories within those classifications, such as problem novels or sonnets. Genre fiction is a term that covers various types of commercial novels such as mystery, romance, western, science fiction or horror.

Ghosting/ghostwriting. A writer puts into literary form the words, ideas or knowledge of another person under that person's name. Some agents offer this service; others pair ghostwriters with celebrities or experts.

Green light. To give the go-ahead to a movie or TV project.

Half-hour. A 30-minute TV show, also known as a sitcom.

High concept. A story idea easily expressed in a quick, one-line description.

Hook. Aspect of the work that sets it apart from others.

Imprint. The name applied to a publisher's specific line of books.

IRC. International Reply Coupon. Buy at a post office to enclose with material sent outside your country to cover the cost of return postage. The recipient turns them in for stamps in their own country.

Log line. A one-line description of a plot as it might appear in *TV Guide*.

Long-form TV. Movies of the week or miniseries.

Mainstream fiction. Fiction on subjects or trends that transcend popular novel categories such as mystery or romance. Using conventional methods, this kind of fiction tells stories about people and their conflicts.

Marketing fee. Fee charged by some agents to cover marketing expenses. It may be used to cover postage, telephone calls, faxes, photocopying or any other expense incurred in marketing a manuscript.

Mass market paperbacks. Softcover book, usually around 4×7, on a popular subject directed at a general audience and sold in groceries and drugstores as well as bookstores.

MFTS. Made for TV series. A series developed for television also known as episodics.

Middle reader. The general classification of books written for readers 9-11 years old.

Midlist. Those titles on a publisher's list expected to have limited sales. Midlist books are mainstream, not literary, scholarly or genre, and are usually written by new or relatively unknown writers.

Miniseries. A limited dramatic series written for television, often based on a popular novel.

MOW. Movie of the week. A movie script written especially for television, usually seven acts with time for commercial breaks. Topics are often contemporary, sometimes controversial, fictional accounts. Also known as a made-for-TV-movie.

Multiple contract. Book contract with an agreement for a future book(s).

Net receipts. One method of royalty payment based on the amount of money a book publisher receives on the sale of the book after the booksellers' discounts, special sales discounts and returned copies.

Novelization. A novel created from the script of a popular movie, usually called a movie "tie-in" and published in paperback.

Novella. A short novel or long short story, usually 7,000 to 15,000 words. Also called a novelette.

Option. Also known as a script option. Instead of buying a movie script outright, a producer buys the right to a script for a short period of time (usually six months to one year) for a small down payment. At the end of the agreed time period, if the movie has not begun production and the producer does not wish to purchase the script, the rights revert back to the scriptwriter.

Option clause. A contract clause giving a publisher the right to publish an author's next book.

Outline. A summary of a book's contents in 5 to 15 double-spaced pages; often in the form of chapter headings with a descriptive sentence or two under each one to show the scope of the book. A script's outline is a scene-by-scene narrative description of the story (10-15 pages for a ½-hour teleplay; 15-25 pages for 1-hour; 25-40 pages for 90 minutes and 40-60 pages for a 2-hour feature film or teleplay).

Over-the-transom. Slang for the path of an unsolicited manuscript into the slush pile.

Packaging. The process of putting elements together, increasing the chances of a project being made. See also *book packager*.

Picture book. A type of book aimed at the preschool to 8-year-old that tells the story primarily or entirely with artwork. Agents and reps interested in selling to publishers of these books often handle both artists and writers.

Pitch. The process where a writer meets with a producer and briefly outlines ideas that could be developed if the writer is hired to write a script for the project.

Proofreading. Close reading and correction of a manuscript's typographical errors.

Property. Books or scripts forming the basis for a movie or TV project.

Proposal. An offer to an editor or publisher to write a specific work, usually a package consisting of an outline and sample chapters.

Prospectus. A preliminary, written description of a book, usually one page in length.

Query. A letter written to an agent or a potential market, to elicit interest in a writer's work.

Reader. A person employed by an agent or buyer to go through the slush pile of manuscripts and scripts and select those worth considering.

Release. A statement that your idea is original, has never been sold to anyone else and that you are selling negotiated rights to the idea upon payment.

Remainders. Leftover copies of an out-of-print or slow-selling book purchased from the publisher at a reduced rate. Depending on the contract, a reduced royalty or no royalty is paid on remaindered books.

Reporting time. The time it takes the agent to get back to you on your query or submission.

Reprint rights. The rights to republish your book after its initial printing.

Royalties. A percentage of the retail price paid to the author for each copy of the book that is sold. Agents take their percentage from the royalties earned as well as from the advance.

SASE. Self-addressed, stamped envelope; should be included with all correspondence.

Scholarly books. Books written for an academic or research audience. These are usually heavily researched, technical and often contain terms used only within a specific field.

Screenplay. Script for a film intended to be shown in theaters.

Script. Broad term covering teleplay, screenplay or stage play. Sometimes used as a shortened version of the word "manuscript" when referring to books.

Serial rights. The right for a newspaper or magazine to publish sections of a manuscript.

Simultaneous submission. Sending a manuscript to several agents or publishers at the same time. Simultaneous queries are common; simultaneous submissions are unacceptable to many agents or publishers.

Sitcom. Situation comedy. Episodic comedy script for a television series. Term comes from the characters dealing with various situations with humorous results.

Slush pile. A stack of unsolicited submissions in the office of an editor, agent or publisher.

Spec script. A script written on speculation without expectation of a sale.

Standard commission. The commission an agent earns on the sales of a manuscript or script. For literary agents, this commission percentage (usually between 10 and 20 percent) is taken from the advance and royalties paid to the writer. For script agents, the commission is taken from script sales; if handling plays, agents take a percentage from the box office proceeds.

Story analyst. See reader.

Storyboards. Series of panels which illustrates a progressive sequence or graphics and story copy for a TV commercial, film or filmstrip.

Subagent. An agent handling certain subsidiary rights, usually working in conjunction with the agent who handled the book rights. The percentage paid the book agent is increased to pay the subagent.

Subsidiary. An incorporated branch of a company or conglomerate (e.g., Alfred Knopf, Inc. is a subsidiary of Random House, Inc.).

Subsidiary rights. All rights other than book publishing rights included in a book publishing contract, such as paperback rights, bookclub rights, movie rights. Part of an agent's job is to negotiate those rights and advise you on which to sell and which to keep.

Synopsis. A brief summary of a story, novel or play. As a part of a book proposal, it is a comprehensive summary condensed in a page or page and a half, single-spaced. See also *outline*.

Tearsheet. Published samples of your work, usually pages torn from a magazine.

Teleplay. Script for television.

Terms. Financial provisions agreed upon in a contract.

Textbook. Book used in a classroom on the elementary, high school or college level.

Trade book. Either a hard cover or soft cover book; subject matter frequently concerns a special interest for a general audience; sold mainly in bookstores.

Trade paperback. A softbound volume, usually around 5×8, published and designed for the general public, available mainly in bookstores.

Translation rights. Sold to a foreign agent or foreign publisher.

Treatment. Synopsis of a television or film script (40-60 pages for a 2-hour feature film or teleplay).

Turnaround. When a script has been in development but not made in the time allotted, it can be put back on the market.

Unsolicited manuscript. An unrequested manuscript sent to an editor, agent or publisher.

Young adult. The general classification of books written for readers age 12-18.

Young reader. Books written for readers 5-8 years old, where artwork only supports the text.

Contributors to the Insider Reports

IAN BESSLER

Ian Bessler is a production editor for *Poet's Market* and the *Guide to Literary Agents*, and is a fiction writer and musician.

JOANNE MILLER

Joanne Miller's interviews with Arthur Golden, Isabel Allende and Ron Carlson have appeared in *Novel & Short Story Writer's Market*. She is the author of the comprehensive guidebooks *Pennsylvania Handbook* (1998) and *Maryland-Delaware Handbook* (1999—both by Moon Publications).

ANNA OLSWANGER

Anna Olswanger's work has appeared in *Book Links, Children's Book Insider, Children's Writer's & Illustrator's Market, Cricket Magazine, Writer's Digest Magazine* and online. Her story "Shlemiel Crooks" won the 1999 Society of Children's Book Writers & Illustrators Magazine Merit Award for Fiction. She teaches business writing workshops for the Johns Hopkins University Center for Training and Education.

ALICE POPE

Alice Pope is the editor of *Children's Writer's & Illustrator's Market* and regional advisor for the Southern Ohio Chapter of Society of Children's Book Writers and Illustrators.

BRAD VICE

Brad Vice's fiction has appeared in *The Georgia Review, The Southern Review, Hayden's Ferry Review* and *New Stories From the South*. His nonfiction has appeared in *Guide to Literary Agents, Novel & Short Story Writer's Market* and *Fiction Writer Magazine*.

TRICIA WADDELL

Tricia Waddell is the production editor for *Novel & Short Story Writer's Market* and *Artist's & Graphic Designer's Market*. Her interviews have also appeared in *Photographer's Market, Children's Writer's & Illustrator's Market* and *Songwriter's Market*.

Agencies Indexed by Openness to Submissions

We've ranked the agencies according to their openness to submissions. Some agencies are listed under more than one category.

☐ NEWER AGENCIES ACTIVELY SEEKING CLIENTS

Nonfee-charging agents
Amber Literary
Bookmark Literary Agency
Grace Literary Agency, Carroll
JLA Literary Agency
Real Criminals
Taylor, Literary Agent, Rebecca
Travis Literary Agency, Susan
United Tribes

Fee-charging agents
Buchan Literary Service, Jim
Creative Literary Agency
Renaud, Literary Agent, Janis
Scherf, Inc. Literary Management

Script
Chadwick & Gros Literary Agency
CS International Literary Agency
JLA Literary Agency
Larchmont Literary Agency
Magnetic Management
Renaud, Literary Agency, Janis
Vegas Literary Agency

☑ AGENCIES SEEKING BOTH NEW AND ESTABLISHED WRITERS

Nonfee-charging agents
Acacia House Publishing Services
Agents Inc. for Medical and Mental Health
  Professionals
Allen Literary Agency, Linda
Allred and Allred Literary Agents
Altair Literary Agency
Amber Literary
Amster Literary Enterprises, Betsy
Amsterdam Agency, Marcia
Appleseeds Management
Authentic Creations Literary Agency
Baldi Literary Agency, Malaga
Barrett Books Inc., Loretta
Bent, Literary Agent, Jenny
Bernstein & Associates, Inc., Pam
Bernstein Literary Agency, Meredith

Bial Agency, Daniel
BigScore Productions Inc.
Black Literary Agency, David
Bleecker Street Associates
Book Deals, Inc.
Boston Literary Group, The
Brown Associates Inc., Marie
Brown Limited, Curtis
Browne Ltd., Pema
C G & W Associates
Carvainis Agency, Inc., Maria
Castiglia Literary Agency
Circle of Confusion Ltd.
Clausen, Mays & Tahan, LLC
Client First—A/K/A Leo P. Haffey Agency
Cohen, Inc. Literary Agency, Ruth
Cohen Literary Agency Ltd., Hy
Coover Agency, The Doe
Cypher, The Cypher Agency, James R.
Darhansoff & Verrill Literary Agents
Daves Agency, Joan
Dawson Associates, Liza
DH Literary, Inc.
DHS Literary, Inc.
Donadio and Olson, Inc.
Donovan Literary, Jim
Ducas, Robert
Dystel Literary Management, Jane
Educational Design Services, Inc.
Elek Associates, Peter
Ellenberg Literary Agency, Ethan
Ellison Inc., Nicholas
ES Talent Agency
Everitt Literary Agency, Inc., Charles
Feigen/Parrent Literary Management
Fernandez Agent/Attorney, Justin E.
Finesse Literary Agency
First Books
Fitzgerald Literary Management
Flannery Literary
Fleury Agency, B.R.
ForthWrite Literary Agency
Franklin Associates, Ltd., Lynn C.
Fredericks Literary Agency, Inc., Jeanne
Gartenberg, Literary Agent, Max
Gibson Agency, The Sebastian
Gislason Agency, The
Goodman-Andrew-Agency, Inc.
Greenburger Associates, Inc., Sanford J.
Greene, Literary Agent, Randall Elisha

Harris Literary Agency
Heacock Literary Agency, Inc.
Henshaw Group, Richard
Herman Agency LLC, The Jeff
Herner Rights Agency, Susan
Hill Associates, Frederick
Hopkins Literary Associates
Jabberwocky Literary Agency
James Peter Associates, Inc.
JCA Literary Agency, Inc.
Joy Literary Agency
Kern Literary Agency, Natasha
Ketz Agency, Louise B.
Kidde, Hoyt & Picard
Kleinman, Esq. of Graybill & English L.L.C.,
  Jeffrey M.
Knight Agency, The
Kraas Agency, Irene
Lake Agency, The Candace
Larkin, Sabra Elliott
Larsen/Elizabeth Pomada Literary Agents, Michael
Lasher Agency, The Maureen
Levant & Wales, Literary Agency, Inc.
Levine Literary Agency, Inc., Ellen
Levine Literary Agency, Paul S.
Lindstrom Literary Group
Literary Group, The
Madsen Agency, Robert
Mann Agency, Carol
Manus & Associates Literary Agency
McBride Literary Agency, Margret
McDonough, Literary Agent, Richard P.
McHugh Literary Agency
Michaels Literary Agency, Inc., Doris S.
Mura Enterprises, Inc., Dee
Nathan, Ruth
National Writers Literary Agency
Nazor Literary Agency, Karen
New Century Literary Agency
New England Publishing Associates, Inc.
Nine Muses and Apollo
Nolan Literary Agency, The Betsy
Norma-Lewis Agency, The
Otitis Media
Paton Literary Agency, Kathi J.
Pevner, Inc., Stephen
Pinder Lane & Garon-Brooke Associates, Ltd.
Preferred Artists Talent Agency
Priest Literary Agency, Aaron M.
Quicksilver Books-Literary Agents
Rees Literary Agency, Helen
Reichstein Literary Agency, The Naomi
Rhodes Literary Agency, Jodie
Rinaldi Literary Agency, Angela
Robbins Literary Agency, BJ
Roghaar Literary Agency, Inc., Linda
Rosenkranz Literary Agency, Rita
Roth, Literary Representation, Carol Susan
Rotrosen Agency LLC, Jane
Rowland Agency, The Damaris
Rubenstein Literary Agency, Inc., Pesha
Russell & Volkening
Sagalyn Agency, The
Sage Acre Marketing & Publishing Solutions
Sanders Literary Agency, Victoria

Sandum & Associates
Schiavone Literary Agency, Inc.
Schwartz Agency, Laurens R.
Sedgeband Literary Associates
Seligman, Literary Agent, Lynn
Seymour Agency, The
Shepard Agency, The
Shepard Agency, The Robert E.
Simenauer Literary Agency, Jacqueline
Skolnick Literary Agency, Irene
Snell Literary Agency, Michael
Sobel Weber Associates
Spectrum Literary Agency
Sternig & Byrne Literary Agency
Straus Agency, Inc., Robin
Suite A Managment
Sunshine Literary Agency
Sydra Techniques Corp.
Talbot Agency, The John
Taylor, Literary Agent, Rebecca
Toad Hall, Inc.
Tobias—A Literary Agency for Children's Books, Ann
Treimel New York, S©ott
2M Communications Ltd.
United Tribes
Valcourt Agency, Inc., The Richard R.
Van Der Leun & Associates
Vines Agency, Inc., The
Ware Literary Agency, John A.
Watkins Loomis Agency, Inc.
Watt & Associates, Sandra
Waxman Agency, Inc., Scott
Wecksler-Incomco
West Coast Literary Associates
Witherspoon & Associates, Inc.
Wonderland Press, Inc., The
Wright Representatives, Ann
Writers' Productions
Zachary Shuster Agency
Zeckendorf Assoc. Inc., Susan

Fee-charging agents
AEI/Atchity Editorial/Entertainment International
Ahearn Agency, Inc., The
Alp Arts Co.
Author Author Literary Agency Ltd.
Author's Agency, The
Authors' Marketing Services Ltd.
Brinke Literary Agency, The
Buchan Literary Service, Jim
Cambridge Literary Associates
Catalog Literary Agency, The
Creative Literary Agency
Crown International Literature and Arts Agency,
  Bonnie R.
CS International Literary Agency
Devereux Company, The Wilson
Dickens Group, The
Fenton Entertainment Group, Inc.
Fran Literary Agency
GEM Literary Services
Gladden Unlimited
Gusay Literary Agency, The Charlotte
Hamilton's Literary Agency, Andrew
Independent Publishing Agency

Jenks Agency, Carolyn
Johnson Warren Literary Agency
Literary Group West
Magnetic Management
McKinley, Literary Agency, Virginia C.
McLean Literary Agency
Pelham Literary Agency
Pelham-Heuisler Literary Agency
Pell Agency, William
PMA Literary and Film Management, Inc.
Puddingstone Literary Agency
Raintree Literary Agency, Diane
Scherf, Inc. Literary Management
SLC Enterprises
Stern Agency, Gloria
Taylor Literary Agency, Dawson
Toomey Associates, Jeanne
Tornetta Agency, Phyllis
Total Acting Experience, A
Visions Press
Wolcott Literary Agency
Write Therapist, The
Zitwer Agency, Barbara J.

Script
AEI/Atchity Editorial/Entertainment International
Allred and Allred, Literary Agents
Amato Agency, Michael
Amsterdam Agency, Marcia
Bulger and Associates, Kelvin C.
Buscher Consultants
Cameron Agency, The Marshall
Circle of Confusion Ltd.
Client First—A/K/A Leo P. Haffey Agency
Douroux & Co.
Epstein-Wyckoff and Associates
ES Talent Agency
Esq. Management
Feigen/Parrent Literary Management
Filmwriters Literary Agency
FitzGerald Literary Management
Fleury Agency, B.R.
Freed Co., The Barry
Freedman Dramatic Agency, Inc., Robert A.
Gage Group, The
Gelff Agency, The Laya
Gibson Agency, The Sebastian
Graham Agency
Hudson Agency
International Leonards Corp.
Johnson Warren Literary Agency
Kay Agency, Charlene
Kjar Agency, Tyler
Lake Agency, The Candace
Larchmont Literary Agency
Levine Literary Agency, Paul S.
Madsen Agency, Robert
Miller Co., The Stuart M.
Momentum Marketing
Monteiro Rose Agency
Montgomery-West Literary Agency
Mura Enterprises, Inc., Dee
Oscard Agency, Inc., Fifi
Panda Talent
Perelman Agency, Barry

Pevner, Inc., Stephen
Picture of You, A
Pinkham Literary Agency
PMA Literary and Film Management, Inc.
Preferred Artists Talent Agency
Redwood Empire Agency
Silver Screen Placements
Sorice Agency, Camille
Stanton & Associates Literary Agency
Suite A Management
Sydra Technique Corp.
Talent Source
Tantleff Office, The
Toad Hall, Inc.
Toomey Associates, Jeanne
Vegas Literary Agency
Wardlow and Associates
Wauhob Agency, Donna
Whittlesey Agency, Peregrine
Wright Concept, The

◖ AGENCIES PREFERRING TO WORK WITH ESTABLISHED WRITERS, MOSTLY OBTAIN NEW CLIENTS THROUGH REFERRALS

Nonfee-charging agents
Acacia House Publishing Services Ltd.
Acme Talent & Literary
Alive Communications, Inc.
Allen, Literary Agent, James
Andrews & Associates Inc., Bart
Authors Alliance, Inc.
Authors and Artists Group, Inc.
Balkin Agency, Inc.
Bedford Book Works, Inc., The
Boates Literary Agency, Reid
Books & Such
Borchardt Inc., Georges
Boston Literary Group, The
Bova Literary Agency, The Barbara
Brady Literary Management
Brandt & Brandt Literary Agents Inc.
Brown Associates Inc., Marie
Brown Literary Agency, Inc., Andrea
Buck Agency, Howard
Casselman Literary Agency, Martha
Charisma Communications, Ltd.
Cohen Agency, The
Collin Literary Agent, Frances
Communications and Entertainment, Inc.
Congdon Associates, Inc., Don
Connor Literary Agency
Cornfield Literary Agency, Robert
Crawford Literary Agency
Curtis Associates, Inc., Richard
Diamond Literary Agency, Inc.
Dijkstra Literary Agency, Sandra
Donovan Literary, Jim
Doyen Literary Services, Inc.
Elmo Agency Inc., Ann
Evans Inc., Mary

Freedman Dramatic Agency, Inc., Robert A.
French, Inc., Samuel
Greene, Arthur B.
Hodges Agency, Carolyn
Hogenson Agency, Barbara
Howard Agency, The Eddy
Infinity Management International
International Creative Management
Kallen Agency, Leslie
Major Clients Agency
Palmer, Dorothy
Redler Entertainment, Dan
Renaissance Literary Agency
Robinson Talent and Literary Management
Scagnetti Talent & Literary Agency, Jack
Schulman, A Literary Agency, Susan
Shapiro-Lichtman-Stein
Sherman & Associates, Ken
Soloway Grant Kopaloff & Associates
Talent Source
Toad Hall, Inc.
Windfall Management
Wright Representatives, Ann
Writers & Artists Agency

◎ AGENCIES HANDLING ONLY CERTAIN TYPES OF WORK OR WORK BY WRITERS UNDER CERTAIN CIRCUMSTANCES

Nonfee-charging agents
Authors & Artists Group, Inc.
Bookmark Literary Agency
Books & Such
Brown Associates Inc., Marie
Brown Literary Agency, Inc., Andrea
Bykofsky Associates, Inc., Sheree
Cadden, Fuller & Burkhalter LLP
Candace Lake Agency, The
Casselman Literary Agency, Martha
Charisma Communications, Ltd.
Core Creations, Inc.
DHS Literary, Inc.
Educational Design Services, Inc.
Fleming Agency, Peter
Ghosts & Collaborators International
Hopkins Literary Associates
Kidd Agency, Inc., Virginia
Kirkland Literary Agency, The
Paraview, Inc.
Perkins, Rubie & Associates
Real Criminals
Roth, Literary Representation, Carol Susan
Schulman, A Literary Agency, Susan
Scovil Chichak Galen Literary Agency
Shepard Agency, The Robert E.
Suite A Managment
Toad Hall, Inc.
Treimel New York, S©ott

Fee-charging agents
Alp Arts Co.
Brinke Literary Agency, The

Buchan Literary Service, Jim
Crown International Literature and Arts Agency, Bonnie R.
Devereux Company, The Wilson
Gusay Literary Agency, The Charlotte
Hamilton's Literary Agency, Andrew
Mumford Literary Agency, Inc., The
Visions Press

Script
Camejo & Assoc., Suzanna
Cedar Grove Agency Entertainment
Charisma Communications, Ltd.
Dade/Schultz Associates
Dramatic Publishing
Hudson Agency
Kohner, Inc., Paul
Lake Agency, The Candace
Miller Co., The Stuart M.
Schulman, A Literary Agency, Susan
Toad Hall, Inc.

⊘ AGENCIES NOT CURRENTLY SEEKING NEW CLIENTS

Nonfee-charging agents
Abel Literary Agent, Carole
Altshuler Literary Agency, Miriam
Axelrod Agency, Inc., The
Bach Literary Agency, Julian
Barber Literary Agency, Inc., Virginia
Basch, Margaret
Bijur, Vicky
Book Peddlers, The
Brann Agency, Inc., The Helen
Broadway Play Publishing
Burger Associates, Ltd., Knox
Chelius Literary Agency, Jane
Childs Literary Agency, Inc., Faith
Cole, Literary Agent, Joanna Lewis
Columbia Literary Associates, Inc.
Dunow Literary Agency, Henry
Dwyer & O'Grady, Inc.
Edelstein Literary Agency, Anne
Fallon Literary Agency
Fox Chase Agency, Inc.
Fuhrman Literary Agency, Candice
Goldin, Frances
Grayson Literary Agency, Ashley
Groffsky Literary Agency, Maxine
Hanson Literary Agency, Jeanne K.
Harden Curtis Associates
Jackson Agency, Melanie
Janklow & Nesbit Associates
Kirkland Literary Agency, The
Krichevsky Literary Agency, Inc., Stuart
Lazin, Sarah
Leavitt Agency, The Ned
Marcil Literary Agency, Inc, The Denise
Marton Agency, Elisabeth
Matson Co. Inc., Harold
Mattes, Inc., Jed
McCauley, Gerard
McClellan Associates, Anita D.

Geographic Index

Some writers prefer to work with an agent in their vicinity. If you're such a writer, this index offers you the opportunity to easily select agents closest to home. Agencies are separated by state. We've also arranged them according to the sections in which they appear in the book (Nonfee-charging, Fee-charging or Script). Once you find the agency you're interested in, refer to the Listing Index for the page number.

ARIZONA

Fee-charging
Pelham-Heuisler Literary Agency

Script
Momentum Marketing

CALIFORNIA

Nonfee-charging
Agents Inc. for Medical and Mental Health
   Professionals
Allen Literary Agency, Linda
Allred and Allred Literary Agents
Amster Literary Enterprises, Betsy
Andrews & Associates Inc., Bart
Appleseeds Management
Books & Such
Brown Literary Agency, Inc., Andrea
C G & W Associates
Cadden, Fuller & Burkhalter LLP
Casselman Literary Agency, Martha
Castiglia Literary Agency
Cohen, Inc. Literary Agency, Ruth
Dijkstra Literary Agency, Sandra
ES Talent Agency
Feigen/Parrent Literary Management
Fleming Agency, Peter
ForthWrite Literary Agency
Fuhrman Literary Agency, Candice
Fullerton Associates, Sheryl B.
Gibson Agency, The Sebastian
Grayson Literary Agency, Ashley
Halsey North, Reese
Harris Literary Agency
Heacock Literary Agency, Inc.
Hill Associates, Frederick
Infinity Management International
Lake Agency, The Candace
Larsen/Elizabeth Pomada Literary Agents, Michael
Lasher Agency, The Maureen
Lawyer's Literary Agency, Inc.
Levine Literary Agency, Paul S.
Madsen Agency, Robert
McBride Literary Agency, Margret
McDonough, Literary Agent, Richard P.
McGrath, Helen
Nazor Literary Agency, Karen

Nonfiction Publishing Projects
Pevner, Inc., Stephen
Preferred Artists Talent Agency
Renaissance Literary Agency
Rhodes Literary Agency, Jodie
Rinaldi Literary Agency, Angela
Robbins Literary Agency, BJ
Robinson Talent and Literary Management
Roth, Literary Representation, Carol Susan
Scagnetti Talent & Literary Agency, Jack
Sebastian Literary Agency
Shepard Agency, The Robert E.
Suite A Managment
Teal Literary Agency, Patricia
Travis Literary Agency, Susan
Watt & Associates, Sandra
West Coast Literary Associates
Writers House

Fee-charging
AEI/Atchity Editorial/Entertainment International
Brinke Literary Agency, The
Gladden Unlimited
Gusay Literary Agency, The Charlotte
Johnson Warren Literary Agency
Literary Group West
Nelson Literary Agency & Lecture Bureau, BK
Stern Agency, Gloria
Total Acting Experience, A
Visions Press
Windfall Management
Write Therapist, The

Script
Above the Line Agency
Acme Talent & Literary
AEI/Atchity Editorial/Entertainment International
   Agency, The
Allred and Allred, Literary Agents
Bennett Agency, The
Bohrman Agency, The
Brown Agency, Bruce
Camejo & Assoc., Suzanna
Cinema Talent International
Dade/Schultz Associates
Douroux & Co.
Epstein-Wyckoff and Associates
ES Talent Agency

Esq. Management
Feigen/Parrent Literary Management
First Look Talent and Literary Agency
Freed Co., The Barry
Gage Group, The
Gelff Agency, The Laya
Gibson Agency, The Sebastian
Infinity Management International
International Creative Management
Johnson Warren Literary Agency
Kallen Agency, Leslie
Kjar Agency, Tyler
Kohner, Inc., Paul
Lake Agency, The Candace
Larchmont Literary Agency
Levine Literary Agency, Paul S.
Madsen Agency, Robert
Major Clients Agency
Miller Co., The Stuart M.
Monteiro Rose Agency
Panda Talent
Perelman Agency, Barry
Pevner, Inc., Stephen
Preferred Artists Talent Agency
Quillco Agency, The
Redler Entertainment, Dan
Redwood Empire Agency
Renaissance Literary Agency
Robinson Talent and Literary Management
Scagnetti Talent & Literary Agency, Jack
Shapiro-Lichtman-Stein
Sherman & Associates, Ken
Soloway Grant Kopaloff & Associates
Sorice Agency, Camille
Stone Manners Agency
Suite A Management
Vegas Literary Agency
Wardlow and Associates
Windfall Management
Wright Concept, The

COLORADO
Nonfee-charging
Alive Communications, Inc.
Buck Agency, Howard
Core Creations, Inc.
Diamond Literary Agency, Inc.
National Writers Literary Agency
Rein Books, Inc., Jody

Fee-charging
Alp Arts Co.
Pelham Literary Agency

Script
Hodges Agency, Carolyn

CONNECTICUT
Nonfee-charging
Brann Agency, Inc., The Helen
Evans Inc., Mary
Fredericks Literary Agency, Inc., Jeanne

J de S Associates Inc.
New England Publishing Associates, Inc.
Van Der Leun & Associates
Writers' Productions

Fee-charging
Independent Publishing Agency
McLean Literary Agency
Mews Books Ltd.
Toomey Associates, Jeanne

Script
Toomey Associates, Jeanne

DISTRICT OF COLUMBIA
Nonfee-charging
Bent, Literary Agent, Jenny
Goldfarb & Associates
Kleinman, Esq. of Graybill & English L.L.C.,
    Jeffrey M.
Literary and Creative Artists, Inc.
Ross Literary Agency, The Gail
Tobias—A Literary Agency for Children's Books, Ann
Wolf Literary Agency, Audrey A.

FLORIDA
Nonfee-charging
Bova Literary Agency, The Barbara
Fleury Agency, B.R.
Grace Literary Agency, Carroll
Kellock Company, Inc., The
Schiavone Literary Agency, Inc.
Sunshine Literary Agency

Fee-charging
Collier Associates
Magnetic Management
Taylor Literary Agency, Dawson

Script
Cameron Agency, The Marshall
Fleury Agency, B.R.
Legacies
Magnetic Management

GEORGIA
Nonfee-charging
Authentic Creations Literary Agency
Knight Agency, The
Pelter, Rodney
Taylor, Literary Agent, Rebecca

Script
Talent Source

HAWAII
Nonfee-charging
Fogelman Literary Agency, The

IDAHO
Nonfee-charging
McHugh Literary Agency

Fee-charging
Author's Agency, The

ILLINOIS
Nonfee-charging
Basch, Margaret
Book Deals, Inc.
Finesse Literary Agency
Joy Literary Agency
Multimedia Product Development, Inc.

Fee-charging
SLC Enterprises
Steinberg Literary Agency, Michael

Script
Bulger and Associates, Kelvin C.
Communications Management Associates
Dramatic Publishing
Silver Screen Placements

INDIANA
Script
Agapé Productions
International Leonards Corp.

IOWA
Nonfee-charging
Doyen Literary Services, Inc.

KANSAS
Fee-charging
Baranski Literary Agency, Joseph A.
Wolcott Literary Agency

KENTUCKY
Nonfee-charging
Greene, Literary Agent, Randall Elisha

Fee-charging
Dickens Group, The

LOUISIANA
Fee-charging
Ahearn Agency, Inc., The

Script
Chadwick & Gros Literary Agency

MARYLAND
Nonfee-charging
JLA Literary Agency
Sagalyn Agency, The

Fee-charging
Devereux Company, The Wilson

Script
JLA Literary Agency

MASSACHUSETTS
Nonfee-charging
Axelrod Agency, Inc., The
Balkin Agency, Inc.
Boston Literary Group, The
Coover Agency, The Doe
Everitt Literary Agency, Inc., Charles
McClellan Associates, Anita D.
Raymond, Literary Agent, Charlotte Cecil
Rees Literary Agency, Helen
Riverside Literary Agency
Snell Literary Agency, Michael
Stauffer Associates, Nancy
Stuhlmann, Author's Representative, Gunther
Zachary Shuster Agency

Fee-charging
Cambridge Literary Associates
Jenks Agency, Carolyn

Script
Pinkham Literary Agency

MICHIGAN
Fee-charging
Creative Literary Agency
Fenton Entertainment Group, Inc.

MINNESOTA
Nonfee-charging
Book Peddlers, The
Gislason Agency, The
Hanson Literary Agency, Jeanne K.
Lazear Agency Incorporated
Otitis Media

MISSOURI
Nonfee-charging
Flaherty, Literary Agent, Joyce A.

NEVADA
Fee-charging
Scherf, Inc. Literary Management

Script
Baskow Agency
Wauhob Agency, Donna

NEW HAMPSHIRE
Nonfee-charging
Crawford Literary Agency
Dwyer & O'Grady, Inc.

NEW JERSEY
Nonfee-charging
Boates Literary Agency, Reid
Dawson Associates, Liza
Ghosts & Collaborators International
James Peter Associates, Inc.
March Tenth, Inc.
Marshall Agency, The Evan
Millard Literary Agency, Martha
Seligman, Literary Agent, Lynn
Siegel, International Literary Agency, Inc., Rosalie
Simenauer Literary Agency, Jacqueline
Smith-Skolnik Literary
Tiersten Literary Agency, Irene
Weiner Literary Agency, Cherry

Fee-charging
Howard Agency, The Eddy
Puddingstone Literary Agency

Script
Howard Agency, The Eddy

NEW MEXICO
Nonfee-charging
Fitzgerald Literary Management
Kraas Agency, Irene

Script
FitzGerald Literary Management

NEW YORK
Nonfee-charging
Abel Literary Agent, Carole
Altair Literary Agency
Altshuler Literary Agency, Miriam
Amsterdam Agency, Marcia
Authors Alliance, Inc.
Authors & Artists Group, Inc.
Bach Literary Agency, Julian
Baldi Literary Agency, Malaga
Barber Literary Agency, Inc., Virginia
Barrett Books Inc., Loretta
Bedford Book Works, Inc., The
Bernstein & Associates, Inc., Pam
Bernstein Literary Agency, Meredith
Bial Agency, Daniel
Bijur, Vicky
Black Literary Agency, David
Bleecker Street Associates
Bookmark Literary Agency
Borchardt Inc., Georges
Brandt & Brandt Literary Agents Inc.
Broadway Play Publishing
Brown Associates Inc., Marie
Brown Limited, Curtis
Browne Ltd., Pema
Buck Agency, Howard
Burger Associates, Ltd., Knox
Bykofsky Associates, Inc., Sheree
Carvainis Agency, Inc., Maria

Charisma Communications, Ltd.
Chelius Literary Agency, Jane
Childs Literary Agency, Inc., Faith
Circle of Confusion Ltd.
Clausen, Mays & Tahan, LLC
Cohen Agency, The
Cohen Literary Agency Ltd., Hy
Cole, Literary Agent, Joanna Lewis
Columbia Literary Associates, Inc.
Congdon Associates, Inc., Don
Connor Literary Agency
Cornfield Literary Agency, Robert
Curtis Associates, Inc., Richard
Cypher, The Cypher Agency, James R.
Darhansoff & Verrill Literary Agents
Daves Agency, Joan
DH Literary, Inc.
Donadio and Olson, Inc.
Ducas, Robert
Dunow Literary Agency, Henry
Dystel Literary Management, Jane
Edelstein Literary Agency, Anne
Educational Design Services, Inc.
Elek Associates, Peter
Ellenberg Literary Agency, Ethan
Ellison Inc., Nicholas
Elmo Agency Inc., Ann
Evans Inc., Mary
Fallon Literary Agency
Farber Literary Agency Inc.
Flannery Literary
Fogelman Literary Agency, The
Foley Literary Agency, The
Franklin Associates, Ltd., Lynn C.
Freymann Literary Agency, Sarah Jane
Gartenberg, Literary Agent, Max
Gelfman Schneider Literary Agents, Inc.
Goldin, Frances
Goodman Associates
Greenburger Associates, Inc., Sanford J.
Greene, Arthur B.
Groffsky Literary Agency, Maxine
Grosvenor Literary Agency, The
Harden Curtis Associates
Harris Literary Agency, Inc., The Joy
Hawkins & Associates, Inc., John
Henshaw Group, Richard
Herman Agency LLC, The Jeff
Herner Rights Agency, Susan
Hochmann Books, John L.
Hoffman Literary Agency, Berenice
Hogenson Agency, Barbara
Hopkins Literary Associates
International Creative Management
Jabberwocky Literary Agency
Jackson Agency, Melanie
Janklow & Nesbit Associates
JCA Literary Agency, Inc.
Ketz Agency, Louise B.
Kidde, Hoyt & Picard
Kirchoff/Wohlberg, Inc., Authors' Representation
   Division
Klinger, Inc., Harvey
Konner Literary Agency, Linda
Koster Literary Agency, LLC, Elaine

Kouts, Literary Agent, Barbara S.
Krichevsky Literary Agency, Inc., Stuart
Lampack Agency, Inc., Peter
Larkin, Sabra Elliott
Lazin, Sarah
Leavitt Agency, The Ned
Lescher & Lescher Ltd.
Levine Communications, Inc., James
Levine Literary Agency, Inc., Ellen
Lieberman Associates, Robert
Lipkind Agency, Wendy
Literary Group, The
Lord Literistic, Inc., Sterling
Love Literary Agency, Nancy
Lowenstein Associates, Inc.
Lukeman Literary Management Ltd.
Maass Literary Agency, Donald
Maccoby Literary Agency, Gina
Mann Agency, Carol
Manus & Associates Literary Agency
Marcil Literary Agency, Inc, The Denise
Markson Literary Agency, Elaine
Marton Agency, Elisabeth
Matson Co. Inc., Harold
Mattes, Inc., Jed
McCauley, Gerard
Menza Literary Agency, Claudia
Merrill, Ltd., Helen
Michaels Literary Agency, Inc., Doris S.
Moran Agency, Maureen
Morhaim Literary Agency, Howard
Morris Agency, Inc., William
Morrison, Inc., Henry
Mura Enterprises, Inc., Dee
Naggar Literary Agency, Jean V.
Nathan, Ruth
Nine Muses and Apollo
Nolan Literary Agency, The Betsy
Norma-Lewis Agency, The
Ober Associates, Harold
Oscard Agency, Inc., Fifi
Paraview, Inc.
Parks Agency, The Richard
Paton Literary Agency, Kathi J.
Pelter, Rodney
Perkins, Rubie & Associates
Pevner, Inc., Stephen
Pinder Lane & Garon-Brooke Associates, Ltd.
Pine Associates, Inc., Arthur
Priest Literary Agency, Aaron M.
Protter Literary Agent, Susan Ann
Quicksilver Books-Literary Agents
Raines & Raines
Real Criminals
Rittenberg Literary Agency, Inc., Ann
Robbins Office, Inc., The
Roberts, Flora
Rosenkranz Literary Agency, Rita
Rosenstone/Wender
Rotrosen Agency LLC, Jane
Rubenstein Literary Agency, Inc., Pesha
Russell & Volkening
Sage Acre Marketing & Publishing Solutions
Sanders Literary Agency, Victoria
Sandum & Associates

Schulman, A Literary Agency, Susan
Schwartz Agency, Laurens R.
Scovil Chichak Galen Literary Agency
Seymour Agency, The
Sheedy Agency, Charlotte
Shepard Agency, The
Shukat Company Ltd., The
Singer Literary Agency Inc., Evelyn
Skolnick Literary Agency, Irene
Sobel Weber Associates
Spectrum Literary Agency
Spieler Agency, The
Spitzer Literary Agency, Philip G.
Straus Agency, Inc., Robin
Swayne Agency Literary Management & Consulting
Sydra Techniques Corp.
Talbot Agency, The John
Targ Literary Agency, Inc., Roslyn
Treimel New York, S©ott
2M Communications Ltd.
United Tribes
Valcourt Agency, Inc., The Richard R.
Vicananza, Ltd., Ralph
Vigliano Literary Agency, David
Vines Agency, Inc., The
Wald Associates, Inc., Mary Jack
Wallace Literary Agency, Inc.
Ware Literary Agency, John A.
Wasserman Literary Agency, Harriet
Watkins Loomis Agency, Inc.
Waxman Agency, Inc., Scott
Wecksler-Incomco
Weil Agency, Inc., The Wendy
Weingel-Fidel Agency, The
Weyr Agency, Rhoda
Wieser & Wieser, Inc.
Witherspoon & Associates, Inc.
Wonderland Press, Inc., The
Wright Representatives, Ann
Writers House
Writers' Representatives, Inc.
Yost Associates, Inc., Mary
Zachary Shuster Agency
Zeckendorf Assoc. Inc., Susan

Fee-charging
Backman, Elizabeth H.
Crown International Literature and Arts Agency, Bonnie R.
CS International Literary Agency
Fort Ross Inc. Russian-American Publishing Projects
McKinley, Literary Agency, Virginia C.
Nelson Literary Agency & Lecture Bureau, BK
Pell Agency, William
PMA Literary and Film Management, Inc.
Raintree Literary Agency, Diane
Strong Literary Agency, Marianne
Tornetta Agency, Phyllis
Zahler Literary Agency, Karen Gantz
Zitwer Agency, Barbara J.

Script
Amato Agency, Michael
Amsterdam Agency, Marcia

Authors Alliance Inc.
Berman Boals and Flynn Inc.
Charisma Communications, Ltd.
Circle of Confusion Ltd.
CS International Literary Agency
First Look Talent and Literary Agency
Freedman Dramatic Agency, Inc., Robert A.
French, Inc., Samuel
Graham Agency
Greene, Arthur B.
Hogenson Agency, Barbara
Hudson Agency
Mura Enterprises, Inc., Dee
Oscard Agency, Inc., Fifi
Palmer, Dorothy
Pevner, Inc., Stephen
PMA Literary and Film Management, Inc.
Schulman, A Literary Agency, Susan
Sydra Technique Corp.
Tantleff Office, The
Whittlesey Agency, Peregrine
Wright Representatives, Ann
Writers & Artists Agency

OHIO

Nonfee-charging
Fernandez Agent/Attorney, Justin E.

Fee-charging
GEM Literary Services
Hamilton's Literary Agency, Andrew

Script
Picture of You, A

OREGON

Nonfee-charging
First Books
Kern Literary Agency, Natasha
Reichstein Literary Agency, The Naomi

PENNSYLVANIA

Nonfee-charging
Allen, Literary Agent, James
Amber Literary
BigScore Productions Inc.
Collin Literary Agent, Frances
Fox Chase Agency, Inc.
Kidd Agency, Inc., Virginia
Lincoln Literary Agency, Ray
Schlessinger Agency, Blanche
Toad Hall, Inc.

Fee-charging
Hartline Literary Agency

Script
Sister Mania Productions, Inc.
Toad Hall, Inc.

SOUTH CAROLINA

Script
Buscher Consultants

TENNESSEE

Nonfee-charging
Client First—A/K/A Leo P. Haffey Agency
Roghaar Literary Agency, Inc., Linda

Script
Client First—A/K/A Leo P. Haffey Agency

TEXAS

Nonfee-charging
DHS Literary, Inc.
Donovan Literary, Jim
Kirkland Literary Agency, The
Lewis & Company, Karen
New Century Literary Agency
Sedgeband Literary Associates

Fee-charging
Fran Literary Agency
Mumford Literary Agency, Inc., The

Script
Stanton & Associates Literary Agency

UTAH

Script
Montgomery-West Literary Agency

VERMONT

Nonfee-charging
Brady Literary Management
Rowland Agency, The Damaris

VIRGINIA

Nonfee-charging
Communications and Entertainment, Inc.
Lindstrom Literary Group

Script
Communications and Entertainment, Inc.
Filmwriters Literary Agency

WASHINGTON

Nonfee-charging
Goodman-Andrew-Agency, Inc.
Levant & Wales, Literary Agency, Inc.

Fee-charging
Catalog Literary Agency, The
McLean Literary Agency

Script
Cedar Grove Agency Entertainment

WISCONSIN
Nonfee-charging
Sternig & Byrne Literary Agency

CANADA
Nonfee-charging
Acacia House Publishing Services Ltd.
Northwest Literary Services
Slopen Literary Agency, Beverley

Fee-charging
Author Author Literary Agency Ltd.
Authors' Marketing Services Ltd.
Renaud, Literary Agent, Janis
Kay Agency, Charlene

FOREIGN
Script
Brodie Representation, Alan

Agents Index

This index of agent names was created to help you locate agents you may have read or heard about even when you do not know which agency they work for. Agent names are listed with their agencies' names. Check the Listing Index for the page number of the agency.

AGENTS INDEX

Listing Index

Agencies that appeared in the 1999 *Guide to Literary Agents* but are not included this year are identified by a two-letter code explaining why the agency is not listed: **(ED)**—Editorial Decision, **(NS)**—Not Accepting Submissions/Too Many Queries, **(NR)**—No (or Late) Response to Listing Request, **(OB)**—Out of Business, **(RR)**—Removed by Agency's Request, **(UF)**—Uncertain Future, **(UC)**—Unable to Contact, **(RP)**—Business Restructured.

Agencies that appeared in the 1999 *Guide to Literary Agents* but are not included this year are identified by a two-letter code explaining why the agency is not listed: **(ED)—Editorial Decision, (NS)—Not Accepting Submissions/Too Many Queries, (NR)—No (or Late) Response to Listing Request, (OB)—Out of Business, (RR)—Removed by Agency's Request, (UF)—Uncertain Future, (UC)—Unable to Contact, (RP)—Business Restructured.**

Agencies that appeared in the 1999 *Guide to Literary Agents* but are not included this year are identified by a two-letter code explaining why the agency is not listed: (ED)—Editorial Decision, (NS)—Not Accepting Submissions/Too Many Queries, (NR)—No (or Late) Response to Listing Request, (OB)—Out of Business, (RR)—Removed by Agency's Request, (UF)—Uncertain Future, (UC)—Unable to Contact, (RP)—Business Restructured.